Empire, Colony, Genocide

Studies on War and Genocide

General Editors: Omer Bartov, Brown University and A. Dirk Moses, University of Sydney

Volume 1
The Massacre in History
Edited by Mark Levene and Penny Roberts

Volume 2
National Socialist Extermination Policies: Contemporary German Perspectives and Controversies
Edited by Ulrich Herbert

Volume 3
War of Extermination: The German Military in World War II, 1941/44
Edited by Hannes Heer and Klaus Naumann

Volume 4
In God's Name: Genocide and Religion in the Twentieth Century
Edited by Omer Bartov and Phyllis Mack

Volume 5
Hitler's War in the East, 1941–1945
Rolf-Dieter Müller and Gerd R. Ueberschär

Volume 6
Genocide and Settler Society: Frontier Violence and Stolen Indigenous Children in Australian History
Edited by A. Dirk Moses

Volume 7
Networks of Nazi Persecution: Bureaucracy, Business, and the Organization of the Holocaust
Edited by Gerald D. Feldman and Wolfgang Seibel

Volume 8
Gray Zones: Ambiguity and Compromise in the Holocaust and Its Aftermath
Edited by Jonathan Petropoulos and John K. Roth

Volume 9
Robbery and Restitution: The Conflict over Jewish Property in Europe
Edited by M. Dean, C. Goschler and P. Ther

Volume 10
Exploitation, Resettlement, Mass Murder: Political and Economic Planning for German Occupation Policy in the Soviet Union, 1940–1941
Alex J. Kay

Volume 12
Empire, Colony, Genocide: Conquest, Occupation, and Subaltern Resistance in World History
Edited by A. Dirk Moses

Volume 13
The Train Journey: Transit, Captivity, and Witnessing in the Holocaust
Simone Gigliotti

Volume 14
The 'Final Solution' in Riga: Exploitation and Annihilation, 1941-1944
Andrej Angrick and Peter Klein

Empire, Colony, Genocide

Conquest, Occupation, and Subaltern Resistance in World History

Edited by

A. Dirk Moses

Berghahn Books
New York • Oxford

First published in 2008 by

Berghahn Books

www.berghahnbooks.com

First paperback edition published in 2010

Library of Congress Cataloging-in-Publication Data

Empire, colony, genocide : conquest, occupation, and subaltern resistance in world history / edited by A. Dirk Moses.
p. cm. – (Studies on war and genocide ; v. 12)
Includes bibliographical references.
ISBN 978-1-84545-452-4 (hardback : alk. paper) 1. Genocide–History. 2. Crimes against humanity–History. I. Moses, A. Dirk.
HV6322.7.E46 2008
364.15'1–dc22 2008008207

British Library Cataloguing in Publication Data

A catalogue record for this book is available from the British Library.

ISBN 978-1-84545-452-4 hardback

CONTENTS

Preface

This book was inspired by a conference called "Genocide and Colonialism" that I hosted at the University of Sydney in July 2003. The conference was, as far as I can determine, the first held on this topic. Eight of the chapters published here first saw the light of day on that occasion, while two of the papers from the conference were published elsewhere: Michael Rothberg, "The Work of Testimony in the Age of Decolonization: *Chronicle of a Summer*, Cinema Verité, and the Emergence of the Holocaust Survivor," *PMLA* 119, no. 5 (2004): 1231–46; and Norbert Finzsch, "'It is Scarcely Possible to Believe that Human Beings could be so Hideous and Loathsome': Discourses of Genocide in Eighteenth- and Nineteenth-century America and Australia," *Patterns of Prejudice* 39, no. 2 (2005): 97–116 (reprinted in A. Dirk Moses and Dan Stone, eds., *Colonialism and Genocide* [London: Routledge, 2007]). I commissioned the balance of the chapters in order to cover as much of the globe as possible.

Even with nineteen chapters, of course, the book only scratches the surface of world history. No claim to comprehensiveness is made. *Empire, Colony, Genocide* presents case studies of genocide in colonial and imperial contexts in order to stimulate an underrepresented research agenda in the field of genocide studies. To date, the field has been dominated by social scientists who, understandably enough, rely on secondary literature and focus on the twentieth century. The authors in this book are overwhelmingly historians of the early modern and modern periods with detailed knowledge of the archival sources in their area of research. By embedding their empirical expertise in the transnational approach of comparative colonialism and genocide studies, as well as uncovering the colonial roots of the genocide concept itself, they are trying to operationalize Raphael Lemkin's original but ignored insight that genocides are intrinsically colonial and that they long precede the twentieth century. The history of genocide is the history of human society since antiquity.

Although most of the cases studied here cover European encounters with non-Europeans, it is not the intention of the book to give the impression that genocide is a function of European colonialism and imperialism alone. Lemkin himself was interested in many cases, such as the Athenian, Roman, Mongol, and Ottoman empires. We hope to revive interest in his research program and humanitarian view of world history.

No book like this can be produced without the help of friends, colleagues, and institutions. The Humanities Research Centre and the Herbert and Valmae Freilich Foundation at the Australian National University sponsored and largely financed the conference. The School of Philosophical and Historical Inquiry and the Faculty of Arts at the University of Sydney also chipped in. Ann Curthoys and John Docker at the ANU encouraged me along the way, gave papers at the conference, and wrote chapters for this book. My colleagues in the Department of History were most supportive, particularly Robert Aldrich, Alison Bashford, Stephen Garton, and Richard Waterhouse.

I completed some of the work for this project as a Charles H. Revson Fellow at the Center for Advanced Holocaust Studies at the United States Holocaust Memorial Museum, and I am grateful to its staff for their assistance during my months in Washington, DC. The book was finalized while on teaching relief funded by the Australian Research Council (ARC), whose grant on genocide and colonialism allowed me to conduct broader research on this topic. Every Australian academic who has been given time to research and write thanks to ARC teaching relief is a model of productivity and gratitude. I am also indebted to Omer Bartov, the editor of the series in which this book appears, and to the publisher Marion Berghahn for supporting the project and consenting to late changes and endless delays with grace and good humor. Unfortunately, I cannot name the colleagues who acted as anonymous referees, but their erudition and professionalism needs to be acknowledged. My thanks are extended to Marianne Ehrhardt for preparing the index, and to Patrick Wolfe for advice on various matters.

Mustering so many authors and shepherding them towards completion more or less according to plan was no easy task—for them or myself. I thank those who joined the project late in the day for their forbearance in the face of my unremitting strictures regarding form and content, as well, above all, the early contributors who waited patiently for years for the book to appear. I hope they, and readers generally, think that the wait was worthwhile.

These chapters have been anonymously peer reviewed.

ADM, Sydney, November 2007.

– *Section I* –

Intellectual History and Conceptual Questions

– *Chapter 1* –

EMPIRE, COLONY, GENOCIDE

Keywords and the Philosophy of History

A. Dirk Moses

> If we demonstrate by our behavior that we consider the native population merely as an obstacle to be circumvented or smashed, if by our rule we bring them not well-being and enlightenment but destruction, then the only issue between the two races will be that of life and death. Sooner or later Algeria will become the bloody arena for a mortal combat between these two peoples with mercy neither offered nor accepted. In such a struggle, one or the other would have to die. May God forbid that this be our destiny.
>
> —Alexis de Tocqueville[1]

> Thus we constantly approach the South American Indian with both the attitude of the scientific researcher, trying to be objective, and the consciousness of being part of a civilization that has committed a kind of unpardonable sin—in my opinion the greatest sin ever committed in the history of humanity, which is to have destroyed or attempted to destroy half of the richness of humankind.
>
> —Claude Levi-Strauss[2]

Introduction

Empire," "colony," and "genocide" are keywords particularly laden with controversial connotations. Few are the societies that were not once part of empires, whether its core or periphery. Few are the societies that are not the product of a colonization process, whether haphazard or planned. Many are the genocides that have marked imperial conquest through the ages. What is more, the first two of these terms are generally viewed through the lens of their nineteenth and twentieth century relatives, imperialism and colonialism, words of implicit opprobrium because they connote European domination of the non-European world. Imperialism was coined in the middle of the nineteenth century to criticize ambitions for domination and expansion. A century later, to accuse a country of colonialism was to condemn it for enslaving and exploiting another.[3]

These keywords imply an interpretation of world history—indeed, human history tout court—shared by both proponents and critics of this European hegemony. Thus F. A. Kirkpatrick of Cambridge University referred to "colonization" and "empire" rather than "colonialism" or "imperialism" when he told his audience in 1906: "Down to the fifteenth century our ancestors were confined to this little Europe, and knew nothing of empty or half-empty countries inviting their occupation beyond the seas. Modern colonization and empire means the spread of Europe over the world."[4] Writing almost twenty years earlier, the future US president Theodore Roosevelt attributed the expansion of civilization solely to the "English-speaking Peoples." Unlike the Spanish colonists who intermarried with Indigenes in the Americas, Anglophone settlers had retained the conquering prowess and racial purity of their Germanic ancestors: "The average Englishman, American, or Australian of today who wishes to recall the feats of power with which his race should be credited in the shadowy dawn of its history, may go back to the half-mythical glories of Hengist and Horsa, perhaps to the deeds of Civilis the Batavian, or to those of the hero of the Teutoburger fight." Roosevelt also distinguished the English Teuton from the Spanish and French by the nature of his ruthless nation building. "The English had exterminated or assimilated the Celts of Britain, and they substantially repeated the process with the Indians of America."[5] The cause of progress assuaged the conscience. Writing between the world wars, the English soldier, collector, and archaeologist George Henry Lane-Fox Pitt-Rivers advised that when a "superior race" overwhelmed an inferior race, "humanitarian sentiments [are] often irrelevant and for the most part quite unreasonable . . . there should be no reason for members of a superior race to regret the gradual extinction of an inferior race if only the future enrichment and welfare of the world is considered."[6]

Critical observers shared such frank recognition about the price of civilization, but without the celebration. The French anthropologist Georges Balandier noted somberly in 1951: "One of the most striking events in the recent history of mankind is the expansion throughout the entire world of most European peoples. It has brought about the subjugation and, in some instances, the disappearance of virtually every people regarded as backward, archaic, or primitive."[7]

Frantz Fanon, the Martinican psychiatrist who wrote influential books on "third world" liberation, essentially concurred, turning Hegel upside down: "The West saw itself as a spiritual adventure. It is in the name of the spirit, in the name of the spirit of Europe, that Europe has made her encroachments, that she has justified her crimes and legitimized the slavery in which she holds four-fifths of humanity."[8] Although they were writing soon after the United Nations passed the "Convention on the Punishment and Prevention of Genocide" in 1948, Balandier and Fanon did not use this neologism, invented during World War II by Raphael Lemkin (1900–1959), to describe the fate of "people regarded as backward, archaic, or primitive." Nonetheless, the link between human catastrophes and the metanarrative of human progress was clearly in the minds of Europeans and non-European intellectuals at this time.

What precisely this link was and is has bitterly divided debate on the three keywords of this book because the moral legitimacy of Western civilization is at stake, as well, by implication, as the legitimacy of anti-colonial struggles of national liberation, especially in light of the anti-imperial rhetoric of postcolonial dictators. Contributors to the debate pose a number of conflicting questions. Was the expansion of the West—that, is, European colonialism and imperialism since the late fifteenth century—inherently genocidal and generally criminal?[9] Or were non-European societies so nasty and brutish that they screamed out for the milk of European civilizational uplift?[10] And did not genocide and totalitarianism really inhere less in European empires than in their negation, the anti-imperial, anti-Western "liberation movements," of Islamism, Pan-Arabism, the "third world socialism" of the Khmer Rouge and Afrocommunism, even National Socialism?[11]

If these terms seem improbably stark, anachronistic, even crude, consider discussions in the first decade of the twentieth-first century by supposedly subtle intellects. Benny Morris, the Israeli historian whose assiduous archival work helped dispel myths about the "Birth of the Palestinian Refugee Problem" in 1948, nonetheless defended ethnic cleansing and genocide as integral to the formation of (some) nation states and march of human progress. "Even the great American democracy could not have been created without the annihilation of the Indians," he told an interviewer in 2004. "There are cases in which the overall, final good justifies harsh and cruel acts that are committed in the course of history."[12] Also weary of leftist anticolonialism, antiracism, and anti-Zionism, the French philosopher Alain Finkielkraut sought to trump the victim narratives of the non-European colonized with his own:

> I was born in Paris, but I'm the son of Polish immigrants. My father was deported from France. His parents were deported and murdered in Auschwitz. My father returned from Auschwitz to France. This country deserves our hatred: What it did to my parents was much more violent than what it did to Africans.

> What did it do to Africans? It did only good. It put my father in hell for five years. . . . I think that the lofty idea of "the war on racism" is gradually turning into a hideously false ideology. And this anti-racism will be for the 21st century what communism was for the 20th century. A source of violence. Today, Jews are attacked in the name of anti-racist discourse: the separation fence, "Zionism is racism."[13]

What these stances show is that, in the wake of the so-called "war on terror" after 11 September 2001 in particular, the debate about empire, colony, and genocide is marked by a phallic logic. Commentators shout, "my trauma is bigger than yours" in order to defend or attack the theodicy that the brutal extermination and disappearance of peoples over the centuries is redeemed by human progress in the form of the Western-dominated global system of nation-states.[14]

Instead of indulging in speculation about the philosophy of history, scholars can offer their readers more than these simplistic polarizations by asking middle-range questions that are amenable to empirical scrutiny.[15] The following are apposite: What did the founder of "genocide studies," Lemkin, have to say about the links between empires, colonies, and genocides? What can one say more generally about their interrelationship? And how is the Holocaust linked to them? Posing these questions allows us to ponder whether colonial wars of conquest and counterinsurgency are qualitatively different to genocides in Europe. Indeed, whether "colonial genocide" or "indigenocide" should be a subcategory of analysis distinct from genocide proper.[16] Or whether colonial logics inhere in all genocides. Must the state be the perpetrator in cases where settlers killed indigenous people without official authority? Conversely, can indigenous people commit genocide against the settler colonizer? And, finally, is any consistency or pattern discernible in the relations between our three keywords and in phenomena so complex and riddled with contradictions as empires, with their bewildering array of governing modes and varying types of enlistment of subject peoples in their projects?[17]

In answering these questions, historians would do well to consider a pitfall inherent in genocide studies.[18] Because genocide was originally conceived as a legal concept and crime in international law, the temptation is great to "catch a crook" rather than "write a book."[19] If the moral and emotional satisfaction of identifying and excoriating the evil-doers strikes a symbolic blow for surviving victim communities, writing as a hanging judge brings with it the danger of oversimplifying the historical record by casting each genocidal conjuncture as a tidily organized drama of passive victims, wicked perpetrators, and craven bystanders.[20] The complexities of empire, such as the tensions between indirect rule and authoritarian administration, resource exploitation and economic modernization, settler foundations and cultural adaptation cannot be reduced to the single question: was there a genocide? There are as many ways of studying these phenomena as there are instances of colonies and empires.[21]

At the same time, neither ought the cultural and physical destruction that attended the foundation of colonies and expansion of empires be played down by conservatives in the name of Western self-congratulation and Edwardian nostalgia, or ignored by the unintentionally quietist, postcolonial fascination with the construction of identities and intricate networks of cultural circulation.[22] Notwithstanding the different political intentions between these two positions, they share a desire to disrupt the binaries of colonizer/colonized, dominator/dominated, and center/periphery in order to view empires and colonies in less rigid terms. Together, they see

> colonialism as often being a source of creativity and experiment, and while certainly not being without pain, colonial encounters cause the dissolution of values on all sides, creating new ways of doing things in a material and social sense. A stress on creativity takes us away from notions such as fatal impact, domination and resistance or core and periphery, emphasizing that colonial cultures were created by all who participated in them, so that all had agency and social effect, with colonizer and colonized alike being radically changed by the experience.[23]

This is a view of colonization and empire that does not really admit the possibility of genocide. But need the historiography be a zero-sum game? Investing agency in the colonized does not mean empire needs to be seen as a symmetrically structured opportunity for cultural exchange. Remaining faithful to the complexity and contingency of the past need not entail abandoning the search for patterns or logics. It means that the object of inquiry is the sum total of economic, social, and political relations between people in a colonial situation; the various bids for power and the resistances to them; the processes of escalation brought on by real, contrived, or perceived security crises; the success of the colonial state in "pacifying" and either absorbing or expunging the "native"; the conscription of parts of indigenous society in such projects; as well, equally, as the failure of metropoles to realize their ambitions. The right note has been sounded by Donald Bloxham, who observed in relation to the Armenian genocide that "it may be said categorically that the killing did constitute genocide . . . but recognizing this fact should be a 'by-product' of the historian's work, not its ultimate aim or underpinning."[24] Genocide is to be explained as the outcome of complex processes rather than ascribable solely to the evil intentions of wicked men. It is the job of historians to trace how highly structured relationships between geopolitics and states, states and subaltern groups, elites and their bureaucracies become incarnated in and are themselves affected by the agency of individuals in particular situations.[25]

Raphael Lemkin, the Polish-Jewish lawyer who coined the term *genocide* in 1944 and campaigned for its criminalization in international law, wrestled with the dilemma of judging the past.[26] Historians, he thought, were in thrall to the Rankean fascination with interstate relations at the expense of "the role of the human group and its tribulations."[27] "Maybe . . . historians are somewhat guilty because they are used to present history in most cases from the point of view of wars for territorial expansion, of royal marriages, but they did not stress enough the death of civilizations as a result of genocide."[28] It was time to regard history in terms of human group survival, he thought, because "the fight against the destruction of the human group has a more profound moral significance than the fight between states."[29] Lemkin's intention to reorient historical study was therefore explicitly activist: historical knowledge was to serve consciousness-raising in the present. Consequently, the study of genocide was to be scientific, and he drew on the scholarship of his day to develop his concept and write his analyses. For that reason, any analysis of colony, empire, and genocide should commence with his body of ideas.

Lemkin, Genocide, and Empire

Demonstrating that genocide had been a recurring feature of human history was at the heart of Lemkin's public campaign to outlaw genocide in international law in the late 1940s and 1950s. Before his death in 1959, he had almost completed a book on genocide in world history but, unfortunately, publishers were uninterested in his manuscript.[30] Apart from his book manuscript, he also wrote about genocide in the press. Here is a typical statement from his publications at the time of his campaign: "The destruction of Carthage, the destruction of the Albigenses and Waldenses, the Crusades, the march of the Teutonic Knights, the destruction of the Christians under the Ottoman Empire, the massacres of the Herero in Africa, the extermination of the Armenians, the slaughter of the Christian Assyrians in Iraq in 1933, the destruction of the Maronites, the pogroms of Jews in Tsarist Russia and Romania—all these are classical genocide cases."[31] Many of these cases occurred in colonial and imperial contexts, or were instances of colonization as with the "Teutonic Knights and the Prussian Pagans" in the thirteenth century where "partial physical and total cultural genocide" occurred.[32] In fact, most of his case studies from the Eurasian land mass were taken from continental empires: the Roman Empire, the Mongols, the Ottoman Empire, Charlemagne and the spread of German peoples eastwards since the Middle Ages.[33]

Extra-European colonial cases also featured prominently in this projected global history of genocide. In "Part III: Modern Times," he wrote the following numbered chapters: (1) Genocide by the Germans against the Native Africans; (3) Belgian Congo; (11) Hereros; (13) Hottentots; (16) Genocide against the American Indians; (25) Latin America; (26) Genocide against the Aztecs; (27) Yucatan; (28) Genocide against the Incas; (29) Genocide against the Maoris of New Zealand; (38) Tasmanians; (40) S.W. Africa; and finally, (41) Natives of Australia.[34] And he thought carefully about the modalities of genocide in situations where the Europeans were usually outnumbered by the indigenous inhabitants. "It must be clarified here that subjected groups may be a majority controlled by a powerful minority *as in the case in colonial societies*. If the majority cannot be absorbed by the ruling minority and is considered a threat to the minority's power, genocide is sometimes the result (i.e., the American Indian)."[35]

But Lemkin did not just write about genocide in colonial contexts; he defined the concept as intrinsically colonial. On the first page of the relevant chapter in his book, *Axis Rule in Occupied Europe*, he wrote: "Genocide has two phases: one, destruction of the national pattern of the oppressed group: the other, the imposition of the national pattern of the oppressor. This imposition, in turn, may be made upon the oppressed population which is allowed to remain, or upon the territory alone, after removal of the population and the *colonization* of the area by the oppressor's own nationals."[36]

While Lemkin's linking of genocide and colonialism may surprise those who think that his neologism was modeled after the Holocaust of European Jewry, an investigation of his intellectual development reveals that the concept is the culmination of a long tradition of European legal and political critique of colonization and empire.[37] Indeed, the new discipline of "genocide studies" is a continuation of the long-standing European debate about the morality and legality of occupying and dominating other peoples. As Andrew Fitzmaurice shows in this volume, European theologians, philosophers, and lawyers have been debating the morality of occupation since the Spanish conquest of the Americas in the sixteenth century. These Spanish intellectuals—in particular by Bartolomé de Las Casas and Francesco de Vitoria—based their case on natural law that invested rights in Indigenous peoples. Hugo Grotius, Samuel Pufendorf, Emeric de Vattel, and Christian Wolff continued this line of critique. It was incarnated in different ways in the nineteenth and twentieth centuries by humanitarians who assailed the mistreatment of "native peoples" by colonial authorities and settlers.[38]

Twentieth-century jurists who defended indigenous rights, like Charles Solomon and Gaston Jèze, studied Vitoria carefully in making out their views. So did Lemkin, who likely knew Jèze in the 1920s. But Las Casas was his hero: his "name has lived on through the centuries as one of the most admirable and courageous crusaders for humanity the world has ever known."[39] Lemkin explicitly appropriated Las Casas' viewpoint in his study of the "Spanish Colonial Genocide." He called his book on the Nazi empire *Axis Rule in Occupied Europe* in order to place it in the tradition of criticizing brutal conquests. Genocide for Lemkin, then, was a special form of foreign conquest and occupation. It was necessarily imperial and colonial in nature. In particular, genocide aimed to permanently tip the demographic balance in favor of the occupier. In relation to the Nazi case, he wrote that "in this respect genocide is a new technique of occupation aimed at winning the peace even though the war itself is lost."[40] Any doubt that the roots of the genocide concept lie in the five-hundred-year tradition of natural law-based critique of imperialism rather than in Lemkin's reaction to the Armenian genocide or Holocaust can be dispelled by his own words:

> The history of genocide provides examples of the awakening of humanitarian feelings which gradually have been crystalized in formulae of international law. The awakening of the world conscience is traced to the times when the world community took an affirmative stand to protect human groups from extinction. Bartolomé de las Casas, Vitoria, and humanitarian interventions, are all links in one chain leading to the proclamation of genocide as an international crime by the United Nations.[41]

Anticolonialism and Anti-imperialism?

Although himself a liberal, Lemkin did not share the affirmation of empire by liberals like Alexis de Tocqueville, who passionately endorsed the violent French conquest of Algeria.[42] Lemkin was shocked by the dismal record of subaltern suffering at the hands of occupiers, just as a postliberal like Jean-Paul Sartre was incensed by the French reprisals in the Algerian town of Setif and the bombing and shelling of Muslim civilians nearby that killed perhaps many thousands of Arabs in 1945, episodes that the Algerian government now regards as genocidal.[43] Indeed, Lemkin shared with such postliberal anti-imperialists a vision of a noncoercive human group interaction. If Aimé Césaire famously denounced colonialism because it did not enable an authentic blending of "different worlds,"[44] he and Lemkin doubtless would have affirmed what the historian Richard White calls the "middle ground": spaces in which peoples traded and negotiated with one another in mutually created forms of accommodation that were not reducible to the simple binary relationships of domination and subordination.[45] Drawing on Bronislaw Malinowski's theory of cultural change, Lemkin favored what he called "cultural diffusion" via intercultural exchange. It comprised

> gradual changes occur[ing] by means of the continuous and slow adaptation of the culture to new situations. The new situations arise from physical changes, creative energies within the culture and the impact of outside influences. Without them the culture becomes static; if they appear but are not met with adaptation of the whole culture pattern, the culture becomes less integrated. In either case, it becomes weaker and may disintegrate entirely when exposed to strong outside influences. The rise and fall of civilizations have been explained on this general basis.[46]

But whereas Césaire thought that "no one colonizes innocently," Lemkin, like Las Casas, did not oppose colonization or empire per se.[47] Empires, humanely governed, contributed to human progress through "diffusion," he implied. Like Malinowski, Lemkin thought that cultural change was induced by exogenous influences, as weaker societies adopt the institutions of more efficient ones or become absorbed by them because they better fulfill basic needs. "Diffusion is gradual and relatively spontaneous," Lemkin wrote, "although it may lead to the eventual disintegration of a weak culture."[48] He would not have opposed the Phoenician colonization of the western Mediterranean, where a "coming to terms with and utilization of the indigenous population" and fruitful cultural interaction resulted in their assimilation within two generations.[49] An empire that promoted diffusion governed by "indirect rule," Malinowski argued, because it supposedly enabled the autonomous indigenous acquisition of European institutions.[50] Lemkin agreed with this assessment, as we will see below.

What is more, Lemkin possessed a liberal faith in international law that he regarded as the central civilizational instrument to combat genocide. For genocide, in his view, was a reversion to barbaric times when no laws of war existed to protect civilians. Since Western imperialism, however brutal at times, had spread this international law, Lemkin did not share the outright anti-imperialism of leftist intellectuals like Sartre and Fanon, for whom all empires, at least capitalist ones, entailed the exploitation and degradation of the indigenous people.[51] As we have seen, Fanon had no truck with such liberal self-narrations of moral or ethical progress, which he regarded as inevitably taking place at the expense of non-Europeans.

Genocide and Culture

Lemkin was disturbed by occupations like German colonial rule in Africa that ultimately culminated in genocide in German Southwest Africa and German East Africa between 1904 and 1907. "In the German colonies no attempt was made to respect native tribal customs or to invest the chiefs with their former dignity and authority. The chiefs were deprived of their privileges and the only authority permitted them was that delegated to them by the German officials, such authority being solely used for the purpose of recruiting forced labour. If the chiefs failed to cooperate in everything demanded of them, they were systematically ill-treated, flogged and imprisoned, even for the most trivial offenses."[52] This quotation gives us clues to Lemkin's conception of genocide. He was more concerned with the loss of culture than the loss of life. In his correspondence with the Nuremberg prosecutors, he urged them to amend the indictment of the Nazi leaders to include genocide. He wrote,

> It appears in light of this evidence that the term genocide is a correct one since the defendants aimed to destroy, cripple, or degrade entire nations, racial and religious groups. The terms mass-murder or mass-extermination in the light of hitherto produced evidence seems to be inadequate since they do not convey the racial and national motivation of the crime. [M]ass-murder or extermination do not convey the elements of selection and do not indicate the losses in terms of culture represented by the nation's victims. If all the 125 000 Islanders will be killed off, this would mean a disappearance not only of 125 000 human beings but also a disappearance of the Islandic culture with its old language, institutions, national aspirations and all contributions which the Islandic nation made or is able to make to mankind in the future.[53]

Why was culture so central to Lemkin's conception of genocide? Drawing on the functionalist anthropology of Sir James Frazer and Malinowski, he argued that culture, which he called "derived needs" or "cultural imperatives," was as constitutive for human group life as individual physical well-being (i.e., basic needs). Culture integrated society and enabled the fulfillment of individual basic needs. These "so-called derived needs," Lemkin wrote, "are just as necessary to their existence as the basic physiological needs." He elaborated this point thus: "These needs find expression in social institutions or, to use an anthropological term, the culture ethos. If the culture of a group is violently undermined, the group itself disintegrates and its members must either become absorbed in other cultures which is a wasteful and painful process or succumb to personal disorganization and, perhaps, physical destruction."[54] For these reasons, he concluded, "the destruction of cultural symbols is genocide." To destroy their function "menaces the existence of the social group which exists by virtue of its common culture."[55]

Herewith, we come to the thorny issue of "cultural genocide," an issue central to the study of colonialism because it so often involved projects of indigenous assimilation. Lemkin has been fundamentally misunderstood by scholars of genocide who contend that he did not support the concept of cultural genocide. In fact, he wanted cultural genocide included in the 1948 convention. Referring to the Secretariat's draft convention of 1947 that included a section on cultural genocide, he wrote that "Cultural Genocide is the most important part of the Convention."[56] He only reluctantly acceded to its eventual exclusion on tactical grounds.[57] Even so, it is difficult to obtain a clear answer about his own definition of the term from his many statements on the topic. Was forced religious conversion genocidal? At times, he suggested it was: for instance, in the actions of Spanish priests in the Americas.[58] At others, he denied it: "cultural genocide need not involve the substitution of new culture traits (such as forced conversion), but may maliciously undermine the victim group to render its members more defenseless in the face of physical destruction."[59] In *Axis Rule*, he suggested that terms like "denationalization" or "Germanization"—the imposition of the conqueror's "national pattern" on the conquered people—were unsatisfactory because "they treat mainly the cultural, economic, and social aspects of genocide, leaving out the biological aspects, such as causing the physical decline and even destruction of the population involved."[60] Was he hopelessly confused?

Closer inspection of his writings reveals that, true to his concept of group life, he did not consider cultural destruction in isolation from attacks on the physical and biological elements of a group. In the cases of genocide he studied, attacks on culture were inextricably interwoven with a broader assault encompassing the totality of group existence: "Physical and biological genocide are always preceeded by cultural genocide or by an attack on the symbols of the group or by violent interference with religious or cultural activities. In order to deal effectively with the crime of Genocide one must intervene at the very inception of the crime."[61] Nazi mass murder, too, could not be separated from their attack on culture. "Side by side with the extermination of 'undesirables' went a systematic looting of artworks, books, the closing of universities and other places of learning, the destruction of national monuments."[62]

We can encapsulate Lemkin's position on genocide by regarding it as a "total social practice" that affected all aspects of group life.[63] Certainly, it could not be reduced to mass killing, as it is so often in popular consciousness and even genocide studies. "Like all social phenomena," he wrote, "it represents a complex synthesis of a diversity of factors."[64] It was, therefore, "an organic concept of multiple influences and consequences."[65] As a total social practice, genocide comprised various techniques of group destruction. In *Axis Rule*, he outlined eight techniques used by the Nazis. They warrant listing in full because they illustrate his holistic conception of genocide, and demonstrate that mass killing was only one of a number of methods of group destruction. They are discussed here briefly in the order given by Lemkin.[66]

Political techniques refer to the cessation of self-government and local rule, and their replacement by that of the occupier. "Every reminder of former national character was obliterated."

Social techniques entail attacking the intelligentsia, "because this group largely provides the national leadership and organizes resistance against Nazification." The point of such attacks is to "weaken the national, spiritual resources."

Cultural techniques ban the use of native language in education, and inculcate youth with propaganda.

Economic techniques shift economic resources from the occupied to the occupier. Peoples the Germans regarded as of "related blood," like those of Luxembourg and Alsace-Lorraine, were given incentives to recognize this kinship. There were also disincentives: "If they do not take advantage of this 'opportunity' their properties are taken from them and given to others who are eager to promote Germanism."

Biological techniques decrease the birth rate of occupied. "Thus in incorporated Poland marriages between Poles are forbidden without special permission of the Governor (*Reichsstatthalter*) of the district; the latter, as a matter of principle, does not permit marriages between Poles."

Physical techniques mean the rationing of food, endangering of health, and mass killing in order to accomplish the "physical debilitation and even annihilation of national groups in occupied countries."

Religious techniques try to disrupt the national and religious influences of the occupied people. In Luxembourg, the method entailed enrolling children in "pro-Nazi youth organizations" so as to loosen the grip of Roman Catholic culture. Alternatively, in Poland, where no such assimilation was possible, the Germans conducted "the systematic pillage and destruction of church property and persecution of the clergy," in order to "destroy the religious leadership of the Polish nation."

Moral techniques are policies "to weaken the spiritual resistance of the national group." This technique of moral debasement entails diverting the "mental energy of the group" from "moral and national thinking" to "base instincts." The aim is that "the desire for cheap individual pleasure be substituted for the desire for collective feelings and ideals based upon a higher morality." Lemkin mentioned the encouragement of pornography and alcoholism in Poland as an example.

Genocide, Assimilation, and Indigenous Survival

The congruence of these techniques with those of many instances of European colonial rule is striking. Food rationing, forced conversion, inculcation of the new ruling culture, marriage and reproduction restrictions, the sequestration of economic resources, and introduction of European addictions have visited terrible cultural and physical devastation on indigenous peoples. London critics of British settlers listed abuses that largely replicate Lemkin's techniques of genocide. The *Report of the Select Committee on Aborigines (British Settlements)* in 1837 complained that "Too often, their [Aborigines'] territory has been usurped; their property seized; their numbers diminished; their character debased; the spread of religion impeded. European vices and diseases have been introduced amongst them, and they have been familiarized with the use of our most potent instruments for the subtle or the violent destruction of human life, viz. Brandy and gunpowder."[67]

Not for nothing do the perceptions of indigenous people about their experiences accord with Lemkin's phenomenology of genocide. Consider this summary by an Australian indigenous leader.

> While the 1788 invasion was unjust, the real injustice was the denial by [Governor] Phillip and subsequent governments of our right to participate equally in the future of a land we had managed successfully for millenniums [*sic*]. Instead, the land was stolen, not shared. Our political sovereignty was replaced by a virulent form of serfdom; our spiritual beliefs denied and ridiculed; our system of education undermined. We were no longer able to inculcate our young with the complex knowledge that is acquired from intimate engagement with the land and its waterways. The introduction of superior weapons, alien diseases, a policy of racism and enforced biogenetic practices created dispossession, a cycle of slavery and attempted destruction of our society. The 1997 report *Bringing Them Home* highlighted the infringement of the UN definition on genocide and called for a national apology and compensation of those Aborigines who had suffered under laws that destroyed indigenous societies and sanctioned biogenetic modification of the Aboriginal people.[68]

One of the issues raised by the *Bringing Them Home* report was whether forcible assimilation was tantamount to cultural genocide.[69] Lemkin's statements above and his unpublished studies on colonial behavior, especially his aversion to forced religious conversion, suggest that he equated the two. But he was also a pragmatist. In order to ensure that cultural genocide survived the objections to its inclusion in the various UN committees in 1947, he suggested that it be limited to "acts which are disapproved or incriminated [*sic*] by all national, penal courts such as arson, burning of books, destruction of churches and schools" rather than legal administrative measures, i.e., forcible assimilation by lawful means.[70] In other words, he limited cultural genocide to "acts of violence which are qualified as criminal by most of the criminal codes."[71] Legal assimilation was not cultural genocide, then, a conclusion that advantaged states which sought to assimilate their indigenous populations and other minorities after World War II. Lemkin's residual faith in Western civilization as the source of international humanitarian law may also have encouraged this narrower reading of cultural genocide. But in the end, even this restriction of cultural genocide's meaning was unsatisfactory for most UN delegates, who understood the Secretariat's draft convention as equating the closing of libraries with mass murder. Cultural genocide was eventually dropped from the final version of the convention.[72]

Lemkin's equivocation on forcible assimilation may be linked to his unwitting participation in the discourse on indigenous extinction common in the cultural evolutionism of anthropology since the nineteenth century.[73] In keeping with this view, he tended to regard the encounter between European and Indigene as grossly asymmetric, thereby playing down both indigenous agency and the often-tenuous European grip on power, particularly in the initial stages of colonization. In German Southwest Africa, for instance, he did not see that the German governor was initially reliant on local chiefs. In fact, such reliance was most likely the norm, because collaboration with indigenous elites made imperial rule both cheap and efficient. In such cases, the imperial overlords cooperated with these elites rather than trying to Europeanize local culture, although it goes too far to describe these dynamics as "empire by invitation."[74] In fact, indirect rule often disrupted indigenous polities as well by promoting chiefly authority at the expense of other social actors or by fetishizing ethnic differences ("tribes"), which programmed these societies for genocidal conflict after decolonization, as in the case of Rwanda.[75] Nor did Lemkin appreciate that the Herero survived the German genocide of 1904/05 because, as one scholar put it, he "just saw the Herero as helpless victims whose fate was sealed for all time."[76]

Such pessimism about the "disappearing savage" and "fatal impact" of Western colonization conveniently left the Europeans in sole occupation of the land, and worked against the interests of indigenous groups who survived genocidal assaults and later made claims for recognition and recompense. Recent research contests the myth of the "disappearing savage" by arguing that indigenous peoples creatively adapted to new circumstances. The Natick Indians, contrary to the well-known assertions of de Tocqueville that Indian society dissolved upon contact with the settlers, successfully maintained an Indian dimension to the land. A little over a century after first contact, in 1767, 82 percent of them had married outside the community, and they sold property as individuals.[77]

Lemkin's blindness to the question of survival and adaptation was rooted in his particular concept of culture. Despite his anthropological reading, he seems to have equated national culture with high culture. Consider how he regarded the matter in this quotation:

> All our cultural heritage is a product of the contribution of all nations. We can best understand this when we realize how impoverished our culture would be if the people doomed by Germany such as the Jews had not been permitted to

> create the Bible or give birth to an Einstein, a Spinoza; if the Poles had not had the opportunity to give the world a Copernicus, a Chopin, a Curie; the Greeks a Plato and a Socrates, the English a Shakespeare, the Russians a Tolstoy and a Shostakovich, the Americans an Emerson and a Jefferson, the Frenchmen a Renan and a Rodin.[78]

In this statement, the value of culture inhered in its elites who made contributions valuable for humanity as a whole. Recall that the social technique of genocide usually targeted cultural bearers, such as the intelligentsia and priestly class. Genocide could occur when they were exterminated, and when libraries, houses of religious worship, and other elite institutions of cultural transmission were destroyed, even if the mass of the population survived and continued some hybrid popular culture. Here is what Lemkin wrote about the Maya in twentieth-century Mexico centuries after their ravaging at the hands of the Spanish: "While the condition of the Indians has been improving since then, under a more progressive Mexican administration, their lot is still hard and their *cultural heritage has been irrevocably lost.* One million Indians still speak Maya dialect today. They still till the land as their forefathers had done but they have lost their civilized habits, their remarkable skills and knowledge long ago."[79] Clearly, this view is untenable today. Only white perceptions that "real" Indians must be "pure" prevented Europeans seeing that "Indianness" was retained even while Indians adapted their culture and intermarried with others. Lemkin does not seem to have considered the possibility that genocide could be attempted, that much destruction could take place, and that cultural diffusion occurred nonetheless.

The Question of Intention

Even if genocide cannot be reduced to mass killing, the conservative case against the colonial essence of genocide is that Lemkin, in *Axis Rule*, mentions a "coordinated plan of different actions" that attacks groups "with the aim of annihilating" them.[80] Indeed, what kind of plan can be discerned in processes so haphazard and uncoordinated as imperial and colonial expansion, particularly on frontiers that extended beyond the reach of the state? Yet in his writings on colonial cases, Lemkin never spoke of a plan, but he did try to identify the "intent" of the colonists. With regard to the Spanish conquest of the Americas, he wrote that their intent was, in the case of "the empire of Peru," to "take possession of it as their lawful territory and to convert the Peruvians to the true faith."[81] The officially announced will of the Spanish Crown manifested an intention, such as the proclamation to the Maya about the Spanish right to their country: "If you do not ['recognize the Church and his Majesty the king as your rulers'], we will war on you, take your wives and children away, dispose of your property and harm you as much as we can 'as to vassals who will not obey and refuse to receive their lord.'"[82] The reading of the Spanish sovereignty proclamation, whether natives were present or understood it, Lemkin observed, "seemed quite sufficient, in the eyes of the Spaniards, to produce obedience and justify genocide."[83] Lemkin did not take this claim on face value, regarding such announcements as "a mere fiction" because the preemptive massacres committed by Cortes were obviously "intended."[84] Elsewhere he wrote that the "motivation" of the Spanish in killing "rebellious Indians" was the "self-righteous attitude towards the Indians as Spanish property."[85]

The Spanish assumption of sovereignty was ultimately a pretext to kill, a posture inherited by subsequent English thinkers such as John Locke, who wrote that rebellious natives had "declared war against all mankind, and therefore may be *destroyed as a lion or tiger, one of those wild savage beasts with whom men can have no society or security.* And upon this is grounded that great law of Nature, 'Whoso sheddeth man's blood by man shall his blood be shed.' Also Cain was so fully convinced that every one had a right to destroy such a criminal, that, after the murder of his brother, he cries out, 'Every one that findeth me shall slay me,' so plain was it writ in the hearts of all mankind."[86] Lemkin was effectively arguing that occupations and settlements conducted on terms that neither recognized indigenous rights nor engaged in subsequent negotiations were bound to issue in genocide because resistance and its brutal suppression was inevitable.[87] The Nazis, too, fitted this pattern for Lemkin. He thought that Hitler regarded the Russian partisan warfare as but a pretext to "eradicate everyone who opposes us."[88]

Lemkin held individuals responsible for acts of genocide. Thus he found various Spanish leaders in the Americas guilty of genocidal acts.[89] Individual settlers could be guilty of genocidal acts as well, even if they were not authorized by the state. Lemkin never stipulated that genocide was solely a crime of state, and the UN convention concurred in naming individuals as well as state officials as potential perpetrators. Nonetheless, the illusion that genocide is tantamount to the Holocaust continues. Consider the following by an Australian historian:

> The wild times, which ended around 1850, spelt tragedy for Aboriginal people. However, it was not a story of genocide, as is often claimed, at least not according to the formal meaning of the word—that is, of official, intentional, premeditated killing. Intentional killing was carried out by settlers on a private and local level, however, leading to perhaps hundreds of deaths. Other deaths came from impulse and rage over property losses felt by possessive and fearful men. But there was never an official policy of killing Aborigines. Indeed, the British Government that held power during the era abhorred such violence and vainly tried to end it.[90]

In fact, this *is* a story of genocide because of the intentional killing of hundreds of Aborigines. No "official policy" is necessary for genocide to occur according to Lemkin's definition. An unofficial one is sufficient.

Lemkin also considered the issue of what might be called "unintended consequences." Discussing Nazi concentration and labor camps that were not death factories per se but that experienced very high rates of mortality, he postulated that genocidal intent could be inferred where mass death was not explicitly intended but where it was highly probable and reasonably foreseeable. "This is the phenomenon of wasting somebody else's life on a mass scale. This wanton relationship to human life was a natural result of the basic concept of genocide." The camp director was guilty because he "does not object in his mind and agrees with the eventuality of such destruction. In the criminal law of civil law countries such an intent is called 'dolus eventualis.'"[91]

This legal doctrine presents an interesting question for scholars of genocide and colonialism, because there is abundant evidence that Europeans were well aware of the devastation that their colonization wrought on indigenous populations. Robert Brown noted in 1873, for instance, that to save them one would need to keep "away from them . . . for where one is benefited and ameliorated by civilization a thousand are ruined . . . resulting sooner or later in . . . utter extinction."[92] To be sure, Europeans usually ascribed the inevitability of extinction to the supposed weakness of the "native" peoples, and they were well aware of the fatal factors: violence, disease, and fertility decline. But they were also confident that the value of their own civilization was sufficiently great to justify the destruction of the indigenous ones, howsoever caused.[93] President Andrew Jackson's annual address in 1830 exhibited this belief very clearly:

> Humanity has often wept over the fate of the aborigines of this country, and Philanthropy has been long busily employed in devising means to avert it, but its progress has never for a moment been arrested, and one by one many powerful tribes disappeared from the earth. To follow to the tomb the last of his race and to tread on the graves of extinct nations excite melancholy reflections. But true philanthropy reconciles the mind to these vicissitudes as it does the extinction of one generation to make room for another.[94]

Whether Lemkin would ascribe a genocidal intention in these terms to settler colonialism in particular is probably impossible to say, but it is an important question to consider in light of recent jurisprudence in international law.[95] In the case of Radislav Krstic in 2001, the International Criminal Tribunal for the Former Yugoslavia held the accused not guilty of genocide because he had not been directly involved in the massacre of seven thousand Bosnian men and boys at Srebrenica. But his knowledge of the genocidal intention of his comrades and their use of his troops was sufficient to convict him for participating in their "joint criminal enterprise," that is, the secondary offence of aiding and abetting genocide.[96] The tribunal's use of the law of conspiracy, complicity, and incitement means that international jurisprudence is catching up with social scientists who realized long ago that narrow, black-letter interpretations of the convention's stipulations regarding genocidal intention cannot do justice to the messy reality in which such intentions evolve. For all that, the tribunal's distinctions also help students of genocide and colonialism differentiate types of intention in collective projects like colonialism.

Whether colonialism is a joint criminal enterprise is not a question that is scientifically answerable. Who is to judge? Lemkin was caught on the horns of a dilemma. The (modern) empires he scrutinized for committing genocide were also those that spread civilization by the sword as well as the plough. Arguing that measures like forced assimilation, for instance, were only genocidal if considered illegal by civilized nations begs the question, because civilized nations were the states who engaged in such forced assimilation. The subaltern answer to the implicit theodicy has been given by Césaire: "They talk to me about progress, about 'achievements,' diseases cured, improved standards of living. *I* am talking about societies drained of their essences, cultures trampled underfoot, institutions undermined, lands confiscated, religions smashed, magnificent artistic creations destroyed, extraordinary *possibilities* wiped out."[97]

Nazi Imperialism and Colonialism

If Lemkin viewed colonies and empires as the heart of genocide, did he include Nazism and the Holocaust? In some respects, yes; in others, no. This is how he linked the issues in an unpublished draft manuscript:

> The Nazi plan of Genocide was related to many peoples, races, and religions, and it is only, because Hitler succeeded in wiping out 6 million Jews, that it became known predominantly as a Jewish case.
>
> As a matter of fact, Hitler wanted to commit G. against the Slavic peoples, in order to colonize the East, and to extend the German Empire up to the Ural mts. Thereupon after the completion of the successful war he would have turned to the West and to subtract from the French people the 20 million Frenchmen he promised in his conversation with Rauschning. Thus the German Empire would have reached from the Ural Mts. to the Atlantic Ocean. Nazi Germany embarked upon a gigantic plan to colonize Europe, and since there are no free spaces local populations had to be removed in order to make room for Germans. Nazi Germany did not have a fleet to protect overseas possessions. Moreover Germany had never good experiences in the past with overseas colonization. It was thus much simpler to colonize the European continent.

> Hitler's plan covered the Poles, the Serbs, the Russians, the Frenchmen. . . . The main purpose of the Nazis was a commission of a G. against nations in order to get hold of their territory for colonisation purposes. This was the case of the Poles, and the Russians and the Ukrainians.[98]

It is evident that Lemkin did not think that genocide was restricted to the Jewish case. The Nazi empire and its colonization plans were central to its genocidal policies. At the same time, he distinguished the treatment of Europeans Jews and Roma from that of Slavs and colonization.

> The case against the Jews and the Gypsies was not based upon colonisatery [*sic*] but upon racial considerations. . . . The case against the Jews and Gypsies was of a purely racial rather than emotional political nature. The race theory served the purpose of consolidating internally the German people. The Germans had to be shown that they are racially valuable Nordics. Their favorable racial classifications could be understood better by comparing them with those who were called and classified as vermin of the earth—the Jews and the Gypsies.[99]

Given this distinction—if we cannot explain the Holocaust of European Jewry and genocide of the Roma in colonial terms—do we reach a conceptual limit in the linking of colony, empire, and genocide? To answer this question, we need to consider these keywords more generally.

Empire, Imperialism, Colony, Colonization, Colonialism

The vocabulary of our subject comes from the Roman Empire. The historian Sallust is apparently the first to refer to the Roman state as *Imperium* in the first century BCE. Settlements of soldiers on territory it conquered were called *colonia*. As noted already, empire and colonization have been associated with global European domination. With characteristic Eurocentrism, F. A. Kirkpatrick wrote a century ago that "the story of empire, of dominion over rich and populous cultures, apart from any considerable European emigration, deals chiefly with the commercial and political conquest of India and other Asiatic lands by Europeans; the study of colonization deals mainly with the migration of Europeans into the New World."[100] This view may also suit anti-Orientalists for whom Europe is the root of all evil, but the fact is that empires of one type or another have dominated the political organization of humanity for thousands of years:[101] from the Nuba in North Africa, Assyrians in the Middle East, Manchus in China, and Zulus in Africa, to the tribute systems of Mesoamerica, Mongols of Central Asia, Mughals in India, Safavids in Iran, and multinational land empires of the Ottomans, Habsburgs, and Romanovs, not to mention the "blue water" modern empires of Great Britain, France, Belgium, and Germany. Not that Western empires wanted to admit they had acquired territory by violent conquest. That is what rivals did.[102]

Can we conceptually clarify terms so laden with ideological and historical baggage? Are they irredeemably contaminated with political connotations? Careful differentiation is necessary. There is consensus that empire means the domination of one society by another, usually backed by military force. Imperialism is a process and set of policies to acquire such domination whether by annexation or through less formal means.[103] The imperial relationship to colonies has historical precedents. Empires customarily engaged in settlement and resettlement, colonizing frontier regions with loyal subjects. Russian monarchs, for example, encouraged Germans to settle in the Lower Volga in the eighteenth century because their serfs were immobile. By 1914, 1.7 million ethnic Germans lived in east-central Europe, vulnerable to Russian paranoia about their loyalties in the looming war with Germany.[104] Nonetheless, settlement does not necessarily imply colonization. The German settlements were not colonies of imperial Germany. Neither were the early Phoenician settlement colonies in this sense, nor English Puritans in North America, because they were autonomous migrations rather than outposts of a metropolitan center.

Agreement breaks down when colonialism is added to the mix. How does it relate to the other keywords? If Edward Said thought "imperialism was the theory, colonialism the practice of changing the uselessly unoccupied territories of the world into useful new versions of the European metropolitan society," others simply equated the two.[105] Another viewpoint sees the relationship reversed: "Imperialism is a special case of colonialism where there are colonies tied together into one political structure."[106] Still another group of scholars distinguish colonialism from imperialism by insisting that the former entails colonization—the permanent migration of settlers to new territories—whereas the latter does not.[107]

The problem with these articulations of the relationship between the terms is that they omit consideration of colonial rule. Empire can exist without colonization or colonialism. Thus Ottoman rule in Egypt was not colonial because of the large measure of local self-administration and absence of permanent settlers. India was not an English colony for similar reasons. In practice, the sovereignty of empires was not as absolute as supposed by theories of empire.[108] Colonialism, by contrast, is a specific form of rule, and as a process supplements colonization. It means the occupation of societies on terms that robs them of their "historical line of development" and that transforms them "according to the needs and interests of the colonial rulers."[109] Colonial rule can radically alter the structure of, even dismember, an indigenous society.

The distinction between colonization and colonialism is apparent in the difference between two related concepts, internal colonization and internal colonialism. The former is the settlement of peoples, usually in frontier areas, loyal to the metropole to ensure security and encourage economic development of semi- or unoccupied land within a national or imperial territory. The resettlement of Muslim Slavs from former Ottoman territory in the Balkans to the core territories of the empire in the leadup to the First World War, as described by Donald Bloxham in this volume, represents a version of internal colonization.[110] By contrast, the concept of internal colonialism, which originated with Lenin, first meant the Russian metropole's economic exploitation of the periphery, that is, of the country by the towns. The sociologist Alvin Gouldner thought that Stalinism embodied this capitalist economic formation in a socialist context: "Here, internal colonialism refers to the use of the state power by one section of society (the Control Center) to impose unfavorable rates of exchange on another part of the same society (e.g., the Subordinate Remotes), each being ecologically differentiated from the other. The control center governs by using the state to impose unequal exchange. . . . Where these routine mechanisms fail, the control center uses force and violence against the remote subordinates."[111] In the 1970s in particular, Marxist scholars employed the concept of internal colonialism to explain the underdevelopment of certain geographical regions. Drawing on Immanuel Wallerstein's distinction between core and periphery, they were interested in mapping the congruence between cultural and economic divisions of labor.[112]

The turn to cultural history in subsequent decades has seen scholars focus on other dimensions of internal colonialism. It is said to represent the "civilizing project" advanced by the center and its dominant ethnicity over other peoples in remote areas, which contrasts with the usual combination of military conquest and cultural pluralism of the Mesoamerican empires, for instance.[113] Nation building in France in the nineteenth century could be seen under this aspect.[114] Recent research in Chinese history has combined this new approach with a focus on biopolitics, namely the efforts of the state to categorize and map the social class, gender, ethnicity, and nationality of a region in order to better govern peoples and establish borders—indeed, to constitute the nascent nation in the first place.[115]

The nature of colonial rule is significant because governance and cultural autonomy are central to the question of genocide. In light of Lemkin's elaborate techniques of genocide, the proposition can be ventured that the greater the intensity of colonial rule, the greater the likelihood that it is genocidal. As Dominik Schaller shows in this volume, German colonialism in Africa is of particular interest to scholars precisely because its relative lateness meant that the state was intimately involved in creating highly authoritarian and racially segregated societies. German immigrants ruled over deracinated Africans whose political, cultural, and economic independence had been smashed in order to transform them into a helot class of workers for German agriculture.[116]

Lemkin himself identified this kind of direct rule as genocidal. But what about other modalities of colonialism? As might be expected, the demographic question is uppermost in the minds of indigenous leaders and intellectuals. In 1978, Aimé Césaire condemned the French encouragement of emigration to the West Indies as "genocide through substitution."[117] The fact is that disease most likely accounted for the vast majority of indigenous deaths as much as immigration issued in the growth of European populations around the world. One historian likened this astonishing population substitution to a "demographic takeover." This phenomenon occurred in colonies—North America, South America, Australia, and New Zealand—that were less densely populated than Asia and Africa, and where diseases threatened locals rather than the colonists.[118] Even if this population decimation was not solely attributable to "natural causes" (indigenous populations were most vulnerable to disease when they were experiencing dislocation due to colonization and colonial rule), it is hard to make the case that disease was deliberately spread in most cases.[119] Unfortunately, Lemkin hardly reflected on the question of disease in colonial situations.[120]

These societies of "demographic takeover" did not just succeed because of passive population substitution, however. Well before state-led "scientific" colonialism, settlers and pastoralists managed to destroy indigenous societies by other less systematic means. "The destruction of nomadic societies, and their succession by relatively prosperous settler societies," Donald Denoon observed, "has occurred in temperate North America as well as temperate South America, in Siberia as well as Australia and southern Africa."[121] Here was a continuation of the transformation, since the early modern period, of pastoral societies displacing nomadic ones on the Eurasian continent. Denoon holds this displacement to be inevitable. "The coexistence of commercial farming and nomadism was impossible everywhere in the long run." Arguing along similar lines, Patrick Wolfe holds that settlers' interest in the land rather than labor of the nomads means that a logic of elimination characterizes settler colonialism: the nomads' connections to the land needed to be vitiated by their absorption into or expulsion from the new society.[122]

Conflict between "steppe and sown" had not been a zero-sum game in medieval central Asia. Although contemporaries regarded the Khazars, Pecenegs, and Western Oguz as aggressors, such mobile societies did not in fact seek to despoil sedentary ones, because they were needed for trade. The limitations of the nomadic economy, based on herds of stock, meant that luxury and other goods had to be extracted from agricultural societies—whether by "trade or raid"—with which they lived in tense symbiosis.[123] This coexistence was possible because the interrelations were not colonial.

Wolfe's pattern certainly holds true when a "middle ground" became a colony. For instance, in British Columbia, approximately symmetrical relations of trade between British and Indians obtained until the 1850s, when it became a formal colony and land acquisition was the central determinant of interaction. The customary pattern of events unfolded. The British military tried to keep the peace, but imperatives for local rule and economizing in London meant that land policies were ultimately decided by settler politicians. They enclosed common land and legislated exclusive property rights over multiple usage so as to ensure that investments could be made good.[124] Indians could resist by moving, submitting petitions, and not cooperating with the new dispensation, but state and settler violence underwrote the eventual victory of the British social system.[125]

This victory was not always total. Indigenous agricultural communities were better able to resist settlers than nomads, often serving as a source of labor. Not all Indigenes "disappeared."[126] Indeed, the story is anything other than genocidal in many colonial contexts. Where was genocide in plantation and trading colonies: for instance, in the British occupation of Singapore (1819), the Falkland Islands (1833), Aden (1839), Hong Kong (1842), and Lagos (1861)?[127] The distinction between types of imperial rule was made well by Alexis de Tocqueville: "There are two ways to conquer a country; the first is to subordinate the inhabitants and govern them directly or indirectly. That is the English system in India. The second is to replace the former inhabitants with the conquering race. This is what Europeans have almost always done. The Romans, in general, did both. They seized the country's government, and in several parts of it they founded colonies that were nothing other than far-flung little Roman societies." He recommend a combination of the two approaches in Algeria: domination of the interior so the coast could be settled.[128] As we shall see, it is not only cases of settler colonialism that are potentially genocidal.

Genocide and "Savage Wars of Peace"

Colonial and imperial wars are not usually considered genocidal. Once regions are "pacified"—that is, armed resistance is broken—the occupiers settle down to the business of governing. This rather benign view of such conflicts precludes the question of genocide by equating it with the Holocaust of European Jewry: where no death camps can be found, genocide cannot be said to have occurred. Leaving aside the issue of whether the

Holocaust unfolded in the clockwork fashion entertained in popular consciousness, and whether it can be understood apart from the Nazi imperial and colonial project in Europe, colonial conquest and warfare possess a number of potentially genocidal dimensions. In the first place, the aim of the colonizer was not just to defeat military forces but also to annex territory and rule over a foreign people. War aims were not limited, as they customarily were in intra-European wars; they were absolute. "Colonial conquerors came to stay." Second, the colonizer often ended up waging war against the entire population because it was difficult to distinguish between civilians and combatants, especially when guerilla-style resistance ensued. The often flat political structures of indigenous peoples meant that the colonizer could not easily identify leaders and "decapitate" the local polity.[129] Colonial war could mean total war on a local scale.

In the main, imperial troops prevailed over numerically superior opponents because they were regularly paid, well supplied, and trained. The ability to concentrate forces at one point was more decisive than technological superiority alone, especially if indigenous agents could be conscripted, such as the Native Mounted Police in colonial Queensland.[130] Such asymmetry did not always obtain, however. Consider the case of the Karifuna in the Antilles in the seventeenth century. The Spanish had smashed indigenous resistance by the middle of the seventeenth century and enslaved the inhabitants in agriculture and mining, but they were followed by French and English colonists on neighboring islands who wanted the land and to continue the slave economy. Difficulties in subduing the Karifuna on Antigua resulted in dozens of English deaths in the 1620s and 1630s, which led to a joint French and English effort on St. Kitts to kill and drive off as many of the natives as possible. Their survival and mingling with escaped African slaves led to calls in the 1670s for the extermination of the "Carib Indians." But the apathy of plantation owners and divisions between French and British authorities meant that such rhetoric remained hollow. Only the eventual hegemony of the British by the late eighteenth century enabled the roundup and depositing of the survivors on an inhospitable island off Honduras, where a third of them starved within four months.[131]

Equally difficult to subdue were the Indians of the Argentine frontier in the nineteenth century. Their experience demonstrates not only the tenacity of indigenous resistance, but also that neat models of invasion/resistance cannot capture the complexity of the colonial encounter. Well-armed and excellent horsemen, Indians prospered in the pampa, where their mobile lifestyle rendered them less vulnerable to the disease that devastated those who attempted agriculture. Roaming Spanish patrols made little inroads into the region in the early eighteenth century, so the imperial authorities were forced to ally themselves with certain tribes against others. Tribute was paid to some of them for peace and information. A "middle ground" was achieved at this point with rough parity between different groups. The Roman model of settling soldiers on the frontier failed in the face of resistance by ranchers and plutocratic governments loathe to give away land. Domestic Argentine imperatives in the 1830s led to the demand for more grazing land and a military solution, but 50 percent of the badly paid and trained soldiers and militia were casualties of frontier service. By the 1850s, alternative policies to propitiate Indians by granting them land allotments had also failed, with Indians driving off ranchers and settlers. Other efforts in the 1870s to integrate Indians into frontier society by winning them from their raiding/tribute economy also failed. Anxious about the interests of neighboring Chile in the region, a hardline military solution was suggested in 1875 by Julio A. Roca, chief of frontier forces. "In my judgment, the best system to finish the Indians, that is, exterminating them or removing them beyond the Rio Negro, is an offensive war," by which he meant lightning strikes by mobile forces. With the telegraph, railroad, and better-armed troops, his offensives in 1878 were successful. Thousands were killed, with survivors driven to Chile. Missions were built in the place of destroyed villages.[132]

Imperial thinkers devoted considerable thought to the problem of "small wars," with their pattern of conquest followed by resistance. Although they advised against exasperating the conquered population, the destruction of villages and crops was countenanced if necessary. Certainly French and Russian authorities were happy to indulge in such scorched-earth tactics in their respective North African and Caucasian conquests during and after the 1830s.[133] Alexis de Tocqeville's liberal scruples were not shared by many French in Algeria, as he reported in 1833. On one view,

> to subjugate the Arabs, we should fight them with the utmost violence and in the Turkish manner, that is to say, by killing everything we meet. I have heard this view supported by officers who took it to the point of bitterly regretting that we have started to take prisoners in some places, and many assured me that they encouraged their soldiers to spare no one. For my part, I returned from Africa with the distressing notion that we are now fighting far more barbarously than the Arabs themselves. For the present, it is on their side that one meets with civilization.

At the same time, he regarded burning harvests, emptying silos, and interning civilians as "unfortunate necessities, but ones to which any people that wants to wage war on the Arabs is obliged to submit." The reason was because war was being waged on populations, not governments.[134]

Indeed, such tactics were a feature of imperial rule generally. In 133 BCE the Romans destroyed Numantia on the Iberian Peninsula for defying

Roman rule, as they had Carthage thirteen years earlier. Even the late sieges and subsequent destruction of Jerusalem between 70 and 136 CE can be seen in this light. In the euphemistically termed "Harrying of the North," William I ("the Conqueror"), who invaded England in 1066, put down serious Saxon resistance around Yorkshire by destroying all villages and livestock between York and Durham, causing famine and the starvation of up to one hundred thousand people. The aim was to destroy the local society so that it could not provide sustenance to rebels, who hid in marshes and forests, and so that it could not serve as a base for future Danish attack. The country was largely uninhabited for a century thereafter.[135] Continuing the tradition of vicious reprisals, the Elizabethan conquest and colonization of Ireland, which was contemporaneous with significant contact of Englishmen with Native Americans in the sixteenth century, saw the slaughter of men, women, and children where English conquest was resisted. The women and children were considered fair game because they sustained the men, and because the Irish were regarded as pagan.[136] The violent Cromwellian quelling of Catholic uprisings in Ireland in the next century, such as the massacre of Drogheda in 1649, followed the same logics, as did the Spanish counterinsurgency against the Yucatec Mayan uprising of 1761.[137] This pattern was repeated in the Anglo-Zulu war in 1879, when British forces used scorched-earth tactics and massacred wounded fighters and prisoners in their desperate efforts to put down Zulu resistance to imperial rule.[138]

Likely, no power surpassed the Mongols in the extent and violence of their reprisals. Chinggis Khan was pitiless towards disloyalty, exterminating the Merkit in 1217 for attacks on his forces years before. Although they were more interested in booty than conquest, the Mongols were prepared to launch bloody war where sedentary peoples would not hand over their goods. Cities that resisted were razed, and devastated regions took generations to recover. Samarkand was reduced in population by 75 percent in the first decades of the thirteenth century. When Chinggis died in 1227, the mourning army slaughtered the entire population of Zhongxing city.[139] All these cases would be considered genocide under international law today.[140]

Imperial and national elites were constantly worried about security on their peripheries.[141] In 1914, the imperial Russian army deported up to one million Jews living in its western borderlands because they were suspected of disloyalty and potential espionage for the Germans.[142] Between 1935 and 1938, similar paranoia led Soviet authorities to deport nine nationalities away from sensitive border areas. During the Second World War, they violently deported Chechen and Ingush people of the North Caucasus, some of whose number had allegedly collaborated with the invading Germans. In the early 1930s, the famine in the Ukraine had been precipitated by anxieties that it might secede from the union.[143]

The security syndrome led to mass deaths in violent counterinsurgency. The contemporaneous Italian subjugation of Cyranaica in Libya resulted in the deaths of over 6,000 local fighters and the internment in camps of some 76,000 people, about half the total population.[144] In 1952, British authorities in colonial Kenya interned hundreds of thousands of supposed insurgents, killed up to 20,000 in combat, hanged over 1,000, and tortured many others. One historian claims up to 100,000 Mau Mau insurgents died in the camps.[145] Much of the murderous radicalization of the Pol Pot regime in mid-1978 was driven by regime paranoia about rebellious eastern border cadres and other Cambodians thought to be tainted by Vietnamese influence. The Cham nationality, which was targeted for destruction, was likewise considered "rebellious."[146]

The common motivation for deporting or destroying subnational groups is the accusation that they are rebellious, supporting rebellions, or cooperating with enemies across borders, such as the Ottoman Armenians in 1915.[147] The genocide in Darfur is also a counterinsurgency unfolding according to this pattern.[148] What these cases show is that real or imagined resistance to imperial or national rule can radicalize a policy of conquest or "pacification." Resistance leads to reprisals and counterinsurgency that can be genocidal when they are designed to ensure that never again would such resistance occur.[149] In the words of one scholar, such practices possess a "strategic logic" that can culminate in "final solutions."[150]

Subaltern Genocide

If security anxieties have led to genocidal measures of military coercion, another policy option has been to colonize one's own borderlands. Imperial Germany's concerns about Polish population growth within its eastern border led to various schemes to counter "Polonization" with "Germanization," including the purchase of Polish-owned estates and their distribution to German peasant colonists. The sociologist Max Weber was one of many who advocated such measures.[151] The Sri Lankan government engaged in rural colonization schemes to displace Tamils.[152] The government of the Dominican Republic tried to counter the "pacific invasion" of Haitians by "colonizing" the border areas with Dominican peasants in the first decades of the twentieth century.[153]

What these examples show is that the perception of being colonized by outsiders leads to colonization projects of one's own. As might be expected, such perceptions are highly subjective. Thus nationalist Czechs in the first half of the twentieth century regarded Germans who had lived in Bohemia and Moravia for hundreds of years as colonists, while German nationalists regarded those Germans as a beleaguered minority subject to an oppressive colonial rule.[154] Ukrainian nationalists saw themselves as subject to Polish colonial rule in the eastern borderlands of the interwar Polish state. Poles settled those expelled by the Ukrainians on their western border with Germany in order to colonize that vulnerable region. Ukrainians redistributed the lands of "former Polish colonists" to their compatriots.[155] In Rwanda, Hutus regarded themselves as indigenous and Tutsis as colonists from North Africa.

These points lead to broader questions: Can the founding of empires can be linked to the experience of a society's having been colonized and subjected to imperial conquest and rule? Are empires created to ensure that never again is that society dominated by another? Does the impulse for empire—the desire for invulnerability—come from previous feelings of abjection: empire both as security and compensation for past humiliations? Does, in other words, empire have an indigenous origin?

The beginning of the Spanish Empire in the Americas in the late fifteenth century is a case in point. It came in the wake of the *reconquista*, the Christian reconquest, conducted under Papal aegis, of the Iberian peninsula from the Moors who had occupied the area since the eighth century. Christians were settled in reconquered land.[156] Some view the continuation of the *reconquista* in the Americas as the beginning of Europe's poisoned gift to the world: the catastrophe of the ethnically and ideologically homogeneous nation-state that replaced the multicultural utopia of Islamic rule in Spain, with its harmonious coexistence of the three monotheistic faiths.[157] It can also be seen as chain in the continuity of conquest, reconquest, and yet more conquest that has marked human group interaction for thousands of years.

A contemporaneous example is imperial Russia. The Mongol invasions of the thirteenth century were overthrown by the Muscovite princes in the later fifteenth century in a Russian *reconquista*.[158] Within one hundred years, the Tsars, who were centralizing control of their lands, began to conquer the Mongol successor states of Kazan, Astrakhan, and Sibir (later Siberia) on the southeastern boundary. Expansion into the Caucasus and central Asia, at times genocidal as Robert Geraci's chapter in this book shows, ensued in the eighteenth and nineteenth centuries.[159]

That indigenous people would resist colonization did not always seem obvious to Europeans, who thought their gift of civilization would or should make them welcome. In the wake of Palestinian Arab riots against Jewish settlement in 1920 and 1921, Vladimir Jabotinsky berated Labor Zionist leaders for believing their presence would be tolerated by the "natives":

> Every reader has some idea of the early history of other countries which have been settled. I suggest that he recall all known instances. If he should attempt to seek but one instance of a country settled with the consent of those born there he will not succeed. The inhabitants (no matter whether they are civilized or savages) have always put up a stubborn fight. Furthermore, how the settler acted had no effect whatsoever. The Spaniards who conquered Mexico and Peru, or our own ancestors in the days of Joshua ben Nun behaved, one might say, like plunderers. But those "great explorers," the English, Scots and Dutch who were the first real pioneers of North America were people possessed of a very high ethical standard; people who not only wished to leave the redskins at peace but could also pity a fly; people who in all sincerity and innocence believed that in those virgin forests and vast plains ample space was available for both the white and red man. But the native resisted both barbarian and civilized settler with the same degree of cruelty.[160]

Jabotinksy's mention of cruelty raises the issue of the ritualized excess that often characterized indigenous resistance to colonialism, especially in decolonization struggles. Certainly, racism and oppression by the Other are factors in generating murderous fantasies.[161] But racism and oppression do not account for the atrocities in indigenous revenge. The reason for the excess, I suggest, is that the genocidal impulse and national liberation impulse are effectively the same: to preserve the endangered genus or ethnos against an Other that supposedly threatens its existence. This is the origin of what we might call *subaltern genocide:* the destruction of the colonizer by the colonized.

Examples abound of anxieties that one's people will be extinguished or erased by demographic supplanting or mortally endangered by security threats. Thus in 1804, a Haitian slave revolt targeted the island's entire white population.[162] In 1937, fifteen thousand ethnic Haitians in border areas were slaughtered by Dominicans who thought they were endangering the nation.[163] Many Serbs (especially those in Bosnia and Kosovo), still traumatized by the genocidal experience of the Second World War, felt demographically threatened in the early 1990s because 25 percent of Serbs lived outside of Serbia; they wanted a state to defend their ethnicity. The paranoia exhibited by the Khmer Rouge in their self-understanding as liberators of the homeland from foreign influence demonstrates this point in a gruesome manner.[164] The genocidal violence perpetrated against civilians in the Balkans was so grotesque because they were not held to be innocent, but dangerous bearers of a nationality that vitiated the identity of the other.[165] What is more, the subaltern "millenarian rebellions" against exploitative colonial rule were directed against perceived foreign elements that were threatening the survival of the indigenous people—just as in classical cases of imperial genocide.[166]

The connection between genocidal fantasies and national liberation movements has been made by anti-imperial thinkers who have blamed subaltern genocide on imperialism. Writing of the so-called Indian Mutiny, Karl Marx thought the "infamous" conduct of the "sepoys" was "only the reflex, in a concentrated form, of England's own conduct in India, not only during the epoch of the foundation of her Eastern Empire, but even during the last ten years of a long-settled rule. . . . There is something in human history like retribution; and it is a rule of historical retribution that its instruments be forged not by the offended, but by the offender himself."[167] Writing in the same vein, Jean-Paul Sartre noted that "In Algeria and Angola, Europeans are massacred at sight; it is the moment of the boomerang; it is the third stage of violence; it comes back on us, it strikes us, and we do not realize any more than we did the other times that it's we who have launched it."[168] Fanon agreed: "The violence of the colonial regime and the counter-violence of the native balance each other and respond to each other in an extraordinary reciprocal homogeneity."[169] The Tunisian Jew Albert Memmi was also attracted to the Marxist proposition that colonialism produced its own negation by bringing forth an utterly alienated colonized population whose only prospect of dignified life was the "complete liquidation of colonization."[170]

If an alienated "native" issued from colonialism, how was this alienation generated? These Francophone anticolonial thinkers in particular pointed out that the foundational binary between settler and native was a colonial product. In such a "Manichean world" (Fanon) of colonialism, in which the settler cast the native as the incarnation of absolute evil, the native had to invert this value hierarchy for his or her own self-respect. "Colonialism creates the patriotism of the colonized," wrote Sartre.[171] Memmi explained the source of this nativism in his famous book from 1957, *The Colonizer and the Colonized*. His basic message was also that "being considered and treated apart by colonialist racism, the colonized ends up accepting this Manichaean division of the colony and, by extension, of the whole world." Consequently, "in the eyes of the colonized, all Europeans in the colonies are *de facto* colonizers."[172]

What is more, the practical impossibility of assimilation—because of the colonizer's refusal and because of the self-denial entailed—meant that the native inevitably resorted to traditional values as a compensatory orientation. But these values, usually familial and religious, had become petrified by colonial pressure, and did not promote social progress. Nativism was reactionary. By ontologizing collectives in the same way as the settler, and "condemning each individual of that group," the colonized became "a xenophobe and racist."[173]

Sartre and Memmi did not applaud the chauvinism and racism of anticolonialist struggles, and Fanon's aversion to nativism is well known.

Racism and "a legitimate desire for revenge" could not "sustain a war of liberation," he thought. Memmi eventually left Tunis for Paris because, as a Jew, he found life impossible in postcolonial Muslim Tunisia.[174] As Marxists, they were cosmopolitan internationalists who preferred a popular front of anticolonialists that included sympathetic settlers, some closer to the liberation ideal than the Africans or Arabs. National liberation entailed transcending the terms of settler/native to create a new socialist nation of equal citizens. The colonial system needed to be transformed by expropriating the collaborating indigenous bourgeoisie, rather than simply expelling settlers.[175] They wished decolonization to be the assertion of freedom when the newly constituted people could gain political agency, enter history, and create its own authentic civilization, not just a variation of the colonizer's.[176]

At the same time, these writers told their European reading publics that their expectation of a nonviolent, nonracist, anticolonialist struggle was unrealistic.[177] Violent and racist anticolonialism was a predictable phase through which colonized peoples had to pass, even if it entailed "tragic mishaps."[178] Fanon himself was ambivalent, famously praising this violence as a "cleansing force" through which "the native frees himself from his inferiority complex and from his despair and inaction; it makes him fearless and restores his self-respect." This redemptive nationalism was necessary to assert the new postcolonial national culture: "the most elementary, most savage, and the most undifferentiated nationalism is the most fervent and efficient means of defending national culture."[179] Sartre supported Fanon's rendition of the struggle with some stirring quotations: the struggle's "irrepressible violence is neither sound and fury, nor the resurrection of savage instincts, nor even the effect of resentment: it is man recreating himself."[180] For all the romanticization evident here, these thinkers both expressed and explained the revolutionary violence of the colonized as the moment of salvation. It is genocidal in character.

Even by the time he died prematurely in 1961, Fanon was aware that, far from being a transitional political emotion, racism was being used by the "national bourgeoisie" to secure its own position in the postcolonial order. Rather than constructing a new nation beyond race, these elites were allowing precolonial tribal rivalries to recur.[181] Moreover, the new state appeared to the liberated populations less as their own democratic creation than as a distant apparatus that was milked by a dominant, rival ethnic grouping for its own benefit. Their security and identity was therefore more likely to inhere in pre-independence traditional ethnic attachments than in a chimerical supratribal national identity.[182] The catastrophe of postcolonial African political stability, civil war, and genocide has been blamed on this failure to transcend race during and after decolonization. Writing in the tradition of the Francophone intellectuals, the historian Mahmood Mamdani has blamed this failure on colonialism: "That greater crime was to politicize indigeneity, first as a settler libel against the native, and then as a native self-assertion."[183]

Colonialism, Subaltern Genocide, and National Socialism

Postcolonial chaos was not the only problem these thinkers blamed on European colonialism. They also held fascism in general, and National Socialism in particular, to be its poisoned fruit. Consistent with their Marxism, they saw colonialism as the apogee of capitalist exploitation. In a memorable phrase, Marx wrote of colonialism that "the profound hypocrisy and inherent barbarism of bourgeois civilization lies unveiled before our eyes, turning from its home, where it assumes respectable forms, to the colonies, where it goes naked."[184] Lenin had written of imperialism as the highest stage of capitalism, and Rosa Luxemburg continued this line of thinking, fearing "the triumph of imperialism" would mean "the destruction of all culture, and, as in ancient Rome, depopulation, desolation, degeneration, a vast cemetery." She is the source of the now well-known trope that Europe's criminal exploitation of the non-European world would be dialectically imported in heightened form into Europe itself: "It was clear to everyone, therefore, that the secret underhand war of each capitalist nation against every other, on the backs of Asiatic and African peoples must sooner or later lead to a general reckoning, that the wind that was sown in Africa and Asia would return to Europe as a terrific storm, the more certainly since increased armaments of the European states was the constant associate of these Asiatic and African occurrences. . . ."[185]

Of course, Luxemburg did not live to witness the Holocaust. It was the Francophone thinkers who applied the lesson to Nazism, regarding it as the culmination of both colonialism and capitalism. Nazism was intra-European colonialism.[186] In his famous *Discourse on Colonialism* of 1955, Césaire saw liberalism and capitalism as the essence of Nazism, which was less genocidal than exploitative and generally murderous. Writing fifteen years after the end of the Second World War, Fanon, who drew heavily on Césaire, connected colonialism, capitalism, and Nazism in the same way: "Deportations, massacres, forced labor, and slavery have been the main methods used by capitalism to increase its wealth, its gold or diamond reserves, and to establish its power. Not long ago, Nazism transformed the whole of Europe into a veritable colony."[187]

Fanon himself was ambivalent about who was the greater victim of this system, Jews or blacks—at one point likening the persecution and extermination of Jews to "little family quarrels" (among Europeans), at another proclaiming his indignation and empathy because he could not disassociate himself "from the future that is proposed for my [Jewish] brother."[188] Even the latter formulation is an undialectical equation of experiences that he may have learned from older, diasporic black intellectuals like Oliver Cox and W. E. B. Du Bois, who associated Nazism with slavery and white racism. Du Bois, for instance, wrote in *The World and Africa* in 1947 that "there was no Nazi atrocity—concentration camps, wholesale maiming and murder, defilement of women or ghastly blasphemy of children—which the Christian civilization of Europe had not long been practicing against coloured folks in all parts of the world in the name of and for the defense of a Superior Race born to rule the world."[189] This kind of thinking, while understandable in a context when Europeans still ruled most of Africa, and African Americans were being lynched, participates in the phallic logic of trauma competition mentioned above and is not particularly helpful for understanding complex historical processes.[190]

Despite such limitations, these thinkers warrant mention not only because they represent a subaltern intellectual tradition that continues to influence anti-imperialist writers today.[191] In its more sophisticated moments, this tradition provides important insights into the relation of modern genocides to broader processes and structures by positing a theory of system radicalization. Hannah Arendt drew on them in her *The Origins of Totalitarianism*, which is receiving growing attention in the literature on colonialism and genocide because one-third of her book deals with imperialism.[192] Consider Césaire's work, which echoes many of Arendt's key arguments regarding imperialism. Colonialism demoralized the colonizer, making a mockery of European humanism. In colonialism, capitalism produced its own negation in the form of a barbarized system that returned to its source to destroy Europe. Nazism was therefore not simply any colonialism, but "the supreme barbarism that sums up all the daily barbarisms." He also advanced a theory about the phenomenon that Arendt later called "the banality of evil." The greatest criminal was not the ideological fanatic, but the European bourgeois, "the 'decent fellow' across the way," because he tolerated colonial abuses for over a century: the wars, the torture, and mass death, approving the hard line measures of politicians.[193]

Arendt and Césaire did not have to infer the link between Nazism and imperialism. Hitler self-consciously placed his movement in the tradition of European imperialism:

> We have the so-called white race that since the collapse of Antiquity has over around 2,000 years taken on a leading position in the world. I cannot understand the economic dominance of the white race over the rest of the world unless

> I related it closely to a political dominance that the white race possesses naturally for hundreds of years and that it has projected outwards. Think of any area; consider India: England has not won India with justice and law but with regard for the desires, aspirations or laws of the natives, and it has when necessary maintained its dominance with the most brutal measures [*Rücksichtslosigkeit*]. Just as Cortez or Pizarro claimed Central America and the northern states of South America not on the grounds of some legal basis but out of the absolute, inherited feeling of dominance of the white race. The settlement of the north American continent succeeded just as little from some democratic or international conception of legal claims, but out of a sense of justice that is rooted only in the conviction of superiority and with that the right of the white race.[194]

Having exhausted the prospects of "domestic (*innere*) colonization," he thought, it was necessary to colonize Europe itself.[195]

Hitler drew on the imperial experiences of other European nations in formulating his vision of Nazi German imperialism. British India provided the model for German ambitions in Ukraine: a thin layer of military and civilian administrators could occupy a vast landmass and population.[196] North America was a model of settler colonialism. "There is only one duty—to Germanise the country by immigration of Germans and to look upon the natives as redskins."[197] These quotations (and others could be adduced) give clues to Hitler's imperial vision. He wanted both an extractive/tribute empire in the manner of the British in India, but also settler colonies like North America. In Hitler, the imperial models of centuries of human history crystallized into a single, total, imperial fantasy of genocidal conquest and exploitation.[198] Indeed, an increasing body of research is bearing out Lemkin's insight into the imperial and colonial nature of Nazi rule in Europe.[199]

But why the enthusiasm for conquest and colonial rule at all? As Maria Klotz has shown in her analysis of the film *Die Weltgeschichte als Kolonialgeschichte* of 1926, a film sponsored by colonial revisionist groups that lobbied for the return of Germany's empire, Europeans at the time plotted the course of world history in colonial terms. *Kulturvölker* enter history by conquering and colonizing other nations and peoples. The defining distinction between nations was that of colonizer or colonized. Only the former was a participant in world history, in progress, civilization, in uplift. Preventing colonization was tantamount to relegation to an object rather than subject of history, indeed a denial of the right to existence. An examination of Hitler's philosophy of history reveals that he thought very much in these terms. He was convinced that conquest drives world history and human progress, and he spoke often about how the German destruction of Jewry and Bolshevism would rescue western civilization for the good of humanity.[200]

But even if the Nazis established an empire and subjected conquered peoples to colonial rule, can the Holocaust of European Jewry be explained in terms of imperial and colonial logics? Lemkin himself did not think so, referring to race hatred of Jews and Roma as the motivating force of their persecution, which has been a feature of "intentionalist" explanations of the Holocaust for decades.[201] What if we take a transnational or global approach that situates the Holocaust in processes that are universal in imperial and colonial situations? There are four aspects to such an approach:

1. The Nazi genocidal policies against Slavic peoples in occupied Poland and Ukraine stood in the tradition of imperial conquests since antiquity. It was never the intention of the Nazis to exterminate Poles or Ukrainians in their entirety, just as it was not the intention of European colonial powers in Africa to exterminate the Africans and Asians they occupied. The "natives" were needed for labor, although it should not be forgotten that the Nazis envisaged the starvation of tens of millions of "superfluous" people in their plans for the region. During the contingencies of total war, however, as David Furber and Wendy Lower demonstrate in their chapter here, utopian plans of Slavic expulsion and German settlement had to be shelved in favor of food production and stability. The vicious partisan warfare that developed in occupied Eastern Europe stood in the continuity of colonial wars, as well.[202]

2. The extermination of Europeans Jews, by contrast, needs to be understood, to begin with, in terms of subaltern genocide. The Nazis regarded Germans as an indigenous people who had been colonized by Jews, principally from Poland, the perceived home of world Jewry. From the time of Jewish emancipation, anti-Semites in Germany (and not just in Germany) had complained of a "Judaization" of public life, a term equating "Jewish rule" with capitalist modernization and social liberalization. Typical was Wilhelm Marr, the inventor of the term "anti-Semitism," who in 1879 likened Jewish emancipation to the might of the Roman Empire. "With the entire force of its armies, the proud Roman Empire did not achieve that which Semitism has achieved in the West and particularly in Germany."[203] Hitler thought in these terms. A careful reading of *Mein Kampf* reveals that he thought Germany had been under foreign occupation—that is, Jewish domination—since the middle years of the First World War, when the war industry supposedly fell into Jewish hands. For Hitler, "the Jew robbed the entire nation and pressed it under his rule."[204] He was wont to speak of Jews in terms of colonists, mixing bacteriological and colonial metaphors: "Never was a State founded by peaceful economy, but always only by the instincts of preserving the species, no matter whether they are found in the field of heroic virtues or sly cunning; the one results then in Aryan states of work and culture, the other in Jewish colonies of parasites."[205]

The colonization trope is also a feature of the notorious 1940 Nazi propaganda film *Der Ewige Jude*. Jews are depicted as a people with "Asiatic and Negroid" elements that enter central Europe by parasitically attaching themselves to previous empires. Maps of the globe show their spread.

> Everywhere they made themselves unwelcome. In Spain and France the people rose openly against them in the thirteenth and fourteenth centuries, and they wandered on, mainly to Germany. From there they followed the path of the Aryan culture–creative Germans, colonizing the East—until they finally found a gigantic, untapped reservoir in the Polish and Russian sections of eastern Europe.

And from there the Jews colonized the world, that is, the African, American, and Australian continents.[206]

What is more, his perception that Jews were undermining German nationality is couched in terms strikingly similar to Lemkin's eight techniques of genocide. Jews undermined German morality through prostitution, its strength through pacifism, its national spirit via the cosmopolitan press, and so on. Writing in the early 1920s when Germany was in the grip of the inflation crisis and paying massive reparations, Hitler concluded that "the [Weimar] Republic is a slave colony of foreign countries and has no citizens, but at best subjects." The internal enemy serving foreign interests was "the Jew." This situation spelled the end for his beloved Germany: "Carthage's fall is the horrible picture of such a slow self-earned execution of a nation."[207]

The perception that Germany was occupied was widespread in the early Weimar years in particular, as African French troops were stationed in the Rhineland to enforce the reparations stipulations of the Versailles treaty. A hysterical and largely successful propaganda campaign, focused especially on alleged rapes by the troops, was waged by rightwing activists who accused the western powers of betraying the white race by using their non-European troops to occupy and suppress a *Kulturvolk*, the Germans. This occupation, combined with the sequestration of German colonies by the Treaty of Versailles and League of Nations, reinforced the German impression that they had been cast outside the privileged community of colonizers and had become the colonized. Four hundred of the so-called Rhineland Bastards, the offspring of African soldiers and German women, were sterilized under the Nazi regime.[208]

The relentless drive to exterminate the Jews entirely, then, is best explained in terms of the subaltern's racist nationalism. The Nazis thought of themselves as a national liberation movement, a self-consciousness that continued the German policy during the First World War of supposedly liberating central European nations from Russian domination. If the Nazis' anti-Semitism was "redemptive," its particular intensity at this historical conjuncture cannot be read from centuries of anti-Semitism, which had not resulted in genocide like this before.[209] In the Nazi mind, the Second World War was a war of national liberation, and redemption inhered in the elimination of foreign Jewish rule. Understanding this version of anti-Semitism in light of both the political emotions common in central European nationalisms since the nineteenth century, and later anticolonial movements allows us to contextualize the Holocaust in broader, transnational trends. The racist rage of the subaltern subject was not confined to the non-European world.

3. The uncompromising nature of the Jewish persecution by the Nazis cannot be understood solely in terms of subaltern genocide, however.[210] That persecution also shared elements of the security syndrome of other empires. Although it was a fantastical belief, the vehemence of the Nazi conviction that Jews and socialists were responsible for Germany's defeat in 1918 and subsequent civil chaos needs to be appreciated more fully. The racial hatred that congealed in the paranoia around "Judeo-Bolshevism" was all too real. But if Jews were the primary target in this syncretistic formulation rather than Bolsheviks, this racial hatred cannot solely be read from centuries-long traditions of popular anti-Semitism either. The hatred was directed towards an Other that was not only the threatening colonizer, but also, paradoxically, a deadly security threat in the manner of civil and colonial wars. The nationalist trauma of 1918 to 1920—the military defeat and communist uprisings in Germany—drove many Germans to extreme measures to ensure that, like in so many other genocides, never again would inner enemies undermine the nation and war effort.[211] In fact, in this instance, the genocide would *preempt* insurgency and red terrorism. *Einsatzgruppen* shot Jewish men as potential partisans in the summer of 1941, and this measure was expanded to women and children soon thereafter, a "prophylactic" measure that the Soviets also used to eliminate perceived "unreliable elements" before they could foment rebellion and betray the state.[212] Heinrich Himmler articulated the link between the murder of the Jews and preemptive counterinsurgency in his notorious Posen speech in 1944: "In our history this is an unwritten and never-to-be-written page of glory, for we know how difficult we would have made it for ourselves if today—amid the bombing raids, the hardships and the deprivations of war—*we still had the Jews in every city as secret saboteurs, agitators, and demagogues. If the Jews were still ensconced in the body of the German nation, we probably would have reached the 1916–17 stage by now.*"[213]

4. Finally, the Nazis also viewed the eastern Jews they encountered in Poland and the Ukraine in terms of the traditional colonial Other: dirty, lazy, stateless, uncivilized.[214] They were treated in the customary colonial

manner: labor, food, and security considerations combined to determine their fate. Once areas were conquered and secured, surviving Jewish men were put to work until they were no longer needed. Women and children were murdered immediately by German forces because they were held to be "useless eaters." Food shortages led German civilian authorities to mass execution of ghettoized Jews in Poland. The extent and consistency of this pattern of exploitation and murder is striking, contingencies and exceptions notwithstanding.[215]

Conclusion

The phobic consciousness responsible for this genocide continues to baffle historians because, in the main, they have confined their search to European sources.[216] The recent interest in colonial genocides, stimulated in part by the rediscovery of Hannah Arendt's writing on imperialism, goes some way to situating the Nazi project in global patterns. But the Holocaust was no colonial genocide in the common understanding of the term. It was an event, or multitude of events, that united four different, even contradictory imperial and colonial logics into one terrible paranoid mentality and praxis borne of a frustrated imperial nation struggling against a perceived colonizer.

Acknowledgment

My thanks go to Robert Aldrich, Donald Bloxham, Geoff Eley, Wendy Lower, Mark McKenna, Bernard Porter, Pia Solberg, Lorenzo Veracini, and Natasha Wheatley for helpful comments on drafts of this chapter.

Notes

1. Quoted in Melvin Richter, "Tocqueville on Algeria," *Review of Politics* 25, no. 3 (1963): 367.
2. Marcello Massenzio, "An Interview With Claude Levi-Strauss," *Current Anthropology* 42, no. 3 (2001): 419.
3. Richard Koebner and Helmut Dan Schmidt, *Imperialism: The Story and Significance of a Political Word, 1840–1960* (Cambridge, 1964); Philip D. Curtin, "Introduction: Imperialism as Intellectual History," in *Imperialism*, ed. Philip D. Curtin (London, 1971); Rupert Emerson, "Colonialism: Political Aspects," in *International Encyclopedia of*

the Social Sciences, ed. David L. Sills, 10 vols. (New York, 1968), 2:1; Hans Daalder, "Imperialism," in ibid., 7:101. Symptomatic is Robert Strausz-Hupe and Harry H. Hazard, eds., *The Idea of Colonialism* (New York, 1958).

4. F. A. Kirkpatrick, *Lectures on British Colonization and Empire* (London, 1906), 1.
5. Theodore Roosevelt, *The Winning of the West*, 4 vols. (New York and London, 1889), 1:6, 11–12.
6. George Henry Lane-Fox Pitt-Rivers, *The Clash of Culture and the Contact of Races* (London, 1927), 17. I thank Jon Lane from bringing this quotation to my attention.
7. Georges Balandier, "The Colonial Situation: A Theoretical Approach (1951)," in *Social Change: The Colonial Situation*, ed. Immanuel Wallerstein (New York, 1966), 34.
8. Frantz Fanon, *The Wretched of the Earth*, preface Jean-Paul Sartre, trans. Constance Farrington (New York, 1963), 313.
9. Enrique Dussel, *The Invention of the Americas: Eclipse of "The Other" and the Myth of Modernity*, trans. Michael D. Barber (New York, 1995).
10. This view characterizes writers in neoconservative journals like *New Criterion*.
11. Yves Santamaria, "Afrocommunism: Ethiopia, Angola, and Mozambique," in *The Black Book of Communism: Crimes, Terror, Repression*, ed. Stéphane Courtois et al. (Cambridge, MA, 1999), 683–704. Drawing a link between Nazism and Islamism in order to valorize American modernity is Paul Berman, *Terror and Liberalism* (New York, 2003).
12. Benny Morris and Ari Shavit, "Survival of the Fittest," *Ha'aretz*, 9 January 2004; Morris, *The Birth of the Palestinian Refugee Problem Revisited*, 2nd ed. (Cambridge, 2004).
13. Dror Mishani and Aurelia Smotriez, "What sort of Frenchmen are they?" *Ha'aretz*, 17 November 2005; Alain Finkielkraut, "J'assume," *Le Monde*, 26 November 2005: "The intention of the Enlightenment was ambiguous. This ambiguity must keep us from aligning colonialism in purely criminal company. To integrate men in the catholicity of the Enlightenment is something different than a will to extermination. That can have, here or there, positive effects." A study in this vein praising W. E. B. Du Bois for being one of the few African American leaders to recognize the primacy of Jewish suffering over black suffering is Harold Brackman, "'A Calamity Almost Beyond Comprehension': Nazi Anti-Semitism and the Holocaust in the Thought of W. E. B Du Bois," *American Jewish History* 88 (2000): 53–93. For an alternative approach that highlights mutual recognition rather than hierarchy, see Michael Rothberg, "W. E. B. Du Bois in Warsaw: Holocaust Memory and the Color Line, 1949–1952," *Yale Journal of Criticism* 14, no. 1 (2001): 169–89.
14. After the end of the Cold War, a discourse of empire has accompanied one on globalization in relation to North American ascendancy: Niall Ferguson, *Colossus: The Rise and Fall of the American Empire* (New York, 2004); Bernard Porter, *Empire and Superempire: Britain, America and the World* (New Haven, CT, 2006); Charles S. Maier, *Among Empires: American Ascendancy and its Predecessors* (Cambridge, MA, 2006); Pratap Bhanu Metha, "Empire and Moral Identity," *Ethics & International Affairs* 17, no. 2 (2003): 49–62; David Cannadine, "'Big Tent' Historiography: Transatlantic Obstacles and Opportunities in Writing the History of Empire," *Common Knowledge* 11, no. 3 (2005): 375–92; Linda Colley, "Some Difficulties of Empire—Past, Present and Future," *Common Knowledge* 11, no. 2 (2005): 198–214. A study influenced by Edward Said that claims the "post-9/11" world is structured by colonial logics is Derek Gregory, *The Colonial Present* (Oxford, 2004).
15. Victoria E. Bonnell, "The Uses of Theory, Concepts and Comparison in Historical Sociology," *Comparative Studies in Society and History* 22, no. 2 (1980): 156–73.

16. Jürgen Zimmerer, "Kolonialer Genozid? Vom Nutzen und Nachteil einer historischen Kategorie für eine Globalgeschichte des Völkermordes," in *Enteignet,Vertrieben, Ermordet: Beiträge zur Genozidforschung*, ed. Dominik J. Schaller et al. (Zürich, 2004), 109–29; Alison Palmer, "Colonial and Modern Genocide: Explanations and Categories," *Ethnic and Racial Studies* 21, no. 1 (1998): 89–115; Raymond Evans, "'Crime Without a Name: Colonialism and the Case for 'Indigenocide,'" in this volume.
17. For important studies, see Tony Barta, "Relations of Genocide: Land and Lives in the Colonization of Australia," in *Genocide and the Modern Age*, ed. Isidor Wallimann and Michael Dobkowski (Westport, CT, 1987), 237–52; Barta, "Discourses of Genocide in Germany and Australia: A Linked History," *Aboriginal History* 25 (2001): 37–56; Barta, "Mr. Darwin's Shooters: On Natural Selection and the Naturalizing of Genocide," *Patterns of Prejudice* 39, no. 2 (2005): 116–137; Norbert Finzsch, "'It is Scarcely Possible to Conceive that Human Beings Could be so Hideous and Loathsome': Discourses of Genocide in Eighteenth- and Nineteenth-Century America and Australia," ibid., 97–115; Jürgen Zimmerer and Joachim Zeller, eds., *Völkermord in Deutsch-Südwestafrika: Der Kolonialkrieg (1904–1908) in Namibia und seine Folgen* (Berlin, 2003); Ann Curthoys and John Docker, "Introduction–Genocide: Definitions, Questions, Settler Colonies," *Aboriginal History* 25 (2002): 1–15; A. Dirk Moses, ed., *Genocide and Settler Society: Frontier Violence and Stolen Indigenous Children in Australian History* (New York and Oxford, 2004); Moses, ed. (with Dan Stone), *Colonialism and Genocide* (London, 2007); Richard H. King and Dan Stone, eds., *Hannah Arendt and the Uses of History: Imperialism, Nation, Race, and Genocide* (Oxford and New York, 2007).
18. There is more detailed discussion in A. Dirk Moses, "The Holocaust and Genocide," in *The Historiography of the Holocaust*, ed. Dan Stone (Houndmills, UK, 2004), 533–55.
19. See Evans, "Crime Without a Name," 138, for this pithy formulation.
20. Symptomatic of this danger are Peter Balakian, *The Burning Tigris: The Armenian Genocide and America's Response* (New York, 2003), and Samantha Power, *"A Problem from Hell": America in the Age of Genocide* (New York, 2002).
21. Frederick Cooper, *Colonialism in Question: Theory, Knowledge, History* (Berkeley, CA, 2005).
22. For example, Niall Ferguson, *Empire: How Britain Made the Modern World* (London, 2004); David Cannadine, *Ornamentalism: How the British Saw their Empire* (London, 2002); Alan Lester, *Imperial Networks: Creating Identities in Nineteenth Century South Africa and Britain* (London and New York, 2001); Nicholas Thomas, *Colonialism's Culture: Anthropology, Travel, and Government* (Cambridge, 1994). Robert J.C. Young avers that his book assumes the subject position of the subaltern intellectual but the index does not contain the word genocide: *Postcolonialism: An Historical Introduction* (Oxford, 2001).
23. Chris Gosden, *Archaeology and Colonialism: Cultural Contact from 5000 BC to the Present* (Cambridge, 2004), 25.
24. Donald Bloxham, "The Armenian Genocide of 1915–1916: Cumulative Radicalization and the Development of a Destruction Policy," *Past and Present*, no. 181 (November 2003): 189.
25. An exemplary recent contribution is Mark Levene, *Genocide in the Age of the Nation State*, 2 vols. (London, 2005).
26. See the special issue of the *Journal of Genocide Research* 7, no. 4 (2005) devoted to Lemkin as historian. See also John Docker's chapter in this volume.
27. Raphael Lemkin, "War Against Genocide," *Christian Science Monitor*, 31 January 1948, 2.

28. "Genocide (the Newest Soviet Crime)," as discussed by Professor Raphael Lemkin and Joseph P. Burns, WHHC-TV College Roundtable, 30 January 1953. Jacob Rader Marcus Center of the American Jewish Archives, Collection 60, Box 4, Folder 2.
29. Lemkin, "War Against Genocide," 2.
30. The chapters remain in the archives. Most of Lemkin's papers are contained in three places: the Manuscripts and Archive Division of the New York Public Library (LCNYPL), 42nd Street, New York; The American Jewish Historical Society (AHJS), 15 West 16th Street, New York; and The Jacob Rader Marcus Center of the American Jewish Archives (JRMCAJA), 3101 Clifton Avenue, Cincinnati, Ohio. His chapter on Tasmania is now published: Raphael Lemkin, "Tasmania," *Patterns of Prejudice* 39, no. 2 (2005): 170–96; For commentary, see Ann Curthoys, "Raphael Lemkin's 'Tasmania': An Introduction," ibid., 162–69.
31. Lemkin, "War Against Genocide," 2.
32. Cultural genocide was perpetrated by forced conversion and the coercive use of the German language, Lemkin argued. The knights dominated the sparsely settled inhabitants economically and socially by colonizing the area with peasants and towns people. JRMCAJA, Collection 60, Box 7, Folder 14. See Roger Bartlett and Karen Schönwälder, eds., *The German Lands and Eastern Europe* (London, 1999).
33. Eg. Raphael Lemkin, "Charlemagne," American Jewish Historical Society, P-154, Box 8, Folder 6. On the Mongols: JRMCAJA, Collection 60, Box 7, Folder 6. Lemkin was very interested the Pan-German interest in colonizing Poland in the nineteenth century: JRMCAJA, Collection 60, Box 6, Folder 13.
34. Raphael Lemkin "Description of the Project," LCNYPL, Reel 3, Box 2, Folder 1.
35. Raphael Lemkin, "The Concept of Genocide in Sociology," LCNYPL, Box 2, Folder 2. Emphasis added.
36. Raphael Lemkin, *Axis Rule in Occupied Europe* (Washington, DC, 1944), 79. Emphasis added.
37. A good recent discussion of the genocide concept is Martin Shaw, *What is Genocide?* (Cambridge, 2007).
38. Andrew Fitzmaurice, "Anti-Colonialism in Western Political Thought: The Colonial Origins of the Concept of Genocide." Cf. Tzvetan Todorov, *The Conquest of America: The Question of the Other* (New York, 1984), 146–82.
39. Raphael Lemkin, "Spain Colonial Genocide," AJHS, P-154, Box 8, Folder 12. For analysis, see Michael A. McDonnell and A. Dirk Moses, "Raphael Lemkin as Historian of Genocide in the Americas," *Journal of Genocide Research* 7, no. 4 (2005): 501–29.
40. Lemkin, *Axis Rule*, 81.
41. Raphael Lemkin, "Proposal for Introduction to the Study of Genocide," LCNYPL, Reel 3, Box 2, Folder 1.
42. Alexis de Tocqueville, *Writings on Empire and Slavery*, ed. Jennifer Pitts (Baltimore, MD and London, 2001); Jennifer Pitts, "Empire and Democracy: Tocqueville and the Algeria Question," *Journal of Political Philosophy* 8, no. 3 (2000): 295–318; Cheryl B. Welch, "Colonial Violence and the Rhetoric of Evasion: Tocqueville on Algeria," *Political Theory* 31, no. 2 (2003): 235–64;
43. Jean-Paul Sartre, *Colonialism and Neo-Colonialism*, preface Robert C. Young, ed. Azzedine Haddour, Steve Brewer, and Terry McWilliams (London and New York, 2001); James McDougall, "Savage Wars: Codes of Violence in Algeria, 1830s–1990s," *Third World Quarterly* 26, no. 1 (2005): 117–31; "Row with France," *Dreiser Studies* (June 2006): 5.
44. Aimé Césaire, *Discourse on Colonialism*, trans. Joan Pinkham (New York, 1972 [1955]), 11.

45. Richard White, *The Middle Ground: Indians, Empires, and Republics in the Great Lakes Region, 1650–1815* (Cambridge, 1991).
46. Raphael Lemkin, "The Concept of Genocide in Anthropology," LCNYPL, Box 2, Folder 2. He cited Bronislaw Malinowski, *A Scientific Theory of Culture and Other Essays* (Chapel Hill, NC, 1944); Arthur Toynbee, *A Study of History* (London, 1947); Ruth Benedict, *Patterns of Culture* (London, 1935); Leo Louis Snyder, *Race: A History of Modern Ethnic Theories* (New York, 1939); Herbert Seligmann, *Race Against Man* (New York, 1939).
47. Césaire, *Discourse on Colonialism*, 17.
48. Lemkin, "The Concept of Genocide in Anthropology."
49. C.R. Whittaker, "The Western Phoenicians: Colonisation and Assimilation," *Proceedings of the Cambridge Philological Society* CC (1974): 77–78.
50. Paul T. Cocks, "The King and I: Bronislaw Malinowski, King Sobhuza II of Swaziland and the Vision of Culture Change in Africa," *History of the Human Sciences* 13, no. 4 (2000): 25–47.
51. For an analysis of the different strains of British anti-imperialism, see Bernard Porter, *Critics of Empire: British Radical Attitudes to Colonialism in Africa 1895–1914* (London, 1968).
52. Raphael Lemkin, "The Germans in Africa," JRMCAJA, Collection 60, Box 6, Folder 9. Lemkin's views were similar to those of the leftist critics of German colonialism in Imperial Germany. They did not oppose colonial rule per se, but its abuses. For such criticisms, see Helmut Walser Smith, "The Talk of Genocide, the Rhetoric of Miscegenation: Notes on Debates in the German Reichstag Concerning Southwest Africa, 1904–14," in *The Imperialist Imagination: German Colonialism and Its Legacy*, ed. Sara Friedrichsmeyer, Sara Lennox, and Susanne Zantorp (Ann Arbor, 1998), 107–23.
53. Memorandum from Raphael Lemkin to R. Kempner, 5 June 1946. United States Holocaust Memorial Museum, R. Kempner Papers (RS 71.001). My thanks to Jürgen Matthäus for drawing my attention to this document.
54. Raphael Lemkin, "The Concept of Genocide in Anthropology."
55. Ibid.
56. Raphael Lemkin, "Memorandum on the Genocide Convention," AHJS, P-154, Box 6, Folder 5. Representative of this misunderstanding is Helen Fein, *Genocide: A Sociological Perspective* (London, 1993), 9–11.
57. William A. Schabas, *Genocide in International Law: The Crime of Crimes* (Cambridge, 2000), 179–85.
58. McDonnell and Moses, "Raphael Lemkin as Historian of Genocide in the Americas."
59. Lemkin, "The Concept of Genocide in Anthropology."
60. Lemkin, *Axis Rule*, 80. Emphasis added.
61. Lemkin, "Memorandum on the Genocide Convention." I have corrected his spelling of "proceeded." Because attacks on cultural symbols were embedded in a general attack, "where cultural genocide appears to be merely a step towards physical extermination, there will certainly be no difficulty in distinguishing it from diffusion." Lemkin, "The Concept of Genocide in Anthropology."
62. Raphael Lemkin, *Raphael Lemkin's Thoughts on Nazi Genocide: Not Guilty?*, ed. Steven L. Jacobs (Lewiston, NY, 1990), 299, 303. See Robert Bevan, *The Destruction of Memory: Architecture at War* (London: 2006) for an argument highlighting the destruction of the buildings as a signpost for ethnic cleansing and genocide.
63. I am adopting Patrick Wolfe's term "total cultural practice" that he himself adapted from Marcel Maus, who wrote of "total social phenomena": Patrick Wolfe, "On Being

Woken Up: The Dream Time in Anthropology and in Australian Settler Culture," *Comparative Studies in Society and History* 33, no. 2 (1992): 198.

64. Raphael Lemkin, "The Concept of Genocide in Sociology," JRMCAJA, Collection 60, Box 6, Folder 13, 1.
65. Raphael Lemkin "Description of the Project," LCNYPL, Reel 3, Box 2, Folder 1.
66. This discussion of the eight techniques is taken from Lemkin, *Axis Rule*, 82–90. Lemkin was probably not thinking in terms of the "microphysics of colonial rule" that postcolonial historians have laid bare in their studies of the intimate spheres of colonialism. Cf. Ann Laura Stoler, *Carnal Knowledge and Imperial Power: Race and the Intimate in Colonial Rule* (Berkeley, CA, 2002).
67. Cited in Porter, *Critics of Empire*, 22. Cf. Elizabeth Elbourne, "The Sin of the Settler: The 1835–36 Select Committee on Aborigines and Debates Over Virtue and Conquest in Early Nineteenth-Century British White Settler Empire," *Journal of Colonialism and Colonial History* 4, no. 3 (2003).
68. Patrick Dodson, "Short-Term Fix Demeans Nation: We Have Proved Incapable of Confronting Our Past," *The Australian*, 26 May 2006. On Dodson, see Kevin Keeffe, *Paddy's Road: Life Stories of Patrick Dodson* (Canberra, 2003). The *Bringing them Home* report and various policies of "removing" mixed-descent indigenous Australian children from indigenous mothers are discussed in chapters by Robert Manne, Anna Haebich, and Russell McGregor in Moses, *Genocide and Settler Society.*
69. Robert van Krieken, "Rethinking Cultural Genocide: Aboriginal Child Removal and Settler-Colonial State Formation," *Oceania* 7, no. 2 (2005): 125–51. For an important study of French assimilation practices from the early modern period, see Saliha Belmessous, "Assimilation and Racialism in Seventeenth- and Eighteenth-Century French Colonial Policy," *American Historical Review* 110, no. 2 (2005): 322–49.
70. Raphael Lemkin, "Memorandum on the Genocide Convention," AHJS, P-154, Box 6, Folder 5. I have corrected Lemkin's spelling of "disapproved."
71. Raphael Lemkin, "Genocide as Crime under International Law," United Nations Bulletin 15 (January 1948): 71.
72. Matthew Lippman, "The Drafting of the 1948 Convention on the Prevention and Punishment of the Crime of Genocide," *Boston University International Law Journal* 3, no. 1 (1985): 45.
73. On that discourse, see Maximilian C. Forte, "Extinction: The Historical Trope of Anti-Indigeneity in the Caribbean," *Issues in Caribbean Amerindian Studies* 6, no. 4 (August 2004–August 2005); Patrick Brantlinger, *Dark Vanishings: Discourse on the Extinction of Primitive Races, 1800–1930* (Ithaca, NY, 2003); John W. Burton, "Disappearing Savages? Thoughts on the Construction of an Anthropological Conundrum," *Journal of African and African Studies* 34, no. 2 (1999): 199–209.
74. Ronald Robinson, "Non-European Foundations of European Imperialism: Sketch for a Theory of Collaboration," in *Studies in the Theory of Imperialism*, ed. Roger Owen and Bob Sutcliffe (London, 1972), 117–41; Geir Lundestad, "Empire by Invitation? The United States and Western Europe, 1945–1952," *Journal of Peace Research* 23, no. 3 (1986): 263–77.
75. Mahmood Mamdani, "Historicizing Power and Responses to Power: Indirect Rule and Its Reform," *Social Research* 66, no. 3 (1999): 859–86; Leroy Vail, "Introduction: Ethnicity in Southern African History," in *The Creation of Tribalism in Southern Africa*, ed. Leroy Vail (Berkeley, 1989), 1–19; C. S. L. Chachage, "British Rule and African Civilization in Tanganyika," *Journal of Historical Sociology* 1, no. 2 (1988): 199–223; Archie Mafeje, "The Ideology of 'Tribalism'," *Journal of Modern African Studies* 9, no. 2 (1971): 253–61; cf. Michael Crowder, "Indirect Rule: French

and British Style," *Africa: Journal of the International African Institute* 34, no. 3 (1964): 197–205.

76. Dominik J. Schaller, "Raphael Lemkin's View of European Colonial Rule in Africa: Between Condemnation and Admiration," *Journal of Genocide Research* 7, no. 4 (2005): 534; Tess Lea, Emma Kowal, and Gillian Cowlishaw, eds., *Moving Anthropology: Critical Indigenous Studies* (Darwin, 2006).
77. Frederic W. Gleach, *Powhatan's World and Colonial Virginia: A Conflict of Cultures* (Lincoln, Neb., 1997); Jean M. O'Brien, *Dispossession by Degrees: Indian Land and Identity in Natick, Massachusetts, 1650–1790* (Cambridge, 1997); Noenoe K. Silva, *Aloha Betrayed: Native Hawaiian Resistance to American Colonialism* (Durham, NC, 2004).
78. Memorandum from Raphael Lemkin to R. Kempner, 5 June 1946. United States Holocaust Memorial Museum, R. Kempner Papers (RS 71.001). I have corrected spelling and punctuation in this quotation.
79. Raphael Lemkin, "Yucatan," AJHS, P-154, Box 8, Folder 12. Emphasis added.
80. Lemkin, *Axis Rule*, 79; cf. Steven T. Katz, *The Holocaust in Historical Context* (Oxford, 1994).
81. Raphael Lemkin, "Incas," JRMCAJA, Collection 60, Box 7, Folder 7/1.
82. Lemkin, "Yucatan."
83. Ibid. On the theory of universal monarchy, see Anthony Pagden, *Lords of All the World: Ideologies of Empire in Spain, Britain, and France, c. 1500–1800* (New Haven, CT, 1995), chap. 2.
84. Raphael Lemkin, "Aztecs," AJHS, P-154, Box 8, Folder 12.
85. Lemkin, "Yucatan."
86. John Locke, *Two Treatises on Civil Government* (London, 1884), 196–97 [para. 2:11]. Emphasis added. For an analysis of the English reception of the Spanish debates on colonialism, see Andrew Fitzmaurice, *Humanism and America* (Cambridge, 2003).
87. Lemkin, "Aztecs." His research notes taken on Native North American conflicts and massacres begin with some kind of Indian uprising.
88. Lemkin, *Thoughts on Nazi Genocide*, 196–97.
89. See McDonnell and Moses, "Lemkin as Historian of Genocide in the Americas."
90. Richard Broome, *Aboriginal Victorians* (Sydney, 2005), 84.
91. Lemkin, "The Concept of Genocide in Sociology," 2.
92. Brantlinger, *Dark Vanishings*, 9.
93. I discuss the nature of this theodicy in A. Dirk Moses, "Conceptual Blockages and Definitional Dilemmas in the Racial Century: Genocide of Indigenous Peoples and the Holocaust," *Patterns of Prejudice* 36, no. 2 (2002): 7–36.
94. Quoted in Patrick Brantlinger, "Forgetting Genocide: or the Last of the Last of the Mohicans," *Cultural Studies* 12, no. 1 (1998): 19–20.
95. See the chapters in this volume of John Docker and Ann Curthoys for arguments that such acceptance of indigenous destruction is tantamount to genocide.
96. Mark Drumbl, "Prosecutor v Radislav Krstic: ICTY Authenticates Genocide at Srebrenica and Convicts for Aiding and Abetting," *Melbourne Journal of International Law* 5, no. 2 (2004): 434–50.
97. Césaire, *Discourse on Colonialism*, 21–22. Emphasis in the original.
98. Raphael Lemkin, "Hitler Case-Outline." Jacob Rader Marcus Center of the American Jewish Archives, Collection 60, Box 7, Folders 12 and 13. I have corrected spelling in this quotation. Thanks to Steven L. Jacobs and Dan Stone for furnishing me with a copy. For commentary, see Dan Stone, "Raphael Lemkin on the Holocaust," *Journal of Genocide Research* 7, no. 4 (2005): 539–50.

99. Lemkin, "Hitler Case-Outline."
100. Kirkpatrick, *British Colonization and Empire*, 5–6.
101. Anthony Pagden, *Peoples and Empires: Europeans and the Rest of the World from Antiquity to the Present* (London, 2001), 8–10.
102. Anthony Pagden, "Fellow Citizens and Imperial Subjects: Conquest and Sovereignty in Europe's Overseas Empires," *History and Theory* 44 (December 2005): 28–34; Peter C. Perdue, "Comparing Empires: Manchu Colonialism," *International History Review* 20, no. 2 (1998): 255–61.
103. See the lucid discussion in Ronald Grigor Suny, "The Empire Strikes Out: Imperial Russia, 'National' Identity, and Theories of Empire," in *A State of Nations: Empire and Nation-Making in the Age of Lenin and Stalin*, ed. Ronald Grigor Suny and Terry Martin (Oxford, 2001), 23–66; also Ross Hutchings, "Empire and the State: a Critical Theoretical Assessment," *Australian Journal of International Affairs* 60, no 3 (2006): 429–38. I leave aside the question of the reasons for imperialism expounded in Marxist theories.
104. James W. Long, *From Privileged to Dispossessed: The Volga Germans, 1860–1917* (Lincoln and London, 1988); Eric Lohr, *Nationalizing the Russian Empire: The Campaign against Enemy Aliens during World War I* (Cambridge, MA, 2003).
105. Edward Said, *The Question of Palestine* (New York, 1979), 78; Michael Doyle, *Empires* (Ithaca, NY, 1986), 31.
106. Gosden, *Archaeology and Colonialism*, 5. Cf. Young, *Postcolonialism*.
107. Ronald J. Horvath, "A Definition of Colonialism," *Current Anthropology* 13, no. 1 (1972): 45–51; Herbert Lüthy, "Colonization and the Making of Mankind," *Journal of Economic History* 21 (1961): 483–95.
108. Frederick Cooper, "Empire Multiplied: A Review Essay," *Comparative Studies in Society and History* 46, no. 2 (2004): 247.
109. Jürgen Osterhammel, *Colonialism: A Theoretical Introduction*, trans. Shelley L. Frisch (Princeton, NJ, 1997), 15. Cf. D.K Fieldhouse, who is far less critical of European colonial rule but comes close to this definition: Fieldhouse, *Colonialism 1870–1945: An Introduction* (London, 1983), 12–15.
110. Peter Calvert, "Internal Colonisation, Development and Environment," *Third World Quarterly* 22, no. 1 (2001): 51–63; Donald Bloxham, "Internal Colonization, Inter-Imperial Conflict, and the Armenian Genocide," in this volume.
111. Alvin W. Gouldner, "Stalinism: A Study in Internal Colonialism," *Telos*, no. 34 (1978): 5–48; David Goodman, "Guizhou and the People's Republic of China: The Development of an Internal Colony," in *Internal Colonialism: Essays around a Theme*, Monograph No. 3, Developing Areas Research Group, Institute of British Geographers, ed. David Drakakis-Smith and Stephen Wyn Williams (Edinburgh, 1983), 107–28
112. Michael Hechter, *Internal Colonialism: The Celtic Fringe in British National Development, 1536–1966* (London, 1975); Mervyn C. Hartwig, "Capitalism and Aborigines: The Theory of Internal Colonialism and its Rivals," in *Essays in the Political Economy of Australian Capitalism*, 4 vols., ed. Edward L. Wheelwright and Ken Buckley (Sydney, 1978), 3:119–41; *Ethnic and Racial Studies* 2, no. 3 (1979) special issue on internal colonialism; Colin W. Mettam and Stephen Wyn Williams, "Internal Colonialism and Cultural Divisions of Labour in the Soviet Republic of Estonia," *Nations and Nationalism* 4, no. 3 (1998): 363–88.
113. Steven Harrell, "Introduction: Civilizing Projects and the Reaction to Them," in *Cultural Encounters on China's Ethnic Frontier*, ed. Steven Harrell (Seattle and London, 1995).

114. Eugene Weber, *From Peasants to Frenchmen: The Modernization of Rural France, 1870–1914* (Palo Alto, CA, 1976), 485. Thanks to Lorenzo Veracini for drawing my attention to this reference.
115. Dru C. Gladney, *Dislocating China: Muslims, Minorities, and other Subaltern Subjects* (Chicago, 2004), 360–66; Laura Hostetler, *Qing Colonial Enterprise: Ethnography and Cartography in Early Modern China* (Chicago and London, 2001). Historians of China have been inspired by historians of colonialism: Emma Teng, *Taiwan's Imagined Geography: Chinese Colonial Travel Writing and Pictures, 1683–1895* (Cambridge, MA, 2004); James A. Millward, *Beyond the Pass: Economy, Ethnicity, and Empire in Qing Central Asia, 1759–1864* (Stanford, CA, 1998); Daniel McMahon, "Identity and Conflict on a Chinese Borderland: Yan Ruyi and the Recruitment of the Gelao During the 1795–97 Miao Revolt," *Late Imperial China* 23, no. 2 (2002): 53–86; Peter C. Perdue, "Empire and Nation in Comparative Perspective: Frontier Administration in Eighteenth-Century China," *Journal of Early Modern History* 5, no. 4 (2001): 282–304; Perdue, "Boundaries, Maps, and Movement: Chinese, Russian, and Mongolian Empires in Early Modern Central Eurasia," *International History Review* 20, no. 2 (1998): 263–86; Perdue, "Military Mobilization in Seventeenth and Eighteenth-Century China, Russia, and Mongolia," *Modern Asian Studies* 30, no. 4 (1996): 757–93.
116. Dominik Schaller, "From Conquest to Genocide: Colonial Rule in German Southwest Africa and German East Africa," in this volume.
117. Cited in Mireille Rosello, "The 'Césaire Effect', or How to Cultivate One's Nation," *Research in African Literatures* 32, no. 4 (2001): 86–87. See generally Robert Aldrich and John Connell, *France's Overseas Frontier* (Cambridge, 1992), 108.
118. Alfred Crosby, *Germs, Seeds, and Animals: Studies in Ecological History* (Armonk, NY, and London, 1994), 29–30.
119. A good critique of Crosby's fatalistic downplaying of human agency is Tom Griffiths, "Ecology and Empire: Towards an Australian History of the World," in *Ecology and Empire: Environmental History of Settler Societies*, ed. Tom Griffiths and Libby Robin (Melbourne, 1997), 2–3. See also McDonnell and Moses, "Lemkin as Historian of Genocide in the Americas," 519.
120. McDonnell and Moses, "Lemkin as Historian of Genocide in the Americas," 517–20.
121. Donald Denoon, *Settler Capitalism: The Dynamics of Dependant Development in the Southern Hemisphere* (Oxford, 1983), 1.
122. Ibid., 26. See Patrick Wolfe, "Structure and Event: Settler Colonialism, Time, and the Question of Genocide," in this volume. For literature on settler colonialism, see Andrew Armitage, *Comparing the Policy of Aboriginal Assimilation: Australia, Canada, and New Zealand* (Vancouver, 1995); Lynette Russell, ed., *Colonial Frontier: Indigenous-European Encounters in Settler Societies* (Manchester, 2001); Ronald Weitzer, *Transforming Settler States: Communal Conflict and Internal Security in Northern Ireland and Zimbabwe* (Berkeley, CA, 1990); Kate Darian-Smith, Liz Gunner and Sarah Nuttall, eds., *Text, Theory, Space: Land, Literature and History in South Africa and Australia* (London and New York, 1996); David Trigger and Gareth Griffiths, eds., *Disputed Territories: Land, Culture and Identity in Settler Societies* (Hong Kong, 2003); Tim Murray, *The Archaeology of Contact in Settler Societies* (Cambridge, 2004); Moses, *Genocide and Settler Society*.
123. Michael Adas, ed., *Agricultural and Pastoral Societies in Ancient and Classical History* (Philadelphia, 2001); Peter B. Golden, "Nomads and their Sedentary Neighbors in Pre-Cinggisid Eurasia," *Archivum Eurasiae Medii Aevi* 7 (1991): 41–81; Denis Sinor, "Inner Asian Warriors," *Journal of the American Oriental Society* 101, no. 2

(1981): 133–44; Nicola Di Cosmo, "Ancient Inner Asian Nomads: Their Economic Basis and its Significance in Chinese History," *Journal of Asian Studies* 52, no. 4 (1994): 1092–1126. My thanks to Fiona Kidd for these references. For a critique of agricultural societies, see Hugh Brody. *The Other Side of Eden. Hunter-Gatherers, Farmers, and the Shaping of the World* (London 2000).

124. Cf., Norbert Finzsch, "'The aborigines . . . were never annihilated, and still they are becoming extinct': Settler Imperialism and Genocide in Nineteenth Century America and Australia," in this volume; and John C. Weaver, *The Great Land Rush and the Making of the Modern World, 1650–1900* (Montreal and Kingston, 2003).

125. Cole Harris, "How Did Colonialism Dispossess Comments from an Edge of Empire," *Annals of the Association of American Geographers* 94, no. 1 (2004): 165–82. See also his *Making Native Space: Colonialism, Resistance, and Reserves in British Columbia* (Vancouver, 2002). Harris is influenced by Wolfe's concept of "logic of elimination," as are the editors of *Settler Colonialism in the Twentieth Century: Projects, Practices, Legacies*, ed. Caroline Elkins and Susan Pedersen (London, 2005). On Canada, Colin Samson, *A Way of Life that Does Not Exist: Canada and the Extinguishment of the Innu* (London, 2003). On colonial enclosures, Lance van Sittert, "Holding the Line: The Rural Enclosure Movement in the Cape Colony, 1865–1910," *Journal of African History* 43, no. 1 (2002): 95–118.

126. Denoon, *Settler Capitalism*, 27.

127. Timothy Parsons, *The British Imperial Century, 1815–1914: A World History Perspective* (Lanham, MD, 1999), 2.

128. De Tocqueville, *Writings on Empire and Slavery*, 61, 65.

129. H. L. Wesseling, "Colonial Wars: An Introduction," in *Imperialism and War: Essays on Colonial Wars in Asia and Africa*, ed. J. A. de Moor and H. L. Wesseling (Leiden, 1988), 3; Peter Paret, "Colonial Experience and European Military Reform at the End of the Eighteenth Century," in *Warfare and Empires*, ed. Douglas M. Peters (Aldershot, UK, 1997), 357–70.

130. Michael Howard, "Colonial Wars and European Wars," in de Moor and Wesseling, *Imperialism and War*, 218–23; George Raudzens, "Why did the Amerindian Defences Fail? Parallels in the European Invasions of Hispaniola, Virginia and Beyond," *War in History* 3, no. 3 (1996): 331–52; Luke Godwin, "The Fluid Frontier: Central Queensland, 1845–63," in *Colonial Frontiers: Indigenous-European Encounters in Settler Societies*, ed. Lynette Russell (Manchester, UK, 2001), 112.

131. Hilary Beckles, "The Genocide Policy in English-Karifuna Relations in the Seventeenth Century," in *Empire and Others: British Encounters with Indigenous Peoples, 1600–1850*, ed. Martin Daunton and Rick Halpern (London, 1999), 280–302. The Carib population of 8,000 fell to 630 by 1730, recovering to 900 by the mid-twentieth century. It comprised 1,136 in 1960 out of a total population of nearly 60,000, and nearly 2000 in 1978.

132. Richard W. Slatta, "'Civilization' Battles 'Barbarism': The Limits of Argentine Indian Frontier Struggle," in *The Military and Conflict between Cultures: Soldiers at the Interface*, ed. James C. Bradford (College Station, TX, 1997), 131–46.

133. C. E. Callwell, *Small Wars: A Tactical Textbook for Imperial Soldiers*, 3rd ed. (London, [1906] 1990), 26–27, 45, 145; Holquist, "To Count, to Extract, and to Exterminate."

134. De Tocqueville, *Writings on Empire and Slavery*, 70, 87.

135. Peter Rex, *The English Resistance: The Underground War against the Normans* (Stroud, UK, 2004), 87–105.

136. Nicholas P. Canny, "The Ideology of English Colonization: From Ireland to America," *William and Mary Quarterly*, 3rd series, 30, no. 4 (1973): 582–83.

137. Katie Kane, "Nits Make Lice: Drogheda, Sand Creek, and the Poetics of Colonial Extermination," *Cultural Critique*, no. 42 (1999): 81–103; Robert Path, "Culture, Community, and 'Rebellion' in the Yucatec Maya Uprising of 1791," in *Native Resistance and the Pax Colonial in New Spain*, ed. Susan Schroeder (Lincoln and London, 1998), 67–83.
138. Michael Lieven, "'Butchering the Brutes All Over the Place': Total War and Massacre in Zululand in 1879," *History* 84 (October 1999): 614–32.
139. David Christian, *A History of Russia, Central Asia, and Mongolia*, vol. 1, *Inner Eurasia from Prehistory to the Mongol Empire* (Oxford, 1998), 396–406.
140. For analyses of recent jurisprudence about genocidal intention and the question of how much of a group needs to be destroyed to constitute genocide, see Drumbl, "Prosecutor v Radislav Krstic"; and Cecile Aptel, "The Intent to Commit Genocide in the Case Law of the International Criminal Tribunal for Rwanda," *Criminal Law Forum* 13, no. 3 (2002), 273–91.
141. Michael Freeman, "Genocide, Civilization and Modernity," *British Journal of Sociology* 46, no. 2 (1995): 207–23.
142. Eric Lohr, "The Russian Army and the Jews: Mass Deportations, Hostages, and Violence during World War One," *Russian Review* 60, no. 2 (2001): 404–19.
143. Terry Martin, "The Origins of Soviet Ethnic Cleansing," *Journal of Modern History* 70 (December 1998): 813–861; N. F. Bugai and A. M. Gonov, "The Forced Evacuations of the Chechens and Ingush," *Russian Studies in History* 4, no. 2 (2002): 43–61; Nick Baron, "Stalinist Planning as Political Practice: Control and Repression on the Soviet Periphery, 1935–1938," *Europe-Asia Studies* 56, no. 3 (2004): 439–62.
144. John Gooch, "Re-Conquest and Suppression: Fascist Italy's Pacification of Libya and Ethiopia, 1922–39," *Journal of Strategic Studies* 28, no. 6 (2005): 1021; Nicola Labanca, "Colonial Rule, Colonial Repression and War Crimes in the Italian Colonies," *Journal of Modern Italian Studies* 9, no. 3 (2004): 300–13.
145. David Anderson, *Histories of the Hanged: Britain's Dirty War in Kenya and the End of Empire* (London, 2004); Caroline Elkins, *Britain's Gulag: The Brutal End of Empire in Kenya* (London, 2004).
146. Ben Kiernan, *The Pol Pot Regime: Race, Power, and Genocide in Cambodia under the Khmer Rouge, 1975–79* (New Haven, CT, 1996), 399, 428.
147. Donald Bloxham, *The Great Game of Genocide: Imperialism, Nationalism, and the Destruction of the Ottoman Armenians* (Oxford, 2005).
148. Alex de Waal, "Counter-Insurgency on the Cheap," *London Review of Books* 26, no. 15 (5 August 2004).
149. Benjamin A. Valentino, Paul Huth, and Dylan Balch-Lindsay, "'Draining the Sea': Mass Killing and Guerrilla Warfare," *International Organization* 58 (Spring 2004): 375–407. Thanks to Carter Johnson for supplying me with this reference.
150. Benjamin A. Valentino, *Final Solutions: Mass Killing and Genocide in the Twentieth Century* (Ithaca, NY, 2004).
151. William W. Hagen, *Germans, Poles, and Jews: The Nationality Conflict in the Prussian East, 1772–1914* (Chicago and London, 1980), 134–35; Wolgang J. Mommsen, *Max Weber and German Politics, 1890–1920* (Chicago, 1974), 26–28.
152. Chelvadurai Manogaran, "Space-Related Identity in Sri Lanka," in *Nested Identities: Nationalism, Territory and Scale*, ed. G.H. Herb and D.H. Kaplan (Lanham, MD, 1999), 199–216.
153. Richard Lee Turtis, "A World Destroyed, A Nation Imposed: The 1937 Haitian Massacre in the Dominican Republic," *Hispanic American Historical Review* 82, no. 3 (2002): 589–635.

154. Tara Zahra, "Looking East: East Central European 'Borderlands' in German History and Historiography," *History Compass* 3 (2005): 10; Eagle Glassheim, "National Mythologies and Ethnic Cleansing: The Expulsion of Czechoslovak Germans in 1945," *Central European History* 33, no. 4 (2000): 463–86.
155. Timothy Snyder, "The Causes of Ukraine-Polish Ethnic Cleansing, 1943," *Past and Present*, no. 179 (2003): 197–234.
156. Elena Lourie, "A Society Organised for War: Medieval Spain," in Lourie, *Crusade and Colonisation: Muslims, Christians, and Jews in Medieval Aragon* (Aldershot, UK, 1990), 54–76; Pagden, *Lords of All the World*, 74.
157. Dussel, *The Invention of the Americas*, 13: "After centuries of experimentation in Andalusia, this victimization and sacrificial violence parading as innocence began its long destructive path." See also John Docker, *1492: The Poetics of Diaspora* (London and New York, 2001), 190, 201; and Ronald Wright, *Stolen Continents: Five Hundred Years of Conquest and Resistance in the Americas* (Boston and New York, 1992).
158. Mark Ferro, *Colonization: A Global History* (London, 1997), 2.
159. Robert Geraci, "Genocidal Fantasies and Impulses in Imperial Russia," in this volume; Michael Rywkin, ed., *Russian Colonial Expansion to 1917* (London, 1988); Michael Khodarkovsky, *Russia's Steppe Frontier: The Making of a Colonial Empire, 1500–1800* (Bloomington and Indianapolis, IN, 2005); Michael Khodarkovsky, "Of Christianity, Enlightenment, and Colonialism: Russia in the North Caucasus, 1550–1800," *Journal of Modern History* 71, no. 2 (1999): 394–431; Theodore R. Weeks, *Nation and State in late Imperial Russia: Nationalism and the Russification of the Western Frontier, 1863–1914* (Dekalb, IL, 1996); Jeff Sahadeo, "Conquest, Colonialism, and Nomadism on the Eurasian Steppe," *Kritika: Explorations in Russian and Eurasian History* 4, no. 4 (2003): 942–54; Dominic Lieven, "Dilemmas of Empire, 1850–1918: Power, Territory, Identity," *Journal of Contemporary History* 34, no. 2 (1999): 163–200; Keziban Acar, "An Examination of Russian Imperialism: Russian Intellectual and Military Descriptions of the Caucasians during the Russo-Turkish War of 1877–1878," *Nationalities Papers* 32, no. 1 (2004): 7–21; John P. Ledonne, *The Russian Empire and the World, 1700–1917: The Geopolitics of Expansion and Containment* (New York, 1996); W. Bruce Lincoln, *The Conquest of a Continent: Siberia and the Russians* (New York, 1994). Older literature: Richard A. Pierce, *Russian Central Asia, 1867–1917: A Study in Colonial Rule* (Berkeley, CA, 1960); Terence Armstrong, *Russian Settlement in the North* (Cambridge, 1965); Donald W. Treadgold, *The Great Siberian Migration: The Government and Peasant Resettlement from Emancipation to the First World War* (Princeton, NJ, 1957).
160. Zev Jabotinsky, "An Iron Wall (We and the Arabs)," in *Zionism: Background Papers for an Evaluation*, vol. 4, ed. Eliezer Schwied et al. (Jerusalem, n.d.), 67.
161. Nicholas A. Robins, *Native Insurgencies and the Genocidal Impulse in the Americas* (Bloomington and Indianapolis, IN, 2005).
162. Philippe R. Girard, "Caribbean Genocide: Racial War in Haiti, 1802–1804," *Patterns of Prejudice* 39, no 2 (2005): 137–61.
163. Richard Lee Turtis, "A World Destroyed, A Nation Imposed: The 1937 Haitian Massacre in the Dominican Republic," *Hispanic American Historical Review* 82, no. 3 (2002): 589–635.
164. See the chapters by Ben Kiernan and Alexander L. Hinton in this volume.
165. Jacques Semelin, "Analysis of a Mass Crime: Ethnic Cleansing in the Former Yugoslavia, 1991–1999," in *The Specter of Genocide: Mass Murder in Historical Perspective*, ed. Robert Gellately and Ben Kiernan (Cambridge, 2003), 353–370; Bette Denich, "Dismembering Yugoslavia: Nationalist Ideologies and the Symbolic Revival

of Genocide," *American Ethnologist* 21, no. 2 (1994): 367–90; Robert M. Hayden, "Imagined Communities and Real Victims: Self-Determination and Ethnic Cleansing in Yugoslavia," *American Ethnologist* 23, no. 4 (1996): 783–801; Damir Mirkovic, "The Historical Link between the Ustasha Genocide and the Croato-Serbian Civil War: 1991–1995," *Journal of Genocide Research* 2, no. 3 (2000): 363–73; Anthony Oberschall, "The Manipulation of Ethnicity: From Ethnic Co-operation to Violence and War in Yugoslavia," *Ethnic and Racial Studies* 23, no. 6 (2000): 982–1001.

166. Mike Davis, *Late Victorian Holocausts: El Nino Famines and the Making of the Third World* (2001), 177–210.
167. Karl Marx, *Karl Marx on Colonialism and Modernization*, ed. and intro. Shlomo Avineri (New York, 1969), 224
168. Jean-Paul Sartre, "Preface," in Fanon, *Wretched of the Earth*, 20.
169. Fanon, *Wretched of the Earth*, 88.
170. Albert Memmi, *The Colonizer and the Colonized*, intro. Jean-Paul Sartre (Boston, [1957] 1965), 151. Liah Greenfeld writes similarly of resentment—hate and envy—as the source of nationalism. See her *Nationalism: Five Roads to Modernity* (Cambridge, MA, 1992), 16.
171. Fanon, *Wretched of the Earth*, 93; Jean-Paul Sartre, "Introduction," in Memmi, *The Colonizer and the Colonized*, xxviii; Abdul R. JanMohamed, *Manichean Aesthetics: The Politics of Literature in Colonial Africa* (Amherst, MA, 1983), 4.
172. Memmi, *The Colonizer and the Colonized*, 130–31.
173. Ibid., 130, 139. Memmi's insight is very close to the theory of social regression advanced by Vamik Volkan. See his *Bloodlines: From Ethnic Pride to Ethnic Terrorism* (Boulder, CO, 1997); Volkan, *Blind Trust: Large Groups and their Leaders in Times of Crisis and Terror* (Charlottesville, VA, 2004); Volkan, "Traumatized Societies," in *Violence or Dialogue? Psychoanalytic Insights on Terror and Terrorism*, ed. Sverre Varvin and Vamik D. Volkan (London, 2003), 217–36.
174. Albert Memmi, *Jews and Arabs* (Chicago, 1975).
175. Fanon, *Wretched of the Earth*, 146, 158; Benita Parry, "Resistance Theory/Theorising Resistance or Two Cheers for Nativism," in *Colonial Discourse/Postcolonial Theory*, ed. Francis Barker, Peter Hulme, and Margaret Iversen (Manchester, UK, 1994), 172–191.
176. Cf. Steven T. Katz, *Historicism, The Holocaust, and Zionism: Critical Studies in Modern Jewish Thought and History* (New York and London, 1992), 299.
177. Memmi, *The Colonizer and the Colonized*, 134–37; Sartre, "Preface," in Fanon, *Wretched of the Earth*, 18, 21.
178. Fanon, *Wretched of the Earth*, 148.
179. Ibid., 94, 24.
180. Sartre, "Preface," in ibid., 22. "The native cures himself of colonial neurosis by thrusting out the settler through force of arms. When his rage boils over, he rediscovers his lost innocence and he comes to know himself in that he himself creates himself."
181. Fanon, *Wretched of the Earth*, 156–59.
182. Clifford Geertz, "The Integrative Revolution: Primordial Sentiments and Civil Politics in the New States," in *Old Societies and New States: The Quest for Modernity in Asia and Africa*, ed. Clifford Geertz (New York, 1963), 109–19.
183. Mahmood Mamdani, "Beyond Settler and Native as Political Identities: Overcoming the Political Legacy of Colonialism," *Comparative Studies in Society and History* 43, no. 4 (2001): 651–64.
184. Marx, in *The Marx-Engels Reader*, ed. Robert C. Tucker, 2nd ed. (New York, 1972), 663.

185. Rosa Luxemburg, "The Junius Pamphlet: The Crisis in the German Social Democracy," in *Rosa Luxemburg Speaks*, ed. and intro May-Alice Waters (New York, 1970), 269, 281.
186. I give a more detailed analysis in A. Dirk Moses, "Colonialism," in *The Oxford Handbook of Holocaust Studies*, ed. Peter Hayes and John K. Roth (Oxford, 2009).
187. Fanon, *Wretched of the Earth*, 101.
188. Frantz Fanon, *Black Skin/White Masks*, trans. Charles Lam Markmann (New York, 1967), 115, 89.
189. Cited in Richard H. King, *Race, Culture, and the Intellectuals, 1940–1970* (Washington, DC and Baltimore, MD, 2004), 47.
190. Representative of this kind of equation or trumping is Ward Churchill, *A Little Matter of Genocide* (San Francisco, 1997).
191. For instance, Marianna Torgonvik, *Gone Primitive: Savage Intellects, Modern Lives* (Chicago, 1990), 9, 13.
192. Pascal Grosse, "From Colonialism to National Socialism: Hannah Arendt's Origins of Totalitarianism," *Postcolonial Studies* 9, no. 1 (2006): 35–52; King and Stone, *Hannah Arendt and the Uses of History*. I discuss Arendt and imperialism in "Moses, "Conceptual Blockages and Definitional Dilemmas in the 'Racial Century,'" 31–33.
193. Césaire, *Discourse on Colonialism*, 14–27; Hannah Arendt, *Eichmann in Jerusalem: A Report on the Banality of Evil* (London, 1963).
194. Adolf Hitler, *Hitler Reden und Proklamationen, 1932–1945*, vol. 1, *Triumph (1932–1938)*, ed. Max Domarus (Würzburg, 1962), 74–75. He argued against the doctrine of peaceful economic conquest by referring to the British Empire: "No nation has more carefully prepared its economic conquest with the sword with greater brutality and defended it later on more ruthlessly than the British": Hitler, *Mein Kampf* (New York, 1940), 189. See also the lucid discussion of Dan Stone, *History, Memory and Mass Atrocity* (London, 2006), chapter ten.
195. Hitler, *Mein Kampf*, 172–81. "If a people limits itself to domestic colonization, at a time when other races cling to greater and greater surfaces of the earth's soil, it will be forced to exercise self-restriction even while other nations will continue to increase," 174.
196. See David Furber and Wendy Lower, "Colonialism and Genocide in Nazi-Occupied Poland and Ukraine," in this volume.
197. See for instance, *Hitler's Table Talk, 1941–44*, ed. Hugh-Trevor Roper (London, 1973), 617.
198. Wendy Lower, *Nazi Empire-Building and the Holocaust in Ukraine* (Chapel Hill, NC, 2005), 25–26.
199. Jürgen Zimmerer, "The Birth of the Ostland Out of the Spirit of Colonialism: A Postcolonial Perspective on the Nazi Policy of Conquest and Extermination," *Patterns of Prejudice* 39, no. 2 (2005): 202–24; Moses, "Conceptual Blockages and Definitional Dilemmas in the 'Racial Century'; Enzo Traverso, *The Origins of Nazi Violence* (New York and London, 2003); Benjamin Madley, "From Africa to Auschwitz: How German South West Africa Incubated Methods Adopted and Developed by the Nazis in Eastern Europe," *European History Quarterly* 33, no. 3 (2005): 429–64. German scholars Götz Aly and Susanne Heim have been arguing that the Holocaust had its origins in a "territorial solution" to the "Jewish question" in east-central Europe in the context of Nazi plans for a more general "ethnic reordering" of the region for German settlers: Aly and Heim, *Architects of Annihilation: Auschwitz and the Logic of Destruction* (London, 2002); David Furber, "Near as Far in the Colonies: The

Nazi Occupation of Poland," *International History Review* 26, no. 3 (2004): 541–79; Dieter Pohl, "War, Occupation, and the Holocaust in Poland," in Stone, *The Historiography of the Holocaust*, 88–119; Rolf-Dieter Müller, 'From Economic Alliance to a War of Colonial Exploitation," in *Germany and the Second World War*, vol. 4, *The Attack on the Soviet Union*, ed. Horst Boog, et al. (Oxford, 1998), 118–224.

200. Marcia Klotz, "Global Visions: From the Colonial to the National Socialist World," *European Studies Journal* 16, no. 2 (1999): 37–68.
201. I discuss this question in A. Dirk Moses, "Structure and Agency in the Holocaust: Daniel J. Goldhagen and his Critics," *History and Theory* 37, no. 2 (1998): 194–219.
202. Ben Shepherd, "*Wehrmacht* Security Regiments in the Soviet Partisan War, 1943," *European History Quarterly* 33, no. 4 (2003): 493–529; Mark Mazower, "Military Violence and National Socialist Values: The Wehrmacht in Greece 1941–1944," *Past and Present*, no. 134 (1992): 129–158; Truman Anderson, "Incident at Baranivka: German Reprisals and the Soviet Partisan Movement in Ukraine, October-December 1941," *Journal of Modern History* 71, no. 3 (1999): 585–623.
203. Wilhelm Marr, "The Victory of Judaism over Germandom (1879)," in *The Jew in the Modern World: A Documentary History*, ed. Paul Mendes-Flohr and Jehuda Reinharz, 2nd ed. (New York and Oxford, 1995), 332.
204. Hitler, *Mein Kampf*, 252.
205. Ibid., 140.
206. See the analysis in Klotz, "Global Visions," 44.
207. Hitler, *Mein Kampf*, 590, 969.
208. See the discussion in Jared Poley, *Decolonization in Germany: Weimar Narratives of Colonial Loss and Foreign Occupation* (Oxford, 2005), 151–76.
209. Cf. Saul Friedländer, *Nazi Germany and the Jews*, vol. 1, *The Years of Persecution* (New York, 1997).
210. This is how Mahmood Mamdani reads the Nazis in *When Victims Become Killers: Colonialism, Nativism, and the Genocide in Rwanda* (Princeton, NJ, 2001), 9–11.
211. Levene, *Genocide in the Age of the Nation State*, vol. 1, 187; vol. 2, 225.
212. Christian Gerlach, "The Wannsee Conference, the Fate of the German Jews, and Hitler's Decision in Principle to Exterminate All European Jews," *Journal of Modern History* 70 (December 1998): 759–812; Peter Holquist, "To Count, to Extract, and to Exterminate: Population Statistics and Population Politics in Late Imperial and Soviet Russia," in *A State of Nations*, ed. Ronald Grigor Suny and Terry Martin (Oxford, 2001), 111–44.
213. Lucy Dawidowicz, ed., *A Holocaust Reader* (West Orange, NJ, 1976), 133.
214. See Furber and Lower, "Colonialism and Genocide in Nazi-Occupied Poland and Ukraine."
215. Ulrich Herbert, ed., *National Socialist Extermination Policies* (New York, 2000).
216. See the nominalism of Traverso, *Origins of the Nazi Violence*.

– *Chapter 2* –

ANTICOLONIALISM IN WESTERN POLITICAL THOUGHT

The Colonial Origins of the Concept of Genocide

Andrew Fitzmaurice

Introduction

Most chapters in this book are concerned by the degree to which the term "genocide," coined by Raphael Lemkin in 1944 and adopted by the United Nations in 1948, can be used to understand the devastation wrought by colonization over the past five hundred years.[1] This chapter will invert that question: that is, it will show that Lemkin's understanding of genocide developed out of a critique of colonization that had its origins in the sixteenth century and was sustained by successive generations of writers on natural and human rights.

In order to understand that the concept of genocide is itself a product of the history of colonization, we must first excavate the anti-imperial tradition to which it belongs. It is a tradition that has been obscured by a generation of scholarship. Since at least the 1980s, scholars have sought to demonstrate that the dispossession of indigenous peoples and the destruction of indigenous societies proceeded within European legal frameworks. "A will to empire," as Robert M. Williams has put it, "proceeds most effectively under a rule of law."[2] Liberalism has been shown to have blood on its hands.[3] Or, rather, key figures in the liberal canon have been shown to have been apologists for colonization (even though few of them would have described themselves as "liberals"). It is argued that the idea of rights in the writings of thinkers including Francesco de Vitoria, Hugo Grotius, John Locke, and Emeric de Vattel developed in step with the rationalization of empire. In this chapter, I argue that these "revisionist" accounts have buried a profound scepticism in the history of Western legal thought about the justice of colonization. Ironically, the revisionist account has also obscured the problems of responsibility. If all Europeans were united in their moral and legal certainty about the justice of colonizing and, indeed, if all peoples possess a "will to empire," then they can be said to have been responsible only in terms of having been a cause, but not in terms of having made a choice.[4]

I will argue that opposition to conquest and colonization can be traced in Western political thought from the beginning of European expansion in the early sixteenth century through to the twentieth century. This opposition amounted to no less than a tradition. It was based upon systematically articulated principles, and it was self-referential. Each generation of critics was conscious of participating in a polemic that had a history, and they were profoundly knowledgeable about that history. While liberalism or, more broadly, Western political thought bears great responsibility for colonial devastation, the responsibility is all the greater when we understand that Western political thought simultaneously supported a sustained political critique of that devastation for over four hundred years.

The Aristotelian Critique

Prior to the conquest of the Americas, medieval Europeans conducted a long and detailed debate, which found direct inspiration in the Crusades, on whether it was lawful to conquer heathen peoples.[5] They asked whether non-Christian peoples held *dominium*, or property in their persons, goods, and lands. This debate was conducted between two poles. One view, represented by the twelfth-century theologian Alanas Anglicus, held that all dominion was based upon belief in the true God and that earthly rulers receive their power and legitimacy from the Church.[6] The other view, articulated by the Aristotelian philosophers at the University of Paris, led by Thomas Aquinas (1225–1274), used natural law to argue that property is based on the use of reason, and not belief in God, and that infidels are therefore equally capable as Christians of exercising dominion.[7] Already in this medieval debate there was profound uncertainty about the legitimacy of non-European societies.

The uncertainty about the rights of infidels was to be amplified enormously in writings on the legitimacy of the Spanish conquests of America initiated in 1492. Concern about the legal status of the conquests was articulated over the course of the sixteenth century by the writers of the "School of Salamanca," and particularly by Francesco de Vitoria (1485–1546), their most influential figure.[8] Vitoria was trained as a Scholastic philosopher, a Thomist (a follower of Aquinas) or Aristotelian, at the University of Paris. He accepted the Prime Chair of Theology at the University of Salamanca in 1526. In the 1530s, partly at the instigation of the Spanish Crown, Vitoria began a detailed consideration of the justice of the Spanish conquests, which he delivered in his lectures at the university. His "On the American Indians" are the most important of these lectures. Vitoria's arguments are well known, but worth reiterating in some detail because they had, as we shall see, a tremendous impact on anti-imperial thinking through to the twentieth century.

Vitoria's Dominican order was charged with administering the Inquisition into religious orthodoxy. Rumors had been circulating in Europe that the conquistadors had justified their conquests with the argument that the civilizations of the Aztecs and Incas were ungodly and therefore justly dispossessed. The argument that the only just society was a godly society was a Protestant heresy, and therefore fell within the concern of the Inquisition and under Vitoria's moral authority. In response to this context, Vitoria set himself a simple question: namely, what is a justly constituted society? From this point, he could provide the grounds upon which a conquest would be just, and he could determine the legality of the arguments already used to justify the conquests. To these problems Vitoria provided a characteristically Thomist and Aristotelian answer. The world, he argued, was created by God (and is governed) according to laws that are universal. These laws are latent in nature and are thereby known as natural laws. The laws of nature exist in potential, and it is the purpose (and distinguishing feature) of humans to release that potential through the exploitation of nature. Humans must use reason to transform the material world into chairs, tables, houses, roads, bridges, and cities. But they must also transform the moral potential of nature, so that friendship and natural community, for example, can be transformed into social and political institutions including marriage, the family, religion (Christian or otherwise), commerce, laws, and civil society. Where these outward signs of the exploitation of nature are evident, it is clear that justly constituted societies have been established.

Vitoria then pointed out that the societies of the Americans that had been conquered by the Spaniards were self-evidently such just societies because their domain was not, as he put it in terms of Roman law, *res nullius*: that is, it was not a thing void of use.[9] The "Indians" had, he argued, "some order in their affairs: they have properly organised cities, proper marriages, magistrates and overlords, laws, industries, and commerce, all of which require the use of reason. They likewise have a form of religion, and they correctly apprehend things that are apparent to other men, which indicates the use of reason."[10]

It remained, therefore, to consider the legality of the titles by which the Spanish had claimed their American possessions. Vitoria dismissed the 1493 Donation whereby Pope Alexander VI had given the non-Christian world to the west of the Atlantic to the Spanish, and the East to the Portuguese, because he did not accept the Church's pretensions to temporal jurisdiction.[11] The claim that the American peoples were ungodly and therefore justly dispossessed was dismissed as heretical.[12] He likewise dismissed the claim that possession could be "by right of discovery"—that could only apply where goods, or land, have no owner, and here he observed, "we need not argue long" because the "barbarians possessed true public and private dominion."[13] He raised the possibility that the "barbarians" could be madmen or infantile, which could justify their protection (although not stealing their goods), but he pointed out again that he had clearly shown that they have "order in their affairs."[14] He then arrived at the extraordinary conclusion that "it is clear from all that I have said that the Spaniards, when they first sailed to the land of the barbarians, carried with them no right at all to occupy their countries."[15] At this point, as Anthony Pagden has observed, Vitoria appeared, at least on paper, to have robbed the Spanish king of *dominium* (the right to property), and to have endangered his *imperium* (or sovereignty), in America.[16]

Having delegitimized the conquest, Vitoria then inquired upon what basis Spaniards might legally be able to go to the Americas (albeit not as conquistadors). Again, here his answer was characteristically Aristotelian in that it was based upon the assumption of human sociability. Humans, Vitroria argued, are sociable animals; they have a natural inclination to live in communities. The natural fellowship of humanity requires that all peoples should welcome others amongst them as part of the natural communication and partnership between "man and man."[17] Forms of natural communication include the activities of missionaries and peaceful commerce. Should any people reject this right to move amongst the human community, they would be understood to have violated natural law and may have established a just cause for war.

Many historians have claimed that with these arguments Vitoria provided a secular justification for conquest.[18] Indeed, Vitoria did provide material for justifications of conquest by subsequent generations. Future generations would argue that Amerindians and other colonized peoples had not established dominion through the exploitation of nature, and they also demanded the natural right of communication, including the right to trade and to preach. But Vitoria did not himself describe Amerindian societies in these terms, nor did he claim that fellowship had been denied. Rather he insisted that it was the Spanish, and not the Amerindians, who had violated the natural rights of communication.[19] He believed that the fate of the American peoples was closely tied to that of Europeans. As a leader of the Inquisition, he did not want to see the universalist claims of the church nor the heretical argument about just societies being godly societies rebound on European states. Nor did he want to see people holding just dominion stripped of their rights to property. His concerns were prescient—Europe was sliding into two centuries of bloody war fought over precisely these questions.

Vitoria was not an isolated figure. His natural law theories and his discomfort with the American conquests were amplified by subsequent generations at Salamanca, from his celebrated pupil Domingo de Soto through to the Jesuits Luis de Molina and Francisco Suárez. They were also echoed in Bartolomé de Las Casas' famous denunciation of Spanish cruelty. Importantly, this natural law tradition, with its scepticism of conquest, would form the foundation for modern discussions of natural and, later, "human" rights.

Grotius and Pufendorf

European colonizers and trading empires were acutely conscious of the writings of the Salamanca School and the problems they presented for the legitimacy of continuing conquest and colonization. When the Dutch attempted to establish trade in the East Indies, they found themselves blocked by the activities of the Portuguese, who claimed prior rights of discovery and the legitimacy conferred by the Donation of Alexander. The Dutch East India Company employed Hugo Grotius (1583–1645), one of the most precocious intellects of his generation, to respond to the Portuguese case. Among his achievements, Grotius has been viewed as the founder of the theory of international law as well as a founder of the "modern" school of natural law (basing natural laws on the universality of self-interest rather than upon human sociability). Grotius' understanding of American conquest was that large tracts of the continent were sparsely inhabited and underexploited, although he condemned the conquest of societies that appreciate the operation of natural law.

In his writings on the East Indies, however, particularly in *The Free Sea (Mare Liberum)*, his views were hardly distinguishable from Vitoria's polemic. Following Vitoria, Grotius demolished each of the Portuguese and Spanish claims to *dominium* and *imperium* in the Indies, devoting a chapter to each claim: first, the claim to dominion based upon discovery, then by the "Pope's gift," then "by title of war" or conquest, and finally by religion. In response to the claim to "title by invention," or discovery, Grotius followed Vitoria's reasoning that the "Indians" "have, and always had, their kings, their commonwealth, their laws, and their liberties": that is, lawful society was already constituted in a manner demonstrating that the "Indians" understood the operation of natural law.[20] Moreover, he pointed out, discovery never provides title "for to find [i.e., possess] is not to see a thing with the eyes but to lay hold of it with the hands."[21] He concluded: "Vitoria therefore rightly saith that the Spaniards got no more authority over the Indians for this cause than the Indians had over the Spaniards if any of them had come formerly into Spain."[22] Grotius also offered the possibility, again raised by Vitoria, that the Indians could be "out of their wits and unsensible" but concluded that they were "ingenious and sharp witted."[23]

On Pope Alexander's donation of the East Indies to the Portuguese, Grotius noted first of all that "our Lord Christ had rejected all earthly government" so that he could not have "translated" temporal power either to "Peter or the Church of Rome." Again he concluded by the authority of "the opinion of Cajetanus and Vitoria . . . that it is not a sufficient title against the Indians . . . [simply] because the Pope gave those provinces."[24] On the question of just war, Grotius declared: "there were no cause truly that they should pretend war. For they who pursue the barbarians with war, as the Spaniards do the people of America, are wont to pretend two things: that they are hindered from trading with them, or because they will not acknowledge the doctrine of true religion. As for trading, the Portugalls obtained it of the Indians, so that in this behalf they have no reason to complain."[25] On "the other pretence," namely that of conquest in the name of religion, he cited Cajetan on the doctrine that Vitoria adopted: namely, that for infidel countries, "the lords thereof, although infidels, are lawful lords, whether they be governed by regal or political government, neither are they deprived of dominion of the lands or goods for their infidelity."[26]

Consistent with the direction of postcolonial political thought, recent studies of Grotius have argued not only that he was the founder of international law, but that he was an apologist for the expansion of Europe, an "imperialist thinker."[27] Thus the foundations of international law were cast in a colonial mold. The polemical purpose of *The Free Sea* was not merely to challenge Portuguese colonization in the East, but to establish trading rights for the Dutch.[28] Those trading rights have been understood to be the thin edge of a colonial wedge. At the same time, it is clear that at no time did Grotius claim *dominium* and, far less, *imperium* for the Dutch in the East. One cannot help wondering that, as for Vitoria, his writing has been understood anachronistically in the light of subsequent events.

The critique of European colonial practices becomes even more pronounced when we turn from Grotius to Pufendorf (1632–1694), one of the greatest natural law writers of the seventeenth century. Pufendorf was a native of Saxony, educated in the Grotian school of moral and political philosophy. One of the striking differences between Grotius and Pufendorf is in how they read Vitoria. Whereas Grotius understood Vitoria to have been attacking the Spanish conquests, Pufendorf interpreted Vitoria as an apologist for empire and developed his own profound critique of colonial rationalizations. According to Pufendorf, "Franciscus a Victoria, *Relectiones de Indis*, Pt.V, § 3, does not win many to his position when he discusses the adequate grounds on which the Spaniards felt themselves entitled to subdue the Indians."[29] He continued: "It is crude indeed to try to give others so indefinite a right to journey and live among us, with no thought of the number in which they come, their purpose in coming, as well as the question of whether . . . they propose to stay but a short time or settle among us permanently."[30] Pufendorf was able to put Vitoria's discussion of the rights of "natural communication" in doubt because, in common with the "modern" natural law writers, his understanding of natural law rested less upon the supposition of a universal human fellowship and more upon the notion of the universal rule of self-interest.

He had very little further to say in explicit reference to peoples conquered by Europeans, but he proceeded to critique the legal arguments based upon "use" that had come to support European colonial ventures. God's command that men should "use the products of the earth" (which was a staple justification of colonial ventures) was not, Pufendorf argued, the "immediate cause of dominion."[31] Dominion, he argued, arises from consent, from the agreement of the community about the nature and limits of ownership. Thus, he pointed out, a community may decide legitimately to employ proprietorship whereby individuals possess things for their own use, or they may rather hold some or all of the goods and land in "positive community": that is, in a communal ownership. In *both* cases, Pufendorf insists, all claims by outsiders to those goods are excluded. He implicitly rejected here the argument used by colonizers that native peoples who had not established individual proprietorship had failed to establish dominion. Following this argument, Pufendorf mounted a powerful defence of the differences between peoples, arguing that ownership and sovereignty could be based upon a variety of different relationships to the land. God, he declared, "gave men an indefinite right" to the "earth and its products," "yet the manner, intensity, and extent of this power were left to the judgement and disposition of men; whether, in other words, they would confine it within certain limits, or within none at all, and whether they wanted every man to have a right to everything, or only to a certain and fixed part of things, or to be assigned his definite portion with which he should rest content and claim no right to anything else."[32] He added: "Yet it was far from God to prescribe a universal manner of possessing things, which all men were bound to observe. And so things were created neither proper nor common (in positive community) by any express command of God, but these distinctions were later created by men."[33]

The English Colonization of America

How did Pufendorf arrive at this dramatically different understanding of the implications of natural law for colonization? And how did he come to see Vitoria as an apologist for European expansion? Between the writing of Grotius' *Mare Liberum* (1609) and Pufendorf's *De Jure Naturae* (1672), the character of European colonization and the ideological justifications for colonization had undergone dramatic change. Nowhere was this change more evident than in the English colonization of America. English colonizers had absorbed the implications of the Salamanca School writers, and of Vitoria in particular, and as a result they had altered radically the polemical force of those writers. The Virginia Council's plans to establish a colony in America, realised in 1607, were greatly troubled by the writings of the Salamanca School. When the Virginia Council met in its first years its members debated whether they should promote their colony. The notes for one meeting record a debate on whether "some form of justification of our plantation might be conceived and pass . . . into many hands." After long deliberation, the members decided against publishing a justification for the colony for a number of reasons. Above all, it was observed that when the Spanish king had subjected the Spanish conquest to the consideration of the "Casuists and Confessors" (namely, the Salamanca School), the consequence was that they "declyn'd him from that severe and unjust course." According to the Virginia Council minutes, the Salamanca writers "gathered for him [the Spanish king] no title, of Dominion or property, but only a Magistracy and Empire [i.e. *imperium*]." Certainly, here Vitoria was still being read with the meaning he intended. Remarkably, the Council members concluded: "Because therefore, we shal be putt to defend our title, not yet publiquely quarrelled, not only comparatively to be as good as the Spaniards . . . *but absolutely to be good against the Naturall people*: some thought it better to abstayne from this unnessisary way of provocation, and reserve ourselves to the defensive part." [34] Reading Vitoria led the Virginia Council to believe that they "would be putt," that they would find it difficult, to justify their title in America "against the Naturall people," i.e., the Indians. Put baldly, the English people who established the first permanent English colony in America believed that there was a strong probability that they had no sovereign rights there and that their colony would unjustly dispossess the indigenous inhabitants. And they were led to this conclusion through reading the most important early modern natural law discussions about the idea of natural rights. These colonial interests did not allow such anxieties to stop them.[35]

It is clear, however, that at this point in time, as under the Spanish empire, the tradition of thinking about political rights was understood to be antagonistic to colonization. This English anxiety about dispossession was expressed repeatedly throughout the following expansion of English settlement in North America. English writers frequently acknowledged that Native Americans lived in legitimate political societies and they denied any intention to dispossess these peoples.[36] Accordingly, English colonizers routinely acknowledged the natural law principle that "a Christian may take nothing from a heathen against his will. . . . We will take nothing from the Savages by power nor pillage, by craft nor violence, neither goods, lands nor libertie, much lesse life."[37]

How, then, were the English able to reconcile colonization with recognition of the Indians as civilized peoples in full possession of natural rights? They were not able to. They were obliged either to acknowledge the injustice of their actions, or to redescribe native peoples as uncivil and therefore holding only rudimentary rights. Here the problems of Vitoria's defense of the peoples conquered by Spain became apparent (as did the reasons for Pufendorf's later rejection of many of those principles). Vitoria's defense, based upon the exploitation of the laws of nature, was a double-edged sword. A change of empirical description was all that was required to deny conquered peoples of their rights. "Who will think," William Strachey argued, "it is an unlawful act, to fortefye, and strengthen our selves (as Nature requires) with the best helpes, and by sitting down with Guards, and forces about us, in the wast and vast, unhabited groundes of their amongst a world of which not one foot of a thousand, do they either use or know how to turne to any benefit, and therefore lyes so great a Circuit vayne and idle before them?"[38] Native Americans were no longer civil. The law of nature was central to this redescription; as the metaphysical poet and Dean of St Paul's, John Donne, argued in his sermon to the Virginia Company: "In the law of Nature and Nations, a land never inhabited, by any, or utterly derelicted and immemorially abandoned by the former Inhabitants, becomes theirs that will possesse it. So also is it, if the inhabitants doe not in some measure fill the Land, so as the Land may bring forth her increase for the use of men."[39]

In addition to employing natural law to describe Native Americans as uncivil, the English passed through the door of "communication" that Vitoria had left open. They claimed rights of community and trade. The Indians, they argued, could not deny the natural law rights of humans to move freely amongst each other, and commerce was clearly an extension of this right. Accordingly, William Strachey declared: "the Law of Nations . . . admits yt lawfull, to trade with any manner of People . . . the Salvages themselves may not impugne, or forbid the same in respect of Common fellowship and Community betwixt man and man."[40] In this manipulation of Salamanca doctrines we find one reason why Pufendorf found it necessary to attack Vitoria's arguments concerning trade and fellowship.

Through these means the English arrived at a justification of colonization pursued through commerce, which they distinguished from the Spanish empire that was based upon conquest.[41] Where the Spanish had expanded with the sword, the English, so they argued, expanded through cultivation and resorted to military means only as a matter of defense. This justification of English colonization received its most celebrated formulation in John Locke's *Two Treatises of Government*, in particular, in his essay "Of Property" in the second treatise. Indeed, Locke (1632–1704) is often seen as the originator of the justification of colonization by cultivation (known as the "agriculturalist argument"), although the essential pieces of the argument were in place, as we have seen, more than seventy years before he wrote the treatises. In much-cited passages, Locke argued that though the earth was given by God in common "to all men, yet every man has a *Property* in his own *Person*." It followed that the "*Labour* of his Body, and the *Work* of his Hands, we may say, are properly his." Whatsoever a man "hath mixed his *Labour* with," and so "joined" it to himself, "he thereby makes it his *Property*."[42] Although an admirer of Pufendorf, Locke had absolutely no doubt that property was based in use. Moreover, the greater the use, or exploitation, of nature, the stronger the hold on property. For this reason, the claims of a people that hold property in common will be "overbalanced" by those who pursue the "*Property of labour*." Indeed, Native Americans were guilty of not profiting from the gifts of nature: "An Acre of Land that bears here Twenty Bushels of Wheat, and another in *America*, which, with the same Husbandry, would do the like, are, without doubt, of the same natural, intrinsick Value. But yet the Benefit Mankind receives from the one, in a Year, is worth 5 *l.* and from the other possibly not worth a Penny, if all the Profit an *Indian* received from it were to be valued, and sold here: at least, I may truly say, not 1/1000."[43]

There is no question about the depth of Locke's involvement in the colonization of Carolina, which extended beyond his office as secretary of the lords proprietors of Carolina. Nor is there any doubt that the defense of English colonization was an important purpose of Locke's *Two Treatises*.[44] Indeed, much of the revisionism in postcolonial political thought has focused upon Locke, for the dual reasons that he remains one of the most important figures for liberalism and because his apology for colonization was unambiguous.

Emeric de Vattel and Christian Wolff

I have isolated two common responses to the tension between natural law doctrines and colonization. One was the description of colonized peoples as uncivil, and Locke made the classic statement in that genre. The other was to declare dispossession unjust. Discussions of the rights of indigenous peoples have frequently been trapped between these poles. They have often demonstrated an ambiguity that betrays an awareness that the tradition of thinking about rights had been used as vigorously to defend indigenous peoples as it had to attack them. This tension is evident even in some of the most dramatic attacks upon the rights of colonized peoples. Emeric de Vattel's *Droit des Gens* (1758) is regarded widely as a statement of Lockean principles and it was more widely cited in eighteenth- and nineteenth-century discussions of the rights of colonized peoples than was Locke's *Two Treatises*. Vattel (1714–1767) argued repeatedly that the North American Indians had been justly dispossessed because they claimed more land than they could use: "The people of those extensive tracts rather ranged than inhabited them."[45] He endorsed the argument that cultivation of the soil established the strongest claim to property in the land. While it is true, however, that Vattel articulated the agriculturalist argument, he lacked Locke's unflinching certainty that the dispossession of peoples who were believed to be at earlier stages of historical development was justified by natural law. Like Vitoria and Grotius, he disdained the European doctrine of discovery whereby navigators claimed title in the name of their sovereigns by virtue of having "erected some monument."[46] He agreed that the "conquest of the civilized empires of Peru and Mexico was a notorious usurpation." And for this reason, he praised the "moderation" of the New England Puritans who "purchased off the Indians the land."[47] And, later in Book II, he made the ambiguous observation that

> Families wandering in a country, as the nations of shepherds, and ranging through it as their wants require, possess it in common: it belongs to them to the exclusion of all other nations; and we cannot, without injustice, deprive them of the tracts of country of which they make use. . . . The savages of North America had no right to appropriate all that vast continent to themselves; and since they were unable to inhabit the whole of those regions, other nations might, without injustice, settle in some parts of them, provided they left the natives a sufficiency of land.

Vattel's caution increased as he went on to claim that no nation has a right to narrow the boundaries of the "pastoral Arabs" unless "she be under want of land" or "in a case of pressing necessity."[48] This was a marked retreat from Locke's invitation to exploit nature's excess capacity, which depended in no way on the pressures upon the colonizer.

Vattel's departure from Locke is attributable partly to the impact of Christian Wolff (1679–1754), the most eminent writer on international law in the first half of the eighteenth century. Vattel was a conscientious student of Wolff's thought. Wolff had articulated the clearest defense since Vitoria of the sovereign rights of non-European peoples, particularly those regarded as not living in civil society. Indeed, while Vitoria was at pains to defend the subjects of Spanish conquest, he did so because he believed them to be civil. Wolff plugged the gap, created by Vitoria, whereby non-European peoples could be redescribed as uncivil. He established first that "unknown lands inhabited by a nation may not be occupied by foreign nations."[49] He also acknowledged that "certainly separate families dwelling in the same land are to be distinguished from nations, nor can those things be applied to them which have been proved concerning the right and duties of nations."[50] He then turned to the question of "separate families dwelling together in a certain territory." He argued repeatedly that:

> if the families have no settled abode but wander through the uncultivated wilds, in that case, nevertheless, they are understood to have tacitly agreed that the lands in that territory in which they change their abodes as they please, are held in common, subject to the use of individuals, and it is not to be doubted but that it is their intention that they should not be deprived of that use by outsiders. Therefore they are supposed to have occupied that territory as far as concerns the lands subject to their use, and consequently to have jointly acquired ownership of those lands, so that the use of them belongs to all without distinction. Therefore those lands are subject to a mixed community-holding.[51]

He conceded that "things are occupied for the sake of their use," but responded that "if, indeed, separate families should be accustomed to wander about after the manner of the Scythians [the classic early modern example of barbarity] through uncultivated wilds . . . the intention of wandering, which is governed by that intended use gives sufficient evidence of the occupation of the lands subject to their use, although they have not established a permanent abode on them."[52]

Wolff even questioned the centrality of "use" (so important for Locke) in the understanding of property, moving closer to Pufendorf's understanding that ownership has its basis in consent. Having said that things are occupied for their use, he was then able to declare, in complete opposition to Locke, that "ownership is not lost by a non-user."[53] In what was a devastating critique of seventeenth- and eighteenth-century colonial practice, he argued that the lands of "separate wandering families" "can be occupied by no one coming into the territory inhabited by these families, even if at the time those who inhabit the territory are not using those lands."[54] Wolff reached the inevitable conclusion that the *imperium*, or sovereignty, claimed by contemporary colonizers was invalid insofar as it was based upon what we have come to call the agriculturalist argument. In the chapter "Whether separate families can be subject to civil sovereignty," he simply concluded "no one has the right to subject separate families to civil sovereignty." "By nature all men are free," he argued, and "therefore, since a right born with him can be taken from no man, but since it certainly is taken away in part, if any are subjected to civil sovereignty against their will; in either hypothesis no one has the right to subject to civil sovereignty separate families dwelling in a certain territory."[55]

The Late-Eighteenth-Century Attack on Empire

These remarkable sentiments developed the recognition, already found in Pufendorf, that each society's claims to ownership had to be measured at least to some degree in their own terms. This natural law defence of the rights of indigenous peoples——with its relativism—was to be developed into a powerful late-eighteenth-century attack on European empire. Vitoria, and many of those he influenced, challenged the justice of European empire on the basis that universal laws of behavior exist and that, according to those laws, non-European peoples conformed sufficiently to the norms of humanity such that it would be unjust to dispossess them. Eighteenth-century writers, referred to as "Enlightenment thinkers," developed the natural law critique of empire into something very different. They opposed empire on the basis of a moral relativism—that is, on the basis that humanity is constituted through its *mores* and that the *mores* of different peoples are incommensurable. This shift from universalism to relativism had begun in Pufendorf and Wolff's writings, partly in response to the colonial manipulation of natural law universalism. Writing on the late eighteenth century, Sankar Muthu has recently revealed the depth of this anti-imperial thinking and its basis in what he refers to as "cultural" understandings of humanity (although, as Muthu points out, "culture" was not a term used in this sense in the eighteenth century).[56] Muthu's illuminating analysis concentrates on Denis Diderot (1713–1784), Immanuel Kant (1724–1804), and Johann Gottfried Herder (1744–1803), although he claims mistakenly that anti-imperial thought was exceptional to the second half of the eighteenth century.

In anonymous passages in the Abbé Raynal's *Histoire philosophique et politique des établissements et du commerce des Européens dans les deux Indes* (1770), Diderot made impassioned attacks upon European expansion reminiscent of the writings of Las Casas: "Savage Europeans! You doubted at first whether the inhabitants of the regions you had just discovered were not animals which you might slay without remorse because they were black, and you were white. . . . In order to re-people one part of the globe that you have laid waste, you corrupt and depopulate another."[57] Similarly, Kant, who in his early career had been a member of the Wolffian philosophical school that dominated German philosophy in the mid-eighteenth century, deplored the tyranny of European colonizing powers. He declared:

> It can still be asked whether, when neither nature nor chance but just our own will brings us into the neighborhood of a people that holds out no prospect of a civil union with it, we should not be authorized to found colonies, by force if need be, in order to establish a civil union with them and bring these human beings (savages) into a rightful condition (as with the American Indians, the Hottentots and the inhabitants of New Holland [i.e. Australia]); or (which is not much better), to found colonies by fraudulent purchase of their land, and so become owners of their land, making use of our superiority without regard for their first possession.[58]

And Herder insisted on the relativism that nourished this abhorrence of colonization: "Let justice be done to other ways of life, which, from the constitution of the Earth, hath been destined, equally with agriculture, to contribute to the development of humankind. . . . If nature has anywhere attained her end, she attained it everywhere. The practical understanding of human beings was intended to blossom and bear fruit in all its varieties: and hence such a diversified Earth was ordained for so diversified a species."[59]

There is a widely held view that the notion of natural and, therefore, universal rights became dormant from the outset of the nineteenth century and remained so until after World War II.[60] Following the French Revolution, the natural rights tradition mutated into a concern with "human" rights that, through the strength of nineteenth-century nationalism, retreated into specific national preoccupations. According to this view, the "rights of man became increasingly political rights," which meant they were confined to certain kinds of political regimes, namely "civilized" societies.[61] Maintaining its distinctive rights became the concern of each particular regime. Accordingly, concern for colonized peoples came to be expressed throughout the nineteenth century, as Anthony Pagden puts it, as a "duty" and not in terms of the intrinsic rights of those peoples. This is a common understanding of nineteenth- and early twentieth-century arguments defending indigenous peoples: such arguments are characterized as "philanthropic," or "humanitarian," sentiments that were more often than not expressed by missionaries.[62] These "humanitarians" were motivated by their own Christian duty rather than by an appreciation of the natural rights tradition.[63]

The understanding of the nineteenth century as void of a language of universal rights is mistaken. The natural rights tradition continued to flourish in the nineteenth and early twentieth century. This should at least be evident from the fact that the "agriculturalist" argument, which was fundamentally a natural law doctrine, was used vigorously to *deny* that indigenous peoples had rights. The attack upon the rights of indigenous peoples had to be mounted from the perspective of universal rights, and the canon of rights theorists (more often Vattel than Locke) was mobilized for that attack. But the universal rights tradition was also used in a positive sense, throughout the nineteenth century, to defend colonized peoples and to attack the arbitrary power wielded by colonizers. There is space here only to explore two illustrative cases.

The Nineteenth Century—Saxe Bannister

Saxe Bannister (1790–1877) was in many ways typical of what has been described as the "humanitarian" nineteenth-century opposition to colonization. Bannister was certainly enthusiastic about the virtues of "civilization," and he accordingly supported the idea of a civilizing mission. But he was a vociferous critic of the reality of colonization and particularly of the dispossession of indigenous peoples. There were "humanitarian" elements to his thought and he was closely associated with the antislavery campaign. "Humanitarian," however, was a term that was often used vituperatively rather than in self-description, which should lead to more caution in its historical use.[64] Bannister's opposition to colonization can be described more accurately as participating in the tradition of anti-imperialist political thought. He was immensely knowledgeable about the history of colonization, about the history of colonial abuses, and the history of opposition to colonization, and he employed that knowledge in his own campaigns. He wrote several accounts, in his own words, of the "whole course of British colonial history." He also wrote a *Defense of the Indians of North America* as well as separate studies of South Africa, North Africa, and Australia, and numerous biographical essays including, notably, one on Herder.[65]

Importantly, while Bannister deplored the violence and crimes of settlers on the colonial frontier, he identified the cause of colonial abuses to be the administration of the colonial office in London, and he campaigned for the reform of that office. He also had a claim to base his writings on the direct experience of colonization. In 1823, he was sent to Canada as a commissioner responsible for the reform of the Indian Department.[66] From 1823 to 1826, he served as the first Attorney General of New South Wales. In that role, he apparently alienated himself from further government service. Subsequently, according to his own claims, in 1836 he "originated" the Aborigine's Protection Society in London, which played an important role in critiquing the treatment of indigenous peoples, and he made submissions to the 1837 Parliamentary Select Committee Inquiry into the treatment of Aboriginal peoples.[67]

In many of his writings, Bannister accepted the fait accompli of colonial sovereignty and concerned himself with questions of *dominium*, or property. He argued consistently against the dispossession of indigenous peoples. But at times Bannister also challenged the *imperium* of the colonizing powers, particularly where he could see that colonization was being initiated rather than already accomplished. For example, in his *Appel en faveur d'Alger et de l'Afrique du Nord*, now an apparently unread work judging from the absence of citations, Bannister attacked the colonization attempt being launched by the French in Alger and in North Africa more generally. He published this appeal in French and at Paris to be sure that he reached his intended audience.[68] Bannister urged the French government not to pursue what he described as a "project of extermination": "New plans are nevertheless proposed everyday to enrich France at the expense of Alger. Without examining all of them, we will recall the project of extermination (E) proposed against the millions of people to whom the country belongs with as much right as Paris belongs to the French."[69] He then declared: "We claim, on the contrary, independence for the North Africans in the real meaning of the word and such as the proclamation has announced; and to establish it, we request that the native people of the country be called to declare in the face of Europe their opinions on the most suitable form of government. It belongs to them to determine this form: it is up to Europe, and especially to France, to support them with wisdom and honor. France has to become the friend of a *free* Africa."[70]

Bannister was careful to assure his French audience that he was not deploring their colonial abuses while being blind to those of his own country: "We should not allow England to forget that the humiliations imposed on the peoples of North Africa are just a repetition of the humiliations England is imposing upon the peoples of South Africa. Floods of African blood shed without provocation in Cafrerie in 1828 (H); arbitrary acts which have been left without compensation on the borders of the Cape of Good Hope; cold blooded massacres committed in Australian in 1826 (I), without regard to all the laws, impose too eloquently silence on the English government."[71] Importantly, Bannister based his hopes not upon philanthropy or humanity but in a language of "rights" and an appeal to "*législation internationale*" or international law.[72]

It is important at this point to consider why opponents of European colonization mounted such passionate attacks on the violations of the rights of colonized peoples. There is no doubt that there was a high-minded element to their objections. Clearly, many opponents were motivated by the belief in a common humanity and by a concern for human dignity. But the motive of high-mindedness is insufficient an explanation for the sustained opposition over five hundred years that constitutes an anti-imperial tradition. The "expansion" of Europe conducted over those five hundred years was paralleled, and to some degree driven, by the creation of the modern European state.[73] The creation of the state was, by definition, the consolidation of sovereign power over a territory and its population. This creation of "territorial competence" provoked a response from European subjects who were anxious to define the limits and regulation of sovereign power (particularly in relation to the issues of property and religious conscience).[74] One of the principal political languages employed to define those limits was the language of rights that was developed largely from theories of natural (and Roman) law.[75] Protection from the abuses of sovereign power demanded universal laws regarding the nature of sovereign power and the status of subjects. Vitoria, Pufendorf, Wolff, and Kant are best known as several of the foundational writers on the concept of rights in Western political thought. Many of these writers, both renowned and obscure, who proclaimed and developed the theories of natural (and later "human") rights, made the question of the rights of colonized peoples central to their discussions. If the laws regarding sovereigns and subject were universal, then the failure by a European sovereign, or his or her agents, to respect the rights of a colonized people was theoretically equivalent to the violation of European subjects' rights. It has to be remembered that these authors conducted their discussions of rights over centuries in which Europe was immersed in conflicts between sovereigns with absolutist pretensions and subjects demanding basic rights. Saxe Bannister, for example, was writing against the background of Chartism and the pressure to extent the franchise in England. It is important to note that he wrote extensively not only on colonial reform, but also on the reform of the British government and British education system. In this context, the threat posed by these writers to the imperial grandeur or the colonial profits of their sovereigns was for them a minor consideration.

To the concern about the political rights of Europeans we must add a second and related context that motivated European writers on the rights of colonized peoples. Throughout the colonial period, Europe experienced successive wars of occupation, from the wars of religion in the sixteenth and seventeenth centuries, to the Napoleonic wars and the First and Second World Wars. The problems of the laws of occupation during war were very similar and in many ways identical to those prevailing in colonies (although belligerent occupation did not always, of course, lead to settlement). European writers concerned with colonial occupation often stressed that conquering armies in Europe, while possessing *imperium*, had no rights of dominion and were obliged to respect the laws of the occupied country.[76]

Similarly, in international law, colonization, despite the best efforts of promoters, was often difficult to distinguish from conquest pursued by war (and, indeed, this was precisely the judgment of Chief Justice Marshall in the United States in 1823). Such were the parallels between the two contexts that the term "occupation" was applied in both cases and the same body of international law was applied to explain both situations.

The Anti-imperial Response to the 1884/85 Conference at Berlin

Against this background, it is possible to argue, of course, that the universalism of the natural rights theorists had a very particular and self-interested motivation. That theories of the rights of colonized peoples were provoked by European concerns is evident from Charles Salomon's *L'Occupation des Territoires sans Maître* (1887), a treatise on the rights of colonized peoples and on the powers of colonizers. Salomon (1862–1936), a Doctor of Law in Paris, belonged to the final anti-imperial genre that I wish to consider. He was careful to trace the development of theories on the rights of colonized peoples from a detailed examination of Vitoria through the history of European colonization. Central to his inquiry was the problem of whether sovereignty gives rights over property, observing that: "it was believed for a long time . . . that sovereignty was a right of property." He responded that "this dangerous conception . . . which was adopted by absolute monarchy, was completely rejected from the public law of modern states by the French Revolution."[77] This response reveals clearly what was at stake in the discussion of indigenous rights: the conflict between powerful states with prerogative powers, absolute or otherwise, and the demands for liberty by European subjects.

Salomon's defense of indigenous rights belongs to a host of treaties written on the same question following the 1884/85 Conference at Berlin between the colonizing powers. The immediate aim of the conference was to establish "rules" that should apply in the rapidly unfolding colonization of Africa. These rules stated that a colonizer's sovereignty in Africa would only be recognized on the basis of "effective occupation" (that is, not on the basis of "discovery" or flag-raising). Nonetheless, the act agreed on at Berlin provoked numerous responses from writers on international law. Many were disturbed by the legally arbitrary manner in which the colonizers were proceeding. Others, while not disputing the principles agreed on at Berlin, were unhappy with the implementation of those principles in practice. The consequence was a series of works on the limits of imperial powers, on the conditions in which a territory can be occupied, and on the rights of occupied peoples.[78]

Gaston Jèze (1869–1953) was in many ways typical of these authors. In his *Étude Théorique et Pratique sur L'occupation* (1896), Jèze acknowledged the criticism of the Berlin conference: "However, we would be told, the Powers had in 1884, during the Berlin Conference, a good opportunity to show, in the highest way, their generous intentions and to proclaim in the face of the world their absolute respect for the sovereign rights of the barbarian peoples. And yet, the Declaration does not contain, neither explicitly nor implicitly, anything of that kind."[79] Jèze, however, disagreed with this judgment. He argued that the Berlin Act contained enough substance to protect the sovereignty and property of indigenous Africans, and that the subsequent abuses of those rights had arisen from the states and companies acting without regard to the agreement.[80] Reviewing the anti-imperial tradition Jèze observed: "As Vitoria already said in the sixteenth century, civilized powers have no more right to seize the territories of savages than savages have to occupy the European continent. The law of nations does not admit any distinction between the barbarians and the so-called civilized: men of all races, white or black, yellow or red, however unequal they are in fact have to be considered equal in the law."[81] He then turned to Kant, whose anti-imperial thoughts have been said to have been forgotten in the nineteenth century: "The theory is not new, but it is not before the end of the eighteenth century that it started recruiting numerous followers. One of the first, the philosopher Kant, exposed it in excellent terms in his *Metaphysical Elements of the Doctrine of Law* . . . we do not 'without a specific contract' have the right to colonize the land of another people."[82] He notes Kant's observations on the limits that colonizers must observe when settling near another people, and cites Kant's stipulation that "if we are concerned with pastoral or hunting peoples (like the Hottentots, the Tongouses and most of the American nations) whose lifestyles demand vast and empty regions, we cannot resort to violence, but one needs to obtain a contract, and even then it is not allowed to take advantage of these aboriginals' ignorance concerning the cession of their lands."[83] He added the exclamation by Gérard de Reyneval, the first French ambassador to the United States, that "the European conquests in the Indies, Africa and America have violated all the principles of natural law and the law of nations."[84] Delivering his own view, Jèze summarized: "On better reflection, we decide in favor of the absolute right of the indigenous peoples. We believe the opposite theory does nothing but establish, on the pretext of civilization, the maxim 'might is right' and violates, under the appearance of legality, the fundamental rule of racial equality."[85]

Jèze had a long career and acted upon his convictions. When the Italians under Mussolini invaded Ethiopia, he offered his services as an eminent international lawyer to Haile Selassie, the King of Ethiopia, and represented

Ethiopia's challenge to the legitimacy of the Italian conquest in the League of Nations.[86] His action attracted "virulent" demonstrations from the French monarchist and nationalist right in late 1935 and 1936. From January to March 1936, the demonstrators, including the young François Mitterand, prevented Jèze from delivering his lectures at the University of Paris. Similarly, during World War II, Jèze challenged the powers of the occupying German army over the French Jewish community. The two cases were connected—as Jèze well understood, the laws of occupation applied in colonies and in European wars.

The German occupation of Europe produced precisely the kinds of violations of Europeans' rights that writers on colonization had anticipated. One of the most important writers to denounce those violations was, of course, Raphael Lemkin. Lemkin took "The Laws of Occupation" to be a central question of *Axis Rule in Occupied Europe*. As a writer on international law, he was familiar with the literature on the laws of colonial occupation.[87] In unpublished manuscripts, Lemkin wrote at length on the Spanish conquests of America, examining in detail the Spanish actions in Mexico, Peru, and Yucatan.[88] The judgements of Las Casas in particular, and also Vitoria, were central to his account of that history. In Lemkin's proposal for the unpublished book *Introduction to the Study of Genocide*, among the seven grounds he listed for the "importance of the project" was "international law and relations." Here Lemkin made clear his understanding that the concept of genocide as he had developed it was drawing on a tradition of anti-colonial writings that had Vitoria and Las Casas at its foundations:

> The history of genocide provides examples of the awakening of humanitarian feelings which gradually have been crystalized in formulae of international law. The awakening of the world conscience is traced to the times when the world community took an affirmative stand to protect human groups from extinction. Bartolome de las Casas, Vitoria, and humanitarian interventions, are all links in one chain leading to the proclamation of genocide as an international crime by the United Nations.[89]

Lemkin died before he could write the volume in which he would examine this anticolonial tradition in greater detail and reveal further the place of his own thought in that tradition.

It is a moot point whether the word "genocide" can be meaningfully used to describe the horrors of colonization in the centuries that preceded the context in which Lemkin coined the term. But if we turn this problem on its head, we can ask some penetrating questions, such as, what impact did colonization have upon the concept of genocide? It would appear that the development of the concept of genocide drew not simply upon the immediate context of the German occupation of Europe, but upon the history of colonization, and specifically upon the tradition of anticolonial political and legal thought that was strongly represented in writing on international law in the generation before Lemkin wrote *Axis Rule*. It was for this reason that Lemkin conducted extensive research on colonial occupations, which he examined for what he regarded as instances of genocide.[90] Plainly, Lemkin was trying to extend the application of his neologism "genocide" to contexts beyond the German occupation of Europe. He was trying to read the colonial past from the perspective of the European present. But clearly he also understood that colonial history formed an important context for the development of the idea of genocide, so that on another level he was retracing his intellectual steps into the colonial past. The concept of universal human rights, which was fundamental to understanding genocide as a crime, had developed largely in debates over the status of colonized peoples.[91] Lemkin's education in international law taught him that one side of that debate was constituted by a tradition of anti-imperial thinking. He would have appreciated that the dispossession and destruction of occupied peoples in colonies had been conducted against the opposition of outspoken critics of successive generations. He would have appreciated also that he was taking his own place in that anti-imperial tradition. It is as a part of that tradition that his work must now be understood.

Notes

1. Convention on the Prevention and Punishment of the Crime of Genocide, adopted by Resolution 260 (III) A of the United Nations General Assembly on 9 December 1948, Article 2; Raphael Lemkin, *Axis Rule in Occupied Europe: Laws of Occupation, Analysis of Government, Proposals for Redress* (Washington, DC, 1944).
2. Robert A. Williams, *The American Indian in Western Legal Thought* (Oxford, 1990), 325.
3. There are numerous studies in this genre. See, for example, Williams, *American Indian*; James Tully, *An Approach to Political Philosophy: Locke in Contexts* (Cambridge, 1993); Bhikhu Parekh, "Liberalism and Colonialism: A Critique of Locke and Mill," in *The Decolonization of Imagination: Culture, Knowledge and Power*, ed. Nederveen Pieterse and Bhikhu Parekh (London, 1995); Barbara Arneil, *John Locke and America: The Defence of English Colonialism* (Oxford, 1996); Richard Tuck, *The Rights of War and Peace: Political Thought and the International Order from Grotius to Kant* (Oxford, 1999); Duncan Ivison, Paul Patton, and Will Sanders, eds., *Political Theory and the Rights of Indigenous Peoples* (Cambridge, 2000); Anthony Pagden, "Human Rights, Natural Rights, and Europe's Imperial Legacy," *Political Theory* 31, no. 2 (April 2003): 171–99; David Armitage, "John Locke, Carolina, and the Two Treatises of Government," *Political Theory* 32, no. 5 (October 2004): 602–27.

4. Henry Reynolds makes a similar point in the context of missionary opposition to colonial abuses in nineteenth and early twentieth century Australia. See Henry Reynolds, *This Whispering in Our Hearts* (Sydney, 1998). On the need for a broad interpretation of intention, see A. Dirk Moses, "Genocide and Settler Society in Australian History," in *Genocide and Settler Society. Frontier Violence and Stolen Indigenous Children in Australian History*, ed. A. Dirk Moses (New York, 2004), 23–30.
5. For the pre-1492 legal status of heathen peoples, see James Muldoon, *Popes, Lawyers, and Infidels: The Church and the Non-Christian World, 1250–1550* (Philadelphia, 1979); James Muldoon, ed., *The Expansion of Europe: The First Phase* (Philadelphia, 1977); and Williams, *American Indian*, ch.1.
6. Williams, *American Indian*, 40.
7. Ibid., 45. See also Annabel Brett, *Liberty, Right and Nature. Individual Rights in Later Scholastic Thought* (Cambridge, 1997).
8. The following account of Vitoria's thought draws heavily upon Anthony Pagden, *The Fall of Natural Man: The American Indian and the Origins of Comparative Ethnology*, 2nd ed. (Cambridge, 1986); and Francesco de Vitoria, *Political Writings*, ed. Anthony Pagden and Jeremy Lawrance (Cambridge, 1991).
9. Vitoria, "On the American Indians" in *Political Writings*, 280. The use of Roman law doctrine was not accidental. It was one of Vitoria's principal aims to show that Roman law reflected natural law principles.
10. Ibid., 250.
11. Ibid., 258–64.
12. Ibid., 265–72.
13. Ibid., 264.
14. Ibid., 250.
15. Ibid., 264.
16. Ibid., xxvii–xxviii.
17. Ibid., 278–86.
18. See, for example, Tully, *Approach to Political Philosophy*, 142–43; Williams, *American Indian*, 105–7.
19. Vitoria, "Letter to Miguel de Arcos, 8 November 1534," in *Political Writings*, 331–33.
20. Hugo Grotius, *The Free Sea,* trans. Richard Hakluyt, with William Welwod's *Critique and Grotius's Reply*, ed. David Armitage (Indianapolis, IN, 2004), 13–15.
21. Grotius, *Free Sea*, 13. Grotius is commonly regarded as having understood property to arise from consent and compact, but as this passage shows, and as Barbara Arneil points out, he clearly also acknowledges an important role for use. See Arneil, *Locke and America*, 46–54.
22. Grotius, *Free Sea*, 15.
23. Ibid., 15.
24. Ibid., 16–17.
25. Ibid., 18.
26. Ibid., 18–19. See also Vitoria, "On the American Indians," 263–64.
27. Sankar Muthu, *Enlightenment Against Empire* (Princeton, NJ, 2003), 277; see also 7, 17, and 268. Richard Tuck, *Natural Rights Theories: Their Origins and Development* (Cambridge, 1979), 62; Arneil, *Locke and America*, 46–54.
28. Notably, Grotius later argued against English trading rights to the East in the spiralling of European commercial rivalry in the region.
29. Samuel Pufendorf, *De Jure Naturae et Gentium Libri Octo*, vol. 2, translation of the edition of 1688 by C.H. Oldfather and W.A. Oldfather (Oxford, 1934), 364.
30. Ibid., 364–65.

31. Ibid., 536.
32. Ibid., 536.
33. Ibid., 536.
34. "A justification for planting in Virginia" in *The Records of the Virginia Company of London*, ed. S.M. Kingsbury, 4 vols. (Washington, DC, 1906–35), 3: 1–3, printed from Tanner Manuscripts, XCIII, folio 200, Bodleian Library, Oxford. Emphasis added. For an extended discussion of the use of natural law arguments to debate the rights of Native Americans, see Andrew Fitzmaurice, "Moral Uncertainty in the Dispossession of Native Americans," in Peter Mancall, ed., *The Atlantic World and Virginia, 1550–1624* (Chapel Hill, NC, 2007), 383–409.
35. Although, see Andrew Fitzmaurice, *Humanism and America: An Intellectual History of English Colonization, 1500–1625* (Cambridge, 2003) on ideological anxieties impeding English expansion.
36. See, for example, Alexander Whitaker, *Good Newes From Virginia* (London, 1613), 26–27.
37. William Crashaw, *A Sermon Preached Before Right Honourable the Lord Lawarre* (London, 1609), [D3]v–D4v. See also Robert Gray, *A Good Speed to Virginia* (London, 1610), [C4]r.
38. William Strachey, *The Historie of Travell into Virginia Britannia (1609–1612)*, ed. Louis B. Wright and Virginia Freund (London, 1953), 25.
39. John Donne, *A Sermon Preached to the Honourable Company of the Virginian Plantation* (London, 1622), 25–27.
40. Strachey, *Historie of Travell*, 22–23. See also *A True Declaration of the Estate of the Colonie in Virginia*, 6–7.
41. For an elaboration of this argument, see Anthony Pagden, *Lords of All the World: Ideologies of Empire in Spain, Britain and France c. 1500–1800* (New Haven, CT, 1995).
42. John Locke, *Two Treatises of Government*, ed. Peter Laslett (Cambridge, 1988), 287–88.
43. Ibid., 298.
44. David Armitage has recently revealed the depth of that colonial preoccupation. See: Armitage, "John Locke, Carolina and the Two Treatises." Cf. Stephen Buckle, "Tully, Locke and America," *British Journal for the History of Philosophy* 9, no. 2 (2001): 245–81.
45. Emeric de Vattel, *The Law of Nations or Principles of Natural Law*, intro. Albert de Lapradelle, trans. Charles G. Fenwick (Washington, DC, 1916), I: 81; "their unsettled habitation in those immense regions cannot be accounted a true and legal possession" so that "the people of Europe . . . were lawfully entitled to take possession of it."
46. Ibid., I, 208.
47. Ibid., I, 209.
48. Ibid., II, 97.
49. Christian Wolff, *Jus Gentium Methodo Scientificia Pertractatum*, 2 vols., trans. Joseph H. Drake (Oxford, 1934), 2: 156. Henry Reynolds has also noted Wolff's concerns about the justice of colonization, see Reynolds, *The Law of the Land* (Melbourne, 1987 and 2003), 19–22.
50. Wolff, *Jus Gentium*, 157.
51. Ibid., 158.
52. Ibid.
53. Ibid., 159.
54. Ibid.
55. Ibid.

56. Muthu, *Enlightenment Against Empire.*
57. Guillaume-Thomas Raynal, *Histoire Philosophique et Politique des Établissements et du Commerce des Européens dans les Deux Indes*, 10 vols (Geneva, 1780), 8: 22; cited from Muthu, *Enlightenment Against Empire*, 93.
58. Cited from Muthu, *Enlightenment Against Empire*, 188. Muthu is silent on Wolff's anti-imperialism and its impact upon Kant.
59. Johann Gottfried Herder, *Outlines of a Philosophy of the History of Man*, trans. T. Churchill and J. Johnson (London, 1800), 208; cited from Muthu, *Enlightenment Against Empire*, 244.
60. See, for example, Pagden, "Human rights," 190–91; Michael Ignatieff, *Human Rights as Politics and Idolatry*, ed. Amy Gutman (Princeton, NJ, 2001).
61. Pagden, "Human rights," 190–91.
62. See, for example, Alan Lester, "British Settler Discourse and the Circuits of Empire," *History Workshop Journal* 54 (2002): 25–48; Reynolds, *This Whispering in our Hearts;* John Gascoigne, *The Enlightenment and the Origins of European Australia* (Cambridge, 2002), 153–59.
63. Gascoigne, *Enlightenment*, is an exception within this scholarship insofar as he places "humanitarian" sentiments in the context of "enlightenment" languages of rights.
64. Cf. Lester, "British Settler Discourse."
65. Saxe Bannister, *Mr Bannister's Claims* (London, 1853), 11–14.
66. Ibid., 15.
67. Ibid.
68. Ibid., 14.
69. Saxe Bannister, *Appel en Faveur d'Alger et de l'Afrique du Nord* (Paris, 1833), 9 (my translation): "De nouveaux plans n'en sont pas moins proposés tous les jours pour enrichir la France aux dépens d'Alger. Sans les passer ici tous en revue, nous rappelerons le projet d'extermination (E), proposé contre les millions d'hommes à qui le pays appartient d'aussi bon droit que Paris appartient aux Français." Bannister's footnote "E" cites M.Gaëtan de la Rochefoucauld in the Chambre des Députés on 8 March 1833, declaring: "Remember that many writers stated that succeeding the Turks with security in Alger could only be achieved by governing like them; that civilizing the Arabs was impossible, and that using terror was the only way to maintain them in peace; and, finally, that putting colonisation into practice would be possible just once the country would be entirely evacuated of indigenous people" (my translation): "Souvenez-vous que, dans de nombreux écrits, on disait qu'on ne pouvait, à Alger, succéder aux Turcs avec sûreté qu'en gouvernant comme eux; qu'il était impossible de civiliser les Arabes, et qu'on ne pouvait les maintenir en paix que par la terreur, et qu'enfin la colonization ne serait praticable que lorsque le pays serait entièrement évacué par les indigènes. Voilà, messieurs, les opinions qui ont induit en erreur le gouvernement." Turning to the record of the debate in the Chambre des Députés, it is clear that Rochefoucauld was not arguing against the colonization of North Africa, but rather against the imposition of a military rather than civilian administration. See: Archives de l'Assemblée Nationale, Paris, Chambre des Députés, 8 mars 1833, 711–17.
70. Ibid., 9–10 (my translation): "Nous réclamons au contraire, pour les Africains du Nord, l'indépendance dans le vrai sens de ce mot et telle que l'annonce la proclamation; et pour l'établir, nous demandons que les naturels du pays soient appelés à déclarer, à la face de l'Europe, leurs opinions sur la forme de gouvernement la plus convenable. C'est à eux qu'il appartient de déterminer cette forme: c'est à l'Europe et principalement à la France à les soutenir avec sagesse et honneur. La France doit devenir l'amie de l'Afrique libre."

71. Ibid., 11 (my translation): "Il ne faut pas laisser oublier à l'Angleterre que les vexations imposées aux peuples de l'Afrique du Nord ne sont qu'une répétition de celles qu'elle exerce sur ceux de l'Afrique du Sud. Les torrens de sang africain versés sans provocation dans la Cafrerie en 1828 (H); les actes d'arbitraire qui sont restés jusqu'à ce moment sans réparation sur les frontières du cap de Bonne-Espérance; les massacres de sang-froid commis dans l'Australie en 1826 (I), au mépris de toutes les lois, imposent trop éloquemment silence au gouvernement anglais."
72. Ibid., 11, his emphasis.
73. On the links between state formation and European expansion, see Armitage, *Ideological Origins*; David Armitage, "Greater Britain: A Useful Category of Historical Analysis," *American Historical Review* 104, no. 2 (April 1999); Michael J. Braddick, *State Formation in Early Modern England, c. 1550–1700* (Cambridge, 2000); and Elizabeth Mancke, "Empire and State," in *The British Atlantic World 1500–1800*, ed. David Armitage and Michael J. Braddick (Basingstoke, UK, 2002), 175–95. See also James Muldoon, *Empire and Order: The Concept of Empire 800–1800* (London, 1999); and Christine Daniels and Michael Kennedy, eds., *Negotiated Empires: Centres and Peripheries in the Americas, 1500–1820* (New York, 2002).
74. The term is Braddick's in *State Formation*.
75. In England, the "Ancient Constitution" was also an important source of the understanding of rights.
76. See, for example, Henry Bonfils, *Manuel de Droit International Public*, 7th ed. (1894; Paris, 1914), 375–400, and 819–41.
77. Charles Salomon, *L'Occupation des Territoires Sans Maître* (Paris, 1887), 7 (my translation): "on a cru longtemps . . . que la souveraineté était un droit de propriété. . . . Cette conception dangereuse . . . adoptée par la monarchie absolue, a été définitivement écartée du droit public des Etats modernes par la Révolution française."
78. See, for example, Bonfils, *Manuel de Droit*; Gaston Jèze, *Étude Théorique et Pratique sur l'Occupation* (Paris, 1896); Salomon, *L'Occupation des Territoires Sans Maître*; Frantz Despagnet, *Cours de Droit International Public*, 4th ed. (Paris, 1910). In this group we can include two treatises from the 1860s, before the Berlin Conference: Pasquale Fiore, *International Law Codified*, translated from the 5th Italian edition by Edwin M. Borchard (New York, 1918), 423–25; and M.P. Pradier-Fodéré, *Vattel's le Droit des Gens* (Paris, 1863).
79. Jèze, *Étude Théorique et Pratique sur l'Occupation*, 131 (my emphasis): "Mais, nous dira-t-on, les Puissances avaient en 1884, lors de la conférence de Berlin, une belle occasion de manifester hautement leurs intentions généreuses et de proclamer à la face du monde leur respect absolu pour les droits de souveraineté des peuples barbares. Et cependant, la Déclaration ne contient ni expressément, ni implicitement, rien de semblable."
80. Ibid., 131–56.
81. Ibid., 103 (my translation): "Comme le disait déjà Victoria au XVIe siècle, les puissances civilisées n'ont pas plus le droit de s'emparer des territoires des sauvages que ceux-ci n'ont le droit d'occuper les continent [*sic*] européens. Le droit des gens n'admet pas de distinction entre les barbares et les prétendus civilisés: les hommes de toutes les races, blanches ou noires, jaunes ou rouges, si inégaux qu'ils puissent être en fait doivent être considérés comme égaux en droit."
82. Ibid., 104–5 (my translation): "La théorie n'est pas nouvelle; mais ce n'est guère qu'à partir de la fin du XVIIIe siècle qu'elle recrute des adeptes nombreux. L'un des premiers, le philosophe Kant, dans ses «Eléments métaphysiques de la doctrine du Droit», l'expose en excellents termes: « on ne peut avoir, «sans un contrat particulier,

. . . [le droit de] colonization sur le sol d'un autre peuple».” Cf. Muthu, *Empire Against Enlightenment*, 5: “The anti-imperialist writings of the latter half of the eighteenth century failed to rally later thinkers to the cause of exposing imperialist injustices, defending non-European peoples against imperial rule, and attacking the standard rationales for empire.”

83. Jèze, *Étude Théorique et Pratique sur l'Occupation*, 104–5 (my translation): “Si l'on a affaire à des peuples pasteurs ou chasseurs (comme les Hottentots, les Tongouses et la plupart des nations américaines), dont le genre de vie exige des contrées vastes et désertes, on ne peut avoir recours à la violence, mais il faut obtenir un contrat, et même il n'est pas permis de profiter de l'ignorance de ces indigènes relativement à la cession de leurs terres.”
84. Ibid., 105 (my translation): “Les conquêtes des Européens dans les Indes, en Afrique et en Amérique, ont violé tous les principes de loi naturelle et du droit des gens.” The quotation is from Gérard de Rayneval, *Institutions du Droit de la Nature et des Gens* (Paris, 1803). See also Rayneval, *Institutions du Droit de la Nature et des Gens*, 2 vols. 3rd ed. (Paris, 1851), 367–69 for the extent of Rayneval's anticolonial thought.
85. Jèze, *Étude Théorique et Pratique sur l'Occupation*, 112 (my translation): “Après mûres réflexions, c'est en faveur du droit absolu des indigènes que nous nous décidons. La théorie contraire, croyons-nous, ne fait que consacrer, sous prétexte de civilisation, la maxime «la Force prime le Droit», et violer, sous des apparences juridiques, la règle fondamentale de l'égalité des races.”
86. Pierre Péan, *Une Jeunesse Française. François Mitterrand, 1934–1947* (Paris, 1994), 45–61.
87. It is interesting to note that both Lemkin and Jèze wrote on international financial movements—one of the most troubling issues of the interwar years. Lemkin's *La Réglementation des Paiements Internationaux* (Paris, 1939) does not cite Jèze's *Les Paiements Internationaux* (Paris, 1926), but the authors' parallel interests indicate one of the contexts within which early twentieth century authors thought about rights.
88. American Jewish Historical Society, New York, Box 8, Folder 12, “Spanish colonial genocide”; Box 7, Folder 1, “Incas”; Box 8, Folder 12, “Yucatan.” My thanks to Dirk Moses for his generosity in providing copies of these manuscripts.
89. New York Public Library, Reel 3, Box 2, Folder 1, “Proposal for Introduction to the Study of Genocide.” Note that Lemkin places the term “humanitarian” in the context of international law.
90. On Lemkin's colonial writings, see also John Docker, “Are Settler-Colonies Inherently Genocidal? Re-reading Lemkin,” in this volume; and Ann Curthoys, “Raphael Lemkin's ‘Tasmania’: An Introduction,” *Patterns of Prejudice* 39, no. 2 (2005): 162–69.
91. It is true that Lemkin distinguished the crime of genocide from the violation of human rights. His understanding of genocide was based upon group or collective rights, whereas since the fifteenth century the rights tradition had been dominated by a concern with individual rights. Moreover, he was mounting a strategic defence of the genocide treaty within the UN (See, for example, Raphael Lemkin, “Memorandum on the Genocide Convention,” 3, Collection 60, Box Number 4, Folder No. 4/6, Jacob Rader Marcus Center of the American Jewish Archives, Hebrew Union College, Cincinnati, OH). Some UN delegates thought that existing “legislation” on human rights covered the crimes under the genocide treaty and that therefore it was not necessary to have the separate crime of genocide. Having said that, Lemkin was fully aware of the genesis of the concept of genocide within the rights tradition, regarding the Genocide Convention as a distinct branch from that tradition.

– *Chapter 3* –

ARE SETTLER-COLONIES INHERENTLY GENOCIDAL?

Re-reading Lemkin

John Docker

> Our whole cultural heritage is a product of the contributions of all peoples. We can best understand this if we realize how impoverished our culture would be if the so-called inferior peoples doomed by Germany, such as the Jews, had not been permitted to create the Bible or to give birth to an Einstein, a Spinosa [*sic*]; if the Poles had not had the opportunity to give to the world a Copernicus, a Chopin, a Curie, the Czechs a Huss, and a Dvorak; the Greeks a Plato and a Socrates; the Russians, a Tolstoy and a Shostakovich.
>
> —Raphael Lemkin, "Genocide—A Modern Crime"[1]

> . . . colonialism cannot be left without blame.
>
> —Raphael Lemkin, "Introduction to the Study of Genocide"[2]

In this chapter, I will explore the conjoining of genocide and colonialism in the writings of Raphael Lemkin, the brilliant Polish-Jewish jurist (1900–1959). I will highlight three aspects of his thought: First, that the concept of genocide as created by Lemkin offers the groundwork for the delineation and discussion of different kinds of genocide in history—for example, genocide as episode or genocide as a more extended process. Second, that Lemkin's concept of genocide links settler-colonies and genocide in a constitutive and inherent relationship. Finally, that Lemkin, in his published work, but more powerfully in his unpublished manuscripts, developed a methodology that permits the possibility of subtle, intricate, and multifaceted analyses of settler-colonial histories in relation to genocide as an extended process that may also involve more sharply destructive episodes and events.

I will be stressing throughout the importance to Lemkin of the notion of cultural genocide. In his illuminating, unfinished autobiography, "Totally Unofficial Man," written shortly before he died in 1958, Lemkin regrets that he could not persuade the relevant UN committee meeting in Paris after World War II to include an article in the final convention on "cultural genocide": "I defended it successfully through two drafts. It meant the destruction of the cultural pattern of a group, such as the language, the traditions, the monuments, archives, libraries, churches. In brief: the shrines of the soul of a nation. But there was not enough support for this idea in the Committee. . . . So with a heavy heart I decided not to press for it." He had to drop an idea that, as he put it, "was very dear to me."[3]

Strengths of Lemkin's Definitions

Lemkin's thinking about genocide began well before the German unleashing of World War II. In 1933, he was a young public prosecutor in Warsaw, already immersed in his life project to have certain egregious crimes outlawed. Hitler had just been elected to the government in Germany. Lemkin was at the last moment prevented by the Polish government, fearful he would embarrass it, from leaving Poland to present a paper at a League of Nations conference on the unification of penal law held in Madrid.[4] The paper, presented in his absence, proposed the creation of the crimes of barbarity and vandalism as new offences against the law of nations, that is, against the whole international community. Acts of barbarity—which he also calls acts of extermination—undermine the fundamental basis of an ethnic, religious, or social collectivity. They are acts that, taken as a whole, range from massacres and pogroms to the ruining of the economic existence of the members of a collectivity, as well as "all sorts of brutalities" that attack the "dignity of the individual" as part of the campaign of extermination of the group. Lemkin also proposed for the same conference the crime of vandalism, the destruction of the cultural heritage of a collectivity as revealed in the fields of science, arts, and literature. Lemkin noted that the contribution of any particular collectivity to "world culture" forms the wealth of all humanity, even while exhibiting unique characteristics. Thus the destruction of any work of art of any nation must be regarded as an act of vandalism directed against world culture. Such acts, Lemkin said, reveal an asocial and destructive spirit that shocks the conscience of humanity, while generating extreme anxiety about the future.[5]

What is notable is that already in 1933, under the heading of barbarity and vandalism, Lemkin had assembled many of the features of his now-famous definition of genocide in his 1944 book *Axis Rule in Occupied*

Europe.[6] In particular, we can note the breadth of his 1933 formulations, that barbarity and vandalism involve a systematic and organized destruction of the social order of a collectivity, in terms that may involve direct killing as well as actions that are economic, moral, intellectual, and cultural. In his 1944 definition, he again says that genocide is composite and manifold, that it signifies a coordinated plan of different actions aiming at the destruction of the essential foundations of life of a group. Such actions can, but do not necessarily entail mass killing. They involve considerations that are political, social, legal, intellectual, spiritual, economic, biological, physiological, religious, and moral. Such actions involve health, food, and nourishment, of family life and care of children, and of birth as well as death, in relation to genocide and as part of genocide. Such actions involve consideration of the honor and dignity of peoples, and the future of humanity as a world community.[7]

The continuity between 1933 and 1944 concerns the wide range of destructive acts against a group. Yet there is also something significantly new added in 1944, when Lemkin says that genocide may involve two phases, that it is a two-fold process. Here is the key passage from the opening page of chapter nine of *Axis Rule*: "Genocide has two phases: one, destruction of the national pattern of the oppressed group; the other, the imposition of the national pattern of the oppressor. This imposition, in turn, may be made upon the oppressed population which is allowed to remain, or upon the territory alone, after removal of the population and the colonization of the area by the oppressor's own nationals."[8] Whereas in 1933 Lemkin had focused on genocide as an episode or act or event, now he writes that genocide can also be a process, a process that describes and entwines genocide and settler-colonialism.

Explorations of an Idea

Nonetheless, in his published work Lemkin never seems to have discussed genocide in relation to European settler-colonies as part of a world-historical process. In *Axis Rule* Lemkin refers to how the German "occupant," in order to impose its national pattern, "organized a system of colonization" in areas that Germany wished to incorporate, including western Poland, Luxemburg, and Alsace-Lorraine: "The Polish population have been removed from their homes in order to make place for German settlers who were brought in from the Baltic States, the central and eastern districts of Poland, Bessarabia, and from the Reich itself. The properties and homes of the Poles are being allocated to German settlers; and to induce them to reside in these areas the settlers receive many privileges, especially in the way of tax exemptions."[9] In an April 1945 essay, "Genocide—A Modern Crime," he again refers to colonization, writing with irony that where "the people, such as the Poles, could not achieve the dignity of embracing Germanism, they were expelled from the area and their territory (western Poland) was to be Germanized by colonization."[10] It seems clear that during World War II, Lemkin conceived his idea of linking genocide and colonization chiefly from the example of Nazi colonization of western Poland.[11]

Lemkin was deeply concerned not only with contemporary events, however momentously catastrophic, but also with historical genocides. In "Totally Unofficial Man," he says that from his "very young days" he was interested in historical accounts of examples of extermination of national, racial, and religious minorities. Lemkin here writes that he always "felt that history is much wiser than are lawyers and statesmen." He confides that from an early age he "took a special delight in being alone, so that I could think and feel without outer disturbances," and that "loneliness" became the essential condition of his life. History, it appears, was his lifelong companion. As is well known, during the postwar years he worked tirelessly in the fledgling UN circles to persuade influential people to bring about a UN convention criminalizing genocide.[12] Lemkin reflects that even during the most stressful days and nights he would read or re-read history books to keep himself "articulate and determined," and he persuaded delegates to read historical cases of genocide: "Let history," he wrote, "make a plea to them." He realized, he continued, that just showing *Axis Rule* to committees and delegates was not enough, because it drew only on one criminal experience alone, the Nazis. It was necessary to "draw on all available experiences of the past." He started digesting historical cases of genocide and submitting them to delegates in the form of memoranda.[13]

In the autobiography, Lemkin relates the examples of genocide that stirred him from an early age, examples drawn from antiquity through to modern times. They include the destruction of the Christians by Nero; the Mongol hordes overrunning Russia, Poland, Silesia, and Hungary in 1241; the persecution of Jews in Russia by Tzar Nicholas I; the destruction of the Moors in Spain; and the devastation of the Huguenots. When in 1941 Lemkin and other refugees reached Japan on the way to exile and haven in the United States, he reflected on the atrocious persecution of 30,000 Japanese Catholics in the seventeenth century, who had been converted by Portuguese and Spanish missionaries.[14]

In a footnote to chapter nine of *Axis Rule*, Lemkin refers to classical examples of wars of extermination in which nations and groups of a population were completely or almost completely destroyed, including the destruction of Carthage in 146 BC and of Jerusalem by Titus in AD 72; the religious wars of Islam and the Crusades; the massacres of the Albigenses and Waldenses; and the siege of Magdeburg in the Thirty Years' War. And wholesale massacres occurred in the wars waged by Genghis Khan and Tamerlane.[15]

From his published work, in *Axis Rule*, and in his essays and autobiography, it would seem clear that the historical instances of genocide, though many and extensive, which inspired Lemkin's lonely, lifelong quest to have genocide indicted in international law, did not include the European settler-colonies of the Americas, or southern Africa, or Australia. However, in his unpublished research and writings during the 1940s and 1950s and until his death in 1959, Lemkin did not confine genocide to European history, and he also pondered with subtlety and insight the difficult problem of intention in relation to genocide and settler colonial societies.[16]

Lemkin's Manuscripts: A Book Takes Shape

The American Jewish Historical Society in New York contains boxes of Lemkin manuscripts with titles like (I preserve Lemkin's spelling here) "German Massacre at Herrero (Southwest Africa) General Assembly Report, Essay and Pamphlets"; "British Treatment of Ireland"; "Charlemagne"; "German Oppression of Slavs and East Europeans"; "German Oppression of Slavs and East Europeans (Polish)"; "History of Genocide Projected Book and North American Indian Research Correspondence"; and "Spanish Treatment of South American Indians"; and research index cards with headings that include "Moriscos," "North American Indians—Enslavement," "North American Indians—European Expropriation of Land," "North American Indians—Extermination," "North American Indians—Forced Relocation," "North American Indians—Miscellany," "Spaniards—American Indians," "Spaniards—Peruvian Indians," "Spaniards—Yucatan Indians," and a more general card title, "Psychology and Sociology of Genocide."[17]

Upon inspection, it becomes readily apparent that Lemkin in the 1940s was working on a book, with the help of student research assistants, on the history of global genocide. Some chapters were evidently to concern genocide in antiquity, as with the cases of genocide that the Assyrians committed against peoples in the ancient world, including the Hebrews and Babylonians (Subseries 2, Box 8, Folder 1). In Box 8, Folder 6, there is an evocation of Charlemagne, whom Lemkin foregrounds as one of history's more prominent "genocidists" (Lemkin's own term): in 772, Lemkin notes here, Charlemagne inaugurated a war of conquest against the pagan Saxons who resided on the eastern frontier of the Frank dominions, a bloody war that continued for over thirty-three years. Lemkin refers to Charlemagne's determination in 774 either to compel the Saxons to embrace the Christian religion or to exterminate them.[18] Another folder concerns early modern Europe, as with the persecutions of Catholics under Elizabeth in the sixteenth century (Box 8, Folder 4) or British treatment of Ireland (Box 8, Folder 5), especially by Cromwell and his "Plantation regime, whereby land was taken away from the Irish, Catholics could hold no land, positions, nor could they vote. A scheme of 'transplantation' (like the similar Turkish efforts) was inaugurated, former land-owners were kicked out and their holdings taken over by imported land lords." There is mention here of "economic" and "cultural" genocide against the Irish from early modern European to modern times.

Plainly, in these manuscript essays and notes, Lemkin was giving shape to a historical and comparative approach that was based on, yet temporally and spatially extends, his definition of genocide in *Axis Rule*. A scholar who had only just created the very word *genocide* in 1944, was now a few years later creating a method of how to analyze and discuss genocidal situations in the ancient world and European history generally; a method that he also was about to apply to examples of European colonization around the globe.

In 1947, Lemkin was seeking financial assistance to conduct the research for his book on genocide. His application to the Rockefeller Foundation was unsuccessful; Lemkin receiving a chillingly cold rejection letter (Folder 11: Note from a Roger F. Evans, Assistant Director of Social Sciences for the Rockefeller Foundation, dated 6 November 1947). Happily, however, Folder 11 reveals that Lemkin did receive support from another source, the Viking Fund, a foundation for scientific charitable and educational purposes located in New York. In a progress report to Paul Fejos, the director of research for the Viking Fund, he writes that work on the project had began on 1 March 1948, and that the Yale Law School was providing an office and typing facilities and was paying for the expenses of a research assistant. Lemkin tells the fund that data was being collected under "headings covering physical, biological and cultural genocide," with emphasis laid upon the role played by "governments, groups and individuals in the commission of the crime," and that "psychological and sociological factors are also being examined." Lemkin lists the "following genocide cases" as those upon which data was being collected (I preserve his spelling):

1. The Early Christians.
2. The Jews in the Middle Ages; the Jews in Tzarist Russia.
3. The Morescos in Spain.
4. The Indians in Latin America.
5. The Valdenses.

6. The Armenians.
7. The Hugenots.
8. The Greeks in Turkey.
9. The Turks under Greek occupation in 1922.
10. The Indians in North America (in part).

Lemkin adds that part of the research material was being "made available to several members of the United Nations Drafting Committee on Genocide, with whom the author of the project is in constant contact."

There is also close by a letter dated 25 May 1948 from a researcher "Birgit" who relates that since her research for him on Yucatan, she has written material on the sale of liquor and on Indian slavery; on the Plains Indians and the Californian Indians (including forceful eviction from fertile valleys into barren mountains where Indians starved: "Wanton murder and milit. action against Indians who refused to leave, rebelled or returned occasionally to get food"); on the Sandy Creek Massacre of Plains Indians ("worst type of atrocities a [*sic*] la Europe"), the Washita Massacre, and the Wounded Knee Massacre; on the destruction of buffalo to starve Indians; on the prohibition of tribal culture in early reservations and the withholding of food supply; on individual land allotment to destroy tribal life. Birgit writes she "used extensively" John Collier's *The Indians of the Americas* in her research for Lemkin in the Public Library in New York.[19]

In a further letter dated 22 July 1948 to the Viking Fund's Paul Fejos, Lemkin reports that his genocide volume continues to progress, and offers a general reflection on the book as a history: "The historical analysis is designed to prove that genocide is not an exceptional phenomenon, but that it occurs in intergroup relations with a certain regularity like homicide takes place between individuals." Lemkin informs Fejos that owing to the "expansion of the volume and the necessity for additional research," Dean Wesley A. Sturges of the Yale Law School has generously provided funds for five hundred additional hours for his research assistant.

It is clear from the letters in Box 8, Folder 11 that the project was indeed expanding. Additional support fortunately came from another New York funding body, the Lucius N. Littauer Foundation. A letter from Harry Starr, its president and treasurer, acknowledges Lemkin's "written application and the several discussions we have had thereon," and assures him that funds of $5,000 will be made available to the Lemkin Research Fund on Genocide at the Yale University Law School. Starr writes that he understands from Lemkin that the grant will assist in the employment of "several research assistants" necessary for the completion of the manuscript, which is to be published "in two volumes." The project, as Lemkin had outlined to him, would be to examine "every genocide of importance" from ancient times to the present, in its "historical, legal, psychological, political, sociological, economic, religious and cultural aspects." In each case, there would be a survey of the "background and conditions" leading up to the genocide, the "method and techniques used in the commission of the crime," and its "effect upon society through loss of life and destruction of economic resources and cultural values."

Lemkin's book on the study and history of genocide was well on its way, a remarkable achievement considering how much time he must also have been devoting to consulting with and advising UN committee members about the proposed convention banning the crime. As Lemkin had said, the two activities of historical research and contemporary international law proceeded in tandem, feeding into each other.

Lemkin's Methodology

Lemkin continued to work on the book during the 1950s. In a letter in Box 8, Folder 11 dated 26 February 1951 to the Lucius N. Littauer Foundation, he writes to Harry Starr thanking him for the foundation's continued support; he felt that the Foundation's generosity would enable him to finish the book and to "express finally in a scientific way many ideas on the subject of Genocide which tortured my mind for many years." He also confides to Starr that he prefers to "base the research on documents than on books," and for that reason had recently spent some time "in the New York Libraries and in private collections on the search for hitherto unpublished documents concerning the extermination of the gypsies and Armenians."

After these letters, Box 8, Folder 11 included two typed pages headed "Revised Outline for Genocide Cases," which summarize Lemkin's approach to the historical study of genocides, and which probably date from around 1951. I reproduce the diagrammatic outline as follows, retaining his spelling.

REVISED OUTLINE FOR GENOCIDE CASES

1. Background
    - Historical
2. Conditions leading to genocide
    - Fanaticism (religious, racial)
    - Irredentism (national aspirations)
    - Social or political crisis and change
    - Economic exploitation (e.g. slavery)
    - Colonial expansion or milit. conquest
    - Accessability of victim group
    - Evolution of genocidal values in genocidist group (contempt for the alien, etc.)

Factors weakening victim group

3. Methods and techniques of genocide
    - *Physical*:
        - Massacre and mutilation
        - Deprivation of livelihood (starvation, Exposure, etc.—often by deportation)
        - Slavery—exposure to death
    - *Biological*:
        - Separation of families
        - Sterilization
        - Destruction of foetus
    - *Cultural*:
        - Desecration and destruction of cultural symbols (books, objects of art, religious relics, etc.)
        - Loot
        - Destruction of cultural leadership
        - Destruction of cultural centers (cities, churches, monasteries, schools, libraries)
        - Prohibition of cultural activities or codes of behavior
        - Forceful conversion
        - Demoralization
4. The Genocidists
    - Responsibility
    - Intent
    - Motivation
    - Feelings of guilt
    - Demoralization
    - Attitude towards victim group
    - Opposition to genocide within genocidist group
5. Propaganda
    - Rationalization of crime
    - Appeal to popular beliefs and intolerance; sowing discord (divide and rule)
    - Misrepresentation and deceit
    - Intimidation
6. Responses of victim group
    - *Active*:

Submission	Polit. subordination
Escape (suicide, hiding, etc.)	Assimilation
Disguise	Resistance
Emigration (planned)	Demoralization

    - *Passive (emotional, mental)*
        - Terror
        - Conceptions of genocidist and his crimes
7. Responses of outside groups
    - Opposition to genocide
    - Indifference to "
    - Condonement of "

Collaboration in "
Demoralization (exploitation of genocide situation)
Fear as potential victims
8. Aftermath
Cultural losses
Population changes
Economic dislocations
Material and moral deterioration
Political consequences
Social and cult. changes

In the next folder, Box 8, Folder 12, Lemkin evokes examples of genocide drawn from the Americas, where he puts into practice and continuously deploys the categories of analysis of the diagrammatic summary. Notable here is that Lemkin does not exculpate the colonizers in terms of death by illness. In "Spanish Treatment of South American Indians Essay, n.d.," Lemkin, drawing in particular on the observations of Las Casas, successively evokes "Methods of Genocide—Physical," which include massacre, slavery, and deprivation of livelihood; family life was disregarded, bread made of root-meal was often the only food; when the slaves fell sick, they were left to die or at best sent home. The treatment of Indian women constituted an aspect of biological genocide, the "death of the race." Slave mothers, exhausted with hunger and fatigue, could not nurse their babies. Children were not infrequently carried off by the Spanish; some Indian women were not only violated indiscriminately but also taken to "fill the Harems of the Spanish colonists." In terms of physical genocide, the population of the islands catastrophically fell. In the Bahamas, the population dropped from fifty thousand to nearly zero. The population of Nicaragua was almost entirely wiped out; in fourteen years more than six hundred thousand had died as beasts of burden. Lemkin says Las Casas claimed that the total of Indians killed in Spanish America exceeded twenty million. Lemkin adds that this number does not include those who died from overwork, the slaves killed in the mines, or the Indians killed during active combat, nor the prisoners who were executed.

Cultural genocide could occur in many ways. Cultural centers were destroyed. Religion was important. Lemkin refers to the "subtle kind of cultural genocide" committed by the Spanish missions that abounded in Mexico, California, Louisiana, and elsewhere. He notes that "while most of the Indians may not have been converted by actual force, it may well be assumed that they had little idea of either Christianity or the life and burdens in store for them after baptism." Once they yielded to the admonitions of the fathers, their fate was sealed; they could no longer escape from the reach of the church, or the mission. The missionaries, for example in a church in San Francisco, gave mass in Latin and Spanish, and made no effort to learn the native tongue. Corporal punishment was inflicted on Indians of both sexes who failed in their religious duties; if an Indian escaped from the mission village, he was brought back by soldiers and lashed.

Continuing to apply his method, Lemkin evokes and gives examples of other categories of genocide—from economic to political. There was looting and pillaging of Indian wealth. There was destruction of Indian leadership in the murder of one chief or king after another. Under the heading of "Responsibility," he argues that with few exceptions the colonists of New Spain were guilty of genocide: "the colonists were guilty on all counts." The colonists and their supporters at court in Spain firmly resolved to frustrate all efforts at stopping the genocide, including not enforcing the royal orders against slavery and other abuses, and keeping vital information from the king; wherever they could, the colonists and their metropolitan supporters tried to frustrate the efforts of Las Casas to gain a hearing in Spain.

Lemkin then discusses further genocidal aspects of Spanish colonization under headings like "Motivation," including a mordant account of the motives of Columbus, which included not only greed for gold and riches but also a desire, stated to Queen Isabella, to convert the masses of the Orient to Catholicism. He is highly critical of Columbus and the historical example he set for the future of colonization in the Americas:

> After his discovery of the West Indies and the first flush of excitement at finding such peaceful and friendly natives in a charming country, Columbus hardened to become a model to the later colonists. He may have been disappointed at not discovering the riches he had hoped for. At any rate he mismanaged his colony and tolerated all kinds of genocidal crimes. To atone for the growing stories of poor discoveries and of his mismanagement, he sent Indian slaves to Spain. Natives to him constituted the principal wealth of the island and he wanted to impress the crown with them and derive a profit in turn. Thus he set the infamous example for what was to become the shame and scandal of Spanish conquest in the New World . . .

Lemkin suggests an aspect of colonization and imperial domination of others (upon which Hannah Arendt also reflected): "the impact of sudden wealth and power" leads to the demoralization or degeneration of the moral standards of the Europeans—the colonizers, the conquerors, the genocidists.[20]

Nevertheless, Lemkin does not present the motivations and ethical thinking of the genocidist group as uniform, and here his discussions are indeed subtle and far-reaching for the general history of European colonizing, with implications for the ethical conduct and capacities of humanity itself. In particular, he distinguishes between metropolitan society and colonial settlers. In terms of relationships between the European metropole and colonies across the seas, Lemkin observes under the heading "Opposition from Within" that the Spanish government never authorized slavery in New Spain. In 1500, Queen Isabella ordered governor Bobadilla to respect the liberty and safety of the Indians, but Bobadilla, who had many Indian slaves, paid no attention to the royal order. In the face of such persistent violation of the crown's orders, Queen Isabella instituted a new system called *encomienda*, which was to take the place of the notorious slave system and serve for the protection as well as the voluntary and peaceful conversion of the Indians to Christianity. However, the colonists quickly took advantage of the new situation, using *encomienda* as a cloak for renewed slavery, now rendered more odious by the hypocrisy involved. Lemkin generalizes sociologically that genocide is "largely a function of interest," and that particular groups, while enforcing genocide against one group or a number of groups, will declare themselves opponents of genocide against another group or other groups. Queen Isabella, he reflects, while she became a patron of the Indians and sought to protect their liberty and welfare against colonial abuses, had herself "just committed outrageous genocide against the Moors of Spain, both physical and cultural."

Lemkin argues that the relationship between oppressor and victim in history is always unstable. He points to the "strange transformation of genocidal victim into genocidists," as with the Protestant Germans, who had left Europe because of cultural genocide directed against them, but had then perpetrated physical genocide in Venezuela for profit. Once persecuted as heretics, the Germans who now colonized Venezuela in the sixteenth century "were no less cruel than the Spanish." Nonetheless, Lemkin warns against perceiving either genocide or opposition to genocide as "motivated purely by selfish considerations, or group loyalties," for there is often the surprising appearance of individuals whose opposition goes beyond personal or group interest or who ignore such interests entirely: "Thus Las Casas went much beyond the ordinary ecclesiastic opposition to genocide in the Indies; he preached a doctrine of humanitarianism which was actually beyond the values of his own time." Perhaps, I thought as I read this salute to Las Casas, we can say the same of Lemkin himself in his passionate intellectual and legal opposition to genocide in history.

Lemkin then considers the Spanish colonization of the Americas in terms of his other categories: Rationalization and Misrepresentation (the Indians possessed, says Lemkin, a "high degree of culture" in such places as Yucatan, Mexico, and Peru, but the early Spanish conquerors spread stories among the people of Spain that the Indians were subhuman and cannibalistic; Las Casas's reputation was "constantly sullied by those who wished to protect the cause of genocide"). He discusses Responses of Victims (submission, escape, family and mass suicide, resistance, dread of

Christianity). There is also an essay here on Yucatan in which again Lemkin's analysis carries out his wide-ranging method of genocide research, outlining through various categories the destruction and death of a whole way of life, of the foundations of a group's existence.

Recurring Features

In Subseries I, Box 7, Folder 2, in a typescript essay defining the "Nature of Genocide," Lemkin observes that the "techniques of physical genocide have repeated themselves through history." Such recurring techniques include "mass mutilations" as an "essential element of the crime of genocide." Another recurring technique is evident in the Spanish treatment of the Moriscos: their deportation from Spain where they were loaded on ships in "unbearable sun," with thousands dying from sunstroke. He compares this technique of deportation under lethal sun to the deportation and forced march of 1,200,000 Armenians, with only ten per cent surviving. Another recurring technique in terms of biological genocide is an attack on the family, with the separation of men and women and the taking away of the opportunity of procreation; Lemkin here refers to situations that have variously involved Turks, Quakers, Greeks, Slavs, Albigenses, and Huguenots. Another recurring technique is the transfer of children: "The children can be taken away from a given group for the purpose of educating them within the framework of another human group, racial, religious, national or ethnical." In this regard, Lemkin cites many instances in history, the Huguenots, Albigenses, Turkey; Jewish children were transferred in Russia under the Tsars.[21] He also includes the genocide of political groups as a recurrent feature.

In Series III, Subseries I, Folder 7, Lemkin expands on the theme of the removal of children in history. He quotes from a lecture given by a Professor A.N. Tairintanes, Faculty of Law, Athens University, on the occasion of the inauguration of the Save the Children Campaign, Athens, 29 May 1949. In the reign of Sultan Selim and afterwards, Turkish abductors, their ears plugged so that the wailings of the bereaved mothers would not reach their hearts, entered Greek villages to take children. In the twentieth century, Communist guerrillas have taken away Greek children, some 28,000 of them in northern Greece, and removed them behind the iron curtain.

Death through illness, hunger, and disease may be recurring features, and the colonizers cannot be considered blameless, as if they are mere bystanders. Lemkin in Folder 10 of Series III, Subseries I raises the issue of genocide and disease. Referring to Collier's *Indians of the Americas*, Lemkin argues that the bringing of Indians into settlements was censurable as genocide inasmuch as this social dislocation, the removal of the Indians from their own lands, exposed them to epidemic diseases due to overcrowding.

Lemkin points to the difficulty of establishing intention. In Folder 10 there is a copy of a handwritten letter, originally in the British Museum, from Geo. Croghan, Fort Pitt, April 1763 to His Excellency Sir Jeffery Amherst. Along with the quoting from this notorious letter urging the spreading of smallpox among "this Execrable Race," there is a note by Lemkin: "Information to be checked at the British Museum." He requests a researcher to find out if the plan had ever been carried out and if there were any other plans by the British at the time for mass extermination. Lemkin suggests here that even if a genocidal intention can be established, research still has to confirm that it was carried out, reminding one of Claude Rawson's distinction in *God, Gulliver and Genocide* (2001) between a *velleity* that does not wish to be acted on and a *desire* that does seek historical realization.[22]

North America

Reading over the Research Index Cards in Subseries 3, Box 9, Folders 1–21, dated 1948/49, we can see Lemkin focusing on aspects of genocide perpetrated by the English, French, and postindependence Americans that constitute a comprehensive historical process over a number of centuries, including deep into the nineteenth century: dispossessing indigenous peoples of their land (with or without permission of central authorities), kidnapping, enslavement, removal, and deportation often involving forced marches, taking of children, disease through overcrowding on reservations with inadequate food and medicine, self-destruction brought on by introduction and sale of liquor, curtailing and deprivation of legal rights, cultural genocide (as in re-education of children in boarding schools, cutting off of braids, forbidding of native languages, prohibitions on Indian culture and banning of religious ceremonies, forcing children to become Christians), and mass death.

On a card entitled "North American Indians—Enslavement," Lemkin links slavery with cultural genocide: "Slavery may be called cultural genocide par excellence. It is the most effective and thorough method of destroying a culture, and of de-socializing human beings" (Card 11). Lemkin here refers to slavery in New England with captives taken in the Pequot War, in Massachusetts, New Plymouth, and Connecticut; also slavery in the mid-seventeenth century of Indians in Virginia, North Carolina, and Maryland.

In Box 9, Folder 12 of Series III, Subseries 3, Lemkin makes an interesting distinction between "cultural change" and "cultural genocide." The

Indians were forced to accept, after the loss of their hunting grounds, "the economic and social system of the white man," and such may be referred to as "cultural change" of a "radical and perhaps inhumane type (considering the misery of the generations undergoing the change)." Such severe cultural change only "becomes cultural genocide (and physical genocide)" when no adequate measures were taken to facilitate the charge from nomadic to agricultural life, with the Indians through cession and warfare being left "landless and foodless."

Even when (Lemkin notes in the same place) Indian peoples were already "agriculturalized," as with the five Southern tribes, there was "forcible removal to western territory under deplorable conditions," which was both "cultural and physical genocide": "There was here no question of purchasing uncultivated land and of 'civilizing' the Indian. The only intent was the expulsion of the Indian to make room for whites." I consider the distinction between cultural change and cultural genocide below.

In Box 9, Folder 12 of Series III, Subseries 3, on a card entry entitled "Collier. Cultural Genocide Against Plains Indians," Lemkin refers to the use of "concentration camps" as part of the white attempts to defeat them, which also included starvation and systematic slaughtering of food sources like the buffalo. The deployment of the term "concentration camps" is interesting if we think of Hannah Arendt's contention that a distinguishing feature of twentieth-century totalitarianisms, of the Nazis and Stalin's Russia, is the presence not just of the detention but the *concentration* camp; in the concentration camp, Arendt argued passionately, an attack is made on the existential conditions necessary for human life: "a present in which to think, a space in which to act," an enforced denial of the spatial and temporal requirements of freedom.[23] For Arendt, the concentration camp represented an unprecedented attack on human freedom in modernity, an unprecedented *total dominion* over human life. For Lemkin, it would appear from such references to North American colonization, concentration camps and their constituent total dominion were a recurring feature of historical genocide, including the history of Western colonialism.[24]

Lemkin's cards present harrowing reading. Such is particularly so in Lemkin's evocation of the forced removal and deportations of Indians, who always mourned the loss of their homelands. Series 3, Subseries 3, Box 9, Folder 14 refers, for example, to the deportation of the Cherokee from Georgia. The Choctaw deportation of the early 1830s involved great suffering, including a deportation insisted on by the authorities in winter, with Lemkin commenting: "I do not understand why they were not made to leave in the spring or summer." Many deportees, poorly clad, died from exposure, demoralization, and cholera. Lemkin points out that the Choctaw were deeply soil-bound and unwilling to emigrate. In the Creek removal, warrior prisoners were chained together in a ninety-mile march, the warriors followed by the old and infirm, in intense heat, with infectious diseases rampant; the sick were transported on overcrowded boats. There was destitution and misery. Lemkin observes that physical genocide was carried out on the remaining Creeks. While the Creek warriors were enlisted for service against the Seminole, their families remained east in "concentration camps": again the use of a term usually associated with the kind of twentieth-century phenomenon Lemkin himself studied at length.

Cultural Change and Cultural Genocide

The New York Public Library contains material from Lemkin that seems to refer to his thinking about genocide in the middle or latter 1950s. In an essay "Introduction to the Study of Genocide," in Reel 3, Box 2, Folder 1, from which I have already quoted for my second epigraph and that appears to be a description of his project for a grant or for a publisher, Lemkin characteristically defines genocide in a wide-ranging way. It is an "organic concept of multiple influences and consequences," and has "always existed in history": "genocide followed humanity through history and . . . the last centuries have been particularly abundant in genocide cases." In a section entitled "Scope of Project," Lemkin again lists the "categories" that constitute his methodology for the still-unfinished book (including "Psychosociological reactions" of Victims, Perpetrators, and Outside World), and outlines his chapter plan, with chapter headings for a section entitled Modern Times where he instates "Tasmanians" and, in pencil, "Natives of Australia," as well as "Maoris of NZ."[25] There is an essay here of some one hundred typed pages on American Indians and genocide.

There are also extended and careful observations on the distinction between cultural change and cultural genocide. In Reel 3, Box 2, Folder 1, Lemkin writes that cultural genocide "must not be confused with the gradual changes a culture may undergo," occurring "by means of the continuous and slow adaptation of the culture to new situations," where a very common type of adaptation is to "outside influences" and the "assimilation of certain foreign culture traits." Lemkin refers to such adaptation as "the process of cultural diffusion," and then asks: "What then is the exact distinction between diffusion and genocide?" His answer is that genocide involves complete and violent change, "that is, the destruction of a culture . . . the premeditated goal of those committing cultural genocide." In the section Lemkin entitled "Scope of the Project," he refers to the "basic changes" that have occurred in societies "through the gradual disintegration of culture and through the cultural exhaustion of various societies."

Again, genocide is only involved when there are "surgical operations on cultures and deliberate assassination of civilizations."

In his "Introduction to the Study of Genocide," Lemkin refers to his aim of examining in the projected book the "etiology and the reasons motivating the crime of genocide" in different historical periods and in different cultures. He thinks cultural anthropology will play a part in explaining the ways genocide can be "explained as resulting from a cultural conflict," for example in the "encounter between migratory nomadic societies and sedentary ones."[26] Such an observation could be applied to the way migratory nomadic societies of the Spanish and British Empires, the white colonizers/migrants coming from afar, across the seas, from 1492 onwards, invaded the lands of "sedentary" indigenous groups in the Americas or Australia, sedentary within their particular territories and nations and civilizations even if as traditional peoples they moved about within those territories; their homes, for example in Australia or North America, may not have been individual houses, but their territories were nevertheless their sedentary world, involving profound attachment to and imbrication in a nurturing cosmos.[27]

Cosmos is a term Lemkin himself deploys. In Reel 3, Box 2, Folder 1, he writes that the philosophy of the Genocide Convention is based on the "formula of the human cosmos": "This cosmos consists of four basic groups: national, racial, religious and ethnic." Such groups are to be protected by the convention "not only by reasons of human compassion but also to prevent draining the spiritual resources of mankind."

Conclusions

We can only mourn the fact that Lemkin's manuscript writings were not published as he hoped, for in them the inherent and constitutive relationship between genocide and settler-colonialism is argued strongly, given subtle, intricate methodological form, and brought descriptively to life.[28] In the ways he formulates his theory and presents his historical consciousness of crimes against humanity, Lemkin was concerned that humanity should establish a duty of care to all the world's peoples and cultures, as when he writes that the loss of the culture of any disintegrated or crippled group,[29] to employ his own metaphors, is a loss to world culture, to the human cosmos; or when in his autobiography he avers that from his time as a refugee fleeing Poland, he wished his life to proceed by "enlarging the concept of my world-awareness, or rather of the oneness of the world."[30] A notion of world culture necessitates a notion of world history: that is what Lemkin's unfinished and unpublished book somberly promised to the world.

Lemkin certainly does not posit a comforting narrative of progress for the Christian West. He writes in the preface to *Axis Rule* that the extremely inhuman treatment in occupied Europe of the Jews promoted the "anti-Christian idea" of the inequality of human beings and of German racial superiority.[31] Yet in the historical examples he mentions in both his published and unpublished work, there are appalling instances of Christian persecution of Jews, Moors, and those regarded as the wrong kind of Christian. Further, when discussing in his unpublished essay "Introduction to the Study of Genocide" (in New York Public Library, Lemkin papers, Reel 3, Box 2, Folder 1) how to explain why genocide might occur in history, he feels that in situations of "conflict of cultures," for example the encounter between "migratory nomadic societies and sedentary ones," such conflict was "particularly violent when the ideas of the absolute appeared in the course of the encounter of various religions." Here Lemkin seems to be suggesting that monotheism in history is particularly productive of violence including genocidal violence.

Lemkin is also clearly profoundly uneasy about Western law, in particular, that throughout the 1930s it did not include provision for crimes against the destruction of human groups. He always regretted that the 1933 Madrid conference did not enact his proposals in international law. Had his proposals been ratified by the countries represented there, the new laws could have inhibited the rise of Nazism by declaring attacks upon national, religious, and ethnic groups as international crimes and that the perpetrators of such crimes could be indicted whenever they appeared on the territory of one of the signatory countries.[32]

We ignore Lemkin's wide-ranging definition of genocide, inherently linked with colonialism, at our peril. In his autobiography, he wrote: "After a war is lost, a nation may rebuild its technical and financial resources, and may start a new life. But those who have been destroyed in genocide have been lost for ever. While the losses of war can be repaired, the losses of genocide are irreparable."[33] Lemkin's definition can stir us to the understanding and passion we need to oppose the genocidal destruction of groups and collectivities that will continue to occur in history as a permanent potential of what human groups do to other human groups.

Notes

1. Raphaël Lemkin, "Genocide – A Modern Crime," *Free World – A Magazine devoted to the United Nations and Democracy* (April 1945), 39–43, accessed at http://www.preventgenocide.org/lemkin/freeworld1945.htm. This essay is a development of my

paper "Are Settler-Colonies Inherently Genocidal? Some Thoughts on Lemkin," Genocide and Colonialism, ANU Humanities Research Centre conference held at The University of Sydney, 18–20 July 2003. A shorter version of the chapter was given as "Raphael Lemkin's History of Genocide and Colonialism," paper for United States Holocaust Memorial Museum, Center for Advanced Holocaust Studies, Washington, DC, 26 February 2004. For helpful discussion and interest I would like to thank Ann Curthoys, Ned Curthoys, Jim Fussell, Ben Kiernan, Wendy Lower, Dirk Moses, Aron Rodrigue, and Jürgen Zimmerer. See also Ann Curthoys and John Docker, "Defining Genocide," in *The Historiography of Genocide*, ed. Dan Stone (Houndmills, 2008).

2. Lemkin Papers, New York Public Library, Reel 3, Box 2, Folder 1.
3. Raphael Lemkin, "Totally Unofficial Man," in *Pioneers of Genocide Studies*, ed. Samuel Totten and Steven Leonard Jacobs (New Brunswick, NJ, 2002), 393. Cf. A. Dirk Moses, "Genocide and Settler Society in Australian History," in *Genocide and Settler Society: Frontier Violence and Stolen Indigenous Children in Australian History*, ed. A. Dirk Moses (New York, 2004), 22.
4. Lemkin, "Totally Unofficial Man." 373.
5. Lemkin's 1933 proposals can be accessed at http://www.preventgenocide.org/lemkin/madrid/1933-english.htm. See also Samantha Power, *"A Problem from Hell": America and the Age of Genocide* (New York, 2002), 21–23, and Moses, "Genocide and Settler Society," 21.
6. See also A. Dirk Moses, "The Holocaust and Genocide," in *The Historiography of the Holocaust*, ed. Dan Stone (London, 2004), 537.
7. Lemkin, *Axis Rule in Occupied Europe: Laws of Occupation, Analysis of Government, Proposals for Redress* (Washington, DC, 1944), chap. 9, "Genocide," 79–95; Ann Curthoys and John Docker, "Introduction—Genocide: Definitions, Questions, Settler-Colonies," *Aboriginal History* 25 (2001): 5–11.
8. Lemkin, *Axis Rule*, 79.
9. Ibid., 82–83.
10. Lemkin, "Genocide—A Modern Crime."
11. Cf. David Furber, "Near as Far in the Colonies: The Nazi Occupation of Poland," *International History Review* 26, no. 3 (2004): 541–79. For the relationship between Nazism and colonialism more generally, see Jürgen Zimmerer, "Colonialism and the Holocaust: Towards an Archaeology of Genocide," in Moses, *Genocide and Settler Society*, 49–76. See also Wendy Lower, *Nazi Empire Building and the Holocaust* (Chapel Hill, NC, 2005).
12. See Power, *"Problem from Hell,"* chaps. 1–5.
13. Lemkin, "Totally Unofficial Man," 366–69, 387–92.
14. Ibid., 366, 370, 379–80, 387–88.
15. Lemkin, *Axis Rule*, 80, note three. Concerning the Roman destruction of Carthage, see Ben Kiernan, "Le premier génocide: Carthage, 146 A.C.," *Diogène*, no. 203 (2003): 32–48; apropos Magdeburg, see Mark Levene and Penny Roberts, eds., *The Massacre in History* (New York, 1999), 100, 235.
16. For an excellent discussion of intention, see Tony Barta, "Relations of Genocide: Land and Lives in the Colonization of Australia," in *Genocide and the Modern Age: Etiology and Case Studies of Mass Death*, ed. Isidor Wallimann and Michael N. Dobkowski (New York, 1987), 237–43, 246–49, and Moses, "Genocide and Settler Society," 28–30. See also Tanya Elder, "What You See Before Your Eyes: Documenting Raphael Lemkin's Life by Exploring his Archival Papers, 1900–1959," *Journal of Genocide Research* 7, no. 4 (2005): 469–99.

17. Helen Fein, *Genocide: A Sociological Perspective* (London, 1993), 11, writes that in his unpublished work Lemkin's examples of genocide include: "Albigensians, American Indians, Assyrians in Iraq, Belgian Congo, Christians in Japan, French in Sicily (c. 1282), Hereros, Huguenots, Incas, Mongols, the Soviet Union/Ukraine, Tasmania." In a footnote, Fein thanks Rabbi Steven L. Jacobs for showing her an inventory of Lemkin's unpublished papers (1942–1959) held at the American Jewish Archives in Cincinnati, Ohio, and an inventory of the New York Public Library collection of Lemkin correspondence and writings; the citation of examples is "from the NYPL collection, box 2."
18. Cf. Ann Curthoys and John Docker, *Is History Fiction?* (Sydney, 2005), chap. 6, comparing Lemkin here with Leopold von Ranke's *History of Latin and Teutonic Nations* (1824) in relation to Charlemagne.
19. See John Collier, *Indians of the Americas: The Long Hope* (1947; New York, 1948). Collier's book covers American Indian "prehistory" and also history both south and north of the Rio Grande. My thanks to Jim Fussell for his present of a copy of Collier's book.
20. Cf. Hannah Arendt's comment that imperialism from 1884–1914 was a formative influence on the twentieth-century development of totalitarianism including National Socialism: *The Origins of Totalitarianism* (London, 1967), 123. Cf. Ned Curthoys, "The Politics of Holocaust Representation: The Worldly Typologies of Hannah Arendt," *Arena Journal*, no. 16 (2000/1): 49–74. See also Michael A. McDonnell and A. Dirk Moses, "Raphael Lemkin as Historian of Genocide in the Americas," *Journal of Genocide Research* 7, no. 4 (2005): 501–29.
21. Cf. Isabel Heinemann, "'Until the Last Drop of Good Blood': The Kidnapping of 'Racially Valuable' Children and Nazi Racial Policy in Occupied Eastern Europe," in Moses, *Genocide and Settler Society*, 244–66.
22. See Claude Rawson, *God, Gulliver, and Genocide: Barbarism and the European Imagination, 1492–1945* (Oxford, 2001), passim; see also the review by John Docker in *Journal of Genocide Research* 5, no. 1 (2003): 161–65.
23. Elizabeth Young-Bruehl, *Hannah Arendt: For Love of the World* (New Haven, CT, 1982), 204, 210–11, 253.
24. Zimmerer, "Colonialism and the Holocaust," 66, refers to notorious "concentration camps" maintained by the Germans in Southwest Africa to intern Herero and Nama men, women, and children; he points out in an endnote, 76, note 89, that the term was first used by the Spanish during their campaign in Cuba in 1896, later by the Americans in the Philippines, the British in South Africa, then the Germans in Southwest Africa.
25. Ann Curthoys has edited Lemkin's long essay on the Tasmanian genocide, on Reel 3 of the New York Public Library Lemkin collection, for publication in *Patterns of Prejudice* 39, no. 2 (2005) 170–196; see also Ann Curthoys, "Genocide in Tasmania: The History of an Idea," in this volume. Cf. David B. MacDonald, "Daring to Compare: the Debate about a Maori 'Holocaust' in New Zealand," *Journal of Genocide Research* 5, no. 3 (2003): 383–403.
26. Dan Stone has drawn on anthropology to explore aspects of the Holocaust. See his *History, Memory and Mass Atrocity: Essays on the Holocaust and Genocide* (London and Portland, OR, 2006).
27. See Ann Curthoys, "Whose Home? Expulsion, Exodus, and Exile in White Australian Historical Mythology," *Journal of Australian Studies*, no. 61 (1999): 1–18.
28. See also Curthoys and Docker, "Introduction—Genocide," 14.
29. For "disintegration" of group life, see Lemkin, "Genocide—A Modern Crime" (and another metaphor in this essay, when Lemkin refers to a "coordinated plan aimed at

destruction of the essential foundations of the life of national groups so that these groups wither and die like plants that have suffered a blight"); see Lemkin, "Genocide as a Crime under International Law," *American Journal of International Law* 41, no. 1 (1947): 145–51, for the phrase "to cripple permanently a human group."

30. Lemkin, "Totally Unofficial Man," 377.
31. Lemkin, *Axis Rule*, xi.
32. Ibid., xiii, 92–93. See also Lemkin, "Genocide under International Law," 147: "On November 22, 1946, during the discussion of genocide in the United Nations General Assembly, Sir Hartley Shawcross, United Kingdom Attorney General and delegate declared that the failure of this proposal made it impossible to punish some of the serious Nazi crimes."
33. Lemkin, "Totally Unofficial Man," 366.

– *Chapter 4* –

STRUCTURE AND EVENT

Settler Colonialism, Time, and the Question of Genocide

Patrick Wolfe

A Logic of Elimination

Introducing his first collection in this series, Dirk Moses had favorable things to say about the term "logic of elimination," which I coined some years ago to express the essential characteristic of the settler-colonial project.[1] I offered this term, rather than "genocide," to mark both the specificity of settler colonialism and its positive dimensions, in particular the multifarious procedures whereby settler-colonial societies have sought to eliminate the problem of indigenous heteronomy through the biocultural assimilation of indigenous peoples. Whatever else one may wish to say about this approach, it does seem to beg the question of genocide. Thus Moses took it as one among a number of alternative approaches to the historical analysis of genocide.[2] Gratifying though it is, therefore, his endorsement is also a calling to account. Why add to our conceptual vocabulary? Does the logic of elimination express anything significant that is not already encompassed in genocide? Such questions are of much more than academic significance. Genocide is a crime under international law, the crime of crimes, with sanctions and penalties to match, so playing fast and loose with its definition could fatally diminish the redress available to its victims. By the same token, our attempts to understand genocide, like attempts to understand other global scourges, are valuable to the extent that they offer the possibility of prevention. Genocide must go the way of smallpox. That is why we study it.

Moses favored my approach because, to him at least, it suggested a way into the question of genocidal agency that avoids both the Scylla of reified social systems and the Charybdis of spontaneous individual voluntarism.

The logic of elimination is a primary motivation or agenda of settler colonialism that distinguishes it from other forms of colonialism, such as chattel slavery on the US model or franchise colonialism on the British-India model. Whereas the latter depend on native labor, settler colonialism is first and foremost a territorial project, whose priority is replacing natives on their land rather than extracting an economic surplus from mixing their labor with it. Within a given colonial society, different colonial relationships usually coexist. In the US, for instance, Indians were generally cleared from their land rather than being put to work on it, to be replaced by enslaved Black people who provided the labor to be mixed with the land. In Australia, something comparable could be said about the relationship between coerced convict labor and Aboriginal dispossession in the south, or about the role of indentured Pacific Islander labor in the northeast. Thus settler colonialism has both negative and positive dimensions. Negatively, it strives for the dissolution of native societies. Positively, it erects a new colonial society on the expropriated land base. As I put it, settler-colonizers come to stay—invasion is a structure not an event.[3] In its positive aspect, elimination is an organizing principle of settler-colonial society, rather than a one-off (and superseded) occurrence. In the wake of the crudely homicidal eliminationism of the frontier, settler societies characteristically devise a number of often coexistent strategies to eliminate the threat posed by the survival in their midst of irregularly dispossessed social groups who were constituted prior to and independently of the normative basis on which settler society is established.[4] These strategies include expulsion and other forms of geographical sequestration, as well as programs of incorporation that seek to efface the distinguishing criteria—biology, culture, mode of production, religion, etc.—whereby native difference is constructed in settler discourse. Positively, therefore, the outcomes of the logic of elimination can include officially encouraged miscegenation, the breaking down of native title into alienable individual freeholds, native citizenship, child abduction, religious conversion, and a whole range of cognate biocultural assimilations. All these strategies, including frontier homicide, are characteristic of settler colonialism. Some of them are more controversial in genocide studies than others.

These eliminatory strategies all reflect the centrality of land, which is not merely a component of settler society but its basic precondition. No amount of good intentions or improved racial theorizing can alter this fundamental fact if they are not accompanied by territorial (re-)cession. So long as it persists with its claim to colonial territory, therefore, the metropolitan power cannot distance itself from the ostensibly unauthorized activities of frontier land grabbers. The logic of elimination unites the diplomatic niceties of the law of nations and the maverick rapine of the squatters' posse within a cohesive project that implicates individual and nation-state, official and unofficial alike. This, I think, is what Moses found appealing in the approach:

> In their clamor for government protection and the implementation of exterminatory policies, the Europeans on the frontier articulated the logic of the colonization process in its most pure form: driven by international market forces, they seized the land of Aboriginal groups without compensation or negotiation, and excluded them from their sources of food. A struggle for survival ensued in which, from the European perspective at the time, the Aborigines had to be subdued, and, if necessary, exterminated. For if the settlers did not get their way and were forced to abandon the land, the economic system would collapse and with it the colonization project itself. In these circumstances, the structure or objective implication of the process became consciously incarnated in its agents, and this is the moment when we can observe the development of the specific genocidal intention that satisfies the UN definition.[5]

This excerpt expresses something of the structural complexity of settler colonialism. Frontier individuals' "clamor for government protection" not only presupposed a commonality—based on incessantly refurbished discursive elements such as race, nation, civilization, etc.—between the private and official realms. In most cases (Queensland was a partial exception), it also presupposed a global chain of command linking remote colonial frontiers to London. Behind it all lay the driving engine of international market forces, which linked Australian wool to Yorkshire mills and, complementarily, to cotton produced under different colonial conditions in India, Egypt, and the slave states of the Deep South. As Cole Harris put it in relation to the dispossession of Indians in British Columbia, "combine capital's interest in uncluttered access to land and settlers' interest in land as livelihood, and the principal momentum of settler colonialism comes into focus."[6] The Industrial Revolution, misleadingly figuring in popular consciousness as an autochthonous metropolitan phenomenon, required colonial land and labor to produce its raw materials just as centrally as it required metropolitan factories and an industrial proletariat to process them, whereupon the colonies were further required as a market.

In its modern (which is to say, post-Columbian) form, the settler-colonial logic of elimination partakes of the structural complexity of the global system, reconciling individual motivations to the overarching imperatives of statecraft and capitalist expansion. Yet this is not the only sense in which I term it a structure rather than an event. As already suggested, in addition to its complexity as a social formation, settler-colonial discourse is continuous over time. In this regard, I find Moses's reading of my approach too limited to the frontier. There is irony in this, since he finds my "structuralist schema" too static and unable to account for historical change, in particular for "how and why the settler-colonial system radicalizes from assimilation to destruction."[7] I do not wish to defend my approach for the mere sake of it, but it seems to me that some important issues for the relationship of settler colonialism and genocide are involved. First, I detect an implicit teleology in the assumption that settler colonialism will radicalize from assimilation to destruction rather than, say, the other way around. Second, I regard assimilation as itself a form of destruction. Third, the confinement of eliminatory discourse to frontier homicide limits the equivalence between genocide and settler colonialism to the settler-colonial strategy in which that equivalence is most straightforwardly manifest. This inhibits—possibly even precludes—investigation of the relationship between genocide and other eliminatory strategies that are characteristically deployed in settler-colonial societies. With apologies for pushing my own barrow, therefore, I feel bound to insist that my account explicitly set out to situate the changing historical modalities of the logic of elimination in both Australia and the US. In Australia, this logic subtends the overlapping historical phases that I term confrontation, confinement, and assimilation, the latter phase extending into the present in the form of the deceptively emancipatory provisions of native title legislation. In the US, a strikingly similar set of strategies is somewhat complicated by the even-more deceptive construction of Indian sovereignty presupposed in measures such as allotment and tribal registration.[8] In short, the logic of elimination not only refers to the summary liquidation of indigenous people, though it includes that. It also refers to a structural feature of settler-colonial society that is historically continuous. It is in both foregoing senses—as a complex social formation and as a continuity through time—that settler colonization is a structure rather than an event, and it is on this basis that I shall consider its relationship to genocide.[9]

The Tide of History

To start at the top, with the European sovereigns who laid claim to the territories of non-Christian (or, in later secularized versions, uncivilized) inhabitants of the rest of the world: justifications for this claim were derived from a disputatious arena of scholarly controversy that had been prompted by European conquests in the Americas and is misleadingly referred to, in the singular, as the doctrine of discovery.[10] Though a thoroughgoing diminution of native entitlement was axiomatic to discovery, the discourse was primarily addressed to relations between European sovereigns rather than to relations between Europeans and natives.[11] Competing theoretical formulas were designed to restrain the endless rounds of war-making over claims to colonial territory that European sovereigns were so prone to indulge in. The rights accorded to natives tended to reflect the balance between European powers in any given theater of colonial settlement. In Australia, for instance, where British dominion was effectively unchallenged by other European powers, Aborigines were accorded no rights to their territory, informal variants on the theme of *terra nullius* (*pace* Henry Reynolds) being taken for granted in settler culture. In North America, by contrast, treaties between Indian and European nations were premised on a sovereignty that reflected Indians' capacity to permute local alliance networks from among the rival Spanish, British, French, Dutch, Swedish, and (in the west) Russian presences.[12]

Even where native sovereignty was recognized, however, ultimate dominion over the territory in question was held to inhere in the European sovereign in whose name it had been "discovered." Through all the diversity among the theorists of discovery, a constant theme is the clear distinction between dominion, which inhered in European sovereigns alone, and natives' right of occupancy, also expressed in terms of possession or usufruct, which entitled natives to pragmatic use (understood as hunting and gathering rather than agriculture)[13] of a territory that Europeans had discovered. The distinction between European dominion and native occupancy illuminates both the inclusive cohesion of the settler-colonial project and its groundedness in the elimination of native societies.

Through being the first European to visit and properly claim a given territory, a discoverer acquired the right, on behalf of his sovereign and vis à vis other Europeans who came after him, to buy land from the natives. This right, known as preemption, gave the discovering power (or, in the US case, its successors) a monopoly over land transactions with the natives, who were prevented from disposing of their land to any other European power. On the face of it, this would seem to pose little threat to people who did not wish to dispose of their land to anyone. Indeed, this semblance of native voluntarism has provided scope for some limited judicial magnanimity in regard to Indian sovereignty.[14] In practice, however, the corollary did not apply. Preemption sanctioned European priority but not indigenous freedom of choice. As Harvey Rosenthal observed of the concept's extension into the US constitutional environment, "the American right to buy always superseded the Indian right not to sell."[15] The mechanisms of this priority are crucial. Why should ostensibly sovereign nations, residing in territory solemnly guaranteed to them by treaties, decide that they are willing, after all, to surrender their ancestral homelands? More often than not (and nearly always up to the wars with the Plains Indians, which did not take place until after the Civil War), the agency that reduced Indian peoples to this abjection was not the US Cavalry or some other official instrument, but irregular, greed-crazed invaders who had no intention of allowing the formalities of federal law to impede their access to the riches available in, under, and on Indian soil.[16] If the government notionally held itself aloof from such disreputable proceedings, however, it was never far away. Consider, for instance, the complicity between bayonet-wielding troops and the "lawless rabble" in this account of events immediately preceding the eastern Cherokee's catastrophic "Trail of Tears," one of many comparable 1830s removals whereby Indians from the southeast were displaced west of the Mississippi to make way for the development of the slave-plantation economy in the Deep South:

> Families at dinner were startled by the sudden gleam of bayonets in the doorway and rose up to be driven with blows and oaths along the weary miles of trail that led to the stockade [where they were held prior to the removal itself]. Men were seized in their fields or going along the road, women were taken from their wheels and children from their play. In many cases, on turning for one last look as they crossed the ridge, they saw their homes in flames, fired by the lawless rabble that followed on the heels of the soldiers to loot and pillage. So keen were these outlaws on the scent that in some instances they were driving off the cattle and other stock of the Indians almost before the soldiers had fairly started their owners in the other direction. Systematic hunts were made by the same men for Indian graves, to rob them of the silver pendants and other valuables deposited with the dead. A Georgia volunteer, afterward a colonel in the Confederate service, said: "I fought through the civil war and have seen men shot to pieces and slaughtered by thousands, but the Cherokee removal was the cruelest work I ever knew."[17]

On the basis of this passage alone, the structural complexity of settler colonialism could sustain libraries of elaboration. A global dimension to the frenzy for native land is reflected in the fact that, as economic immigrants, the rabble were generally drawn from the ranks of Europe's landless. The cattle and other stock were not only being driven off Cherokee land; they were being driven into private ownership. Once evacuated, the Red man's land would be mixed with Black labor to produce cotton, the white gold of the Deep South. To this end, the highest echelons of the formal state apparatus fused seamlessly with the disorderly pillaging of a nomadic horde who may or may not have been "lawless," but who were categorically White. Moreover, in their indiscriminate lust for any value that could be extracted from the Cherokee's homeland, these racialized grave-robbers are unlikely to have stopped at the pendants. The burgeoning science of craniology, which provided a distinctively post-eighteenth-century validation for their claim to a racial superiority that entitled them to other people's lands, made Cherokee skulls too marketable a commodity to be overlooked.[18] In its endless multidimensionality, there was nothing singular about this one sorry removal, which all of modernity attended.

Rather than something separate from or running counter to the colonial state, the murderous activities of the frontier rabble constitute its principal means of expansion. These have occurred "behind the screen of the frontier, in the wake of which, once the dust has settled, the irregular acts that took place have been regularized and the boundaries of White settlement extended. Characteristically, officials express regret at the lawlessness of this process while resigning themselves to its inevitability."[19] In this light, we are in a position to understand the pragmatics of the doctrine of discovery more clearly. Understood as an assertion of indigenous entitlement, the distinction between dominion and occupancy dissolves into incoherence. Understood processually, however, as a stage in the formation of the settler-colonial state (specifically, the stage linking the theory and the realization of territorial acquisition), the distinction is only too consistent. As observed, preemption provided that natives could transfer their right of occupancy to the discovering sovereign and to no one else. They could not transfer dominion because it was not theirs to transfer; that inhered in the European sovereign and had done so from the moment of discovery. Dominion without conquest constitutes the theoretical (or "inchoate") stage of territorial sovereignty.[20] In US Chief Justice John Marshall's words, it remained to be "consummated by possession."[21] This delicately phrased "consummation" is precisely what the rabble were achieving at New Echota in 1838. In other words, the right of occupancy was not an assertion of native rights. Rather, it was a pragmatic acknowledgment of the lethal interlude that would intervene between the conceit of discovery, when pompous navigators proclaimed European dominion over whole continents to trees or deserted beaches, and the practical realization of that conceit in the final securing of European settlement, formally consummated in the extinguishment of native title. Thus it is not surprising that native title had hardly been asserted in Australian law than Mr. Justice Olney was echoing Marshall's formula, Olney's twenty-first-century version of consummation being the "tide of history" that provided the pretext for his notorious judgment in the Yorta Yorta case.[22] As observed, the logic of elimination continues into the present.

In sum, then, settler colonialism is an inclusive, land-centered project that coordinates a comprehensive range of agencies, from the metropolitan center to the frontier encampment, with a view to eliminating indigenous societies. Thus its operations are not dependent on the presence or absence of formal state institutions or functionaries. Accordingly—to begin to move toward the issue of genocide—the occasions on or the extent to which settler colonialism conduces to genocide are not a matter of the presence or absence of the formal apparatus of the state. A failure to recognize this can lead to unfortunate conclusions. For instance, Paul Bartrop has compared the 1843 Warrigal Creek massacre of Kurnai (Gunnai) people in what is now eastern Victoria, Australia, to the better-known 1864 massacre of Cheyenne people in Sand Creek, Colorado, concluding that the Sand Creek massacre amounted to genocide while the Warrigal Creek one did not.[23] This is an extremely grave conclusion to inscribe, since it amounts to an assertion that, while descendants of the massacred Cheyenne should be entitled to genocide redress, descendants of the massacred Kurnai may not be. Thus it is disturbing to find that Bartrop bases his conclusion on the inadequate (and anyway misleading) ground that the formal apparatus of the state was involved in the Sand Creek massacre but not in the Kurnai one. There is no question as to the involvement of the state in the Sand Creek massacre, which was carried out by the Third Colorado Volunteers under the command of Colonel John Chivington, who had received orders from state governor John Evans. When it comes to Warrigal Creek, however, Bartrop relies on the fact that, at the time the massacre was committed, the Crown Lands Commissioner had yet to arrive in the area in person, so law and order (i.e., the White man's) "existed solely in name."[24] In consequence, though a genocidal intent to destroy the Kurnai was unquestionably present "if measured by the settlers' murderous standards,"

> their standards cannot be applied, owing to the existence of a higher authority in the land that proscribed their actions and worked (sometimes resolutely, sometimes not) to nullify their behavior. It is that authority, the colonial government, that must be assessed when bringing the charge of genocide, because it was the ultimate legal arbiter of right and wrong throughout the land. And there is no evidence that demonstrates the government sought the destruction of the [Kurnai].[25]

Thus the government was not present, but its law applied "throughout the land." How could this law apply at all under the circumstances that Bartrop depicts, even if "solely in name"? The reason is, of course, that, three-quarters of a century earlier, Captain James Cook had asserted British dominion over the land of the Kurnai. Bartrop wants this aspect of the state to be present throughout the land but, at the same time, he wants to avoid the implications of that dominion being consummated by the tide of history that his murderous settlers represented. In the event, the colonial state retrospectively endorsed the settlers' activities by way of extant fee-simple titles to Kurnai land whose provenance Bartrop does not consider.

Race, Colonialisms, and Difference

Attempts, such as Bartrop's, to lose responsibility for indigenous deaths in an extra-state vacuum that nonetheless ends up being formally incorporated into the state would seem to be the prompt for Alison Palmer's distinction between "society-led" and "state-led" genocides.[26] So far as settler colonialism is concerned, this understandable distinction is not necessary. Moreover, while it is clearly the case, as Zygmunt Bauman has argued, that the pace, scale, and intensity of certain forms of modern genocide require the centralized technological, logistical, and administrative capacities of the modern state,[27] this does not mean that settler-colonial discourse should be regarded as pre- (or less than) modern. Rather, as a range of thinkers—including, in this particular connection, W.E.B. Du Bois, Hannah Arendt, and Aimé Césaire—have argued, some of the core features of modernity were pioneered in the colonies.[28]

It is a commonplace that the Holocaust gathered together the instrumental, technological, and bureaucratic constituents of Western modernity. Accordingly, despite the historiographical energy that has already been devoted to the Holocaust, the genealogical field available to its historian remains apparently inexhaustible. Thus we have recently been informed that its historical ingredients included the guillotine and, for the industry-scale processing of bodies, the techniques of Chicago cattle-yards.[29] Yet the image of the dispassionate genocidal technocrat that the Holocaust certainly spawned is by no means the whole story. Rather, as Dieter Pohl, Jürgen Zimmerer, and others have pointed out, a substantial number of the Nazis' victims, including Jewish and "Gypsy" (Sinti and Rom) ones, were murdered not in camps but in deranged shooting sprees that were more reminiscent of sixteenth-century Spanish behavior in the Americas than of Fordism, while millions of Slav civilians and Soviet soldiers were simply starved to death in circumstances that could well have struck a chord with late-eighteenth-century Bengalis or mid-nineteenth-century Irish people.[30] This is not to suggest a partition of the Holocaust into, say, modern and atavistic elements. It is to stress the modernity of colonialism.

I have already pointed to colonialism's centrality to the global industrial order. This means that the expropriated Aboriginal, enslaved African American, or indentured Asian is as thoroughly modern as the factory worker, bureaucrat, or flaneur of the metropolitan center. The fact that the slave may be in chains does not make him or her medieval. By the same token, the fact that the genocidal Hutus of Rwanda often employed agricultural implements to murder their Tutsi neighbors en masse does not license the racist assumption that, because neither Europeans nor the latest technology were involved, this was a primordial (read "savage") blood-letting. Rwanda and Burundi are colonial creations—not only so far as the obvious factor of their geographical borders is concerned, but, more intimately, in the very racial boundaries that marked and reproduced the Hutu/Tutsi division. As Robert Melson has observed in his sharp secondary synopsis of it, "the Rwandan genocide was the product of a postcolonial state, a racialist ideology, a revolution claiming democratic legitimation, and war—all manifestations of the modern world."[31] The mutual Hutu/Tutsi racialization on which this "post" colonial ideology was based was itself an artifice of colonialism. In classic Foucauldian style, the German and, above all, Belgian overlords who succeeded each other in modern Rwanda had imposed a racial grid on the complex native social order, co-opting the pastoral Tutsi aristocracy as a comprador elite who facilitated their exploitation of the agriculturalist Hutu and lower-order Tutsis. This racial difference was elaborated "by Belgian administrators and anthropologists who argued—in what came to be known as the 'Hamitic Hypothesis'—that the Tutsi were conquerors who had originated in Ethiopia (closer to Europe!) and that the Hutu were a conquered inferior tribe of local provenance."[32] Shades of the Franks and the Gauls. In their inculcation with racial discourse, Rwandans were integrally modern. Even the hoes with which some Hutus murdered their Tutsi compatriots symbolized the agriculture that not only encapsulated their difference from their victims. As such, these hoes were also the instruments of the Hutus' involvement in the global market.

The issue of race is a constant companion of both genocide and modernity as a whole. European xenophobic traditions such as antisemitism, islamophobia, or negrophobia are considerably older than race, which, as many have shown, became discursively consolidated fairly late in the eighteenth century.[33] But the mere fact that race is a social construct does not of itself tell us very much. As I have argued, different racial regimes encode and reproduce the varied relationships of inequality into which Europeans coerced the populations concerned. For instance, Indians and Black people in the US have been racialized in opposing ways that reflect their antithetical roles in the development of US society. Black people's enslavement produced an inclusive taxonomy that automatically enslaved the offspring of a slave and anyone else. In the wake of slavery, this taxonomy became fully racialized in the "one-drop rule," whereby any amount of African ancestry, no matter how remote, and regardless of phenotypical appearance, makes a person Black. For Indians, in stark contrast, non-Indian ancestry compromised their indigeneity, producing "half-breeds," a regime that persists in the form of blood-quantum regulations. As opposed to enslaved people, whose reproduction augmented their owners' wealth, indigenous people obstructed settlers' access to land, so their increase was counterproductive. In this way, the restrictive racial classification of Indians straightforwardly furthered the logic of elimination. Thus we cannot simply say that elimination, genocide, or any other racially framed practice is targeted at a given race, since a race cannot be taken as given. It is made in the targeting.[34]

Black people were racialized as slaves; slavery constituted their blackness. Correspondingly, the original owners of the land were removed, killed, romanticized, assimilated, fenced in, bred White, and otherwise eliminated *as Indians*. Roger Smith has missed this point in seeking to distinguish between victims murdered for where they are and victims murdered for who they are.[35] So far as indigenous people are concerned, where they are *is* who they are, and not by their reckoning alone. As Deborah Bird Rose has pointed out, to get in the way of settler colonization, all the native has to do is stay at home.[36]

Good, Dead, and Other Indians

The question remains, though: to get in the way of what? We have yet to come to grips with the insatiable dynamic whereby settler colonialism always needs more land. The answer that springs most readily to mind is agriculture, though it is not necessarily the only one. The whole range of primary sectors can motivate the project. In addition to agriculture, therefore, we should think in terms of forestry, fishing, pastoralism, and mining (the last straw for the Cherokee was the discovery of gold on their land.) With the exception of agriculture, however (and, for some peoples, pastoralism,), none of these is sufficient in itself. You cannot eat lumber or gold; fishing for the world market requires canneries. Moreover, sooner or later, miners move on, while forests and fish become exhausted or need to be farmed. Accordingly, while the fact that agriculture springs most readily to mind no doubt reflects its sovereign place in the Western imaginary (where it goes on echoing the Neolithic revolution, endlessly re-enacted by Ceres and Apollo, Cain and Abel, etc.), agriculture is central to settler colonialism in an objective sense. It not only supports the other sectors. It is inherently sedentary and, therefore, permanent. In contrast to extractive industries, which rely on what happens to be there, agriculture is a rational means/end calculus that is geared to vouchsafing its own reproduction, generating capital that projects into a future where it repeats itself (hence the farmer's dread of being reduced to eating seed stock). Moreover, as John Locke never tired of pointing out, agriculture supports a larger population than nonsedentary modes of production.[37] In settler-colonial terms, this means that an agricultural population can be expanded by continuing immigration at the expense of native lands and livelihoods. The inequities, contradictions, and pogroms of metropolitan society ensure a recurrent supply of fresh immigrants—especially, as noted, from among the landless. In this way, individual motivations dovetail with the global market's imperative for expansion. Through its ceaseless expansion, agriculture (including, for this purpose, commercial pastoralism) progressively eats into indigenous territory, a primitive accumulation that turns native flora and fauna into a dwindling resource and curtails the reproduction of indigenous modes of production. In the event, indigenous people are either rendered dependent on the introduced economy or reduced to the stock raids that provide the classic pretext for colonial death squads (Moses's "genocidal moments").

None of this means that indigenous people are by definition nonagricultural. Whether or not they actually do practice agriculture, however (as in the case of the Indians who taught Whites to grow corn and tobacco,), natives are typically represented as unsettled, nomadic, rootless, etc., in settler-colonial discourse. In addition to its objective economic centrality to the project, agriculture, with its life-sustaining connectedness to land, is a potent symbol of settler-colonial identity. Accordingly, settler-colonial discourse is resolutely impervious to glaring aporias such as sedentary natives or the fact that the settlers themselves have come from somewhere else. Thus it is significant that the feminized, finance-oriented (or, for that matter, wandering) Jew of European antisemitic mythology should assert an aggressively masculine agricultural self-identification in Palestine.[38] The reproach of nomadism renders the native removable. Moreover, if the natives are not already nomadic, then the reproach can be turned into a self-fulfilling prophecy through the burning of corn or the uprooting of olive trees.

But if the natives are already agriculturalists, then why not simply incorporate their productivity into the colonial economy? At this point, we begin to get closer to the question of just who it is (or, more to the point, who they are) that settler colonialism strives to eliminate—and, accordingly, closer to an understanding of the relationship between settler colonialism and genocide. To stay with the Cherokee removal: when it came to it, the factor that most antagonized the Georgia state government (with the at least tacit support of Andrew Jackson's federal administration) was not actually the recalcitrant savagery of which Indians were routinely accused, but the Cherokee's unmistakable aptitude for civilization. Indeed, they and their Creek, Choctaw, Chickasaw, and Seminole neighbors, who were also targeted for removal, figured revealingly as the "Five Civilized Tribes" in Euro-American parlance. In the Cherokee's case, two dimensions of their civility were particularly salient: they had become successful agriculturalists on the White model, with a number of them owning substantial holdings of Black slaves, and they had introduced a written national constitution that bore more than a passing resemblance to the US one.[39] Why should genteel Georgians wish to rid themselves of such cultivated neighbors? The reason why the Cherokee's constitution and their agricultural prowess stood out as such singular provocations to the officials and legislators of the state of

Georgia—and this is attested over and over again in their public statements and correspondence—is that the Cherokee's farms, plantations, slaves, and written constitution all signified *permanence*.[40] The first thing the rabble did, let us remember, was burn their houses.

Brutal and murderous though the removals of the Five Nations generally were, they did not affect each member equally. This was not simply a matter of wealth or status. Principal Cherokee chief John Ross, for example, lost not only his plantation after setting off on the Trail of Tears. On that trail, one deathly cold Little Rock, Arkansas, day in February 1839, he also lost his wife, Qatie, who died after giving her blanket to a freezing child.[41] Ross's fortunes differed sharply from those of the principal Choctaw chief Greenwood LeFlore, who, unlike Ross, signed a removal treaty on behalf of his people, only to stay behind himself, accept US citizenship, and go on to a distinguished career in Mississippi politics.[42] But it was not just his chiefly rank that enabled LeFlore to stay behind. Indeed, he was by no means the only one to do so. As Ronald Satz has commented, Andrew Jackson was taken by surprise when "thousands of Choctaws decided to take advantage of the allotment provisions [in the treaty LeFlore had signed] and become homesteaders and American citizens in Mississippi."[43] In addition to being principal chiefs, Ross and LeFlore both had White fathers and light skin. Both were wealthy, educated and well connected in Euro-American society. Many of the thousands of compatriots who stayed behind with LeFlore lacked any of these qualifications. There was nothing special about the Choctaw to make them particularly congenial to White society—most of them got removed like Ross and the Cherokee. The reason that the remaining Choctaw were acceptable had nothing to do with their being Choctaw. On the contrary, it had to do with their *not* (or, at least, no longer) being Choctaw. They had become "homesteaders and American citizens." In a word, they had become individuals.

What distinguished Ross and the removing Choctaw from those who stayed behind was collectivity. Tribal land was tribally owned—tribes and private property did not mix. Indians were the original communist menace. As homesteaders, by contrast, the Choctaw who stayed became individual proprietors, each to his own, of separately allotted fragments of what had previously been the tribal estate, theirs to sell to White people if they chose to. Without the tribe, though, for all practical purposes they were no longer Indians (this is the citizenship part.) Here, in essence, is assimilation's Faustian bargain: have our settler world, but lose your indigenous soul. Beyond any doubt, this is a kind of death. Assimilationists recognized this very clearly. On the face of it, one might not expect there to be much in common between Captain Richard Pratt, founder of the Carlisle boarding school for Indian youth and leading light of the philanthropic "Friends of the Indian" group, and General Phil Sheridan, scourge of the Plains and author of the deathless maxim, "The only good Indian is a dead Indian." Given the training in individualism that Pratt provided at his school, however, the tribe could disappear while its members stayed behind, a metaphysical variant on the Choctaw scenario. This would offer a solution to reformers' disquiet over the national discredit attaching to the Vanishing Indian. In a paper for the 1892 Charities and Correction Conference held in Denver, Pratt explicitly endorsed Sheridan's maxim, "but only in this: that all the Indian there is in the race should be dead. Kill the Indian in him and save the man."[44]

Group Death

But just what kind of death is it that is involved in assimilation? It will not do to slip in a metaphor to usurp the reality of genocide. As we know, the etymology of "genocide" combines the senses of killing and of grouphood. Both are indispensable, and there is no priority between them. As we also know, the term "homicide" combines the senses of killing and of individuality. So far as I know, when it comes to killing an individual, there is no alternative to terminating their somatic career.[45] Yet, when Orestes was arraigned before the Furies for the murder of his mother Clytemnestra, whom he had killed to avenge her murder of his father Agamemnon, he was acquitted on the ground that, in a patrilineal society, he belonged to his father rather than to his mother, so the charge of matricide could not stand. Now, without taking this legend too seriously, it nonetheless illustrates (as legends are presumably meant to) an important point. Orestes' beating the charge did not mean that he had not actually killed Clytemnestra. It meant that he had been brought before the wrong court (the Furies dealt with intrafamily matters that could not be resolved by the mechanism of feud). Thus Orestes may not have been guilty of matricide, but that did not mean he was innocent. It meant that he might be guilty of some other form of illegal killing—one that could be dealt with by the blood feud or other appropriate sanction (where his plea of obligatory revenge may or may not have succeeded.) In other words, as in those languages where a verb is inflected by its object, the nature of a justiciable killing depends on its victim. There are seemingly absolute differences between, say, suicide, insecticide, and infanticide. For judicial purposes, genocide refers to the intentional destruction, in whole or in part, of a group. "Group" is more than a purely numerical designation. *Genos* refers to a denominate group with a membership that persists through time (Raphael Lemkin translated it as "tribe"). It is not simply a random collectivity, such as, say, the passengers on a bus. Accordingly, with respect to Robert Gellately and Ben Kiernan (concerning both the title of their excellent book and their reference, in this context, to 9/11), the strike on the World Trade Center is an example of mass murder, but not, in my view, of genocide. Certainly, the bulk of the victims were US citizens. On the scale of the whole, however, not only was it an infinitesimal part of the group "Americans" (which, strictly, is not a consideration), but it was a one-off event.[46] This does not mean that the perpetrators of 9/11 are not guilty. It means that a genocide tribunal is the wrong court to bring them before. Mass murders are not the same thing as genocide, though the one action can be both. Thus genocide has been achieved by means of summary mass murder (to cite examples already used) in the frontier massacring of indigenous peoples, in the Holocaust, and in Rwanda. But there can be summary mass murder without genocide, as in the case of 9/11, and there can be genocide without summary mass murder, as in the case of the continuing postfrontier destruction, in whole and in part, of indigenous *genoi*. Lemkin knew what he was doing when he used the word "tribe."[47] Richard Pratt and Phillip Sheridan were both practitioners of genocide. The question of degree is not the definitional issue.

Vital though it is, definitional discussion can seem insensitively abstract. In the preceding paragraph, part of what I have had in mind has, obviously, been the term (which Lemkin favored) "cultural genocide." My reason for not favoring the term is that it confuses definition with degree. Moreover, though this objection holds in its own right (or so I think), the practical hazards that can ensue once an abstract concept like "cultural genocide" falls into the wrong hands are legion. In particular, in an elementary category error, "either/or" can be substituted for "both/and," from which genocide emerges as either biological (read "the real thing") or cultural—and thus, it follows, not real. In practice, it should go without saying that the imposition on a people of the procedures and techniques that are generally glossed as "cultural genocide" is certainly going to have a direct impact on that people's capacity to stay alive (even apart from their qualitative immiseration while they do so). At the height of the Dawes-era assimilation program, for instance, in the decade after Richard Pratt penned his Denver paper, Indian numbers hit the lowest level they would ever register.[48] Even in contemporary, post–native-title Australia, Aboriginal life expectancy clings to a level some twenty-five percent below that enjoyed by mainstream society, with infant mortality rates that are even worse.[49] What species of sophistry does it take to separate a quarter "part" of the life of a group from the history of their elimination?

Clearly, we are not talking about an isolated event here. Thus we can shift from settler colonialism's structural complexity to its positivity as a structuring principle of settler-colonial society across time.

Bioculture

The Cherokee Trail of Tears, which took place over the winter of 1838–39, presupposed the Louisiana Purchase of 1803, when Thomas Jefferson had bought approximately one-third of the present-day continental United States at a knockdown price from Napoleon.[50] The greatest real estate deal in history provided the territory west of the Mississippi that successive US governments would exchange for the homelands of the eastern tribes, whom they were bent on removing. For various reasons, these removals, which turned eastern tribes into proxy invaders of Indian territory across the Mississippi, were a crude and unsatisfactory form of elimination. In particular, they were temporary, it being only a matter of time before the frontier rabble caught up with them.[51] When that happened, as Annie Abel resignedly observed in concluding her classic account of the removals, "titles given in the West proved less substantial than those in the East, for they had no foundation in antiquity."[52] Repeat removals, excisions from reservations, grants of the same land to different tribes, all conducted against a background of endless pressure for new or revised treaties, were the symptoms of removal's temporariness, which kept time with the westward march of the nation. In the end, though, the western frontier met the one moving back in from the Pacific, and there was simply no space left for removal. The frontier had become coterminal with reservation boundaries. At this point, when the crude technique of removal declined in favor of a range of strategies for assimilating Indian people now that they had been contained within Euro-American society, we can more clearly see the logic of elimination's positivity as a continuing feature of Euro-American settler society.

With the demise of the frontier, elimination turned inwards, seeking to penetrate through the tribal surface to the individual Indian below, who was to be co-opted out of the tribe, which would be depleted accordingly, and into White society. The Greenwood LeFlore situation was to be generalized to all Indians. The first major expression of this shift was the discontinuation of treaty making, which came about in 1871.[53] Over the following three decades, an avalanche of assimilationist legislation, accompanied by draconian Supreme Court judgments that notionally dismantled tribal sovereignty and provided for the abrogation of existing treaties,[54] relentlessly sought the breakdown of the tribe and the absorption into White society of individual Indians and their tribal land, only separately. John Wunder has termed this policy framework "the New Colonialism," a discursive formation based on reservations and boarding schools that "attacked every aspect of Native American life—religion, speech, political freedoms, economic liberty, and cultural diversity."[55] The centerpiece of this campaign was the allotment program, first generalized as Indian policy in the Dawes Severalty Act of 1887 and subsequently intensified and extended, whereby tribal land was to be broken down into individual allotments whose proprietors could eventually sell them to White people.[56] Ostensibly, this program provided for a cultural transformation whereby the magic of private property ownership would propel Indians from the collective inertia of tribal membership into the progressive individualism of the American dream. In practice, not only did Indian numbers rapidly hit the lowest level they would ever record, but this cultural procedure turned out to yield a faster method of land transference than the US Cavalry had previously provided. In the half century from 1881, the total acreage held by Indians in the United States fell by two-thirds, from just over 155 million acres to just over 52 million.[57] Needless to say, the coincidence between the demographic statistics and the landownership ones was no coincidence. Throughout this process, reformers' justifications for it (saving the Indian from the tribe, giving him the same opportunities as the White man, etc.) repeatedly included the express intention to destroy the tribe in whole.[58] With their land base thus attenuated, US citizenship was extended to all Indians in 1924. In 1934, under the New Deal Indian Reorganization Act, allotment was abandoned in favor of a policy of admitting the tribe itself into the US polity, only on the condition that its constitution be rewritten into structural harmony with its US civic environment. A distinctive feature of the model constitutions that the Secretary of the Interior approved for tribes that registered under the 1934 act was blood quantum requirements, originally introduced by Dawes Act commissioners to determine which tribal members would be eligible for what kind of allotments.[59] Under the blood quantum regime, one's Indianness progressively declines in accordance with a "biological" calculus that is a construct of Euro-American culture. [60] Juaneño/Jaqi scholar Annette Jaimes has termed this procedure "statistical extermination."[61] In sum, the containment of Indian groups within Euro-American society that culminated in the end of the frontier produced a range of ongoing complementary strategies, whose common intention was the destruction of heterodox forms of Indian grouphood. In the post–World War II climate of civil rights, these strategies were reinforced by the policies of termination and relocation, held out as liberating individual Indians from the thralldom of the tribe, whose compound effects rivaled the disasters of allotment.[62] A major difference between this and the generality of noncolonial genocides is its sustained duration.

I have previously rehearsed the continuity of the logic of elimination through postfrontier Australian society at some length, and more than once, so I shall leave it as read here.[63] Nonetheless, it is important to reiterate the fundamentally destructive nature of assimilation programs. In an excess of voluntarism that mistakes responsible officials' (in the main, Paul Hasluck's) expressions of intent for the fullness of state activity, Russell McGregor has asserted that, because officials talked publicly of preparing Aborigines for assimilation into full membership of mainstream Australian society, post–World War II Aboriginal assimilation was cultural as opposed to biological and, therefore, not genocidal.[64] Apart from the fact that Hasluck-era policy sought to elevate Aborigines from out of their group and into mainstream Australian society as individuals (a strategy aimed at eliminating the group), and from the fact that, however it may be ideologically rationalized, child abduction is child abduction, the unexamined assumption that "culture" and "biology" are discrete categories is untenable.[65] In the Australian context alone, many scholars apart from myself have recognized that "the genetic and cultural codes recapitulated each other."[66] To take an example from genocide's definitional core, Article II (d) of the UN Convention on Genocide, which seems to have been relatively overlooked in Australian discussions, includes among the acts that constitute genocide (assuming they are committed with intent to destroy a target group in whole or in part) the imposition of "measures intended to prevent births within the group." Given that child abduction, assuming it is "successful", brings about a situation in which second-generation offspring are born into a group that is different from the one from which the child/parent was originally abducted, there is abundant evidence of genocide being practised in postwar Australia on the basis of Article II (d) alone. Yet it is impossible to draw simple either/or lines between culture and biology in cases such as this. Though a child was physically abducted, the eventual outcome is as much a matter of a social classification as it is of a body count. Nonetheless, the intentional contribution to the demographic destruction of the "relinquishing" group is unequivocal.

Structural Genocide

Why, then, logic of elimination rather than genocide? As stated at the outset, settler colonialism is a specific social formation and it is desirable to retain that specificity. So far as I can tell, an understanding of settler colonialism would not be particularly helpful for understanding the mass killings of, say, witches in medieval Europe, Tutsis in Rwanda, enemies of the people in Cambodia, or Jews in the Nazi fatherland (the *Lebensraum* is, of course, another matter). By the same token, with the possible exception of the witches (whose murders appear to have been built into a great social transition,) these mass killings would seem to have little to tell us about the long-run structural consistency of settler colonizers' attempts to eliminate native societies. In contrast to the Holocaust, which was endemic to Nazism rather than to Germany (which was by no means the only—or even, historically, the most—antisemitic society in Europe) settler colonialism is relatively impervious to regime change. The genocide of American Indians or of Aboriginal people in Australia has not been subject to election results. So why not a special kind of genocide?—Raymond Evans' and Bill Thorpe's etymologically deft "indigenocide," for instance,[67] or one of the hyphenated genocides ("cultural genocide," "ethnocide," "politicide," etc.)[68] that have variously been proposed? The apparently insurmountable problem with the qualified genocides is that, in their very defensiveness, they threaten to undo themselves. They are never quite the real thing, just as patronizingly hyphenated ethnics are not fully Australian or fully American. Apart from this categorical problem, there is a historical basis to the relative diminution of the qualified genocides. This basis is, of course, the Holocaust—the nonparadigmatic paradigm that, being the indispensable example, can never merely exemplify. Keeping one eye on the Holocaust, which is always the unqualified referent of the qualified genocides, can only disadvantage indigenous people because it discursively reinforces the figure of lack at the heart of the non-Western. Moreover, whereas the Holocaust exonerates antisemitic Western nations who were on the side opposing the Nazis, those same nations have nothing to gain from their liability for colonial genocides. On historical as well as categorical grounds, therefore, the hyphenated genocides devalue indigenous attrition. No such problem bedevils analysis of the logic of elimination, which, in its specificity to settler colonialism, is premised on the securing—the obtaining and the maintaining—of territory.[69] This logic certainly requires the elimination of the owners of that territory, but not in any particular way. To this extent, it is a larger category than genocide. For instance, the style of romantic stereotyping that I have termed "repressive authenticity," which is a feature of settler-colonial discourse in many countries, is not genocidal in itself, though it eliminates large numbers of empirical natives from official reckonings and, as such, is often concomitant with genocidal practice.[70] Indeed, depending on the historical conjuncture, assimilation can be a more effective mode of elimination than outright killing, since it does not involve such a disruptive affront to the rule of law that is ideologically central to the cohesion of settler society.[71] When invasion is recognized as a structure rather than an event, its history does not stop (or, more to the point, become relatively trivial) when it moves on from the era of frontier homicide. Rather, narrating that history involves charting the continuities, discontinuities, adjustments, and departures whereby a logic that initially informed frontier killing transmutes into different modalities, discourses, and institutional formations as it undergirds the historical development and complexification of settler society. This is not a hierarchical procedure.

Despite these and other advantages that my term seems to offer, however, in the end I cannot get around Robert Gellately and Ben Kiernan's salutary admonition that tampering with the definition of genocide could lead to some of its victims being found ineligible for redress.[72] After all, as recent Australian experience has shown, there is no shortage of influential cultural players who are only too willing to deny, distort, and suppress information on the issue.[73] Thus the problem becomes one of how to retain the specificity of settler colonialism without downplaying its impact by resorting to a qualified genocide. I suggest that, to express settler colonialism's genocidal dimension, the term "structural genocide" avoids the questions of degree (and, therefore, of hierarchy among victims) that are entailed in qualified genocides, while retaining settler colonialism's structural induration (it also lets in the witches, whose destruction, as Charles Zika has shown, was closely linked to the coeval transatlantic destruction of Native Americans[74]). Given a historical perspective on structural genocide, we can recognize its being in abeyance (as, mercifully, it seems to be in contemporary Australia) rather than being a thing of the past—which is to say, we should guard against the recurrence of what Moses terms "genocidal moments" (social workers continue to take Aboriginal children in disproportionate numbers, for example.[75]) Focusing on structural genocide also enables us to appreciate some of the concrete empirical relationships between spatial removal, mass killings, and biocultural assimilation. For instance, where there is no space left for removal (as occurred on the demise of the frontier in the US and Australia, or on the Soviet victory on Nazi Germany's eastern front), mass killings or assimilation become the only eliminatory options available. Under these circumstances, the resort to mass killings can reflect the proclaimed inassimilability of the victim group, as in the case of Jews in relation to the "Aryan" bloodstock.[76] Correspondingly, assimilation programs can reflect the ideological requirements of settler-colonial societies, which characteristically cite native advancement to establish their egalitarian credentials to potentially fractious groups of immigrants.[77]

The demise of the frontier was not, however, a local phenomenon. As J.A. Hobson and, following him, V.I. Lenin so influentially noted, imperialism had been central to the expansion of industrial capitalism.[78] Once the space for further colonization of the extra-European world had been effectively exhausted, the expanded universe of European imperialism turned back in on itself, bringing the contest over existing imperial possessions to the point of world war. Oversimplified as it is (though not thereby inaccurate), this generalization is enough, for our purposes, to underline the crucial point, in relation to settler colonialism and genocide, that Germany emerged from World War I effectively bereft of overseas imperial possessions. As a number of scholars have noted, the push for German living space (*Lebensraum*) in western Poland, which involved clearing that region of Jewish, Slav, and other supposedly non-German populations, evinced many of the characteristic features of settler colonialism, in particular mass killings, removals (until precluded by the Soviets), and the assimilation of Poles alleged to look like Aryans.[79] It is important to note that territorial separation was not involved here. Nothing that I have said about settler colonialism requires there to be a spatial hiatus (or "blue water") between metropole and colony.[80] Settler colonization occurs and persists to the extent that a population sets out to replace another one in its habitation, regardless of where the colonizing population originated.

How, then, might any of this help to predict and prevent genocide?

Indications

In the first place, it shows us that settler colonialism is an indicator. Unpalatable though it is (to speak as a member of a settler society), this conclusion has a positive aspect, which is a corollary to settler colonialism's temporal dimension. Since settler colonialism persists over extended periods of time, structural genocide should be easier to interrupt than short-term genocides. For instance, it seems reasonable to credit the belated UN/Australian intervention in East Timor with warding off the likelihood of a continued or renewed genocidal program. Realpolitik is a factor, however. Thus the relief of Timor would not seem to hold out a great deal of hope for, say, Tibet.

Since settler colonialism is an indicator, it follows that we should monitor situations in which settler colonialism intensifies or in which societies that are not yet or not fully settler-colonial take on more of its characteristics. Israel's progressive dispensing with its reliance on Palestinian labor would seem to present an ominous case in point.[81] Colin Tatz has argued, conclusively in my view, that, while Turkish behavior in Armenia, Nazi behavior in Europe, and Australian behavior toward Aborigines (among other examples) constitute genocide, the apartheid regime in South Africa does not. His basic reason is that African labor was indispensable to apartheid South Africa, so it would have been counterproductive to destroy it. The same can be said of African American slavery. In both cases, the genocide tribunal is the wrong court.

The US parallel is significant because, unlike in South Africa, the formal apparatus of oppression (slavery) was overcome but Whites remained in power.[82] On emancipation, Blacks became surplus to some requirements and, to that extent, more like Indians. Thus it is highly significant that the barbarities of lynching and the Jim Crow reign of racial terror should be a postemancipation phenomenon.[83] As valuable commodities, slaves had only been destroyed *in extremis*. Even after slavery, Black people continued to have value as a source of super-cheap labor (providing an incitement to poor Whites), so their dispensability was tempered.[84] Today in the US, the blatant racial zoning of large cities and the penal system suggests that, once a colonized people outlives its utility, settler societies can fall back on the repertoire of strategies (in this case, spatial sequestration) whereby they have also dealt with the native surplus. There could hardly be a more concrete expression of spatial sequestration than the East Jerusalem, and West Bank walls. There again, apartheid also relied on sequestration. Perhaps Colin Tatz, who insists that Israel is not genocidal,[85] finds it politic to allow an association between the Zionist and apartheid regimes as the price of preempting the charge of genocide. It is hard to imagine that a scholar of his perspicacity can have failed to recognize the Palestinian resonances of his statement, made in relation to Biko youth, that "they threw rocks and died for their efforts."[86] Nonetheless, as Palestinians become more and more dispensable, East Jerusalem, Gaza and the West Bank become less and less like Bantustans and more and more like reservations (or, for that matter, like the Warsaw Ghetto).

All this and more follows, it seems to me, from the recognition that settler-colonial invasion is a structure rather than an event.

Acknowledgment

My thanks to Dirk Moses for his helpful editorship and to Zora Simic for her comments. A different version of the analysis presented in this chapter has been published as "Settler Colonialism and the Elimination of the Native," *Journal of Genocide Research* 8, no. 4 (2006): 387–409.

Notes

1. Patrick Wolfe, "Nation and MiscegeNation: Discursive Continuity in the Post-Mabo Era," *Social Analysis* 36 (1994): 93–152; Wolfe, *Settler Colonialism and the Transformation of Anthropology: The Politics and Poetics of an Ethnographic Event* (London, 1999); Wolfe, "Land, Labor, and Difference: Elementary Structures of Race," *American Historical Review* 106 (2001): 865–905.

2. A. Dirk Moses, "Genocide and Settler Society in Australian History," in *Genocide and Settler Society: Frontier Violence and Stolen Indigenous Children in Australian History,* ed. A. Dirk Moses (New York, 2004), 30–35.
3. Wolfe, *Settler Colonialism,* 2; idem, "Nation and MiscegeNation," 96.
4. A pioneering expression of a comparable perspective in the Australian context was Tony Barta, "Relations of Genocide: Land and Lives in the Colonization of Aboriginal Australia," in *Genocide and the Modern Age: Etiology and Case Studies of Mass Death,* ed. Isidor Wallimann and Michael N. Dobkowski (Westport, CT, 1987), 237–52.
5. Moses, "Genocide and Settler Society," 34.
6. Cole Harris, "How Did Colonialism Dispossess? Comments from an Edge of Empire," *Annals of the Association of American Geographers* 94 (2004): 179.
7. Moses, "Genocide and Settler Society," 32.
8. For Australia, see for example Wolfe, "Nation and MiscegeNation." For Australian and US policies together, see idem, "The Limits of Native Title," *Meanjin* 59, no. 3 (2000): 129–44; idem, "Land, Labor, and Difference."
9. My approach shares ground with Raphael Lemkin's two phases of genocide: "One, destruction of the national pattern of the oppressed group; the other, the imposition of the national pattern of the oppressor. This imposition, in turn, may be made upon the oppressed population which is allowed to remain, or upon the territory alone, after removal of the population and colonization of the area by the oppressor's own nationals." *Axis Rule in Occupied Europe: Laws of Occupation, Analysis of Government, Proposals for Redress* (New York, 1944), 79.
10. For varying analyses and discussions of the principal formulations of the doctrine of discovery, see for example Anthony Anghie, "Francisco de Vitoria and the Colonial Origins of International Law," in *Laws of the Postcolonial,* ed. Eve Darian-Smith and Peter Fitzpatrick (Ann Arbor, MI, 1999), 89–107; Andrew Fitzmaurice, *Humanism and America. An Intellectual History of English Colonisation, 1500–1625* (Cambridge, 2003); David Kennedy, "Primitive Legal Scholarship," *Harvard International Law Journal* 27 (1986): 1–98; Mark F. Lindley, *The Acquisition and Government of Backward Territory in International Law* (London, 1926); Robert A. Williams, Jr., *The American Indian in Western Legal Thought: The Discourses of Conquest* (Oxford, 1990), esp. 233–86.
11. This observation unites almost all commentators, whatever their political inclination. Cf. for example Anthony Anghie, "Finding the Peripheries: Sovereignty and Colonialism in Nineteenth-Century International Law," *Harvard International Law Journal* 40 (1999): 69; L.C. Green, "Claims to Territory in Colonial America," in *The Law of Nations and the New World,* ed. L.C. Green and Olive P. Dickason (Edmonton, 1989), 125.
12. See for example Wilcomb E. Washburn, ed., *History of Indian-White Relations* (Washington, DC, 1988); William C. Sturtevant, ed., *Handbook of North American Indians,* 11 vols. (Washington, DC, 2001), 4: 5–39.
13. As Mr. Justice Johnson put it in his concurrence with Chief Justice Marshall's judgment in *Cherokee v. Georgia,* "the hunter state bore within itself the promise of vacating the territory, because when game ceased, the hunter would go elsewhere to seek it. But a more fixed state of society would amount to a permanent destruction of the hope, and, of consequence, of the beneficial character of the pre-emptive right." *Cherokee v. Georgia* (30 *US* [5 Peters] 1, 1831), 23.
14. The judgments most often cited in this connection are *Worcester v. Georgia,* 31 *U.S.* 515 (6 Peters 1832); Ex parte *Crow Dog,* 109 *U.S.* 556 (1883); and *Williams v. Lee,*

358 *U.S.* 217 (1959). I present a critique of the limitations of these judgments, and of the limitations of US-style Indian sovereignty as a whole, in an article entitled "Against the Intentional Fallacy: Marking the Gap between Rhetoric and Outcome in US Indian Law and Policy," under consideration by a journal.

15. Harvey D. Rosenthal, "Indian Claims and the American Conscience: A Brief History of the Indian Claims Commission," in *Irredeemable America: The Indians' Estate and Land Claims*, ed. Imre Sutton (Albuquerque, NM, 1985), 36.
16. The classic accounts from a well-established literature include Annie H. Abel, "The History of Events Resulting in Indian Consolidation West of the Mississippi River," in *American Historical Association Annual Report for 1906*, 2 vols. (Washington, DC, 1906), 2: 233–450; Angie Debo, *A History of the Indians of the United States* (Norman, OK, 1970); Foreman, *Indian Removal*; Helen Hunt Jackson, *A Century of Dishonor: A Sketch of the United States Government's Dealings with Some of the Indian Tribes* (New York, 1885).
17. James M. Mooney, *Historical Sketch of the Cherokee* (Chicago, 1975 [1900]), 124.
18. The most lively source on the ghoulish enterprise of craniology/craniometry remains Stephen J. Gould, *The Mismeasure of Man* (Harmondsworth, UK, 1981). For a superbly written account with an Australian focus, see Helen MacDonald, *Human Remains: Episodes in Human Dissection* (Melbourne, 2005).
19. Wolfe, "Limits of Native Title," 144.
20. Williams, *American Indian*, 269.
21. *Johnson v. McIntosh*, 21 U.S. 543 (8 Wheaton 1823), 573.
22. For discussion of Olney's "tide of history" concept, see Jackie Delpero, "'The Tide of History': Australian Native Title Discourse in Global Context" (MA thesis, Victoria University of Technology, 2003); David Ritter, "The Judgement of the World: The Yorta Yorta Case and the 'Tide of History,'" *Australian Historical Studies* 123 (April 2004): 106–21.
23. Paul R. Bartrop, "Punitive Expeditions and Massacres: Gippsland, Colorado, and the Question of Genocide," in *Genocide and Setter Society*, 194–214.
24. Ibid., 199.
25. Ibid., 203.
26. Alison Palmer, *Colonial Genocide* (Adelaide, 2000), 199.
27. Zygmunt Bauman, *Modernity and the Holocaust* (Cambridge, 1989).
28. In 1902, the renowned English liberal J.A. Hobson expressed the fear "that the arts and crafts of tyranny, acquired and exercised in our unfree Empire, should be turned against our liberties at home." *Imperialism: A Study* (London, 1902), 160. For Du Bois, see Hannah Arendt, *The Origins of Totalitarianism* (New York, 1966). On Césaire, see Lorenzo Veracini's chapter in this book.
29. Enzo Traverso, *The Origins of Nazi Violence*, trans. Janet Lloyd (New York, 2003); Charles Patterson, *Eternal Treblinka: Our Treatment of Animals and the Holocaust* (New York, 2002).
30. "The [Central Government-region Jewish] ghetto clearings amounted to wild, day-long shooting sprees in particular sections of cities, at the end of which bodies were lying in the main streets leading to train stations." Dieter Pohl, "The Murder of Jews in the General Government," in *National Socialist Extermination Policies: Contemporary German Perspectives and Controversies*, ed. Ulrich Herbert (New York, 2000), 99. See also the discussion in Stephen R. Welch, "A Survey of Interpretive Paradigms in Holocaust Studies and a Comment on the Dimensions of the Holocaust," Yale Center for International and Area Studies Working Paper, no. GS17 (New Haven, CT, 2001), 9, n. 24, 25; Jürgen Zimmerer, "Colonialism and the Holocaust: Towards an Archaeology

of Genocide," in Moses, *Genocide and Settler Society*, 48–76. On colonial starvations and the "New Imperialism," see Mike Davis, *Late Victorian Holocausts: El Niño Famines and the Making of the Third World* (London, 2001).

31. Robert Melson, "Modern Genocide in Rwanda: Ideology, Revolution, War, and Mass Murder in an African State," in *The Specter of Genocide*, ed. Robert Gellately and Ben Kiernan (Cambridge and New York), 326.
32. Ibid., 327–28.
33. See for example Collette Guillaumin, "The Idea of Race and its Elevation to Autonomous Scientific and Legal Status," in *Racism, Sexism, Power and Ideology* (London, 1995), 61–98; Ivan Hannaford, *Race: The History of an Idea in the West* (Baltimore, MD, 1996); Kenan Malik, *The Meaning of Race: Race, History and Culture in Western Society* (London, 1996); George L. Mosse, *Toward the Final Solution: A History of European Racism* (Madison, WI, 1985); Tzvetan Todorov, *On Human Diversity: Nationalism, Racism, and Exoticism in French Thought* (Cambridge, MA, 1993). For discussion, see my "Race and Racialisation: Some Thoughts," *Postcolonial Studies* 5, no. 1 (2002): 51–62.
34. Robert Manne misses this point ("Aboriginal Child Removal and the Question of Genocide," in *Genocide and Settler Society*, 219–20). Responding to a question posed in 1937 by Western Australian Aboriginal affairs functionary A.O. Neville ("Are we going to have a population of 1,000,000 blacks in the [Australian] Commonwealth, or are we going to merge them into our white community and eventually forget that there ever were any aborigines in Australia?"), Manne suggests that, in order to "grasp the genocidal implications" of the question, "we need only replace the words 'blacks' and 'Aborigine' [*sic*] with the word 'Jew'" and locate the posing of the question in Berlin rather than Canberra. Apart from its contrivedness, this analogy fails because the Nazi racialization of Jews did not conduce to their assimilation. Rather, the reverse was the case. As Robert Gellately has observed, "Although we can point to some similarities in Nazi plans and actions for Jews and Slavs, there was, and remains one crucial difference: in principle Jews could never be saved, never convert, nor be assimilated." "The Third Reich, the Holocaust, and Visions of Serial Genocide," in *Specter of Genocide*, 262.
35. Roger W. Smith, "Human Destructiveness and Politics: The Twentieth Century as an Age of Genocide," in *Genocide and the Modern Age*, 31.
36. Deborah Bird Rose, *Hidden Histories: Black Stories from Victoria River Downs, Humbert River and Wave Hill Stations* (Canberra, 1991), 46.
37. "For the provisions serving to the support of humane life, produced by one acre of inclosed and cultivated land, are (to speak much within compasse) ten times more, than those, which are yeilded [*sic*] by an acre of Land, of an equal richnesse, lyeing wast in common." John Locke, *Two Treatises of Government* (Cambridge, 1963 [1698]), 312.
38. See, for instance, the Adi Nes photograph used as publicity for the Jewish Museum of New York's 1998/99 "After Rabin: New Art from Israel" show. www.thejewishmuseum.org/site/pages/content/exhibitions/special/rabin/rabin_zoom/rabinL1.html. The "New Jew" is an established Zionist theme. In introducing his terrorist memoir, for instance, future Israeli prime minister Menachim Begin announced that, in addition to his Jewish readers, he had also written the book for Gentiles, "lest they be unwilling to realise, or all too ready to overlook, the fact that out of blood and fire and tears and ashes a new specimen of human being was born, a specimen completely unknown to the world for over eighteen hundred years, 'the FIGHTING JEW.' " *The Revolt*, Samuel Katz, trans. (London, 1979), xxv, capitals in original.

39. "[John] Ross—the successful self-made Cherokee entrepreneur—was really what white Georgians feared. Their biggest obstacle to acquiring the Cherokee lands was the cultivator's plow and overseer's whip—not the war club, bow, and scalping knife." Sean M. O'Brien, *In Bitterness and in Tears: Andrew Jackson's Destruction of the Creeks and Seminoles* (Westport, CT, 2003), 229. For the Constitution of the Cherokee Nation, see *The Cherokee Phoenix*, 28 February 1828.
40. The capacity to achieve permanence was typically put down to European ancestry, as in Andrew Jackson's exasperated disparagement of the "designing half-breeds and renegade white men" who had encouraged Chickasaw reluctance to cede land. Theda Perdue, *"Mixed Blood" Indians: Racial Construction in the Early South* (Athens, GA, 2003), 70, 95–96. With particular reference to the Cherokee, Governor George Gilmer of Georgia responded to Ross's organization of the *Cherokee v. Georgia* Supreme Court case with the assertion that real Indians were incapable of civilized improvements: "Upon examination, it will be found that the Aboriginal [*sic*] people are as ignorant, thoughtless, and improvident, as formerly . . . that the chief [Ross,] the president of the council, the judges, marshals and sheriffs, and most of the persons concerned in the administration of the [Cherokee] Government, are the descendants of Europeans." *Sketches of Some of the First Settlers of Upper Georgia* (Baltimore, MD, 1965), 294, 296.
41. Foreman, *Indian Removal*, 310.
42. Perdue, *"Mixed Blood" Indians*, 68.
43. Ronald N. Satz, *American Indian Policy in the Jacksonian Era* (Lincoln, NE, 1975), 83.
44. From Richard H. Pratt, "The Advantages of Mingling Indians with Whites" [1892], in Francis P. Prucha, ed., *Americanizing the American Indians: Writings by the "Friends of the Indian", 1880–1900* (Cambridge, MA, 1973), 261. As this article was going off to the publishers, Ward Churchill's *Kill the Indian, Save the Man: The Genocidal Impact of American Indian Residential Schools* (San Francisco, 2004) arrived in Australia. Apart from recommending this book, I cannot comment on it adequately in a footnote, so I am putting it off until another time.
45. Apart, that is, from conceivable vegetative states that modern medicine may be able to induce and sustain, but of which I remain thankfully unaware.
46. So far, at least. If al-Qaeda were to repeat the procedure a sufficient number of times, then 9/11 could emerge as the onset of a genocide. Definitionally, in other words, as in the case of other patterned or cumulative phenomena, genocide can obtain retrospectively.
47. He had alternatives. Liddell and Scott give "race, stock, family" as primary meanings of *genos*, with secondary meanings including offspring, nation, caste, breed, gender (!), and "class, sort, kind." "Tribe" is listed as a subdivision of *ethnos* ("a number of people living together, a company, body of men . . . a race, family, tribe"). Henry G. Liddell and Robert Scott, *Greek-English Lexicon* (Oxford, 1869), 314, 426. Cf. Lemkin, *Axis Rule*, 79.
48. Russell Thornton, *American Indian Holocaust and Survival: A Population History Since 1492* (Norman, OK, 1987), 133.
49. "In 1998–2000, life expectancy for Aboriginal and Torres Strait Islander peoples was shorter by 21 years for males and 20 years for females, compared with the total population. . . . In 1998–2000, the death rate for Indigenous infants was around four times the rate in the total population." Australian Bureau of Statistics, *Australian Social Trends: Health—Mortality and Morbidity: Mortality of Aboriginal and Torres Strait Islander Peoples* (Canberra, 2002), 1. See also House of Representatives Standing Committee on Family and Community Affairs, *Health is Life: Report on the Inquiry into Indigenous Health* (Canberra, 2000); Neil Thomson, "Trends in Aboriginal Infant Mortality," in *A*

Matter of Life and Death: Contemporary Aboriginal Infant Mortality, ed. Alan Gray (Canberra, 1990), 1–8.

50. What Jefferson bought was French dominion. The rawly unsettled nature of the Purchase territory (at least, outside New Orleans and its environs and outpost settlements such as Detroit and St. Louis) was illustrated by the rapid commissioning of Lewis and Clark's 1803 expedition to chart it.
51. This was the reality behind the mushrooming frontier demographies. "In the decade before 1820, the population of the new state of Alabama increased by a startling 1,000 per cent." O'Brien, *In Bitterness and in Tears*, 221. For an illuminating catalogue of Creek responses to this invasion, see Richard S. Lackey, comp., *Frontier Claims in the Lower South. Records of Claims Filed by Citizens of the Alabama and Tombigbee River Settlements in the Mississippi Territory for Depredations by the Creek Indians During the War of 1812* (New Orleans, 1977).
52. Abel, "Indian Consolidation," 412.
53. "No Indian nation or tribe within the territory of the United States shall be acknowledged or recognized as an independent nation, tribe, or power with whom the United States may contract by treaty." 16 *Stat.*, 566 (Act of 3 March 1871), c. 120, s. 1. For discussion, see Vine Deloria, Jr. and David E. Wilkins, *Tribes, Treaties, & Constitutional Tribulations* (Austin, TX, 1999), 60–61; Francis P. Prucha, *The Great Father: The United States Government and the American Indians*, abridged ed. (Lincoln, NE, 1986), 165.
54. In particular, *US v. Kagama*, 118 U.S. 375 (1886); *Lone Wolf v. Hitchcock*, 187 U.S. 553 (1903).
55. John R. Wunder, *"Retained By The People": A History of American Indians and the Bill of Rights* (New York, 1994), 39, 17.
56. The best source on this campaign remains the authoritative report that found its way into the House hearings preceding the Indian Reorganization Act of 1934: D.S. Otis, *The Dawes Act and the Allotment of Indian Lands*, ed. Francis P. Prucha (Norman, OK, 1973 [1934]).
57. *Statistical Abstract of the United States* (US Bureau of the Census, Department of Commerce, 1955), 180.
58. See, for example, Frederick E. Hoxie, *A Final Promise: The Campaign to Assimilate the Indians, 1880–1920* (Cambridge, 1989); Prucha, *Americanizing the American Indians*, passim.
59. Thomas J. Morgan, "What Is an Indian?", *Sixty-Fifth Annual Report of the Commissioner for Indian Affairs* (Washington, DC, 1892), 31–37.
60. "Thus the key factor in colonial and 'post'-colonial race relations is not, as some have argued, simple demographic numbers, since populations have to be differentiated before they can be counted. Difference, it cannot be stressed enough, is not simply given. It is the outcome of differentiation, which is an intensely conflictual process." Wolfe, "Land, Labor, and Difference," 894.
61. M. Annette Jaimes, "Federal Indian Identification Policy: A Usurpation of Indigenous Sovereignty in North America," in *The State of Native America: Genocide, Colonization, and Resistance* (Boston, 1992), 137. Patricia Limerick is almost as succinct: "Set the blood quantum at one quarter, hold to it as a rigid definition of Indians, let intermarriage proceed as it has for centuries, and eventually Indians will be defined out of existence. When that happens, the federal government will finally be freed from its persistent 'Indian problem.'" *The Legacy of Conquest: The Unbroken Past of the American West* (New York, 1987), 338.

62. Donald L. Fixico, *Termination and Relocation. Federal Indian Policy, 1945–1960* (Albuquerque, 1986); Charles F. Wilkinson and Eric R. Biggs, "The Evolution of the Termination Policy," *American Indian Law Review* 5 (1977): 139–84.
63. Wolfe, "Nation and MiscegeNation"; idem, *Settler Colonialism*, chapter 6.
64. Russell McGregor, "Governance, Not Genocide: Aboriginal Assimilation in the Post-war Era," in *Genocide and Settler Society*, 290–311.
65. In attaching a temporal correlate (roughly, World War II) to his insulation of these two categories, McGregor misrepresents my discussion of the policy of Aboriginal assimilation, citing it as an example of the mistaken claim that the "foundations of a national assimilation policy" were laid at the 1937 Canberra Conference on Aborigines ("Governance, Not Genocide," 294, n. 15). Technically, that conference did provide such a foundation, since state Aboriginal policies had not previously been coordinated on the national (Commonwealth) level. To accommodate this consideration, and to express the coordinated nature of the resolution, on the page that McGregor cites (Wolfe, *Settler Colonialism*, 11), I stated that the policy was "standardized" in 1937. I nowhere stated that it was "founded" anything like as late as that. On the contrary, in a number of places, I explicitly asserted 1886 as the founding date (e.g., "the 1886 Victorian [Aborigines] Act was the first official expression of the national policy of assimilation," 181. See also, *inter alia*, 31, 175). It would seem that more than mere carelessness is involved here. In the same footnote, McGregor includes Stuart Macintyre in the same misrepresentation. On the page before the one that McGregor cites, Macintyre states that the policy of absorbing Aborigines was "first adopted in Victoria in 1886 and followed elsewhere by 1912." Macintyre, "Assimilation," in *The Oxford Companion to Australian History*, ed. Graeme Davison, John Hirst, and Stuart Macintyre (Melbourne, 1998), 41f. On the following page, the one that McGregor cites, Macintyre accurately states that the 1937 Conference representatives "declared that the destiny of the mixed-race [Aboriginal] population was to be absorbed into the white population." There is no suggestion that this was the first time that such a policy had been declared and, here again, no mention of foundations.
66. Wolfe, "Nation and MiscegeNation," 111; idem, *Settler Colonialism*, 180. Scholars who have made this point subsequently are too numerous to mention. Among those who made it before my 1994 discussion, see for example Jeremy Beckett, "The Past in the Present, the Present in the Past: Constructing a National Aboriginality," in *Past and Present: The Construction of Aboriginality* (Canberra, 1988), 191–217; Gillian Cowlishaw, "Colour, Culture and the Aboriginalists," *Man* 22 (1988): 221–37; Andrew Lattas, "Aborigines and Contemporary Australian Nationalism: Primordiality and the Cultural Politics of Otherness," in *Writing Australian Culture*, ed. Julie Marcus (special issue of *Social Analysis* no. 27 1990.), 50–69.
67. Raymond Evans and Bill Thorpe, this volume, also "The Massacre of Aboriginal History," *Overland* 163 (2001): 36.
68. For examples (some of which are actually hyphenated), see Katherine Bischoping and Natalie Fingerhut, "Border Lines: Indigenous Peoples in Genocide Studies," *Canadian Review of Social Anthropology* 33 (1996): 484–85; Robert K. Hitchcock and Tara M. Twedt, "Physical and Cultural Genocide of Various Indigenous Peoples," in *Genocide in the Twentieth Century*, ed. Samuel Totten, William S. Parsons, and Israel W. Charny (New York, 1995), 498–501. For "politicide" ("a process that covers a wide range of social, political, and military activities whose goal is to destroy the political and national viability of a whole community of people"), see Baruch Kimmerling, *Politicide: Ariel Sharon's War Against the Palestinians*, rev. edn (London, 2006).

69. Ever alert to the damaging implications in this connection of Israel's invasion of Palestinian territory, Colin Tatz belittles the significance of "a contest for land and what the land held" as merely "explain[ing] away" colonial ethnocide (*With Intent to Destroy: Reflecting on Genocide* [London, 2003], 180). Lower down the same page, however, he observes that "We need to remember that Aboriginal Australians were deemed expendable not just because they were considered 'vermin', or because they sometimes speared cattle or settlers, but because they failed the Lockean test of being a people capable of a polity and a civility, to wit, they couldn't or wouldn't exploit the land they held, at least not in the European sense."
70. Wolfe, "Nation and MiscegeNation," 110–18; idem, *Settler Colonialism*, 168–90. For US examples, see for example Robert F. Berkhofer, Jr., *The White Man's Indian. Images of the American Indian from Columbus to the Present* (New York, 1979); Hugh Honour, *The New Golden Land: European Images of America from the Discoveries to the Present Time* (New York, 1975). For responses to the phenomenon, see for example Fergus M. Bordewich, *Killing the White Man's Indian. Reinventing Native Americans at the End of the Twentieth Century* (New York, 1996); Ward Churchill, *Indians Are Us? Culture and Genocide in Native North America* (Monroe, ME, 1994).
71. Thus we need not detain ourselves with wondering, counterfactually, why settlers should have refrained from killing every last Aboriginal person (or, as the question has been put more generally by Tim Rowse: "How Did a Liberal Tradition of Respect for Indigenous Rights Survive at All in Twentieth-Century Australia?" in *After Mabo: Interpreting Indigenous Traditions* [Melbourne, 1994], 24). Even apart from the question of indigenous resistance, settler colonialism has, as observed, two principal aspects—not only the removal of native society but also its concomitant replacement by settler institutions. This latter, positive aspect involves the establishment and legitimation of civil hegemony, a project that would be pointlessly complicated by the openly irregular slaughter of people who no longer have the capacity seriously to obstruct the formation of settler society. The logic of elimination is not simply killing for its own sake but elimination for a purpose, and by a variety of strategic means. As I put it in 1994, "Since the requirement for legitimacy rendered massacres relatively inefficient, [child] abduction represents a purer solution to the same social imperative." ("Nation and MiscegeNation," 117).
72. "To contest categorization of a genocide may even serve to deny victims of such an event the legal remedy to which they have legitimate resort." Gellately and Kiernan, ed., *Specter of Genocide,* 379–80.
73. With courageous persistence, Robert Manne has pursued the inconsistencies and misrepresentations of this group, who are well financed and litigious: "In Denial: The Stolen Generations and the Right," *Australian Quarterly Essay* 1 (2001): 1–113; Manne, ed., *Whitewash: On Keith Windschuttle's Fabrication of Aboriginal History* (Melbourne, 2003). Ward Churchill has a comparable, if less judicious, record in the USA. See *A Little Matter of Genocide: Holocaust and Denial in the Americas, 1492 to the Present* (San Francisco, 1997).
74. Charles Zika, "Fashioning New Worlds from Old Fathers: Reflections on Saturn, Amerindians and Witches in a Sixteenth-century Print," in *Dangerous Liaisons: Essays in Honour of Greg Dening,* ed. Donna Merwick (Melbourne, 1994), 249–81; idem, "Cannibalism and Witchcraft in Early-Modern Europe: Reading the Visual Images," *History Workshop Journal* 44 (1997): 77–105.
75. "At June 2002, 22% (4,200) of children in out-of-home care were Aboriginal or Torres Straight [*sic*] Islander children. This represented a much higher rate of children

in out-of-home care among Indigenous children than non-Indigenous children (20.1 per 1,000 compared with 3.2 per 1,000)." An indication of the progress that Indigenous people in Australia have achieved since the darkest days of the assimilation policy is contained in the sentence that follows this excerpt: "In all jurisdictions, the Aboriginal Child Placement Principle outlines a preference for Indigenous children to be placed with other Aboriginal or Torres Straight [*sic*] Islander peoples, preferably within the child's extended family or community," in Australian Bureau of Statistics, *Australia Now* (Canberra, 2004), s. 2, "Australian Social Trends, 2003: Family and Community-Services: Child Protection."

76. Given the matrilineal transmission of (and relative difficulty of conversion to) Judaism, this factor indicates vigilance in relation to Palestine.
77. "Assimilated natives would be proof positive that America was an open society, where obedience and accommodation to the wishes of the majority would be rewarded with social equality." Hoxie, *Final Promise*, 34. See also George P. Castile, "Indian Sign: Hegemony and Symbolism in Federal Indian Policy," in *State and Reservation. New Perspectives on Federal Indian Policy*, ed. George P. Castile and Robert L. Bee (Tucson, AZ, 1992), 176–83.
78. Hobson, *Imperialism*; N. [V.I.] Lenin, *Imperialism, the Highest Stage of Capitalism* (Moscow, 1970 [1916]). For discussion, see Wolfe, "History and Imperialism: A Century of Theory, from Marx to Postcolonialism," *American Historical Review* 102 (1997): 389–93.
79. Isabel Heinemann, "'Until the Last Drop of Good Blood': The Kidnapping of 'Racially Valuable' Children and the Nazi Racial Policy in Occupied Eastern Europe," in *Genocide and Settler Society*, 244–66; Jürgen Zimmerer, "The Birth of the *Ostland* Out of the Spirit of Colonialism: A Postcolonial Perspective on the Nazi Policy of Conquest and Extermination," *Patterns of Prejudice* 39, no. 2 (2005): 197–219; Zimmerer, "Colonialism and the Holocaust."
80. For the Blue Water Thesis, whereby the United Nations accepted a definition of "colony" as geographically separate from its administering nation, see Ward Churchill, *Perversions of Justice. Indigenous Peoples and Angloamerican Law* (San Francisco, 2004), 51.
81. A drive to replace Palestinian labor with cheap immigrant labor began in the early 1990s in response to the first Intifada. Though this policy was officially abandoned as it generated its own problems, around eight percent of Israel's population continues to be made up of illegal immigrants (who are, by definition, non-Jewish). See Shmuel Amir, "Overseas Foreign Workers in Israel: Policy Aims and Labor Market Outcomes," *International Migration Review* 36 (Spring 2002): 41–58; Eric Beauchemin, "Illegal in Israel," Radio Netherlands broadcast, 16 November 2004: www.radionetherlands.nl/humanrights/illegalinisrael; Leila Farsakh, "An Occupation that Creates Children Willing to Die. Israel: An Apartheid State?" *Monde Diplomatique* (English language edition, 4 November 2003). http://mondediplo.com/2003/11/04apartheid. Distinguished Hebrew University of Jerusalem sociologist the late Baruch Kimmerling prognosticated ominously of the Israeli regime: "The escalating racist demagoguery concerning the Palestinian citizens of Israel may indicate the scope of the crimes that are possibly being considered, perhaps planned, and which wait only for the proper time for them to be implemented." *Politicide*, 30.
82. Even though formal legislative power was, for a time, exercized by Blacks in Black-majority Southern states during Reconstruction. See Thomas C. Holt, *Black Over White: Negro Political Leadership in South Carolina during Reconstruction* (Urbana, IL, 1977).

83. W. Fitzhugh Brundage, *Lynching in the New South: Georgia and Virginia, 1880–1930* (Urbana, IL, 1993); Leon F. Litwack, *Trouble in Mind: Black Southerners in the Age of Jim Crow* (New York, 1998); Joel Williamson, *The Crucible of Race: Black-White Relations in the American South Since Emancipation* (Oxford, 1984), 180–223.
84. "Slave labor could be analyzed in economic, social, and political terms [in traditional histories,] but free labor was often defined as simply the ending of coercion, not as a structure of labor control that needed to be analyzed in its own way." Thomas C. Holt, Rebecca J. Scott, and Frederick Cooper, *Beyond Slavery: Explorations of Race, Labor, and Citizenship in Postemancipation Societies* (Chapel Hill, NC, 2000), 2–3.
85. Though he is too scrupulous a scholar not to acknowledge that "Israeli actions may become near-genocidal." *With Intent to Destroy*, 181.
86. "[C]apital punishment being an unquestioned, routine penalty for chucking stones at Israelis." Robert Fisk, *The Great War for Civilisation: The Conquest of the Middle East* (London, 2005), 546. Quote in text from Tatz, ibid., 117. I have chosen not to patronize Professor Tatz by quoting approvingly from his otherwise excellent book, on account of our fundamental divergence over the issue of Zionism, which I wholeheartedly oppose, and, in particular, of my disdain for his attempts to confuse anti-Zionism with antisemitism (e.g., 19; 27; 127). Apart from anything else, these attempts do grave injustice to the real victims of antisemitism.

– *Chapter 5* –

"Crime Without a Name"

Colonialism and the Case for "Indigenocide"

Raymond Evans

> My father said the truth is a rabbit in a bramble patch. And all you can do is circle around it and point and say it's somewhere in there. But you can't put your hand on it and touch it. You can't put your hand on that furry, quivering body. All you can say is it's somewhere in there.
>
> —Pete Seeger[1]

> Suppose the truth was awful, suppose it was just a black pit, or like birds huddled in the dust of a dark cupboard? Suppose only evil were real, only it was not evil since it had lost even its name?
>
> —Iris Murdoch[2]

The Problem with the Concept of Genocide for Colonialism

The "composite mathematician" Nicolaus Bourbaki, in developing a range of theorems across some two-dozen volumes of the *Éléments de Mathematique*, invented a symbol that has the appearance of a large, bold 'Z' with rounded corners—rather like a roadside warning sign. It is inserted helpfully into texts to denote points at which argument becomes potentially slippery or contentious. This symbol is called a *tournant dangereux:* a precarious corner in the evolution of an argument's logic. At noisy meetings of the Bourbakis (as the French mathematicians engaged upon the grand project were called) it was common for speakers, enunciating faulty theorems, to be challenged by loud cries of "coconut tree!" from the floor. This cry reflected the Polynesian custom of maintaining one's position near the top of a tree while others shook it from below, in order to test one's ongoing prowess. The Bourbakis' expletive thereby denoted a challenge to the tenacity of one's theoretical grasp. A careful examination of the literature of genocide, particularly in reference to its purported colonial manifestations, cannot fail to discern that it is littered with points at which *tournant dangereux* signs require honest insertion or "coconut trees" might fruitfully be implanted.[3]

An abiding difficulty in the literature is the now familiar lack of fit between the United Nations genocide definition of 1948 and analysis of the disastrous process of indigenous dispossession occasioned by settler colonialism. On the one hand, it is posited that the dispossession process is insufficient to the demands of the definition. This has largely been the position of those scholars who regard the Nazi Holocaust as paradigmatic. The "coconut tree" here is that this "unspeakable" trauma of sudden, calculated annihilation of millions is presented as both the "standard form" of the phenomenon and the unrivalled one—as simultaneously representative and untouchable in its malignancy.[4]

On the other hand, it has also been maintained (largely by proponents of the concept of "colonial genocide") that the official definition—specifying certain destructive processes but omitting others, and requiring overly rigid standards of proof—is insufficient to the requirements of the dispossession experience that, in the long range, has been at least as potentially devastating upon its target populations as the concentrated shock of the Holocaust itself. The *tournant dangereux* here are numerous and include definitional authority, the dangers of definitional dilution, the determination of intentional and unintended consequences, and the difficulty of discriminating between colonial procedures and specifically genocidal ones.[5]

Scholars have approached this problem in a number of ways. Ward Churchill, for instance, has adopted a combative stance, advocating the Americas rather than Europe as the site of preeminent, unparalleled tragedy—i.e., of a "mega-genocide" attacking "hundreds of discrete cultures" for generation after generation rather than an intense, time-concentrated assault upon a "handful of cultures." In doing so, he makes a uniqueness claim of his own: "The American holocaust was and remains unparalleled, both in terms of its magnitude and the degree to which its goals were met, and in terms of the extent to which its ferocity was sustained over time by not one but several participating groups."[6] This type of approach is unlikely to advance the discussion, for comparative measuring is fraught.

By contrast, A. Dirk Moses has called for an end to competitive, hierarchical ways of viewing mass-lethal processes, whenever or wherever they occur, and advocates instead the study of linkages between potentially genocidal phenomena that remains sensitive to their historically distinctive features. Most pertinently, he emphasizes the connection between the consequences of Western imperial expansionism and the precisely targeted campaign of Nazi terror. Invoking Hannah Arendt's thesis in her *Origins of Totalitarianism*, he views the two as coupled in "a single modernizing process of accelerated violence related to nation-building that commenced in the European colonial periphery and culminated in the Holocaust."[7]

Yet even this broadly encompassing approach does not entirely escape the problems of hierarchy and primacy. For although Moses is sensitive to expanding Western technological capacities for human carnage, he still views the Holocaust as the "culmination" of an "upwardly spiralling violence" swelling across time from "periphery" to center. Imperial actions heralding and overspreading the non-European world during "the racial century" of 1850 to 1950 are considered "largely haphazard" in their noxious effect, whereas Nazi policies are executed with lethal deliberation and near "flawless" perfection. Western colonialism still appears thereby as precursive and arbitrary, with Holocaust processes as ultimate in a mushrooming enlargement of potentially genocidal acts.[8]

Logically, the accuracy of this view ultimately rests upon one's chosen vantage point. The colonial world is only marginal from a European perspective, and imperialism's violence is arguably only "upwardly spiralling" towards the Holocaust if it is simply measured in terms of volume proportional to timeframe. For the targets of Western expansionism, however, their assailed territory becomes the pivotal locale of suffering; indeed, their lengthy ordeal under the exactions of colonialism tends to produce, either proportionally or in real numerical terms, a vaster demographic collapse over time than the dramatic Nazi onslaught. As historian Bill Thorpe indicates, for instance, crude estimates of Australian Aborigines' decline under colonialism, directly consequent upon processes of population intrusion and land dispossession, reach mortality levels above ninety percent in certain regions.[9]

What is more, the Nazis were rapidly arrested in their horrific campaign, many punished, and their deeds widely and graphically publicized by their conquerors. By contrast, the imperial deeds of expansionist Western nations that defeated Hitler's Germany have not been similarly dealt with, and according to some highly plausible analyses, never have been so halted nor brought fully to account for any ongoing global devastations they inflicted. In fact, neocolonialism is making a comeback today in the form of authors who advocate an explicitly imperial mission for the United States in world affairs, an approach that entails rehabilitating the reputation of recent, past world empires, above all, the British one.[10] A trajectory of progressively mounting horrors from distant frontiers to Central European death camps only tends to make interpretive sense if the growths of technological sophistication and Western bureaucracy are to be the principal foci of analysis. But should they be if our object of inquiry is colonialism and imperialism outside Europe?

Over and over again in genocide research, all roads tend to lead back to the 1948 UN formulation and its template, the German occupation of Europe and war of extermination. Although, as Raphael Lemkin's own work makes clear, other atrocities, like the pogroms he witnessed, the texts he read of cruelties of antiquity, and the contemporary impact of the Armenian genocide by the Young Turks, were all powerful motivations in the evolution of his thinking about "barbarity" and "vandalism," in the end it was the Nazis' genocidal occupation of Europe itself and its intimate, searing assault upon his own extended family and other Jews that molded his formulation of the new term *genocide*.[11] In subsequent, unpublished writings, Lemkin went on to draw out further connectives between Nazi ethnic cleansing and expansionism, and earlier imperialistic actions of a destructive nature in the Americas, Africa, Ireland, and Australia (specifically Tasmania).[12] Arguably, the seeds of a theory of historical interconnectivity between global colonialism and the European Holocaust were being tentatively sown here, as John Docker's chapter in this book demonstrates. But rather than from Lemkin's ecumenical thinking, it was from the passage of the term "genocide" through the mills of the United Nations bureaucracy—where it was debated and refashioned by various committees into a final draft that was, in turn, hammered in the General Assembly into internationally consensual *and* compromised shape—that a specific, itemized definition emerged. Few words have ever received such portentous consideration, and in the long passage from conception to birth it was invested with a tremendous gravitas and jurisdictional power, which tends to solidify it prodigiously in terms of its ultimate meaning and use.[13]

It was no longer merely Lemkin's word, evolving from an expanding historical consciousness. It was now a global indictment—a definition that specified "the single international and local standard against which charges of genocide must be measured." And such charges in turn denoted "the most odious international crime." It remains thus the only explanation of the term upon which prosecutions can proceed.[14] Yet as subsequent scrutiny has demonstrated amply, it was also a severely flawed definition—a product of the compromises of incipient Cold War realpolitik, couched within the arraignment of a disgraced and defeated power by its conquerors, themselves imperialist powers.

Thus it specifies genocide's victims as "national, ethnical, racial or religious," but not as political or social. It itemizes features of destructive biological and mental assault, but not environmental or cultural ones, despite Lemkin's favoring of "cultural genocide." It establishes as criminal the forcible transfer of children away from a victim group, but does not incorporate the severing and mass removal of peoples of any other age from their territories or kin. Although it refers to inflicting "serious bodily . . . harm" with a massively destructive intent, in its largely patriarchal gloss it says nothing about the systematic sexual abuse of subject populations. Until the recent international criminal tribunals on Rwanda and Yugoslavia, systemic rape, for instance, had remained unconsidered.[15] Whereas an "intention to destroy" receives primacy motivationally, the enabling ideologies that underpin, promote, and excuse destruction are never profiled. And although the definition is adamant upon the matter of precise perpetrator agency, it offers nothing helpful about the potential agency of the target groups in combating and resisting genocide. For instance, do retributive acts of physical opposition to perpetrator violence in any way nullify a genocide charge being laid? Must the thrust of genocidal action, in short, always occur within the context of "one-sided" infliction?[16]

Scholarly attempts to expand or clarify the master definition, or to qualify its difficult demand for ultimate proof of intentionality are all logically checked by its "definitive jural meaning."[17] No matter how often individual private scholars take another crack at it with their own unauthorized formulations, "genocide" remains precisely as it was enunciated by the United Nations—an inviolable legal precept rather than simply a useful, heuristic research tool. Documented proof of exterminatory intent is demanded within a construct of bringing culprit individuals or groups to task before a national or international penal tribunal.

Scholars in this field need to remain vigilant of the perilous slippage between undertaking delicate research into contingent historical "truths" and mounting binding legal cases for the prosecution. Historians researching other projects are rarely required to produce such hard evidence of intention, which in effect must amount to finding overt, self-incriminating admissions of guilt upon preserved documentation, in order to construct plausible interpretations of past events. Rather they are meant to be skilled at the reproduction of time-faded scenarios and a subtle, empathetic appreciation of causation, motivation, and relational outcomes. They are not trained detectives or forensic experts nosing out corpses, clues, suspects, or "smoking guns." They are neither prosecuting attorneys preparing clinching legal indictments, nor jurists or judges convicting or passing sentence on apprehended criminal parties. The search for evidence of "aforethought to commit a crime," especially when enunciated as official policy preserved somehow for posterity's judgment, is by and large self-defeating. As far as colonial history is concerned, it also seems largely futile to be out there still looking for "smoking guns" when these guns usually ceased smoking long ago and massacre scenes were rarely treated contemporaneously as crime scenes for the collection of incriminating evidence. In general, too, all the intellectual perils of constructing "advocacy histories" are well known.

The essential question, to put it bluntly, ought to be: "Are you catching a crook or writing a book?"

The usual substitute phrase, "colonial genocide," does not in turn offer an acceptable solution either—for, like a Trojan horse, its unreconstructed terminology keeps conveying the essential definitional dilemmas of 1948 right back into the analysis. "Colonial genocide," in short, merely carries the difficulties of a rigidly defined concept into new historical settings. Although Alison Palmer asserts that "it is essential to use a more comprehensive definition of genocide . . . pinpointing its basic and most crucial elements," she remains preoccupied with establishing (albeit only imperfectly) solid evidence of clear perpetrator intent: evidence that was, in any case, never systematically gathered or preserved at the time the violence occurred.[18] The historian, Henry Reynolds, in his book on genocide in Australia also appears caught in the bind of establishing "colonial genocide" as "pre-eminently a crime of state" (even though private initiatives are also officially specified in the UN formulation); for how otherwise, he writes, would it be possible to judge the "percentage of a population's involvement . . . required before the society itself can be considered to be genocidal?"[19] One envisages here the absurdist scenario of compiling admissions en masse of individual intentions in order to lodge a composite arraignment of societally led assaults. Clearly a Gordian knot requires cutting.

Other commentators, such as Raimond Gaita and Robert Manne, have called for new terminology[20] and, more recently, Martin Krygier and Robert Van Krieken have concluded: "Even if we agree that for the most effective use of the concept of genocide, we should exclude its application to . . . [colonialism] this does not dispose of the issue. . . . It simply generates a need to find some other word or idea."[21]

Colonialism, Destruction, and Responsibility

Although extermination of indigenous people in colonialism was not always actively pursued, invariably it was agreeably countenanced and openly anticipated. "Annihilation," "extinction," and "extermination" predictions are rife in colonial literature.[22] "Incitement" and "complicity" to encourage it were habitual in the colonial press, among private individuals, and in certain political and administrative sanctums. In the absence of incriminating documentation, intention also might be inferred readily in the act of pressing ahead regardless with unwelcome occupations, even though the odious outcomes may be easily foreseeable in advance, observable in process, and regrettably admitted to in retrospect—then later, simply repeated in new settings. "Earth-hunger" or "greed of country" here preempts all other considerations as though colonialism was an inevitable, unstoppable force.[23]

For instance, in the colonization of Queensland, Australia, what was likely to occur was already clear from what had eventuated in earlier acts of dispossession; and, while the fatal processes were in train, they were anticipated, encouraged, reported upon, and exposed *ad finitum*, despite transparent official disclaimers. Between 1850, when a British private served a short sentence for firing into a peaceful Aboriginal encampment in Brisbane, and 1883 when a white male in Townsville was imprisoned for raping an Aboriginal child, the law was effectively "a dead letter" in successfully prosecuting *any* European aggressions against Aborigines in the colony. And this was precisely the key period of land grabbing and intense frontier conflict in which many hundreds of incomers and many thousands of Aborigines violently perished. Indeed, no European was punished in this colony for actually killing an Aborigine until 1888—around the same time as Aboriginal testimony became admissible in colonial courts.[24] Throughout the expansionist phase, colonial politicians and other official functionaries (who were often the direct material recipients of the acquired land) lied and dissembled about the carnage, while British imperial authorities virtually washed their hands of it. Yet in 1901, with the land all virtually secured, the *Official Queensland Year Book* reported cheerfully: "First and foremost, let the public be once and for all assured the regime of the Native Police is now a thing of the past . . . with the result that since then [i.e., 1897] not a single 'dispersal'—i.e., by bullet, has taken place."[25] Even this claim was misleading, as Native Mounted Police patrols continued in northern regions into the early years of the First World War. But just four years prior to the *Official Year Book*'s frank admission, the home secretary, Horace Tozer, still had been insisting that claims of "wholesale murderous slaughter on the part of the Native Police" were merely the "conjured up visions" of "highly imaginative persons."[26]

Instead of pursuing largely futile researches after the will-o'-the-wisp of historically camouflaged intentions, it might be more helpful to examine and debate degrees of responsibility: responsibility for the deleterious impact of land annexation and transformation; responsibility for a priori expectation of mass deaths, while pushing ahead regardless[27]; responsibility for the release of decimating pathogens; responsibility for the technological range of eradication employed; responsibility for forced removals and enervative institutional concentrations; responsibility for the promulgation of ideas that promote, excuse, and camouflage the devastation; responsibility for the political withholding of sheltering rights and the professional denial of legal protection and/or medical prophylaxis. Western settler colonialism was both advantageous and malign, but it was neither an immutable nor an inexorable force. Rather it was one adopted and pursued by choice, premeditation, and acquisitive will. The lure of territory always took precedence over the problems of assailed people. To advance thus with clear cognizance of massively baleful effects was equivalent to proceeding with a sense of "malice aforethought," despite the many rationalizations that colonizers offered to explain away their usurpative actions.

The twin despoilers of disease and violence both provide analytical difficulties. Instead of conceptualizing these simply as "either/ors"—the one "unavoidable" and the other purposive—it might be more realistic to identify their connections: for instance, how mass violence, terror, and trauma provide context for the spread and reception of epidemic illness; and how the confiscation of land and livelihood undermines physical, emotional, and spiritual well-being, actively advancing disease by disrupting food supplies and a stable socio-cultural environment.[28] Debilitative "survival" conditions following upon land deprival and the imposition of patterns of "racial feeding" are directly contributive.[29] Furthermore, it is feasible that the spread of infection sometimes might be either a calculated or a blithely cavalier infliction; and that denying otherwise available medical interventions may be an act of violence comparable in its effect to the spray of bullets. The racial history of health and disease in Australia has scarcely begun to be written.[30]

Secondly, the pattern of violence attached to a colonial struggle for territory and resources is a two-sided one. Dispossession encourages indigenous resistance to a degree that Western participants habitually regard the contest as a kind of warfare, and Aborigines often find themselves fighting in ways not previously countenanced. Although the conflict is increasingly disproportional, invaders as well as defenders continually fall victim. Does a manner of warfare thereby cancel any charge of attempted extermination? Whereas genocide may be effected "in time of war," it is not usually considered "an act *of* war." On the contrary, it has been normally restricted to "purposive actions that fall outside the recognized conventions of legitimate warfare."[31] But what if the war is not "legitimate," but rather undeclared and unstructured, without agreed rules of engagement or settlement treaties and indemnities? What if its conduct falls outside the orbit of fair play (as defined by the Geneva accords) and is pursued with an arbitrariness and an escalating intensity of reprisal, often propelling it inexorably towards extremes? Sorties can and do segue into massacres, and battle fields become killing fields. The entire process becomes widely recognized as it unfolds as a "war of extermination."[32] Does this mean that this kind of colonial warfare can be considered sequentially coeval with genocidal outcomes?

Indigenocide

It was in this cautionary vein that, in 2001, Bill Thorpe and I decided to "do a Lemkin" ourselves and coin a new term *indigenocide*. We adopted this new term not because we sought a softer word to assuage easily bruised white Australian sensibilities, but because we wanted to formulate a more incorporative, exacting, and penetrative one.[33] It is an attempt to incorporate the cataclysmic impact of settler colonialism upon host cultures, particularly the lethal effects of imperial migration, intrusion, and land seizure upon the lives and fates of indigenes like the Australian Aboriginal peoples. The formal genocide definition was both providing too little and demanding too much. Although settler colonialism and indigenocide are hardly identical concepts, their affinity is substantial as the logic of the one feeds inexorably into the trauma of the other. We defined indigenocide in the following way:

> First . . . indigenocide usually occurs when an invading group *intentionally* invades and colonizes another group or groups who are the "first peoples" of that region, or who have proof of such origins. . . . Secondly, the invaders must conquer the Indigenes and maintain their advantages over them as long as is necessary or possible. Thirdly, as conquerors, the invaders must kill sufficient numbers of Indigenes, or render their ways of sustaining meaningful life so difficult that they come close to extinction and may disappear altogether. . . . Fourthly, and this reinforces the actively *genocidal* aspects, the invaders must classify the Indigenes as "the lowest form of humanity," rather like Eichmann classified Jews as a "garbage nation," who deserve to be exterminated. Fifthly, indigenocide, notably with Native Americans and Aboriginal Australians, involves destroying, or attempting to destroy, Indigenous religious systems and imposing binaries between the material and spiritual realms. Above all, indigenocide implies in theory and practice that Indigenous people are *less valued* than the land they inhabit and which the invaders desire.[34]

The essential precondition of indigenocide, then, lies not so much in any detected expression of murderous intent, either by private individuals or the state. Rather it inheres in the very process of forcibly usurping occupied territory and perpetuating that takeover by conquering, holding, and repopulating it in blatant disregard of the consequences upon its dispossessed occupiers, *whatever those consequences may be.* The term communicates an interdependent, three-way onslaught upon lives, land, and culture. Although it has been inferred that biological assault upon human bodies should always be prioritized as more dangerous than either environmental or cultural erasure, it should be realized that this is an entirely Western reading of precedence. Collapsing the biological, the environmental, and the cultural into one equally damaging offensive is only an occlusion in many Western eyes. From an indigenous (and, to a degree, Lemkin's own) perspective, however, life, land, and spirit/culture are integrative and codependent vectors. No one of these essentials makes proper functional or metaphysical sense or thrives independently of the others. Here we are prioritizing the ecological body, vitally attached to its natural milieu, rather than the atomistic Newtonian/Cartesian body that is ostensibly alienated from it.[35] Thus it may be suggested that indigenocide—which literally conveys a sense of an encompassing lethal or malignant attack upon those "born to that place"—operates to combine elements of the officially defined genocidal impulse (i.e., of peoplehood destruction) with those of ecocide and ethnocide (i.e., environmental and cultural destruction).

The Australian white settlement story combines acute aspects of all three of these tendencies. Ecocide in Australia for instance reflects a settler initiative more environmentally detrimental than in other comparable global actions, and a higher concentrated destruction of flora and fauna than elsewhere: i.e., some 126 plant and animal species eliminated in 200 years, half the forests destroyed as well as presently among the highest salinity levels, and the highest per capita rates of land clearance and of greenhouse gas emission in the world. Overall, Australia, which represents one of the richest regions of megadiversity, has also experienced probably the most severe ecological assault from imperial expansionism.[36] Add to this the totalizing effect of Western land acquisition—a historically unique example of territorial seizure without due historical consideration (until very recently) of *any* prior indigenous rights—and the baleful effects of ecocide and "earth hunger" upon human decline become apparent. Traducing and transforming ecosystems, sundering territories from people, and peoples from territory in an excruciating dual display of "geographical violence" (to paraphrase Edward Said) reveals a crucial aspect of settler colonialism's destructive project.[37]

In fact, Lemkin himself in 1944 delineated the mise en scène for genocide as first the "destruction of the national pattern of the oppressed group" and then the "imposition of the pattern of the oppressor" either upon people left territorially fixed or upon territory cleared of its inhabitants to allow for "colonization of the area by the oppressor's own nationals," in order "to destroy or cripple the subjugated people in their development."[38] This appears very close to definitions of settler colonialism, such as that provided by anthropologist, Richard Horvath, envisaging it as:

1. Domination over territories and behaviors of other groups by the migration of permanent settlers.
2. Exploitation of the dominated territory's natural and/or human resources for extraction and profit.
3. An enforced culture-change process involving destruction of indigenous life-ways.[39]

In his unpublished research, Lemkin too was moving decidedly in this direction, as his focus on the Herero genocide in German Southwest Africa, the colonial destruction of Tasmanian peoples, the English colonization of Ireland, and dispossession in the Americas (particularly the British Army's use of the smallpox virus upon American Indians) makes plain.[40] Given the perversion of Lemkin's thinking in the UN convention definition, indigenocide may well accord more faithfully with his actual intentions.

It is undoubtedly unduly partisan to view colonialism's effects upon host populations as entirely invidious. Yet it is nevertheless substantially so. As race relations sociologist, E. Ellis Cashmore, notes of the colonized: "For all the benefits they might have received in terms of new crops, technologies, medicine, commerce and education, they inevitably suffered: human loss in the process of conquest was inestimable; self-sufficient economies were obliterated and new relationships of dependence were introduced; ancient traditions, customs, political systems and religions were destroyed."[41] Such obliterations—human, social, and cultural—were not simply unintended byproducts of an otherwise distracted system of territorial acquisition. Rather, to use Moses' words, they were "inherent in the structure and logic of the colonial project." Moses, however, goes on to insist that "genocide is not an inevitable process of European penetration," and that discrimination, slaveholding, and apartheid were not necessarily "exterminatory."[42] Yet even these manifestations could still be described as lethally destructive "in whole or in part" by the escalation of either rapid or slow death/killing through the imposition of harsh oppressions and physically enervative "conditions of life" upon the colonized.

A similar gloss may be cast over the impact of cultural genocide or ethnocide. Officially excluded from the United Nations definition, this form of genocide was initially incorporated in Lemkin's original formulation. Australian Aboriginal cultures were regarded by Westerners as the sine qua non of savagery and/or barbarity—and virtually seen for considerable periods as "non-cultures." They were thereby crushed, remolded, and assimilated with unabashed disdain as dominant colonial discourses became "human-blind" towards Aboriginal peoples. Scientific racist analysis classified them as a subhuman linkage to other mammal species, and Australian folk racism was thereby suffused with imagery melding Aboriginality with animality.[43] "Suprahuman edicts" against subhuman targets legitimated aggression and provided distinctive alibis for abiding atrocity.[44] What is thereby referenced here is what Frantz Fanon in 1967 termed "the death and burial of . . . local cultural originality" in a discussion further preferencing the cultural/spiritualized body over the atomized/civilized one.[45] The pseudointellectual "debate" in Australia in the first years of the twenty-first century about levels of frontier violence and the degree of overt, extralegal killing provides little explanation for a catastrophic demographic plunge among host populations of an order of 90 to 95 percent over large territories.[46] In order to encompass such a mammoth tragedy, indigenocide clearly needs to confront substantially more than massacres.

Conclusion

Indigenocide therefore addresses situations of intentional invasion, seemingly unconcerned with the dire consequences of its own exorable progress. The subsequent pattern of conquest over territories, cultures, and usually resistant peoples is buoyed and excused by a profound sense of cultural entitlement and land hunger. Such entitlement blatantly declassifies former occupiers as beings of fully human worth and thereby opens them to all manner of harmful abuse, with little or no legal redress and a minimal sense of moral outrage from the perpetrator group over the tragedy of this singular, ongoing destruction. In settler colonies, the colonial "end," in short, always predetermined the decimating "means." Such demolition, in turn, is a thoroughgoing one, targeting land, lives, livelihoods, and lifeways in a composite, integrated onslaught upon and usurpation of an ecosphere and its cohabitants. In its very persistence and comprehensiveness, it represents an unprecedented eliminative act, not encompassed by such narrower formulations as "genocide" or even "colonial genocide."

Acknowledgement

My gratitude to Ann Curthoys, John Docker, A. Dirk Moses, Jahara Rhiannon, Bill Thorpe, and Joanne Watson for their help and encouragement in writing this piece.

Notes

1. Larry Long and Pete Seeger, "Well May the World Go," in *The Songs of Pete Seeger*, vol. 2, track 16 (Appleseed Recordings APR CD 1055, 2001).
2. Iris Murdoch, *The Time of the Angels* (London, 1966), 163.
3. Nicholaus Bourbaki, *Éléments de Mathematique* (Paris, 1940); Rachel Hartman and Jim Ottooiani, "Bourbaki for Beginners" in *SPX2000* (Bethesda, MD, 2002), unpaginated. See also www.gt-labs.com/bourbaki/.
4. See the analysis in Dan Stone, *Constructing the Holocaust* (London, 2003).

5. Alison Palmer, *Colonial Genocide* (Adelaide, 2000), 34–36.
6. Ward Churchill, *A Little Matter of Genocide: Holocaust and Denial in the Americas 1492 to the Present* (San Francisco, 1997), 4, passim.
7. A. Dirk Moses, "Conceptual Blockages and Definitional Dilemmas in the 'Racial Century': Genocides of Indigenous People and the Holocaust," *Patterns of Prejudice* 36, no. 4 (2002): 7–36. See also Moses, "Genocide and Settler Society in Australian History," in *Genocide and Settler Society: Frontier Violence and Stolen Indigenous Children in Australian History*, ed. A. Dirk Moses (New York and Oxford, 2004), 3–48.
8. Moses, "Conceptual Blockages."
9. Claire Williams and Bill Thorpe with Carolyn Chapman, *Aboriginal Workers and Managers. History, Emotional and Community Labour and Occupational Health and Safety in South Australia* (Adelaide, 2003), 6–8. See also Gary Foley, "Australia and the Holocaust: A Koori Perspective," The Koori History Website, Essay 8, http://www.kooriweb.org/foley/essays/essay_8.html, 4–5. Foley points out that around 57 percent of the total prewar Jewish population of Europe perished in the Holocaust, but that percentages reached as high as 88 percent in occupied regions like Poland, which was analogous to earlier colonized territories. See especially, David Furber, "Near as Far in the Colonies: The Nazi Occupation of Poland," *The International History Review* 26, no. 3 (2004): 541–79.
10. Niall Ferguson, *Empire: The Rise and Demise of the British World Order and the Lessons for Global Power* (London, 2003); idem, *Colossus: The Price of America's Empire* (New York, 2004).
11. Raphael Lemkin, *Axis Rule in Occupied Europe* (Washington, DC, 1944); idem, "Genocide as a Crime under International Law," *American Journal of International Law* 41, no. 1 (1947): 147.
12. See the Lemkin Papers, American Jewish Historical Society, New York, P–154, especially Box 8, Folders 5, 11, 12; Raphael Lemkin, "War against Genocide," *The Christian Science Monitor*, 31 January 1948, 2; Jacob Radner Center of the American Jewish Archives, Cincinnati, OH, Collection 60, Box 6, Folders 6/6, 6/9, 6/12, 7/1, 7/11. I am indebted to A. Dirk Moses for making these sources available to me.
13. Roman S. Stocky, "The Genocide Convention," *The Ukrainian Quarterly* 2 (1949): 144–63; Matthew Lippman, "A Road Map to the 1948 Convention on the Prevention and Punishment of the Crime Genocide," *Journal of Genocide Research* 4, no. 2 (2002): 177–95; Lawrence J. LeBlanc, *The United States and the Genocide Convention* (Durham, NC, 1991).
14. Palmer, *Colonial Genocide*, 29; Henry Reynolds, *An Indelible Stain? The Question of Genocide in Australia's History* (Melbourne, 2001), 18.
15. Sherrie L. Russell-Brown, "Rape as an Act of Genocide," *Berkeley Journal of International Law* 21 (2003): 350–74.
16. Frank Chalk and Kurt Jonassohn, eds., *The History and Sociology of Genocide* (New Haven, CT, 1990), 23.
17. Reynolds, *An Indelible Stain?*, 25
18. Palmer, *Colonial Genocide*, 30.
19. Reynolds, *An Indelible Stain?*, 96, 119.
20. Raimond Gaita, *A Common Humanity: Thinking About Love and Truth and Justice* (Melbourne, 1999); Robert Manne, "In Denial: The Stolen Generation and the Right," *Australian Quarterly* 1 (2001): 1–13.
21. Martin Krygier and Robert van Krieken, "The Character of the Nation," in *Whitewash: On Keith Windschuttle's Fabrication of Aboriginal History*, ed. Robert Manne (Melbourne, 2003), 97.

22. Patrick Brantlinger, *Dark Vanishings: Discourse on the Extinction of Primitive Races, 1800–1930* (Ithaca, NY, 2003).
23. Ibid.; Peter Gay, *The Cultivation of Hatred. The Bourgeois Experience, Victoria to Freud*, 3 vols. (New York, 1993), 3: 59.
24. Raymond Evans, "'Plenty Shoot 'Em': The Destruction of Aboriginal Societies along the Queensland Frontier," in Moses, *Genocide and Settler Society*, 167–68; idem, "Racial Assaults," in *Radical Brisbane. An Unruly History*, ed. Raymond Evans and Carole Ferrier (Melbourne, 2004), 33–40; Palmer, *Colonial Genocide*, 64.
25. W.E. Roth, "Aboriginal Natives: Their State and Treatment," in *Official Queensland Year Book* (Brisbane, 1901), 412.
26. Raymond Evans, Kay Saunders, and Kathryn Cronin, *Race Relations in Colonial Queensland. A History of Exclusion, Exploitation and Extermination* (Brisbane, 1993), 133.
27. Moses, "Conceptual Blockages," 29–31; Ann Curthoys' chapter in this volume.
28. Raymond Evans, *Fighting Words: Writing About Race* (Brisbane, 1999), 28; Pamela Lukin Watson, "Passed Away? The Fate of the *Kurawali*," in Moses, *Genocide and Settler Society*, 174–93.
29. Evans, Saunders, and Cronin, *Race Relations*, 85–101; Jan Kociumbas, "Genocide and Modernity in Colonial Australia, 1788–1850," in Moses, *Genocide and Setter Society*, 79–82.
30. Judy Campbell, *Invisible Invaders: Smallpox and Other Diseases in Australian History, 1780–1880* (Melbourne, 2002); E. Hunter, " ' . . . the Deep Sleep of Forgetfulness': Reflecting on Disremembering," Presentation to the Third World Conference for the International Society for Traumatic Stress Studies (Melbourne, 2000), 1–20
31. Reynolds, *An Indelible Stain?*, 15, 25; Martin Shaw, *War and Genocide: Organized Killing in Modern Society* (Malden, MA, 2003).
32. Evans, *Fighting Words*, 23–24; Evans, Saunders, and Cronin, *Race Relations*, 77–80; Raymond Evans, "Across the Queensland Frontier," in *Frontier Conflict: The Australian Experience*, ed. Bain Attwood and S.G. Foster (Canberra, 2003), 66–67.
33. Raymond Evans and Bill Thorpe, "Indigenocide and the Massacre of Aboriginal History," *Overland* 163 (2001): 21–40.
34. Ibid., 37.
35. Jinki Trevillian, "Talking with the Old People. Histories of Cape York Peninsula, 1930s to 1950s" (Ph.D. diss., Australian National University, 2003), 241.
36. William J. Lines, *Taming the Great South Land. A History of the Conquest of Nature in Australia* (Sydney, 1991); Geoffrey Bolton, *Spoils and Spoilers. Australians Make Their Environment, 1788–1980* (Sydney, 1981); Bill Thorpe, *Colonial Queensland. Perspectives on a Frontier Society* (Brisbane, 1996), 76–132; Vincent Serventy, *A Continent in Danger* (London, 1966); A. J. Marshall, ed., *The Great Extermination: A Guide to Anglo-Australian Cupidity, Wickedness and Waste* (London, 1966); "Our Hall of Shame," *Courier Mail* [Brisbane], 1 April 1995, 1–2.
37. Edward W. Said, *Culture and Imperialism* (London, 1993), 1–15.
38. Lemkin, *Axis Rule*, xi, 79.
39. Richard Horvath, "A Definition of Colonialism," *Current Anthropology* 13, no. 1 (1972): 46.
40. See especially Lemkin's research cards, American Jewish Historical Society, New York, P–154, Box 8, Folder 12; Raphael Lemkin, "The Hereros," Jacob Rader Center of the American Jewish Archives, Collection 60, Box 6, Folder 6/12. My thanks to A. Dirk Moses for these references.
41. E. Ellis Cashmore, *Dictionary of Race and Ethnic Relations* (London, 1988), 59.

42. Moses, "Conceptual Blockages," 26–27.
43. Evans, *Fighting Words*, 41–43; Evans, Saunders, and Cronin, *Race Relations*, 74–79; Henry Reynolds, *Frontier: Aborigines, Settlers and Land* (Sydney, 1987), 111–13, 117–18. As early as 1793, Spanish visitors to Port Jackson described Aborigines as appearing "to occupy the last grade of man before passing on to the ape family"; Michael Duffy, *Men of Honour: John Macarthur—Duellist, Rebel, Founding Father* (Sydney, 2003), 103.
44. Evans, "Across the Queensland Frontier," 70; Jonathan Glover, *Humanity: A Moral History of the Twentieth Century* (London, 2001), 337–39; Gay, *Cultivation of Hatred*, 40–48.
45. Frantz Fanon, *The Wretched of the Earth* (Harmondsworth, UK, 1967), 83–85.
46. Stuart Macintyre and Anna Clark, *The History Wars* (Melbourne, 2003), 142–70. Some recent studies showing the massive death rate include Williams and Thorpe, *Aboriginal Workers and Managers*, 6–8, 20; Patrick Collins, *Goodbye Bussamarai: The Mandandanji Land War, Southern Queensland, 1842–1852* (Brisbane, 2003); Tony Roberts, *Frontier Justice: A History of the Gulf Country to 1900* (Brisbane, 2005); Deborah Bird Rose, *Hidden Histories: Black Stories from Victoria River Downs, Herbert River and Wave Hill Stations* (Canberra, 1991).

– *Chapter 6* –

Colonialism and Genocides

Notes for the Analysis of a Settler Archive

Lorenzo Veracini

The Settler Archive of the European Imagination

In this chapter I propose to consider a Western settler consciousness as a discursive and ideological practice utilizing a "settler archive" that was constituted through numerous passages of political, religious, and colonial histories during the last five centuries. Whereas the archeology of a number of other types of colonial imagination has been approached authoritatively already, the settler consciousness of the European gaze has yet to find its Edward Said. This archive—constantly tested, updated, added to, in progress, and continuously transforming through time—was (and is) readily available to be mobilized in different contexts and for different objectives.[1] I propose to understand a settler mentality and its ultimately ethnocidal racism not as a full-fledged ideology—neither as a coherent conceptual system, nor as a discourse—but as a practice in which one can enter, slide, pause, and from which one can also depart in different moments. Individuals, groups, cultural and political movements, and obviously states have adopted this practice throughout history for purposes, in contexts, and with consequences extremely diverse.

Still today, remaining settlers aside and despite momentous intellectual shifts, decolonization, and the emergence of postcolonial perspectives, this archive and practice can be adopted effectively in some public domains. Recent examples of this include US Christian fundamentalist groups and their unswerving support for Israeli policies in the Occupied Territories, and the British and Australian exceptional and disproportionate interest in Zimbabwean affairs. The need to force an ethnocentric assimilation upon the indigenous peoples of settler nations or the non-European migrants to former colonial metropolises can also be mentioned in this context.[2] One could suggest that even the ambiguities the postapartheid South African administration is expressing when dealing with the AIDS epidemics may be related to the legacy of a settler routine. In its otherwise difficult to interpret reluctance to accept a medicalizing gaze over the communities that bore the brunt of the apartheid regime, the South African government may *also* be expressing an unwillingness to allow the official return of an apartheid-related typology of social intervention: a mindset that pathologizes, segregates, racializes, and invariably constructs black and poor as one category "at risk"—a type to be surveyed, sedated, and dealt with in a pharmaceutical way.[3]

The settler archive that this ideological and discursive practice mobilizes is a repertoire of images, notions, concepts, narratives, stereotypes, and thoughts (i.e., "the empty/unused lands," the "dying races," the "Manifest Destinies," etc.) that was accumulated and precipitated together in the European imagination at least since the Protestant Reformation and since the Irish Plantation of the sixteenth century.[4] While Calvinism has played a fundamental role in the early settler experiences of the European expansion in Ulster, New England, and especially in South Africa (a long-lasting workshop of the settler archive), a Calvinist sensibility has traditionally focused on self-supporting, borders-drawing, ethnically, and religiously cohesive communities.[5]

These conceptualizations have sedimented through various forms of popular and scientific racism, and around a specific interpretative tradition of the biblical book of Exodus—where a divinely elected people takes over a promised land and disperses the original Canaanite inhabitants.[6] The settler archive of the European imagination has benefited from the most diverse and exotic colonial experiences: a specific library of the colonial imagination (Said, for example, refers to a comprehensive cultural system of "structures of attitude and reference") was formed thanks to a collection of authors, works and texts (anonymous, collective, individual, literary, medical, political, philosophical, scientific—among them one could name a specific reading of Darwin, Renan, Kipling, Gobineau, and, alternatively, Conrad's denunciation) and through a number of events, only sometimes associated with the history of European colonialism proper.[7] The Protestant Reformation, the subsequent wars of religion, the displacements of communities around Europe; the French Revolution and especially its Haitian reverberations; the new emergence of anti-Semitic tendencies and milieus; and the growing appeal of genocidal impulses (Bacon noted that every "plantation" demands an "extirpation") have all added to this archive in different passages, and became in time constituent parts of its practice.[8]

Yet although they in many ways overlap and utilize similar ideological constructs, it should be noted that a settler practice constitutes an autonomous routine vis-à-vis other colonial archives and typologies. In fact, settler and other colonial projects often operate in contradiction with each other: one ultimately envisaging, even in its more humanitarian versions, the disappearing (cultural and/or biological) of the indigenous "other"; the others reproducing a gaze that permanently reestablishes/reinforces a colonial hierarchy.[9] These archives constantly borrow from and blur into each other, sharing borderlands that characterize their operational registers; yet they remain quite separate, their contradictions often resurfacing in the history of colonial enterprises and their governance—at least since Bartolomé de Las Casas famous indictment.[10] (It should be also noted that, contrary to other colonial experiences, a settler mentality has hardly ever allowed for the formation of hybrid identities, and that, in the case of settler societies, the surveillance of colonial boundaries has been especially attended to and periodically reinforced).[11]

While dialogically operating as a counterpoint to each other and constantly communicating, the dialectics between a settler consciousness and other typologies of colonial projects have produced outcomes as diverse as Fiji's neotraditional and colonially sponsored state indigenism, or, at the other end of the spectrum, Australia's recurring reaffirmations of *terra nullius* doctrines despite London's possible original recognition of indigenous land rights.[12] In practice, however, the settler imagination was continuously capable of mustering a hegemonic reading of local developments and of informing metropolitan and colonial public opinions as well as government perceptions. Only occasionally have settler interests been limited or qualified by other colonial projectualities. One exception to this pattern is the Boer War, when an antisettler rhetoric was mobilized in order to rally the public opinion behind the imperial effort. However, even this display was remarkably short lived and a prosettler current of opinion never disappeared from the British public domain.[13]

There is also a left-wing typology of a settler mindset, constructed, for example, around a Soviet rhetoric of pioneering efforts and its derivative versions, or around the regenerative and redemptive capacity of kibbutzim life, a mythology so remarkably effective that even after its substantial demise it continues to inform public perceptions of Israel.[14] Yet this tradition is much older. Earlier versions of this tendency included Italy's representations as *la grande proletaria* during the 1911 war against Turkey for the control of Libya, which was expected to become a colony of settlement, and a substantial Saint-Simonian tradition, capable of considerably influencing French colonial experiences during the nineteenth and early twentieth centuries.[15] Only at a later stage did the debate on the "colonial question" in the socialist parties of Europe before WWI move from original denunciation to embrace. This happened both in England, where the Fabians were essential in the successful attempt to sanitize colonial domination for the political left, and in Germany, where Social Democratic leader Eduard Bernstein ended up stressing that "the right of savages to the soil they occupy" is not an "unconditional right."[16] Coherently with this trend, one pre-WWI international socialist congress even moved a motion asserting the "the right of the inhabitants of civilized countries to settle in lands where the population is at a lower stage of development."[17]

More specifically, one should consider the emergence of colonial projects especially geared for the creation of a number of "New Europes" devoid of the flaws associated with modernity and industrialism, or what were perceived as the more "degenerative" aspects of the "chaotic" and egalitarian development of the North American frontiers of European expansion (i.e., Edward Gibbon Wakefield's inspired projects for New Zealand and South Australia).[18] One should also add to this list the long tradition of European colonization schemes associated with religious and political utopianisms, and the many attempts to establish communities in various parts of the planet—from Puritan New England to William Lane's Paraguay, from the sixteenth century to the twentieth.[19]

One should also approach this archive with an assessment of the impact on the European imagination of phenomena related to the epidemiological history of the world and what has been defined as "ecological imperialism," the substitution of a largely European biota for a native one in extensive areas of temperate regions.[20] The recurrence of colonial famines also added to this archive, reproducing a Malthusian gaze over colonial demographics and assisting an interpretation of colonial phenomena associated with the inevitability (and indispensability) of settler enterprises.[21]

As well, one should appraise the impact on a settler archive of foundational and survivalist narratives that coagulate around the victorious repression of indigenous resistances. These episodes often acquire a quasi-mythological status in settler narratives, and are represented as the moment in which the community of Europeans, perceiving itself as both outnumbered and isolated, is saved from destruction and secures its right to exist. The Orangist celebration of the Battle of the Boyne, the Afrikaner interpretation of the Battle of Blood River, Caldoche renditions of the war of 1878 in New Caledonia, and Israeli narratives of the War of 1948, for example, all share a common template of interpretative refrains.[22] (Yet this list could certainly be further extended, perhaps encompassing sometimes fictional yet recurring images of pioneering caravans trekking westward being attacked by marauding Indians, defending themselves to the last man and woman before being rescued by a providential Hollywood-style cavalry charge).

Conversely, there are also a number of interpretative tropes relating to the decolonization of settler societies—when settler projects had to be abandoned and the settler community did not stand the military, demographical, racial, and political test of its survival—exchanging an actual (counter)exodus for a mythical one (i.e., Algerian *pied-noirs*, the settlers of Lusophone Africa, Kenyan and Rhodesian settlers, etc.). Jungles, thickets, their impenetrability, and most of all the lack of "visibility" of some "adverse" environments have all had a special place in colonial constructions of settler failure.[23] Since Algeria's successful liberation, casbahs, which always had a special place in Orientalist constructions of the Arab "other," have also constituted a particularly sore spot of the settler imagination, including the Israeli one, which naturally incorporated part of this imagery via the immigration/settlement of Jewish *pied-noirs*.[24] This narrative framework, which De Gaulle dubbed *"l'Algérie de papa"* (the Algeria of nostalgia), is also part of the settler archive and is epitomized by Edith Piaf's refrain that the repatriated *pied-noirs* sang while abandoning their "lost country": *"je ne regrette rien"* (I have no regrets).[25]

Indeed, perhaps resulting from the recent demise of Euro-centered historiographies, a comparative analysis of the processes of European expansion (and its interaction with a settler archive) is a remarkably neglected area of scholarly research. Nevertheless, the settler archive should not be overdrawn: not all the "frontiers" of European expansion witnessed the mobilization of a settler imagination and the establishment of a settler practice. The example of the Argentinean wheat expansion during the latter part of the nineteenth century, of a settlerless frontier filled with temporary migrants—the *golondrinas* (swallows), southern European peasants who crossed the Atlantic in the off season and could earn their return fare in a fortnight—is an example of how diversified processes of frontier extension can be and a reminder that the "opening" of "new" territory is not necessarily accompanied by the mobilization of a settler ethos.[26]

What is generally referred to as "decolonization," the passages and events that have left a mark on the settler archive and the ideological practices that mobilize it but have not erased it from the imagination of the West, demonstrates its inadequacy vis-à-vis this archive's remarkable capacity to endure. The analysis of the indigenous/settler equation and its archive is especially sensitive because this relationship has often been a way to test the conscience of the West.[27] In this context, one should also consider the romantic notion of a positive indigenous "other," continuously present in the European imagination and yet constantly reformulated through time. The mythology of the "noble savage" and its more localized versions—the "Aryan Maori" for example—are all constructions that have become a constituent part of a settler archive and contributed to the formation of its imagery. The settler/indigenous equation has functioned, one would say, as "part for the whole": a metaphor and symbol that Europe utilizes to think about itself, especially its vices and its virtues (i.e., Alexis de Tocqueville's voyages in America and Frederick Jackson Turner's notion of "frontier" and its impact on US and other historiographies).[28]

Colonial Genocides to Genocidal Colonialism

Scholarly inquiry into the settler archive is also essential because its operational registers and evolution are surprisingly similar to another of the archives of the European imagination that deal with difference: the anti-Semitic one. The two practices and their respective archives have grown side by side, sometimes feeding on each other, always interwoven, and, in the specific junction of the extermination of the European Jewry, short-circuiting, becoming one. It is perhaps no coincidence that both archives were developed especially after 1492; however, perhaps due to an intellectual tradition that insisted on the nationalist and social origins of European fascisms and neglected their colonial interface, the interaction between the two practices has been largely ignored.[29]

And yet, Antillaise poet Aimé Césaire had very well detected this overlap already in 1955, and had insisted on the need to see fascism as a colonial form that had engulfed Europe at a time when the outward expansion of imperial colonialism had encountered its final limits: "What the very Christian bourgeois of the twentieth century cannot forgive Hitler for is not the crime in itself, the crime against humanity, not the humiliation of humanity itself, but the crime against the white man . . . ; it is the crime of having applied to Europe the colonialist actions as were borne up till now by the Arabs, the Coolies of India and the negroes of Africa."[30] Framed in this perspective, genocide and colonialism appear interpenetrating and obviously closer than generally allowed.[31] Scholarship that insists on the uniqueness of the Shoah should be integrated with a study of the genealogy of this overlap. While this is a line of inquiry that has rarely been pursued within the context of Holocaust studies, the mere fact that Israel is also a colonialist society that claims a special relationship with the history of the Shoah adds a further complicating element to this interpretative context and further disincentivizes such a line of inquiry.[32]

While the association between Rousseau and Hegel as ideological precursors of twentieth-century totalitarianism and genocidal impulses has been the subject of sustained academic attention, the Anglophone lineage anticipating the same phenomena is much less explored.[33] And yet, there is a direct contiguity and cross-fertilization between English neoidealism and

German biologism during the second part of the nineteenth century. It is useful to quote from Marc Ferro's work on this trajectory:

> The Empire—naturally the British Empire—was thus viewed as the highest stage of the social organization [by the neo-idealists of Oxford]. Spencer Wilkinson was one of the main eulogists of this notion of Empire. His pronouncements made their mark on men like Alfred Milner, Toynbee and Haldane in England, and the disciples of the historian Ranke in Germany. . . . As a matter of course, British historians saw the British Empire as a historic fulfillment. Interestingly they set up against the Marxists, and especially against the German Franz Mehring, a parallel and different model of historical development. While the Marxists, in their analysis of historical development, defined the stages of slavery, feudalism and capitalism as the harbingers of socialism, the English imperialists—notably J. R. Seely, but above all J. A. Cramb in *The Origin and Destiny of Imperial Britain*—emphasized other stages of historical development: the city-state, the feudal state, the class state, the national democratic state. The British state was thus the crowning achievement of a history in conformity with the ideals of freedom and of tolerance that were born during the Reformation.[34]

Crucially, this was no Prussian state, which is characterized in the Hegelian tradition through "Reason" in a dialectic that largely but not entirely ignores colonial issues.[35] This is Lord Milner's "Empire"; in these works, the British Empire is exalted purely through its capacity of exercising colonial domination and as a direct function of its unmatched capacity of transplanting "energetic" (white) settler ("free") "democracies" in colonial settings, an ability that almost all other colonial powers explicitly and sorely missed.

As Ferro has noted, this cultural tradition highlights the genocidal/colonial interface during the second half of the nineteenth century and emphasizes the ways in which genocidal impulses were eventually transplanted within the boundaries of metropolitan Europe:

> [t]o this [neoidealistic] trend of opinion was added a vision of man which tended to the glorification of exploits, of action, such as is found in the *Lebensphilosophie* eulogized by William Dilthey, Oswald Spengler and Max Scheler. All three were imperialists and, like Nietzsche, endorsed the idea of a form of social Darwinism directed against the outside world. In the wake of this biological trend followed scientists, sociologists, eugenists who returned to and took up the ideas of Gobineau. Like Gidding, they glorified the *Übermensch* of tomorrow. In this manner they brought about a fusion of predominantly British neo-idealism with predominantly German biologism. This process was stimulated by Houston Chamberlain—the Britisher who became a subject of Kaiser Wilhelm II—who acted as a go-between.[36]

The Nazis then were not the first in successfully shifting to Europe crucial aspects of the colonial dynamic, obliterating a boundary that had protected metropolitan Europe from the pattern of relationships it established in the colonial world.[37]

Previously, the intrinsic discrimination separating colony and metropolis had been attentively and constantly reinforced/surveilled throughout multiple passages of colonial history, and the juridical status of an individual or the acceptability of certain acts had crucially depended on the location of the individual and on whether these acts had been committed within the borders of metropolitan Europe. The 1787 case of a fugitive slave who had reached Britain before being recaptured by his owner and was set free after a judge had failed to detect in England any law or custom that sanctioned the practice of slavery, epitomizes this differentiating trend.[38] Yet during the nineteenth century this boundary had become blurred, especially in British colonial practice and in British academic circles. (More practically, the British India Criminal Castes Act 1871 and Criminal Castes Act 1911, where entire groups were designated as "criminal tribes," can be seen as predecessors in the explicit and legal criminalization of entire social groups because of their social identity, which anticipates the persecutory practice of the Bolshevik and Nazi regimes).[39]

This is not to say that a genocidal outcome was unavoidable, that colonial genocides were the result of a predetermined process. Colonial policy makers and colonial agents on the ground were full protagonists and actively shaped these events. Yet an available and mobilizable settler archival background facilitated their actions and made colonial genocides thinkable and possible. While these sequences should not be understood as chain reactions in which each rung necessarily presupposes the following one, these were passages in which each successive incident would not have been possible without the previous one. In the end, the project of transplanting European settlers outside of Europe had produced practices that were eventually relocated right in the heart of Europe.[40] With the Shoah, the cycle had come full circle; Bartolomé De Las Casas' original prophecy on the inhumanity of colonialism had been fulfilled.

Racism, antisemitism, and the colonial imagination all fed on a common cultural history and on a shared collection of tropes, both at the level of colonial ideology and cultural production, and at the level of colonial practice. A survey of the parallel development (and current availability) of an anti-Semitic archive and of a settler/colonial one is essential in order to approach the contiguities between these two practices.[41] The nonavailability of a colonial outlet in post–WWI Germany may have contributed to the fatal and final collapse of the two practices.[42] After the trauma of 1870/71, France had been capable of effectively projecting colonial fantasies of a Greater France *d'outre mer* and rebuilding a vast colonial empire. Bismarck himself, for example, saw that France would get Tunisia, not the

Italians.[43] Whereas at the turn of the century France had been the epicenter of Western European antisemitism, after WWI, this shifted decisively to Germany. The colonial factor in these trajectories has been dramatically overlooked.[44]

On the contrary, after defeat Germany was denied the possibility of a colonial scenario. This was seen and understood as an especially violent and unwarranted rupture, especially because the perception that Germany's record as a colonial power had been remarkably positive was one specific feature of Germany's colonial consciousness. Even if comparatively limited, its colonial tradition had been extremely diversified and had encompassed a broad range of colonial practices and engagements. Its colonial experience had included "neofeudal" relations in Samoa and the Pacific, proto-"social democratic" engagement in Tanganyika, more traditional systems of forced labor extraction in New Guinea, and outright genocidal action in South-West Africa (itself, quite significantly, a site for a settler project).[45] A dynamic colonial tradition and its imagination were abruptly and traumatically terminated at Versailles; Belgium possessed a colossal empire, even Denmark had Greenland. At the apex of Europe's apparently irresistible colonialist ascendancy, Germany had become the only Western European body politic incapacitated of actually exercising a specific set of colonizing fantasies.

Deprived of the promises of modernity associated with the possibility of entertaining colonial imaginings (which in turn necessitate the actual exertion of colonial enterprises), sections of Germany's colonial imagination inclined toward more millenarian and premodern versions of a colonial ethos. Hitler explicitly noted that it:

> . . . cannot be tolerated any longer that the British nation of 44,000,000 souls should remain in possession of fifteen and a half million square miles of the world's surface. They pretend to have obtained it from God and are not prepared to give it away. Likewise the French nation of 37,000,000 should own more than three and a half million square miles, while the German nation with 80,000,000 should only possesses about 230,000 square miles.[46]

It was a perspective that crucially collapsed the traditional distinction between colonial and European domains. In this specific evolution of a colonial imagination, Templar knights replaced the colonial trading companies, the eastern *Lebensraum* in Ukraine replaced the tropical settings and the aristocratic aloofness of colonial officials: the eastward expansion of a German sphere finally superseded dreams of a German *Mittelafrika*. While Mussolini was allowed to toy with the "sword of Islam", Hitler would project his colonial fantasies on a colony of settlement that should emerge after the Jews had been exterminated and the population economy of a reinvented "colonial" scenario comprehensively reshaped.[47] The

Italian fascists had been the first in using chemical weapons of mass destruction against civilians in Abyssinia, yet did not finally break the distinction between colony and metropolis. As Sven Lindqvist has argued in *History of Bombing*, it was the German fascists that perpetrated for the first time in Europe actions typical of a colonial setting and crucially ignored this boundary (Raphael Lemkin also consistently notes this throughout his work).[48]

The movement with which typically colonial forms infiltrated the European space concerns a number of elements of the "total war" that had applied for a long time to colonial subjects before flooding the European space: these include the concentration camp, the machine gun (developed in time to participate in the final stages of the Indian wars and then used against striking workers in the US), but also fingerprints, as Carlo Ginzburg has demonstrated, originally conceived in Bengal and eventually deployed within the metropolitan space with the strategic purpose of distinguishing between "laborious" and "dangerous" classes.[49]

Lenin's notion that it was imperialism and WWI that had finally removed the barriers between (European) national question and (colonial) anti-imperialist struggles may be seen in a new light.[50] According to Lenin, the imperialistic practices characteristic of non-European scenarios were bound to eventually enter the metropolitan theater in the final stage of imperialism, and indeed they had. The Shoah vindicated Lenin's intuition as well as Las Casas'. Most importantly, Lenin's *Imperialism* was also based on a reading of the later Marx, which deals extensively if not systematically with the colonial question, and on Hobson's idea that the dynamics of the colonial relation were the mainspring of historical development.[51]

Notes

1. Richard J. Perry, *From Time Immemorial* (Austin, TX, 1996); and Daiva Stasiulis, and Nira Yuval-Davis in *Unsettling Settler Societies* (London, 1995).
2. For a sophisticated analysis of the dialectics between a colonial metropolis, its settler impulses, and an immigrant population from former colonial polities see Abdelmalek Sayad, *La double absence: des illusions de l'émigré aux souffrances de l'immigré* (Paris, 1999).
3. For an analysis of the role of medical science in the establishment of a segregationist practice in South Africa and elsewhere in colonial contexts, see, for example, Marc Ferro, *Colonization: A Global History* (London, 1997), 131–34.
4. See, for example, the classical Roland Herbert Bainton, *The Age of the Reformation* (Malabar, FLA, 1984 [1956]).
5. See Timothy J. Keegan, *Colonial South Africa and the Origins of the Racial Order* (London, 1996).

6. Edward W. Said, "Michael Walzer's *Exodus and Revolution*: A Canaanite Reading," in *Performance & Reality: Essays from "Grand Street,"* ed. Ben Sonnenberg (New Brunswick, NJ, 1989), 97–117. See also Regina M. Schwartz, *The Curse of Cain: The Violent Legacy of Monotheism* (Chicago, 1997); and John Docker, *1492: The Poetics of Diaspora*, (London, 2001), especially 130–50. For an analysis of the impact of *Exodus* in Australian popular white mythology, see Ann Curthoys, "Expulsion, Exodus and Exile in White Australian Historical Mythology," *Journal of Australian Studies* 61 (1999): 2–18.
7. See Edward W. Said, *Culture and Imperialism* (London, 1994), 62; and Sven Lindqvist, *"Exterminate All the Brutes"* (London, 1998).
8. Cyril Lionel Robert James, *The Black Giacobins: Toussaint L'Overture and the San Domingo Revolution* (New York, 1963), Francis Bacon, *Of Plantations*, quoted in Deirdre Coleman, *Romantic Colonization and British Anti-Slavery* (Cambridge, 2005), 162–63.
9. See Nicholas Thomas, *Colonialism's Culture: Anthropology, Travel and Government* (Melbourne, 1994).
10. See Michael Hardt and Antonio Negri, *Empire* (Cambridge, 2000), especially 114–59.
11. On "hybridity," see Homi K. Bhabha, "DissemiNation: Time, Narrative and the Margins of the Modern Nation," and "Signs Taken for Wonders: Questions of Ambivalence and Authority under a Tree outside Delhi," in *The Location of Culture* (London, 1994); and Robert Young, *Colonial Desire: Hybridity in Theory, Culture and Race* (London, 1995).
12. See John D. Kelly, and Martha Kaplan, *Represented Communities: Fiji and World Decolonization* (Chicago, 2001); and Henry Reynolds, *The Law of the Land* (Melbourne, 1987).
13. See the classical Ronald Edward Robinson, *Africa and the Victorians: The Official Mind of Imperialism* (London, 1961).
14. See Zeev Sternhell, *The Founding Myths of Israel: Nationalism, Socialism and the Making of the Jewish State* (Princeton, NJ, 1999).
15. See, for example, Isabelle Merle, *Expériences coloniales: La Nouvelle Calédonie (1853–1920)* (Paris, 1995).
16. Quoted in Tariq Ali, *Bush in Babylon: The Recolonisation of Iraq* (London, 2003), 178–82.
17. Ibid., 181.
18. See Miles Fairburn, *The Ideal Society and its Enemies: The Foundations of Modern New Zealand Society, 1850–1900* (Auckland, 1989).
19. See Howard Zinn, *A People's History of the United States* (New York, 1980), which presents an unorthodox reading of US history; Francis Jennings, *The Creation of America: Through Revolution to Empire* (Cambridge and New York, 2000), which insists on the "imperial" consciousness of Puritan settlers; Michael Wilding, *The Paraguayan Experiment* (Melbourne, 1984); and Anne Whitehead, *Paradise Mislaid: In Search of the Australian Tribe of Paraguay* (Brisbane, 1997).
20. Jared M. Diamond, *Guns, Germs and Steel: A Short History of Everybody for the Last 13,000 Years* (London, 1998); Alfred W. Crosby, *Ecological Imperialism* (New York, 1986); Tim Flannery, *The Future Eaters: An Ecological History of the Australasian Lands and People* (Melbourne, 1994); Tim Flannery, *The Eternal Frontier: An Ecological History of North America and its Peoples* (Melbourne, 2001); and Geoff Park, *Ngā Uruora, The Groves of Life: Ecology and History in a New Zealand Landscape* (Wellington, 1995).
21. Mike Davis, *Late Victorian Holocausts: El Niño, Famines and the Making of the Third World* (New York, 2002).

22. See, among others, Oliver MacDonagh, *States of Mind: A Study of Anglo-Irish conflict, 1780–1980* (London, 1983); Leonard M. Thompson, *The Political Mythology of Apartheid* (New Haven, CT, 1985); Bronwen Douglas, *Across the Great Divide: Journeys in History and Anthropology* (Amsterdam, 1998), especially 193–217; and Avi Shlaim, *The Iron Wall: Israel and the Arab World* (London, 2000).
23. For an assessment of "visibility" as a necessary condition for the establishment of a settler gaze (and how the open landscapes of Australia were an especially conducive location for the development of a settler project), see Paul Carter, *The Road to Botany Bay* (London, 1987), 230–60.
24. According to Baruch Kimmerling's notion of "frontierity," the most significant factor in determining settler/indigenous relations is population density, with a high density of indigenous population preventing frontier-like conditions and unchecked dispossession. Baruch Kimmerling, *Zionism and Territory* (Berkeley, CA, 1983).
25. Ferro, *Colonization*, 131.
26. A highly comparative analysis of frontier experiences can be found in Charles Alistair Michael Hennessy, *The Frontier in Latin American History* (London, 1978). For an analysis of Argentina's frontier experience, see especially 89–92.
27. See, for example, Daniel Francis, *The Imaginary Indian: The Image of the Indian in Canadian Culture* (Vancouver, 1992); James Belich, *Making Peoples: A History of the New Zealanders from Polynesian Settlement to the End of the Nineteenth Century* (Auckland, 1996); and Belich, "Myth, Race and identity in New Zealand," *New Zealand Journal of History* 31, no. 1 (1997): 9–22.
28. The literature on this subject is notably vast. Departing points can be: Alexis de Tocqueville, *Democracy in America* (New York, 2000); Cheryl B. Welch, *de Tocqueville* (Oxford, 2001); Frederick Jackson Turner, "The Significance of the Frontier in American History," in *The Early Writings of Frederick Jackson Turner*, ed. Everett E. Edwards (Madison, WI, 1938); and Richard W. Etulain, ed., *Writing Western History: Essays on Major Western Historians* (Reno, NV, 2002).
29. See George L. Mosse, *The Nationalization of the Masses: Political Symbolism and Mass Movements in Germany from the Napoleonic Wars through the Third Reich* (New York, 1975); Zeev Sternhell, *Ni droite, ni gauche: l'idéologie fasciste en France* (Brussels, 1987); and Zeev Sternhell, Mario Sznajder, and Maia Ashéri, *Naissance de l'idéologie fasciste* (Paris, 1989).
30. Quoted in Ferro, *Colonization*, x.
31. Even earlier, African American scholar and activist W. E. B. Du Bois had emphasized this connection: "There was no Nazi atrocity—concentration camps, wholesale maiming and murder, defilement of women or ghastly blasphemy of childhood—which the Christian civilization of Europe had not been practicing against colored folk in all parts of the world in the name of and for the defense of a Superior Race born to rule the world." See W. E. Burghardt Du Bois, *The World and Africa: An inquiry into the part which Africa has played in world history* (New York, 1965), 23.
32. See, for example, Dan Stone, ed., *The Historiography of the Holocaust* (London and New York, 2004).
33. For examples, see Hannah Arendt, *The Origins of Totalitarianism* (New York, 1951); Jacques Derrida, *De l'esprit: Heidegger et la question* (Paris, 1987), which insists on the intrinsic violence of Hegel's logic; and James Kaye and Bo Stråth, eds., *Enlightenment and Genocide: Contradiction of Modernity* (Brussels, 2000).
34. Ferro, *Colonization*, 21–22.
35. An analysis of the link between Hegel's production and Haiti's revolution can be found in Susan Buck-Morss, "Hegel and Haiti," *Critical Inquiry* 26, no. 4 (2000): 821–65.

36. Ferro, *Colonization*, 22.
37. See Enzo Traverso, *The Origins of Nazi Violence* (New York, 2003).
38. See Ferro, *Colonization*, 175. It should be noted that the sentence that had freed this former slave had insisted on the obligation of English courts to acknowledge the contracts relating to slave ownership in the colonies. In fact, the Somerset case had reinforced the distinction between colonial circumstances and metropolitan contexts. For a thorough discussion of the Somerset case, see David Brion Davis, *The Problem of Slavery in the Age of Revolution* (Ithaca, NY, 1975), 470–74.
39. See Ferro, *Colonization*, 21.
40. An argument highlighting the ways in which imperial powers repatriated from the colonies practices of generalized violence and mass murder is presented in Norman M. Naimark, *Fires of Hatred: Ethnic Cleansing in Twentieth-Century Europe* (Cambridge, MA, 2001).
41. It should be noted that Hannah Arendt had already proposed a very similar approach. Arendt, however, had focused on an imperialistic tradition rather than a specifically colonial one. See Arendt, *Origins*. See also Mark Mazower, *Dark Continent: Europe's Twentieth Century* (London, 1998), and Benjamin Stora, *Le transfert d'une mémoire: De l'«Algérie française» au racisme anti-arabe* (Paris, 1999), which explores the ways in which a settler memory from French Algeria was displaced to France and became a constitutive foundation of right wing and neofascist discourse.
42. See Raphael Lemkin, *Axis Rule in Occupied Europe* (Washington, DC, 1944). Lemkin, the originator of the concept of genocide, interpreted German behavior against some Eastern European populations as typically colonial.
43. On the colonial experience of the Third Republic, see Robert Aldrich, *Greater France: A History of French Overseas Expansion* (London, 1996). On the evolution of French colonial theories, see Raymond F. Betts, *Assimilation and Association in French Colonial Theory, 1890–1914* (New York, 1961).
44. See Woodruff D. Smith, *The German Colonial Empire* (Chapel Hill, NC, 1978); Smith, *The Ideological Origins of Nazi Imperialism* (New York, 1986); and Sara Friedrichsmeyer, Sara Lennox, and Susanne Zantop, eds., *The Imperialist Imagination: German Colonialism and Its Legacy* (Ann Arbor, MI, 1998). See also Jürgen Zimmerer, "Colonialism and the Holocaust: Towards an Archeology of Genocide," in *Genocide and Settler Society: Frontier Violence and Stolen Indigenous Children in Australian History*, ed. A. Dirk Moses (New York and Oxford, 2004), 49–76.
45. See John A. Moses and Paul M. Kennedy, eds., *Germany in the Pacific and Far East 1870–1914* (Brisbane, 1977); and Jürgen Zimmerer, *Deutsche Herrschaft über Afrikaner: Staatlicher Machtanspruch und Wirklichkeit im kolonialen Namibia*, 3rd ed. (Hamburg, 2003).
46. Cited in Norman G. Finkelstein, *Image and Reality of the Israel-Palestine Conflict* (London, 2003), 234.
47. See Angelo Del Boca, Nicola Labanca, *L'impero africano del fascismo* (Rome, 2002), 52. See also Wendy Lower, "New Ordering of Space and Race: Nazi Colonial Dreams in Zhytomyr Ukraine, 1941–1944," *German Studies Review* 25 (2002): 227–44.
48. See John Docker in this volume, and Sven Lindqvist, *A History of Bombing* (London, 2001).
49. Carlo Ginzburg, "Spie: Radici di un paradigma indiziario," in *Miti emblemi spie: Morfologia e storia* (Turin, 2002), 189–90.
50. See Vladimir Ilich Lenin, *Imperialism the Highest Stage of Capitalism: A Popular Outline* (London, 1934).

51. Karl Marx, *Notes on Indian History (1664–1858)* (Moscow, 1960); Karl Marx and Friedrich Engels, *The First Indian War of Independence 1857–1859* (Moscow, 1968); Karl Marx, *Marx on China, 1853–1860: Articles from the New York Daily Tribune*, ed. Dona Torr (London, 1951); Karl Marx, *Karl Marx on Colonialism and Modernization: His Dispatches and other Writings on China, India, Mexico, the Middle East and North Africa* (Garden City, NY, 1968); and John Atkinson Hobson, *Imperialism: A Study* (London, 1902).

– *Chapter 7* –

Biopower and Modern Genocide

Dan Stone

Introduction

Two striking quotations—from Michel Foucault and Giorgio Agamben—provide my starting point. They illustrate the "biopolitical approach," that is to say, they emphasize the need to understand genocide as a result of the modern state's control over the life and death of its citizens:

> The existence in question is no longer the juridical existence of sovereignty; at stake is the biological existence of a population. If genocide is indeed the dream of modern powers, this is not because of a recent return of the ancient right to kill; it is because power is situated and exercised at the level of life, the species, the race, and the large-scale phenomena of population.[1]

> The Jew living under Nazism is the privileged negative referent of the new biopolitical sovereignty and is, as such, a flagrant case of a *homo sacer* in the sense of a life that may be killed but not sacrificed . . . the Jews were exterminated not in a mad and giant holocaust but exactly as Hitler had announced, "as lice," which is to say, as bare life. The dimension in which the extermination took place is neither religion nor law, but biopolitics.[2]

I would like to compare the approach set out so powerfully by Foucault and Agamben to an approach that, while apparently less radical in terms of its critique of post-Holocaust society, may in the end turn out to be even more of a warning than that presented by the two eminent philosophers.

One of the notable splits within Holocaust scholarship is that between those who stress the fundamentally rational, technocratic, or bureaucratic nature of the Nazi genocide—often associated with the metaphor of "industrial killing," which compares the gas chambers to modern factory-line production—and those who see the murder of the Jews as the result of a bizarrely irrational, though historically explicable, ideology founded on the fear of a Jewish conspiracy to enslave the world. In this chapter, I will show that the literature on biopolitics lends credence to the former approach, but only at the expense of overlooking some essential elements of the Holocaust. By setting the Holocaust into the longer-term context of colonial genocide, one can see that biopolitical explanations of genocide go a long way to helping us in our quest for understanding. Nevertheless, the need to account for the impetus to carry out policies of mass atrocity remains, for these cannot adequately be encompassed within schemes of bureaucratic administration.

Scholars of the Holocaust are familiar with the divide between "intentionalists" and "functionalists." Intentionalists believe that the murder of the Jews was a logical realization of Hitler's ideas, which he set out in *Mein Kampf* (if not earlier), and that the Nazi state was geared to putting Hitler's plans into practice. Functionalists, or structuralists, on the other hand, while they do not necessarily deny the significance of anti-Semitism—though some dismiss it as mere crowd-mobilizing rhetoric—argue that the Holocaust occurred not as the actualization of a long-held intent, but as the step-by-step slide into increasingly radical policies, a "cumulative radicalization" that was driven largely by the circumstances in which the Nazi leaders found themselves during the war. The former view stresses the role of ideology, especially anti-Semitism, and of hatred and violence. The latter places more emphasis on bureaucracy, the means-ends rationality that characterizes "modernity," and the threat to individuals' lives posed by the surveillant state. It subscribes to an understanding of events that sees them as driven less by conscious agency and more by social dynamics that are unleashed through institutions such as bureaucracies.[3] The limitations of both schools of thought have been helpfully set out by William Hagen:

> Both interpretive schools are capable of conveying rich insights, but the first approach [functionalism] suffers from having to treat values or motives, including ideologies such as anti-Semitism, even when "scientized" and thus "rationalized", as exogenous to modernity's logic. Yet, upon closer inspection, the rationality of modernity is one of means, not of ends. The second approach [intentionalism] suffers, in its metapsychological versions, from difficulties of empirical verification and dependence on more or less apodictic theories of human psychodynamics. Where it emphasizes "ancient hatreds", it likewise is hard-pressed to explain why they exist, and why they seemingly slumber for long periods, only to break out later in unprecedented new forms. . . . This school of thought is continually in danger of seeing its preferred independent variable—passionate, violence-infused hatred—fall into dependency on social

> conditions, above all, Durkheimian *anomie* and "modernization crises," triggering ideologized aggression against outsiders and scapegoats.[4]

This split between intentionalism and functionalism—which has not been entirely overcome despite the efforts of many scholars to find a framework to reconcile the two positions[5]—is not a new division in scholarly literature. It can be seen as a continuation of an earlier tradition, whereby proponents of race theory in the nineteenth and early twentieth centuries liked to use the language of science to justify the most outrageous slaughters. In other words, even in the nineteenth century, this tension between the "irrational-ideological" and the "structural-bureaucratic" lay at the heart of explanations of the occurrence of colonial genocide, which was amenable to both sorts of approach. In Holocaust studies and in the history of colonial genocide, the stress on structures may be seen as akin to the biopolitical approach, for the logic of modernity's rationality and cold scientific objectification that is central to the functionalist explanation concurs with the biopolitical stress on the enumeration and medicalization of society and—where the state turns genocidal—with a dynamic of destruction that derives irresistibly from impersonal and ostensibly nonideological measures such as registration and identification through to segregation and "eugenic" extermination. And this in turn should be seen as a one-sided version of an explanatory framework used over the last two centuries to explain the terrible consequences of colonialism for indigenous peoples.

Colonial Genocide as Incipient Biopolitics

Charles Darwin famously included a chapter on "The Extinction of the Races of Man" in *The Descent of Man* (1871), and many writers in the mid-nineteenth century justified the "disappearance" of "primitive races" on evolutionary grounds.[6] In New Zealand, Australia, South Africa, Hawaii, and North America, "the inferior organisation makes room for the superior. As the Indian is killed by the approach of civilization, to which he resists in vain, so the black man perishes by that culture to which he serves as a humble instrument."[7] Typical was the view of the great evolutionist Alfred Russel Wallace: "The Red Indian in North America, and in Brazil; the Tasmanian, Australian and New Zealander in the southern hemisphere, die out, not from any one special cause, but from the inevitable effects of an unequal mental and physical struggle. The intellectual and moral, as well as the physical qualities of the European are superior. . . . If my conclusions are just it must inevitably follow that the higher—the more intellectual and moral—must displace the lower and more degraded races."[8]

This was a widely shared view. James Cowles Prichard, author of the major early anthropological study *Researches into the Physical History of Man* (1813) stated baldly: "Wherever Europeans have settled, their arrival has been the harbinger of extermination to the native tribes."[9] A few years later, one author put it rather clinically that "races have only been extinguished, or brought to the verge of extinction, when it has happened that the soil on which they subsisted has been occupied by other races at the same time that their number was in process of diminution through the operation of the same causes to which all races are periodically subject."[10] In somewhat more colourful prose, another noted that "it is only utter savages, whose presence is of no more use to the conqueror than the ferocious beasts of the forest, that disappear before an invader of higher civilization."[11] The examples can be multiplied many times over.

What these claims represent is a kind of incipient biopolitics. They are not simply ideological justifications of extinction, but also clear statements of the modern, civilizing state's right to remove ostensibly backward or primitive elements. The arguments they make are not the same as those made by Agamben about the modern state's regulation and production of life, but nor are they simply "respectable" society's refusal to look at things as they really were. Rather, it is clear that those who put forward such claims firmly believed that the civilized nations had the right and the responsibility to control matters of life and death of "inferior races."

Such statements were by no means typical only of the middle years of the nineteenth century. At the end of the century one Cardiff physiologist and Social Darwinist claimed that "the struggle to survive among the savage tribes of man must be excessive. Whole races come and go, and their survivors fall victims to the privations, disease, or natural enemies, before the white man with his better brain and capacity for adaptation."[12] Paul Topinard, the French author of one of the most influential synthetic works of anthropology of the late nineteenth century, noted simply: "Whether rapid, slow, or scarcely perceptible, this progressive extinction in the presence of new races, relatively superior, and differing in morals and civilization, is an acknowledged fact."[13] And as late as 1909 another medical man, this time a New York ophthalmologist and leading member of the American Association for the Advancement of Science, argued that the world was gradually coming into the control of the superior race—the "blond Aryan occupying the northern part of Europe." The implications for others were severe, according to Charles Woodruff: "All the lower races in civilization, then, are actually a species of animal under domestication, increased in number hugely by the sanitation forced upon them and kept up by the Aryans."[14] In other words, "the extinction of the unfit was merely the obverse of that beneficial law of survival of the fittest that guaranteed the constant elevation and improvement of mankind."[15]

Woodruff, who excused the slavery and extinction of "lower races," also justified the persecution of Jews on similar grounds:

> The Jew, then, is a typical illustration of a commensal race, welcomed as long as he renders a returning benefit, but driven out or killed off as soon as he becomes so numerous that he is a harmful parasite and a national disease. European nations have repeatedly undergone a process of disinfection in this regard. The same law applies to the Jew as applies to a bacillus or any other organism which may be beneficial if few and in place, but deadly if numerous and out of place. . . . The persecution of the Jew, then, is and always has been a natural law, because it is necessary for survival of the supporting organism.[16]

Thus when scholars such as those contributing to this volume identify a trend in the current literature on genocide that stresses on the one hand the genocidal nature of colonialism, and on the other the colonial nature of the Holocaust, we can clearly see that the history of ideas, especially the history of anthropological ideas, will back up that historiographical development: "to colonise and to extirpate are synonymous terms," as an article in the *Popular Magazine of Anthropology* had it in 1864.[17] Or, as Patrick Wolfe put it more recently, "the primary logic of settler colonialism can be characterized as one of elimination."[18]

The importance of the biopolitical approach is shown not only in the example of the development of anthropology, but in the fact that the way of thinking that divided the world into definable and controllable population groups gained in strength throughout the nineteenth and first half of the twentieth century. The control of bodies went hand in hand with a widely held Social Darwinism that explained the movement of history as the progressive victory of the fit. In other words, biopower—"what brought life and its mechanisms into the realm of explicit calculations and made knowledge-power an agent of transformation of human life"—must be seen in the context of "bio-history": "the pressures through which the movements of life and the processes of history interfere with one another," as Foucault explains.[19] In other words, the examples on which I have drawn from the history of anthropology are just one strand of nineteenth-century thought that illustrate the rise to prominence of a Social Darwinism that fed the logic of the modern, technocratic state. This state took it upon itself to undertake the biological administration of its citizenry, from medicalizing society to eliminating those that threatened the attainment of the long-term vision of how society should be shaped. Laws of nature and history came together in a way that demanded the control over people's bodies in the name of steering the direction of historical change.[20]

An excellent example of the need to take control of evolutionary laws is the book, titled quite simply *Bio-Politics*, by the minor English novelist and short-story writer Morley Roberts (1856–1942). The book is an attempt to argue that society should be modeled on the individual organism, which is controlled by the brain: "the somatic assembly of would-be dominating aristocrats, a cerebral senate or House of Lords."[21] The implications of Morley's views are most vividly expressed on the subject of the Jews. Seeing the Jews as "the nearest to being a true race of any people in Europe," Morley argued that they were "too deeply differentiated to be assimilated." This meant that there was "no safe ground on which to establish sufficient tolerance to avoid the phenomenon inevitably associated with any struggle for immunity, though the Jews seem incapable of seeing that on scientific principles a non-immune untolerated body must be ejected, immured, or remain likely to cause social friction and disorder."

Thus despite the notable tolerance of the English, it was "undeniable that the late influx of Jews into England has resulted in reactions which seem remarkably analogous to anaphylactic shock."[22] Morley's book—along with other examples across Europe, such as Iuliu Moldovan's *Biopolitica* (1926), the key text of the Romanian eugenics movement[23]—confirms Peter Holquist's claim that, in the late nineteenth century, "increasingly, threats to the state were defined in prophylactic terms, as threats to health of the social body. . . . [O]ne sees a state continually seeking to sculpt and mold its population according to an applied science of society."[24]

The Limits of Biopower

Agamben's work on the modern state's control over its population's life and death sits in this tradition (as well as others[25]). Although the biopolitical approach cannot simply be assimilated to the functionalist interpretation of the Third Reich and the Holocaust, as I have shown, it shares certain assumptions with it, such as that rational, bureaucratic structures give rise to extraordinary brutality, and a downplaying of the role of ideology or fantasy thinking in human affairs. Agamben's claim that the camps represent "the *nomos* of the modern" is in fact remarkably close to the Frankfurt School analysis that sees the destruction of the Jews as a metaphor for the eradication of difference begun under authoritarianism that would be fully realized under the pseudo-freedom of postwar capitalism (especially in Herbert Marcuse's work). The former argument is based on the normalization of the "state of exception" (Carl Schmitt), while the latter is based on a critique of capitalism, but both focus on the "control" of populations that eradicates difference. Agamben's claim also sounds like an echo of an article written over twenty years ago by an admirer of the Frankfurt School, Ben Agger, who argued that "the kind of absolute integration represented by the concentration camps—where all subjective otherness is quite literally demolished under sway of the 'preponderance of the object', as Adorno called it—is nothing less than the *telos* of the entire Enlightenment, in which the Holocaust and monopoly capitalism are the two most recent stages, themselves dialectically intertwined."[26]

Most theorists now recognize that this Frankfurt School analysis is too essentialist, and the same could be said of Agamben's theory, enormously productive though it is. In his book, Agamben generalizes from the discussion of the "sacred man" (*homo sacer*) as put forward in a minor Latin text by Pompeius Festus to propose a way of understanding the position of the victims of the Holocaust. The "sacred man," according to Agamben, has the status of an outsider who can be killed by anyone, but is not subject to sacrifice or homicide. The extension of this principle under modern conditions of technological control, surveillance, and genetic engineering provides Agamben with the framework for theorizing the Holocaust. The Jews, in Agamben's argument, are the group that is reduced to "bare life" and murdered as such, without any sacrificial significance, in what is merely an "antiseptic operation."

There is no doubt that Agamben's argument is seductive, and provides powerful insights into how mass murder comes about. But historically speaking, can it account for why genocide was unleashed by Germany and not other modern societies? As Dan Diner points out, "it is enough to point to the notorious tradition of eugenics that evolved in both Scandinavia and North America to show the limits of any linkage between Auschwitz and the spirit of social and racial eugenics. . . . In order, then, to grasp the historical *specificity* of Nazi mass murder, we need in the end to return to a sphere of political action and personal accountability: to a specificity resting within the political-historical constellation at the time."[27]

In other words, Foucault's and Agamben's stress on *bare life* cannot account for the fact that in Britain, where eugenics was invented, no eugenic legislation ever even entered onto the statute books, or that in the US, where 30,000 "feeble-minded" people were sterilized, the movement did not end in mass murder. A variable is missing. In Raul Hilberg's formulation, "a primordial impulse had suddenly surfaced among the Western nations; it had been unfettered through their machines."[28] Agamben and Foucault account for the machines, but not for the primordial impulse. Or as sociologist Hans Joas notes, "there is as yet no study that integrates this [bureaucratic side of the Holocaust] with spontaneous violence that can be ascribed to particular individuals."[29] Most importantly, the thrust of the literature on biopolitics—which focuses on identifying the "dark side" of modernity—overlooks the fact that biopolitics led not only to genocide, but also to advances in social welfare, public health, and family policy, even as the aims and vocabulary of welfare advocates and eugenicists were often indistinguishable. Plainly, biopolitics cannot be seen solely as part of the history of genocide, as Edward Ross Dickinson reminds us:

> The investigation of the history of modern biopolitics has enabled new understandings of National Socialism; now we need to take care that our understanding of National Socialism does not thwart a realistic assessment of modern biopolitics. Much of the literature leaves one with the sense that a modern world in which mass murder is not happening is just that: a place where something is not—yet—happening. Normalization is not yet giving way to exclusion, scientific study and classification of peoples is not yet giving way to concentration camps and extermination campaigns. Mass murder, in short, is the historical problem; the absence of mass murder is not a problem, it does not need to be investigated or explained.[30]

Biopolitics, Fantasy, and Violence

Can the bureaucracy of biopolitics be reconciled with the primordial fantasies of violence? In the remainder of this chapter, I point to ways in which these two explanatory strands can be brought closer together.

It is useful to compare Foucault's and Agamben's explanation for the origins of genocide with that offered by Dominick LaCapra, who places more stress on "affective" forces. LaCapra writes of Agamben's work that it "coincides with an often exaggerated emphasis on confined, positivistic, relatively antiseptic notions of biology, medicalization, and eugenics," which chimes in with Foucault's version of biopower and biopolitics. He goes on to say that, while this approach explains one strand of thinking that fueled the Holocaust, it "does not account for Nazi quasi-ritual horror at contamination, elation in victimization, regeneration or redemption through violence, fascination with extreme transgression, and equivocation or even at times ambivalence with respect to the Jew (who was seen as abject—even as a germ or vermin—but to whom erotic energies and incredible powers of world conspiracy were also imputed."[31] Elsewhere he writes of:

> a somewhat crazed sacrificialism and scapegoating, which seems especially uncanny and out of place because it happens within a modernized context, where indeed you do have phenomena such as extensive bureaucratization, industrialization of mass murder, functional imperatives, and so forth. One can see these phenomena and how important they are. But I think there is also scapegoating in a specific sense within contingent historical circumstances, scapegoating related to a horror, an almost ritual and phobic horror, over contamination

> by 'the other.' Within a certain Nazi framework, the Jew was a pollutant or a contaminant literally or figuratively in the *Volksgemeinschaft* that had to be eliminated for the Aryan people to reach its purity and wholeness.[32]

But LaCapra himself does not offer any empirical historical work that shows how the interaction of the bureaucratic and the ritual-phobic-sacrificial worked. Yet many aspects of the Holocaust and other modern genocides, especially Cambodia and Rwanda (and perhaps recent events in the Democratic Republic of Congo and the Darfur region of Sudan), could provide evidence for LaCapra's theory.

Is it possible to bridge the two approaches? Agger notes that "Fascism [= Nazism] was animated by a combination of mythic belief in national 'blood' and an operational efficiency, combining bureaucratic chain-of-command with cost-effective 'production' and disposal techniques in the camps. . . . The Jewish Other did double duty as a mythic figure of anti-Christ and as the symbolic incarnation of the greedy businessman."[33] In each of these dualisms, Agamben has focused on only side of the equation. From the apologists for colonial genocide to the theorists of social anaphylaxis and contemporary theorists of bio-politics and genetic engineering, the stress on the growth of social science and its implications for population control overlooks a less empirically observable but no less vital element for explaining mass murder and genocide: the role of fantasy or magic in modern life.[34] It is to these elements that I now turn.

In the mid-1930s Bronislaw Malinowski described Nazism as a kind of modern magic, and later on these insights were developed by Norbert Elias, who saw Hitler as a kind of shaman.[35] And there were other, "earthier" aspects to the Holocaust than those of domination through rationality. Indeed, Eric Wolf notes that "Jew-baiting often took on carnivalesque dimensions, not in Mikhail Bakhtin's sense of carnival as a means of social protest, but rather as shows of playful aggression directed against 'outsiders.'" I would argue that the real transgressive horror of the Holocaust consisted in the fact that the Jews were not "outsiders," but constituted part of the European "self"; the perpetrators too knew this, and the extreme violence is the result of the operation of a kind of "cynical reason"—the deployment of rational, means-ends thinking for fantastic-utopian ends—that opted for transgressive behavior.[36] In other words, however rationally justified, the project as a whole of murdering the Jews of Europe was carried out in the name of a belief that cannot be understood as a form of technocratic population management: the struggle between Aryan and non-Aryan forces that, for the leading Nazis, defined the movement of history.

While it is possible to explain the mechanics of the Holocaust through examining the massive state agencies that were directed to the task of enumerating, isolating, transporting, and finally murdering the Jews, the history of this process is not sufficient to understand the *impetus* to murder the Jews. For this, one must turn to ideology, in particular the Nazi world view that perceived the world through the lenses of racial struggle and, within this, the necessity of combating the putative Jewish world conspiracy.

Thus, even though we have to bear in mind Foucault's biopolitics that gives rise to "comprehensive measures, statistical assessments, and interventions aimed at the entire social body or at groups as a whole,"[37] and that, according to Ian Hacking, has been "rampant in western civilization from the eighteenth century or earlier," we must remember that this systematic, "*restlose Erfassung*" does not in itself explain genocide.[38] Nazi violence, just as that of the Cambodian or Rwandan genocides, cannot simply be seen in terms of the irresistible spread of modern, technological population control. Rather, one must consider what Léon Poliakov called Hitlerism's "deep essence": "the fact that it was an explosion of hatred and blind fury which, in venting itself on others, in the last analysis turned against itself."[39]

A broader perspective, then, would incorporate the insights of Foucault and Agamben, or Bauman, about modern genocide into one that includes the question of ideology and motivation. For as Elias noted, the two are not incommensurable: "Just like scientifically conducted mass wars, the highly organized and scientifically planned extermination of whole population groups in specially constructed death camps and sealed-off ghettos by starvation, gassing or shooting does not appear to be entirely out of place in highly technicized mass societies."[40] Unlike Bauman et al., however, Elias stressed that this was not a blanket condemnation of modern society; rather, he sought to provide explanations based on his theory of civilizing and decivilizing trends that could explain why the Holocaust originated in Germany, and not in France or Britain. After all, the violence of the Nazis was not simply a state-directed form of ultra-discipline; initially, during the Weimar years, it was an anti-state violence: "The violence of the National Socialist movement, with the aid of privately organized defence associations," Elias noted, " . . . brought about the almost complete dissolution of the monopoly of force—without which a state, in the long term, cannot function—and destroyed the Weimar Republic from within."[41]

Why have there been so few attempts to link the bureaucratic and the ultra-violent aspects of the Holocaust? Perhaps the reason has to do with the argument, dominant within Holocaust historiography for so long, that the genocide of the Jews is a unique event to which other events cannot be compared.[42] Or, if this is too reductionist, it could be that the Holocaust is taken, whether consciously or not, as defining genocide, so that other genocides or examples of "ethnic cleansing" are overlooked—and even sponsored—by those who profess to be dismayed and horrified by genocide.[43] Hence, the Holocaust's history as part of a centuries-long trajectory of violence that encompasses state building, slavery, and colonialism is obscured.[44]

Historians who have recently looked at colonial genocide have uncovered a history of ferocious brutality.[45] This routine violence, at the service of the modern state, was carried over into the Nazi project to reshape the demography of Europe according to their racial dream.[46] Outside of Holocaust studies narrowly defined, this viewpoint is increasingly becoming the norm: "The Holocaust brought to Europe practices developed in colonial Africa, as the genocidal war against the Herero and the role of anthropologists in that war make all too clear."[47] German anthropologists, like their counterparts elsewhere, had been proclaiming the inevitable disappearance of backward races since at least 1870, when the Darwinian, Oscar Peschel, editor of *Das Ausland*, wrote: "Everything that we acknowledge as the right of the individual will have to yield to the urgent demands of human society, if it is not in accord with the latter. The decline of the Tasmanians therefore should be viewed as a geological or paleontological fate: the stronger variety supplants the weaker. This extinction is sad in itself, but sadder still is the knowledge, that in this world the physical order treads down the moral order with every confirmation."[48] And Hitler, though he shifted the geographical focus of the earlier German colonial enterprise, made the connection between colonialism and Nazism quite explicit in *Mein Kampf*:

> And so we National Socialists consciously draw a line beneath the foreign policy tendency of our pre-War period. We take up where we broke off 600 years ago. We stop the endless German movement to the south and west, and turn our gaze towards the land in the east. At long last we break off the colonial and commercial policy of the pre-War period and shift to the soil policy of the future.
>
> If we speak of soil in Europe today, we can primarily have in mind only Russia and her vassal border states.
>
> . . . The great empire in the east is ripe for collapse. . . . We have been chosen by Fate as witness of a catastrophe which will be the mightiest confirmation of the soundness of the *völkisch* theory.[49]

This debate is not only about the realm of ideas. What the notion of "savage races" legitimized was what the Catholic philosopher Jacques Maritain called "a surgical operation that is not even aseptic but, in fact, infected with hate and injustice."[50] The Holocaust, then, should be seen as an extreme example of genocide, not as separate from it. Nazism was a worldview that cultivated a belief in order and stability, but created a reality that was the entire opposite. It sought to use its revolutionary potential to bring about an ahistorical *Volksgemeinschaft*, immune from the ravages of time. This internal contradiction helps explain the extreme violence of Nazism, as Fred Weinstein pointed out two decades ago: "There was no way to resolve this tension in structural terms, except as the war and the concentration camps provided an arena in which both could find integrated expression. The camps became in fact the scene of the wildest, most unrestrained sadistic excesses and also of the methodical mastery of the technical-engineering problems presented by the demands for mass murder."[51]

Colonial genocide also derived from this dynamic between the desire to order the world for certain purposes (trade, racial expansion)—biopower—and the implied release from "civilized" behavior that the colonial project implied—transgression. The Holocaust, then, was to a large extent in the tradition of earlier colonial genocides, and much of the ground on which it built was already prepared in the colonies. Other genocides of the twentieth century—whether they are explained as the result of the collapse of the pre–World War I great power system, as an outcome of the process of nation building, or as the consequence of race-theory—are all characterized by this dilemma of reconciling an ideology of world order with the extreme violence required to realise that vision. Perhaps if Nazism was so extreme (of course, a claim that will no doubt sound odd in some parts of the world) it is because here the ideological dilemma was reversed; unlike, say, Cambodia where the desire for an ordered, simple life unleashed a wave of fury against those who represented a different way of life (the country's town-dwellers or "new people"), in Nazism the ideology was one of "thinking with the blood," of overturning rationalism and the Enlightenment, but the means of attaining this bucolic *Volksgemeinschaft* meant relying, paradoxically, on scientific-technological rationality. Yet as Weinstein also points out, the Nazi dream of autarchy, which encompassed genocide and the ruthless exploitation of subject peoples, "could be regarded as within the bounds of imperialist-chauvinist sentiment as expressed in Europe and elsewhere."[52] If it was true that "the genocidal behavior is accounted for by . . . fantasy thinking,"[53] this is no less true of colonial genocide or politicide than of the Holocaust.

Here we see how the two themes of biopower and fantasy intersect. On the one hand we are confronted with massive projects to reorder the world, projects that require the defining, counting, and marshalling of populations on a grand scale. On the other hand, these projects are often driven by beliefs that are not entirely amenable to bureaucratic accounting, and whose central tenets certainly do not coincide with the means used to achieve them. Milan Hauner noted twenty years ago that Nazism's basic concept was a "racial revolution," which could be seen "almost as the mirror image of the universal class war which had been advocated for some time under the banner of world revolution by the Marxists."[54] He went on to note that this concept meant "the epic transfiguration of man as a biological animal," the demographic and biological restructuring of the world, in a manner redolent of Agamben's or Foucault's notion of biopower. But he also noted that this did not simply signify the triumph of the "taming of chance" or the apogee of modern, state techniques of population surveillance and control. Rather these means of control were placed at the service of, to use Ernst Bloch's term, a thoroughly "non-contemporaneous" ideology: "The peculiar fusion of the ancient "blood and soil" mythology, with a whole range of quite modern elements, helped to create a new political religion, whose function it was, it could be argued, to prepare the chosen people, at the expense of the subhumans (*Untermenschen*), for the conquest of the world."[55] It is in this "political religion" aspect of Nazism—more accurately encompassed in Friedländer's notion of "redemptive anti-Semitism"—that the difference between Nazism and colonial genocides resides. It is certainly true to note, as Mark Mazower does, that "if Europeans would have resented being ruled as the British ruled India, they were shocked at being submitted to an experience closer to that inflicted upon the native populations of the Americas."[56] In other words, Nazism shares a great deal with earlier forms of colonial rule and atrocity; it is the "metaphysical" quality of the Holocaust that distinguishes it from colonial genocides. However, this should not be interpreted as meaning that "blood and soil" mythology is a "premodern" phenomenon that somehow "appears" atavistically in a modern context, as LaCapra suggests. Rather it is very much a product of modernity, and I have argued elsewhere that the structures of modernity, with their denial of the affective life, create and then channel outbursts of mass violence.[57] Thus "redemptive anti-Semitism," for example, is not simply a continuation of "traditional" Christian anti-Judaism; rather it is also an adaptation of Jew hatred under modern conditions of the emancipation of the Jews, the emergence of a homogeneous notion of citizenship in place of a formally stratified society, and, most significantly, the rise to prominence of ways of thinking that stress the eradication of superstition and the superiority of science. Instead of seeing fantasy thinking and means-ends rationality as irreconcilable opposites, it is important to see here how the rationalized structures of modernity can themselves not only channel but even create forms of thinking that are utopian and ultra-violent.[58] What this means is that genocide cannot be seen simply as the result of demographic planning based on ill-perceived reasons of state. In these processes of state building, colonization, and development the role of fantasy, fear of pollution, and what Ronald Aronson calls "social madness" must also be accounted for.[59]

Notes

1. Michel Foucault, *The History of Sexuality, vol. 1: An Introduction*, trans. Robert Hurley (Harmondsworth, UK, 1984), 137. For a discussion of the development of Foucault's ideas on biopower, see Martin Stingelin, ed., *Biopolitik und Rassismus* (Frankfurt am Main, 2003).
2. Giorgio Agamben, *Homo Sacer: Sovereign Power and Bare Life*, trans. Daniel Heller-Roazen (Stanford, CA, 1998), 114.
3. The best introduction is Ian Kershaw, *The Nazi Dictatorship*, 4th ed. (London, 2000).
4. William W. Hagen, "A 'Potent, Devilish Mixture' of Motives: Explanatory Strategy and Assignment of Meaning in Jan Gross's *Neighbors*," *Slavic Review* 61, no. 3 (2002): 472–73.
5. Compare Ulrich Herbert, ed., *National Socialist Extermination Policies: Contemporary German Perspectives and Controversies* (Oxford, 2000) with Peter Longerich, *Politik der Vernichtung: Eine Gesamtdarstellung der nationalsozialistischen Judenverfolgung* (Munich, 1998). See also Christopher R. Browning (with Jürgen Matthäus), *The Origins of the Final Solution: The Evolution of Nazi Jewish Policy, September 1939–March 1942* (London, 2004), for the most authoritative statement by the leading "moderate functionalist."
6. On Darwin, see Tony Barta, "Mr Darwin's Shooters: On Natural Selection and the Naturalising of Genocide," *Patterns of Prejudice* 39, no. 2 (2005): 116–37.
7. *Journal of the Anthropological Society of London*, 2 (1864): lxviii, cited in Christine Bolt, *Victorian Attitudes to Race* (London, 1971), 20.
8. Alfred R. Wallace, "The Origin of Human Races and the Antiquity of Man Deduced from the Theory of 'Natural Selection,'" *Anthropological Review* 2 (1864): clxv, clxix. Wallace, however, was critical of the "civilizing mission" and was less ready than Darwin, Huxley, and others to see the extinction of primitive races as desirable.
9. Dr. Pritchard [*sic*], "On the Extinction of Human Races," *Edinburgh New Philosophical Journal* 28 (1840): 169.
10. T. Bendyske, "On the Extinction of Races," *The Anthropological Review* 2 (1864): cii.
11. John Crawfurd, "On the Commixture of the Races of Man as Affecting the Progress of Civilization (Europe)," *Transactions of the Ethnological Society* 2 (1863): 205. Despite these words, Crawfurd, a doctor and philologist, and President of the Ethnological Society at the time of its split in 1863 (when James Hunt formed the Anthropological Society of London), condemned slavery, though he believed that "negroes" were a separate species.
12. John Berry Haycraft, *Darwinism and Race Progress* (London, 1895), 25.
13. Paul Topinard, *Anthropology*, trans. Robert T.H. Bartley (London, 1894), 413.
14. Charles Edward Woodruff, *Expansion of Races* (New York, 1909), 335, 379.
15. Russell McGregor, *Imagined Destinies: Aboriginal Australians and the Doomed Race Theory, 1880–1939* (Melbourne, 1997), 58.
16. Woodruff, *Expansion of Races*, 382.
17. Cited in Bolt, *Victorian Attitudes*, 20. See also Patrick Brantlinger, "'Dying Races': Rationalizing Genocide in the Nineteenth Century," in *The Decolonization of Imagination: Culture, Knowledge and Power*, ed. Jan Nederveen Pieterse and Bhikhu Parekh (London, 1995), 43–56; idem., *Dark Vanishings: Discourse on the Extinction of Primitive Races, 1800–1930* (Ithaca, NY, 2003); McGregor, *Imagined Destinies*; Henry Reynolds, *An Indelible Stain? The Question of Genocide in Australia's History*

(Melbourne, 2001), 139–54; Barry W. Butcher, "Darwinism, Social Darwinism, and the Australian Aborigines: A Reevaluation," in *Darwin's Laboratory: Evolutionary Theory and Natural History in the Pacific*, ed. Roy Macleod and Philip F. Rehbock (Honolulu, 1994), 371–94; Robert F. Berkhofer, Jr., *The White Man's Indian: Images of the American Indian from Columbus to the Present* (New York, 1979); Richard Drinnon, *Facing West: The Metaphysics of Indian-Hating and Empire-Building* (New York, 1980); Brian W. Dippie, *The Vanishing American: White Attitudes and U.S. Indian Policy* (Lawrence, KS, 1982); Norbert Finzsch, "'It is scarcely possible to conceive that human beings could be so hideous and loathsome': Discourses of Genocide in Eighteenth and Nineteenth-Century America and Australia," *Patterns of Prejudice* 39, no. 2 (2005).

18. Patrick Wolfe, '"Land, Labor, and Difference: Elementary Structures of Race," *American Historical Review* 106, no. 3 (2001): 868. See also Wolfe's *Settler Colonialism and the Transformation of Anthropology: The Politics and Poetics of an Ethnographic Event* (London, 1999).
19. Foucault, *History of Sexuality*, 1: 143.
20. The *locus classicus* for the argument that the Holocaust emerged from a bureaucratic process of means-ends rationality is Zygmunt Bauman, *Modernity and the Holocaust* (Cambridge, 1989).
21. Morley Roberts, *Bio-Politics: An Essay in the Physiology, Pathology and Politics of the Social and Somatic Organism* (London, 1938), 26.
22. Ibid., 84, 165, 166. See also Philip Conford, *The Origins of the Organic Movement* (Edinburgh, 2001), 187–88.
23. On which see Maria Bucur, *Eugenics and Modernization in Interwar Romania* (Pittsburgh, PA, 2002), especially chap. 3.
24. Peter Holquist, "To Count, to Extract, and to Exterminate: Population Statistics and Population Politics in Late Imperial and Soviet Russia," in *A State of Nations: Empire and Nation-Making in the Age of Lenin and Stalin*, ed. Ronald Grigor Suny and Terry Martin (New York, 2001), 124, 133.
25. See the essays in the special issue of *Paragraph* 25, no. 2 (2002), ed. Brian Dillon, devoted to Agamben.
26. Ben Agger, "The Dialectic of Desire: The Holocaust, Monopoly Capitalism and Radical Anamnesis," *Dialectical Anthropology* 8, nos. 1–2 (1981): 76. It is important to note that Agger goes on—dialectically—to propose a view of desire that resists, through remembrance, this totalizing aspect of fascism.
27. Dan Diner, "Historical Experience and Cognition: Juxtaposing Perspectives on National Socialism," in *Beyond the Conceivable: Studies on Germany, Nazism, and the Holocaust* (Berkeley, CA, 2000), 169.
28. Raul Hilberg, *The Destruction of the European Jews*, 3 vols., rev. ed. (New York, 1985), 3:1187.
29. Hans Joas, *War and Modernity* (Cambridge, 2003), 198n16.
30. Edward Ross Dickinson, "Biopolitics, Fascism, Democracy: Some Reflections on Our Discourse About 'Modernity,'" *Central European History* 37, no. 1 (2004): 25.
31. Dominick LaCapra, *Writing History, Writing Trauma* (Baltimore, MD, 2001), 128n14. For a discussion see Florin Lobont and Dan Stone, "Modernization and Antisemitism in Romania,'" *Revista de psihologie aplicată* (Timişoara) 4, no. 2 (2002): 103–14.
32. LaCapra, *Writing History, Writing Trauma*, 165.
33. Agger, "Dialectic," 78.
34. See my discussion of Collingwood, Borkenau, and Kolnai in *Responses to Nazism in Britain, 1933–1939: Before War and Holocaust* (Basingstoke, UK, 2003), chap. 1. See

also Richard Stivers, *Technology as Magic: The Triumph of the Irrational* (London, 2000).

35. See my "Nazism as Modern Magic: The Political Anthropology of Bronislaw Malinowski," *History and Anthropology* 14, no. 3 (2003): 203–18.
36. Cf. my "Genocide as Transgression," *European Journal of Social Theory* 7, no. 1 (2004): 45–65.
37. Foucault, *The History of Sexuality*, 1: 146.
38. Ian Hacking, *The Taming of Chance* (Cambridge, 1990), 22; Götz Aly and Karl Heinz Roth, *Die restlose Erfassung: Volkszählen, Identifizieren, Aussondern im Nationalsozialismus* (Frankfurt am Main, 2000). See also Holquist, "To Count"; Eric D. Weitz, "Racial Politics without the Concept of Race: Reevaluating Soviet Ethnic and National Purges," *Slavic Review* 61, no. 1 (2002): 1–29. Cf. Isabel Heinemann, *"Rasse, Siedlung, deutsches Blut": Das Rasse- und Siedlungshauptamt der SS und die rassenpolitische Neuordnung Europas* (Göttingen, 2003) for the SS's race experts.
39. Léon Poliakov, *Harvest of Hate* (London, 1956), 286.
40. Norbert Elias, *The Germans: Power Struggles and the Development of Habitus in the Nineteenth and Twentieth Centuries* (Oxford, 1996), 303, cited in Eric Dunning and Stephen Mennell, "Elias on Germany, Nazism and the Holocaust: On the Balance between 'Civilizing' and 'Decivilizing' Trends in the Social Development of Western Europe," *British Journal of Sociology* 49, no. 3 (1998): 342. Orig: Elias, *Studien über die Deutschen: Machtkämpfe und Habitusentwicklung im 19. und 20. Jahrhundert* (Frankfurt am Main, 1994), 395.
41. Elias, *The Germans*, 228, cited in Dunning and Mennell, "Elias on Germany," 351; *Studien über die Deutschen*, 299.
42. I have dealt with this elsewhere: "The Historiography of Genocide: Beyond 'Uniqueness' and Ethnic Competition," *Rethinking History* 8, no. 1 (2004): 127–42.
43. For an excellent discussion of this problem see Robert M. Hayden, "Schindler's Fate: Genocide, Ethnic Cleansing, and Population Transfers," *Slavic Review* 55, no. 4 (1996): 727–48.
44. See Michael C. Mbabuike and Anna Marie Evans, "Other Victims of the Holocaust," *Dialectical Anthropology* 25, no. 1 (2000): 1–25; Enzo Traverso, *The Origins of Nazi Violence*, trans. Janet Lloyd (New York, 2003); Mark Levene, *Genocide in the Modern Age. Vol. 1: The Coming of Genocide* (London, 2005).
45. For example, Alison Palmer, *Colonial Genocide* (Adelaide, 2000); Mike Davis, *Late Victorian Holocausts: El Niño Famines and the Making of the Third World* (London, 2001); A. Dirk Moses, ed., *Genocide and Settler Society: Frontier Violence and Stolen Indigenous Children in Australian History* (Oxford, 2004); A. Dirk Moses and Dan Stone, eds., *Colonial Genocide*, special issue of *Patterns of Prejudice* 39, no. 2 (2005).
46. K.-M. Mallmann, Volker Rieß, and Wolfram Pyta, eds., *Deutscher Osten 1939–1945* (Darmstadt, 2003); Michael Burleigh, *Germany Turns Eastwards: A Study of* Ostforschung *in the Third Reich*, 2nd ed. (London, 2002); Götz Aly, *Macht-Geist-Wahn: Kontinuitäten deutschen Denkens* (Frankfurt am Main, 1999).
47. Andrew Zimmerman, *Anthropology and Antihumanism in Imperial Germany* (Chicago, 2001), 245. See also Jürgen Zimmerer and Joachim Zeller, eds., *Völkermord in Deutsch-Südwestafrika: Der Kolonialkrieg 1904–1908 in Namibia und seine Folgen* (Berlin, 2003); Jürgen Zimmerer, *Deutsche Herrschaft über Afrikaner: Staatliche Machtanspruch und Wirklichkeit im kolonialen Namibia*, 3rd ed. (Munster, 2003); Jan-Bart Gewald, *Herero Heroes: A Socio-Political History of the Herero of Namibia 1890–1923* (Oxford, 1999); Isabel V. Hull, "Military Culture and the Production of

'Final Solutions' in the Colonies: The Example of Wilhelminian Germany," in *The Specter of Genocide: Mass Murder in Historical Perspective*, eds. Robert Gellately and Ben Kiernan (Cambridge, 2003), 141–62; Henrik Lundtofte, "'I Believe That the Nation as Such Must Be Annihilated': Radicalization of the German Suppression of the Herero Rising," in *Genocide: Cases, Comparisons and Contemporary Debates*, ed. Steven L. B. Jensen (Copenhagen, 2003), 15–53; Tilman Dedering, "'A Certain Rigorous Treatment of All Parts of the Nation': The Annihilation of the Herero in German South West Africa, 1904," in *The Massacre in History*, ed. Mark Levene and Penny Roberts (Oxford, 1999), 205–22; Helmut Walser Smith, "The Logic of Colonial Violence: Germany in Southwest Africa (1904–1907); the United States in the Philippines (1899–1902)," in *German and American Nationalism: A Comparative Perspective*, ed. Hartmut Lehmann and Hermann Wellenreuther (Oxford, 1999), 205–31; Dan Stone, "White Men with Low Moral Standards? German Anthropology and the Herero Genocide," *Patterns of Prejudice* 35, no. 2 (2001): 33–45. More broadly on the change in German anthropology from liberal to racist, see H. Glenn Penny and Matti Bunzl, eds., *Worldly Provincialism: German Anthropology in the Age of Empire* (Ann Arbor, MI, 2003).

48. Cited in Richard Weikart, *From Darwin to Hitler: Evolutionary Ethics, Eugenics, and Racism in Germany* (Basingstoke, UK, 2004), 8.
49. Adolf Hitler, *Mein Kampf*, trans. Ralph Manheim (London, 1984), 598, translation slightly modified.
50. Jacques Maritain, *Anti-Semitism* (London, 1939), 4.
51. Fred Weinstein, *The Dynamics of Nazism: Leadership, Ideology, and the Holocaust* (New York, 1980), 128f.; cf. Brett R. Wheeler, "Antisemitism as Distorted Politics: Adorno on the Public Sphere," *Jewish Social Studies*, n.s. 7, 2 (2001): 114–48.
52. Weinstein, *Dynamics*, 133. Weinstein provides many of the necessary quotations from Hitler and other leading Nazis to back up this claim.
53. Ibid., 146. The kind of "fantasy thinking" I have in mind here is what Saul Friedländer calls "redemptive anti-Semitism." See his *Nazi Germany and the Jews. Vol. 1: The Years of Persecution 1933–39* (London, 1997), chapter 3.
54. Milan L. Hauner, "A German Racial Revolution?" *Journal of Contemporary History* 19, no. 4 (1984): 676. See also the essays in James Kaye and Bo Stråth, eds., *Enlightenment and Genocide: Contradictions of Modernity* (Brussels, 2000), and on SS "education," Jürgen Matthäus et al., *Ausbildungsziel Judenmord? "Weltanschauliche Erziehung" von SS, Polizei und Waffen-SS im Rahmen der "Endlösung"* (Frankfurt am Main, 2003).
55. Hauner, "A German Racial Revolution?" 677, 679. See also Otto Dov Kulka, "The Critique of Judaism in Modern European Thought: Genuine Factors and Demonic Perceptions"; Saul Friedländer, "'Europe's Inner Demons': The 'Other' as Threat in Early Twentieth-Century European Culture"; and Philippe Burrin, "Nazi Antisemitism: Animalization and Demonization," all in *Demonizing the Other: Antisemitism, Racism and Xenophobia*, ed. Robert S. Wistrich (Amsterdam, 1999), 196–209, 210–22, 223–35; Saul Friedländer, "Ideology and Extermination: The Immediate Origins of the 'Final Solution,'" in *Catastrophe and Meaning: The Holocaust and the Twentieth Century*, ed. Moishe Postone and Eric Santner (Chicago, 2003), 17–33; Claudia Koonz, *The Nazi Conscience* (Cambridge, MA, 2003); Uriel Tal, *Religion, Politics and Ideology in the Third Reich: Selected Essays* (London, 2004).
56. Mark Mazower, *Dark Continent: Europe's Twentieth Century* (London, 1998), 184, cf. 73. See also Jürgen Zimmerer, "Colonialism and the Holocaust: Towards an Archaeology of Genocide," in A. Dirk Moses, ed., *Genocide and Settler Society*, 68, for

the argument that it is "redemptive antisemitism" that distinguishes the Holocaust from colonial genocides.

57. Dan Stone, "Georges Bataille and the Interpretation of the Holocaust," in *Theoretical Interpretations of the Holocaust*, ed. Dan Stone (Amsterdam, 2001), 79–101; Stone, "Modernity and Violence: Theoretical Reflections on the *Einsatzgruppen*," *Journal of Genocide Research* 1, no. 3 (1999): 367–78.
58. See also Theodor W. Adorno and Max Horkheimer, *Dialectic of Enlightenment*, trans. John Cumming, 2nd ed. (London, 1986).
59. Ronald Aronson, "Social Madness," in *Genocide and the Modern Age: Etiology and Case Studies of Mass Death*, ed. Isidor Wallimann and Michael N. Dobkowski, 2nd ed. (Syracuse, NY, 2000), 125–41. See also Mark Levene, "Battling Demons or Banal Exterminism? Apocalypse and Statecraft in Modern Mass Murder," *Human Rights Review* 3, no. 1 (2004): 67–81.

– Section II –

Empire, Colonization, and Genocide

– *Chapter 8* –

EMPIRES, NATIVE PEOPLES, AND GENOCIDE

Mark Levene

Arguing a Case and Doubtless Muddying the Water

Any serious attempt to understand genocide in its broadest dimensions across time and space cannot but involve questions about the origins of violence.[1] This, however, might lead to a broader question still, one arguably encapsulated in the recent plea by A. Dirk Moses that scholars in the field need to "try to imagine genocides of modernity as part of a single process rather than merely in comparative (and competitive) terms."[2] Moses's point is an extremely provocative one, not least because in posing that there might be *a single process,* he almost at one fell swoop challenges an overriding wisdom that has informed the basic working assumptions of genocide studies to date. Certainly, the field is increasingly interested to compare and contrast different genocides; yet each ultimately is nearly always treated as if it were essentially an aberration set against a normative nongenocidal model—which, on closer inspection, turns out to be the liberal democracies of the West, from which the vast majority of genocide scholars happen to hail. The fact that in most of modern and certainly all of contemporary history the West has provided the dominant, indeed hegemonic economic and political framework within which all other polities and societies throughout the world have had to operate, and that this might have some bearing on the sequence and indeed persistence of genocide seems to have been repeatedly—one might opine conveniently—overlooked.

Is genocide aberrant, or is what we are actually considering part of a broader structural dysfunction? To put both thesis and antithesis more roundly, are the genocides committed in the modern world the product of some oddity, whether ideological, cultural, structural or whatever, which disposes or even predisposes particular state-societies towards this very singular outcome and thus entirely against the grain of what is taken to be the normative universe of the ordered, civilized, legally constituted international system of states; or is it actually within that system itself and the historic struggles and interrelationships out of which it emerged that we ought to search for our primary, first cause?

My own position within this debate is unequivocal. Indeed, my own starting point for this contribution would be to posit that if we truly wish to see the forest for the trees, then modern cases of genocide or suspected genocide cannot be isolated in a series of self-contained, or even purely comparative boxes. Nor can they be treated in either limited chronological or spatial contexts. They have to be seen and hence understood within the broadest terms of world-historical reference. Certainly such an argument neither, on the one hand, refutes autonomous factors of environment, culture, and society that are as fundamental to any treatment as are issues of contingency. Nor, on the other, does it start out from an assumption that genocides, including those committed within imperial contexts primarily against indigenous peoples, are functionally inevitable, predetermined, or blanket by-products of the states from which they emanate. What instead this contribution seeks to demonstrate is that a widely geographically dispersed incidence of such exterminatory events on the broad world stage, from the early seventeenth century through to the 1914 watershed, cannot be treated simply as a series of coincidences. Rather, in their totality, they suggest a series of massive destabilizations of human communities and their historic relationships to one another. In turn, moreover, they act as critical harbingers of the end of the premodern world—which paradoxically included a previously "normative" system of self-contained traditional "world empires"—in favor of the crystallization of a global community and political economy of nation-states.[3]

But if this proposition is correct and hence genocide is intrinsic to the gestation of our contemporary international system, this can only reinforce the degree to which it is at deviance from some of the most authoritative comparative readings of the phenomenon to date. For instance, for a number of scholars, genocide not only essentially crystallizes in the twentieth century but also, moreover, primarily within a European or near-European context before it then takes off in a post-1945, third world, postcolonial one. The issues at stake thus become not about empire or colonial settlement as such, but rather are bound up with the onset of modernity and its relationship to the state—most particularly in the form of what are often represented as quite specific utopian projects to engineer society in favor of some ideological totalitarianism and/or toward some ethnic or racial dominance, if not outright homogenization.[4]

This is not to propose that these commentators do not have their own singular approaches to the phenomenon. But by both blocking out the significance of its pre-twentieth-century occurrence and indeed its persistent (though not exclusively) nonmetropolitan enactment, the seminal relationship between genocide, empire, and colonialism is actually implicitly marginalized in these interpretations. Most colonial genocide predated 1914. Spatially, as one would expect, moreover, these were not metropolitan events but ones that took place on imperial or colonial peripheries. To be sure, genocides did take place also in metropolitan cores. The events in the Vendée in 1793/94 was one such event of seminal significance in the emergence of modern genocide. But the Vendée was also quite singular. Nothing remotely comparable happened again, at least in western or central Europe, until the twentieth century.[5]

By contrast, imperial genocides committed by metropolitan states in colonial environs were a notable and sometimes quite endemic feature of the period between the French Revolution and the First World War. Again, we are faced with an interesting but perplexing conundrum: The critical protagonists involved, directly or indirectly, in the explosion of exterminatory assaults on native peoples at colonial peripheries were indeed the builders of modern, avant-garde, metropolitan nation-states. However, they committed these genocides *not* in their nation-state manifestation but in their imperial one.

How should we approach this issue? Hannah Arendt was the first to seriously speculate upon the relationship,[6] and then, arguably both rather unevenly and without notably resolving it.[7] The time is now ripe for reconsideration of the matter. The work of historians such as Anthony Pagden, Niall Ferguson, Dominic Lieven, and others[8] suggest that the study of the concept and practice of empire is both acceptable and indeed respectable in a way that it was not in the aftermath of Western empire three, or even two decades ago. Paradoxically, then, resuscitated interest from different quarters in the subject of empires suggests not just opportunities, but perhaps even an urgent need for fresh historical approaches that seek to explore how events at what we think of as the peripheries of an evolving metropolitan-dominated world not only provided integral signposts to genocides that were to later occur at its heart, but even perhaps a clue as to the ongoing dysfunctionality of our resulting globalized political economy. Major treatments of genocide, however, in a colonial-cum-imperial context—insofar as they exist—do not make this task particularly easy. Two basic trajectories present themselves. The first focuses on single events such as the destruction of the Herero (1904/5) as if these were essentially aberrations at odds with the main thrust of modern imperialism.[9] The second treats specifically Western conquest as an almost unmitigated and relentless history of genocidal violence perpetrated against indigenous peoples, a charge that in recent years has become increasingly amplified by polemical disputes with Holocaust-centric scholars.[10]

The Scylla and Charybdis aspect of these approaches in itself requires some brief commentary. With regard to the latter approach, certainly, empires cannot be created or sustained without a politico-military supremacy emanating from a single source. However, equally, if empires remained inherently genocidal, they would have no subject populations. Indeed, the concept of empire assumes populations as markets for metropolitan goods, and/or as a subservient labor source. Instrumental rationality would seem to dictate that while exploitation, even hyperexploitation (meaning mass suffering and mass death), might be norms of empires, "divide and rule" rather than conscious population extermination is the logical direction by which such polities sustain themselves. Thus, I take it as a basic premise here that "advancing" Western maritime empires—in contradistinction to the position taken by Jean-Paul Sartre, or more recently Sven Lindqvist[11]—were neither founded on nor otherwise characterized by an inherent propensity towards genocide. Similarly, the ongoing multiethnicity of "retreating" world empires right through to 1914 would also seem to negate this verdict.

Yet the multiplicity and range of exterminatory assaults on native people in the pre-1914 imperial context would equally invite attention. Imperial genocide repeatedly and persistently occurred in this fin-de-siècle record even where there was no one single obvious ideological predisposition in this direction. The remainder of this consciously schematic and macrohistorical synopsis from c. 1600 to 1914 thus aims to outline the broad historical dimensions and contours as well as geographical range of such assaults, offer pointers to their interconnectedness, and present brief concluding remarks on their causation.

A final word on our usage of the term "empire." It is easy enough to consider nineteenth-century Britain, France, or Germany as empires, albeit notably in the former case often subcontracting its powers to chartered companies or self-governing colonial administrations. The US equally in its post-1898 acquisitions is clearly imperial. But what then of its transcontinental surge beginning a century earlier? Should we see this phase as the actions of an autonomous nation builder or simply as an extension of British empire building in its North American theater? By the same token, is Argentina in the same category, a nation operating in its own right post-1816 independence, or a more forceful and vigorous "son of Hispanic imperial fathers"? There are only complex answers, I suspect, to these questions—but for my purposes, both examples will fall under the empire-building umbrella just as will the case of Antipodean colonial administrations whose self-determination remained firmly under the aegis of the British crown.

Before we get too focused on these types of cases, however, we forget at our peril that such essentially maritime-based empires are extraordinary late-comers on the historical scene, and that while in the nineteenth century they are increasingly the dominant ones, there remain on the stage four major continental "world empires"—the Qing, Ottoman, Romanov, and Habsburg (albeit in their twilight existence)—which are representatives of a much more traditional imperial norm. Then there is the non-Western empire building of Shaka and other Bantu conquerors in southern Africa.[12] If, in repeating a general Western historical mantra that the primary motor in the creation of a globalized political economy is the rise of West itself, the genocides with which I am concerned here are as much the indirect result of the West's destabilization of the old "world empires," as they struggled to reposition themselves in this new international framework, as they are the direct results of Western avant-garde imperial building through their penetration and control of discrete regions around the globe. As a general rule, by this juncture the general case for imperial genocide as a result of Western diffusion or, put less charitably, global dysfunction is overwhelming.

Plotting trajectories

Let me then propose three basic trajectories or tendencies in modern imperial genocide that I will then delineate further:

1. Tendencies towards direct European settlement in what I will call "the 3 As"—the (north) Americas, Argentina, and the Antipodes—each of which produced a sequence of "frontier genocides" at notable moments in colonial expansion from c.1600 to the closing of their respective frontiers, arguably completed in all three regions by the 1890s (two decades later in Queensland). While the origins of these imperial responses can be traced back to the consolidation of states in their European contexts, the commonality between aspects of genocide in their diverse colonial settings is also noteworthy.
2. A significant bunching of genocidal or subgenocidal events in the 1880–1910 period—with incidents widely spread across nominally conquered or subdued regions of Africa, the Philippines, the Dutch East Indies, and elsewhere—all of which point to a crisis of the advancing Western empires at their apparent apotheosis.
3. By contrast, a further series of genocides or subgenocides perpetrated by the historic but relatively speaking "retreating" world empires: China, Russia, the Ottoman Empire, and Austria-Hungary in the 1860–1915 period—each one, it should be added, still strongly imbued with its own sense of religiously ordained legitimacy and "world" mission. Each episode also

> strongly suggests an imperial effort to cohere and consolidate frontiers in response to the impact of a global Western hegemony, and with once again the crisis efforts of the imperial state leading to collisions with diverse, culturally and religiously very different peoples either on their frontiers or in other new national entities on their imperial peripheries.

Before I develop these trajectories further, however, let me add a rider that, arguably, is particularly pertinent and relevant with regard to our "retreating empires" category. Imperial or colonial genocides, almost by definition, are enacted at the geographical periphery of their respective "metropolitan" states. Remoteness, however, has not ultimately prevented research on the elimination of the Aboriginal tribes of Tasmania or native tribes in California being at least to a degree disseminated to a broader public. The problem for the peoples, say, of Sinkiang or the Caucasus, however, is not only one of geographical obscurity. It is also a question of being located at the extreme margins of a dominant Eurocentric history, to the point of being seriously off any Western cognitive map. Take an example: In the far northwestern reaches of Sinkiang, in the late 1750s, the Mongolian Dzungar tribe some 600,000 in number was physically annihilated by the Qing. The vast majority of those Dzungars who were not directly slaughtered succumbed to starvation and epidemic.[13] In terms of our overall schema, this makes this event not just an extremely important prequel to our third, "retreating empires" trajectory. It is also arguably the eighteenth century genocide par excellence. Yet because little information about the event was recorded at the time, including any memoirs of survivors, there is a very major lacuna in our basic knowledge of the event. The problem, however, is not simply one of a lack of information recovery because the victims were illiterate nomads or because the perpetrators failed to offer a detailed inventory of their extermination. One can find *some* details of the fate of the Dzungars in specialist Russian and Chinese monographs. Rather, the issue is one of what Michel-Rolph Trouillot would call "the production of history."[14] The Dzungar extermination might deserve to be treated as seminal. However, because it has no place—or indeed *value*—within a Western frame of reference, even arguably a genocide-focused one, its marginalization, or more accurately mental obliteration down a giant memory hole, is likely to be perpetuated into the foreseeable future.

The "3 As"

The "3As" arena in the Americas and Antipodes closely follows the contours of Alfred Crosby's geographical concept of neo-Europes.[15] The regions in questions thus are those characterized not just by conquest, but by temperate climatic and agricultural conditions that enabled settlement of large numbers of northern- and western-European incomers. While the French, Spanish, and many other Europeans were involved in this grand colonizing project, not only in two out of our three regions did settlers from British Isles backgrounds come to predominate, but equally significantly under the aegis of "Anglo" political administrations. Equally significantly, and partly antagonistic to Crosby's overall thesis, these regions were also characterized by relatively small native populations—compared, that is, with the number of incomers—who, effects of epidemiological devastation as well as technological disadvantage notwithstanding, were certainly demographically overwhelmed by the sheer weight of the latter and/or their ovine or bovine appendages.[16]

This is not to endorse entirely false assumptions that the native populations in question were either insignificant in number or did not know how to manage or indeed maximize the resource potential of their respective environments.[17] Notions of *vacuum domicilium* or *territorium* or *(res) nullius* were entirely the sophistries of the colonizers.[18] Their repeated invocation, however, highlights a further defining feature of this trajectory: the colonizers' intent was not just to own, but to take direct possession of the totality of the land and its resources for their own increasingly market-dominated interest. Thus, unlike the dominant Iberian pattern of conquest in the central and southern Americas, where the colonizers sought to assimilate and acculturate the indigenous populations (albeit by massive and bloody coercion), in the case of the "3 As," the process was one of conscious disgorgement of the natives with a view to their supersession either by the colonizers themselves or their great stocks of domesticated animals. This pattern had already begun on the "Anglo" colonial frontier in Ireland, arguably extending this sequence back to the late 1500s.[19] As the campaigns to remove the native populations of the Gaeltacht, that is, of the Scottish Highlands, as well as the island of Ireland, were ongoing into the nineteenth century, this also arguably provides for a critical transoceanic linkage between genocidal events in the "3 As" and the margins of Europe.

Indeed, the nature of close Anglo-Scottish settlement in the Gaeltacht might appear superficially to provide us with a strongly functional explanation for both genocide here and in the "3 As." Settlers want land—natives resist; outcome—annihilation. Yet this is not only a one-dimensional portrayal of events in the Gaeltacht, where the process of supersession was never comprehensively enacted despite three hundred years of trying—even in the "3 As," where it was, the exterminatory consequences are similarly very far from continuous or across the board. Rather, in all three regions, it is most obviously what Moses has characterized as "genocidal moments,"[20] specifically with regard to the consolidation of a retreating native frontier within the Australian imperial domain, which offers the best overarching framework for the killing sequence. The plot in Australia is rather clear: Tasmania in the 1820s; the northeastern corner of New South Wales in the late 1830s; the Darling Downs and Upper Brisbane valley in the 1840s; and central and then northern Queensland in succeeding decades.[21] What makes the north Americas significantly different is the much longer time span in the sequence: the first eastern seaboard genocidal moments taking place the 1620s and 1630s, and the last in the Great Plains not for another quarter of a millennium.[22] By contrast, again, a specifically independent Argentinean program of extermination of the Araucanian Indians is telescoped practically into a fifty-year period.[23]

Treating any or all of this purely as a functional by-product of native-settler encounter, however, will not suffice. Genocide is a phenomenon associated with the state. Yet the paradox of the matter is that neither official US, nor colonial Australian, or even Argentinean policy was founded on one of extermination of native peoples per se, but rather of exclusion, or especially latterly, incorporation, of such peoples—forcible where necessary—into the dominant culture. This aspect certainly amounts to a yawning gap between principle and practice, but the fact that in no case was the legal principle entirely abandoned must itself throw attention not just on the searing contradiction between the developmental demands of expansion and misplaced humanitarian obligation, but also on the native response.[24] To put it bluntly, the genocidal potential implicit in frontier encounters thus required and indeed revolved around a very particular dynamic: on the one hand, the refusal of the colonizing state to concede that there might be some limit or restraint on its control and consolidation of a territorial resource—as also staked out and thus treated as an absolute through European concepts of sovereignty—on the other, native unwillingness, not to say obduracy, to play according to the white man's rules, thereby *successfully* acting as an inertial drag where not a serious impediment on that very colonizing agenda.

Outcomes of genocide or subgenocide, in short, in these cases, were not primarily the result of cultural antipathy towards natives, or even racism per se, though these undoubtedly were critical contributory factors. They were because the natives did not do what they were required to do according to the colonizing script—namely give way, preferably by disappearing into the ether. The series of "genocidal moments" in Australia may often have been more localized and widely dispersed than some of the more heavy-duty US federal efforts, for instance, to sweep practically all the remaining native peoples from the eastern seaboard, as in the early 1830s,[25] or for that matter the simultaneous efforts on the Argentine pampas to literally expunge the Araucanian peoples. But there again, some obviously formulaic predetermination to these encounters would be to miss the dialectical nature of each separate confrontation. Each was contingent on the nature and evolution of the crisis itself. It might involve very localized, almost entirely unreported efforts of a tribe acting on their volition, to resist encroachment as in the case of the Yuki in California in the 1850s[26]; it might involve the very public and legal obstructions placed by the Cherokees in the US federal courts to the state of Georgia's efforts to expropriate their lands thirty years earlier[27]; or for that matter, the seriously pan-tribal efforts associated with Pontiac in the Great Lakes region nearly three-quarters of a century before.[28] In each case, however, the brake each placed on the colonizing project precipitated, in somewhat different ways and to different degrees, explosions of colonizer exterminatory overkill.

Certainly, the independent interests or behavior of "frontier" settlers themselves (as opposed to "states") could be a major factor in these equations; one of the most problematic aspects of genocide in the Americans and Antipodes being the role of equally displaced, traumatized, and often thoroughly brutalized Gaelic-speaking Scots and Irish, as well Presbyterian Scots-Irish as primary actors in these confrontations.[29] Equally, the very fact of displacement of often seasonally perambulating peoples from their traditional habitus, thus forcing them into increasingly diminished and degraded as well as unfamiliar spaces (usually alongside other displaced native tribes), poses the degree to which the resulting competition for scarce resources produced black on black, or red on red, as well as simply white on red, or black genocide.[30]

This still leaves some examples where the ensuing dynamics do not necessarily materialize as something we can specifically denote as genocide. New Zealand is one unusual arena, for instance, where an undoubted and extremely unforgiving mid-nineteenth-century military encounter between Maori and Pakeha (i.e., whites) may have been sufficiently symmetrical for long enough—thus paradoxically posing a tribute to Maori martial attributes and military innovation—to actually prevent a wholesale genocidal onslaught against them.[31] By comparison, the virulence of native insurrection in the late 1870s against close and rapid French settlement in New Caledonia proved insufficient to an outcome much more in keeping with "Anglo" genocides in the Americas,[32] though again interestingly at some variance with the general (but by no means unblemished) accommodationist thrust of French/native encounters on that same continent in previous centuries.[33]

If the inference from this grouping of genocides is that the nature and evolution of local social and cultural relationships, not to say the larger imperatives of a state's developmental agenda, offer the potential either for outright violence or an alternative—however fragile—for long-term coexistence, our second grouping of cases offers a much more chronologically straightjacketed but geographically dispersed sequence of genocidal outcomes.

Colonial Genocide at Fin-de-Siècle

This sequence is firmly situated not in the territories of the first maritime empires and their successor states, but rather within the new wave of Western imperial advance, in Africa, Asia, and the Pacific at fin-de-siècle. Settlement is not thus the primary issue in these cases—though certainly it is a factor in some of the genocides, most notably the one that is the focus of most current research, namely, that committed against the Herero, and to a slightly lesser extent against the Nama peoples in South West Africa between 1904 and 1906.[34] The fact that this is a genocide committed by Germans thirty years before the advent of the Nazi regime, and with the inference of some colonial transmission belt from one to the other, seems to be a major factor in the research equation. Interestingly, however, in terms of death toll this is not the nadir of German colonial assaults on native peoples in this period. While by 1906, something approaching 100,000 inhabitants[35]—an estimated sixty percent of the colony's central and southern population—had perished as a direct or indirect result of the German military quelling of the insurrections, the destruction of the pan-tribal Maji-Maji revolt in German East Africa in 1906/7, primarily though military-induced famine, led to a fatality rate of at least two to three times this number, including three-quarters of the Pangwa, and half the Matumbi and Vidunda peoples.[36]

Even then, narrowing the examination to these and other Wilhelmine colonial atrocities would fail to take into account a broader picture of very similar assaults by other imperial parties at fin-de-siècle. These would certainly include:

1. The military extirpation of the Umvukela and Chimurenga revolts in British-controlled Rhodesia 1896/7, in the latter case especially evincing aspects markedly similar to the German destruction of the Herero and Nama peoples.[37]
2. The Dutch campaign against Aceh's insurgent effort to resist incorporation into the Dutch East Indies, a military campaign culminating in a massive counterinsurgency operation by the Dutch commander, van Daalen, against the entire population.[38]
3. The Japanese extirpation of the peasant Tonghak rebellion in Korea's southern Cholla region in the mid-1890s, en route to its seizure of the entire Korean peninsula and in which the anti-Tonghak operation has been described as "a systematic extermination of the civilian base."[39]

4. The extirpation of resistance to the American conquest of the Philippines—centered in South West Luzon—in the early 1900s, with military-induced famine against the entire support population as the chosen strategy. The resulting war-related deaths, primarily through disease and starvation, have been conservatively estimated at 200,000; other writers, however, argue that out of a total Filipino population of 7 million, the fatalities actually amounted to one in seven.[40]

Broadened out somewhat one might wish to add a series of other events that also carry similar, strongly genocidal attributes. These include the British extirpation of the Islamicist Mahdiyya regime in the Sudan in the late 1890s, again using famine as the chosen method;[41] the physical annihilation of the religiously inspired Canudos community in Brazil's Bahia province in this same period, by direct military assault;[42] the orgy of massacres carried out by the international expedition sent to quell the Chinese Boxer uprising in 1900;[43] and the *reconcentrado* system set up by General Weyler to starve out and defeat the Cuban insurgency against Spanish overlordship in 1897.[44] One might even include, in a more limited sense, the British application of a similar form of mass population detention in order to defeat the Boer guerrilla struggle fought from the veld between 1900 and 1902.[45]

Objectively speaking, one might wish to argue that none of the cases, barring possibly the Herero annihilation, should really be treated as "genocide" per se because there was no "intent" involved. On this score, indeed, one might even wish to question the Herero case, as there is no evidence of a German military blueprint at the outset to exterminate them. Rather, it developed and radicalized in the course of the conflict.[46] Yet, this is in fact the unifying factor in all these cases. As with the "3 As," so here again the extent and tenacity of native resistance—blocking off in the process an assumed imperial developmental trajectory—massively ratcheted up the contours of violence, ultimately producing imperial reactions that were massively disproportionate to the purely military task in hand.

The synchronicity of these events also sheds further light on their place within a broader macrohistory. In each case, native insurrection was undoubtedly desperate, often notably millenarian, and certainly fought as a last-ditch effort. In each case, it could only be thus, given the entirely asymmetrical terms of the military encounter. Yet in each case, it was exactly these attributes on the part of the resisters that knocked their opponents so off balance, denting in the process broader national prestige and at a juncture when the imperial self-image was so obviously one of the carriers of some *mission civilisatrice*. Poor, benighted—and certainly racially inferior—natives were required to be dutifully grateful and passive in the face of conquest, not to physically confront or challenge it. Somewhere in the interstices between the hubris and the ignominious reality, the military machines of slighted states lurched into massive, sustained, and blanket retaliation.

Why this happened with some frequency at this fin-de-siècle moment arguably also tells use something of broader relevance. Read Mike Davis's *Late Victorian Holocausts*, and it is clear that the foreclosing of traditional regional and localized economies from c. 1876–1905 in favor of a global market created, determined, and regulated according to the Western laissez-faire doctrine produced an almost unimaginable scale of "Third World" deaths.[47] It ought to remind us that structural, let alone exterminatory violence need not necessarily be preceded by the epithet *genocidal*. Interestingly, one region where the results were particularly extreme falls outside both Davis's study and the examples cited here. The economic asset stripping of the ivory and rubber wealth of the Congo, at the behest of Leopold II's internationally recognized "free-trade" [*sic*] regime, produced a demographic catastrophe far in excess of any murderous military assault elsewhere at fin-de-siècle. True, there were widespread atrocities involving direct punitive raids on communities who resisted the coercive labor demands of the rubber companies. Most mass death, however, occurred without either genocidal intent or even necessarily the dialectic of resistance and retaliation. Hyperexploitation, not genocide per se, was the cause of the immiseration and collapse of the Congo basin population in a matter of decades, from an estimated twenty million to possibly only half that number.[48]

What, however, does link the structural and exploitative violence of this type to the direct exterminatory massacres we are more concerned with here is the broad submergence of native peoples' traditional habitus into an emerging, integrated, Western-dominated world economy. In either case, the consequent dislocation and degradation of peoples' lives was total and irrevocable. Genocides, however, were more likely to occur where populations physically resisted the attempt at integration, that is, sufficiently effective to put a spanner in the works of imperial agendas; insufficiently enough—except in exceptional cases such as the Abyssinian defeat of the Italians at Adowa in 1896[49] (thereby mirroring the Maori achievement in the preceding half-century and more)—to actually prevent exterminatory retaliation.

This certainly leaves a handful of cases that neither chronologically fit neatly into this pattern, nor, for that matter, spatially into that of the "3 As." Settlement on the neo-European, market-orientated model *is*, for instance, the primary motor in French genocidal responses to repeated native resistance to the incorporation of Algeria into metropolitan France in the 1840s, and again in the 1870s.[50] Similarly, Italian efforts to consolidate

Cyrenaica, further along the African coast, in the twenty-year period after attempted occupation in 1911—with a view to filling it with southern Italian peasants—culminated in the incarceration of almost its entire Bedouin hill country population into concentration camps, in an attempt to flush out and exterminate the ongoing resistance to occupation led by the Islamic Sanusi order. At least 60,000 and possibly as many as 100,000 of a total regional population of some 225,000 may have died as a result—mostly in this final concentration camp phase from 1928–31.[51]

Significantly, though products of a specifically Western imperial response to native insurrection, there are parallels in these North African cases with our third "retreating empires" sequence, not least in the religious-cum-national dimensions of resistance to encroaching empire.

Retreating "World Empires"

The geographic range of our final genocidal trajectory is firmly Eurasian, and more specifically along what might be described as a tectonic plate across the spine of central Asia, running from Chinese Turkestan (Sinkiang) in the east through the Caucasus and Eastern Anatolia to a final European terminus in the northern Balkans. As in our second sequence, the timescale is relatively telescoped, though here primarily from the second half of the nineteenth century through to the onset of the First World War. Moreover, while the geographical distances as well as chronological spacing make the four episodes of exterminatory violence distinct, they are all closely interlinked. Yet paradoxically, only one of these—the Armenian massacres of 1894–96—is relatively known in the historical landscape, and this primarily not because it is so much recognized as a genocide in its own right, but more as a prequel to the exterminatory destruction of the majority of Ottoman Armenians in 1915/16. It is this latter event that is often referred to not just as the first contemporary genocide but "the template for most of the genocide that followed in the twentieth century."[52] Yet anything between 80,000 and 200,000 Christian Armenians—mostly in Eastern Anatolia—are estimated to have been killed at Ottoman-Muslim state behest in the episode twenty years prior.[53]

If the events of 1894–96 are in partial shade and obscurity, this however is even more the case in our related three additional episodes:

1. The extirpation of a wide swath of Muslim peoples and communities in Kashgaria and other part of western and northern Sinkiang by the Qing empire in the mid-1870s, albeit an event harbingered by the Qing extirpation of the Dzungar more than a century earlier. In the later event the full weight of

imperial retribution fell particularly on the Uighur peoples. The population loss is unclear but is variously estimated in the region of one million.[54]

2. Midway along the tectonic plate, the ongoing struggle by Romanov Russia to wrest control of the northwest Caucasus, itself a critical flank to its consolidation of the Black Sea, notably ratcheted up in the early 1860s with a full-scale assault on its—again—Muslim Circassian tribes. The specific aim as it crystallized in 1864 seems to have been one of total "ethnic cleansing." In practice, this process was carried through by systematic massacre followed by the literal disgorgement of survivors in unseaworthy, disease-ridden vessels across the Black Sea to the Ottoman Empire. One recent estimate has suggested as many as one to one and a half million deaths as a result, or close to half the Circassian population. [55]
3. At the western end of the tectonic plate and at the chronological culmination of all our three trajectories, in 1915/16 the estimated loss of one-quarter of Serbia's 4.5 million largely Orthodox population, with some 800,000 of those casualties noncombatants, in the context of the state's military destruction by its Austro-Hungarian neighbor.[56] This final case is indeed significantly different than the others for being enacted by an imperial state against another sovereign state-society, but *as if it were* a colonial vassal. What is additionally of note is that this attempted annihilation of at least part of the Serbian population has until very recently been treated as a rather subsidiary and unimportant footnote to the supposedly main parameters of the First World War.[57]

Considered overall, however, what is interesting about this grouping—the Serbian case included—is the degree to which each episode involved a retreating "world empire" attempting to cohere and consolidate its boundaries, primarily in order to stay afloat and intact in response to the impact of direct Western penetration and overall Western hegemony. In each, the resulting crisis efforts of Ottoman, Qing, Romanov, and Habsburg respectively, entailed a collision with a native people or peoples either at the empire's historic frontiers and/or a protean national entity at its periphery. What is doubly interesting is the degree to which the actual points of fracture tended to be geographically situated where two or more of these empires found themselves contiguous with one another, or involved in some other form of geo-strategic contestation, with also potentially severe domestic consequences for one or more of the imperial powers.

As one example, the displacement of surviving Circassians as *muhajirs* (Muslim refugees) from the Russian-occupied Caucasus into Ottoman Eastern Anatolia had a profound, amplifying effect on already-stressed Armenian relations with Kurdish and other peoples in the region.[58] Similarly, many of the Circassian number settled by the crisis-ridden Ottoman authorities in Roumelia were specifically and infamously enrolled as *bashibazouks* (paramilitary auxiliaries) in order to commit retaliatory massacres against insurrection-prone Bulgarian and other Balkan Christians, from

1875 onwards.[59] The immediate result was a spiralling cycle of violence in which not only Muslims and Christians committed atrocities and ethnic cleansing against one another, but Russia found a pretext to intervene.[60] By the same token, this rapidly generalizing Ottoman crisis, especially insofar as its remaining European rump of the empire was concerned, brought Austria and Russia into head-on competition for control of the emerging political vacuum, again with further serious ramifications not just for what remained of the Ottoman Empire in Europe, but for its still notably diverse and ethnically mixed populations.[61]

That, of course, brings us geographically and chronologically much closer to a more familiar and not just Eurocentric break point in world history. As the foreign and domestic tensions of "retreating" empires came to hone in, during the summer of 1914, on the specific issue of Serbia's relations with Austria, from our vantage point they also seem to provide a point of intersection both with the emergence onto the world stage of a new wave of nation-states—both before and after the First World War—and the explosion of twentieth-century genocide in a primarily European locale. Significantly, it is also at this same watershed that the old surviving world empires sought to adapt to, alternatively circumvent, or literally break out from the conditions of the post-1918 restatement of Western global dominance—if not necessarily by overtly refashioning themselves as nation-states within an international system of such states, then certainly by throwing off their religiously grounded universalist pretensions and turning themselves into streamlined. homogeneous polities. As a consequence, if before 1914 the old world empires under their "universalist" umbrella had provided the last remnant of an increasingly precarious and diminishing space within which indigenous peoples were able to maintain an economic and social existence, a culture, a religion, often at marked variance from the metropolitan norm, thereafter modernizing state trajectories in all three imperial ranges seemed to offer only the choice between "voluntary" extinction—in other words, cultural genocide[62]—with the helping hand of the state, or, if the natives refused, then unremitting punitive war with the ongoing potential for actual genocide.

Imperial genocide *tout ensemble*

While this trajectory hardly reached its conclusion in 1914, as we have suggested, its ultimate direction was already well on course long before then. This still arguably leaves in the shade the role played by native peoples themselves—perhaps for obvious reasons, given that they were the ones who were the victims of imperial exterminatory violence. Certainly, the onus has to be ultimately on the perpetrators, though, again as we have suggested, a paradox in all our sequences is that circumventing the possibility of extermination seems to have been the official starting point of all our imperial types. Hoping that difficult natives would somehow assimilate, do obeisance to the dominant power, and learn to accept their place within the imperial frame of things—or failing these then magically disappear—remained, for sure, the general aspiration of harassed colonial administrators, very often even in the face of often steadily increasing geostrategic, resource, or colonizing imperatives emanating from the metropolitan center, or from settlers themselves.

However, neither center nor local administration could ever cope with native peoples who refused to play according to the script. Or worse, failed to conduct themselves according to some preconceived one-dimensional type. Whether resiliently local, pan-tribal, or even pan-national, direct physical resistance of native groups to accelerated imperial agendas was almost bound to turn notions of imperial accommodation—always of course on the empire's own terms—into *failed* policies of accommodation and integration. In our final sequence, one might add, the failure could also be treated almost in terms of "a clash of civilisations,"[63] the bonds of religious solidarity for Muslim Uighurs and Circassians, or Apostolic Armenians, providing a potent counterchallenge to notions of religiously-sanctioned imperial peace and order, this factor also playing some small part in the clash between Orthodox Serbia and the self-consciously Catholic Habsburg throne.[64]

Yet the other side of the coin is the degree to which the breakdown of what, at least in some instances, had been exactly such historic long-term accommodations, can be seen as the consequence of something other than simply a one-dimensional imperial dynamic with a particular native group. The exposure of so many North American peoples on the eastern seaboard to the potentiality of genocide arguably reached its zenith in the context of a *global* eighteenth-century contest between British and French empires, a contest most bitterly played out in this particular hemisphere and with the tribes themselves allotted roles as bit players, ripe for expendability when they had served their purpose. Many of the tribes themselves may have been adept at playing off the imperial contestants one against the other, but their very participation in these dangerous games made them all the more exposed when one of the imperial competitors—the French in this instance—were literally removed from the stage.[65] A century later, Shona in British Rhodesia and Armenians in Ottoman Eastern Anatolia found themselves equally vulnerable to extermination, not just because of the domestic contexts in which some of their number challenged their respective imperial masters, but because by then no self-respecting empire could allow its weakness to be demonstrated to its imperial competitors.

By 1914, indeed, the very social Darwinian nature of the new world order made it impossible for any empire, whether British, French, Chinese, or Ottoman, to negotiate with those who had already been ordained as subordinate and inferior. As a result, implicitly if not explicitly, the geopolitical pressures under which all imperial entities were operating ultimately molded and determined each and every one of their actual interactions with native peoples. Moreover, in such an interconnected world—where every state indeed was now also an onlooker on each and every other one else in the system—to have one's imperial sense of place and mission flouted, one's legitimate and by implication civilized and civilizing authority ignored, avoided, even perhaps, in one's worst nightmares, usurped by untutored, illegitimate, and always by implication "savage" natives posed that dread crisis-moment question: what other options exactly were left but a zero-sum solution?

"During the last four or five years the human life and property destroyed by the Aboriginals in the North totals up to a serious amount. . . . settlement on the land and the development of the mineral and other resources of the country have been in a great degree prohibited by the hostility of the blacks with undiminished spirit," opined an 1879 editorial in the leading Queensland paper.[66] The leader hardly needed to spell out what needed to be done. Retrospectively, a distinguished journalist-cum-historian spoke of the Serbs in the run-up to Sarajevo as "a thorough-going nuisance, a nest of violent barbarians whose megalomania would sooner or later meet the punishment it deserved. There had been several occasions when the rest of Europe fully expected to see Austria lash out and wipe Serbia off the map."[67]

Is this the particular and peculiar story of imperial Austria struggling to maintain its place in an increasingly unforgiving world? Or rather of all empires—indeed all states in a globalizing political economy? The imperatives to compete, to make good, and thereby to survive within its supposedly fixed and unnegotiable parameters—all in the name of that thing we call progress—have determined not only that ordinary human beings the world over are caught up in its deadly treadmill, but that alternative paths towards a gentler, more humane, more latitudinarian development continue to be laughed out of court. Perhaps the final word should be with the philosopher, Giorgio Agamben: "In any modern state there exists a point which marks the moment when the decision on life is transformed into a decision of death and when biopolitics becomes thanatopolitics."[68]

Notes

1. Ben Kiernan, "Cambodia: Comparative History and Relative Justice" (unpublished paper, International Association of Genocide Scholars, University of Galway, Eire, 12 June 2003).
2. A. Dirk Moses, "Conceptual Blockages and Definitional Dilemmas in the 'Racial Century': Genocides of Indigenous Peoples and the Holocaust," *Patterns of Prejudice* 36, no. 4 (2002): 28.
3. Mark Levene, *Genocide in the Age of the Nation- State*, vol. 2, *The Coming of Genocide and the Rise of the West* (London and New York , 2005), for a fuller exposition of this entire theme. The term "world empires" here is consciously borrowed from Immanuel Wallerstein as used, for instance, in his "World System or World Systems?" in *The World System, Five Hundred Years or Five Thousand?*, ed. André Gunder Frank and Barry K. Gills (London and New York, 1993), 292–96.
4. Leo Kuper, *Genocide: Its Political Use in the Twentieth Century* (New Haven, CT and London, 1981); Helen Fein, "Genocide: A Sociological Perspective," *Current Sociology* 38, no. 1 (1990): 1–126; idem, "Accounting for Genocide after 1945: Theories and Some Findings," *International Journal on Group Rights* 1 (1993): 79–106; Barbara Harff and Ted Robert Gurr, "Toward Empirical Theory of Genocides and Politicides: Identification and Measurement of Cases since 1945," *International Studies Quarterly* (1988): 359–71; Eric D. Weitz, *A Century of Genocide, Utopias of Race and Nation* (Princeton, NJ and Oxford, 2003).
5. See Reynauld Secher, *Le Génocide franco-français, La Vendée-Venge*, 4th ed. (Paris, 1992); Peter Paret, *Internal War and Pacification: The Vendée 1789–1796* (Princeton, NJ, 1961). For fuller analysis of the place of the Vendée in European history, see Levene, *Rise of the West*, chap. 3, "The Vendée—A Paradigm Shift?"
6. Hannah Arendt, *The Origins of Totalitarianism*, 2nd ed. (London, 1958). Recently, Enzo Traverso has taken up Arendt's focus on imperialism as a precursor to the Holocaust: *The Origins of Nazi Violence* (London, 2003). Jürgen Zimmerer is working on the issue, too: "Colonialism and the Holocaust: Towards an Archaeology of Genocide," in *Genocide and Settler Society: Frontier Violence and Stolen Indigenous Children in Australian History*, ed., A. Dirk Moses (New York and Oxford, 2004), 49–76.
7. See for instance A. Dirk Moses, "Genocide and Settler Society in Australian History," in idem, *Genocide and Settler Society,* 4f. for critical commentary on Arendt's unwillingness to properly embrace the Anglophone settler societies in her narrative of imperial conquest and atrocity.
8. See notably Anthony Pagden, *Peoples and Empires* (London, 2001); Niall Ferguson, *Empire: How Britain Made the Modern World* (London, 2003); Dominic Lieven, *Empire: The Russian Empire and its Rivals* (London, 2000).
9. See, for example, Henrik Lundtofte, "'Ich glaube, dass die Nation als solche vernichtet werden muss . . . 'Radikaliseringen af den tyske nedkaemelse af hereroostanden 1904," *Den Jyske Historiker* 90 (December 2000): 74–105. One might add that standard histories of British and other empires rarely acknowledge that conflict against, and conquest of native peoples might involve genocidal destruction.
10. See notably David E. Stannard, *American Holocaust: Columbus and the Conquest of the New World* (New York, 1992); Ward Churchill, *A Little Matter of Genocide, Holocaust and Denial in the Americas: 1492 to the Present* (San Francisco, 1997).
11. Jean-Paul Sartre, "On Genocide,'" *Ramparts* (Feb. 1968), 37–42; Sven Lindqvist, *"Exterminate all the Brutes"* (London, 1998).

12. The subject itself is actually one of intense historiographical debate in South Africa. See Carolyn Hamilton, ed., *The Mfecane Aftermath, Reconstructive Debates in Southern African History* (Johannesburg and Pietermaritzburg, 1995).
13. Owen Lattimore, *Pivot of Asia, Sinkiang: The Inner Asian Frontiers of China and Russia* (Boston, 1950), 126.
14. Michel-Rolph Trouillot, *Silencing the Past, Power and the Production of History* (Boston, 1995).
15. Alfred W. Crosby, *Ecological Imperialism: The Biological Expansion of Europe, 900–1900* (Cambridge, 1986).
16. Ibid., chaps. 7–9.
17. See William Cronon, *Changes in the Land: Indians, Colonists and the Ecology of New England* (New York, 1983), for the classic study of native self-sufficiency compared with settler profligacy.
18. Ibid., 56–57 and 77–79. Also see R.H.W. Reece, *Aborigines and Colonists: Aborigines and Colonial Society in New South Wales in the 1830s and 1840s* (Sydney, 1974), 168–69, and John H. Bodley, *Victims of Progress*, 2nd ed., (Palo Alto, CA, 1982), 63–64, for the application of these concepts in Australasia.
19. See notably Nicholas Canny, *Making Ireland British, 1580–1650* (Oxford, 2001); Bruce Lenman, *England's Colonial Wars, 1550–1688* (London, 2001).
20. See A. Dirk Moses, "An Antipodean Genocide? The Origins of the Genocidal Moment in the Colonisation of Australia," *Journal of Genocide Research* 2, no. 1 (2000): 103.
21. Bain Attwood and S.G. Foster, eds., *Frontier Conflict, the Australian Experience* (Canberra, 2003), for a critical overview. More specifically, Henry Reynolds, *The Other Side of the Frontier: Aboriginal Resistance to the European Invasion of Australia* (Sydney, 1981), 84–85.
22. Churchill, *Little Matter*, ch. five, "'Nits Make Lice': The Extermination of North American Indians, 1607–1996," 129–288, provides probably the nearest thing to an overview on this score, if albeit a highly polemical one.
23. Alfredo M. Serres Güiraldes, *La Estrategia del General: Roca* (Buenos Aires, 1979) while unsatisfactory in its strongly nationalistic Argentinean tenor, at least provides some details of these campaigns.
24. See Reginald Horsman, *Expansion and American Indian Policy 1783–1812* (East Lansing, MI, 1967); Bernard W. Sheehan, *Seeds of Extinction, Jeffersonian Philanthropy and the American Indian* (Chapel Hill, NC, 1973), for important excursions on this theme.
25. See Anthony F.C. Wallace, *The Long Bitter Trail, Andrew Jackson and the Indians* (New York, 1993), chap. 4, "The Trail of Tears," for a succinct summary.
26. Lynwood Carranco and Estle Beard, *Genocide and Vendetta: The Round Valley Wars of North California* (Norman, OK, 1981).
27. William G. McLoughlin, *Cherokee Renascence in the New Republic* (Princeton, NJ, 1986) for the full story.
28. Gregory Evans Dowd, *A Spirited Resistance, The North American Indian Struggle for Unity, 1745–1815* (Baltimore, MD and London, 1992), esp. 118–20.
29. See notably Richard White, *The Middle Ground, Indians, Empires and Republics in the Great Lakes Region, 1650–1815* (Cambridge, 1991), 315–17; 340–41, for more specifically on the Scots-Irish. Also Don Watson, *Caledonia Australis: Scottish Highlanders on the Frontier of Australia* (Sydney, 1984), esp. 165–67, where Watson describes the Warrigal Creek massacre of some 100 to 150 of the Brautauolong people of the Gippsland region of South East Australia—itself reputedly one of the largest

single massacres in Australian frontier history—as "certainly a very Scottish affair" perpetrated by a self-styled "Highland brigade."

30. See White, *Middle Ground*, esp.14–15. Jeffrey P. Blick, "The Iroquois Practice of Genocidal Warfare," *Journal of Genocide Research* 3, no. 3 (2001): 405–29, for the impact, too, of native peoples being drawn into European economic imperatives.
31. James Belich, *The New Zealand Wars and the Victorian Interpretation of Racial Conflict* (Auckland, 1986), esp. chap. 14, "The Maori Achievement."
32. Mike Davis, *Late Victorian Holocausts, El Niño Famines and the Making of the Third World* (London and New York, 2001), 98–99.
33. Again see White, *Middle Ground*, for a cautious appraisal on this score. A "dense network of mutual obligation" (15), for instance, did not prevent an attempted French extermination of the Mesquaki ("Fox") people in the protracted war from 1712–30, when the latter failed to do French bidding, nor simultaneously a similarly retributive onslaught further south in the Mississippi region against the Natchez and Yazoos. See Charles J. Balesi, *The Time of the French at the Heart of North America, 1673–1818* (Chicago, 1992), chaps. 9 and 10.
34. Recent studies include Jürgen Zimmerer, *Deutsche Herrschaft uber Afrikaner. Staatlicher Machtanspruch und Wirklichkiet in kolonialen Namibia*, 2nd. ed. (Münster, Hamburg, and London, 2002); Isabel V. Hull, "Military Culture and the Production of 'Final Solutions' in the Colonies: The Example of Wilhelminian Germany," in *The Spectre of Genocide: Mass Murder in Historical Perspective*, ed. Ben Kiernan and Robert Gellately (Cambridge and New York, 2003), 141–62; Tilman Dedering, "'A Certain Rigorous Treatment of all Parts of the Nation': The Annihilation of the Herero in German South West Africa, 1904," in *The Massacre in History*, ed. Mark Levene and Penny Roberts (Oxford, 1999), 205–22.
35. Horst Drechsler, *Let Us Die Fighting: The Struggle of the Herero and Nama against German Imperialism 1884–1915* (London, 1980), 212–14, for a casualty breakdown.
36. J. Iliffe, *Tanganyika under German Rule, 1905–1912* (Cambridge, 1979), chap. 6, "The Maji-Maji Rebellion, 1905–7."
37. See Terence O. Ranger, *Revolt in Southern Rhodesia 1896–97, A Study in African Resistance* (London, 1967); Arthur Kepple-Jones, *Rhodes and Rhodesia. The White Conquest of Zimbabwe 1884–1902* (Kingston and Montreal, 1983), for major studies.
38. See *Perang Kolonial Belanda di Aceh/The Dutch Colonial War in Aceh*, 2nd. ed. (Banda Aceh, Indonesia, 1990), esp. 187–94; Dutch sources referred to in Maarten Kuitenbrouwer, *The Netherlands and the Rise of Modern Imperialism: Colonies and Foreign Policy, 1870–1902*, trans. Hugo Beyer (Oxford, 1991), 321, put the death toll from the 1904 operation at 3,000 villagers, including 1,200 women and children.
39. Davis, *Late Victorian Holocausts*, 125. See also Han Woo-keun, *The History of Korea* (Seoul, 1970); chapter 28, "The Tonghak Revolt."
40. Compare Richard E. Welch, Jr., *The United States and the Philippine-American War, 1899–1902* (Chapel Hill, NC, 1979), 42, with the higher figure in Davis, *Late Victorian Holocausts*, 199.
41. See Davis, *Late Victorian Holocausts*, 133–38.
42. Robert M. Levine, *Vale of Tears: Revisiting the Canudos Massacre in Northeastern Brazil, 1893–1897* (Berkeley and Los Angeles, 1992).
43. Diana Preston, *A Brief History of the Boxer Rebellion, China's War on Foreigners, 1900* (London, 2002); Sabrine Dabrinhaus, "An Army on Vacation? The German War in China, 1900–1901," in *Anticipating Total War, The German and American Experiences, 1871–1914*, ed. Manfred F. Boemeke, Roger Chickering, and Stig Forster (Cambridge, 1999).

44. See Sebastian Balfour, *The End of the Spanish Empire, 1898–1923* (Oxford, 1997), 21–22; Ada Ferrer, *Race, Nation and Revolution, Cuba 1868–1898* (Chapel Hill and London, 1999), 152. The death toll from starvation and mass epidemic in Oriente and Caruaguey provinces where the rural population "reconcentration" occurred was at least 100,000 and possibly as many as 400,000—arguably half the total regional number.
45. S.B. Spies, *Methods of Barbarism: Roberts and Kitchener and Civilians in the Boer Republics, January 1900–May 1902* (Cape Town, 1977), esp. chap. 6, "Kitchener's Initial Measures: December 1900 to March 1901."
46. See Lundtofte, "Ich glaube"; Hull, "Military Culture" for cumulative radicalizations of standard military doctrine in this instance.
47. Davis, *Late Victorian Holocausts,* Parts I and II.
48. Adam Hochschild, *King Leopold's Ghost: A Story of Greed, Terror and Heroism in Colonial Africa* (London, 1998), 233. For a fuller reading of Leopold's state and its atrocities, see Jules Marchal, *L'Etat Libre du Congo, Paradis Perdu, L'Histoire du Congo, 1876–1900,* 2 vols. (Borgloon, Belgium, 1996), esp. vol. 1, Part III, "La Regne de la Terreur."
49. See Bruce Vandervort, *Wars of Imperial Conquest 1830–1914* (London, 1998), 156–64; Romain H. Rainero, "The Battle of Adowa on 1st March 1896: A Reappraisal," in *Imperialism and War, Essays in Colonial Wars in Asia and Africa*, ed. J.A. de Moor and H.L. Wesseling (Leiden, 1989), 189–200, for perspicacious readings of Adowa's specifically Italian and broader significance.
50. See Charles-Robert Ageron, *Histoire de l'Algerie Contemporaine* (Paris, 1964); 10–16, 38–42; M. Emerit, "La Queston Algerienne en 1871," *Revue d'Histoire Moderne et Contemporaine* 19 (1972): 256–64.
51. Giorgio Rochat, "La repressione della resistenza Arabe in Cirenaica nel 1930–31: Nei Documenti dell'Archivo Graziani," *Il Movimento di Liberazione in Italia* 25 (1973): 3–39. Also E.E. Evans-Pritchard, *The Sanusi of Cyrenaica* (London, 1949), esp. 198–99.
52. Peter Balakian, *The Burning Tigris, The Armenian Genocide and America's Response* (New York, 2003), xiv.
53. See Robert F. Melson, *Revolution and Genocide: On the Origins of the Armenian Genocide and the Holocaust* (Chicago, 1992) for careful evaluation of the widely different estimates on fatalities. Jelle Verheij, "Die armenischen Massaker von 1894–1896: Anatomie und Hinterfgrunde enier Krise," in *Die Armenische Frage und die Schweiz (1896–1923)*, ed. Hans-Lukas Kieser (Zurich, 1999), 69–133, for the first full critical study of the 1894–96 massacres in two decades.
54. Francois Thierry, "Empire and Minority in China," in *Minority Peoples in the Age of Nation-States*, ed. Gerard Chailand (London, 1989), 85; Owen Lattimore, *Inner Asian Frontiers of China* (Oxford and New York, 1988 [1940]), 183–87. While somewhat antiquated and obscure, Wen-Djang Chu, *The Moslem Rebellion in North-West China 1862–1878, A Study of Government Minority Policy* (The Hague and Paris, 1966) provides some details of the Qing campaign.
55. Stephen Shenfield, "The Circassians, A Forgotten Genocide?" in *Massacre*, ed. Levene and Roberts, 154. Shenfield's extrapolations are notably high. Another more cautious recent estimate puts the combined mortality from the Russian campaigns and their aftermath at half a million. See Peter Holquist, '"To Count, to Extract and to Exterminate,' Population Statistics and Population Politics in Late Imperial and Soviet Russia," in *A State of Nations, Empire and Nation-Making in the Age of Lenin and Stalin*, ed. Ronald Grigor Suny and Terry Martin (Oxford, 2001), 119.

56. Figures from Tim Judah, *The Serbs, History, Myth and the Destruction of Yugoslavia* (New Haven, CT and London, 1997), 101.
57. See Hew Strachan, *The First World War*, vol. 1, *To Arms* (Oxford, 2003) for the critical shift of emphasis.
58. See Kemal H. Karpat, "Population Movements in the Ottoman State in the Nineteenth Century: An Outline," in *Collections Turcica III, Contributions a l'histoire economique et sociale de l'Empire Ottoman*, ed. Jean-Louis Bacque and Paul Dumont (Louvain, 1983), 400–408; more generally Tessa Hoffman and Gerayer Koutcharian, "The History of Armenian-Kurdish Relations in the Ottoman Empire," *Armenian Review* 39, no. 4 (1986): 1–45.
59. See Januarius A. MacGahan, *The Turkish Atrocities in Bulgaria* (Geneva, 1966), for a contemporary news reporter's first-hand account of the *bashi-bazouk* killings. James J. Reid, "Batak 1876: A Massacre and its Significance," *Journal of Genocide Research* 2, no. 3 (2000): 375–409; Justin McCarthy, *Death and Exile: The Ethnic Cleansing of Ottoman Muslims, 1821–1922* (Princeton, NJ, 1995), 39–60, for further analysis and overview.
60. Though notably polemical, McCarthy, *Death and Exile*, 67–91, offers a strong and convincing case for Muslims as the primary victims of the Russian-assisted Balkan wars of independence in 1877/8.
61. See *The Other Balkan Wars, A 1913 Carnegie Endowment Inquiry in Retrospect with a New Introduction and Reflections on the Present Conflict by George F. Kennan* (Washington, DC, 1993), notably chap. 4, "The War of the Nationalities," for the Balkan wars of 1912/13 denouement.
62. Whether "assisted" cultural disappearance should be interpreted as a facet of genocide per se, however, remains a contested subject. See A. Dirk Moses, "Conceptual Blockages and Definitional Dilemmas in the 'Racial Century': Genocides of Indigenous Peoples and the Holocaust," *Patterns of Prejudice* 36, no. 4 (2002): 22–24, for acute examination of the current debate.
63. This is not to overplay the thesis in Samuel P. Huntington, *The Clash of Civilisations and the Remaking of World Order* (London and New York, 1998), but simply to argue that it has some salience to our argument here.
64. See Robin Okey, "State, Church, and Nation in the Serbo-Croat-speaking Lands of the Habsburg monarchy 1850–1914," in *Comparative Studies on Governments and Non-dominant Ethnic Groups in Europe 1850–1940, Religion, State and Ethnic Groups*, vol. 2, ed. Donal A. Kerr et al., (Dartmouth, NH, 1992), 51–78.
65. See Fred Anderson, *Crucible of War: The Seven Years' War and the Fate of Empire in British North America* (New York, 2000), for a broad overview.
66. Quoted in Reynolds, *Other Side of the Frontier*, 111.
67. Edward Crankshaw, *The Fall of the House of Habsburg* (London, 1963).
68. Giorgio Agamben, *Homo Sacer: Sovereign Power and Bare Life* (London, 1998), 132.

– *Chapter 9* –

Serial Colonialism and Genocide in Nineteenth-Century Cambodia

Ben Kiernan

Introduction

Most genocidal regimes display not only racial or religious hatreds, but other ideological preoccupations as well. Genocidal thinking usually includes expansionist or irredentist territorial demands, an agrarian ideology vaunting supposedly superior land use, and a cult of antiquity envisaging return to a pristine era of ethnic purity, military superiority, or cultural dominance. This combination of ethnic and agrarian visions with military and territorial ambitions makes colonial conquest a common context for genocide.[1] In Cambodia's case, colonialism and genocide are multiply intertwined. In the two centuries before the Khmer Rouge genocide of 1975–79, the country suffered four colonial conquests of varying lengths. These invasions brought external rule and local repression by Vietnamese, Thai, French, and Japanese regimes, respectively. Here I begin by examining the first two of these colonial cases, which together arguably inflicted partial genocide on Cambodia in the 1830s and 1840s.

From around the turn of the nineteenth century, as European colonial powers advanced elsewhere over the globe, the newly resurgent dynasties of Cambodia's neighboring Confucian and Buddhist kingdoms, then known as Đại Việt and Siam, expanded into the country from east and west. They fought each other and Cambodian resistance for the country's territory and its population's labor. For over a decade, as the two invaders' control of Cambodia seesawed, their successive devastations were brutal, and the apparent demographic impact severe, though no population statistics survive to document it. Their violent colonial practices ranged from military suppression and administrative subordination to economic exploitation and cultural assimilation, while proclaiming Confucian paternalism and Buddhist universalism, respectively. Their territorial ambitions and visions of superior agriculture, as well as, in the Vietnamese case at least, preoccupation with ancient (Confucian) models, were consistent with the thinking of other genocidal regimes of various cultures, centuries, and continents.

At the same time, during their resistance to Vietnam's occupation, Cambodian rebels indiscriminately slaughtered ethnic Vietnamese, and even after Vietnam's military withdrawal in the 1840s, Thai forces in Cambodia conducted a genocidal massacre of the Vietnamese population remaining there. These killing campaigns prefigured the Khmer Rouge genocide of Vietnamese civilian residents of Cambodia in 1975–79.

The strength of Cambodian resistance, and the kingdom's recovery in the 1850s after two deadly occupations, were also remarkable. Ironically, it was the French arrival and imposition of a new colonial Protectorate in 1863 that may have posed most urgently the question of Cambodia's national survival. For, now, local resistance to the French presence produced new anticolonial collaboration between ethnic Cambodians and Vietnamese. Though enjoying access to few historical sources about their country's past, Cambodians under French rule increasingly worried for its future status and existence.

Cambodia, Siam, and Đại Việt

From the end of the thirteenth century, the medieval Khmer kingdom of Angkor had faced intermittent Siamese invasions. In the seventeenth century, the southern Vietnamese kingdom also began launching incursions into Cambodia, while ethnic Vietnamese farmers and traders started settling there. Ethnopolitical divisions between Khmers and Vietnamese sharpened in 1750 when Cambodia's king Ang Snguon successfully ordered a genocidal massacre of almost all the Vietnamese residents in the country.[2] After more Vietnamese settled in the Mekong delta, Khmers again slaughtered many in 1769.[3]

Yet at other times, members of the two ethnic groups cooperated. A long Vietnamese civil war that began in 1771 saw the kingdom of Đại Việt first reunified and then conquered by a resurgent Nguyen dynasty in 1802. The victor, who became the new emperor Gia-Long (r. 1802–19), had received aid not only from French forces, a Siamese rebel and a Chinese pirate and their fleets of junks, and twenty thousand Siamese troops, but also from a former Cambodian palace slave who mobilized 5,000 Khmer followers in the Nguyen cause. Collaboration remained an alternative to ethnic conflict. However, by then, as historian Alexander Woodside comments, "ethnic differentiation and stratification were more finely developed in the Vietnamese imperial outlook," than in either Cambodia or Siam.[4]

Vietnam's Nguyen restoration eventually opened the way to its further western expansion into Cambodia. And in 1794, Siam, pursuing its own eastward expansion, occupied Cambodia's northwest provinces, including the temples of Angkor and the province of Battambang, which it held for over a century.[5] In the 1830s and 1840s, contending Vietnamese and Siamese invasions would bring Cambodia to the brink of annihilation.

Gia-Long established a new capital at Hue, on the central coast, and renamed his kingdom Việt Nam ("Southern Viet") in 1804. Despite his initial multiethnic following, Gia-Long believed that "the Vietnamese and the barbarians must have clear borders." He combined this policy with Confucian paternalism and regional pragmatism: "Cambodia is a small country. . . . We will be its mother; its father will be Siam." Cambodia was "an independent country that is the slave of two."[6] Vietnamese paternalism and Siamese suzerainty were both unwelcome in Cambodia, but the closeness of their contention gave it greater room to maneuver. Disenchanted by Siamese power, the Khmer king Chan (r. 1806–35) offered to become Gia-Long's vassal, and the Khmer court moved downriver from Udong to Phnom Penh. Gia-Long ordered his officials in the delta to "separate people of Chinese descent, Chinese merchants, Cambodians, and Malays."[7]

Contention over Cambodia gradually led to yet closer colonial impositions. Siam invaded Cambodia in 1811, clashing with Việt Nam's forces. Withdrawing in defeat, Siamese troops destroyed both the former capital of Udong and the citadel in Phnom Penh, and deported thousands of Cambodians to the Siamese-controlled northwest territories.[8] As Gia-Long restored his country's traditional name Đại Việt in 1813, a 13,000-strong army enforced its protectorate over Cambodia.[9] Gia-Long withdrew Vietnamese residents from there in 1815 to avoid "trouble with Cambodians in the future," and later ordered his officials to "prevent my people from intervening in their lives." Twice a month, the Khmer king had to bow to a tablet inscribed with Gia-Long's name, and a thousand Vietnamese soldiers garrisoned the capital, but their demands and controls on Cambodia were not yet severe. Hue's formal policy was "to strengthen the preservation" of Cambodia. Siamese forces still threatened it, reoccupying the northern provinces in 1814.[10]

Việt Nam tightened its grip on Cambodia. In 1816, Nguyen authorities recruited 5,000 Khmer workers in both kingdoms to dig a canal along the northern edge of the Mekong delta. More laborers joined the project before construction was completed in 1820.[11] In a Buddhist poem composed fifty years later in reflection on this era, the Khmer monk Venerable Pich offered a total estimate of "one hundred thousand Khmer and Vietnamese workers." The digging, Pich wrote, "killed many people and exhausted many others."[12] The workers were paid and supervised by corrupt Vietnamese officials under harsh conditions. An English diplomat who visited Vietnam reported a death toll on the project of ten thousand laborers.[13]

Rule and resistance brought escalating violence. In eastern Cambodia, a Buddhist monk named Kai raised a rebel force in 1820, joined by a Cambodian general whom the Nguyen authorities had demoted.[14] Led by Kai, the rebels "annihilated all the Vietnamese soldiers" sent to arrest him. Vietnamese commanders denounced Kai for "daring to exterminate their compatriots." The rebels continued to massacre ethnic Vietnamese in eastern Cambodia. According to Pich's poem: "The number of dead was high. The soil was bathed in blood. Many abandoned bodies lay on the ground. For the Vietnamese it was a general debacle." Launching a fleet of thirty boats on the Mekong, the rebels sailed on Phnom Penh, but were routed.[15]

Before one engagement, the poem portrays Kai reciting Buddhist sutras and blessing his troops to make them invulnerable. At first it worked. Vietnamese fell "like banana stalks" to Khmer attacks. Kai's followers announced: "We will suffer no misfortune, for we have no guilt." But the poet criticized Kai for his "misdeeds," such as involving monks in violence, contrary to Buddhism. "After what he had done, the merit had faded away, and now he had no special powers. . . . His followers were unable to attack or fire their weapons. So the Vietnamese, Chams and Malays attacked them mercilessly from their boats, with axes, rifles and swords." Many Buddhist monks fell fighting, including some who, Pich suggests, had lost religious merit when they "killed Vietnamese." Vietnamese forces captured and killed Kai, tried and executed the defecting Cambodian general, and beheaded many other rebels.[16]

Pich's poem drew a somber lesson from this revolt and its failure: "People's arms quivered in the cold. So much rain fell all day, all night, that it was impossible to distinguish sunrise from sunset. The weak and the strong alike ran off to hide, and the land was mournful." Gia-Long had died in 1819, and the new Vietnamese monarch, his son Minh-Mang, took a different approach: "Peace has been restored, but there is much to be done in Cambodia, and little has been accomplished."[17]

Minh-Mang's Domestic Policies and Ideology

Vietnamese Emperor Minh-Mang (r. 1820–41) was more aggressive and ideologically rigid than his father. His tragic intervention in Cambodia in 1833–41 fit the pattern of his rule. Repressive and haughty, deeply concerned with agricultural welfare and development, Minh-Mang exhibited a Confucian preoccupation with models from Chinese antiquity, while imposing ethnic assimilation at home and pursuing territorial expansionism in response to conflict abroad. After brutal Siamese intervention in Laos, Minh-Mang annexed parts of that country in 1827–31, and he would soon add Cambodia after a Siamese attack there.[18]

At home, Minh-Mang's reign was wracked by discord and rebellions. In contrast to his father's acceptance of Western advisers at the Vietnamese court, none remained there under Minh-Mang after 1824. He attempted to ban Catholicism the next year, and executed seven Western missionaries in 1833–38, along with Vietnamese Catholics. He ordered northern Vietnamese women to wear trousers instead of skirts, and tried to ban village theater performances, stating: "I hear that a stupendous number of males and females, old people and young people, watch these plays. This must definitely be an evil custom."[19]

Minh-Mang placed similar impositions on domestic ethnic communities. For the Khmer and highland minorities of southern Việt Nam, he abandoned Gia-Long's policy of muted segregation, and insisted on assimilation: "We must hope that their barbarian habits will be subconsciously dissipated, and that they will daily become more infected by Han [Sino-Vietnamese] customs." Significantly, the emperor associated this cultural assimilation with both agriculture and state supervision of the population: "The surveying of land and the erecting of settlements, the promulgation and completion of the quotas and the registers, these things are essential demonstrations of 'using Hsia to change barbarians.'"[20]

The imposition of strict Confucian controls likewise provoked multi-ethnic responses. When a son of the governor of Saigon, Lê Van Khôi, led rebels in a revolt in the Mekong delta in 1833, they were supported by local Khmers, Chinese merchants in Saigon, the leader of the remnant coastal principality of Champa, and by the king of Siam.[21] After crushing Khôi's rebellion in 1834, Minh-Mang proclaimed: "The number of rebels, like herds of dogs and foxes, grew daily, and the revolt became an extremely serious problem. . . . I cannot hide my vexation. . . . how was the disaster able to extend through the six provinces and resist the court for three years?" Minh-Mang did not simply put down the Cham rebellion in 1835; he also finally dissolved the last Champa principality.[22]

As emperor, Minh-Mang also saw himself as a Confucian ruler with Heaven's mandate to be benevolent. He established a genuine agrarian "relief" system to help the poor cope with drought, flood, and fire. He explained: "The relationship between a king and his people is like that of a good father with a young child who does not wait for the child to be cold to put clothes on him." He ordered the rich to hand over two-thirds of their private lands to village communes, and forbade the sale of commune land at a profit.[23]

Minh-Mang's agrarian vision was powerful. Confucian doctrine placed the peasantry second only to the scholar-mandarinate on the social ladder. An 1831 ordinance offered free grants of uncultivated land "to any person who asks for it." Minh-Mang revived the Đại Việt institution of royal land grants in the south to groups of military colonists, for payment in rice and performance of military duties. A French historian credited Minh-Mang with pioneering "a new doctrine" on irrigation. An 1833 edict proclaimed:

> When the rice fields are flooded by the rains and the water-courses are still at a rather low level, it is useful to dig drainage canals and to clear the rice fields of water into the water-courses; in this way one can avoid flooding and the rotting of the summer harvests. Inversely, if the rains are lacking and the rice fields are drying off, and if at the same time the water in the river is rather high, then it is useful to bring the water into the fields by means of small channels. . . . It is thus preferable to entrust the care of all dykes, public and private, to the provincial mandarins, who will maintain them according to the prescribed rules. . . . During the summer and winter crops, they should introduce water from the water-courses, according to whether the rice fields are dry or flooded.[24]

Minh-Mang left 12,000 pages of writings, which include "hundreds of poems and pieces of prose about agriculture and the peasant."[25] The emperor announced a new program of land measurement throughout southern Vietnam in 1836. "It is very important to clarify the borders of fields," his edict stated. Landed property had to be recognized. Minh-Mang overruled his officials to ensure that public lands were not augmented, and he reduced taxes to encourage the clearing and farming of new land. As he put it, "private land has been possessed for a long time, and ownership has already been recognized." Rejecting his mandarins' proposal to "cut away and take their private property," Minh-Mang responded that "it is natural to see the rich provide the land and the poor provide the labor." His main goals were land clearing, rice production, and private property. As he put it, "[I] do not worry whether the amount of rice fields is small for each peasant, . . . [I] only worry that people are not diligent." He required cultivation efforts on the part of landlords, too. It was a crime to accumulate land beyond the owner's capacity to farm. Minh-Mang ordered his officials: "Any owner who has relatively too much land to be able fully to cultivate it, then take half of 30 percent." At the other end of the social scale, convicts who had cleared public lands were to become small landowners: "If they want to stay there . . . give the cleared land to them as the form of private land to live on. If they want to go back home, sell the cleared land to others." The

Hue government provided buffalo, tools, and seeds to individuals setting out to clear new land, and it rewarded or punished local officials on the basis of the area of their region that was brought into cultivation.[26]

The Nguyen administration's cult of antiquity also expressed a special Confucian orthodoxy. As Woodside has pointed out, "The Vietnamese elite's sense of Chinese history was strong. Its faith in Chinese allusions, classical and historical, momentous and trivial, was romantic and unlimited." A performing elephant at Minh-Mang's court in the 1820s, Woodside writes, elicited an allusion to an eighth-century elephant "that had held a goblet in its mouth at the T'ang court." When soldiers digging a gate for the imperial city excavated a skeleton in 1833, Minh-Mang ordered it solemnly reburied on a precedent set by a classical Chinese monarch. He would tell stories at any pretext about the first Ming emperor, "complete with dialogue." Minh-Mang's historical curiosity extended to Cambodia. In a slightly condescending tone, he remarked that the Khmer "have been a nation for over 1,200 years, but we do not know precisely what year they began, in terms of the Vietnamese and Chinese dynasties that were then reigning."[27]

Seeking ritual continuity between past and future, Minh-Mang would survey the heavens for omens, following the tradition of early Chinese emperors and the *Book of Songs*. One day in late 1834, he predicted with optimism: "On every winter solstice day the ancients ascended the Spirit Tower to examine the clouds. . . . Today in the early dawn I saw that the color of the sun was radiant and the cloud ornaments were luxuriant, and I reflected that the peace and happiness of men next spring could be foretold."[28] War over Cambodia, however, would prove him wrong.

Đại Việt's Annexation of Cambodia

A Siamese army marched through Cambodia in 1833, to invade Đại Việt in support of Lê Van Khôi's revolt there. Siam's Cambodia policy was ruthless. The Siamese king Rama III (r. 1824–51) aimed to rule the country through two pro-Siamese Khmer princes, or failing that, to depopulate Cambodia. Thus Rama III explained in 1832 that the objective of Siam's invasion was to secure a Khmer labor force. "Our governors and officials in Battambang are well equipped and ready. Do not let the Khmers cross the line [into Cambodia]. When there is a chance, you must strike it hard. If the Khmers flee, send troops to beat them. . . . Try to bring more people into the [Siamese] kingdom so that we will have more manpower. . . . Arrange for their settlement so that they could start to grow food." More explicitly, Rama III ordered his military commander, Chaophraya Bodin

(1777–1849): "You are to figure out a means of returning Cambodia to [rule from] Bangkok as it used to be. If this is not possible, you should turn Cambodia into forest; only the land, the mountains, the rivers and the canals are to be left. You are to carry off Khmer families to be resettled in Thai territory, do not leave any behind."[29]

Bodin's large expeditionary force marched into Cambodia, headed by shock troops with "a multitude of enormous elephants."[30] The Khmer monk Venerable Pich wrote in an 1855 poem: "The Siamese army invaded the whole country and ravaged towns and villages. Everywhere in the country, from the rural areas to the capital, the population, panicking in fear, were completely terrorized."[31] In the words of a Khmer chronicle, "All the people were surprised to see such a large army, and they trembled with fear." When the Siamese army approached Phnom Penh, its Vietnamese garrison retreated, massacring four hundred ethnic Chinese who had settled there from Vietnam.[32]

Pursuing the offensive, Bodin's army attacked into Vietnam, but met defeat there and had to fall back in early 1834. In Cambodia, Khmer rebels had already begun massacring Siamese forces, and much of its population fled the fighting to take refuge in the forest.[33] Following Rama III's instructions, Bodin sent brutal orders to the Cambodian princes on the march with his retreating forces: "Now the Khmers are revolting in many towns; therefore, it is difficult to retain Cambodia. The army commanders in Phnom Penh must demolish all ramparts, and turn Phnom Penh into a charnel ground." He also instructed them to "transport the Khmer, Indian [Cham], Chinese and others in Phnom Penh to Battambang," the northwest Khmer province under Thai control. Bodin further ordered Siamese commanders in the Cambodian coastal towns of Hatien, Kampot, and Kompong Som "to evacuate the people, to burn down the houses in every town, and to demolish the town, so that only the forest and the rivers are left."[34]

As the poet Pich recalled in 1855, the Siamese army, implementing Bodin's orders in Phnom Penh, "destroyed the palace compound, burning down all the houses of the villagers. Commanders and soldiers plundered and shared out their booty." The situation in the city was "catastrophic."[35] On their withdrawal, the Siamese carried off Khmer and Chinese residents of Phnom Penh, "at least two thousand families," each with children and grandchildren, Pich wrote.[36] Perhaps one-quarter of the deportees escaped on reaching Udong, only to wander, a Vietnamese official asserted, "trembling and afraid in the deep woods."[37] Siamese troops commanded by Bodin's son, mounted on elephants and horses, pursued an opposing force of 1,500 Khmers and came upon the entire population of Samrong Tong district hiding in the forest. According to Pich, the Siamese soldiers spared only the Khmer women. "The men were bound, beaten, and murdered," and over a thousand of their dependents taken prisoner and deported.[38] As the Siamese retreated westward across Cambodia, they rounded up the local populations for resettlement in what is now northeast Thailand. Historian David Chandler writes that the affected provinces "were systematically emptied, either because the populations were carried off, or took refuge in the woods." Cambodian historian Khin Sok asserts that "the majority of the population" of Cambodia was deported to Siam. Reaching the Siamese-controlled Cambodian town of Battambang, Bodin had its citadel destroyed, and forced thousands of local Khmer laborers to dig a moat for a new city, redirecting the Sangker river.[39] The Siamese forces also erected ethnic barriers. Learning that its protégé Khmer princes had taken a large number of Vietnamese captives, Bangkok ordered them not to "hold a single Vietnamese."[40]

Meanwhile Bodin's son, commanding a force of ten thousand and "many huge elephants," marched northward, retreating from Phnom Penh with a large number of Khmer captives. Pich describes him as "cruel like a lion." He "burnt everything in his path," including villages. The Siamese elephant force invested the Khmer provincial town of Kompong Thom. "Many dead lay on the ground. . . . As if on a hunt, the Siamese soldiers pursued the fugitives and decimated a great number of them. There were as many dead on each side. Those hiding in the high grass were run through with lances and many others disappeared in the river." Bodin's son marched back to Siam, leaving his troops a further order to "crush the Khmers."[41]

On retaking Phnom Penh, the Vietnamese hardened their policy, too. At the end of 1834, Minh-Mang formally renamed Cambodia as a Vietnamese province, *Tran tay thanh*, "the citadel of the western protectorate." He also renamed central and southern Laos, and signaled his expansion policy by changing his own kingdom's name from Đại Việt to Đai Nam, "the Great South." Minh-Mang now laid claim to more than the old Viet realm.[42] The 1838 edict announcing the name change to Đai Nam reflected his ambitions: "This dynasty owns the whole southern part. . . . All creatures that move belong to our territory."[43]

A Vietnamese general in northern Cambodia, according to the poet Pich, press-ganged the entire population of Kompong Thom, "some to build fortresses, to dig the earth; the others cultivated rice and transported it into granaries." In the five northern provinces, even top Khmer officials had to perform this labor. "No one dared revolt for fear of the Vietnamese and everyone collaborated."[44]

However, Minh-Mang's viceroy in Cambodia, Truong Minh Giang, quickly encountered problems establishing Vietnamese authority there. He reported to the emperor in 1834: "We have tried to punish and reward the Cambodian officials according to their merits and demerits. We have asked the king [Chan] to help us, but he has hesitated to do so. After studying the situation, we have decided that Cambodian officials only know how to bribe and be bribed. Offices are sold; nobody carries out orders; everyone works for his own account. . . . For the last four months, nothing has been accomplished."[45] Compiling an assessment of Cambodia's resources six years later, Đai Nam officials still complained that "official posts were acquired by paying money," and that, contrary to the Confucian code of patriarchy, Khmer family ties were closer on the maternal than the paternal side. Thus, they reported, "the worst aspect" of Cambodian society was that people "do not know the ethnical codes. Although they accept the supreme power of our country, they still keep their own customs."[46]

Hue also considered that its newly incorporated Cambodian territory lacked appropriate agriculture. A major problem was feeding the occupying forces. An 1834 memorial complained that Cambodia did not practice basic rice and grain storage.[47] In their subsequent assessment of Cambodia's resources, Đai Nam officials wrote: "Land is abundant here and the population is scarce. Only 30–40 percent of the land is under cultivation, mainly for cotton and betel nut and a little rice." The document added: "It is customary here that the king has no granary, and the country has no [standing] army."[48]

So while enjoining Vietnamese officials there to "teach them our customs," Minh-Mang also meant to impose his agrarian vision on the land. He told his viceroy:

> I have heard, for example, that the land is plentiful and fertile, and that there are plenty of oxen . . . but the people have no knowledge of agriculture, using picks and hoes, rather than oxen. They grow enough rice for two meals a day, but they don't store any surplus. . . . Now all these shortcomings stem from the laziness of the Cambodians . . . and my instructions to you are these; teach them to use oxen, teach them to grow more rice, teach them to raise mulberry trees, pigs, and ducks. . . . As for language, they should be taught to speak Vietnamese. [Our habits of] dress and table manners must also be followed. If there is any outdated or barbarous custom that can be simplified, or repressed, then do so.[49]

At first, Minh-Mang's approach was paternalistic and gradualist. "The barbarians have become my children now, and you should help them," he advised his viceroy Giang. "Let the good ideas seep in, turning the barbarians into civilized people. . . . As for winning the hearts of the people, and teaching them, we plan to do this rather slowly." Minh-Mang requested reports from Cambodia on its "customs, people, and agricultural produce. I want to know whether the people are prosperous, and whether or not the Cambodian militia have been trained . . . if the barbarian people have learned Vietnamese ways, and if they are happy."[50]

More ominously, the new requirements of intensive cultivation involved official Vietnamese monitoring of previously mobile populations. Hue's 1834 memorial complained that "the Cambodian territory is broad . . . but up until now its soldiers and adult males have wandered about and have not been registered and controlled." In 1835 alone, Minh-Mang dispatched over a hundred Vietnamese officials to staff the new administration.[51] He also arranged for the deportation of new Chinese immigrants and landless Chinese from Vietnam to Cambodia: "Give them some land, and divide up parcels of land for them to cultivate unused soil. The government will provide those lacking means with seed grain and farming tools."[52] Chams were sent to similar settlements along the Cambodian frontier.[53] Minh-Mang ordered progress reports: "After three years, surmise the number of people, of farming plots; organize the data in record books, and report them." [54] By the late 1830s, Minh-Mang's officials also brought Vietnamese crops to Cambodia and supervised their systematic cultivation. Truong Minh Giang reported: "We have often advised them to till the land diligently and cultivate crops accordingly, to plant beans and rice." However, food shortages now threatened an "emergency" in the area west of Phnom Penh, which was "in very bad shape."[55] Minh-Mang finally complained in 1840 that for six years he had insisted in vain on the measurement of Cambodian cropland and compilation of records on its rainfall, granaries, and irrigation works, and once again he ordered these tasks fulfilled.[56]

In part, Minh-Mang's policy reflected Confucian preoccupations with benevolence, border security, and cultural superiority. When Truong Minh Giang reported in the late 1830s on the distribution of "10,000 measures of rice" to Khmer delta communities, the king replied: "It is right to do that. You should allow your compassion to keep the outside [Cambodia] peaceful so that the inside [Đai Nam] can be comfortable."[57] In establishing Hue's control over Cambodian communities, Minh-Mang also followed China's traditional sinicization policy of regularizing court appointments in minority regions by replacing hereditary chiefs, a process known as changing from "aboriginal" rulers to "circulating" bureaucratic appointees. He thus planned to replace Cambodian province chiefs with Vietnamese, starting from the provinces near Phnom Penh. The replacements officially required a combination of agricultural and military skills. Few if any of these new positions were ever filled.[58]

Đai Nam officials who appear to have shared Minh-Mang's historical perspective wrote around 1840: "Ah! The expansion of the earth goes from north to south." Just as in ancient times, southern China was "deserted and beyond the reach of civilization," so southern Đại Việt, too, had once been "the land of Chams and Khmers." However, "Since our ancestral sages [the early Nguyen] began to open it up, it has now become a superior civilized country." In Cambodia itself, the authors of this assessment wrote, it was also necessary to "open the land up, then to civilize uncouth people with writing, cover fish scales with clothing, turn unhealthy air into good, and transform barbarians into *Hoa* (Vietnamese). . . . Heaven cannot let it be a barbarian wilderness. Now that our country is changing things in a significant way and registering [Khmer] households, the day of transforming old customs into *Hoa* has come!"[59]

Such optimism proved unmerited. At this height of Đại Việt's historical expansion, the kingdom had overreached. Cambodians welcomed neither Vietnamization nor repression, nor the colonial condescension, equally evident in Minh-Mang's description of King Chan: a "fresh wind or the cry of a bird could make him flee." In late 1834, Chan sought his own advice, apparently from Khmer court Brahmins whom viceroy Truong Minh Giang considered "magicians," and they supposedly urged the monarch to take bribes and "let criminals out of jail." Giang had these "magicians" executed, and when Chan died the next year, the viceroy crowned the king's daughter, Mei, as queen.[60]

Đai Nam's repression of Cambodians now intensified. According to Pich's poem, Truong Minh Giang devised "a terrifying plan, for the whole country." After apprehending a leading Khmer official and his family, and torturing them to death, Giang then "gave the order to arrest, in the citadel, all the Khmer dignitaries and to put them to death." One ranking official was locked in a vice, "burned, dismembered and eliminated." At this, Pich claims, Kompong Thom province's "entire Khmer population, stupefied and terrorized, fled into the forest." A Vietnamese force marched north to arrest Nong and Ey, the leading Khmer officials in Kompong Thom. There, Pich writes, "refusing to submit, these two men rapidly mustered troops to massacre the Vietnamese. These massacres began in Kandal province and extended to all the fortresses, from Staung to Baray, and all the populations rose up." Seeing further resistance as hopeless, however, Nong led a large party of Cambodians through the jungle to a Siamese-controlled northern Khmer province, where he and many of the refugees died.[61]

Further scattered Khmer uprisings occurred from 1837 to 1839.[62] Now, Pich asserted, rebels "were murdering the Vietnamese in the whole country." The occupying forces, unable to locate the rebels, "arrested only frightened individuals," incarcerating a thousand prisoners in cages stacked up on top of each other. Truong Minh Giang's intention, according to Pich, was "to dissuade the youths from joining the rebellion." He "eliminated the rebels as if he were uprooting trees." Among hideous tortures Pich recounts, Giang reputedly ordered three children stretched on the ground, "their heads placed around a fireplace. Then the fire was lit and on their heads was placed an enormous iron pot in which other children were boiled."

Prisoners had to dig ditches into which they were thrown; "then they were covered with earth and a fire lit to turn them to ashes."[63]

Minh-Mang took a piqued, personal interest in Cambodia's pacification. Addressing Khmers in an 1838 decree, he complained that they had ignored his "generosity." For instance, "Imperial troops were dispatched to Cambodia, costing millions of coins, and brought you security by destroying the Thai. Troops were stationed to bring peace. This action was like bringing the Cambodian people out of the mud onto a warm feather bed . . . why are there people who hate us and believe the rebels?" A year later, Minh-Mang again complained that Cambodian officials who had all been "given titles from my court" continued inexplicably to use their Khmer titles. "The Cambodians should be told that it is an honor to have titles bestowed on them by this court. In conversation, therefore, they should use our titles." Another Vietnamese official asserted that Cambodians retained excessive power: "Local people collect the taxes that are owed to us, and still rule over one another." Vietnamese personnel finally took over direct administration of Cambodia's provinces in 1840. That June, Minh-Mang demoted Queen Mei and imposed a Vietnamese taxation regime, including new taxes on food products. The arrest of six prominent Khmer officials was followed in August by that of Mei and two princesses. All went off to exile in Saigon.[64] Đai Nam officials explained that the late King Chan had left "no heir and four of his daughters stood equal and could not rule the country. [Our king] thus ordered the army to prepare rice rations and sent them to the [protecting Vietnamese] government, in order to manage the land and set up [district] administrations."[65]

Meanwhile, challenges to Hue's authority proliferated at home. The 1830s saw three major internal rebellions; a fourth broke out in 1841. As Minh-Mang's ambitious land measurement program got underway in southern Vietnam in 1836, he asked a mandarin about popular attitudes in the south. The response was: "All people are shaking and sighing." Minh-Mang's agrarian program was needed to raise more tax revenue to feed the troops in Cambodia. A Vietnamese official reported that the occupation had to support five to six thousand military forces there. Each year, this cost Vietnam seventy to eighty thousand *hoc* of unhusked rice, at a monthly salary of one *hoc* per soldier.[66] Besides tripling tax revenues in rice, land registration facilitated conscription for the Cambodian front. Vietnamese soldiers there were all landowners (tenants were exempt). The proportion of southern Vietnamese men conscripted also tripled, from 7 to 20 percent. After 1836, Hue drafted 21,000 southerners for military service until they reached age 50 or 55. From 1839, wealthy Vietnamese received government rank for donating and delivering over 2,500 *hoc* of unhusked rice to Cambodia or the border. The war increasingly militarized Minh-Mang's regime. By 1839, he was advising his administrators: "All civil officials ideally should be forced to learn the military arts and all military officials should be forced to learn civil business. . . . Civil officials must not consider guns and cannon to be the sphere of responsibility of military bureaucrats."[67]

Đai Nam's problems escalated when serious rebellion erupted in southern and eastern Cambodia in September 1840. According to Pich, the imprisonment of the Khmer princesses and courtiers had provoked Cambodia's officials and population to revolt "against the arrests and the arbitrary exterminations. The rebellion spread to the whole country."[68] Minh-Mang exploded in a letter he wrote to Giang in Phnom Penh: "Sometimes the Cambodians are loyal; at other times they betray us. We helped them when they were suffering, and lifted them out of the mud. . . . Now they are rebellious: I am so angry that my hair stands upright. . . . Hundreds of knives should be used against them, to chop them up, to dismember them." He added in another edict that rebels must be "crushed to powder." Cambodian rebel leaders reciprocated the sentiment: "We are happy killing Vietnamese. We no longer fear them; in all our battles, we are mindful of the three jewels [of Buddhist teaching]—the Buddha, the Law, and the monastic community." Minh-Mang expressed his own view before his death in early 1841: "The Cambodians are so stupid, that we must frighten them. Ordinary moral suasion has no effect." In a sad sign of his dashed hopes for agricultural development of the annexed territory, Minh-Mang ordered the burning of Cambodian orchards and crops.[69]

Another Siamese Invasion

Siam now returned to the offensive, after difficulties with its own Khmer royal protégés. Bangkok had imprisoned one of its favored Cambodian princes, and another defected to the Vietnamese in 1839 with several thousand followers, only to be arrested by Giang in Phnom Penh. The Siamese commander Bodin garrisoned Battambang in 1840 to prepare a new invasion. Once more marching into Cambodia later that year, his 35,000-strong army overran the Vietnamese fort at Pursat, then fell back to Battambang. A Khmer rebel reported difficulties from the interior: "We are unable to continue fighting the Vietnamese. We lack the troops to do so, the rifles, the ammunition, and the supplies." However, their enemies were also chastened. Bodin estimated that 10,000 Khmer rebels were in the field, but the Vietnamese thought they faced 30,000.[70]

The Siamese deported 1,500 Vietnamese overland from Pursat to Siam, and 800 more by boat.[71] When they captured another group of 180, one, a

Vietnamese official from Phnom Penh, told the Siamese: "I heard that Thai and Khmer troops were everywhere. I was so afraid that I and another 160 people decided to flee."[72] A Vietnamese report stated in 1841 that Khmer rebels "appear and disappear at will," avoiding contact unless they had the advantage. "They concentrate their forces where the jungle is thick, and in swampy areas where our troops cannot maneuver." Culturally, the Vietnamese were even more isolated; "we have no intelligence about the enemy, and no guides."[73]

Minh-Mang's death in January 1841 had a pronounced impact. Writing from Bangkok a year later about the situation in Cambodia, a French missionary stated that if Vietnam's "persecution did not quite stop" with Minh-Mang's death, "it has at least greatly slowed."[74] Indeed, Vietnamese forces had by then abandoned Cambodia, under Minh-Mang's successor, emperor Thieu-Tri (r. 1841–47). Late in 1841, viceroy Truong Minh Giang evacuated Phnom Penh's six thousand inhabitants to Vietnam. He accepted responsibility for "losing" Cambodia, and committed suicide.[75]

Now mostly under Siamese control, Cambodia saw no peace after the Vietnamese withdrawal. Bodin ordered "the general massacre" of the "numerous" Vietnamese still resident there. According to a French missionary who arrived a few years later, the Siamese "fell upon Cambodia, rallied the whole population around them, and massacred the Annamites [Vietnamese] dispersed in the country."[76] In the Mekong delta to the south, ethnic consolidation continued, as the Siamese attempted to forcibly round up populations. In 1842, they captured two thousand Chinese-Cambodian refugees apparently fleeing the delta into Siamese-occupied territory. Seizing 250 Khmer inhabitants from three villages in Chaudoc, Siamese forces complained that "six Khmer households and fifty Cham households" had evaded capture. In one mass breakout from Siamese control, a hundred delta Khmers "escaped from the camp."[77] The Siamese forcibly evacuated Khmers from many villages near Phnom Penh. Upriver in eastern Cambodia, officials in four Mekong provinces rounded up their families and fled into the jungle. In messages to Bangkok, Siamese officers reported depopulating the South China Sea coast of its Chinese and Khmer populations, moving the Chinese north along the coast, and also dispatching 134 Vietnamese prisoners to Bangkok.[78]

Beyond population control for counterinsurgency, the Siamese labor deportation campaigns had an agricultural purpose. Bangkok instructed its governor of a border province in 1843 to "effectively organize the Chinese, Laotian and Khmer people to grow more sugar cane than ever before."[79] The Thai historian Puangthong Rungswasdisab has shown that increased rice cultivation was another Siamese goal. She concludes: "The pattern of forced resettlement was designed to meet the growing needs of agricultural production." Siam's depopulation campaigns devastated areas near Vietnam, such as Phnom Penh, and "remarkably diminished the size of Cambodia's population."[80]

However, Siam also confronted some of the same difficulties in Cambodia that had defeated Đai Nam. With a pessimism recalling that of Vietnamese viceroy Truong Minh Giang a decade earlier, Bodin reported to Bangkok in 1843: "We have been in Cambodia for three years without accomplishing anything. We are short of supplies; people are going off into the forest to live on leaves and roots; and nearly a thousand men in our army have died from lack of food." The Siamese abandoned Phnom Penh in 1844, and retreated to Udong. Vietnamese forces again returned to Phnom Penh. A desperate Bodin informed Bangkok that "all the Khmer leaders and nobles, all the district chiefs and all the common people are ignorant, stupid, foolish and gullible." Vietnamese attacks on Udong in 1845 led to peace talks.[81] Bodin wrote to Rama III: "We have decided to avoid the renewal of the war with the Vietnamese. In effect, the Khmer fighters have nearly all perished. The soldiers are afraid of the Vietnamese; the populations have fled into the forest to find food; the fields are uncultivated: Cambodia knows famine. During the recent Vietnamese intervention, a good number of Khmers rallied to Annam [Đai Nam] for the sake of peace."[82] Both sides eventually implemented a mutual withdrawal in 1847. In Udong, Siam's protégé Khmer prince assumed the throne, reigning as King Ang Duang (r. 1848–60). Đai Nam's hold on the country had ended, but Siam annexed Cambodia's northern provinces.[83]

David Chandler writes that Minh-Mang, within his own ideological framework, had "tried hard to be informed about Cambodia, to be fair to its people, and to improve their way of life." His conquest of the country was in fact provoked by a Siamese attack on Vietnam itself, just as his annexation of Lao provinces responded to earlier Siamese depredations there. However, Minh-Mang's ideological preoccupations also included territorial expansion, repressive control, cultural superiority, classical precedent, and agricultural reform, and he was prepared from the start to impose them all, if necessary by force, within Đai Nam as well as in Cambodia. What he shared with the ideological mindset of other colonial perpetrators meant that, in the face of competitive Siamese expansion and relentless Khmer opposition, he finally resorted to policies that could be considered genocidal. This also applies to the brutal orders Siam's Rama III gave to his own army, and to their implementation by the Siamese commander Bodin.

No extant statistical information records the Cambodian death toll resulting from the violence of Đai Nam's occupation and Siam's deportations. Their impact may be gauged only from a Khmer account published sixty years later, looking back on the late 1840s.

> The land was no longer cultivated. The peasants deserted their villages because they were still afraid of the Vietnamese and Siamese who had come to pillage their harvests. Half of the fruit trees in the villages were cut down. As a result villages which had counted up to a hundred and fifty houses no longer had more than fifty or even twenty. In each village the number of people had fallen considerably. . . . Entire villages were abandoned and my grief reached its height at the sight of the widows deprived of everything, incapable of feeding their young children.[84]

The French Colonial Conquest

Cambodia recovered from this disaster during the 1850s.[85] However Ang Duang died in 1860, the year after the French conquest and colonization of Vietnam had begun. France then imposed a protectorate on Cambodia in 1863. In the next two years, Khmer rebellions challenged the regime of Duang's successor, King Norodom (r. 1860–1904), and his French protectors, whom Norodom hoped would shield his kingdom from Siam and Đai Nam. His main dangers proved to be domestic. Moreover, Norodom's rule and early acquiescence to the French presence even resurrected previous traditions of collaboration between Khmer and Vietnamese neighbors. Antiroyalist rebels resembled the multiethnic coalitions once fielded by Gia-Long and Lê Van Khôi. With King Norodom's half-brother, Prince Si Votha, already fomenting revolt against him, two messianic Buddhist monks launched their own rebellions. In 1865, one of them, Pou Kombo, a member of Cambodia's small Kouy minority, recruited a thousand Khmers, three hundred Vietnamese, and a hundred Muslim Chams and tribal Stiengs. By late 1866, Pou Kombo fielded five thousand troops in a single battle, including seven hundred to eight hundred Vietnamese. One thousand French colonial troops marched into Cambodia to help defeat him. Khmer royalist forces killed Pou Kombo the next year, but one of his lieutenants re-emerged five years later with four hundred followers "of every race in Indochina," and another fought on until 1875. Pou Kombo's revolt had again "turned the tiny Khmer kingdom upside down."[86]

Royal repression was severe. After one clash in early 1865, a royal commander reported the capture of thirty-two prisoners, Khmers and Vietnamese, who "were all executed already."[87] Peasants took refuge in the jungles. Campaigning against Pou Kombo in eastern Cambodia in mid-1866, a prominent prince wrote: "I ordered the soldiers to gather every family in every village of Tbaung Khmum province that were in hiding in the forest." He had also sent "2,500 soldiers" to one district, to try to capture Pou Kombo "and all the enemies" there. Royal forces faced similar problems elsewhere, the prince added: "All the families in Romeas Hek province have betrayed [us] since my father's time."[88] A few months later a royal missive ordered officials to assemble "all the people, Khmer, Chinese and Vietnamese" and to conscript "all of the single males in Ba Phnom province, servants, workers, young adults, and those who have just left the monkhood. . . . No one should be left out. Make [them] soldiers to seriously protect all the people." If rebel forces approached, the king's orders were to "chop, stab, shoot, destroy—don't be intimidated by them." The court complained of the carelessness and self-interest of its own commanders: "That is why the royal government has been ruined this much."[89]

It was during this period following the French arrival in Cambodia that the Buddhist poet Venerable Pich added a significant line to a new work that expanded on his 1855 poem: "But I realize that Cambodia is not at peace, that it knows only misfortunes and that the kingdom of Kampuchéa is on the point of disappearance." The new crisis had provoked Pich to recopy and enhance his poem in order "to transmit a heritage" now in danger of being lost. "I write so that our descendants may know the distant past of their ancestors."[90]

Despite the stark memories of Vietnamese rule in the 1830s that Pich recorded, Khmer official orders to royal commanders suggest that the court, like the rebel opposition, saw Cambodia as a multiethnic kingdom. Commanders had to "gather all the families of Vietnamese and Khmer," and "form a troop to protect all the families who came to our side," including "all families of Vietnamese, Khmer, and Stieng, every day." The court aimed to strengthen the kingdom and make it "stable, abundant, and peaceful."[91] However, the turmoil was unceasing. Prince Si Votha launched yet another rebellion in 1876/77. Along with royal forces, four columns of French and Vietnamese colonial troops marched against him and drove the prince off again.[92]

In June 1884, the French governor in Saigon, Charles Thomson, sailed three gunboats up the Mekong to Phnom Penh. He imposed on Norodom and his court France's right to introduce in Cambodia "all the administrative, judicial, financial and commercial reforms" that it judged necessary, including the appointment of French *résidents* in provincial towns, the introduction of property in land, and the outlawing of slavery.[93] Rebellion erupted again in January 1885, and in May five thousand rebels invaded the capital, before French marines and police dispersed them.[94] A two-year nationwide insurgency tied down thousands of colonial troops, who took heavy casualties and caused significant destruction. Also in May 1885, for instance, three hundred Khmers drove the French and Annamese troops from the port of Kampot. Escapees to Siam then reported the retaliation: "The French sent two steamships and two Vietnamese ships to bombard the Khmer rebels. . . . The French then moved in and burned down the town."[95] Colonial forces were able to quell the Cambodian revolt only with cooperation from King Norodom and the loss of over 5,000 troops. Rebel Prince Si Votha fought on until 1889. His death in a remote jungle camp in 1892 ended his thirty-year dissidence. A French source estimated that casualties during the 1885–87 conflict as well as a mass exodus to Cambodia's Siamese-controlled provinces had reduced the protectorate's population by as many as 195,000, or one-fifth of the entire Khmer population. "Around 1879, relying on official information, [the French *Resident-Supérieur*] M. Moura estimated the total figure for the kingdom's population at 945,000 inhabitants. After the period of the insurrection from 1884 to 1887, following the devastation of the country, the diseases and the exceptional mortality, which were the fatal consequences of that period, scarcely more than 750,000 inhabitants were counted."[96]

Conclusion

As in other regions of the shrinking nineteenth-century globe, colonialism proved a strategic, competitive enterprise, even when the competitors' philosophical traditions and political-economic goals differed, as did those of Đai Nam, Siam, and France. Colonial conquests were often bloody, but genocide has more often occurred in cases of settler colonies, involving the forcible seizure of a territory's arable land and the violent dispossession of its inhabitants for the exclusive purposes of colonial agriculture or pastoral settlement. Though none of Cambodia's competing colonial conquerors promoted extensive settler colonization, the expansionism and brutality of all three, the Vietnamese and Siamese preoccupation with land and labor for agriculture, and Minh-Mang's cult of antiquity, are reminiscent of other genocide perpetrators. If all three of Đai Nam, Siam, and France did not commit what we might recognize as classic cases of genocide, their cumulative demographic impact was devastating.

The cultural impact was also catastrophic. In part, these serial colonial disasters set the historical scene for a collective Khmer memory of national subjugation that would fuel the Khmer Rouge genocide of the 1970s. This impact was compounded and distorted, however, by Cambodia's twentieth-century climate of historiographical ignorance, itself a partial result of the early nineteenth-century destruction of Khmer archival records and literary and historical works during the Vietnamese and Siamese invasions, as well as subsequent French colonial neglect of both Cambodia's education system and the study of its modern history.[97]

During the twentieth century, by discouraging discussion of the damage and destruction of the French colonial conquest, by pursuing a policy of divide and rule of its Vietnamese and Khmer subjects, and by highlighting the ancient glory of Cambodia's Angkor empire at the expense of the country's modern history and contemporary problems, France focused Khmer political attention and enmity on Vietnam.[98] This set the intellectual stage for the Pol Pot regime in the 1970s to pursue a postcolonial conflict of genocidal proportions in the name of supposedly ancient racial hatreds. By then Cambodia's nationalist memory had given prominence to Đai Nam's devastation of Cambodia in the 1830s, and spurred the Lon Nol regime in 1970 and the Khmer Rouge regime in 1977 to emulate long-forgotten genocidal massacres that had preceded and followed that devastation, when Cambodia's King Ang Snguon in 1750, and the Thai commander Chaophraya Bodin in the 1840s, each organized the wholesale murder of every Vietnamese resident who could be found in Cambodia.[99]

Notes

1. Ben Kiernan, *Blood and Soil: A World History of Genocide and Extermination from Sparta to Darfur* (New Haven, CT, 2007). I am grateful to Nola Cooke and Li Tana for their help with this chapter. Any errors are mine.
2. M. Piguel à Mgr. Lefebvre, 8 avril 1751, M. d'Azema à M. de Noëlène, undated, quoted in M. J-B. Maigrot à Mgr. de Martiliat, 16 septembre 1751, and d'Azema aux Directeurs du Séminaire des M.-E., Cambodge, 20 juin 1757, in Adrien Launay, *Histoire de la Mission de Cochinchine 1658–1823, Documents Historiques*, vol. 2, *1728–1771* (Paris, 1924), 368, 366, 370; Kiernan, *Blood and Soil*, chap. 4.
3. Victor Lieberman, *Strange Parallels: Southeast Asia in Global Context, c. 800–1830*, vol. 1, *Integration on the Mainland* (New York, 2003), 412.
4. Alexander B. Woodside, *Vietnam and the Chinese Model: A Comparative Study of Nguyen and Ch'ing Civil Government in the First Half of the Nineteenth Century* (Cambridge, MA, 1971), 16–17, 243–44; Choi Byung Wook, *Southern Vietnam under the Reign of Minh Mang (1820–1841): Central Policies and Local Response* (Ithaca, NY, 2004), 42.
5. D.P. Chandler, *A History of Cambodia* (Boulder, CO, 1983), 118; Chandler, "Cambodia Before the French: Politics in a Tributary Kingdom, 1794–1848" (Ph.D. diss., University of Michigan, 1973), 91.
6. Choi, *Southern Vietnam*, 34; Lieberman, *Integration*, 427; Chandler, *History*, 116, 119.
7. Woodside, *Vietnam*, 248, 244; Chandler, *History*, 114, 119–20.
8. Chandler, "Cambodia Before the French," 90.
9. Christopher E. Goscha, *Vietnam or Indochina? Contesting Concepts of Space in Vietnamese Nationalism, 1887–1954* (Copenhagen, 1995), 14; Woodside, *Vietnam*, 248; Choi, *Southern Vietnam*, 53.
10. Choi, *Southern Vietnam*, 34–35; Chandler, "Cambodia Before the French," 90, 93; Woodside, *Vietnam*, 248; Lê Thành Khôi, *Histoire du Vietnam des origines à 1858* (Paris, 1981), 363.

11. D. P. Chandler, "An Anti-Vietnamese Rebellion in Early Nineteenth Century Cambodia: Pre-colonial Imperialism and a Pre-Nationalist Response," *Journal of Southeast Asian Studies* 6, no. 1 (1975): 16–24, 17.
12. Bâtum Baramey Pich, *Sastra voat Kroch khum Kroch srok Prey Chhô khêt Kâmpung Cham* [1869?] ("Manuscript of Kroch pagoda, Kroch subdistrict, Prey Chhor district, Kompong Cham province"), text and translation of an 1875 copy, in Khin Sok, *L'Annexion du Cambodge par les Vietnamiens au XIXe siècle d'après les deux poèmes du Vénérable Bâtum Baramey Pich* (Paris, 2002), 203, 52.
13. John Crawfurd, *Journal of an Embassy from the Governor General of India to the Courts of Siam and Cochinchina* (London, 1830, repr. 1967), 587, cited in Chandler, "Anti-Vietnamese Rebellion," 18n15.
14. Chandler, "Anti-Vietnamese Rebellion," 18.
15. *Sastra voat Kroch khum Kroch srok Prey Chhô khêt Kâmpung Cham*, in Khin Sok, *L'Annexion*, 55–56; Chandler, "Anti-Vietnamese Rebellion," 17–21.
16. Chandler, "An Anti-Vietnamese Rebellion," 21–22; Chandler, *History*, 120–21.
17. Chandler, "An Anti-Vietnamese Rebellion," 22–24.
18. Woodside, *Vietnam*, 249; Lê Thành Khôi, *Histoire du Vietnam*, 364.
19. Woodside, *Vietnam*, 135, 27; Lê Thành Khôi, *Histoire du Vietnam*, 369; Choi, *Southern Vietnam*, 130n5.
20. Woodside, *Vietnam*, 167.
21. Ibid., 249; Chandler, "An Anti-Vietnamese Rebellion," 20n32; Puangthong Rungswasdisab, "War and Trade: Siamese Interventions in Cambodia, 1767–1851" (Ph.D. diss., University of Wollongong, 1995); Choi, *Southern Vietnam*, 141.
22. Choi, *Southern Vietnam*, 96; Lieberman, *Integration*, 430. France annexed Champa's last two provinces to its Cochinchina colony in 1883; E. Aymonier, *Excursions et reconnaissances*, X, (Qui Nhon, Vietnam, June 1883).
23. Jean Chesneaux, *The Vietnamese People: Contribution to a History*, tr. M. Salmon (Sydney, 1966), 51.
24. Chesneaux, *The Vietnamese People*, 62–63.
25. Mai Khac Ung, *Chinh Sach Khuyen Nong Duoi Thoi Minh Mang* ("Emperor Minh Mang's Agriculture Encouraging Policy") (Hanoi, 1996), 459.
26. Choi, *Southern Vietnam*, 175, 182–86.
27. Woodside, *Vietnam*, 13–14; Chandler, *History*, 127; see also Nola Cooke, "The Myth of the Restoration: Dang Trong Influences in the Spiritual Life of the Nguyen Dynasty (1802–1847)," in *The Last Stand of Asian Autonomies: Responses to Modernity in the Diverse States of Southeast Asia and Korea, 1750–1900*, ed. Anthony Reid (New York, 1997).
28. Woodside, *Vietnam*, 14.
29. "Chotmaihet kieokap khmen lae yuan," *Prachum Pongsawadan* Part 68, Vol. 41 (Bangkok, 1969), 244, translation by Puangthong Rungswasdisab; Rungswasdisab, *War and Trade*, 144.
30. Bâtum Baramey Pich, *Sastra voat Kroch*, in Khin Sok, *L'Annexion*, 235, 238.
31. Bâtum Baramey Pich, *Sastra lbaoek rôba khsat phêndey Outeyréachéa Ang Chan* [1855] ("Manuscript relating the lineage of King Ang Chan"), text and translation in Khin Sok, *L'Annexion*, 329–59, 331.
32. Chandler, "Cambodia Before the French," 114–15.
33. Bâtum Baramey Pich, *Sastra voat Kroch*, in Khin Sok, *L'Annexion*, 250.
34. Rungswasdisab, *War and Trade*, 99–100.
35. Bâtum Baramey Pich, *Sastra lbaoek rôba khsat*, in Khin Sok, *L'Annexion*, 332.
36. Pich, *Sastra voat Kroch*, in Khin Sok, *L'Annexion*, 245.

37. Chandler, *History*, 123. Pich, *Sastra voat Kroch*, in Khin Sok, *L'Annexion*, 245, says the Siamese deported "at least two thousand families," each with children and grandchildren.
38. Bâtum Baramey Pich, *Sastra voat Kroch*, in Khin Sok, *L'Annexion*, 238, 243, 21.
39. Chandler, "Cambodia Before the French," 115–16; Khin Sok, *L'Annexion*, 65.
40. Rungswasdisab, *War and Trade*, 144–45.
41. Pich, *Sastra voat Kroch*, in Khin Sok, *L'Annexion*, 246–49.
42. Chandler, *History*, 122–23; Lê Thành Khôi, *Histoire du Vietnam*, 363; Woodside, *Vietnam*, 121, 249–50.
43. Choi, *Southern Vietnam*, 132.
44. Pich, *Sastra lbaoeuk rôba khsat*, in Khin Sok, *L'Annexion*, 333.
45. Chandler, *History*, 124.
46. *Zhenxi fengtu ji* ("The Customs of Tran Tay"), in Chinese, ms. dating from c. 1840; English translation kindly provided by Li Tana, 7 pp., at p. 6.
47. Woodside, *Vietnam*, 145.
48. *Zhenxi fengtu ji*, 6.
49. Chandler, *History*, 126.
50. Ibid., 126–27.
51. Woodside, *Vietnam*, 145, 250.
52. *Đai Nam thuc luc chinh bien, de nhi ky* XIV (1836), Vol. 18, Book 176, 342 (cited as *DNTL* II, 176:12–12b, in Woodside, *Vietnam*, 250), (Hanoi, 1967). Translation by Vy Vu.
53. *Đai Nam thuc luc chinh bien, de nhi ky*, Book 121 (*DNTL* II, 121:28, cited in Woodside, *Vietnam*, 250).
54. *Đai Nam thuc luc chinh bien, de nhi ky*, vol. 18, Book 176, 342.
55. Ibid., XI (1834), Vol. 15, Book 138, 297 (cited as *DNTL* II, 138:27, in Woodside, *Vietnam*, 254.). Translation by Vy Vu.
56. *Đai Nam thuc luc chinh bien, de nhi ky*, vol. 18, Book 176, 342; Chandler, *History*, 129.
57. Ibid., vol. 15, Book 138, 297.
58. Woodside, *Vietnam*, 251; Chandler, *History*, 127–28.
59. *Zhenxi fengtu ji*, 6–7.
60. Chandler, *History*, 122, 124–25.
61. Pich, *Sastra lbaoeuk rôba khsat*, in Khin Sok, *L'Annexion*, 334–39.
62. Chandler, *History*, 128–29.
63. Pich, *Sastra lbaoeuk rôba khsat*, in Khin Sok, *L'Annexion*, 340–41.
64. Chandler, *History*, 130, 127, 125, 129–31.
65. *Zhenxi fengtu ji*, 1.
66. Choi, *Southern Vietnam*, 180, 178, 176, 188, 171n.27.
67. Ibid., 187, 189, 178–79, 171, 190; Woodside, *Vietnam*, 147–49.
68. Chandler, *History*, 128–30; Pich, *Sastra lbaoeuk rôba khsat*, in Khin Sok, *L'Annexion*, 341.
69. Chandler, "Cambodia Before the French," 153–54; Chandler, *History*, 132.
70. Chandler, *History*, 127–28, 132–33.
71. Abbreviated report from Chaophraya Bodin, "Chotmaihet kieokap khmen lae yuan," in *Prachum Pongsawadan* Part 68, Vol. 42, ([1840] Bangkok, 1969), 224. Translation by Puangthong Rungswasdisab.
72. "Chotmaihet kieokap khmen lae yuan," *Prachum Pongsawadan* Part 68, Vol. 42, 244.
73. Chandler, *History*, 132.

74. J.B. Granjean, Bangkok, le 20 janvier 1842, excerpted in Khin Sok, *L'Annexion*, 82n1.
75. Chandler, *History*, 134.
76. Auguste Pavie, "Excursion dans le Cambodge et le Royaume de Siam," *Excursions et Reconnaissances* 7, no. 18 (1884): 405; C.-E. Bouillevaux, *Voyage dans l'Indochine, 1848–1856* (Paris, 1858), 181. See Nola Cooke and Li Tana, *Water Frontier: Commerce and the Chinese in the Lower Mekong Region, 1750–1880* (New York, 2004), 155n42.
77. Thai National Library, Bangkok, *Chotmaihet R.III* cho.so. 1204/1/cho/12, "Report on the War against the Vietnamese in Cambodia"; cho/17, "Copy of the Report on the War against the Vietnamese in Cambodia." *Chotmaihet ruang thap yuan khrang ratchakan thi sam*, Bangkok, Rongphim Sophon Phiphatthanakan, *Cremation volume for General Phraya Singhaseni*, 1933, 6, 8. Translations by Puangthong Rungswasdisab.
78. *Chotmaihet ruang thap yuan khrang ratchakan thi sam*, 28, 48, 16, 20, 134.
79. *Chotmaihet Rama III* cho.so. 1205/20, quoted in Rungswasdisab, *War and Trade*, 149.
80. Rungswasdisab, *War and Trade*, 151, 154.
81. *Chotmaihet Rama III* cho.so. 1206/6 [1844], quoted in Chandler, *History*, 134–35.
82. Quoted in Khin Sok, *L'Annexion*, 87.
83. Chandler, *History*, 135; Khin Sok, *L'Annexion*, 88, 90.
84. Méah, *Roeung Bândam Ta Méah* ("Memoirs of grandfather Méah") [1907], 40 pp., at 5–6, quoted in Khin Sok, *L'Annexion*, 88–89, 64n2.
85. Chandler, *History*, 135–36.
86. Jean Moura, *Le Royaume du Cambodge* (Paris, 1887), 159–61, 170, 172; Lt. Batz, "Historique de l'Occupation Militaire du Cambodge par les Troupes Françaises de 1855 à 1910," *Bulletin de la Société des Etudes Indochinoises* 6, no. 3 & 4 (1931): 175–85, at 180.
87. Neak Oknha Kralahom to Ong Thambien Chhang Bang, Feb.–Mar. 1865, in Papiers Pou Kombo, *Fonds Finot*, Ecole Française de l'Extrême-Orient (EFEO), Paris; translation by Thavro Phim.
88. Samdech Preah Chao Thireach Karnai Keofa to General Ong Thoam Mieng, June–July 1866, ibid.
89. Samdech Preah Ang Keo to Neak Oknha Yumreach and Neak Oknha Chakrei, Oct.–Nov. 1866, ibid.
90. *Sastra Voat Kroch* [copy dated 1875], text and translation in Khin Sok, *L'Annexion*, 203.
91. Neak Oknha Chakrei to Ong Teung Tvin [?], Oct.–Nov. 1866, Papiers Pou Kombo, *Fonds Finot*, EFEO.
92. Batz, "Historique de l'Occupation Militaire," 182.
93. Chandler, *History*, 143.
94. Batz, "Historique de l'Occupation Militaire," 182.
95. *Chotmaihet Phraratkitraiwan Phraratniphon nai Phrarat Somdet Phrachulachomklaochaoyuhua* ("Rama V's Diary"), Part 19 (Bangkok, 1970), 63, 70. Translation by Chalong Soontravanich.
96. Armand Rousseau, *Le Protectorat Français du Cambodge: organisation politique, administrative, et financière* (Dijon, 1904), 169–70; "Introduction," in Ben Kiernan and Chanthou Boua, *Peasants and Politics in Kampuchea 1942–1981* (London, 1982), 2.
97. Ben Kiernan, "Recovering History and Justice in Cambodia," *Comparativ* 14, nos. 5/6 (2004): 76–85.

98. Ben Kiernan, *How Pol Pot Came to Power: Colonialism, Nationalism, and Communism in Cambodia, 1930–75*, 2nd ed. (New Haven, CT, 2004), ix–xx, chap. 1.
99. Ben Kiernan, *The Pol Pot Regime: Race, Power and Genocide in Cambodia under the Khmer Rouge, 1975–1979*, 2nd ed. (New Haven, CT, 2002), 296–98, 423–25; Alexander Laban Hinton, *Why Did They Kill? Cambodia in the Shadow of Genocide* (Berkeley, CA, 2005), 154, 219.

– Chapter 10 –

GENOCIDE IN TASMANIA
The History of an Idea

Ann Curthoys

> The naval armament of the Persians wintered at Miletus, and in the following year proceeded to attack the islands off the coast, Chios, Lesbos, and Tenedos, which were reduced without difficulty. Whenever they became masters of an island, the barbarians, in every single instance, netted the inhabitants. Now the mode in which they practise this netting is the following. Men join hands, so as to form a line across from the north coast to the south, and then march through the island from end to end and hunt out the inhabitants.
>
> —Herodotus, *The Histories* (6.31)

> Our fields and forests, which once furnished us with abundance of vegetable and animal food, now yield us no more; they and their produce are yours. You prosper on our native soil, and we are famishing!
>
> —Paul E. de Strzelecki, 1845[1]

Introduction

It is a paradox of world history that while Tasmania, one of Australia's six states and an island to the south of the Australian mainland, has long and frequently been cited internationally as having witnessed a clear-cut case of genocide, such a characterization is rarely adopted within Australia. The aim of this chapter is to elucidate how this came to be so. In the course of attempting to historicize and explain this paradox, I will explore the complex history of ideas about the rapid decline of indigenous populations in the wake of colonization, and the ways these ideas have been consistently tied to political agendas and broader worldviews, both historically and in the present. I also argue that the separation of and divergence between international and Australian approaches since the 1970s has been deleterious for both genocide studies and Australian historical scholarship. Finally, I make a case for seeing the Tasmanian events as a case of genocide, though not of state planning, mass killing, or extinction.

Although the interpretations of Tasmanian history vary considerably, they generally tell a story of largely peaceful, though sporadically violent, interactions between Europeans and indigenous peoples between 1803 and 1827, when European settlement under direct British government supervision was generally sparse. Matters changed dramatically in the next few years, when British settlement intensified, affecting traditional sources of food. Fierce Aboriginal attacks on European settlement prompted harsh reprisals by settlers and government forces; the result was widespread frontier conflict especially between 1827 and 1830. As conflict continued, and in an attempt to protect both the settlers and the remaining Aboriginal people, Lieutenant-Governor Arthur adopted a policy of land clearance, that is, of removing all Aboriginal people from the island, known until 1852 as Van Diemen's Land, with the hope of confining them to an offshore island. To this end, the government sponsored the "Black Line" of October and November 1830, when soldiers swept the length and breadth of the colony to capture any remaining Aboriginal people, somewhat reminiscent of the Persians "netting" the inhabitants of Greek islands, as evoked by Herodotus. When the Black Line failed in its objectives, the authorities turned to conciliation and persuasion. Aboriginal numbers were by this time already falling rapidly and George Augustus Robinson, working as a government agent, eventually succeeded in persuading the remaining two hundred or so Aboriginal people to move to Flinders Island, just off the Tasmanian coast, in 1830/31. Although Robinson and others had high hopes of here "preserving the race," the numbers continued to drop alarmingly. By the mid 1830s, with just over 120 survivors remaining, and very few births on the island, it seemed clear that as a people they would not survive. By 1847, the numbers on Flinders Island had again fallen, the island was abandoned, and the remnant population of forty-seven people taken to Oyster Cove, about thirty miles from Hobart on the Tasmanian mainland. Their numbers continued to plummet, until in 1876 the last Tasmanian of full descent, Truganini, passed away, widely described as "the last of her race." The extinction of the Aboriginal Tasmanians appeared to be complete.[2]

The Tasmanian case is significant for several reasons. First, Tasmania has long held a particular place in our consciousness of the destruction of indigenous peoples. When French and British maritime explorers first encountered the indigenous people of what was then Van Diemen's Land in the late eighteenth century, the latter had been separated from contact with other human groups since the end of the last ice age, about 8,000–10,000 years before. As geographer and world historian Jared Diamond wrote, we are fascinated by isolated societies. "Tasmania," he says, "holds the record for the longest isolation known in human history."[3] Also striking is their rapid demise in the wake of British colonization. Many indigenous peoples throughout the Americas and Australia met similar fates, and in retrospect we can see that what happened in Tasmania was not unusual in the history of settler colonialism. Yet it has long attracted particular notice, partly because, as Australian historian Charles Rowley pointed out in *The Destruction of Aboriginal Society*, the indigenous Tasmanians' isolation from other indigenous peoples made it especially easy to think of them as an entirely separate people.[4] The disappearance of entire peoples on the mainland, where the boundaries between peoples were unclear to European observers, has been far less evident or obvious. Furthermore, in contrast to the mainland, where a mix of imperial and local settler authorities oversaw the taking of land, the displacement of the indigenous peoples of Tasmania was conducted entirely within the period of British rule. As a result of this long-standing focus on Tasmania, our interest now must lie not only in the historical events themselves but also in the peculiar attention they have received ever since.

Importantly, the terminology has changed over this long period of discourse about the destruction of the indigenous Tasmanians and indigenous peoples generally. In the nineteenth-century discussion of such disappearance, the common terms were *extirpation*, *extermination*, and *extinction*. These three words could be used interchangeably, but they did have slightly distinct meanings: "extirpation" usually denoted a *process* emphasising settler agency; "extinction" described an *outcome* in which no members of a particular human group remained; while "extermination" tended to mean the connection between the two, a process conducted by settlers with extinction as its outcome. Since the Second World War, modern discussions have been both enhanced and made more complicated by the introduction of a new word, *genocide*, which has now largely displaced these earlier terms. The term *genocide* was coined in 1944 by the eminent Polish Jewish jurist, Raphael Lemkin, in his remarkable text, *Axis Rule in Occupied Europe*.[5] Initially concerned by the rise of Nazism in Germany and later by its policies and practices of destroying Jews and Slavs, and replacing them with German settlers in Eastern Europe, Lemkin argued that international law could be developed and invoked to prevent a recurrence of attempts to destroy whole peoples. A new word was needed to describe these crimes: *genocide*, literally, the killing of a people. Importantly for modern historians, Lemkin's aims were not only to establish a new crime, and mechanisms for its prevention, but also to reinterpret the course of human history in light of his new concept. In his published work, but also especially his unpublished work that I consider in this chapter, he hoped that his notion of genocide could be used to interpret past episodes of group destruction through land seizure, the importation of diseases, the taking of women and children, and other ways of removing the very foundations of group life. While the concept of genocide derives much of its modern relevance and impact from the example of Nazi rule in Europe, it was for Lemkin also a way of characterizing long-term instances of genocide in European colonialism. Its dual existence as both a legal and a historical term has been both productive and confusing, as I will explore.

Ideas about Extermination and Extinction in Tasmania, 1820s–1870s

Extinction discourse accompanied settler colonization everywhere. As Patrick Brantlinger points out, discourses of extinction found expression in "art, literature, journalism, sciences, and governmental rhetoric"; it was often elegiac in form, expressing both sorrow at the loss of whole peoples and at the same time a confident belief that the white colonies and nations would arise as savage peoples receded.[6] A strong recurrent feature of extinction discourse—and this was to become particularly true in Tasmania—was a special interest in the last survivor of a given human group. By the 1820s, there were many literary accounts of disappearing races in North America, with the best-known and emblematic example being James Fennimore Cooper's *The Last of the Mohicans*, published in 1826.[7] As the indigenous population of Van Diemen's Land began to fall rapidly from the late 1820s, colonial governors, settlers, and British officials were aware of these American events and discourses and, with varying degrees of concern, contemplating the possibility that the same might happen around them.

The belief that the indigenous peoples of Van Diemen's Land would soon disappear entirely developed around 1830. In response to the report of an Aborigines Committee established by Lieutenant-Governor Arthur to advise him on how to prevent further Aboriginal attacks on settlers, Sir George Murray as secretary of state for the colonies wrote (in an oft-quoted passage) on 5 November 1830 as follows: "The great decrease that has of late years taken place in the amount of the aboriginal population, renders it not unreasonable to apprehend that the whole race of these people may, at a not distant period, become extinct."[8] Three weeks later, and before receiving Murray's dispatch, Arthur expressed a similar view, writing to Murray of his belief that only capture and confinement could protect the colony and arrest "the eventual extirpation of the race itself."[9]

As the 1830s progressed, and as the remaining couple of hundred indigenous people gathered on Flinders Island continued to die and few children were born, the conviction that they would soon completely disappear spread beyond official dispatches to the settler population generally. In 1835, Henry Melville, a journalist, publisher, and writer who had arrived in the colony seven years earlier, wrote that: "It is generally believed that this race of human beings will soon become extinct altogether, as the deaths are common, and the increase nothing equal in proportion."[10] Melville blamed the early settlers of the 1800s and 1810s. Whereas the colonists of his own time had genuinely had something to fear from Aboriginal attacks, he thought, those who came much earlier had attacked without provocation: "Nothing can be offered in extenuation of the conduct of the first Colonists towards these bewildered creatures, and the historian must ever lament that he has to record outrages so inhuman and so unjust on the part of a British community."[11] Melville saw the Aboriginal people of Van Diemen's Land (VDL) as "easy, quiet, good-natured and well-disposed towards the white population," and thought they had been treated worse than American tribes by the Spaniards, deprived of their hunting grounds and other sources of food, and thus driven to retaliate.[12] The Americas continued to influence colonial thinking; a year later, Major Thomas Ryan wrote that unless the government did all it could to "propagate the species," the "race of Tasmania, like the last of the Mohicans, will pine away and be extinct in a quarter of a century."[13]

Meanwhile, a British House of Commons committee in 1835 and 1836 was examining the situation of indigenous people in British settlements around the world. Led by the evangelical abolitionist, Sir Thomas Fowell Buxton, the Christian, liberal, and humanitarian committee had a prior agenda: to protect, civilize, and convert the indigenous peoples in British colonies. The Report of the committee, published in two volumes in 1836/37, argued that indigenous peoples were being morally degraded and physically destroyed through direct violence, alcohol, and introduced diseases. The committee did not think that colonization should or could be slowed or stopped; rather the solution was Christianization. Although the Committee was poorly informed of events in Van Diemen's Land, interviewing few with direct experience of what had happened there, its report concluded that: "Whatever may have been the injustice of this encroachment, there is no reason to suppose that either justice or humanity would now be consulted by receding from it."[14]

Discussion of the fate of the indigenous people of Van Diemen's Land shifted in the mid 1830s from *whether* the people would disappear, to *why*. The great British scientist Charles Darwin was one of those pondering why after he visited Van Diemen's Land in the *Beagle* in February 1836, and learned of the removal a few years earlier to Flinders Island. "Thirty years," he wrote, "is a short period, in which to have banished the last aboriginal from his native island."[15] Darwin pondered the universality of extinction in the wake of European settlement: "Besides these several evident causes of destruction, there appears to be some more mysterious agency generally at work. Wherever the European has trod, death seems to pursue the aboriginal. We may look to the wide extent of the Americas, Polynesia, the Cape of Good Hope, and Australia, and we shall find the same result. . . . The varieties of man seem to act upon each other in the same way as different species of animals; the stronger always extirpating the weaker."[16]

This idea of inevitability and something mysterious being at work took hold in the European imagination, though there were also some, like Colonial Office official Herman Merivale, who in 1840 retorted that there was nothing mysterious about it; there were clear reasons, "appreciable causes," such as the effects of firearms on the destructiveness of intertribal fighting, the loss of food, the effects of alcohol, the disastrous effects of epidemics (especially smallpox), or the effects of a sudden change in habits, which he mentioned specifically in relation to the Aboriginal Tasmanians on Flinders Island.[17] Count Strzelecki, a Polish noble and geologist who visited many colonies of settlement around the world, including the Australian colonies between 1839 and 1843, thought the main reason for Aboriginal depopulation was declining fertility, the result either of sterility from venereal and other diseases or because indigenous women (he thought) who had had sexual intercourse with the settlers could no longer conceive children with men of their own race.[18] As the dying and depopulation continued, settlers developed their own theories and explanations, such as the idea that the indigenous people were dying because they had given up, had lost the will to live.[19]

By the 1860s, in British scientific circles, the Tasmanians (as they were known after 1852) had become the prototypical case. On 19 January 1864, when the Anthropological Society in London debated the extinction of the so-called lower races, the opening speaker, Richard Lee, noted that the "natives of Tasmania are almost, if not quite, extinct. . . . Nowhere has the disappearance of a native race been more complete in modern times than in Tasmania." At the same meeting, T. Bendyshe challenged the idea of inevitable and perhaps mysterious extinction as a consequence of colonization, arguing that the problem was not the "mere presence of the white man," but the taking of a people's land. He asked of those who invoke mystery rather than loss of land: "But how or on what were these people to live *after* their lands were occupied?"[20]

The Tasmanian events had thus come to represent a clear, unambiguous, incontrovertible, and well-documented example of the extermination of an entire people. Although there were differences between different commentators over the facts, explanation, or morality of what had happened, there was no significant deviation between local settler and metropolitan British understandings of events and issues. They were in this period inextricably entwined, as ideas and knowledge moved back and forth from colony to metropole.

James Bonwick's remarkable and still-read book, *The Last of the Tasmanians* (1870), published forty years after the removal of the people from the Tasmanian mainland, told the story of an almost extinct people in considerable detail. Having first become interested in the subject after a visit to the ill-fated Flinders Island settlement in 1859, he worked with colonial government records and interviewed some early settlers. He also used his own knowledge from living in the colony in the 1840s; he writes, for example, that he had "on several occasions heard men declare that they thought no more of shooting a Black than bringing down a bird."[21] Bonwick's explanation for the near-disappearance of the Tasmanians was the British and settler appropriation of indigenous land. After discussing the early visits by maritime explorers, he writes: "The Whites came again. They came not as curious visitors, but to make a home in the land. They came not to share the soil with the dark man, but to appropriate it."[22] He thought it ironic that on the one hand the British authorities instructed Collins to live in amity and kindness with the natives, and to punish offenders against them, and on the other remained "utterly oblivious of their rights to the land."[23] Bonwick thought the "wild man" had two choices: to "prostrate themselves beneath the feet of the usurpers and quietly submit to slavery," or to "refuse to sell their birthright of freedom, and take the consequences." It was no surprise to Bonwick that they chose the latter course.[24] Bonwick noted official attempts to stop the conflict, and their futility. The events in Tasmania, he thought, provided a story like that written by Las Casas in his "Short Account of the Destruction of the Indies." In both cases, the government tried impotently to protect the natives "against the avarice and cruelty of its subjects."[25]

Bonwick stresses not only the direct effects of land loss in frontier conflict, but also the indirect effects; disease, ill health, and lower fertility, in effect an inventory of the effects of colonization on indigenous people. His wide-ranging account was used by Charles Darwin the following year in *The Descent of Man* (1871). In a section entitled "Extinction of the Races of Man," Darwin largely abandons the idea of a "mysterious" disappearance, and explores a large number of possible reasons for indigenous population decline, including loss of land and therefore sustenance, new diseases and spirituous liquors, loss of will to live, and general ill health. After stressing the complexity of the matter, he concludes that fertility decline, a result of being forced "to desert their homes and to change their habits," was especially important in the disappearance of indigenous peoples.[26]

In 1874, another Tasmanian settler, J.E. Calder, listed many of the same causes as Bonwick had, with one important exception: he largely excluded loss of life through direct frontier violence. On the frontiers of settlement, he suggested, it was the Aborigines and not the Europeans who had generally prevailed. "Aggressiveness," he wrote, "was almost always on the side of the blacks; and in this unequal contest the musket of the Englishman was far less deadly than the spear of the savage, at least five of the former dying for one of the latter."[27] The rapid population decline had other causes: "Whole tribes . . . which had probably never had a shot fired at them . . . had absolutely and entirely vanished." His list of alternative explanations included infecundity resulting from prostitution, disease, and the settler's favorite, the loss of will to live.[28] His version of events, minimizing the effects of frontier violence and emphasizing indigenous people's self-destruction, remained long in local Tasmanian, and Australian, historical consciousness.

The Extinction Thesis

Soon after Calder's account appeared, public interest had turned towards the impending death of Truganini, the last known Tasmanian of full descent. Such a death was seen to signify *extinction*, since in nineteenth-century thinking mixed-race descendants did not signify the survival of a people. Accordingly, when Truganini died on 8 May 1876, the Tasmanians were duly pronounced extinct, a conviction that has lasted well into our own time. Indeed, so fixed did the idea of the complete extermination of the Tasmanian Aboriginal people become, that it was not until the 1980s that most Australians learned there were indeed descendants, after all.[29]

The question of extinction became especially important in late nineteenth- and early twentieth-century racial discourse, when belief in white racial superiority and fear of competition from other races reached a peak in Europe, the Americas, and other settler societies. Australian and international (mainly British) understandings continued to be much the same on this issue. Charles Pearson, an Englishman who had spent twenty years in Australia, took indigenous extinctions for granted in his influential book, *National Life and National Character: A Forecast.* He warned that not all "inferior races" were doomed to extinction, distinguishing sharply between the "evanescent" races, such as the Australian Aborigines and American Indians who disappeared wherever Europeans went, and the enduring races, like Indians, Chinese, and Africans ("Negroes") who were "too numerous and sturdy to be extirpated" and who would in time challenge Europeans for world supremacy.[30]

The attribution of extinction to a particular form of racial inferiority lasted well into the twentieth century. In Australia, the story of the extinction of the Tasmanian Aborigines settled into an orthodoxy that was rarely explored in any detail.[31] Aboriginal people had not only (apparently) disappeared from the earth, but from history as well.[32] Some reference to violent conflict did remain, for example in Ernest Scott's immensely popular *A Short History of Australia*, which included three and a half pages on the Tasmanian conflict. One of Australia's first history professors, Scott attributed blame to the settlers, who he said provoked the Tasmanians through frequent cases of "murder and outrage."[33] And a very few still remembered the Tasmanians with understanding. Mary Bennett, a humanitarian who intervened strongly in Aboriginal affairs in the 1930s, wrote an unusually sympathetic book, *The Australian Aboriginal as a Human Being*, where she pointed out that 1930 was the centenary of the Black Line, followed so soon afterwards by the removal of the people to Flinders Island. She recounted how a Mr. Gardiner, who had lived for a long time on Flinders Island while the Aboriginal station was there, had told her father how "old men and women and children were seen in the early morning to ascend Mount Arthur (!) and perch themselves upon the top and wait until the sun lifted the mists from the peaceful ocean, and when the blue mountains of their native land became visible they would raise their swarthy attenuated arms, and with tears rolling down their cheeks, exclaim, 'Country belonging to me!'"[34]

Both inside and outside Australia, the Tasmanians by this time had largely become not real people to be mourned, but simply the cold objects of science. As Lyndall Ryan has related, scientists in England, France, Germany, and Australia debated in the early years of the twentieth century whether the extinct Tasmanian Aborigines, seen as representatives of early Stone Age man, were the missing link between ape and man. It was generally agreed they had been unusually primitive as a result of their long isolation from other peoples, though some also attributed this to a supposed smaller-than-usual brain capacity. For Professor Fred Wood Jones, isolation meant not only a failure to evolve to a higher state, but also the loss of skills previously held, an idea subsequently picked up by archaeologists and popularized.[35]

New Understandings: The Impact of World War II

From the late 1930s, changes in government policy and thinking about the place of Aboriginal people in Australia's future began to have an impact on historical scholarship. World War II, especially as knowledge and understanding grew of the Nazi campaign to exterminate the Jews, also had a profound impact on thinking about race and history. Several specialist studies on Australian Aboriginal history, all involving original research, were completed just before or during the war, though in wartime conditions they took varying amounts of time to appear in print.[36] One of these was by Clive Turnbull, a Tasmanian-born journalist working for the Melbourne *Herald*, whose book *Black War: The Extermination of the Tasmanian Aborigines*, appeared in 1948.[37] So radical a break did it mark that it is worth close examination.

Black War signalled a challenge to the comfortable extinction discourse that had prevailed since the 1870s. It began: "Not, perhaps, before has a race of men been destroyed utterly within 75 years. This is the story of a race which was so destroyed, that of the aborigines of Tasmania."[38] More clearly than anyone since Bonwick, Turnbull attributed this destruction directly to the effects of colonization. He places the blame squarely with the British authorities who made the decision to colonize the island, first as a prison and later as a place of profit: "Either object [prison or profit] might have been, and both were, fatal to the aborigines who were superfluous and, indeed, a hindrance to those achievements. Their fate was written when [Governor] King turned his thoughts toward the island as a penal settlement."[39] Indeed, he wrote on page two: "The extinction of the people of Van Diemen's Land was foreseen from the earliest years of the European settlement but that did not in any degree dissuade the Government from its course."[40] Turnbull writes that while many were "appalled by the atrocities committed upon the natives" the policy of colonization was not abandoned. After all, he says, "the only remedy would have been to deny to the invaders all property rights in the island." This was not done, and instead the authorities attempted "one pious palliative after another," to little effect, until "eventually the aborigines solved the problem in the way most convenient for all by dying."[41]

The idea of a mysterious disappearance in the wake of a meeting of two incompatible cultures was still popular in Australia, and Turnbull set out to refute it. "These people," he wrote, "were not destroyed by a foreign culture. They were destroyed by arms and expatriation as part of a ruthless policy."[42] They were destroyed "not only by a different manner of life but by the ill-will of the usurpers of the race's land."[43] In explanation of what he means by "policy," he says: "It was not so much that there was a general will for the extermination of the aborigines—though that was sometimes expressed—as that there was no general will against it."[44] He concludes: "They were driven from their land because the colonists wished to occupy it; and when they retaliated they were taken from the island to get them out of the way."[45]

Turnbull makes an interesting distinction between active and passive "ill-will"; active ill will was expressed in brutality, while passive ill will "deplored extermination while condoning, and participating in the rewards of, a system which made extermination inevitable."[46] It was the latter that most concerned him, and that he saw at work in the British settlement of Tasmania. He ponders how such indifference to human life could be possible in a civilized community, and we can see here how his thinking about Nazi atrocities against the Jews had influenced his ideas about colonizers and indigenous peoples: "Beyond its [the civilized community's] confines the moral geometry no longer applies. Van Diemen's Land aborigines, Incas, natives of the Congo, 'Non-Aryans,' move in another dimension and it is possible for all imperialist peoples to live in satisfaction and self-esteem by their own rules while conducting, in the extra-moral and extra-racial universe, such adventures as the common quality of rapacity may indicate as desirable."[47]

He concluded his book by reflecting on the long and continuing history of indigenous peoples dying while their conquerors profit. Modern Australians, he pointed out, are the beneficiaries of these long-ago events: "Today the whole wealth of Australia may be ascribed to territories taken from the aborigines."[48] That he was influenced not only by revulsion against Nazi anti-Semitism, but also events closer to home, is clear in the final pages of the book, where he draws attention to what he understood as the impending disappearance of the Aboriginal peoples of Victoria. The attitudes that underlay the original dispossession, he warns, have not disappeared: "The aborigines of Tasmania have gone; the aborigines of Victoria are going, and for the miserable remnant there is from the community at large neither interest nor pity."[49] Attitudes of indifference while indigenous peoples disappear are still with us: "It must not be supposed that the story of the Tasmanian aborigines belongs to a past with which we have no connection, or that their fate, were the colonization of Van Diemen's Land about to take place now, would necessarily be different."[50]

Turnbull does not use the word "genocide," coined by Lemkin just a few years earlier; he had probably not heard of it when writing his book, apparently completed some considerable time before its actual publication in 1948. Nevertheless, it is clear that he, like Lemkin, was at least in part prompted by the horrors of the Second World War, and the example of Nazi Germany in attempting the destruction of an entire people.[51] As Lyndall Ryan argues, it seems that he wanted to use the heightened awareness of the horrors of Nazi policies and practices towards the Jews to shock Australians into recognition of the enormity of their own history.[52]

Unbeknownst to Turnbull, Lemkin himself was at the same time reaching similar conclusions about what had happened in Tasmania. Lemkin in the late 1940s extensively researched and wrote many chapters towards a book, or series of books, on the history of genocide. He never finished the project, and it remained unpublished at the time of his death in 1959, and is unpublished still. Chapter plans, extensive notes, and draft chapters, are, however, held in three different archives in the US.[53] In these plans, notes, and chapters Lemkin covered many genocidal episodes throughout human history: the Albigensians, Carthage, the forced deportation of the Cherokee, the Herero, and many others. One of the forty planned chapters was about Tasmania. His research on Tasmania relied on secondary sources, especially Bonwick, though he also consulted other works by Giblin, Backhouse, Calder, Melville, Merivale, and West. It was written without benefit of Clive Turnbull's *Black War*, which was just appearing on the other side of the world as he wrote.

In this chapter, we see Lemkin applying his own method of analysis to Tasmania. In each case of genocide or suspected genocide, he thought it important to consider the conditions leading to genocide, the methods and techniques used, the question of intent and motivation of the genocidists, the responses of the victim group and of outside groups, and the aftermath. Having given the bare bones of the Tasmanian story, he headed one section with a question: "Intent to Destroy—who is guilty—Government or Individuals?" His answer is both, especially individuals. He places the blame for the destruction of Tasmanian society first on settlers and convicts who attacked the Aboriginal people, provoking them to retaliation, and second on the governing authorities who, while neither planning nor conducting genocide, failed in their basic duty of protection. He also discusses at some length the rapid decline in the birth rate, the result of conditions of warfare, loss of land, and the loss of women to sealers and others. He also had sections on cruelty, legal status, and the effects of liquor and disease, and paid particular attention to the effects of confinement on Gun Carriage, Bruny, and Flinders Islands, which left the people "lifeless and dispirited."[54] In short, his account clearly classes the events in Tasmania as genocide, but he does not see it as state organized or as purely a matter of frontier violence.

Separate Development: Genocide Studies and Australian Historiography

While Lemkin's work on Tasmania remained unknown, his new word *genocide* did not. The older terms *extermination* and *extinction* (*extirpation* had long gone) dropped from historians' and popular vocabulary to be replaced by *genocide*. This change in terminology had some extremely important consequences. Where *extermination*, *extirpation*, and *extinction* placed the Tasmanian events in a long ago past, out there away from the present, *genocide* connected them to an ongoing present, to legal and political as well as historical considerations. To call something "genocide" rather than "extermination" was somehow seen as far more serious for modern Australians; the questions of intent and responsibility were so much closer to home.

The direct connection that "genocide" implied between the past and the present meant, however, that the application of the new term to Tasmania operated quite differently in international scholarship and Australian historiography. Genocide scholarship had really got under way in the 1970s, and grew dramatically in the 1980s, almost wholly generated by scholars educated in the US and writing in English in the US, Canada, and Israel.[55] Among its concerns were the uniqueness of the Holocaust, whether the killing of political groupings could be included in the definition of genocide even though the UN Convention excluded them, and the role of the state and planning in defining genocide. Most scholars in the field wanted to widen the definition from that accepted by the UN to include political groups, but also narrow it by defining genocide as necessarily through mass murder conducted and managed by the state.[56] On the basis of very limited knowledge of Tasmanian history, and interpreting the Black Line and the removal to Flinders Island as an example of a state-led and planned desire to destroy a whole people, these scholars took the view that Tasmania constituted a clear case of genocide.[57]

Furthermore, the idea of Tasmanian genocide spread far beyond the work of specialist genocide scholars, and appears also in a wide range of international scholarly and popular work.[58] The long-standing story of the Black Line, the removal to Flinders Island, and the (supposed) extinction of the Tasmanians, built from a multitude of sources of which Bonwick was possibly the most important, was now redefined as "genocide." Perhaps, in popular consciousness, Tasmania came to be readily accepted as a clear case of genocide for two reasons. First, there seems to be some slippage between two distinct ideas, extinction and genocide; everyone "knew" that Tasmania was a case of colonial *extinction;* therefore it seemed to follow it must be a case of *genocide.* Second, as Henry Reynolds points out, the central role played by government in controlling relations with Aboriginal people in Tasmania (in contrast to mainland Australia, where settlement and its destructive consequences frequently ran far beyond government boundaries of control) fitted in well with, and seemed to exemplify, the emphasis on the role of the state in much genocide theory and scholarship at the time. The extent of Aboriginal resistance to settlement, and attacks on the settlers, was either unknown or ignored.[59] In any case, the term "genocide" quickly replaced "extermination" and "disappearance" in international commentary, slipping in almost unnoticed where the former terms used to be.

In Australia itself, however, international genocide scholarship was little known, and local historiography went in quite a different direction. Although some commentators—legal, historical, and cultural—did apply the concept of genocide to Australian history, they did so only casually and in passing.[60] Indeed, there was not a great deal of historical research into the Tasmanian events for two decades after the publication of *Black War*. Despite the 1950s and 1960s being a period of rapid growth in the writing of Australian history, there were no new specialist monographs on the destruction of Tasmanian society. The general histories produced to meet the growth in university and other study of Australian history had even less Aboriginal material than their predecessors.[61] As a result, Bonwick's *The Last of the Tasmanians* and Turnbull's *Black War* remained the standard texts on the destruction of Tasmanian Aboriginal society for many years.

A number of historians in the 1970s and 1980s began to look at Tasmanian history more closely, investigating hitherto little-used archives and other documentary material. The most comprehensive study was by Lyndall Ryan, who completed her PhD on the history of the Aboriginal Tasmanians in 1976, revised and published as a book in 1981. Using much more extensive archival sources than previous historians, she drew a detailed picture that in general supported Clive Turnbull's story of violence and disregard for human life, and of humanitarian impulses powerless to affect the outcome. She saw the reasons for the decline in Aboriginal population as a mix of the effects of direct frontier violence, loss of women "through exchange with the sealers and stock-keepers," and the conditions on Flinders Island.[62] She explicitly discounted disease as a factor before the people's relocation to Bruny and Flinders Islands, but saw it as of major importance under conditions of incarceration.[63]

She departed from Turnbull significantly, however, in rejecting the notion of extinction. The effects of the loss of women to the sealers she saw as double edged; on the one hand, this loss was an important reason for population decline in certain bands, especially along the north coast, but on the other it "saved Aboriginal Tasmanian society from extinction."[64] She emphasized that modern indigenous Tasmanians are descended from these unions, and traced the history of their descendants in considerable detail. Recognizing the permeability of racial boundaries in a way the traditional extinction thesis did not, Ryan regarded the descendants as they regard themselves, as indications of the survival, against all odds, of the indigenous peoples of Tasmania.

At around the same time, Noel Plomley edited and published Robinson's journals, thus adding enormously to the public availability of relevant records, and also wrote his own historical analyses.[65] He outlined the reasons for decline especially well. There are two prerequisites for living, he wrote, "one an adequate food supply and the other a stable social environment."[66] In Tasmania, the indigenous people lost both, the latter with the "removal of native women from the tribes to enslave them, the stealing of Aboriginal children, and the destruction of the family and social life of the tribe."[67] Though Plomley seemed unaware of Lemkin's work, he was in fact applying Lemkin's wide-ranging criteria to Tasmania and concluding that the circumstances there constituted the destruction of the foundations of life of a human group.[68] He did not, however, call it genocide. He seems to have shared the view of most historians, and indeed of most Australians, that "genocide" was synonymous with the "Holocaust" and therefore inappropriate in discussions of Australian history.[69]

Bringing Genocide Home

If the specialist historians rejected the idea of a Tasmanian genocide, one significant Australian historian did not. A very thoughtful attempt to apply the burgeoning genocide scholarship to Australia came from Tony Barta, in two groundbreaking articles in the mid-1980s. Barta is in fact an Australian expert in German history, with a good general knowledge of Australian colonial history. In the first article, "After the Holocaust: Consciousness of Genocide in Australia," he focused on Lemkin's definition of genocide as no historian working in Australia had done before him. He drew attention to that key section of Lemkin for any discussion of colonialism, contending that genocide proceeds in two phases: "destruction of the national pattern of the oppressed group" followed by "the imposition of the national pattern of the oppressor."[70] Such a definition clearly applied to the Australian case: as he said, "there is no dispute that the basic fact of Australian history is the appropriation of the continent by an invading people and the dispossession, with ruthless destructiveness, of another." There can also be no doubt, he continued, "about the disintegration of Aboriginal society, traditional culture, and religion, the destruction of the Aborigines' economic existence, their languages, their personal security, liberty, health, and dignity." That there was great loss of life cannot be doubted, and he pointed to Tasmania, Victoria, and New South Wales. "If ever a people has had to sustain an assault on its existence of the kind Lemkin described it would seem to have been over the last two hundred years in Australia."

Barta then argued that the problem in seeing Australian history as an example of genocide was, however, that in Australia "genocide" had come to be understood as synonymous with the Holocaust. He commented on the effects: the very restricted sense of the applicability of the concept of genocide means that Australians could and would continue to fail to acknowledge the shadow in their own past. "Whatever took place in our past, it was nothing like that," as he put it. And if it was nothing like that, then it was not so bad. It cannot be called genocide. Barta insists that to describe Australian colonial history as genocide is not to equate it with the Holocaust; the Holocaust was in fact "a policy of genocide pushed to its ultimate extreme."[71]

Another problem with describing the Australian situation as genocide was, of course, the question of intention. In a second intervention three years later, Barta pursued this issue, developing the idea of genocidal *relations* as distinct from genocidal *policy*.[72] Returning to a distinction between a genocidal state and genocidal society that he had started to develop in the first article,[73] he now argued that in the Australian case the appropriation of land, implicitly "a relationship of genocide," was "fundamental to the type of society rather than to the type of state."[74] It was not, Barta wrote, a matter of ill will on either side, but rather "the objective nature of the relationships" between the white capitalist wool producers and black hunter-gatherers, a relationship of land, which constituted the genocidal character of colonialism in the Australian context.[75]

Barta's work gradually had some impact in Australia, though not on the specialist historians of Tasmania. In an article in 1994 entitled "Nation and MiscegeNation," Patrick Wolfe put forward a similar case to Barta's, describing settler colonialism in Australia as having a "logic of elimination," owing to the fact that the colonizers primarily wanted land rather than labor.[76] Raymond Evans and Bill Thorpe, experts on Aboriginal history in Queensland, also took up some of Barta's suggestions, proposing the concept of "indigenocide" as an alternative to the concept of genocide in relation to indigenous peoples.[77]

In the late 1990s, political developments again had an impact on Australian historical scholarship, as they had done in the 1940s and again in the 1970s. The Human Rights Commission's *Bringing Them Home* report of 1997, which reported on the history and effects of Aboriginal child removal in the nineteenth and twentieth centuries, brought the genocide question to public notice. The report contended that Australian child removal practices fell within the definition of genocide used in the UN 1948 Genocide Convention, ratified by Australia in 1949. The convention specifically includes "forcibly transferring children of the group to another group" with the intention of destroying the original group in whole or in part. The report explained: "Genocide is not only the mass killing of a people. The essence of genocide is acting with the intention to destroy the group, not the extent to which that intention has been achieved."[78] But this explanation fell on deaf ears. Most Australians understood genocide to signify mass killing and especially the Holocaust, and were shocked and outraged to find child removal described as genocide.

The *Bringing Them Home* report influenced discussion of genocide and Australia in relation not only to the stolen generations but also to frontier violence and the disappearance of indigenous peoples in the wake of colonization. By 2000, there was a renewed interest in the subject among Australian historians. A. Dirk Moses, like Barta an expert in German history, but as an Australian interested in the question of genocide in Australian history, criticized Barta's notion of genocidal relations, arguing that one cannot do away with intention to this degree. Agency, he insisted, was indispensable. Rather, colonization as an historical process has a genocidal potential that is released in certain circumstances he called "genocidal moments." The evidence showed, he suggested, that the term *genocide* is less appropriately applied to Tasmania (where it is usually thought most relevant) than to Queensland (which has rarely been discussed in this context).[79]

The following year, Henry Reynolds, in his book, *An Indelible Stain? The Question of Genocide in Australia's History*, made a similar case. After outlining the definition of genocide in the UN Genocide Convention of 1948, he assessed a number of historical events in Australia against it and concluded that while the Australian frontier, notably in Queensland, was marked by "genocidal moments," "when settlers and police systematically pursued particular groups of Aborigines with the intention of destroying them," colonial Tasmania did not represent one of these moments.[80] There was no evidence, he suggested, of governmental intent to destroy a people: in his words, although Tasmania's Governor Arthur "was determined to defeat the Aborigines and secure the permanent expropriation of their land . . . there is little evidence to suggest that he wanted to reach beyond that objective and destroy the Tasmanian race in whole or in part."[81]

The gulf between international and national approaches largely remains, though the gap is closing with the appearance of at least two collections of essays, and the publication in the *Journal of Genocide Research* of a number of articles comparing the destruction of Tasmanian society with indigenous genocides elsewhere, in the Americas and southern Africa.[82] Nevertheless, despite this growing conversation, most international genocide scholars still consider the term *genocide* applicable to Tasmania while most specialist scholars on Tasmanian history still do not.[83]

Conclusion: Genocide After All

The separation of Australian from international debates and scholarship has had some deleterious effects for both. Genocide scholars have declared

Tasmania to be a case of state planning and mass killing on the basis of little knowledge of events, while the general avoidance of the "genocide" word within Australia has meant reluctance amongst specialists in Australian history to engage in comparative and conceptual analysis.[84] To engage in both—detailed historical analysis, and conceptual and comparative study—would, I suggest, lead to some new ways to conceptualize both the destruction of indigenous societies on the one hand and the nature of genocide on the other.

Most historians agree that colonization meant the Tasmanians lost the foundations of life—food, reproductive capacity, health, and a homeland. They also agree that the colonizers in Britain and the colony were aware of populations disappearing in the Americas in the wake of colonization. Most agree also that from the beginning, but especially from the 1820s, when two very different societies were competing for land, it was clear to everyone that if colonization continued, the indigenous population would rapidly decline and could possibly disappear. To continue with colonization under these circumstances was, I would argue, to participate knowingly in what later generations came to call a genocidal process. It is a clear case of colonization without sufficient regard for the effects on the indigenous peoples of the removal of the foundations of life, resulting in the replacement of one human group by another. It is genocide.[85]

The insights of earlier scholars such as Bonwick, Turnbull, and Barta seem too often to have been forgotten or rejected. All three had placed the blame for the near destruction of the Aboriginal Tasmanians squarely at the hands of both the British authorities and the British settlers themselves. It seems to me they were absolutely correct to do so. To seek to take land whatever the consequences—and these were in fact either already known or highly predictable from experience in North America and the Caribbean—is surely a genocidal project. By and large, and despite moments of angst within British ruling elites in the 1830s in particular, the British authorities, and later the settler governments that replaced them, not only continued with land seizure and population replacement, but also consistently failed to take sufficiently serious measures to control settler land hunger and violence. Historians need to recognize fully the seriousness of these colonizing decisions, both imperial and local. This is not to reject recognition of indigenous violence, or the importance of the loss of fertility as an explanation for population decline, or the fact of the survival and political claims of the current descendants. It is to say that if we understand genocide to include the taking of actions that are *known to be likely to lead to the destruction of an entire people*, then the colonization of Tasmania must surely be included.

At the same time, international genocide and colonization scholarship needs to exercise greater care. Generalizations have been made about Tasmanian history with little recourse to the detailed Australian studies that demonstrate that it is not a clear and sustained case of state planning or of mass killing, but rather of land seizure undertaken without sufficient regard for the indigenous peoples of the island, characterized by a fairly short period of violent conflict between settlers and indigenous peoples for the land. It was a colonization attended by a wide range of governmental policies, including futile attempts, too little and too late, to protect the indigenous people from settler attack and from the effects of the loss of the necessaries of life itself.

It is time for a more robust exchange between genocide and Tasmanian historical scholarship if we are to understand better just what did happen in Tasmania in the first half of the nineteenth century, how best to conceptualize it, and how to consider what that historical knowledge might mean for us now, morally and intellectually, in the present.

Notes

1. Paul E. de Strzelecki, "On the Aborigines of New South Wales and Van Diemen's Land," in *A Physical Description of New South Wales and Van Diemen's Land* (London, 1845), 356.
2. Lyndall Ryan, *The Aboriginal Tasmanians* (Sydney, 1981), 1996; Henry Reynolds, *The Fate of a Free People* (Melbourne, 1995); Noel Plomley, *The Aboriginal/Settler Clash in Van Diemen's Land, 1803–1831,* Occasional Paper no. 6, Queen Victoria Museum and Art Gallery (Tasmania, 1992); Keith Windschuttle, *The Fabrication of Aboriginal History* (Sydney, 2002).
3. Jared Diamond, "Ten Thousand Years of Solitude," *Discover* 14, no 3 (1993): 50.
4. Charles Rowley, *The Destruction of Aboriginal Society* (Melbourne, 1970), 43; Lyndall Ryan, "The Aborigines in Tasmania, 1800–1974 and their problems with the Europeans" (Ph.D diss., Macquarie University, 1975), 43.
5. Raphael Lemkin, *Axis Rule in Occupied Europe: Laws of Occupation, Analysis of Government, Proposals for Redress* (New York, 1944).
6. Patrick Brantlinger, *Dark Vanishings: Discourse on the Extinction of Primitive Races, 1800–1930* (Ithaca NY, 2003), 3–4.
7. For discussions of this literature see: Robert F. Berkhofer, *The White Man's Indian: Images of the American Indian from Columbus to the Present* (New York, 1978); Brian W. Dippie, *The Vanishing American: White Attitudes and US Indian Policy* (Middletown, CT, 1982); Francis A. de Caro, "Vanishing the Red Man: Cultural Guilt and Legend Formation," *International Folklore Review* 4 (1986): 74–80.
8. Despatch, 5 November 1830, Papers on Van Diemen's Land, 1831, No. 259, 56, as quoted in "Report from the Select Committee on Aborigines (British Settlements) with

the Minutes of Evidence, Appendix and Index," *Great Britain, Parliamentary Papers*, 1836 (538), VII, I, 14.

9. Governor Arthur, Memorandum, Sorell Camp, 20 November 1830, in *Great Britain, Parliamentary Papers, Colonies, Australia*, vol. 4, 244, as quoted in Windschuttle, *Fabrication of Aboriginal History*, 196.
10. Henry Melville, *The History of the Island of Van Diemen's Land from the Year 1824 to 1835* (London, 1835), 121–22.
11. Melville, *History of Van Diemen's Land*, 122.
12. Ibid., 23.
13. Report of Major Thomas Ryan upon the Aboriginal Establishment, Flinders Island, March 1836, Robinson Papers, vol. 24, Mitchell Library, Sydney, Australia, as quoted in Lyndall Ryan, "Extinction Theorists and Tasmanian Aborigines," in *The Future of Former Foragers in Australia and Southern Africa*, ed. Carmel Schrire and Robert Gordon (Cambridge, MA, 1985), 48.
14. Clive Turnbull, *Black War: The Extermination of the Tasmanian Aborigines* (Melbourne, 1965, first published 1948), 241. For the Report's comments on VDL, see Great Britain, *Parliamentary Papers*, 1837 (425), vol. VII: *Report of the Select Committee on Aborigines (British Settlements)*, 13–14. See also Elizabeth Elbourne, "The Sin of the Settler: The 1835–1836 Select Committee on Aborigines and Debates over Virtue and Conquest in the Early Nineteenth-Century British White Settler Empire," *Journal of Colonialism and Colonial History* 4, no. 3, (2003).
15. Charles Darwin, *Journal of Researches into the Natural History and Geology of the Countries Visited During the Voyage of H.M.S. Beagle round the World Under the Command of Capt. Fitzroy* (London, 1839), 447. On Darwin, see Tony Barta, "Mr Darwin's Shooters: On Natural Selection and the Naturalizing of Genocide," *Patterns of Prejudice* 39, no. 2 (2005): 116–37.
16. Darwin, *Journal of Researches*, 520.
17. Herman Merivale, *Lectures on Colonization and Colonies* (London, 1928), 544. The lectures in this book were delivered before the University of Oxford in 1839, 1840, and 1841.
18. Strzelecki, *Physical Description of New South Wales and Van Diemen's Land* (London, 1845), 347.
19. Henry Reynolds points out that the idea of the Tasmanians having lost the will to live appears also in recent texts by Clive Turnbull, Robert Hughes, N.G. Butlin, and Peter Conrad: see Reynolds, *Fate of a Free People*, 189.
20. Richard Lee and T. Bendyshe, untitled papers, *The Anthropological Review* II (1864): xcv–cxiii. See also Sven Lindqvist, *"Exterminate all the Brutes": One Man's Odyssey into the Heart of Darkness and the Origins of European Genocide* (London, 1998), 130–31.
21. James Bonwick, *The Last of the Tasmanians* (London, 1870), 57–58.
22. Ibid., 28.
23. Ibid., 31.
24. Ibid., 28.
25. Ibid., 57. For a more detailed discussion of Bonwick, see my chapter, "The History of Killing and the Killing of History," in *Archive Stories*, ed. Antoinette Burton (Durham, NC, 2005).
26. Charles Darwin, *The Descent of Man and Selection in relation to Sex*, 2nd ed. (London, 1882), 183, 191; see also Russell McGregor, "The Doomed Race: A Scientific Axiom of the Late Nineteenth Century," *Australian Journal of Politics and History* 39, no. 1 (1993): 16–17.

27. J.E. Calder, "Some Account of the Wars of Extirpation, and Habits of the Native Tribes of Tasmania," *The Journal of the Anthropological Institute of Great Britain and Ireland* 3 (1874): 8.
28. Ibid., 28.
29. Ryan, *The Aboriginal Tasmanians*, 218–20. Ryan notes that in fact another Aboriginal Tasmanian woman of full descent, Suke, died on Kangaroo Island, off the South Australian coast, in 1888. Truganini is, nevertheless, still generally regarded as the "last" Tasmanian.
30. Charles Pearson, *National Life and National Character: A Forecast* (London, 1893), 33.
31. See my entry on "Aboriginal History" in *The Oxford Companion to Australian History*, ed. Graeme Davison, John Hirst, and Stuart Macintyre, 2nd ed. (Melbourne, 2002).
32. Stephen Roberts, *History of Australian Land Settlement, 1788–1920* (London, 1969), 181, xiii; RW Giblin, *The Early History of Tasmania*, vol. II, *1804–28* (London, 1938), xxviii.
33. Ernest Scott, *A Short History of Australia* (Melbourne, 1964, [1916]).
34. M.M. Bennett, *The Australian Aboriginal as a Human Being* (London, 1930), 38–39. Another rare mention in the 1930s was William E.L.H. Crowther, "The Passing of the Tasmanian Race, 1803–1876," *Medical Journal of Australia* (3 February 1934).
35. Ryan, "Extinction Theorists and Tasmanian Aborigines," 49–51.
36. See also Edmund Foxcroft, *Australian Native Policy: Its History, Especially in Victoria* (Melbourne, 1941); Paul Hasluck, *Black Australians: A Survey of Native Policy in Western Australia, 1829–1897* (Melbourne, 1942).
37. Clive Turnbull, *Black War: The Extermination of the Tasmanian Aborigines* (Melbourne, 1965, [1948]).
38. Ibid., 1.
39. Ibid., 23.
40. Ibid., 2.
41. Ibid., 24.
42. Ibid., 28.
43. Ibid., 1.
44. Ibid., 28.
45. Ibid., 240.
46. Ibid., 1.
47. Ibid., 2.
48. Ibid., 241.
49. Ibid., 237.
50. Ibid., 238.
51. Given the lack of discussion of the topic within Australia until the late 1970s (and there was little even then), he may still not have been aware of "genocide" when he wrote a short essay entitled "Tasmania: The Ultimate Solution" for Frank Stevens's edited collection, *Racism: The Australian Experience: A Study of Race Prejudice in Australia*, vol. 3 (Sydney, 1972). In this essay, he sounds remarkably like Raphael Lemkin, whose work he seems not to know, when he writes "all of life is diminished by the loss of any part of it," 233.
52. Lyndall Ryan, "The Struggle for Trukanini 1830–1997," *Tasmanian Historical Research Association Papers and Proceedings* 44, no 3 (1977): 153–73.
53. There are archival collections at The Jacob Rader Marcus Center of the American Jewish Archives, Hebrew Union College-Jewish Institute of Religion, Cincinnati, OH

campus; The American Jewish Historical Society, New York; and in the New York Public Library.

54. For a more detailed account of this chapter, and a reproduction of the chapter itself, see Ann Curthoys, "Raphael Lemkin's 'Tasmania': An Introduction," *Patterns of Prejudice* 39, no. 2 (2005): 162–69
55. See Helen Fein, *Genocide: A Sociological Perspective* (London, 1993), 5; Samuel Totten and Steven L. Jacobs, *Pioneers of Genocide Studies* (New Brunswick, NJ, 2002).
56. A. Dirk Moses, "The Holocaust and Genocide," in *The Historiography of the Holocaust*, ed. Dan Stone (London, 2004), 533–55.
57. Henry Reynolds has traced the expressions of this view in works written or edited by the key figures in genocide studies: Reynolds, *An Indelible Stain?* 50–52. Other examples are given by Dirk Moses, "Genocide and Settler Society in Australian History," in *Genocide and Settler Society: Frontier Violence and Stolen Indigenous Children in Australian* History, ed. A. Dirk Moses (New York, 2004), 42, note 75. Examples from the 1990s and 2000s include *The History and Sociology of Genocide: Analyses and Case Studies*, ed. Frank Chalk and Kurt Jonassohn (New Haven, CT, 1990); Ward Churchill, *A Little Matter of Genocide* (San Francisco, 1997), 405; Ian Hernon, *The Savage Empire: Forgotten Wars of the 19th Century* (New York, 2000), 62; David Maybury-Lewis, "Genocide against Indigenous Peoples," and Samuel Totten, Williams S. Parsons, and Robert K. Hitchcock, "Confronting Genocide and Ethnocide of Indigenous Peoples," in *Annihilating Difference: The Anthropology of Genocide*, ed., Alexander L. Hinton (Berkeley, CA, 2002), 45, 61f.
58. A search of the Amazon.com website in mid-2004 gave literally hundreds of examples. Some of the most recent are: *The Specter of Genocide: Mass Murder in Historical Perspective*, ed Robert Gellately and Ben Kiernan (Cambridge and New York, 2003), 55, 378; Stephen Oppenheimer, *The Real Eve: Modern Man's Journey out of Africa* (New York, 2003), 31; Niall Ferguson, *Empire: the Rise and Demise of the British World Order and the Lessons for Global Power* (New York, 2003), 109–10; Stanley Crouch, *Reconsidering the Souls of Black Folk* (Philadelphia, 2003), 183; Robert B. Edgerton, *Africa's Armies: From Honor to Infamy—A History from 1791 to the Present* (Boulder, CO, 2002), 183; Jan Morris, *Heaven's Command: An Imperial Progress* (Fort Washington, PA, 2002), 437; and John Pilger, *Heroes* (Cambridge, MA, 2002), 604.
59. Henry Reynolds, "Genocide in Tasmania?" in *Genocide and Settler Society*, ed. Moses, 145–46.
60. For some references to these casual usages, see Reynolds, *An Indelible Stain?*, 29, and Tony Barta, "Relations of Genocide: Land and Lives in the Colonization of Australia," in *Genocide and the Modern Age*, ed. Michael Dobkowski and Isidor Wallimann (New York, 1987), 237–51, n. 3. Reynolds draws attention to Tom Haydon's 1978 film, *The Last Tasmanian: A Story of Genocide*, and also to Justice Murphy's judgment in *Coe v. Commonwealth of Australia* (1979) to the effect that Aboriginal people were killed or forcibly removed from their land "in what amounted to attempted (and in Tasmania almost complete) genocide." For brief references to genocide in Tasmania by historians such as Robert Hughes and Noel Butlin, see Reynolds, "Genocide in Tasmania?," 127.
61. Curthoys, "Aboriginal History," in *The Oxford Companion to Australian History*, ed. Davison, Hirst, and Macintyre.
62. Ryan, *The Aboriginal Tasmanians*, 176.
63. Ibid., 175.
64. Ibid., 71.

65. N.J.B. Plomley, *Weep in Silence: A History of the Flinders Island Aboriginal Settlement* (Hobart, 1987). See also N.J.B. Plomley, *The Tasmanian Aborigines: A Short Account of Them and Some Aspects of Their Life* (Launceston, Tasmania, 1977).
66. Plomley, *The Aboriginal/Settler Clash*, 5.
67. Ibid., 6–7.
68. See Lemkin, *Axis Rule*, 79.
69. See A. Dirk Moses, "Genocide and Holocaust Consciousness in Australia," *History Compass* 1 (2003) AU 28: 1–11. http://www.history-compass.com
70. Tony Barta, "After the Holocaust: Consciousness of Genocide in Australia," *Australian Journal of Politics and History* 31, no. 1 (1984): 154.
71. Ibid., 155.
72. Barta, "Relations of Genocide," 237–51.
73. Barta, "After the Holocaust," 160.
74. Barta, "Relations of Genocide," 239. Barta defines a genocidal society as "one in which the whole bureaucratic apparatus might officially be directed to protect innocent people but in which the whole race is nevertheless subject to remorseless pressures of destruction inherent in the very nature of the society." He then says: "It is in this sense that I would call Australia, during the whole 200 years of its existence, a genocidal society" (240).
75. A similar argument to Barta's has been developed more recently by Alison Palmer in relation to Queensland. Alison Palmer, *Colonial Genocide* (Adelaide, 2000), 209.
76. Patrick Wolfe, "Nation and MiscegeNation: Discursive Continuity in the Post-Mabo Era," *Social Analysis*, no. 36 (1994): 93–152.
77. Raymond Evans and Bill Thorpe, "Indigenocide and the Massacre of Aboriginal History," *Overland* 163 (Winter 2001): 21–39. See also Evans' chapter in this volume.
78. Australian Human Rights and Equal Opportunity Commission, *Bringing Them Home: a Guide to the Findings and Recommendations of the National Inquiry into the Separation of Aboriginal and Torres Strait Islander Children from Their Families* (Canberra, 1997), 27.
79. A. Dirk Moses, "An Antipodean Genocide? The Origins of the Genocidal Moment in the Colonization of Australia," *Journal of Genocide Research* 2, no. 1 (2000): 91–92. In a later article, Moses shifted his position slightly to argue for a fairly weak criterion of intention; we can, he says, detect it indirectly. When authorities refuse to cease the colonization project even when the drastic effects on indigenous populations are known, they can be held at least partly responsible for the genocidal outcomes: idem, "Conceptual Blockages and Definitional Dilemmas in the Racial Century: Genocide of Indigenous Peoples and the Holocaust," *Patterns of Prejudice* 36, no. 4 (2002): 29–31.
80. Reynolds, *An Indelible Stain?*, 130.
81. Ibid., 78.
82. See the special issue of *Aboriginal History* 25 (2001); Moses, ed., *Genocide and Settler Society;* Benjamin Madley, "Patterns of Frontier Genocide 1803–1910: The Aboriginal Tasmanians, the Yuki of California, and the Herero of Namibia," *Journal of Genocide Research* 6, no. 2 (2004): 167–92; Ashley Riley Sousa, "'They Will be Hunted Down like Wild Beasts and Destroyed!': A Comparative Study of Genocide in California and Tasmania," *Journal of Genocide Research* 6, no. 2 (2004): 193–209.
83. In the political arena, the term *genocide* cannot be used, the National Museum of Australia being explicitly instructed not to use the term in its exhibitions. Speech by Dawn Casey, former Director of the National Museum of Australia, at a conference entitled "Narrating Frontier Families," Australian National University, 5 August 2004.

84. Comparative analysis has come from scholars like Barta, Wolfe, and Moses with expertise in other national histories.
85. For similar arguments, see (for the Karuwali in southwest Queensland) Pamela Lukin Watson, "Passed Away? The Fate of the Karuwali," in Moses, *Genocide and Settler Societies*, 174–93, and Moses, "Genocide and Settler Society in Australian History," in ibid., 28–35.

– Chapter 11 –

"THE ABORIGINES . . . WERE NEVER ANNIHILATED, AND STILL THEY ARE BECOMING EXTINCT"

Settler Imperialism and Genocide in Nineteenth-century America and Australia[1]

Norbert Finzsch

Conceptualization

Genocides in modern history tend to be perceived as chronologically limited occurrences that punctuate time, rather than as repetitive and enduring processes. They paradigmatically culminate in historical *events* like the holocaust of 1941–1945 or the mass killings of Armenians in Turkey between 1915 and 1918, which have a plot and are narratable in a successive manner.[2] Although it is intuitive to perceive genocides in this way, it fails to grasp the implications of far-reaching policies and practices that operate below the threshold of public perception and political debate, but that may be no less genocidal than spectacular eruptions of focused and intense violence.[3] In this chapter, I focus on one enduring development of this type, namely, "settler imperialism."[4] This variety of imperialism is the rhizomatic expansion of settler colonies and settler states, directed against "exterior" indigenous populations, achieved in the context of a democratic and egalitarian society of white, predominantly Protestant Anglo-Saxon settlers organized in farms and family households. I argue that settler imperialism is inherently genocidal, since "an invading group quite literally supplants the indigenous population on its own landbase."[5] It is a variety of imperialism that is not based on the towering role of capitalist industrialism, but rests on a link between agrarian home production on the frontier and rentier capitalism in the cities. In this respect, settler imperialism has no periphery and no core, since the capital-owning elites in the cities and the social actors on the frontier form one complex interactive community.[6] Long-term genocidal tendencies in connection with settler imperialism come into play when agrarian home production and/or demographic factors demand the rapid expansion of settled surfaces. This expansionism is ideal—typically achieved by intrusion into the land of first nations.

The taking possession of the land ("*Landnahme*," according to Carl Schmitt) did not necessarily result in open mass killings of first nations.[7] Rather than single and singular events, settler imperialism entails a series of repetitions of the same (or different) occurrences:[8] settlers transgress the border between colonial and indigenous territories by staking claims, squatting the ground, erecting fences, tilling the soil, clearing the land, and starting to cultivate the ground in an European fashion.[9] Forms of settlement made visible through enclosures, fences, or ploughing represent both aspects of the taking of the land: they were at the same time symbolic and factual.[10] After a certain period, indigenous populations would organize resistance, often in the form of burning crops, stealing provisions, killing animals, and attacking settlers.[11] After a period of low-intensity warfare, bands of settlers, militia corps, mounted police, or the regular army would undertake punitive actions.[12] Indigenous populations would be vanquished, dispersed, or forced to retreat into the hinterland.

In the American variety of settler imperialism, the indigenes would sign treaties with the government, thereby relinquishing tribal lands and being relocated further inland.[13] In every instance of treaties made between 1783 and 1850, these contracts stipulated the loss of land to white settlers or the explicit acknowledgment of American supremacy.[14] Between 1800 and 1860, for instance, federal land agents sold off more than 600.000 square kilometers (roughly 158 million acres, almost the size of Texas or the Ukraine).[15] Between 1823 and 1871, the United States additionally granted land to railroad corporations, canal companies, and the like 570.000 square kilometers (roughly 140 million acres).[16] The indigenous land loss did not stop here: between 1802 and 1866, the federal government also granted land to the individual states to the amount of 480.000 square kilometers (118 million acres). The combined losses of Native American lands between 1800 and 1875 amount to 1.6 million square kilometers (400 million acres). This figure does not include loss through squatting or erosion by illegal logging.

Australia, like the US, was a settler society. This fact implies the intimate link between two narratives, settlement and genocide.[17] As early as the 1790s, in the Hawkesbury River area 80 kilometers northwest of Sydney (settled in 1788), 400 British settlers occupied both banks of the river, thus preventing Aboriginal access to water and food sources. Hostilities erupted and the settlers took matters into their own hands, since troops were not in place. This pattern of conflict persisted during the next century. All over Australia, the desire for land exceeded the means of state control. Where British and colonial London authorities wanted an orderly procedure in which the welfare of the Aborigines would be protected, settlers just proceeded into the interior to pick the land they wanted. If troops were called in, they predictably sided with the settlers.[18] As in the United States, surveyors measured the land and land agents threw it open for preemption, speculation, or general settlement by other settlers.[19]

The reason why this process is best captured by the concept of settler *imperialism* rather than settler *colonialism* is that it could only be implemented in conjunction with "gentlemanly" elites in the cities on the eastern seaboard.[20] Those sequestering the land are thus not just the settlers and squatters on the frontier, but also the state and the financiers who acquired land in order to sell it off to land-hungry farmers or plantation owners.[21] Settler imperialism also highlights that the process is not limited to the colonial phase of a settler society. The United States after 1783 was no longer a settler colony, but a nation-state, and territorial expansion was intrinsic to the idea of American sovereignty.[22]

Previous Definitions

The term "settler imperialism" has a short history, although the phenomenon it denotes is at least three hundred years old.[23] The concept was first developed by Carl Degler, who coined the term "agrarian imperialism" in referring to American hunger for land that resulted in the acquisition of new vast areas during the eighteenth and nineteenth centuries.[24] In a similar vein, the historian Stig Förster has suggested that historians study the effects of settler imperialism on American history before the advent of modern imperialism.[25] It was Karl Marx, however, who initiated this intellectual tradition. Using the concept *avant la lettre*, Marx described settler imperialism as the result of the division of labor and the externalization of parts of the agrarian production into the colonies.[26] Following in his footsteps, the English economic historians P.J. Cain and A.J. Hopkins developed a theory of settler imperialism in the British Empire in which gentlemanly rentiers dominated the empire, while a dependent and collaborating elite ran the dominions.[27] They perceive British history during the early part of the nineteenth century as characterized by a decline of aristocratic influence. Power and prestige passed on to a new "gentlemanly class" arising from the nonindustrial service sector of British capitalism. At its center was the City of London, and by the mid-Victorian period the gentlemanly class increasingly obtained control of the global economy rather than a colonial one. The landed gentry could alleviate its decline only by reaching an adjustment with this new gentlemanly class. The public schools and an "Oxbridge" education gave ideological cohesion to this new, synthetic ruling elite. The most senior British officials, at home or abroad, were drawn largely from its ranks. This elite invested to sustain its "gentlemanly life-style," distanced itself from the productive activities of manufacturing and industry, and became the financiers of British and overseas governments.

Cain's and Hopkins' class distinction highlights the domestic social formation necessary for the spread of British capital. Settler imperialism was not kept alive by investment of rentier capitalists in overseas possessions alone, however. It had to find agents in the colonies and dependent territories in order to function. As much as the assumption of a gentlemanly class helps to understand the machinery of British or American settler imperialism at home, it conceals its workings at the fringes of colonial possessions. Settler imperialism, therefore, is defined not only by the economic and political control of territorial expansion within the metropolises. It requires the existence of a class of landless or land-hungry farmers, plantation owners, and surveyors whose concern is to increase the area under their control and to drive the indigenous populations off the land that they possess.

Comparison

To exemplify my points, I will consider the United States during its late colonial and early national periods until 1860 and Australia after its development into a halfway independent colony in the mid-nineteenth century.[28] I compare American and Australian settler imperialism asynchronously, i.e., as events that were not synchronized in time, because both societies were marked by substantial expansion of white settlers into the hinterland owned by indigenous populations in different time frames.[29] For example, the Australian family farm became the typical unit in rural settlement, ensuring (at least after the land acts of the 1860s and 1870s) a reasonably wide distribution of land ownership. This is similar to the pattern of public land disposal observed in the United States and Canada. The long-run economic consequences were probably momentous—influencing not just the distribution of wealth but the concentration of political power, the timing of the widening of the political franchise, investment in public education, immigration policy, and even the evolution of financial market institutions. Additionally, it should be noted that the comparison undertaken in this study is not only asynchronic, but also asymmetric. For reasons of space and concentration, I refer to the Australian example only in order to comment on the American event horizon.[30]

Land Policies, Surveying, and Elites

A direct comparison between America and Australia is promising because differences abound despite similarities. While in Australia the British Empire maintained its nominal political control over the Australian colonies into the 1850s, in the American case London lost political power after the American Revolution, an event that put political power in the hands of American agrarian elites and merchant capitalists. Whereas in North America, the new nation-state served as a means to reinforce the settlers' thrust into the outback through aggressive nationalism and an ideology of republican agrarianism, in Australia the colonial authorities were not always open to a policy of unconstrained expansion of the settlers. They feared the eruption of open violence and they were not pressured by local voters in regular national and state elections.[31]

The almost complete control by the Imperial Crown affected land policies in Australia. In New South Wales (NSW), for instance, after 1788 and before the establishment of the Department of Land in 1856, Crown land was disposed of in the following manner: due to the principle of *res* (or *terra*) *nullius*, all land was vested in the Crown. The entire responsibility for land policy rested with the residing governor under direction from the British Parliament. In that time, NSW almost could be classed as a department under the Imperial government. The governor was the supreme authority in the colony, equipped with almost autocratic powers. Voter pressure did not exist in this period of Australian history. All correspondence of an important nature that required decision and/or action on the part of the governor was addressed to the colonial secretary. Matters of minor importance or mere detail were directed to the relevant offices.

Considering the similarities in the US and Australia, it is noteworthy that in the United States, land policies were a matter of the federal state, which was in control of the public domain. The Land Ordinance of 1785 had created simple procedures for the acquisition and distribution of public lands. It remained the model for the distribution of land taken from Native Americans for over one hundred years, until the Indian Territory was divided up in 1889: After Indians ceded title to their lands to the federal government, surveyors would mark the land off into giant squares six miles on a side and then subdivide them into sections of one square mile.[32] Each section, in turn, would contain four quarter-sections of 160 acres each. The government would then sell this land at public auction. Any unsold land after the auction could be bought at the land office at a minimum price of $2.00 an acre.[33] After 1799, voices were frequently raised in Congress, demanding open lands in the interest of the frontier people.[34] It is important to note that this happened after the second stage of territorial government was inaugurated in the Northwest Territory, the vast region between the Ohio River in the south and the Mississippi in the west.

William Henry Harrison, like George Washington before him, represents the connection between "gentlemanly elites" in the east and settler desires at the frontier. In 1799, he served as secretary of the Northwest Territory, having previously fought with "Mad" Anthony Wayne as aide-de-camp. Wayne was notorious as the Indian-fighting general who opened the west for white settlement in the Battle of Fallen Timbers in 1794 and the subsequent Treaty of Greenville in 1795, in which the Northwest Indian Confederacy ceded about three-quarters of what was to become the state of Ohio. The next fifteen years after the Treaty of Greenville were a tough period for the Indians of the northwest. Although the treaty had apparently established limits between Indian and white lands in Ohio and Indiana, these lines of demarcation were constantly violated by trappers and settlers. In order to encroach upon additional farmlands, American squatters crossed the treaty lines to clear ground and build cabins in areas that had been guaranteed to the Native Americans. Trappers from Kentucky ranged as far north as the Wabash and Illinois, and in 1801 even William Henry Harrison admitted that:

> The people of Kentucky . . . make a constant practice of crossing over the Indians lands opposite to them every fall to kill deer, bear, and buffalo—the latter from being in great abundance a few years ago is now scarcely to be met with. One white hunter will destroy more game than five of the common Indians—the latter generally contenting himself with a sufficiency for present subsistence—while the other eager after game hunt for the skin of the animal alone.[35]

In addition, the ledgers of Indian traders in the region prove the decline of the pelt trade. Shawnee and Miami trappers still ran their trap lines, but without much success. Once an independent people, the Native Americans now faced scarcity. They no longer had sufficient foodstuff and they could not afford to purchase those trade items on which they depended for survival.[36]

Now, after his resignation from the Army, Harrison pushed through a policy that would enable the settler to purchase land on which to live and earn his livelihood.[37] In addition, the settlers would have preferred land offices close to the land that was to be sold, but often the land that the pioneers wished to purchase was several days' journey from Cincinnati and Pittsburgh, the only places such business could be conducted. This required a long and expensive trip to see the land and select a tract, another long journey to reach the land office where the auction was to be held, and the return journeys. Albert Gallatin once more advocated land for the home-maker and aided Harrison in securing passage of a bill favorable to the settlers. The resultant land law of 1800, sometimes called the "Harrison Land Law," contained all of the above points: (1) a man could purchase as little as a half-section instead of 610 acres; (2) three additional land offices were established in the vicinity of the tracts to be sold; and (3) a liberal system of credit was set up. Under the credit stipulations, payment was spread over a period of four years at a six percent rate of interest.

As in the United States, in Australia the central executive attempted to control land policy. But the picture was a little more complicated, since in Australia both the Imperial government and the various colonial legislatures tried to direct the pace and character of settlement expansion by various modes of land disposal. Bureaucratic decision making had to compete with a large estate, the boundaries of which changed considerably over time. Between 1788 and 1850, divisions or departments did not separate public business. Many branches of the public sector were involved in selling, leasing, and granting Crown land. Much of the work was routine and many tasks were duplicated. Delays stemming from confusion over responsibilities saw land administration fall further and further into arrears.

Sweeping changes regarding the disposal of Crown land were first made under Governor Richard Bourke. The Land Board was abolished in 1831.[38] The government opened land reserves for sale and reduced the inadequate Survey Department. This change marked the shift from a mere convict colony to a settler colony. The governor was ordered to discontinue the practice of giving land instead of pensions or as rewards for services.[39] In January 1831, the practice of land grants was discontinued altogether and was substituted by the Goderich Regulations, which stated that land had to be sold off at public auction. By 1837, the sale of Crown lands by auction with a minimum price of 5s. per acre was firmly put into practice.[40] Further changes occurred when the land policy was again modified in 1840 through the division of New South Wales into three districts, the northern, middle, and southern. Land auctions were restricted to the older settled areas, where much of the land was already alienated. In the outer areas, a fixed price for all land was arranged for. In 1841, the Imperial Parliament passed an act for "Regulation of Sale of Waste Lands in the Australian Colonies." Its main provision was that the control of land was transferred from the Queen to the House of Commons.[41]

Only after Australian self-rule was initiated and Australian voters gained partial control over their administration can one productively compare the land policy in Australia with the United States. In 1850, the Australian Colonies Government Act of the Imperial Parliament not only separated the southeastern Australian district of Port Phillip from New South Wales and established it as the colony of Victoria, but also gave authority to the Legislative Council to prepare a democratic constitution for the colonies.[42] In 1852, the governor handed over the control of land policy and revenue to the Legislative Council. Moreover, the problems confronting the early land administrators in the mid-1800s were rendered more complex by the effects of the gold rush in central NSW, which began in 1851.[43] Prior to 1856, land disposal and settlement in NSW were characterized by the desire of the colonial government to recreate the colony in line with the social and economic system of land use in England and the attempts of the home government to restrain the spread of settlement despite the development of a widespread desire for land.[44]

After the opening of Australia to public settlement in 1816, the ideal of establishing yeoman farmers dominated the public discourse, although the number of farms established was not impressive. In the early 1850s, a concerted effort was made by the old, wool-rich rural elite—the "squattocracy"—to fashion the new constitution in a way that would allow for a heritable upper chamber to curb the democratic extremes of the more popular lower house. This ambition failed because of the British determination to move to the kind of institutional arrangements already emerging in Canada.[45] With the 1855 act of the Imperial Parliament, a responsible government was granted to the colony of NSW. That act transferred the entire management and control of "wastelands" belonging to the Crown to the colonial legislature. The establishment of responsible government in NSW represented a significant departure from the previous administrative framework for decision making and policy making with regard to Crown land. The outcome and impact of this new legislation and policy influenced land settlement patterns for many decades of this early period in Australian settlement.

In North America, British colonial authorities tried to minimize the process of *Landnahme* by setting up the Proclamation Line of 1763. They had learned the hard way that intensive wars against Native Americans during the period 1755 to 1765 were expensive. In Australia, colonial authorities also tried to limit the amount of land that was taken from the Aborigines. In both cases, the half-hearted attempts of the governments failed, in North America because of the Revolution, in Australia because of the advent of responsible government in the separate colonies after 1850.

Genocidal Effects of Settler Imperialism

Settlers simply took matters in their own hands and squatted on land owned by indigenous peoples, using both soft methods (clearing the woods, driving away the animals hunted by Native Americans) and hard methods (poisoning of water resources, tactics of guerrilla warfare) that would prove fatal to the indigenous populations. Settler imperialism may hence be described as a process of constant deterritorialization and reterritorialization, a process that is genocidal in itself, according to Raphael Lemkin's wide definition.[46] In order to analyze settler imperialism, therefore, it is not sufficient to only regard the economic interest of landless farmers as a driving force, but also to understand the discourses and rationales for practices that put settler imperialism in motion. Indigenous populations had to be externalized and exterminated as lawful owners of the land. Before scientific racism (around 1860), other discourses served as justifications for this policy of expulsion. The primitivist discourse, for instance, a "visual ideology," linked the (white male) gaze with concepts of culture and serves thus as a means of assigning indigenous culture a low evolutionary stage without having to refer to biological racism.[47]

One can conceive of settler colonies as "deterritorialized states" constituted by shared economic and political interests between citizens who have settled abroad and "those who control a state apparatus in the home country."[48] The taking of the land consisted of the deterritorialization of indigenous lands and their subsequent reterritorialization within new political borders. Ownership of land was the symbolic as well as effective condition for subsequent political expansion in the form of national territories/new states. Forms of settlement made visible through enclosures, fences, or ploughing represent both aspects of the taking of the land: they are at the same time symbolic and factual.[49] Settlers, as the embodiment of bio-power, are not defined as being beyond or within a border, but settlers *are* the frontier, the border in its advancing and expanding dynamism. As A. Dirk Moses has argued in a seminal article, processes of territorialization and deterritorialization such as expropriation and ethnic cleansing tended to result in "genocidal moments" whenever indigenes resisted these processes. The genocidal moment of colonization passed when the indigenous populations were either wiped out or submitted to the new order.[50]

A second step, however, is required in order to transform the factual frontier into an internationally accepted border. Land occupation by a colonizing power or by settlers differs from the colonization by trading companies or merchants who want to control trading and merchant routes. Both states and settlers are interested in the control of the land itself. If there happened to be powers competing for the control of the land, it was likely that either settlers or states declared their territory to be *terra nullius* retroactively.[51] This is not the same thing as turning the indigenous populations into *homines sacri*, but it means denying them the capacity to be citizens of a sovereign state.[52] *Terrae nullius*, territories without original owners, have no borders because there is no state or sovereign who defines and defends their borders. International conflicts about colonization therefore were only conceivable among colonial powers, but not between indigenous inhabitants and settlers.[53] Hence the settler's real enemy was the indigene. The indigenous enemy had to be de-located ("*entortet*"), which could be achieved through discourses that declare the first nations to be nomads. This was usually the first step, followed by a consecutive extinction or assimilation within the occupying settler society. Reservations and homelands therefore were less relocations than exclusions within a space that has been occupied by settlers: Those areas guaranteed the cultural and corporeal vanishing of the indigenous within the settled space, limiting indigenous culture to the enclaves.

By moving *beyond the line* and exposing himself to skirmishes and colonial warfare with first nations, the settler became the instrument that turned raw facts into legal titles and gave himself a place by de-localizing his enemy, the original owners of the land. This process was by no means an unconscious function of the search for free land, but was a conscious strategy invented and implemented by the gentlemanly elite.[54] Outright wars against the Native Americans (and against the first peoples of Australia, one might add), proved too expensive and inefficient. A cheaper and more effective policy was the territorialization of land and its sale to large numbers of white settlers, a measure that would render it ecologically useless for the Indians. They would then sell or cede it for a low price. The next step would be the controlled shift of the now open border toward the west.[55]

The gentlemanly elite, however, was not the exclusive agent in the hunt for land: pressure for open land also came from within the settler society. Settler imperialism is grounded in the structure of farm households as they developed in the United States after 1800: "Farm households . . . were income-pooling units of production that had to sustain themselves, and husbands and wives had to cooperate in the productive enterprises . . . of the farm."[56] According to econometrician Guillaume Vandenbroucke, endogenous fertility, investment in land, and migration controlled the westward movement. Population growth in the US during the nineteenth century was characterized by high rates of natural increase as well as high rates of national and international migration. The total fertility rate for white women in the United States reached an all-time high between 1800 and 1850.[57] The same is true for Australia between 1845 and 1870.[58] Both the migration and the fertility decisions are linked to land accumulation in the western part of the country.

American inheritance laws and the abolition of the primogeniture system mandated an equal provision of land among the children, including the daughters.[59] This fact led to an exponential increase of land needed for the next generation. If no land could be bequeathed to the children, landless children of farmers had to either work as tenant or agricultural workers or to move on to the west, where cheap land could be had.[60] This mechanism constituted by no means an economic necessity, nor was there an American *lebensraum* discussion because of "overcrowding."[61] Hunger for land was rather a culturally engrained phenomenon. Many farmers bought or acquired additional lands, because it gave them a greater sense of independence in times of economic crises. This attitude was most popular among immigrants who had experienced the European crises of the early nineteenth century. Nevertheless, even American-born farmers kept uncultivated land in reserve. Some used it for speculation, some set it aside in order to provide for their heirs, and others kept it in order to be able to extend the cultivated area at any moment.[62] Population density was low. Around 1820, when American settlers started to move to what was then the "West" (Louisiana, Mississippi, and Illinois), population density in Georgia was lower than two people per square mile. Huge tracts within Pennsylvania were completely unsettled. In 1840, when Americans started to stretch out toward Texas and Mexico, large parts of the former west (central Illinois, western Georgia, the later West Virginia) had not evolved beyond the phase of the frontier.[63] Settler imperialism was characterized by seminomadism, triggered by "excessive individualism. Inability to adapt one's self and one's ideas to the prevailing order of things in any community has made many a 'chronic pioneer,' who has emigrated at short intervals from one settlement to another, until old age has overtaken him."[64]

This seminomadism, however, was closely linked to a capitalist market. Land speculation necessarily included a dependence on capitalist markets. Surplus land could be sold with a handsome profit before any sons or daughters reached an age during which marriage seemed imminent, thus enabling farmers to give daughters a dowry and sons a tract of land. This practice often constituted the only way of providing children with an inheritance. The social costs of this kind of transitory existence were enormous. Land had to be made accessible in rising quantity if the system was supposed to be fail-safe. Growing population figures meant more land at the frontier had to be preempted, squatted, settled, and eventually cultivated. Whereas population density differed widely depending on location and quality of available land, pressure to open western lands for settlement was greatest between the relative peak of population in relation to arable land (1810) and the opening of the western domain after 1830. This pressure coincides with the creation of a land office, which administered the public domain, and the subsequent forceful relocation of Native Americans in the "unsettled" west.[65] During the 1830s, the Amerindian groups of the east had been relocated in the trans-Mississippi west, losing about 35 percent of their population in the process of removal.[66]

Even before the introduction of preemption rights (1830), the federal administration, as well as individual states of the Union, pursued a very active policy of land cessions from the Native Americans. Since the United States accepted ownership of land by Indians and did not treat Indian lands as *terra nullius*, treaties had to be concluded, which resulted in the sale of huge tracts of land by Native Americans.[67]

This detail marks an important difference with the Australian policy.[68] In North America, common law acknowledged Indians' land rights, which were based on possession and occupation of the land rather than founded on a grant from the Crown. This title constituted a burden on the underlying title of the Crown, although it did not derive from the Crown.[69] In the American context, discovery did not constitute a legal title that had to be achieved through the legal purchase or cession, concluded in a treaty between nations.[70] After the Supreme Court decisions *Johnson v. M'intosh* (1823) and *Worcester v. Georgia* (1832), it was standard legal procedure that First Nations retained possession of their lands following discovery and, moreover, that such possession did not amount to site-specific activities such as hunting and fishing but included the right to utilize their traditional lands according to their own discretion and needs.[71] Chief Justice Marshall reasoned that the original inhabitants of North America "were admitted to be the rightful occupants of the soil, with a legal as well as just claim to retain possession of it and to use it according to their own discretion."[72] Despite differences within the American and Australian legal frameworks, therefore, it would be worthwhile to further investigate the connection between family structures of yeoman farms, population growth, and inheritance patterns in both the United States' and Australia's settler societies. This comparative work, however, remains to be done in the future.

Conclusion

Settler imperialisms may differ in legal foundations and chronological sequence, depending on the period of state formation. Their common denominators are the rapid influx of land-hungry settlers into areas inhabited by indigenous populations, the taking of the land as a legal result of indigenous cessions (United States), or the application of the theory of *terra nullius* (Australia). These settlement processes are achieved through the active involvement of the gentlemanly class that is exposed to political pressure by the settlers and profit directly, both economically as landowners and surveyors and politically. Indigenous populations are exposed to and affected by *Landnahme* in different ways, ecologically and economically, resulting in loss of land, forced dislocation and low-intensity warfare, often disguised as "border skirmishes." These long-lasting processes were less visible, but just as deadly as large-scale massacres and genocides.

Notes

1. The quotation is from Ingeborg Bachmann, *"Todesarten"-Projekt*, 5 vols. (Munich, 1995), 2: 230–31. I thank Lilian Friedberg for directing my attention to Bachmann's remarks.
2. The UN definitions emphasizes the criminal act as an event, rather than the endurance and repetition of a social practice. United Nations, Convention on the Prevention and Punishment of the Crime of Genocide, Article II, 9 December 1948. The original definition by Polish jurist Raphael Lemkin was much more open to the composite nature and long-lasting aspect of genocides. Frank Chalk and Kurt Jonassohn, *The History and Sociology of Genocide: Analyses and Case Studies* (New Haven, CT, 1990), 8–9; Ward Churchill was among the first historians to complain about the conceptual rigidity of the genocide definitions. Ward Churchill, *A Little Matter of Genocide: Holocaust and Denial in the Americas 1492 to the Present* (San Francisco, 1997), 71. See also Ann Curthoys and John Docker, "Introduction—Genocide: Definitions, Questions, Settler-Colonies," *Aboriginal History* 25, no. 1 (2001): 1–15.
3. Curthoys and Docker, "Introduction," 10.
4. Alison Palmer differentiates between "state-led" and "societally-led" colonial genocides. For her, the genocidal momentum came from the Queensland frontier rather than the center in Brisbane. Alison Palmer, *Colonial Genocide* (Adelaide, 2000).
5. Churchill, *A Little Matter of Genocide*, 84.
6. Wallerstein claims that even under sixteenth-century Spanish rule, the Crown could not control the settlers in the colonies. Immanuel Wallerstein, *The Modern World-System: Capitalist Agriculture and the Origins of the European World-Economy in the Sixteenth Century* (New York, 1976), 188.
7. Curthoys and Docker, "Introduction," 6.
8. This development seems to have been typical for every frontier except "beachhead frontier" like Sydney, NSW, or Plymouth, Massachusetts. John Connor, *The Australian Frontier Wars, 1788–1838* (Sydney, 2002), 26.
9. Gregory Evans Dowd, *A Spirited Resistance: The North American Indian Struggle for Unity, 1745–1815* (Baltimore, MD and London, 1992), 23. Squatters were a constant source of friction in Australia as well. New South Wales, Legislative Council, and Committee on Police and Goals, *Final Report of the Committee on Police and Goals* (Sydney, 1835). John C. Weaver, "Beyond the Fatal Shore: Pastoral Squatting and the Occupation of Australia, 1826 to 1852," *American Historical Review* 101, no. 4 (1996): 981–1007.
10. Cornelia Vismann, "Terra nullius: Zum Feindbegriff im Völkerrecht," in *Übertragung und Gesetz. Gründungsmythen, Kriegstheater und Unterwerfungstechniken von Institutionen*, ed. Armin Adam and Martin Stingelin (Berlin, 1996), 167.

11. Aboriginal acts of resistance against white expansion started with Pemulwuy in NSW (1790–1802), and continued to the armed resistance in Tasmania in the 1820s and to the bloody skirmishes in NSW and Victoria in the 1830s and 1840s. Paul W. Newbury, *Aboriginal Heroes of the Resistance from Pemulwuy to Mabo* (Sydney, 1999); Eric P. Willmot, *Pemulwuy: The Rainbow Warrior* (Sydney, 1988); Rory Medcalf, *Rivers of Blood: Massacres of the Northern Rivers. Aborigines and Their Resistance to the White Occupation, 1838–1870* (Lismore, NSW, 1993); James Miller, *Koori, A Will to Win: The Heroic Resistance, Survival and Triumph of Black Australia* (London, 1985); Alan Pope, *Resistance and Retaliation: Aboriginal-European Relations in Early Colonial South Australia* (Adelaide, 1989). For North America, publications about Indian resistance are numerous: Robin Brownlie, *A Fatherly Eye: Indian Agents, Government Power, and Aboriginal Resistance in Ontario, 1918–1939* (Don Mills, NY, 2003); Ward Churchill, *Struggle for the Land: Native North American Resistance to Genocide, Ecocide, and Colonization* (San Francisco, 2002); James V. Fenelon, *Culturicide, Resistance, and Survival of the Lakota ("Sioux Nation")* (New York, 1998); Kirsten Fischer, *Suspect Relations: Sex, Race, and Resistance in Colonial North Carolina* (Ithaca, NY, 2002); Cécile Gouy-Gilbert, *Une Résistance Indienne: Les Yaquis Du Sonora* (Lyon, 1983); Richard A. Grounds, George E. Tinker, and David E. Wilkins, *Native Voices: American Indian Identity and Resistance* (Lawrence, KS, 2003); Evelyn Hu-DeHart, *Yaqui Resistance and Survival: The Struggle for Land and Autonomy, 1821–1910* (Madison, WI, 1984); Alvin M. Josephy, *The Patriot Chiefs: A Chronicle of American Indian Resistance* (New York, 1993); Jane B. Katz, *Let Me Be a Free Man: A Documentary History of Indian Resistance* (Minneapolis, 1975); Rupert Norval Richardson, *The Comanche Barrier to South Plains Settlement: A Century and a Half of Savage Resistance to the Advancing White Frontier* (Millwood, NY, 1973); Siobhan Senier, *Voices of American Indian Assimilation and Resistance: Helen Hunt Jackson, Sarah Winnemucca, and Victoria Howard*, (Norman, OK, 2001); William B. Taylor and Franklin G. Y. Pease, *Violence, Resistance, and Survival in the Americas: Native Americans and the Legacy of Conquest* (Washington, DC, 1994).
12. Bain Attwood and S. G. Foster, eds., *Frontier Conflict: The Australian Experience* (Canberra, 2003). In Queensland, the Native Police was one of the most effective agents of genocidal acts. A. Dirk Moses, "An Antipodean Genocide? The Origins of the Genocidal Moment in the Colonization of Australia," *Journal of Genocide Research* 2, no.1 (2000): 99–102.
13. Charles Joseph Kappler, *Indian Affairs: Laws and Treaties* (Washington, DC, 1903–1971), available online http://digital.library.okstate.edu/kappler/, accessed 13 December 2004.
14. Kappler, *Indian Affairs*.
15. United States and Bureau of the Census, *Historical Statistics of the United States, Colonial Times to 1970*, 2 vols. (White Plains, NY 1989). Part 1, "Population," Series J 20: "Public Land Sales: 1800 to 1860," 430.
16. US, *Historical Statistics*, J 21–25, 430.
17. A. Dirk Moses, "Coming to Terms with Genocidal Pasts in a Comparative Perspective," *Aboriginal History* 25 (2001): 104. See also A. Dirk. Moses, ed., *Genocide and Settler Society: Frontier Violence and Stolen Indigenous Children in Australian History* (New York and Oxford, 2004).
18. Moses, "Antipodean Genocide," 95.
19. Paul Wallace Gates, Allan G. Bogue, and Margaret Beattie Bogue, *The Jeffersonian Dream: Studies in the History of American Land Policy and Development* (Albuquerque, NM, 1996), 8.

20. P. J. Cain and A. G. Hopkins, *British Imperialism: Innovation and Expansion, 1688–1914, London* (New York, 1993), 4.
21. Edmund Sears Morgan, *American Slavery, American Freedom: The Ordeal of Colonial Virginia* (New York and London, 1995), 250–70; Lois Kimball Mathews, *The Expansion of New England: The Spread of New England Settlement and Institutions to the Mississippi River, 1620–1865* (New York, 1962), 43–74, 254. This combination of actors implies the possibility that the agents disagreed about the direction and speed of expansion, but such a fact does not undermine the theory of settler imperialism. On the contrary, it underlines analytical value of the concept, since the network of metropolitan and frontier agents functioned to expropriate indigenous peoples despite any internal tensions. See John Law and John Hassard, *Actor Network: Theory and After* (Oxford, 1999).
22. See Churchill, *A Little Matter of Genocide*, 52; Michael Hardt and Antonio Negri, *Empire* (Cambridge, MA, 2000), 165–70.
23. Usage is still rare. Alan Richenberg, "Legacies of Empire," *History Today* 48, no. 3 (1998): 8; Robert Bickers, "Chinese Burns Britain in China 1842–1900," *History Today* 50, no. 8 (2000): 10. See also Joshua Nkomo, "Southern Rhodesia: Apartheid Country," in *Africa Speaks*, ed. James Duffy and Robert A. Manners (Princeton, NJ, 1961), 143.
24. The term *agrarian imperialism* also appears in the context of world systems, although with a different meaning. According to world system theories, agrarian imperialism may be characterized as being marked by the rise and fall of successive multinational empires that thrived on agrarian surplus economies, urban political centers, and capital accumulation through international trade in luxury goods. Majid Tehranian, "Pan-capitalism and Migration in Historical Perspective," *International Political Science Review* 19, no. 3 (1998): 289–304.
25. See his personal homepage where he refers to research of his students, http://www.hist.unibe.ch/foerster.htm, accessed 30 December 2004.
26. "By constantly making a part of the hands 'supernumerary,' modern industry, in all countries where it has taken root, gives a spur to emigration and to the colonization of foreign lands, which are thereby converted into settlements for growing the raw material of the mother country; just as Australia, for example, was converted into a colony for growing wool." Karl Marx, *Das Kapital*, in *Marx Engels Werke*, 43 vols. (Berlin, 1972), 23: 475.
27. Cain and Hopkins, *British Imperialism*. Their aim is to write economic history rather than to explain the effect and the mechanisms of settler imperialism within the dependent areas.
28. Another comparative study is Donald Denoon, *Settler Capitalism: The Dynamics of Dependent Development in the Southern Hemisphere* (Oxford, 1983).
29. On the possibility of comparison see Lilian Friedberg, "Dare to Compare: Americanizing the Holocaust," *American Indian Quarterly* 24, no. 3 (2000): 353–80.
30. The dangers and advantages of asymmetric historical comparisons are discussed in Jürgen Kocka, "Asymmetrical Historical Comparison: The Case of the German *Sonderweg*," *History and Theory* 38, no. 1 (1999): 40–50.
31. "Australia's Status as Independent Nation," in *Final Report of the Constitutional Commission*, ed. Maurice Byers, Enid Campbell, Rupert Hamer, E. G. Whitlam, and Leslie Zines, 2 vols. (Canberra, 1988), 1: section 2, 112–28.
32. US Serial Set, Number 4015, 56th Congress, 1st Session, 648–649: Indian Land Cessions in the United States, 1784–1894, in *A Century of Lawmaking for a New Nation: U.S. Congressional Documents and Debates*, 1774—1875, http://memory.loc.gov/ammem/amlaw/lwss-ilc.html, accessed 25 December 2004.

33. John Clement Fitzpatrick et al., eds., *Journals of the Continental Congress, 1774–1789*, 34 vols. (Washington, DC,1904), 28: 375–81; Gerhard Kollmann, "Revolution und Kontinuität: Eine Untersuchung der Pläne und Ansätze zur Organisation der Gebiete zwischen Appallachen und Mississippi, 1774–1786," 2 vols. (PhD diss., Cologne University 1976), 2: 659–91.
34. Everett Dick, *The Lure of the Land: A Social History of the Public Lands from the Articles of Confederation to the New Deal* (Lincoln, NE, 1970), 9–10.
35. Harrison to the Secretary of War, 15 July 1801, Hyacinth Lasselle Papers, Indiana State Library, Indianapolis.
36. Harrison to the Secretary of War, 15 July 1801, Hyacinth Lasselle Papers, Indiana State Library, Indianapolis. William Burnett to Robert Innes and Co., 20 December 1798, in Wilbur M. Cunningham, *Letter Book of William Burnett: Early Fur Trader in the Land of Four Flags* (St. Joseph, MI, 1967), 112; Burnett to George Gillespie, 30 May 1800, ibid., 129.
37. Freeman Cleaves, *Old Tippecanoe: William Henry Harrison and his Time* (New York and London, 1939), 28–30.
38. Manning H. Clark, *A History of Australia*, 6 vols. (Melbourne, 1963), 2: 105.
39. Frederick Watson, Peter Chapman, *Historical Records of Australia*, 34 vols. (Sydney, 1914–1997), series I, vol. 16, 639.
40. Watson, Chapman, *Historical Records of Australia*, series I, vol. 18, 765.
41. Marjorie Faith Barnard, *A History of Australia* (New York, 1963), 285–86.
42. 13 & 14 Victoriae, Cap. 59, An Act for the Better Government of Her Majesty's Australian Colonies, 5 August 1850.
43. Kerry Cardell and Cliff Cumming, eds., *A World Turned Upside Down: Cultural Change on Australia's Goldfields 1851–2001* (Canberra, 2001), 3.
44. John Jenkins, *Crown Land Administration and Policy in New South Wales, Australia, 1856–1974: Changing Perceptions, Values and Organisational Culture* [Web Page], 2003. Available at: http://www.hicsocial.org/Social2003Proceedings/John%20Jenkins%201.pdf, accessed 3 December 2004.
45. Cain and Hopkins, *British Imperialism*, 237.
46. Gilles Deleuze and Félix Guattari, *What Is Philosophy?* (New York, 1994), 85; Gillian Bottomley, "Anthropologists and the Rhizomatic Study of Migration," *The Australian Journal of Anthropology* 9, no. 1 (1998): 31–44. Lemkin wrote: "Generally speaking, genocide does not necessarily mean the immediate destruction of a nation, *except when* accomplished by mass killing of all the members of the nation. It is intended rather to signify a coordinated plan of different actions aimed at destruction of the essential foundations of the life of national groups, with the aim of annihilating the groups themselves. The objective of such a plan would be the disintegration of the political and social institutions, of culture, language, national feelings, religion, and the economic existence of national groups, and the destruction of personal security, liberty, health, dignity, and the lives of individuals belonging to such groups. Genocide is the destruction of the national group as an entity, and the actions involved are directed against individuals, not in their individual capacity but as members of the national group." Raphael Lemkin, *Axis Rule in Occupied Europe* (Washington, DC, 1944), 79. See also ibid., xi–xii.
47. Norbert Finzsch, "'It is scarcely possible to conceive that human beings could be so hideous and loathsome': Discourses of Genocide in Eighteenth and Nineteenth-Century America and Australia," *Patterns of Prejudice* 39, no. 2 (2005): 97–115.
48. Linda G. Basch, Nina Glick Schiller, and Cristina Szanton Blanc, *Nations Unbound: Transnational Projects, Postcolonial Predicaments, and Deterritorialized Nation-States* (London and New York, 1994), 272.

49. Cornelia Vismann, "Terra nullius: Zum Feindbegriff im Völkerrecht in Übertragung und Gesetz," in *Gründungsmythen, Kriegstheater und Unterwerfungstechniken von Institutionen*, ed. Armin Adam and Martin Stingelin (Berlin, 1996), 167.
50. Moses, "An Antipodean Genocide?," 102; Moses, ed., *Genocide and Settler Society.*
51. Eva Horn, "Partisan, Siedler, Asylant: Zur politischen Anthropologie des Grenzgängers," *Ästhetik & Kommunikation* 29, no. 102 (1998): 39–46.
52. Vismann, "Terra Nullius," 167.
53. Carl Schmitt, *Der Nomos der Erde im Völkerrecht des jus publicum Europaeum* (Cologne, 1950), 100–102.
54. In referring to the Proclamation Line of 1763, with which the British colonial government tried to stall the incursion of settlers into Indian Land, George Washington wrote to William Crawford, a surveyor: It [the proclamation] must fall, of course, in a few years, especially when those Indians consent to our occupying those lands. Any person who neglects hunting out good lands, and in some measure marking and distinguishing them for his own, in order to keep others from settling them will never regain it. If you will be at the trouble of seeking out the lands, I will take upon me the part of securing them, as soon as there is a possibility of doing it and will, moreover, be at all the cost and charges surveying and patenting the same. . . . By this time it be easy for you to discover that my plan is to secure a good deal of land. You will consequently come in for a handsome quantity." Manuscript Division, Library of Congress: *George Washington Papers at the Library of Congress, 1741–1799: Series 5, Financial Papers*; George Washington to William Crawford, 21 September 1767, Account Book 2, 13.
55. Philipp Schuyler, Letters to the President of the Continental Congress, 21 September 1782; 29 July 1783 in *Papers of the Continental Congress, 1774–1789*, ed. John P. Butler, microfilm, 204 reels, Washington, DC, 1959, reel 153 III 593–95, 601–607; George Washington to Duane, 7 September 1783, in *The Writings of George Washington: From the Original Manuscript Sources 1745–1799*, 39 vols., ed. John Clement Fitzpatrick et al. (Westport, CT, 1970), 27: 133–40. These blueprints were subsequently integrated into the Indian policy at the frontier. Walter H. Mohr, *Federal Indian Relations, 1774–1788* (New York, 1971), 94–104; Reginald Horseman, "American Indian Policy in the Old Northwest, 1783–1812," *William and Mary Quarterly* 18 (1961): 36–38; Reginald Horseman, *Expansion and American Indian Policy, 1783–1812* (East Lansing, MI, 1967), 7–14; Kollmann, *Revolution und Kontinuität*, vol. 2, 509–25.
56. Allan Kulikoff, *The Agrarian Origins of American Capitalism* (Charlottesville, VA, 1992), 29–30.
57. Jeremy Greenwood and Guillaume Vandenbroucke, "The Baby Boom and Baby Bust: O.E.C.D. Fertility Data," http://www.econ.rochester.edu/Faculty/GreenwoodPapers, 22 (accessed 3 Dec 2004).
58. Ibid., 2, 29.
59. J. Bradford DeLong, "Bequests: An Historical Perspective," http://www.j-bradford-delong.net/Econ_Articles/Estates/DeLongEstatesMunnell.pdf, 4–6 (accessed 3 December 2004).
60. Lee A. Craig, *To Sow One Acre More: Childbearing and Farm Productivity in the Antebellum North* (Baltimore, MD, 1993); Carl Degler, *Out of Our Past: The Forces that Shaped Modern America* (New York, 1970), 114; Norbert Finzsch, "Genocides against Native Americans between Individualist Agenda and State-Implemented Programs," *Jahrbuch für Historische Friedensforschung* 7 (1999): 48–59.
61. The population index of white people per 1,000 acres of arable land reached its peak in 1810 with 0.848, whereas it dropped increasingly until 1860 and the all-time low

of 0.526. Yasukichi Yasuba, *Birth Rates of the White Population in the United States* (Baltimore, MD, 1962), table V.4, table V.10, 144; 165.

62. Stanley Lebergott, "The Demand for Land: The United States, 1820–1860," *Journal of Economic History* 45 (1985): 181–212.
63. Degler, *Out of Our Past*, 115.
64. Mathews, *Expansion of New England*, 7.
65. Charles Grier Sellers, *The Market Revolution: Jacksonian America, 1815–1846* (New York, 1991), 17. See for example the Cherokee Trail of Tears, 1838–1839, which, although apparently a peaceful resettlement of roughly 14,000 Cherokee from Georgia, Tennessee, and Alabama in the newly assigned Indian Territory (Oklahoma), resulted in estimated 4.000 deaths, caused by starvation, illness, and exhaustion.
66. Michael Paul Rogin, *Fathers and Children: Andrew Jackson and the Subjugation of the American Indians* (New York 1975), 4–5.
67. Charles C. Royce and Cyrus Thomas, *Indian Land Cessions in the United States: Eighteenth Annual Report of the Bureau of American Ethnology to the Secretary of the Smithsonian Institution, 1896–1897* (Washington, DC, 1897), 521–97.
68. Royce, Thomas, *Indian Land Cessions*, 527.
69. *Johnson v. M'Intosh* (1823), 8 Wheaton 543, 21 U.S. 240, 573–74, quoted in Thomas A. Berger and Harry A. Slade, *Delgamuukw, also Known as Earl Muldoe, Suing on His Behalf: Delgamuukw v. Queen*, Court of Appeals, Vancouver; 1991 Dec 3 (CA103770), 6–7.
70. Royce, Thomas, *Indian Land Cessions*, 528.
71. 31 U.S. (6 Pet.) 515 (1832).
72. *Johnson v. M'Intosh* (1823), 8 Wheaton 543, 21 U.S. 240, 573–74.

– *Chapter 12* –

NAVIGATING THE CULTURAL ENCOUNTER
Blackfoot Religious Resistance in Canada (c. 1870–1930)

Blanca Tovías

Introduction

The Blackfoot Confederacy comprised an alliance of of three First Nations, that occupied both sides of the future Canadian-US border zone and shared a common language and culture.[1] Dominating a vast territory with their combined strength and their adoption of the horse and firearms in the first half of the eighteenth century, the Blackfoot, like other Native peoples of the Great Plains, relied on the buffalo for their survival. Each summer, "when the saskatoons were ripe in the thickets along the river," the bands of each tribe camped together, hunted buffalo, and prepared for the most important ceremony of their calendar year, the Sun Dance.[2] Efforts by missionaries and bureaucrats to eradicate this ceremony, seen as an obstacle to "civilization," began in the late 1870s and early 1880s, once the Blackfoot settled into reserves.

The incorporation of the Northwest Territories into the Dominion of Canada in 1870 marked the end of an era for the Blackfoot; the signing of Treaty Seven in 1877 turned them into wards of the state, subject to the provisions of the Indian Act.[3] It was quickly followed by the destruction of the buffalo herds. Without the buffalo to provide sustenance and traditional materials, the Blackfoot became dependent on government rations to avoid starvation. Assimilation into European life-ways accelerated.[4] Having remained hitherto free from interference in their cultural practices, they now faced legislation that proscribed features of their religious praxis deemed unacceptable to bureaucrats and missionaries.

The authorities targeted the Sun Dance. While it was not proscribed per se, they enforced regulations against acts of [self-]torture and the giving away of wealth that took place during its celebration. These efforts aimed to undermine not only the Sun Dance practice, but also Blackfoot cultural reproduction generally in order to pave the way for their "civilization," which non-Native Canadians understood as the disappearance of the Blackfoot as a distinct people by their gradual absorption in the broader population.

Such an ambition raises the question of "cultural genocide." Although omitted from the final draft of the UN Convention on the Prevention and Punishment of the Crime of Genocide in 1948, the concept of genocide as formulated by its inventor, Raphael Lemkin, includes nonlethal "techniques of destruction" that attack the "essential foundations of life of national groups," such as attacks on political self-government, language use, and morality.[5] As John Docker makes clear in his chapter in this volume, Lemkin never relinquished his belief in the conceptual efficacy of cultural genocide. But did he include nonviolent assimilation policies as falling within the rubric of this concept? Lemkin himself distinguished between the adaptation that occurs with the coexistence of different cultures and the desecration of culture that usually attends a violent occupation by a foreign power. Cultural genocide, Lemkin wrote, "must not be confused with the gradual changes a culture may undergo," occurring "by means of the continuous and slow adaptation of the culture to new situations." Here Lemkin appears to have meant the hybridity that attends adaptation to "outside influences" and the "assimilation of certain foreign culture traits." In other words, he continues, "the gradual disintegration of culture . . . through the cultural exhaustion of various societies" is not genocidal. But "surgical operations on cultures and deliberate assassination of civilizations" are genocidal.[6]

In order to see whether the Blackfoot case constitutes cultural genocide, this chapter focuses on the changing environment and the pressures inherent in the colonization of Blackfoot territory during the transition to life on the reserves. The analysis commences with the signing of Treaty Seven: it sketches the background to the legislation proscribing the Sun Dance, the extent of efforts to implement it, and the responses, or repertoire of contention they elicited.

"Civilizing" the Blackfoot

Official attempts to curtail or even eradicate the Sun Dance formed part of a matrix of legislation, bureaucratic programs, and pejorative attitudes and discourses that were deployed by European colonizers throughout the Americas. Their efforts sought the ultimate "disappearance of the Indian" not by physical extermination, but by eradicating their culture. In the

Northwest Territories during the late nineteenth century, government policy aimed at educating the younger generations to reject their own culture "so that, as the older Indians in the course of nature disappear, the task of civilizing becomes more easy."[7] Thus "nature," not human agency, was posited as the mediating force for vanquishing Canadian First Nations' cultures.[8] The discourse of a "vanishing race" gained momentum in the late 1800s and fueled a flurry of "salvage ethnologies" that sought to capture its dying moments.[9] Shifting the blame to nature allowed the colonizers to ignore the destructive effects their own actions imposed on the colonized.

The relationship between the Blackfoot and the Dominion Government was cemented in Treaty Seven, signed by the "Blackfeet, Blood, Piegans," their old allies the "Sarcees," and their traditional foes, the Stoneys, on 27 September 1877. Between 1871 and 1876, Treaties One to Six were signed by other Northwest First Nations. These treaties were calculated to avoid costly wars such as those then taking place in the US. They followed an established British pattern of providing annuities, land reserves, and other benefits in return for land surrender.[10] The Blackfoot had twice requested a treaty, whose guarantees their traditional Cree enemies had already secured. Increasing encroachment by settlers on Blackfoot territory since the arrival of the North-West Mounted Police (hereafter NWMP) in 1874, and the alarming reduction of buffalo herds, fueled their desire to secure similar guarantees.[11]

The Blackfoot were allocated reserves at the time of treaty signing, but the end of their nomadic life-ways began in 1879 when the large herds of buffalo that hitherto had provided their sustenance had been slaughtered to near extinction. While the Blackfoot had been major suppliers of provisions for the fur traders in the mid-1800s,[12] they now became reliant for survival on government-issued rations of beef and flour.[13] As per treaty terms, the Dominion provided them with the rudiments to become farmers within the confines of their reserves, where, under the tutelage of government instructors and Indian Agents, agriculture and cattle farming were gradually adopted by a number of Blackfoot; those who refused remained dependent on rations.[14] In 1879, Canadian officials provided rations and ammunition to able-bodied Blackfoot, and encouraged them to cross the southern border to follow the dwindling buffalo herds. Some of them remained in Montana and returned destitute after two years. Urgent relief was given to those who remained in the reserve.

This was the beginning of a radically different existence. Henceforth, their erstwhile autonomous life-ways became subject to regulation by the Canadian Indian Act. Reliance on rations gave the government leverage to press for the Blackfoot to abandon their cultural and religious practices and to adopt those of the colonizers. This new imperative was often presented as beneficial to First Nations, but the security of settlers and their property was also a powerful motive. At no point was a discourse of physical extermination linked to this imperative in the extant documentation. Soon after the arrival of the NWMP in 1874, Blackfoot traditions such as warring and raiding began to decline, partly through police efforts, but also because the common poverty of the tribes after the disappearance of the buffalo made them forget their old enmities.[15] Across the southern border, which artificially divided the Blackfoot divisions, the Piegan had signed the Judith Treaty in 1855, although a reservation was not set aside for them until 1874. It was the culmination of several years of violence between the Piegan and settlers in Montana that in January 1870 led to the massacre of 173 members of Chief Heavy Runner's peaceful band, badly affected at the time by a smallpox epidemic, including fifty children under twelve years of age, and ninety women. This massacre, perpetrated by troops under Brevet Colonel Eugene M. Baker, needs to be placed under the lens of physical genocide, especially within the broader context of colonization in the US. There was no follow-up to the massacre, which marked the end of Blackfoot armed resistance.[16] The Blackfoot were never at war with the Dominion, and in 1876 they reportedly rejected Sitting Bull's entreaties to join him in a war to exterminate the "whites."[17]

Relative peace did not prevent a contest for cultural supremacy being waged by church and state through evangelization and the imposition of "civilization," often described as the "policy of the Bible and the plough." Christianity was the foundation on which the edifice of "civilization" was to be erected, a goal succinctly described by a common saying: "Destroy the Indian to save the man."[18] While Protestant and Catholic missionaries had been working in the Northwest since the 1840s, some even following the bands during their buffalo hunts, reserve life under the aegis of the Indian Act provided opportunities for proselytizing more forcefully.[19] To fulfill its treaty obligation to send teachers to educate Blackfoot children, the state funded the building of schools and their maintenance, while the church sent missionaries to inculcate Christianity and educate the younger generations according to normative European standards. Young Blackfoot were to be persuaded to embrace Christianity and reject their indigenous beliefs, viewed by most missionaries as a cult to the devil.[20]

Within this context, the Sun Dance, one of the most significant ceremonies of the peoples of the Great Plains and Prairies,[21] and other indigenous customs (such as the Potlatch of the Pacific coastal First Nations), were deemed obstacles to the "civilizing" enterprise and were consequently the target of proscriptive legislation. This "civilizing" project rested on the classic discourse of progress: it was, according to the Governor of the Northwest Territories, Alexander Morris, "opening up to [Native Peoples] a future of promise, based upon the foundations of instruction and the many other advantages of civilized life."[22]

In the Northwest Territories, the role of missionaries at the front line of the "civilizing" project went beyond evangelization and education of the young. They were, according to Protestant missionary John Maclean, "the standing army of the Dominion," preparing "new districts for the advent of the settler."[23] Indeed, missionaries became brokers for the acceptance of cultural and political change by inculcating the superiority of European culture and the fairness of its laws. Prior to the signing of treaties, George McDougall, a Methodist missionary, was commissioned by the Lieutenant-Governor of Manitoba to persuade the Northwest First Nations to place their trust in the government. His son, John McDougall, also a missionary, likewise rendered services in 1874 to prepare the way for the arrival of the NWMP. He was on hand at the signing of Treaties Six and Seven in 1876/77, together with Constantine Scollen, a Catholic oblate priest. Both had submitted reports to the government in 1876 advocating the signing of a treaty with the Blackfoot.[24]

Notwithstanding their rhetoric of benefiting First Nations, the missionaries were instrumental in advancing the colonizing enterprise because they saw it in terms of releasing indigenous inhabitants from a state of savagery. In practice, at least within Catholicism, this notion translated as the replacement of living religions with "magic formulas dear to Christianity" that were to be memorized; among others, "the Large Catechism, the Small Catechism, the Apostles' Creed, the Nicene Creed, and the Ten Commandments."[25] Although professed in the most altruistic terms, their unambiguous belief in the superiority of Christianity was deployed in a manner calculated to disregard utterly the significance of ceremonies such as the Sun Dance, which were not merely concerned with the sacred but which also provided a crucial space for cultural reproduction. Ignorance of Blackfoot culture went hand in hand with its condemnation.[26]

The Blackfoot experience of the colonial encounter differed from that of neighboring First Nations. Insulated from early European influence by their geographical location,[27] their numerical strength and their reputation as fierce warriors who had dominated the Prairies still commanded respect, and perhaps even elicited fear from Whites obliged to negotiate with them face to face. At the same time, Blackfoot dominance of a vast territory had been greatly eroded, they had been weakened by epidemics caused by introduced European diseases, and the whiskey trade had further ravaged them.[28] Nonetheless, their combined number was generally superior to that of other First Nations, listed as 5,050 at the time of treaty signing in 1877. By 1882, the reported number was 8,642, although this figure included all First Nations under Treaty Seven.[29]

Significantly, the strong relationship of the Blackfoot with the NWMP translated into a good relationship with the Dominion. They welcomed police eradication of the bootleggers who had fomented intratribal violence, causing many deaths directly attributable to alcohol consumption.[30] It is worth noting, in passing, that Blackfoot leaders were not averse to availing themselves of educational opportunities, especially reading and writing, for their children as a vehicle for the furtherance of Blackfoot interests, and indeed saw the government-sponsored education of Blackfoot children as a treaty right.[31]

After refusing to join Sitting Bull in a war against Whites in the 1870s, and later the Northwest (Riel) Rebellion in 1885, the Blackfoot were on a comparatively better footing in their dealings with the DIA bureaucracy than their Cree neighbors who had joined Riel.[32] These antecedents influenced the outcomes of Blackfoot dealings with bureaucrats, missionaries, and the NWMP. Furthermore, their interests were represented by able leaders who also gained the respect of Whites, among them chiefs such as Red Crow (Kainai), revered by his people both as a statesman and as a warrior; Crowfoot (Siksika), a consummate diplomat with a reputation as a good provider for those most in need, which earned him the sobriquet of "a father of all his people"; and Old Sun (Siksika), who was a strong religious leader. It befell these leaders, and others whose names are less salient, to guide their followers through the difficult transition to reserve life. At this juncture, their overriding concern was to secure Blackfoot physical survival, an imperative that could be divorced from cultural identity. Under the stress of imposed cultural transformation, the survival of a separate Blackfoot identity could be best ensured through the continuation of the Sun Dance.

Cultural Significance of the Blackfoot Sun Dance

The Sun Dance was emblematic of Blackfoot culture—its eradication would have had the direst consequences. The Sun Dance, a practice shared by many Plains First Nations, may have begun as late as 1700.[33] According to pioneer anthropologist Clark Wissler, it was a "true tribal festival, or demonstration of ceremonial functions, in which practically every important ritual owner and organization had a place."[34] His contemporary Leslie Spier argued that its name, coined by Europeans, "is a misnomer since the dance is by no means connected solely with the sun." The rubric elides the difference between what the Blackfoot call *Ookaan,* the central sacred rite (lasting only four days), and the broader social aspects of the coming together of the bands, which the Blackfoot called *Ako-katssinn* (the time of all people camping together).[35] During the Sun Dance, the All Comrades societies, which functioned to maintain the smooth running of Blackfoot day-to-day life, held their meetings at which initiations took place. Although not the main focus of the Sun Dance, these gatherings underlined its significance.[36] Traditionally, the Blackfoot divisions held separate Sun Dances during which each band occupied a designated place within the circle of lodges, being joined by relatives and friends who came from afar to renew acquaintances. Nor was this an exclusive gathering of Blackfoot; friends from other First Nations were also welcome. This occurred annually "when the wild-fruit is ripe, at the end of July or early in August."[37] The dual significance of the Sun Dance was highlighted by Spier, who described it as a "political unit which functions . . . as a ceremonial unit."[38]

As the largest gathering of the year, the Sun Dance provided the ideal space for cultural transactions and opportunities to attain social prestige not available while the bands camped separately.[39] The requirement that only a married woman—whose virtue must be beyond reproach—could vow to hold a Sun Dance, lent great prestige to the vower, to the male ceremonialist who conducted it, and also to the sponsor. Similarly, males could buttress their social position by recounting past deeds of valor, or "counting coup." This rubric applied to feats such as touching an enemy before striking him the deathblow, and the capture of weapons, shields, or other sacred objects. It was always followed by a distribution of gifts. Thus while counting coup celebrated an individual's success in war, it was also accompanied by a display of generosity towards the less fortunate.[40] These displays impressed upon the young the importance of Blackfoot values and ideals. Socially, the circle camp was ideal for those seeking husbands or wives, and was therefore the time when most marriages were arranged and took place.[41] Within the sacred realm, the Sun Dance provided a link between the present and the mythological past. The vow to hold a Sun Dance was a means to secure divine intervention in cases of extreme need by an individual. Consequently, the Sun Dance became critical at times of hardship.[42] Nor did it lack entertainment value: the reenactment of battles in which the Blackfoot defeated and scalped their most hated enemies, the Crow, would elicit much laughter and applause.[43] Finally, the Sun Dance provided an annual vacation, a time to participate in traditional games and enjoy some respite from the pressures of prairie life: "an excuse for all camping together and having a good time."[44] Such motives then, underlay Blackfoot determination to resist efforts to extirpate the Sun Dance, which, far from being just a religious ceremony, was central to the reproduction of Blackfoot culture and to Blackfoot social cohesion. To forego this practice was tantamount to surrendering their Blackfoot identity.

Rationale for the Sun Dance Extirpation

The authorities viewed the Sun Dance as an obstacle to "civilization" because it provided space for the maintenance of cultural practices deemed incompatible with Christianity. Objections to the Sun Dance were often articulated out of an ostensible concern for the welfare of the practitioners.[45] Religious conversion was seen as the first step to transform the heretofore non-sedentary First Nations of warriors and buffalo hunters into agriculturalists and cattle farmers. Religious concerns were thus inseparable from the secular ones. The link between self-sufficiency and assimilation—which required the adoption of Christianity—is a constant in the extant documentation. For these reasons, the first half-century of reserve life saw the escalation of efforts by the Indian Affairs bureaucracy to eradicate the Sun Dance.[46]

Many bureaucrats regarded the costs associated with reserves as a burden on the public coffers.[47] In 1920, during deliberations of a bill for the compulsory enfranchisement of so-called "civilized Indians," Duncan Campbell Scott, poet, essayist, and Deputy Superintendent General of Indian Affairs, described his goal thus: "I want to get rid of the Indian problem. I do not think . . . that this country ought to continuously protect a class of people who are able to stand alone . . . Our objective is to continue until there is not a single Indian in Canada that has not been absorbed into the body politic, and there is no Indian question, and no Indian Department."[48]

Bureaucrats and missionaries repeatedly alluded to the Sun Dance as an obstacle to progress, a means to detain the Blackfoot in the past, and therefore dependent on government "handouts." Therefore, "the policy of the Department [was] to discourage . . . these dances, as they take the Indians from their work and have a demoralizing effect upon them."[49] In 1914, the new Agent to the Blood complained to Ottawa that the Sun Dance "materially interferes with the progress of the work," suggesting that its duration be limited to two weeks. Commissioner Hayter Reed, referring to other First Nations who also practiced the Sun Dance, summed up the official complaints: "by the Indians congregating in this way for a dance, they lose at least from four to six weeks of the time, in which they should be at work, repairing their fences, and breaking new land, and summer fallowing: besides which it unsettles them from steady work for a longer period."[50]

For an Indian Agent, the successful discharge of his duties was measured in the advance towards "civilization" made by those in his charge. His superiors gauged this progress according to the comparative success of agricultural endeavors: the number of permanent homes built on the reserves, the attendance of children at school, and the absence of conflict between their wards and settlers. Agents blamed the Sun Dance for shortcomings in agricultural production.

The considerable expense involved in sponsoring a Sun Dance contravened the European principle of thrift, and was therefore also specifically targeted by legislation. A Blackfoot testimony c. 1929 itemized the cost of sponsoring a Sun Dance thus:

> [A]ll my best Horses, including my three favorite work Horses . . . my sister contributed ten or fifteen herd Horses, but I gave a lot more. I even paid for the sacred sweatbath . . . It is our custom to pay for every part of a holy initiation. The more sacrifices you make, the more valuable your initiation will be . . . I provided enough Hudson['s] Bay blankets, and other dry goods, to cover the whole path where the Holy Woman and her attendants walked to give out the sacred-tongue-sacrament.[51]

As already indicated, prestige went hand in hand with generosity, the worth of which was lost on Whites, as evident in the report of an uncomprehending Indian Agent: "It is not the sublime religious festival, it is pictured to be. The purposes of the old men are to keep alive the traditions of the past and to be benefited at each Sun Dance to the extent of several horses. In reality, the objects are mercenary."[52]

Apart from the financial costs to sponsor the Sun Dance, the self-torture occurring during the ceremony also came under attack. This self-torture, dubbed the "making of braves," attracted a great deal of White attention and awe. Warriors underwent the ordeal as a reciprocation for the favorable outcome of a plea of aid from the Sun "when ill or in great danger."[53] In the ritual, which never involved more than five warriors, skewers were driven through the muscles of the chest and back and rawhides attached to these were tied to the Sacred Pole, to be torn loose by swinging and surging. George Bird Grinnell describes this part of the Sun Dance as not unlike acts of penance "in our own centers of enlightened civilization."[54] Yet another act of self-torture often took place during the Sun Dance: the ritual cutting of a portion of a finger, again as an offering to the Sun. These rituals were considered at best barbarous, and at worst "heathen" practices that could cause First Nations peoples to revert to their "savage" ways.

Last of all, a seldom-mentioned reason for the prohibition of the Sun Dance relates to the erroneous belief that it was a "war dance," a necessary step for "braves" to be initiated.[55] The Blackfoot habit of carrying rifles and the fact that no law prevented them from purchasing ammunition did nothing to assuage those fears.[56] This impression was evident in the manifest terror of settlers during a Cree "Sun Dance" (Thirst Dance) in neighboring Qu'Appelle, attributed to the "formidable appearance" they presented "in their dancing costumes . . . to individuals unaccustomed to them."[57] In this instance, a NWMP force was promptly dispatched. Such fear was not always unfounded. The Northwest (Riel) Rebellion in 1885 encapsulated the worst concerns regarding the Dominion's control over the Northwest Territories. Large gatherings such as the Sun Dance provided an ideal meeting space to discuss possible alliances against Whites. The fact that the Blackfoot maintained neutrality during the conflict strengthened their position in their subsequent dealings with the DIA.[58]

The rationale for proscribing the Sun Dance was not tempered by the advance of "civilization" on the reserves; measuring and responding to each reserve's progress would have been practically impossible due to their large number. The government's attitude to Indian Affairs seems to have been primarily concerned with a reduction of the cost of fulfilling treaty obligations, especially after 1896, when a new Minister of the Interior, Clifford Sifton, introduced drastic reforms.[59] DIA correspondence leaves no doubt that insofar as the Sun Dance was blamed for the Blackfoot remaining "uncivilized," Indian Agents were pressured to do their utmost to eradicate it.

Measuring Genocidal Intent: Strategies to Eradicate the Sun Dance

Responsibility for the measures undertaken to eradicate the Sun Dance of the Prairies rests on the Dominion Government, and more specifically the DIA, which underwent several reorganizations in the late 1800s and early 1900s. In 1885, the Canadian prime minister himself was the superintendent general of Indian Affairs, but the position was later held by the minister of the interior. Policy-making and administration, however, was usually left to the deputy superintendent.[60] Effectively, these officials presided over efforts to eradicate the Sun Dance. With the exception of Hayter Reed, who served as Indian Agent and rose through the ranks to occupy the deputy's position in 1893, Ottawa bureaucrats had little if any knowledge of those under their charge. In Reed's case, familiarity did not translate into a sympathetic approach.[61] He saw his task in the following terms: "The problem which confronts the department in the territories is a most difficult one: to redeem from a state of partial savagery a horde of Indians dominated by tribal law and aboriginal customs and to transform them into competent agriculturists, ranchers, or mechanics . . . [If] the progress continues as steady in the future, it will not be long before the Indians of the North-[W]est Territories will be able to provide themselves with the necessaries of life."[62]

Not all missionaries opposed to the Sun Dance, but those who did, opposed it vociferously: they lobbied the government, published protests in local newspapers, and generally shaped public opinion.[63]

The most effective tool in the extirpation effort was the education of the young. Where possible, children were separated from their families and prevented from participating in their social and sacred life, including hunting and Sun Dances. This aim was principally accomplished by sending them to boarding schools, where they were at times locked in at night to prevent them from running away.[64] However, as with the implementation of other measures, keeping students from returning home for the summer presented some practical problems, as evinced by the following 1897 report: "the girls in the boarding school did not go out to the [Sun Dance] camp this summer, as formerly. The boys were allowed out by the principal for thirteen days, on account of the assistant principal and matron leaving at the end of the June quarter, and the rest of the staff were released for the holidays."[65]

The hearts and minds of the adults were reached through sermons and other forms of proselytizing. For all that, agents and missionaries did not believe that middle-aged and elderly Blackfoot would abandon their "pagan" beliefs, and so they placed all their hopes in the power of Christian education to prevent continuity of the Sun Dance in the younger generations.[66] That this was contemplated is evident from the following declaration by Duncan Campbell Scott: "The happiest future for the Indian race is absorption into the general population, and this is the object of the policy of our government. The great forces of intermarriage and education will finally overcome the lingering traces of native custom and tradition."[67]

The Sun Dance was first targeted by proscriptive legislation in 1884, although this measure fell short of total prohibition, for which the time was not considered ripe. In other words, the government did not have enough available police should any attempt to impose a complete ban provoke a violent response. Instead, specific features of the Dance were proscribed, as in section 149 of the Indian Act of 1857:[68]

> Every Indian or other person who engages in, or assists in celebrating or encourages either directly or indirectly another to celebrate any Indian festival, dance or other ceremony of which the giving away or paying or giving back of money, goods or articles of any sort forms a part, or is a feature, whether such gift of money, goods or articles takes place before, at, or after the celebration of the dance or who engages or assists in any celebration or dance of which the wounding or mutilation of the dead or living body of any human being or animal forms a part or is a feature, is guilty of an indictable offence and is liable to imprisonment for a term not exceeding six months and not less than two months; Provided that nothing in this section shall be construed to prevent the holding of any agricultural show or exhibition or the giving of prizes for exhibits thereat.[69]

In 1890, Indian Agents were empowered as justices of the peace, designed to increase their control over their charges, and by 1892 the official view was that "more energetic measures can, with safety, be adopted," which if done sooner would have incurred "more or less risk."[70] In 1895, the Potlatch and Sun Dance were subject of further legislation, but the directive to use persuasion rather than force remained.[71] By 1914, all indigenous dances came under attack when Section 149 of the Indian Act was amended as follows:

> Any Indian in the Province of Manitoba, Saskatchewan, Alberta, British Columbia or the Territories who participates in any Indian dance outside the bounds of his own reserve, or who participates in any show, exhibition, performance, stampede or pageant in aboriginal costume without the consent of the Superintendent General of Indian Affairs or his authorized Agency and any person who induces or employs any Indian to take part in such dance, show, exhibition, performance, stampede or pageant, or induces any Indian to leave his reserve or employs any Indian for such a purpose, whether the dance, show, performance, exhibition, stampede or pageant has taken place or not, shall on summary conviction be liable to a penalty not exceeding twenty five dollars or to imprisonment for one month, or to both penalty and imprisonment.[72]

The new measures attempted to check the increased popularity of "Indian" dances among Whites, who were sponsoring Sun Dances. In 1896, a reorganization of the Indian Department by the new Minister for the Interior, Clifford Sifton, ushered in a new era of enforced "civilization." However, decisions remained in the hands of agents.[73] In June 1897, the Indian Commissioner in Regina responded to a Siksika request for assistance to hold a Sun Dance by offering "no interference therewith on this occasion," provided certain conditions were met: the gathering was to last only five days; it would not be compulsory; no torture or giving away of property would take place; there would be no interference with reserve workers, "before, during or after the dance"; children would not be taken away from school; and the Siksika "will engage to fill the existing Schools to their full capacity."[74] The letter is revealing in that the stipulated conditions exceed the power of existing legislation. Less clear is the method deployed to ensure compliance. The limits to DIA authority are set out in a letter to the Chief Inspector of Indian agencies based in Winnipeg in 1913, which suggests that "regulations are good if they could be enforced; but the Department has no authority to impose a penalty for the infraction of any such regulation, consequently it would be useless to formulate and publish them."[75] Consequently, Indian Agents were consistently advised to use persuasion to discourage Sun Dances, legal means being a last resort. In 1921, the Indian Act was again amended to prohibit Sun Dances, Potlatches, or other rituals, instructing Agents and the NWMP to stop them.[76]

It is clear that legislative efforts against the Sun Dance persisted, despite changing conditions on the reserves and many Blackfoot becoming self-sufficient. Prohibition seems to have gathered its own momentum, regardless of changes in circumstances, in particular despite Blackfoot willingness to omit the proscribed activities. Were these measures acts of cultural genocide or assimilation? The answer provided by the documentation suggests a benign form of assimilation, whose purported benefits to Canadian First Nations were a constant in official correspondence. Although the extant records provide only the official version of history, no evidence has emerged to refute this one-sided view. In the absence of such evidence, genocidal intentions, if they existed, cannot be substantiated.

Implementation of the Prohibition

Despite these legislative and administrative efforts to extirpate the Sun Dance, the remoteness from Ottawa made it difficult to supervise the implementation of official policy. Directives were transmitted via a commissioner based in Regina (from 1883 capital of the Northwest Territories), who oversaw Indian agencies and schools until 1898. Thereafter, Indian Agents dealt directly with Ottawa, under the supervision of three inspectors for the entire North-West Territories, who visited the reserves but once a year.[77] Manifestly, the DIA had no means to oversee effectively the implementation of regulations curtailing the Sun Dance. Indian Agents were encouraged to adapt their efforts to local circumstances; consequently, an Agent's attitude carried great weight. The three Blackfoot reserves were administered separately from 1885, such that their circumstances did not always coincide.[78] When disputes arose, the NWMP were called upon to enforce compliance. In the late 1890s, Agent James Wilson prevented the Blood Sun Dance from taking place on several occasions, but the NWMP opposed Wilson and sided with the Blood, who were then able to continue the practice.[79]

Consequently, implementation of the Sun Dance prohibition did not necessarily follow the letter of the legislation, nor was it consistent across reserves. Indian Agents were instructed to suppress the Sun Dance altogether if conditions on their reserves were favorable, even though, strictly speaking, this went beyond the scope of the legislation.[80] The official line from Ottawa was to use dissuasion, rather than coercion, to stop the dancing, but there is extant evidence that the NWMP did intervene to stop Sun Dances, although seldom in the case of the Blackfoot. In 1921, the NWMP attended the Blackfoot Reserve at the behest of Agent Gooderham, yet the Blackfoot were allowed to continue with their Sun Dance.[81] Some Agents took the view that the Sun Dance was destined to disappear of its own accord and saw no reason to forbid it.[82] Systematic reporting on the conduct of Sun Dances by Indian Agents indicates that their endeavors to curtail the celebration were under scrutiny, and such reports should be read as aiming at reassuring their superiors. These reports contain quasi-formulaic predictions of the Sun Dance's imminent demise. They point to dwindling interest and confidently forecast that with the death of the older Blackfoot—those who had experienced the buffalo ways—the practice would become a thing of the past. The official expectation was that education by the missionaries would eventually convince new generations of Blackfoot to accept Christianity and reject their traditional religion. More than reflecting reality, perhaps, these predictions became a topos meant to vouchsafe the Agents' compliance with official policy. The Agent's 1886 report on the Siksika Sun Dance noted: "The sun dance came off as usual . . . but I think the Indians are gradually losing interest in it." Hugh Dempsey offers a different account of the 1886 dance: an "impressive sight" with hundreds of lodges pitched in a great circle.[83] In effect, laws were drafted in Ottawa by bureaucrats who ignored the realities of reserve life, leaving Agents to enforce their unworkable directives.[84] The methods employed by Agents to curtail the Sun Dance are seldom specified in their annual reports. It appears also that some First Nations were uncertain of their rights under the legislation. Ambiguity when responding to requests to hold Sun Dances created the impression that the Sun Dance per se was illegal. A request to Ottawa for permission to hold a Sun Dance by Cree Chief Thunderchild in 1917 elicited the following reply: "the Department cannot sanction any violation of the provisions of the Act, and I may say that, in the interests of the Indians, the Chiefs and Councillors of a band are expected to co-operate with the Indian Agent in his efforts to advance the Indians towards the adoption of the customs of civilisation and to exert their influence in that direction."[85]

That response is ambiguous in its assumption that the Sun Dance would include the forbidden features, but does not specifically say so. Furthermore, the reply reminds Chief Thunderchild of his obligation to cooperate with the DIA. Removal from their positions of chiefs if not deemed "cooperative" was a real possibility.[86] This may explain why in 1888, Chief Crowfoot assisted the Indian Agent with phasing out the self-torture ritual from the Siksika Sun Dance.[87]

From 1886, the DIA sought to replace the Sun Dance by sponsoring alternative events. By 1889, Commissioner Reed reported some success introducing "as a substitute something more profitable in the way of harvest homes."[88] The Piegan and the Blood had agreed, he claimed, "to substitute Dominion Day sports for the objectionable dance." The Blackfoot were "more obdurate and the dance went on, though stripped this year of nearly all its former glory. I do not anticipate its recurrence next year."[89]

In practice, these predictions failed to materialize. Across the southern border, Indian Agents tried "to induce the Blackfeet to observe the Fourth of July instead."[90] A contemporary perspective on Blackfoot attitudes to efforts to eradicate the Sun Dance is provided by North Piegan Chief Brings-down-the-Sun (1905):

> The white race have always cheated and deceived us. They have deprived us of our country. Now they are trying to take away our religion, by putting a stop to the ceremonial sacred to the Sun. Our religion was given to us by the Sun and Moon, and we will never give it up, while the Sun and Moon last. The white people have given us no good reason why they wish to take away our religion. We do not fight, nor drink whisky at our ceremonials, and there is nothing harmful that can come from them. We have been struggling to keep up our religion, in order that our people may be happy, and that they may lead better lives. When I began preparations for a Sun ceremonial this spring, in accordance with the vow, made by one of our women for the healing of her sick son, the agent shut off our rations. He would not allow my family to receive the food, upon which we are dependent. Because of these things my heart has become bitter, and I have made a vow, that I will have nothing more to do with the white race.[91]

Some Indian Agents did not exert pressure against the Sun Dance, placing those who did in an unenviable position.[92] Residents of reserves who could not hold their own Sun Dance had the option of participating in that of another reserve. This was noted by one of the bureaucrats most determined to stamp out the Sun Dance, William Morris Graham, who rose through the ranks to become Indian Commissioner for the Prairie Provinces in 1920. He complained against allowing "those of the Hobbema, Blood and other Alberta Agencies to make the [Sun Dance] an annual practice [because] the Indians of other Bands will probably wish to follow an example which we should not allow."[93] The directives to extirpate the Sun Dance remained in place and the legislation to curtail it was progressively strengthened. Broadening the scope of the legislation, though, was not matched by resources adequate to its implementation, which remained as before in the hands of the Indian Agent, assisted by the NWMP.

The two bureaucracies did not always share a common purpose. In 1889 and 1890, the Blood claimed to have received permission to hold a Sun Dance from Superintendent Deane of the NWMP, though he subsequently denied this. A misunderstanding developed that reached the heads of both services in Ottawa. The Blackfoot divisions were numerous and had been a formidable power in the region during the buffalo days, and some vestigial pride remained. The NWMP had close knowledge of life on the reserves and did not oppose the Sun Dance practice.[94] This may explain why in 1914, after more than two decades of legislated prohibition, the new

Agent at the Blood Reserve, W. J. Dilworth, reported to Ottawa that "[t]he Sun Dance has been held here yearly *no obstacle has been put in its way*."[95] Indeed, the DIA annual reports suggest that (with few exceptions) the Sun Dance continued to take place at the three reserves. Christianity advanced, but at a very slow pace, and most of those who embraced it appear to have done so superficially.[96] Compared with some of their neighboring First Nations, the Blackfoot seem to have endured less interference with their Sun Dance. They were clearly aware that, provided the proscribed activities did not take place, the Agent could not disallow the Sun Dance. A report from the Blood Agent in 1914 indicates that the laws were being respected: "No drinking or other immoral conduct has been indulged in. The grounds have been competently policed at all times day and night. No white visitors have been allowed. The duration of this dance has been the shortest time known to all the old timers; another feature there has been no horses sold as against 208 last year."[97]

In the light of such reports, ongoing harassment of the Sun Dance on the grounds that it retarded progress appears to have lacked foundation. Yet such efforts continued. A pass system had been introduced in 1885 by the then Assistant Indian Commissioner, Hayter Reed, even though it was "hardly supported by any legal enactment." Indeed, the system was in violation of treaty rights, yet it was approved by Reed's superiors post facto because it was perceived "as a necessary weapon in the war against those forces which perpetuated an 'uncivilized' Indian society."[98] A circular to agents suggested prosecution could be attempted under the Vagrant Act (Criminal Code), and recommended using "such means as exist for marking our displeasure towards those who leave without first having obtained passes." The pass system was used extensively to prevent travel to attend Sun Dances and to segregate those living on the reserves from settlers' towns, ostensibly to protect them from bad White influences. Eventually the NWMP refused to enforce passes, because there was no "legal right to arrest any Indian unless he has committed some offence . . . should an illegal arrest be attempted and resistance offered there would be no protection [to the NWMP]. Such a result would be disastrous for our prestige with the Indians."[99] In practice, agents often gave passes to large groups of their charges with instructions to hunt their own food, which tended to weaken the effectiveness of the pass system.[100] To these difficulties must be added the possibility of agents providing travel passes because to deny them would place them in an invidious position, not to mention the susceptibility of any such system to corruption. These factors combined to reduce its effectiveness. In such manner, this system with its potential to harm the Blackfoot social fabric was eventually dismantled. It was a conspicuous failure.

Blackfoot Responses to Prohibition

The Blackfoot were pragmatic in their response to the prohibition of the Sun Dance and reportedly even welcomed some of the curbs. They agreed to eliminate certain features, especially self-torture, but were determined to maintain the practice.[101] Whites wrongly interpreted this feature as being the most crucial part of the Sun Dance. In fact, after warring became a thing of the past, the principal motivation for pledges of that nature was removed. Moreover, Wissler suggests that this feature was probably borrowed from the Arapaho and at the time of prohibition was not "thoroughly adjusted to its place." One informant noted that "[n]one of those taking the cutting [during the Sun Dance] lived to reach old age."[102] Another apparently welcome aspect of the prohibition relates to the use of coercion when choosing new owners of sacred bundles ("catching").[103] However, the Blackfoot resisted the pass system, which prevented them from visiting other reserves,[104] and retaliated against the measure—which had the potential to prevent visitors from attending their Sun Dance—by withdrawing their children from school, arguing that "they do not do any more dancing than their white neighbors and that they see no good reason why they should be singled out in this particular."[105] Their response to the DIA sponsorship of alternative celebrations was to accommodate the new activities without giving up the Sun Dance. It was reported that some Blackfoot wished to see the practice end: "most of the Indians who have taken cattle are against it."[106] Such dissent is to be expected within any large group; evidently, if the Agent was unable to eradicate it, a sufficient number of Blackfoot supported the practice.

The Blackfoot continued to practice their Sun Dance on both sides of the border.[107] In 1897, a letter from the Indian commissioner in Regina suggests that the Blackfoot had boldly requested not merely permission, but even DIA sponsorship, for their Sun Dance. No assistance was granted, but an undertaking not to interfere with the ceremony was made "on account of its religious nature in their eyes and of the representations which have been made." This episode is quite revealing, suggesting as it does that Ottawa was prepared to tolerate the Blackfoot Sun Dance after all. Piegan Chief Bull Plume recorded in his c. 1910 winter count: "Duncan Scott [Deputy Superintendent General of Indian Affairs]. He told me that dancing was not forbidden."[108] Chief Bull Plume had written to Ottawa protesting the prohibition against giving away presents, arguing that "it stands to reason that we should entertain our friends and give them presents and we do not see why The Department should not allow us to do so." On this occasion, Chief Bull Plume cited a donation towards the war effort made by the Piegan. He claimed that presents exchanged with friends were the "same as the present we gave to King George and [the] Government" [of] sixteen hundred dollars in the year 1914."

In 1921, the Blackfoot appropriated some of the discourses regarding the financially detrimental consequences of the Sun Dance for their own ends. Chief Shot in Both Sides requested via telegraph Ottawa's intervention against a directive of the Acting Indian Agent:

> Hunt Blood Agent objects our holding Sundance before treaty day July 14 all Indians wish to hold dance 4 to 13 July then break camp and go for treaty money this will be much better as otherwise Indians would waste treaty money on dance.[109]

This action serves as a reminder that colonized subjects can purposefully appropriate hegemonic discourses and deploy them in their own interest. Blackfoot cultural transformation did not always proceed as dictated by the colonizers. Denying agency to the Blackfoot would be tantamount to endorsing the familiar colonial stereotype of First Nations peoples as neophytes, a discourse often expressed in regard to the Blackfoot by bureaucrats, missionaries, and even Whites who professed to be their friends.[110]

Conclusion: Cultural Genocide or Assimilation?

The progressive strengthening of legislation aimed at weakening and even eradicating this surpassing Blackfoot ceremony hardly seems justified, given the optimistic outlook of DIA annual reports of Blackfoot advances towards self-sufficiency.[111] Clearly, the legislation did not accommodate the circumstances of specific First Nations. The financial costs of fulfilling treaty promises loomed large in the decisions taken by the DIA. Because the development of the Northwest no longer required the cooperation and accommodation of First Nations that had been necessary in the 1870s, the new priority was to reduce expenditure through First Nations self-sufficiency. As a vehicle for social reproduction and the maintenance of a separate Blackfoot identity, the Sun Dance was seen as an obstacle to the integration of the Blackfoot (and other First Nations peoples) into the body politic in accord with Scott's 1921 desiderata: "no Indian question, and no Indian department." Put another way, First Nations were to disappear as separate peoples insofar as their remaining separate involved benefits from the public purse. This was the fundamental rationale for the continuing efforts to eradicate the Sun Dance. The letter of the legislation was not genocidal in its intent, but the instructions emanating from Ottawa regarding its implementation were rather more sinister. In the end, though, the decision was left to individual agents, and there were no mechanisms of compulsion.

During the 1880s, it seems that the DIA was biding its time, and was prepared to allow the Sun Dance to die a natural death, as was so often predicted. It was just a matter of time before those Blackfoot who had known the buffalo times would die and, with them, their traditional beliefs would pass into oblivion. Such was the vain hope of bureaucrats and missionaries. The limited reach of the legislation prohibiting only discrete elements of the Sun Dance would appear to absolve the legislators from any charge of intent to commit cultural genocide. And yet, extant DIA correspondence amply demonstrates that Indian Agents were encouraged by their superiors to go beyond the legislation in order to prevent Sun Dances. Veiled threats and withholding of information seem to have been routine practices by DIA officials.

In the final analysis, this de facto if not de jure prohibition had the potential to cause substantial harm to Blackfoot culture. That such harm was averted was due not only to the machinations of successive bureaucrats in Ottawa not being matched by the resources required to implement them, but also to the determination of Blackfoot leaders to maintain the practice. When overzealous officials such as Hayter Reed and James Wilson attempted to extirpate the Sun Dance, the Blackfoot deployed a wide repertoire of resistance. They compromised with Reed, adopting his "sports days" without abandoning the Sun Dance. By way of illustration, they undermined James Wilson's authority by playing it off against that of the local NWMP superintendent. At the same time, the Blackfoot compromised by eliminating the practices forbidden by the legislation, but on the other hand they demanded the right to practice their religion. The framing of the Sun Dance as a non-negotiable right by Blackfoot political and spiritual leaders within the period covered by this study fits into a pattern pointed out by Jacqueline Gresko (in relation to the Cree) whereby government and missionaries' efforts to transform the First Nations into Christians seemed to elicit a contrary movement of resistance.[112]

The culture of the Blackfoot was radically transformed even prior to face-to-face contact with Europeans through their adoption of the horse and firearms and other trade goods. In the decades following Treaty Seven (1877–1920), they exercised agency by setting the pace of their own cultural transformation. Without rejecting Christianity, the Blackfoot refused to abandon their ancient religion.

How does this complex picture accord with the concept of cultural genocide? The ambitions of the state certainly canvassed the disappearance of the "Indian problem," that is, the disappearance of First Nations as separate peoples. This aim was not to be achieved by a process of "cultural diffusion" that Lemkin equated with assimilation. Nor can the specific circumstances regarding the Blackfoot Sun Dance be equated with what

Lemkin called "surgical operations on cultures and deliberate assassination of civilizations." Prohibition was hardly "surgical" in its execution, allowing plenty of room for Blackfoot agency. There was in fact a great deal of the assimilation in terms of Lemkin's concept of legitimate cultural adaptation, especially when new cultural modes and technologies were seen as beneficial by the Blackfoot. That is how the Blackfoot Sun Dance survived. In the final analysis, the Canadian state only targeted certain features of the Sun Dance. In the specific case of the Blackfoot, it did not deploy force to eradicate the practice. The Blackfoot experience demonstrates that concepts such as cultural genocide must be applied with caution on a case-by-case basis.

Acknowledgements

I thank David Cahill, Fernanda Duarte, Dirk Moses, and Patrick Wolfe for their comments on an earlier draft of this chapter. Any remaining inconsistencies or errors are my sole responsibility.

Notes

1. The tribes are the Kainai ("Many Leaders," also called the Blood); the Pikani (Piegan—Peigan in the USA—divided between the Apatohsipikani in Alberta and Amsskaapipikani in Montana); and the Siksika (Blackfoot, also called Northern Blackfoot). Their traditional territory extended from the Elk River to the Yellowstone. The Blackfoot Gallery Committee (BGC), *Nitsitapiisini: The Story of the Blackfoot People* (Buffalo, NY, 2001), 4–5.
2. Lucien M. Hanks, Jr. and Jane Richardson Hanks, *Tribe Under Trust: A Study of the Blackfoot Reserve of Alberta* (Toronto, 1950), 6.
3. John Leonard Taylor, "Two Views on the Meaning of Treaties Six and Seven," in *The Spirit of the Alberta Treaties*, ed. Richard T. Price (Edmonton, 1999 [1979]), 9–45, 29; Alexander Morris, *The Treaties of Canada with the Indians of Manitoba and The North-West Territories* (Toronto, 1971), 249. The Indian Act "defines Indians . . . as having a status separate and particular from other Canadians with a whole body of law applicable only to them, rendering [them] dependant, incompetent and subject to arbitrary decree in almost every aspect of their economic and political lives": Anthony J. Hall, *The American Empire and the Fourth World: The Bowl with One Spoon* (Montreal, 2003), 481.
4. Oscar Lewis, "The Effects of White Contact upon Blackfoot Culture with Special Reference to the Role of the Fur Trade," in *Monographs of the American Ethnological Society*, ed. A. Irving Hallowell, vol. 6 (Seattle, 1966 [1942]), 18.
5. Raphael Lemkin, *Axis Rule in Occupied Europe* (Washington, DC, 1994), chapter nine.

6. John Docker, "Are Settler Societies Inherently Genocidal? Rereading Lemkin," in this volume.
7. Dominion of Canada. *Annual Report of The Department of Indian Affairs* (hereafter DIA), 1888, 125.
8. See Patrick Brantlinger, *Dark Vanishings: Discourse on the Extinction of Primitive Races, 1800–1930* (Ithaca, NY, 2003); and Brian W. Dippie, *The Vanishing American: White Attitudes and U.S. Indian Policy* (Lawrence, KS, 1982).
9. Edward Curtis, *The North American Indian* (London, 2003 [1907–1930]), 6.
10. Provisions included teachers to instruct children, cattle for raising stock, tools, agricultural implements, planting seed, 2,000 dollars per year for ammunition, and a Winchester rifle for each Head Chief and Minor Chief: John Leonard Taylor, "Canada's Northwest Indian Policy in the 1870s: Traditional Premises and Necessary Innovations"; and "Two Views," in Price, *Alberta Treaties,* 3–8 and 9–45. The Blood signed a separate treaty in 1883: Hugh Dempsey, *Red Crow, Warrior Chief* (Saskatoon, SK, 1980), 134; Treaty Seven transcript at: http://www.treaty7.org/Article.asp?ArticleID=1.
11. John McDougall, *Opening the West: Experiences of a Missionary in 1875–76* (Calgary, 1970), 18; Sir Cecil E. Denny, *The Law Marches West,* ed. W. B. Cameron (Toronto, 1939), 99, and 122; and Hugh A. Dempsey, *Crowfoot: Chief of the Blackfeet,* Civilization of the American Indian Series, vol. 122 (Norman, OK, 1989), 90. Despite their willingness to sign the treaty, Blackfoot interpretation of its contents remains to this day at variance with that of the Canadian Government. See DIA, 1881, 40; BGC, *Nitsitapiisini,* 68–79; and Dempsey, *Crowfoot,* 106.
12. Guy Gibbon, *The Sioux: The Dakota and Lakota Nations* (Malden, MA, 2003), 113–14; and Lewis, "Effects of White Contact," 28–29.
13. During the winter of 1879 the Blackfoot suffered a great famine and were eating grass to keep themselves alive. Indian Commissioner Edgar Dewdney personally brought temporary relief of flour, tea, and beef to Blackfoot Crossing: Dempsey, *Crowfoot,* 112–13; and Denny, *The Law,* 143.
14. By 1901, 123 Blood owned c. 2,000 heads of cattle; the Piegan owned c. 2,200; and the Siksika c. 800: DIA, 1901, xxiii.
15. Denny, *The Law,* 41, and 133.
16. Lewis, "Effects of White Contact," 64–5; Ewers, *The Blackfeet: Raiders of the Northwestern Plains* (Norman, OK, 1958), 246–53.
17. Denny, *The Law,* 98; Dempsey, *Crowfoot,* 90; and DIA, 1881, 37.
18. Hana Samek, *The Blackfoot Confederacy 1880–1920: A Comparative Study of Canadian and U.S. Indian Policy* (Albuquerque, NM, 1987), 123. It is a variant of the often-quoted phrase by US Indian fighter Richard Henry Pratt, founder of the Carlisle Indian School in Pennsylvania, who claimed the school's job was to "kill the Indian to save the man," Benjamin Capps, *The Great Chiefs,* in The Old West Series (New York, 1975), 92.
19. Gaston Carrière, OMI, "The Early Efforts of the Oblate Missionaries in Western Canada," *Prairie Forum (PF)* 4, no. 1 (1979): 10–14.
20. John McDougall defended the Sun Dance: Samek, *Blackfoot Confederacy,* 127; J. Hugonard, Principal, Red Deer Industrial School, was totally against it: DIA, 1896, 347; and Jacqueline Gresko, "White 'Rites' and Indian 'Rites': Indian Education and Native Responses in the West, 1870–1910," in *Western Canada Past and Present,* ed. Anthony W. Rasporich (Calgary, 1975), 168.
21. Leslie Spier, "The Sun Dance of the Plains Indians: Its Development and Diffusion," *Anthropological Papers of the American Museum of Natural History [AMNH]* 16, no. 7 (1921): 453–527.

22. Morris, *Treaties of Canada,* Preface.
23. Hall, *American Empire,* 193, n.157, citing Maclean, *The Indians: Their Manners, Their Customs* (Toronto, 1889).
24. Morris, *Treaties of Canada,* 247–9; and McDougall, *Opening the West,* 15n4, 27, and 42.
25. Vine Deloria Jr., *For this Land: Writings on Religion in America*, ed. James Treat (New York, 1999), 23.
26. The role of missionary education in Canada and USA has been the subject of book-length studies, although further analysis based on the Blackfoot specific circumstances remains to be undertaken. For a Canadian-wide view see J. R. Miller, *Shingwauk's Vision: A History of Native Residential Schools* (Toronto, 2003). A controversial interpretation of the residential schools is Ward Churchill, "Genocide by Any Other Name: North American Residential Schools in Context," in *Genocide, War Crimes and the West: History and Complicity*, ed. Adam Jones (London, 2004), 78–115.
27. The Blackfoot's hunting ground extended from the Red Deer River in the north to the Missouri River in the south, and from the Cypress Hills in the east to the Rocky Mountains in the west: Hugh Dempsey, *Indians of the Rocky Mountain Parks* (Calgary, 1998), 81.
28. Major smallpox epidemics occurred in 1781 (which killed half their number); 1837–38 (when an estimated 6,000 died); 1845, 1857/58; and 1869 (when 1,400 deaths were reported among the Southern Piegan alone). Hugh A. Dempsey, *Indian Tribes of Alberta,* (Calgary, 1979), 12; Alfred W. Crosby, "Virgin Soil Epidemics as a Factor in the Aboriginal Depopulation of America," *The William and Mary Quarterly*, 3rd Series, 33, no. 2 (1976): 289–99.
29. For Blackfoot population changes in this transitional phase see Blanca Tovías, "Colonialism and Demographic Catastrophes in the Americas", paper presented at the Congress of Historical Sciences, Sydney, 10 July 2005; Treaty figures cited are in DIA, 1877, 171 and 1882, 257.
30. Dempsey, *Crowfoot,* 103.
31. Samek, *Blackfoot Confederacy,* 125; for Chief Red Crow's attitude to residential schools, see Dempsey, *Red Crow,* 207.
32. For attitudes to the Cree, see NAC, RG10—Indian Affairs, vol. 3826, f. 60511–3: Telegram 12 June 1916 from Poundmaker [and] Little Pine to J. D. McLean and reply from Rowland dated June 15.
33. D. B. Shimkin, "The Wind River Shoshone Sun Dance," Smithsonian Institution Bureau of American Ethnology Bulletin 151, *Anthropological Papers* 41 (1947): 407.
34. DIA, 1885, 74; Clark Wissler, "The Sun Dance of the Blackfoot Indians," *AMNH* 16, no. 3 (1918): 229.
35. Other names are: "Abstaining from Water Dance" (Plains Cree), often shortened to "Thirst Dance": Spier, "Sun Dance," 459–63.
36. The societies were age graded and functioned "to preserve order in the camp, during the march, and on the hunt; to punish offenders against the public welfare; to protect the camp by guarding against possible surprise by an enemy; to be informed at all times as to the movements of the buffalo herds and secondly by inter-society rivalry to cultivate the military spirit, and by their feasts and dances to minister . . . social recreation." Clark Wissler, "Societies and Dance Associations of the Blackfoot Indians," *AMNH* 11, no. 4 (1913): 359–460, esp. 367 and 430.
37. John Maclean, *The Blackfoot Sun Dance* [Microform], Copp. Clark, 1889, 1.
38. Spier, "Sun Dance," 459.

39. Clark Wissler, "The Social Life of the Blackfoot Indians," *AMNH* 7, no. 1 (1911): 1–64, and "Sun Dance of the Blackfoot."
40. George Bird Grinnell, *Blackfoot Lodge Tales* (Lincoln, NE, 2003 [1892]), 245–9; Calf Robe, Siksika, 40, recounts that Three Suns, a wealthy Siksika, would distribute two wagons of stores after counting *coup*.
41. Glenbow Alberta Archive (GA)—Hanks Papers, M8458, f. 9, Crooked Meat Strings via Mary White Elk.
42. DIA, 1888, 95: "It not unfrequently [*sic*] happens, that in cases of severe illness an Indian's relations will promise, in case of his recovery, a dance to the sun."
43. Maclean, *Sun Dance*, 4.
44. NAC RG18—NWMP, vol. 3290, f. HQ-1034-K.1, Corporal Harper's Report, 27 July 1921, ("K" Division, Lethbridge).
45. NAC, RG18—NWMP, 205, f. 136–01, James A. Smart, Deputy Minister of the Interior to Fred White, Comptroller NWMP, 30 January 1901.
46. DIA, 1885, 74.
47. E. Brian Titley, *A Narrow Vision: Duncan Campbell Scott and the Administration of Indian Affairs in Canada* (Vancouver, 1986), 56.
48. Ibid., 50. The Blackfoot were excluded from this Bill, which was designed for eastern First Nations.
49. NAC, RG10—Indian Affairs, vol. 3826, f. 60,511–3, J. D. Dilworth to Assistant Deputy and Secretary, 10 March 1914; and response 23 March 1914.
50. NAC, RG10—Indian Affairs, vol. 3876, f. 91749, Hayter Reed to Superintendent General, 21 June 1892; and vol. 3826, f. 60511–3, J. D. McLean to Indian Agent, Blood Agency, 23 March 1914.
51. Ben Calf Robe, with Adolf and Beverly Hungry Wolf, *Siksika: A Blackfoot Legacy* (Invermere, BC, 1979), 44.
52. NAC, RG10—Indian Affairs, vol. 3826, f. 60511–3, Indian Agent, Blood Agency, 2 February 1917; and 60511–4A, James McDonald to Assistant Deputy and Secretary, 14 February 1918.
53. Samuel Henry Middleton, *Kainai Chieftainship: History, Evolution and Culture of the Blood Indians: Origin of the Sun Dance* (Lethbridge, AB,1954), 88–90; and Wissler, "Sun Dance," 262–3.
54. Grinnell, *Lodge Tales*, 259.
55. DIA, 1888, lviii.
56. DIA, 1879, 283; 1885, 76; and NAC, RG18—NWMP, vol. 1354 f. 76, NWMP Calgary to Commissioner NWMP, Regina, 14 May 1896.
57. DIA, 1884, xii.
58. DIA, 1885, 74.
59. D. J. Hall, "Clifford Sifton and Canadian Indian Administration 1896–1905," *PF* 2, no. 2 (1977): 129–30.
60. Lawrence Vankoughnet filled the post until 1893. His successor Hayter Reed was replaced with James A. Smart in 1896. In 1902 Frank Pedley was given the deputy position and remained there until 1913.
61. Reed designed the pass system: F. Laurie Barron, "The Indian Pass System in the Canadian West, 1882–1935," *PF* 13, no. 1 (1988): 29.
62. DIA, 1893, xvii.
63. NAC, RG10—Indian Affairs, vol. 3826, f. 60511–3, J. Hugonard [Reverend], Principal, Indian Industrial School, Qu'Appelle, to Secretary, DIA, 20 November 1913, requesting "steps be taken to abolish Indian dances."

64. NAC, RG18—NWMP vol. 112, f. 665, S. B. Steele, Sup. NWMP to Commissioner NWMP, Regina, 5 October 1895.
65. DIA, 1897, 133–34.
66. DIA, 1887, 27.
67. Titley, *Narrow Vision*, 34.
68. 47 Vic. cap. 28; NCA, RG10—Indian Affairs, vol. 3825, f. 60,511–1, Hayter Reed, to C. C. Chipman, Commissioner, Hudson Bay Company, 9 July 1895: "the time is not considered right for suppressing them by law"; Robert J. Surtees, "Canadian Indian Policies," in *Handbook of North American Indians*, ed. Wilcomb E. Washburn, 20 vols. (Washington, DC, 1988), 4: 81–95, and 92. In the US the Sun Dance became a punishable offense of the Courts of Indian Offenses, 1883 and was banned until 1934. Piercing was not permitted until 1952 or later: Clyde Holler, *Black Elk's Religion: The Sun Dance and Lakota Catholicism* (Syracuse, NY, 1995), 110.
69. NAC, RG10—Indian Affairs, vol. 3826, f. 60511–3, J. D. McLean to Reverend Ross, 15 March 1917.
70. DIA, 1892, xix.
71. Sec. 114 of "An Act to further amend the Indian Act," 22 July 1895, *Statutes of Canada*, 58–59 (Victoria, BC, 1895), p. 121; Dempsey, *Red Crow*, 207; and NAC, RG10—Indian Affairs, vol. 3825, f. 60,511–1, F. H. Paget to Indian Agent, Birtle, Telegram 9 June 1896.
72. NAC, RG10—Indian Affairs, vol. 3826, f. 60511–3, Asst. Deputy and Secretary DIA, 17 June 1914.
73. E. Brian Titley, "W. M. Graham: Indian Agent Extraordinaire," *PF* 8, no. 1 (1983): 29.
74. NAC, RG10—Indian Affairs, vol. 3825, f. 60511–1, Indian Commissioner, Regina to Indian Agent, Blackfoot Agency, 3 June 1897.
75. NAC, RG10—Indian Affairs, vol. 3826, f. 60511–4–1, Asst. Deputy and Secretary, J. D. McLean to Glen Cambell, Chief Inspector, 8 August 1913.
76. GA—Gooderham Papers, M4738, f. 9.
77. Ibid., f. 1.
78. Denny, *The Law*, 204.
79. Dempsey, *Red Crow*, 206–14, DIA, 1900, 224 for a mention of the controversy between the police and the agent.
80. NAC, RG10—Indian Affairs, vol. 3826 f. 60511–3, J.D. McLean, Assistant Deputy and Secretary, 23 March 1914.
81. NAC RG18—NWMP, vol. 3290, f. HQ–1034–K.1, Report 27 July 1921 ("K" Division, Lethbridge).
82. NAC, RG10—Indian Affairs, vol. 3826, f. 60511–4 part 1, Indian Agent, Brocket, 14 June 1917.
83. DIA, 1886, 138; and Dempsey, *Crowfoot*, 199–200.
84. Denny, *The Law*, 204.
85. NAC, RG10—Indian Affairs, vol. 3826, f. 60511–4–1, J. D. McLean, 2 June 1917.
86. NAC, RG18—NWMP, vol. 302, f. 658–05. Supt. P. C. Primrose, to Commissioner RNWMP, 5 August 1905.
87. DIA, 1888, lxvii.
88. DIA, 1889, 172.
89. DIA, 1896, 301–2.
90. Samek, *Blackfoot Confederacy*, 131.
91. Walter McClintock, *The Old North Trail or Life, Legends and Religion of the Blackfeet Indians* (Lincoln, NE, 1992 [London, 1910]), 384–85.

92. DIA, 1886, 122.
93. NAC, RG10—Indian Affairs, vol. 3826, f. 60,511–4A, Commissioner Graham to Deputy Supt. General, July 1920; and f. 60,511–4 part 1, 31 May 1915 (original on 427,000–11).
94. In 1902, the good conduct of those attending (250 teepees) a Sun Dance was commended. NAC, RG18—NWMP, vol. 205, f. 136–01, Correspondence Blood Sun Dance.
95. NAC, RG10—Indian Affairs vol. 3826, f 60511–3, W. J. Dilworth, 10 March 1914. My emphasis.
96. DIA, 1914, Census for the Year Ended 31 March 1914: c. 25 percent of Blackfoot listed their religion as Christian: Bloods, 300 out of 1154; Siksika, 235 out of 737; and Piegan, 92 out of 436.
97. NAC, RG10—Indian Affairs vol. 3826, f. 60511–3.
98. Barron, "Pass System," 26–30, links the pass system with apartheid measures. The penalty for traveling without a valid pass was thirty days in jail: BGC, *Nitsitapiisini*, 69.
99. NAC, RG18—NWMP, vol. 1354, 75–1895–3, Correspondence Blood Sun Dance.
100. Dempsey, "Native Peoples and Calgary," in *Centennial City. Calgary*, ed. University of Calgary (1994), 27, n.8.
101. DIA, 1889, Part I, 167.
102. Wissler, "Sun Dance," 263.
103. GA—Hanks Papers, M8458, f. 48, Old Bull via Mary White Elk.
104. NAC, RG18—NWMP, vol. 1382, f. 75–1897, Superintendent Deane, NWMP to Commissioner NWMP Regina, 7 May 1897, Correspondence Blood Sun Dance.
105. NAC, RG10—Indian Affairs, vol. 3826, f. 60511–3, Extract from J. A. Markle, Inspector, Crowfoot Boarding School, 14 February 1916.
106. DIA, 1897, 133–34.
107. Samek, *Blackfoot Confederacy*, 131.
108. GA, M–8188, Bull Plume's winter count; see also NCA, RG 10—Indian Affairs, vol. 3826, f. 60511–3
109. NCA, RG10—Indian Affairs, vol. 3826, f. 60511–4A, Chief Shot in Both Sides to Commissioner Indian Affairs, Telegram 24 June 1921.
110. Grinnell, *Lodge Tales*, xvii–xviii.
111. Denny, *The Law*, 289.
112. Gresko, "White 'Rites,'" 164.

– *Chapter 13* –

FROM CONQUEST TO GENOCIDE

Colonial Rule in German Southwest Africa and German East Africa

Dominik J. Schaller

Introduction

The German colonial enterprise faced a deep crisis in 1907. Major revolts had seriously threatened colonial rule in German Southwest Africa (GSWA; present-day Namibia) and German East Africa (GEA; present-day Tanzania). The German state had to mobilize vast resources to suppress these uprisings, including the deployment of more than 14,000 German soldiers in GSWA alone. The human costs of the wars in the two colonies were also high. Whereas about 1,500 German soldiers lost their lives, about 60,000 Herero, 10,000 Nama and up to 250,000 Ngoni, Ngindo, Matumbi, and members of other ethnic groups were either directly killed or starved to death.[1] The socioeconomic and political structures of the Africans were laid waste, and their reconstruction took several decades.

Most damaging to the Germans were the financial costs of these wars. The military campaign against the Herero and Nama alone swallowed 585 million Reichsmark.[2] Opponents of Germany's imperialist enterprise like Matthias Erzberger (1875–1921), a leading figure in the Catholic Center Party and later minister in governments of the Weimar Republic, perceived the disastrous outcome of the colonial wars as symptomatic of the mismanagement in the colonies generally. Furthermore, politicians in Berlin were afraid that the reputation of Germany as a *Kulturnation* (nation of culture) might suffer since the oppression of the Africans had been received internationally as exceptionally ruthless.[3]

Consequently, a majority of the members of the German *Reichstag* (parliament) rejected the chancellor's wish for supplementary credits for the wars in Africa. Although Wilhelm II dissolved the *Reichstag* and called for re-election in January 1907 (the so-called Hottentots election), colonial administration was reformed.[4] Formerly belonging to the Department of Foreign Affairs (*Auswärtiges Amt*), the colonial office became an independent ministry of its own: the *Reichskolonialamt*.[5] Significantly, the first director of this newly structured department, Bernhard Dernburg (1865–1937), had been a banker specializing in the revitalization of ailing firms.[6] Stronger civilian control of colonial affairs would not only prevent further scandals, corruption and mismanagement. It would lead to fundamental policy change. "Henceforth, the native is the most important object (*Gegenstand*) in the process of colonization," Dernburg proclaimed. Instead of exterminating the indigenous population, he aimed at introducing an "efficient" and "scientific" way of colonization.[7]

It thus seems that German colonial rule as a whole was not inherently genocidal, and that the bloody suppression of indigenous resistance in GSWA and GEA 1904–08 was an unfortunate episode.[8] Indeed, even high-ranking colonial officials and members of the civilian administration in Berlin perceived the murder of a large part of the indigenous population as a grave "accident" that might endanger the economic development in the colonies. Paul Rohrbach (1869–1956), commissioner on settler affairs (*Ansiedlungskommissar*) in GSWA and one of the most influential public intellectuals in Germany, condemned the radical warfare in the colony and its economic consequences and stated that "Southwest Africa with natives was of much more value . . . than without."[9]

To be sure, Europeans normally did not envisage exterminating or expelling the African population. Although both GSWA and GEA were settler colonies or were at least designated for more extensive future settlement by Germans, their conquest and settlement did not inevitably lead to the expulsion and/or annihilation of the natives as was the case with "New England-type" settler colonies in Northern America and Australia.[10] European settlement in Africa followed the establishment of colonial rule and administration, so that the settlers' influence and ability to fight and expel the Africans on their own was more restricted than in the "New England" model of settler colonies in North America and elsewhere. What is more, the colonial states were still weak in their first decades, and their power relied on the cooperation with indigenous chiefs.[11]

Moreover, Europeans were dependent on indigenous labor power. The colonizers' aim was to gain control over African land and labor at the same time. And the securing of indigenous labor was crucial since "the dark continent" was all but an attractive destination for emigrants. Most Europeans associated Africa (and perhaps still do) with incurable illnesses, dangerous animals, cannibalism, and tribal warfare. The tropical climate in large parts of Africa did not suit Europeans well either. There were just not enough

European or Asian immigrants (in contrast to Northern America and Australia) who could have replaced the Africans as indentured servants or contract workers.[12] Therefore, the indigenous population—together with land—was the most important "resource" for the colonizers. In contrast to American Indians and the Aborigines in Australia, Africans did not figure as a "dying race" in the eyes of the Europeans, and were considered to be fit for labor.[13]

And yet, closer inspection of German colonial rule raises the question whether genocidal violence remained structurally implied in postwar German colonial rule, though in a more subtle and creeping way. Raphael Lemkin (1900–1959), who created the term and concept of genocide and was the leading lobbyist for the UN convention, adumbrated nine techniques of genocide that bear striking resemblance to those of the German colonial project in GSWA and GEA. His depiction of Nazi genocides as imperialist and colonial invites the conclusion that the *situation coloniale* in GSWA and GEA was also genocidal. The envisaged incorporation of the indigenous population as wage laborers in a capitalist system was genocidal, this chapter argues, because Europeans tried to overcome the Africans' reluctance to relinquish their land coercively: through negative incentives like penal taxation and means of force and harassment. Massive expropriation of indigenous land was a common method not only in the German colonies to have the Africans abandon their subsistence economy.[14] The colonizers did not shrink from attempting to destroy the indigenous social, political, and religious structures (i.e., fundamental elements of the Africans' culture) in order to acquire control over labor.

Then there is the question of the genocidal wars between 1904 and 1908. If colonial officials and even German farmers and planters were well aware that a large reservoir of indigenous workers was a necessary prerequisite for the development of a modern and efficient infrastructure and economic growth in GSWA and GEA, why did the suppression of indigenous resistance in these two colonies degenerate into wholesale slaughter? Were the Germans' motives purely ideological (i.e., racist) or did situational elements, like the course of war, lack of infrastructure, and fear of losing the control in the colonies feed a disastrous process of radicalization? I seek to answer these questions by presenting the historical development in both GSWA and GEA from the beginning of German colonization to the time of the great wars 1904–08 and the subsequent dismembering of indigenous societies.

The German Conquest of Southwest Africa

When Southwest Africa became a German dependency in April 1884, a handful of powerful Herero chiefs competed with each other for the rank of the paramount chief. Although the Herero were originally pastoralists, they depended in the first half of the nineteenth century almost solely on hunter-gathering and horticulture for their subsistence. But while the Herero fought successful trade wars and secured their position of power in Namibia, they started building up huge cattle herds and soon became to be known as *the* outstanding cattle breeders in Southwest Africa.[15]

The economy of the Nama peoples in southern and central Namibia relied likewise on cattle, but mainly on trade with farmers from the Cape Colony. Northern Namibia—inhabited by the Ovambo—remained for the most part untouched by the Germans, although this region was officially part of their colony. The Ovambo lived in centralized and highly stratified kingdoms that depended economically on agriculture, fishery, and trade with other Ovambo groups in Portuguese Angola.[16] Due to the lack of reliable data it is difficult to estimate the exact population figures. However, most historians agree that about 80,000 Herero, 20,000 Nama, and 450,000 Ovambo were living in the region the Germans claimed as their colony.

German rule was hampered by three factors. In the first place, the colonizers could not legitimize their claim to power by pointing to the argument of the alleged culturelessness of the indigenous population.[17] Namibia had for a long time been connected economically and historically to the emerging frontier society of the Cape Colony. Herero and especially the Nama had contact with European ideas, values, and, not least, technologies. Most Nama wore Western clothes and had modern rifles at their disposal. The most important intermediaries of Western culture were several mission societies who had established stations throughout the region from the 1850s onwards.[18]

Second, the *res nullius* argument failed in Southwest Africa because both Nama and Herero practiced sophisticated and intensive animal husbandry that depended on grasslands. European travellers and early colonists were impressed by the size of the herds that the Herero had built up. It was impossible, therefore, to seize the indigenous lands in Southwest Africa on the grounds that they were not being cultivated or utilized, as indigenous lands had been in Australia and parts of North America.

Third, the desire to pursue imperialist policies and to conquer overseas territories was not matched by the readiness to invest necessary resources. Bismarck's original hopes that concession companies would promote the colonial development in the newly acquired territories were not fulfilled, and the German Empire had to assume the whole political and financial responsibility for the colonial project.[19] Despite significant colonial enthusiasm in German nationalism, German politicians were not ready to spend huge sums for what they perceived as matter of prestige. The grossly insufficient equipment of the colonial administrations in Africa as well as lack of experience in colonial affairs made the conquest and "pacification" of these territories at once so violent and tenuous.

The German conquest of Southwest Africa did not unfold according to a careful plan. In May 1885, three government officials arrived in the region and signed "protection treaties" with indigenous chiefs. The Herero soon cancelled the treaties and expelled the small German administration under *Reichskommissar* Heinrich Göring to the British enclave Walvisbay. The official German response was half hearted. Only twenty men were sent to Southwest Africa 1889 with instructions to avoid the outbreak of an expensive war with the Herero and Nama.[20] But the new commander, Curt von François, did not follow orders. Instead of a "pacification" through peaceful means (i.e., through the signing of protection treaties and negotiations), he deliberately provoked both the Herero in central and the Nama in southern Namibia, and started a war against them in 1893. Von François waged an extraordinarily ruthless campaign against the Nama, committing several atrocities against noncombatants. Uncowed, the Nama resorted to an efficient guerrilla warfare and almost defeated the German commander.

Because German rule in Southwest Africa was in real danger, the government in Berlin replaced von François with Theodor Leutwein (1849–1921), who became the first official governor of GSWA in 1896, remaining in office until 1904. Loyal to Berlin, he was better suited to governing than the belligerent von François who embroiled Germany in expensive colonial conflict. In his memoirs, Leutwein described his mission as follows: "The aim of our colonization was without doubt the creation of a colony inhabited by whites, but without toughness and the use of force."[21] In contrast to von François, Leutwein realized that the conquest and "pacification" of the colony would only be possible through alliances with indigenous chiefs and that the German claim to power could initially only be guaranteed through a system of indirect rule.[22] Leutwein found an ideal partner in Samuel Maharero (1856–1923).[23] Maharero's claim to the position of paramount chief of all the Herero was widely contested and therefore he willingly accepted the German intervention on his behalf in the dispute of succession.[24]

If von François represented a genocidal moment of counterinsurgency, Leutwein and the colonial authorities in Berlin represented genocidal administration, at least in intention. Cooperation with indigenous chiefs was only a temporary expedient. The system of indirect rule should step by step be replaced by direct and unrestricted German rule. Leutwein knew that the complete political dissolution of the indigenous societies was a necessary precondition for undisputed German supremacy.[25] And he therefore tried to limit the power of the indigenous chiefs gradually and to abolish the political institution of chiefdoms.

Economic dependency was to accompany the political subjugation of the Herero and Nama. Colonial authorities as well as German settlers agreed that the Africans should have become a politically and economically dependent lower class, a compliant mass of workers for the colonial economy.[26] Furthermore, the land of the indigenous populations should be seized and handed over to settlers and colonial land companies. The Africans should put up with restricted reservations.[27] The Germans planned to make a settler colony inhabited predominantly by whites, a "new African Germany."[28]

These grandiose plans seemed rather utopian in the obtaining conditions. After all, in the 1880s and early 1890s, the indigenous societies were militarily and economically still stronger than the small European settler community, which counted only about two thousand persons (of whom about five hundred were officials and soldiers) in 1896.[29] Although the indigenous population of GSWA was portrayed in German colonial literature as primitive natives fighting with spears and shields, neither the Herero nor the Nama were heavily outgunned; they had horses and modern rifles. Neither did the Herero depend economically on German capital for wage labor, because their own cattle herds far outnumbered those of the Germans. In fact, German settlers had an interest in trade relations with the Herero when they tried to build up or enlarge their own herds.

Despite these obstacles, the Germans managed to strengthen their position in Southwest Africa in the late 1890s. Natural disasters like drought or flooding have regularly facilitated the European penetration of large parts of the world and the corresponding development of a worldwide capitalist style economy in the age of imperialism.[30] The rinderpest (cattle disease), which reached Namibia in 1897, changed the balance of power and the social equilibrium in favor of the German colonizers irretrievably. Whereas German settlers managed to have their cattle vaccinated, most Herero lost the bulk of their herds.[31] The cattle disease was finally followed by a malaria epidemic that hit the Herero who had already been enfeebled through the lack of milk.[32]

These events led to a far-reaching economic and cultural crisis of the Herero society. To secure their livelihood, the Herero had to sell their land to settlers, traders, and land companies. Furthermore, many Herero were forced into wage labor for the first time, representing a crucial stage in the establishment of a capitalist economy. Many chiefs encountered difficulty maintaining their extravagant lifestyles and therefore sold large parts of their communities' ancestral land at extortionately low prices to German traders and settlers. A large number of Herero were thus transformed from once proud and autonomous pastoralists to weak and dependent proletarians. This significant and far-reaching socioeconomic change took place within the space of a few months and inverted the hierarchy of power between Africans and Europeans.[33] This development resulted in an increasingly ruthless and even cruel behavior of the Germans towards the Africans.[34] Ever more, German farmers treated their new indigenous workers ill and displayed racist arrogance.[35]

Whereas the Herero were gradually deprived of power in central Namibia and faced a crisis of collective self-esteem, the European community expanded incessantly and prospered. Almost five thousand Germans, Boers, and English inhabited GSWA before the outbreak of the war 1904.[36] Already in 1902, several hundred settlers owned as many cattle as the Herero altogether (44,490).[37] The construction of a railway line from Swakopmund to Windhoek promised sustained economic growth in the colony. A dynamic frontier society had developed in Southwest Africa.[38] The economic weakness of the Herero and the sudden flourishing of the European community dazzled both colonial authorities and settlers. The belief was widespread that Southwest Africa would soon become "White Man's Land" and the natives would play an inferior role as disenfranchised workers.

These confident expectations were challenged with the anticolonial uprising in 1904. Their military and economic infrastructure in their colony still underdeveloped, the Germans realized that their project—the creation of an African Germany—was in real danger. This frustration, accompanied with existential fear, partly explain the brutalization of German warfare in Southwest Africa.

Genocidal Warfare against the Herero and Nama

German settlers' expectations had been ambivalent for several years. On the one hand, they had been waiting for an opportunity to eliminate both Herero and Nama as autonomous actors by breaking their economic and political backbone. On the other, European settlers were afraid that the Africans might opt for a military conflict too early in the process of colonization. There was thus a constant fear of an indigenous revolt in the air.[39] There is convincing evidence that it was the Germans' paranoid fright of a Herero uprising and an accumulation of misunderstandings that triggered off the war on 12 January 1904 in the town of Okahandja. A gathering of Herero chiefs in this town made the clumsy German officer Zürn believe that the Herero were preparing an insurrection. In turn, Zürn's panicked reaction terrified the Herero and confirmed their fear that the Germans wanted to subjugate them militarily and realize their plans of turning Southwest Africa into a purely German colony. The start of the hostilities can hence be understood as a self-fulfilling prophecy.[40]

If German settlers had been waiting for an ideal occasion to gain total political and economic control over the Africans, their hopes were disappointed during the first months of the war. They even had to fear for their own existence as the Herero plundered remote German farms and felled telegraph poles. Whereas the Herero took the initiative, German settlers reacted more or less in a headless way while governor Leutwein and the bulk of the *Schutztruppe* were in the south of the colony. The colonizers' existential fear in GSWA met with the German government's anxiety for the loss of national prestige, and this combination provided the background for the most radical solution. In the following, the decisive phases of this radicalization, which resulted in wholesale genocide, will be shown.

At first, German government officials started looking for a scapegoat and found it in governor Leutwein.[41] The gradual reduction of Leutwein's influence in GSWA contributed decisively to an extension and brutalization of the war.[42] The governor's original aim was to persuade the Herero to surrender and to turn the ringleaders over to the German authorities. The chance to put an end to the war was realistic, as Leutwein had a good relationship with Samuel Maharero, but Leutwein's initiative did not meet with the approval of the government. On the contrary, he was ordered to stop all negotations and not to undertake any decisive military or nonmilitary steps until the arrival of the newly appointed supreme commander for GSWA, Lothar von Trotha (1848–1920).[43]

The new commander was an experienced colonial soldier, having participated in several colonial wars in Tanzania and in China, where his racist worldview had developed.[44] He justified his envisaged radical warfare by pointing to his "rich" colonial experience:

> My exact knowledge of many Central-African tribes, Bantu and others, has shown me the convincing necessity that the negro doesn't submit to contracts but only to raw violence. . . . This uprising [of the Herero] is and remains the beginning of a racial fight.[45]
>
> I know enough tribes in Africa. They all resemble each other as that they only shrink back from violence. The exercise of violence with crass terrorism and with cruelty is my policy. I annihilate the rebellious tribes with streams of blood and with streams of money. Only on this seed can something new emerge, which will remain.[46]

Lothar von Trotha was directly subordinate to the emperor and the general staff in Berlin and—what was even more important—enjoyed the unrestricted backing of both institutions. Therefore, von Trotha did not run into difficulties when he declared a state of war in the colony on 19 May 1904. Leutwein remained officially civil governor of GSWA, but he lost all his executive power to von Trotha.[47] Since the German chief of general staff von Schlieffen shared the racist worldview of his subordinate, von Trotha finally had the opportunity to wage the war against the Herero according to his ideas.

After the arrival of sufficient reinforcements from Germany, the supreme commander of GSWA attacked the Herero, who had gathered with their families and herds in the Waterberg region, on 11 August 1904. The Herero were militarily defeated at this battle, but the bulk of the Herero managed to break through the ring of besieging forces and flee to the Omaheke desert. The paths to British Botswana through this desert and the most important watering places were known to the Herero because they were traditional trade roads. But the available capacity of the few water holes was far from being sufficient for the numerous refugees and their herds.[48] The unexpected break out of the Herero of Hamakari prompted von Trotha to resort to genocidal methods and to achieve a "final solution." The German general ordered the persecution of the fleeing Herero as well as the establishment of a cordon of the almost waterless Omaheke.[49] Driving the Herero into the desert and letting them die of thirst had not been planned originally by Lothar von Trotha.[50] On 2 October 1904, the military commander of GSWA issued his infamous genocide order (*Schiessbefehl*):

> I the great General of the German troops send this letter to the Herero people. The Herero are no longer German subjects. . . . The Herero people must leave the country. If the nation doesn't do this I will force them with the *Groot Rohr* [cannon]. Within the German borders, every Herero, with or without gun, with or without cattle will be shot. I will no longer accept women and children, I will drive them back to their people or I will let them be shot at.[51]

In a supplement that was only designated for the *Schutztruppe*, von Trotha added: "Shooting at women and children has to be understood as shooting above their heads, which will make them run away. I assume categorically that this order will result in taking no more male prisoners, but will not degenerate into atrocities against women and children."[52] This additional explanation was not an act of clemency. It meant driving the Herero women and children back to the desert where they faced death from starvation and exhaustion.[53]

The term genocide is undoubtedly appropriate to describe the German actions in the war against the Herero. Violence was targeted at one and the same time against combatants and noncombatants. And Lothar von Trotha's overall aim was not only the suppression of the indigenous uprising, but the complete annihilation of the Herero as such. Undoubtedly, these facts meet the criteria of the UN definition of genocide. Furthermore, Raphael Lemkin left two manuscripts on German colonial rule in Africa and made it quite clear that he considered the war in GSWA as genocidal.[54]

German policy makers debated the aims of the war as well as the questions how to conduct and how to end it. The German chancellor von Bülow and his ministers did not consider Lothar von Trotha as the ideal supreme commander for GSWA because the general was willful and disrespected civilian authorities. Instead of the potentially insubordinate von Trotha, von Bülow would have preferred a loyal and calculable commander who would have respected the aims of the government to end the war in Southwest Africa quickly and with minimum expenses. Furthermore, the government was afraid that von Trotha's ruthless advancement would damage Germany's image as a "good colonizer." The reason why von Trotha was chosen for the post in GSWA lies in the outstanding influence the German military high command enjoyed at the time. Emperor William II had a marked preference both for "brave" soldiers and military recklessness. He exhibited this characteristic, for example, when he delivered his infamous "Hun Speech" on 27 July 1900 in Bremerhaven to German troops who were departing to fight against the "Boxers" in China: "Should you encounter the enemy, he will be defeated! No quarter will be given! Prisoners will not be taken! Whoever falls into your hands is forfeited."[55]

Dissension between political actors, military leaders, and different lobbies was not restricted to the political arena in Berlin. Although colonial officials, settlers, and soldiers stood together when the existence of the colony was in danger during the first weeks of the war, this solidarity soon broke. At first, most settlers welcomed von Trotha's rigorous steps because they hoped that the new commander would consolidate the situation in the colony and subjugate the Africans once and for all. The realization of a "German Africa" consisting of a European ruling class and an African proletarian or helot class came into reach. But von Trotha's genocidal intentions threatened to endanger this project and the economic prospect of the colony.

The settlers' lobbies and the civilian government in Berlin finally managed to convince the Emperor and the general staff that the survival of indigenous workers was essential for the future of the colony, and that Lothar von Trotha's ravage would badly damage Germany's reputation as a *Kulturnation*.[56] Subsequently, the general was advised to repeal his genocide order and to cooperate with the Rhenish Mission, which had offered to act as an intermediary because it was afraid to lose its right of existence in the colony if the African population were completely exterminated.[57] The missionaries started setting up assembly camps for the surviving Herero. From there, the prisoners of war—men, women, and children alike—were transported to concentration camps maintained by the *Schutztruppe*.[58]

Unfortunately, although the missionaries' aim was to save the Africans from wholesale extermination, the deportation to and the placement of the prisoners in camps, where malnutrition, insufficient hygienic conditions, and forced labor were the norm, resulted in the deaths of thousands of Africans. This result met the approval of leaders of the *Schutztruppe* who still favoured a radical solution to end the war in spite of the official repeal of von Trotha's genocide order.[59]

The same kind of radicalism was characteristic for the German warfare against the Nama. The defeat of the Herero did not mean the end of the colonial war in GSWA. During the campaign against the Herero, Hendrik Witbooi had actively supported the Germans. But in October 1904, the Nama themselves turned against the colonizers and launched a war that lasted three years. The Namas' motives are still insufficiently researched, but what is sure is that the outbreak of another war in GSWA put the military and political leadership in the colony under immense pressure.[60] They were expected to nip the Nama uprising in the bud. The Nama had learned from the Herero's defeat and avoided any open battle. Instead, they resorted to a highly efficient guerrilla warfare and launched systematic attacks to German infrastructure. Cutting off the supply of the guerrilla fighters—i.e., a policy of scorched earth—was the strategy applied by the *Schutztruppe*. And the Nama population was deported to concentration camps. Most Nama prisoners were taken to Shark Island near Lüderitz. The hard climate and conditions at the Atlantic coast were jointly responsible for the death of more than the half of the inmates. The German colonizers deliberately inflicted conditions of life on both Herero and Nama calculated to bring about them their physical destruction in whole or at least in part.[61]

The Maji-Maji-War 1905–07: Genocide in German East Africa?

If the war against the Nama in GSWA has been neglected in historiography and public memory, the so-called Maji-Maji-War in German East Africa (GEA) in 1905–07 has been completely forgotten outside Tanzania. The war had no less devastating consequences for the indigenous societies in GEA as for the Herero and Nama in GSWA. Nonetheless, the commemoration of the 100th anniversary of the outbreak of this war in 2005 did not attract as much international attention as the remembrance of the murder of the Herero one year earlier. It is possible that this neglect lies in the fact that only fifteen Europeans were killed in GEA from 1905–07 while the war in GSWA caused the deaths of more than one thousand German soldiers.[62] A further reason is that historians hesitate calling the events in GEA genocide.[63]

Whereas the demographic and ethnographic situation in Southwest Africa was more or less easy to grasp, the demography of the territory the

Germans claimed in East Africa was much more diverse. According to the first official German census in 1899, almost 5,500,000 Africans lived in GEA.[64] Swahili-speaking groups dominated the coastal regions, and the inland was inhabited by several hundred Bantu speaking groups. There were huge differences in the ways these groups were socioeconomically and politically organized. The Arabic Sultanate of Zanzibar and the kingdoms in the Great Lakes Region (present day Rwanda and Burundi) were highly centralized and their societies characterized through social stratification and division of labor. African societies between the coast and the Great Lakes showed a less-developed degree of organization. Nevertheless, these societies were far from being "primitive" or without political influence. The Ngoni and the Hehe, for example, had successfully adopted the Zulu style of warfare and were thus able to establish hegemonic rules in Southern Tanzania. Precolonial East Africa was not a remote region disconnected from any contact with the outside world. Zanzibar had for a long time been integrated into the trade networks of the Indian Ocean. Arab, Indian, and Persian traders had established posts at the East African coast. When the West African slave trade was disrupted by the British proscription of 1807, East Africa, and especially the Sultanate of Zanzibar, became the new center of the international slave trade.

Unlike in GSWA, Germans saw Africans living in the inland of GEA as politically and economically backward savages not entitled to keep their ancestral lands unless they modernized. And although the Swahili communities at the coast were obviously "highly civilized" and belonged to a scriptural religion, the Germans perceived them categorically as ruthless slave drivers. The colonization of East Africa was thus portrayed as an important step in the modernization of Africa and the international struggle against slave trade.

From the outset, the establishment of German rule in Tanzania was violent. German colonization began with a private company, the "Society for German Colonization." Until 1887, the society established several outposts and tried to stretch its economic and military influence as far as possible in mainland Tanzania.[65] But it had only limited resources at its disposal and soon encountered difficulties. The Swahili-speaking coastal inhabitants persistently resisted the German colonization.[66] Consequently, Bismarck felt constrained to buy the shares of the colonial society and to provide a colonial army. A loss of the East African territory would have been a national disgrace. A German sphere of interest from 1885 onwards, Tanzania became an official colony in 1891.[67]

The German newly appointed governor Julius von Soden faced the same problems as Theodor Leutwein in GSWA. His superiors at the colonial office in Berlin expected him to establish German rule over the territory without expensive wars. As might be expected, this order turned out to be an illusion. The small *Schutztruppe* consisting of a few hundred men managed to secure nothing but small islands of dominance. German rule was rather more symbolic than real in most parts of the country.[68] Only around the turn of the century and after a fierce war against the Hehe under Makwawa did the Germans control more or less most parts of the colony.[69] Thereafter, the colony was divided into twenty-four districts with varying governing modes. In some districts, Africans were to a greater extent involved in the colonial administration than in others.[70] A further characteristic of the colonial administration in GEA was its militarization. Until 1906, the army provided half of all the district officials in the colony.[71] The long distances from the different administrative centers to the seat of the colonial government in Dar-es-Salaam, and the resultant lack of social control led to despotic rule of many officials in the periphery of GEA.[72] Furthermore, the *Schutztruppe*, consisting mainly of African mercenaries, backed these local reigns of terror and regularly committed sexual violence and atrocities against the autochthonous population.[73]

Although GEA did not have the same value in the dreams and utopias of colonial enthusiasts as Namibia, it attracted increasing numbers of European settlers from 1900 onwards.[74] In 1905, the year the war broke out, 1,900 Europeans lived in GEA.[75] What the settlers needed for their plantations was land and cheap labor. Because the conditions on these plantations were brutal (corporal punishment was the norm) and the wages more than modest, Africans were uninterested in working for the Europeans. The destruction of the indigenous cultural, economic, and political systems and the integration of Africans into a European system of wage labor was therefore the settlers' aim.[76] The colony was ruled from 1901 onwards by a governor who was fully in favour of the settlers' interests. Hoping to let the indigenous societies abandon their traditional economy, von Götzen imposed several taxes on the Africans, forced village societies to communal labor, and restricted their hunting customs.[77] The Christian missions were mobilized to play a crucial role in this envisaged process of forced assimilation.[78] African societies in southern Tanzania suffered particularly under the colonial power's regulation. The situation was further aggravated by the increasing economic marginalization of this region from 1904 onwards.[79]

The message of a supposed prophet called Kinjikitile began to spread at this time. Not much is known about his life and background, but the impact of his prophecy in southern Tanzania was enormous.[80] Kinjikitile's message promised the reversal of the existing order and the end of foreign rule. What is more, the prophet and his followers provided the faithful with a special medicine called *Maji* (Swahili for water) that was supposed to render the indigenous warriors bulletproof. Although the Maji-Maji warriors soon recognized their new medicine's ineffectiveness after the start of hostilities in July 1905, they continued fighting against the Germans. Often regarded as an irrational or even primitive expression of African religion, the Maji-Maji cult had an integrative function by uniting twenty culturally and politically different societies in a common struggle. African politicians and historians therefore understand the "Maji-Maji War" as birth of a Tanzanian national identity.[81]

The simultaneous wars in GSWA influenced the situation in GEA. The military campaigns against the Herero and Nama swallowed huge sums and resources. And Lothar von Trotha's genocidal warfare resulted in an upswing of German colonial criticism and, internationally, in a loss of German prestige. Both the civilian government and the colonial authorities in Berlin therefore wanted to avoid another theatre of colonial war. Consequently, officials in the colonies received orders to prevent of indigenous uprisings. The administration in GEA was thereafter reorganized and the position of the military thereby strengthened.[82] Yet the further militarization of the colonial administration only exacerbated the situation. Whereas the Africans understood the German measures as an attempt to enhance the colonizers' power, the Germans perceived the Africans' disaffection as clear signs of a forthcoming uprising. This fatal dynamic had a deep impact on both the colonizers' and the Africans' decision making processes.

The course of war in East Africa resembled the one in GSWA very closely. The German *Schutztruppe*—consisting of only 588 men in the south of the colony—were initially at a disadvantage.[83] The Germans sent punitive expeditions to the various trouble spots only with the arrival of reinforcements. Like the Nama in GSWA, the Africans avoided open-field battles by conducting guerrilla warfare. Political and military leaders in GEA were under heavy pressure. Politicians in Berlin expected nothing else than a quick end of the war. Both political pressure and the helplessness of the colonizers resulted in the application of a scorched-earth policy of unprecedented dimensions. The civilian population was systematically targeted: entire villages, fields, and granaries were burnt. Hunger was thus used as weapon to bring the guerrilla fighters to their knees.[84] The consequences for the indigenous population were devastating: fighting, hunger, and diseases that went with it caused the deaths of up to 250,000 Africans. Whole areas were depopulated.[85]

Was the suppression of the Maji-Maji movement in GEA genocide? It is often argued that the German military campaign in Tanzania cannot be called genocide because the murder of hundreds of thousands of Africans or even the entire population in the colony was never the intentional goal of German warfare.[86] And indeed, there was no order like Lothar von Trotha's *Schiessbefehl*. Looking back a few years later, former governor von Götzen stated 1909 that the brutal warfare was just a means to an end, and he had never aimed at annihilating the African population of GEA as such:

> As in all wars against uncivilised nations the systematic damage to hostile people's good and chattels was indispensable in this case. The destruction of economic values like the burning of villages and food supplies might seem barbaric. If one considers, however, on the one hand, in what short time African negro-huts are erected anew and the luxuriant growth of tropic nature gives rise to new field crops, and, on the other hand, the subjugation of the enemy was only possible through a procedure like this, then one will consequently take a more favourable view of this "dira necessitas" [hard necessity].[87]

Far from exculpating von Götzen from genocidal responsibility, his statement makes it quite clear that he and his subordinates had exactly known what the consequences of their scorched-earth policy would be. Although the deaths of hundreds of thousands of Africans were not directly intended, it was reasonably foreseeable and accepted approvingly by the colonial administration. The heavy African losses during the German East African War of 1905–07 were thus more than "collateral damage." While the legal definition of genocide requires intentionality, social scientists have recently stressed that genocides are much more complex and have to be understood as processes of radicalization.[88] It is often difficult, if not even impossible to prove the original intentionality of a genocidal act. In this respect, it is doubtlessly appropriate—probably even important—to understand the German suppression of the Maji-Maji Revolt as genocidal.

Why Genocide?

As noted in the introduction, German settlers and officials regarded the Africans as the most important and contested resource in the colonies. Although economic modes in GSWA and GEA differed, both German farmers in Southwest Africa and plantation owners in East Africa depended on indigenous labor. From this perspective, suppressing "uprisings" by genocidal warfare seems counterproductive, even irrational. But why then did genocides occur in these two German colonies?

Answers can first be found on an institutional level. It is a commonplace now that the arrival of Lothar von Trotha in GSWA was a decisive step towards genocide. What political circumstances made the appointment of such an extremist possible? I have noted that the outstanding influence of the German military high command in political affairs and the Emperor's preference for energetic commanders and drastic solutions can partly explain the development in the colonies. However, this explanation is not sufficient, as it emphasizes solely German political peculiarities and fades out the fact that the British, French, and Spanish resorted to genocidal methods as well during colonial wars.[89] It is thus necessary to place the radicalization processes in GSWA and GEA in a global context. At the fin-de-siècle, most colonial wars (in the Philippines, Cuba, and South Africa, for example) saw the replacement of more or less adequate warfare by radical solutions and moderate colonial officials by hardliners. The reasons for these radicalizations were that colonial powers perceived indigenous resistance as a threat not only to their ambitions in the colonies, but to their imperial project as such, because a possible failure would expose them as weak and degenerate in the eyes of their European rivals.[90]

Massacres and genocidal acts may be ordered or approved by generals and colonial authorities; but they are committed by "ordinary soldiers"—by men on the spot. The debate between Christopher Browning and Daniel Jonah Goldhagen in Holocaust historiography about the motivation of "ordinary Germans" to commit massacres has shed light to the behavior of immediate perpetrators and group dynamics that contribute to radicalization processes.[91] The focus on "ordinary" settlers and colonial soldiers is thus indispensable for an understanding of unbounded violence during colonial wars.

In their memoirs and letters home, colonial soldiers justified violence against noncombatants by referring to Social-Darwinist theories. They portrayed the extinction of the Africans as a predetermined, natural process and themselves as instruments of a numinous force. Werner Freiherr Schenk von Stauffenberg, officer of the *Schutztruppe*, wrote in a letter: "We see the Herero perish as the man in the tragedy. And although we are involved in it, we feel uninvolved. . . . The rich, masterful and warlike Herero will be annihilated and the race struggle has to overflow the rules and norms that cultures and religions have established."[92] Yet racism cannot sufficiently explain the readiness of settlers and colonial soldiers to resort to genocidal warfare. The reference to racist theories was more a retrospective justification than a driving factor. Germans did not commit massacres in the colonies because they were in a strong position and had the power to decide on life or death of the indigenous population. On the contrary, German settlers felt unsafe and were afraid to lose their existence. Most reinforcements from Germany did not exactly know what to expect in GSWA and GEA. Furthermore, they were not at all familiar with the climate and they were afraid of tropical diseases. They just did not cope with the new surrounding and the situation. What is more, the colonizers overestimated the power of the Africans. A constant fear of ambushes was omnipresent. And rumors about African women committing mutilations were widespread. Situational factors, such as fear, the course of war, and group dynamics have to be considered as well. The behavior of ordinary soldiers was influenced by factors that are best explained by a social-psychological approach. So far, this literature has not been sufficiently applied to the colonial case.

Genocide as a Structural Phenomenon of German Rule in Africa

As I have shown so far, the genocidal wars in GSWA and GEA were the results of radicalization processes. Since the mass murder of the Africans was in principle inconsistent with the superior aims of the colonizers, the radicalization had to come to an end as soon as the Germans thought that they had regained control over the situation. Lothar von Trotha, for example, was first ordered to repeal his genocide order, and in 1905 he had to hand the supreme command over to a new civilian government and return to Germany. But that did not mean Germans had abandoned genocidal intentions. Although genocide is widely understood as a synonym for the Holocaust of European Jewry—that is, as the attempt to exterminate a targeted group physically—Lemkin defined the term much more broadly. It was the systematic "disintegration of the political and social institutions, of culture, language, national feelings, religion and the economic existence" of a specific group.[93] Furthermore, Lemkin understood genocides as processes and distinguished between two phases: "one destruction of the national pattern of the oppressed group; the other, imposition of the national pattern of the oppressor."[94] To be sure, Lemkin did not think of assimilation as automatically genocidal, nor the cultural change stimulated by intergroup contact. He called the latter "cultural diffusion." But cultural change was genocidal if the measures taken by the colonizers were intended not only to destroy an entire way of life, but also to ensure that the victim group had no appreciable collective life at all. As Dirk Moses and John Docker show, Lemkin regarded the dismemberment of indigenous cultures as genocidal if it was imposed by physical or structural violence.[95] Lemkin thus understood genocide as a "total social practice" (Moses) that affected all aspects of group life and differed between several techniques of group destruction: political (cessation of self-government and destruction of political institutions), social (annihilation of national leadership, attack on legal system), cultural (ban on the use of language), economic (destruction of the foundation of the economic existence), biological (decreasing the birth rate), physical (mass murder, endangering of health), religious (disruption of religious influence, destruction of religious leadership), and moral (creation of an atmosphere of moral debasement).[96] If Lemkin's broad understanding of genocide is taken as point of departure, the conclusion is obvious that not only were the wars in GSWA and GEA 1904–08 genocidal, but also the German colonial project as such. From the beginnings of German rule until its end in 1918, it was the colonizers' aim to forcibly dissolve the indigenous political, socioeconomic and religious foundations in order to establish a capitalist-style economy.

One of the driving forces of colonial expansion was the European powers' desire to extend their economic influence and to control and dominate as many regions as possible within a capitalist economy. Regions located at the periphery of the world system, such as Africa, were seen as a reservoir for important raw materials. And the indigenous populations were designated to plant, extract, or process these raw materials as cheap laborers and to consume European low-grade products. In their racist sense of superiority, European colonizers did not consider this system as exploitation, but as modernization of allegedly backward societies.[97]

In that respect, the German colonial project was no different from that of other European nations. From the onset of colonization, the colonizers embarked on the strategy of destroying the Africans' economic independence. The imposition of taxes and compulsory labor were means to realize this goal. The governor of GEA, Adolf Graf von Götzen, even considered the destruction of the Africans' food reserves.[98] What is more, even the thinking of the "natives" had to be changed. The imposition of a colonial working morale on the Africans was task of missionaries in particular. Thus, the Europeans considered the elimination of traditional cultures and lifestyles, as for example nomadism, as a crucial precondition for the establishment of a "modern" economic system. Although the Germans did not envisage the physical annihilation of the Africans, these plans and concepts are, according to Lemkin's concept, genocidal because the goal of the colonizers was the destruction of the traditional African societies as such.

These plans were concretely elaborated by colonial authorities both in Berlin and in the overseas territories, experts in colonial economy, and men on the spot, such as settlers' spokesmen.[99] The popular writings of Carl Peters, the conqueror of GEA, and of Paul Rohrbach, one of the most prominent public intellectuals in Germany of his time, had a huge impact on the corresponding colonial discourses and policy making. In his influential guide to German colonial economy, Rohrbach made clear what position was reserved for the Africans in colonial society:

> Only the necessity of losing their free national barbarianism and of becoming a class of servants for the whites provides the natives—historically seen—with an internal right of existence. . . . The idea that the Bantus would have the right to live and die according to their own fashion is absurd. It is true for peoples as well as for individuals that their existence is only justified if they contribute to

> general progressive development. There is no proof that national independence, national property and political organization among the tribes of Southwest Africa would be an advantage for the evolution of humankind in general or the German people in particular.[100]

Rohrbach—who was a strong opponent of Lothar von Trotha's policy of extermination—thus pleaded for the transformation of the Africans into a class of identity-less helots without any form of high culture, living in ghettos apart from the white population. These ideas can be seen as precursors of an apartheid policy that determined the political and socioeconomic situation in Southern Africa until the 1990s.[101]

As I have shown in the overviews on the German conquest of Southwest and East Africa, these plans were hardly or only partly realizable. The colonizers did not have sufficient means to fully subjugate the indigenous societies. Certainly, the consequences of the rinderpest in GSWA and governor von Götzen's incessant interference with indigenous political and economic customs shifted the balance of power slowly in favor of the colonizers. But it was the outcomes of the wars that worked as a catalyst and provided them with the opportunity to arrange their colonies politically and socioeconomically according to their oppressive plans.

In GSWA, the systematic legal disenfranchisement and expropriation of the indigenous population began even before the end of the war. In July 1905, deputy governor Tecklenburg stated that all tribal organization ought to come to an end.[102] In the same year, the indigenous land was seized, and two years later the colonial government issued decrees aiming at controlling the Africans in a totalitarian way.[103] The Africans' freedom of movement was highly restricted, and from the age of seven they were forced to carry a tiny identity badge around the neck.[104] Not only Herero and Nama suffered under the Germans' claim to absolute dominance. Until the end of German rule in SWA 1915, the *Schutztruppe* regularly hunted the nomadic San ("Bushmen") and forced them to a settled way of life in permanent villages.[105] The colonial authorities soon remarked that the consequences of their policy of forced assimilation were lethal. A doctor employed by the government just stated laconically: "I believe that the capture of the San will result in the deaths of a great number of them due to the different living conditions."[106] Although the colonizers came to the conclusion that the "domestication" of the San might turn out to be impossible, they continued this practice and willingly approved the deadly outcome of it.

Despite the totalitarian character of these regulations, the colonizers did not manage to destroy indigenous identity or culture in Southwest Africa completely. The Africans found subtle ways to resist the colonizers' intentions.[107] And African resistance and social reorganization led the

Germans to think of ever more radical methods. Since forced laborers regularly escaped from farms and threw their "native badges" away, settlers demanded that all Africans should be tattooed.[108]

Although both Herero and Nama were militarily defeated, GSWA was not fully "pacified." The situation in the south of the colony remained unsafe for a long time. Several Nama groups operated from the Cape Colony, and regularly launched attacks to German infrastructure. The fear of another large-scale African uprising was widespread among German settlers and officials. Therefore, colonial authorities in Berlin and Windhoek resorted to methods of social engineering, and seriously considered the deportation of the Herero and the Nama to the German colonies in Cameroon and even Papua New Guinea. The outbreak of World War I averted the further planning of this idea. Although these plans did not intend the physical extermination of the Herero and Nama, their implementation would at least have resulted in the irretrievable destruction of these societies.[109] This example shows drastically how persistent and influential genocidal thinking was among German settlers and colonial officials until the end of their rule in Southwest Africa.

The political and economic development in GEA was slightly different. In 1906, Albrecht von Rechenberg, a supporter of Dernburg's reformist course, replaced Götzen as governor. Rechenberg was of the opinion that GEA, and the Africans as its most valuable resource, could only recover from the war if GEA became a trade colony and the settlers' influence were reduced. Settlers were therefore deprived of the generous governmental aid with which they had been provided. Land expropriations were partly cancelled and regulations on forced labor were loosened.[110] It thus seems that Dernburg's reform program had a decisive impact on the Africans' socioeconomic and political situation in GEA in clear contrast to GSWA, where the administration was dominated by hardliners who widely ignored the colonial minister's directives. It should be noted, however, that Chancellor von Bülow had only appointed von Rechenberg because he wanted to appease oppositional forces that wanted to make political capital out of the public's concern about scandals and mismanagement in the colonies. Von Rechenberg's position both in Berlin and in the colony was thus not really strong. And indeed, plantation companies and German settlers put up a bitter and successful fight through their lobbies in Berlin. In spite of the governor's opposition, the number of European settlers in GEA increased from 1,800 in 1905 to 5,300 in 1913.[111] What the German newcomers needed was cheap African labor. Lack of plantation laborers became thus a permanent phenomenon in the whole colony. As a result, ruthless recruiters organized proper slave hunts and regularly ravaged African villages. The governor tried to prevent these excesses, but failed.

In 1912, Rechenberg himself was replaced by a governor who was completely in favor of the settlers' interests. Again, systematic forced labor and ill treatment of African workers became common in the colony, and the colonial administration's prime duty was the establishment of an almost total social, economic, and political control over the Africans' and their "education for work" (*Erziehung zur Arbeit*). In this task, the authorities were assisted by missionaries, whose aim was the elimination of traditional African religions and customs, as for example polygamy. The forced imposition of wage work and migratory labor on the indigenous communities led to the depopulation of whole regions. The German missionary Pater van der Burgt estimated in 1913 that the African population of his district had declined almost 50 percent (i.e., 200,000 people) within a very short period of time.[112] One of the devastating results of this development was the increasing dissolution of several indigenous institutions, most notably of clan structures and the traditional family. Furthermore, migrant work led to the wide-ranging spread of diseases—for example, worm sickness, tuberculosis, and syphilis—that affected African societies throughout the colony.

For all that, the colonizers' control over the Africans in GEA had not been as sophisticated and totalitarian as in GSWA. This difference can partly be explained by the fact that GSWA played a more important role as a projected "New Germany in Africa" in the fantasies of German colonial enthusiasts because of its favorable climate conditions that suited Europeans better. But the main reason for the temporarily different developments in these two colonies lies in the fact that the postwar administration in GSWA was in the hands of hardliners who sought to realize their radical prewar conceptions of a white settler community dominating an African helot class, whereas a reformist (Rechenberg) ruled GEA for five years. As might be expected, then, colonial authorities in GEA resorted to more oppressive and drastic methods as soon as the reformists had lost their influence around 1912. And if Germany had not lost East Africa after World War I, it would have become "a white man's country" exclusively dominated by German settlers.[113]

Conclusion

The term "colonial genocide" has been questioned increasingly in the last years. The sociologist Alison Palmer states that the distinction between "colonial" and "modern genocides" is unsatisfactory because some cases of genocide, like the destruction of the Herero, is simultaneously "modern" and "colonial." Palmer pleads instead for the use of the categories "state genocide" (e.g., the murder of the Herero, the genocide against the Armenians, and the Holocaust) and "societal genocide" (e.g., the murder of Aborigines in Queensland, 1840–1897).[114] Jürgen Zimmerer rejects these kinds of categorizations. He notes that the distinction between "colonial" and "modern" genocides strengthens the assumption that genocides committed in the various "New Worlds" and intra-European genocides like the Holocaust were conceptually completely different from each other. By referring to the colonial aspects of the National Socialists' population and extermination policy in Eastern Europe during World War II, Zimmerer concludes that there were "only" colonial genocides.[115] The analysis in this chapter shows that not only are genocides always colonial, but colonial rule and colonialism as such are constantly genocidal. Whenever colonizers aim at imposing economic modes and/or specific patterns of life on a dominated population, either by physical or structural violence, colonialism is—be it internal or external—inherently genocidal.[116]

Notes

1. For a discussion of the death tolls, see Horst Drechsler, *Südwestafrika unter Deutscher Kolonialherrschaft. Der Kampf der Herero und Nama gegen den deutschen Imperialismus (1884–1915)* (Berlin (DDR), 1966), 252; Ludger Wimmelbücker, "Verbrannte Erde. Zu den Bevölkerungsverlusten als Folge des Maji-Maji-Krieges," in *Der Maji-Maji-Krieg in Deutsch Ostafrika 1905–1907*, ed. Felicitas Becker and Jigal Beez (Berlin, 2005), 87–99.
2. Helmut Bley, *Kolonialherrschaft und Sozialstruktur in Deutsch-Südwestafrika 1894–1914* (Hamburg, 1968), 197.
3. After World War I, the British justified the seizure of German colonies by referring to the fate of the Herero and Nama under German rule. See Jürgen Zimmerer, "Von der Bevormundung zur Selbstbestimmung. Die Pariser Friedenskonferenz und ihre Auswirkungen auf die britische Kolonialherrschaft im südlichen Afrika" in *Versailles 1919: Ziele—Wirkungen—Wahrnehmung*, ed. Gerd Krumeich (Essen, 2001), 145–58. Major Thomas Leslie O'Reilly was authorized in September 1917 to compile atrocities committed by the German *Schutztruppe* during the war against the Herero and Nama. The report was published in 1918: Union of South Africa, *Report on the Natives of South-West Africa and their Treatment by Germany* (London, 1918). Despite of the propagandist intention of the editors, the "Blue Book" is a valuable source containing first-hand accounts by surviving Herero and Nama. See Reinhart Kössler, "Sjambok or Cane? Reading the Blue Book," *Journal of Southern African Studies* 30, no. 3 (2004): 703–8. It has recently been re-edited and commented: Jeremy Silvester and Jan-Bart Gewald, eds, *Words Cannot Be Found. German Colonial Rule in Namibia. An Annotated Reprint of the 1918 Blue Book* (Leiden, 2003).
4. See, for example, Ulrich van der Heyden, "Die 'Hottentottenwahlen' von 1907," in *Völkermord in Deutsch-Südwestafrika. Der Kolonialkrieg (1904–1908) in Namibia und seine Folgen*, ed. Jürgen Zimmerer and Joachim Zeller (Berlin, 2003), 97–102.

5. Horst Gründer, *Geschichte der deutschen Kolonien*, 4th ed. (Paderborn, 2000), 241–43; Harald Sippel, "Die Kolonialabteilung des Auswärtigen Amtes und das Reichskolonialamt," *Kolonialmetropole Berlin. Eine Spurensuche*, ed. Ulrich van der Heyden and Joachim Zeller (Berlin, 2002), 29–32; Andreas Eckert and Michael Pesek, "Bürokratische Ordnung und koloniale Praxis. Herrschaft und Verwaltung in Preussen und Afrika," in *Das Kaiserreich transnational. Deutschland in der Welt 1871–1914*, ed. Sebastian Conrad and Jürgen Osterhammel (Göttingen, 2004), 87–106
6. On Bernhard Dernburg see Werner Schiefel, *Bernhard Dernburg 1865–1937. Kolonialpolitiker und Bankier im wilhelminischen Deutschland* (Zurich and Freiburg, 1974).
7. Bernhard Dernburg, *Zielpunkte des Deutschen Kolonialwesens. Zwei Vorträge* (Berlin, 1907), 6–9.
8. Gründer, *Geschichte*, 242; This argument is also the central thread of the following popular scientific book: Gisela Graichen and Horst Gründer, *Deutsche Kolonien. Traum und Trauma* (Berlin, 2005). For a well-founded critique on this approach, see Jürgen Zimmerer, "Nicht mal 'nen Neger?" *Süddeutsche Zeitung*, 24 November 2005.
9. Paul Rohrbach, *Um des Teufels Handschrift. Zwei Menschenalter erlebter Weltgeschichte* (Hamburg, 1953), 64. Theodor Leutwein, governor of GSWA until 1904, came to a similar conclusion in his memoirs. See Theodor Leutwein, *Elf Jahre Gouverneur in Deutsch-Südwestafrika* (Berlin, 1906), 525, 542.
10. Different types of settler colonies can be distinguished: "New England-type," where the settlers are not dependent on native labor; "African-type," where settlers and planters rely on cheap indigenous labor; and "Caribbean-type," where slaves are imported from outside. See Jürgen Osterhammel, *Kolonialismus. Geschichte, Formen, Folgen*, 3rd ed. (Munich, 2001), 18–19.
11. Christoph Marx, "Siedlerkolonien in Afrika—Versuch einer Typologie," in *Rassenmischehen-Mischlinge-Rassentrennung. Zur Politik der Rasse im deutschen Kolonialreich*, ed. Frank Becker (Stuttgart, 2004), 85–86.
12. The recruitment of Chinese workers (*Kulis*) for the colonies and even for German agriculture was intensively discussed, but only carried out on a trial base. See Sebastian Conrad, "'Die Sehnsucht nach Chinesen'. Chinesische Arbeiter in der preussischen Landwirtschaft?," in *"Macht und Anteil an der Weltherrschaft." Berlin und der deutsche Kolonialismus*, ed. Ulrich van der Heyden and Joachim Zeller (Berlin, 2005), 215–21; Sebastian Conrad, *Globalisierung und Nation im Deutschen Kaiserreich* (Munich, 2006), 168–228.
13. Patrick Wolfe, "Land, Labor, and Difference: Elementary Structures of Race," *American Historical Review* 106, no. 3 (2001): 866–67.
14. Kenneth Good, "Settler Colonialism: Economic Development and Class Formation," *The Journal of Modern African Studies* 14, no. 4 (1976): 603.
15. Jan-Bart Gewald, *Herero Heroes. A Socio-Political History of the Herero of Namibia 1890–1923* (Oxford 1999), 10–26.
16. Harri Siiskonen, *Trade and Socioeconomic Change in Ovamboland, 1850–1906* (Helsinki, 1990).
17. On the role of anthropologists within the German colonial project, see Andrew Zimmerman, "'What Do You Really Want in German East Africa, *Herr Professor?*': Counterinsurgency and the Science Effect in Tanzania," *Comparative Studies of Society and History* 48, no. 2 (2006): 419–61.
18. On the activity of German missionaries in Southwest Africa, see Gustav Menzel, *Die Rheinische Mission* (Wuppertal, 1978); Nicole Glocke, *Zur Geschichte der Rheinischen*

Missionsgesellschaft in Deutsch-Südwestafrika unter besonderer Berücksichtigung des Kolonialkrieges von 1904 bis 1907 (Bochum, 1997). It took the missionaries a long time to convince the indigenous peoples of the "advantages" of the Christian faith. Only after fourteen years did Carl Hugo Hahn manage to baptize the first African. See Gesine Krüger, *Kriegsbewältigung und Geschichtsbewusstsein. Realität, Deutung und Verarbeitung des deutschen Kolonialkriegs in Namibia 1904 bis 1907* (Göttingen, 1999), 39.

19. On German and foreign concession companies in GSWA, see Horst Drechsler, *Südwestafrika unter Deutscher Kolonialherrschaft. Die grossen Land- und Minengesellschaften* (Stuttgart, 1996).
20. Curt von François was an experienced colonial soldier who had previously served in King Leopold's "Congo Free State." As Jan-Bart Gewald has recently shown, many German colonial soldiers learned their trade in the Belgian Congo, where they had participated in atrocities against the indigenous population: "In the same manner that the Congo explorer Hermann von Wissmann founded the *Schutztruppe* in German East Africa, so too his assistant and fellow Congo explorer, Curt von François founded the *Schutztruppe* in German Southwest Africa. In both instances, their experiences and activities in the Congo were of influence and import upon the manner in which they believed that the forces under their command in GEA and GSWA should act." Jan-Bart Gewald, "Learning to Wage and Win Wars in Africa: A Provisional History of German Military Activity in Congo, Tanzania, China and Namibia," Paper presented at the conference "Genocides: Forms, Causes, Consequences. The Namibian War (1904–08) in Historical Perspective" (Berlin, 14 January 2005), 8.
21. Leutwein, *Elf Jahre*, 271.
22. The concept of "indirect rule" was widely used by the British in their African colonies. It goes back to the colonial official Lugard. According to this concept, the colonial administration should exercise power through traditional indigenous institutions. See Frederick John D. Lugard, *The Dual Mandate in British Tropical Africa* (London, 1922).
23. Samuel Maharero was the son of Tjamuaha Maharero (d. 1890), who established the hegemony of the Herero in central Namibia. On Samuel Maharero's family and youth, see Gerhard Pool, *Samuel Maharero* (Windhoek, 1991), 9–55.
24. Samuel Maharero's claim was challenged not least because of his conversion to Christianity. On the Herero dispute of succession, see Gewald, *Herero Heroes*, 29–60.
25. Jürgen Zimmerer, *Deutsche Herrschaft über Afrikaner. Staatlicher Machtanspruch und Wirklichkeit im kolonialen Namibia* (Hamburg, 2001), 27–28.
26. Bley, *Kolonialherrschaft*, 151–52.
27. Especially the representatives of the Rhenish Mission demanded the establishment of reservations of inalienable Herero land. German settlers and members of the *Schutztruppe*, however, opposed these plans. They were afraid of losing the opportunity to get hold of cheap land. See Gewald, *Herero Heroes*, 144.
28. On these colonial imaginations in the German public discourse, see Birthe Kundrus, *Moderne Imperialisten. Das Kaiserreich im Spiegel seiner Kolonien* (Cologne, 2003), 8–9, 58–77.
29. Udo Kaulich, *Die Geschichte der ehemaligen Kolonie Deutsch-Südwestafrika (1884–1914). Eine Gesamtdarstellung* (Frankfurt am Main, 2001), 353.
30. Mike Davis, *Late Victorian Holocausts. El Niño Famines and the Making of the Third World* (London, 2001).
31. The pandemic wiped out approximately 90 percent of the cattle owned by the Herero. See Drechsler, *Kampf*, 119.

32. Approximately 8–10 percent of the Herero fell ill. Bley, *Kolonialherrschaft*, 165. The German missionary Irle estimated that about 10,000 Herero died as a result of this epidemic. Irle, *Herero*, 127.
33. Gewald, *Herero Heroes*, 133.
34. The murder of Chief Zacharias' daughter and the exoneration of the German culprit by the colonial justice were symptomatic of this development. Drechsler, *Kampf*, 154–55. Furthermore, German traders began collecting outstanding debts in a rather brutal manner because Governor Leutwein had forbidden the lending business with the Africans. Ibid., 147–48.
35. Although Governor Leutwein welcomed the shift of the balance of power, he was aware that the desperation of the indigenous population might threaten the envisaged pacification of the colony by "peaceful" means. He therefore condemned excesses committed by German settlers or traders and complained that GSWA became an attractive destination for weak-charactered and failed adventurers. Report by Theodor Leutwein to the Colonial Office of the Foreign Office, 17 June 1904, Bundesarchiv Berlin Lichterfelde (German Federal Archive, Berlin Lichterfelde), R1001/2115, 65–66.
36. Kaulich, *Geschichte der ehemaligen Kolonie Deutsch-Südwestafrika*, 353.
37. Drechsler, *Kampf*, 129.
38. Winfried Speitkamp, *Deutsche Kolonialgeschichte* (Stuttgart, 2005), 81–82.
39. It has been debated in the historiography whether the Herero had thoroughly planned the war with the colonizers or whether the beginnings of the animosities were rather spontaneous. For a summary of this discussion, see Dominik J. Schaller, "Kolonialkrieg, Völkermord und Zwangsarbeit in 'Deutsch-Südwestafrika,'" in *Enteignet-Vertrieben-Ermordet: Beiträge zur Genozidforschung*, ed. Dominik J. Schaller et al. (Zurich, 2004), 163–64.
40. Gewald, *Herero Heroes*, 142–56. Gesine Krüger offers a different interpretation. She argues that the Germans in the colony ignored the signs of a forthcoming rebellion due to their sense of superiority and arrogance. Krüger, *Kriegsbewältigung*, 46.
41. Especially the German defeat in Oviumbo on 13 April, where Leutwein had to order a humiliating retreat, made his superior authorities believe that he would not be able to regain control over GSWA. See Drechsler, *Kampf*, 174; Kriegsgeschichtliche Abteilung des Grossen Generalstabes, ed., *Die Kämpfe der deutschen Truppen in Südwestafrika, Band I: Der Feldzug gegen die Hereros* (Berlin, 1906/07), 110.
42. Kristin Zirkel, "Militärische Struktur und politischer Führung im Deutsch-Südwestafrika-Krieg 1904–07" (MA thesis, Heinrich Heine-University Düsseldorf, 1989), 106.
43. Leutwein, *Elf Jahre*, 511–10; Bley, *Kolonialherrschaft*, 194; Gewald, *Herero Heroes*, 167–68; Drechsler, *Kampf*, 175.
44. On Lothar von Trotha's personal background, see Pool, *Samuel Maharero*, 243–45; Isabel V. Hull, *Absolute Destruction. Military Culture and the Practices of War in Imperial Germany* (Ithaca, NY, 2005), 25–27.
45. Trotha to Schlieffen, 4 October 1904 (Unless otherwise indicated, all translations are my own).
46. Quotation in Drechsler, *Kampf*, 180.
47. Bley, *Kolonialherrschaft*, 200.
48. Krüger, *Kriegsbewältigung*, 51. The escape routes of the Herero are described in Gewald, *Herero Heroes*, 175–81.
49. The colonial veteran Ludwig von Estorff was entrusted with the persecution of the Herero in the desert. He described the event openly and pitilessly in his memoirs. See

idem, *Wanderungen und Kämpfe in Südwestafrika, Ostafrika und Südafrika 1894–1910*, ed. Christoph-Friedrich Kutscher (Wiesbaden, 1968), 116–17.

50. This interpretation is supported by the German historian Horst Drechsler and has been influential for a long time. See idem, *Kampf*, 182–83. Isabell V. Hull has recently called it "a tenacious myth of German military omnicompetence." Idem, *Absolute Destruction*, 37.
51. Proclamation by Lothar von Trotha (copy), 2 October 1904, Bundesarchiv Berlin Lichterfelde, R1001/2098, 7–8.
52. Ibid.
53. For a discussion on von Trotha's motivation to issue the genocide order, see Hull, *Absolute Destruction*, 59–61. Hull had access to von Trotha's diaries.
54. On Lemkin's manuscripts on the colonial war in GSWA, see Dominik J. Schaller, "Raphael Lemkin's View of Colonial Rule in Africa: Between Condemnation and Admiration," *Journal of Genocide Research* 7, no. 4 (2005): 531–38.
55. English translation provided by "German History in Documents and Images" (GHDI): http://germanhistorydocs.ghi-dc.org/sub_document.cfm?document_id=755 (accessed 20 August 2006).
56. Bülow to Emperor Wilhelm II., 14 November 1904, Bundesarchiv Berlin Lichterfelde, R1001/2089, 8–11.
57. Bülow to von Trotha, 14 January 1905, National Archives of Namibia, ZBU/D.IV. m.2, 52.
58. Zimmerer, *Deutsche Herrschaft*, 42–48; Gewald, *Herero Heroes*, 185–90.
59. Until 1907, 7,682 prisoners died in the concentration camps. Report on the mortality in the camps by the command of the Schutztruppe, Bundesarchiv Berlin Lichterfelde, R1001/2140, 161.
60. The German war against the Nama has not received much attention yet in historiography. For a discussion on the causes and the course, see Bühler, *Namaaufstand*; Werner Hillebrecht, "Die Nama und der Krieg im Süden," in Zimmerer and Zeller, *Völkermord*, 121–33.
61. The historian Jürgen Zimmerer has adequately called the treatment of the Africans in the camps as continuation of von Trotha's policy of extermination. See idem, "Kriegsgefangene im Kolonialkrieg. Der Krieg gegen die Herero und Nama in Deutsch-Südwestafrika (1904–1907)," in *In der Hand des Feindes. Kriegsgefangenschaft von der Antike bis zum Zweiten Weltkrieg*, ed. Rüdiger Overmans (Cologne, 1999), 277–94. In present-day Namibia, political leaders of the Herero claim that only their people fell victim to genocide, whereas the Nama were solely "affected by the war." It is the aim of Herero leaders to transform moral capital resulting from the widely acknowledged status as "main victims of German colonialism" to concrete political capital. As the French sociologist Jean-Michel Chaumont has noted, competition among victim groups in the arena of memory politics is nowadays a widespread phenomenon: Jean-Michel Chaumont, *La concurrence des victimes. Génocide, identité, reconnaissance* (Paris, 1997).
62. John Iliffe, *A Modern History of Tanganyika* (Cambridge, 1979), 200.
63. Michael Mann, for example, discusses the murder of the Herero in his broad study on genocide and ethnic cleansing, but completely omits the war in GEA. Mann, *The Dark Side of Democracy: Explaining Ethnic Cleansing* (Cambridge, 2005), 100–107.
64. Rainer Tetzlaff, *Koloniale Entwicklung und Ausbeutung. Wirtschafts- und Sozialgeschichte Deutsch-Ostafrikas 1885–1914* (Berlin, 1970), 287.
65. Reinhard Klein-Arendt, "Ein Land wird gewaltsam in Besitz genommen. Die Kolonie Deutsch-Ostafrika," in Becker and Beez, *Maji-Maji-Krieg*, 28–48, 30–31.

66. On the so-called "Arab Revolt", see Bückendorf, *Schwarz-weiss-rot*, 350–64; Martin Baer and Olaf Schröter, *Eine Kopfjagd. Deutsche in Ostafrika* (Berlin, 2001), 37–45.
67. Bückendorf, *Schwarz-weiss-rot*, 365–452.
68. Michael Pesek sees in these islands of dominance "Potemkin villages." See Pesek, *Koloniale Herrschaft in Deutsch-Ostafrika. Expeditionen, Militär und Verwaltung seit 1880* (Frankfurt am Main, 2005), 190–266.
69. Between 1891 and 1897, the Germans carried out sixty-one "punitive expeditions" in GEA. See Gründer, *Geschichte*, 154. On the war against the Hehe, see Baer and Schröter, *Kopfjagd*, 49–60; Alison Redmayne, "Mkwawa and the Hehe Wars," *Journal of African History* 9, no. 3 (1968): 409–36.
70. Rainer Tetzlaff, *Koloniale Entwicklung und Ausbeutung. Wirtschafts- und Sozialgeschichte Deutsch-Ostafrikas 1885–1914* (Berlin, 1970), 40f.; Juhani Koponen, *Development for Exploitation. German Colonial Policies in Mainland Tanzania, 1884–1914* (Münster, 1995), 112–42.
71. Klein-Arendt, *Ein Land*, 35.
72. Ibid., 36; Detlef Bald, *Deutsch-Ostafrika 1900–1914. Eine Studie über Verwaltung, Interessengruppen und wirtschaftliche Erschliessung* (Munich, 1970), 68.
73. Erick J. Mann, *Mikono ya damu: "Hands of Blood". African Mercenaries and the Politics of Conflict in German East Africa, 1888–1904* (Frankfurt am Main, 2002).
74. On the growth of white settlement from 1900–1906, see Koponen, *Development*, 251–58.
75. Tetzlaff, *Koloniale Entwicklung*, 106.
76. Klein-Arendt, *Ein Land*, 46.
77. Tetzlaff, *Koloniale Entwicklung*, 209f; Koponen, *Development*, 215–23.
78. Anton Markmiller, *"Die Erziehung des Negers zur Arbeit." Wie die koloniale Pädagogik afrikanische Gesellschaften in die Abhängigkeit führte* (Berlin, 1995), 89–118.
79. Newly established trade routes did not lead through the southern districts anymore. See Patrick Krajewski, "Dampfer und Dhaus. Küstenhandel und Landwirtschaft vor dem Krieg (1880–1905)," in Becker and Beez, *Maji-Maji-Krieg*, 49–58.
80. For a discussion on the origins of the Maji Cult and its peculiarities, see Marcia Wright, "Maji Maji Prophecy and Historiography," in *Revealing Prophets. Prophecy in Eastern African History*, ed. David Anderson and Douglas H. Johnson (London, 1995), 124–42; Jigal Beez, *Geschosse zu Wassertropfen. Sozio-religiöse Aspekte des Maji-Maji-Krieges in Deutsch-Ostafrika, 1905–1907* (Cologne, 2003).
81. See, for example, Karl Martin Seeberg, *Der Maji-Maji-Krieg gegen die deutsche Kolonialherrschaft. Historische Ursprünge nationaler Identität in Tansania* (Berlin, 1989). On the memory of the Maji-Maji War in Tanzania, see Felicitas Becker, "Für einige Zeit wiederbelebt. Das Gedenken an den Maji-Maji-Krieg in Tansania, in Becker and Beez, *Maji-Maji-Krieg*, 171–178. The terms "Maji-Maji War" or "Maji-Maji Uprising" are most unfortunate because they imply alleged African irrationality. It would make more sense to speak of the German East African War of 1905–07.
82. Detlef Bald, *Deutsch-Ostafrika 1900–1914. Eine Studie über Verwaltung, Interessengruppen und wirtschaftliche Erschliessung* (Munich, 1970), 64–67.
83. For a description of the events, see Iliffe, *Modern History of Tanganyka*, 168–202.
84. The term "scorched-earth policy" was first used by Gilbert Gwassa to describe the German warfare in GEA. See idem, "German Intervention and African Resistance in Tanzania," in *A History of Tanzania*, ed. Isaria N. Kimambo and Arnold J. Temu (Nairobi, 1969), 85–122.

85. Iliffe, *Modern History of Tanganyka*, 200. In the case of GEA, an estimate of the death is difficult due to the lack of reliable statistics. See Wimmelbücker, "Verbrannte Erde."
86. See, for example, Hull, *Absolute Destruction*, 156–57.
87. Gustav Adolf Graf von Götzen, *Deutsch-Ostafrika im Aufstand 1905/06* (Berlin, 1909), 248
88. See, for example, Christian Gerlach, "Nationsbildung im Krieg: Wirtschaftliche Faktoren bei der Vernichtung der Armenier und beim Mord an den ungarischen Juden," in *Der Völkermord an den Armeniern und die Shoah*, ed. Hans-Lukas Kieser and Dominik J. Schaller (Zurich, 2002), 347–422, esp. 351; Dominik J. Schaller, "Genozidforschung: Begriffe und Debatten," in Schaller, *Enteignet*, 14; Gerd Hankel, "Was heisst eigentlich Völkermord? Überlegungen zu einem problematischen Begriff," *Mittelweg 36* 14, no. 4 (2005): 70–81; Mann, *Dark Side of Democracy*, 140–4.
89. See the contributions in Thoralf Klein and Frank Schumacher, eds., *Kolonialkriege: Militärische Gewalt im Zeichen des Imperialismus* (Hamburg, 2006).
90. Mark Levene, *Genocide in the Age of the Nation State*, vol. 2, *The Rise of the West and the Coming of Genocide* (London, 2005), 266–74.
91. On the Browning-Goldhagen debate and social-psychological approaches to genocidal massacres, see Harald Welzer, *Täter: Wie aus ganz normalen Menschen Massenmörder werden* (Frankfurt am Main, 2005).
92. Quoted from Gertrud Marchand-Volz, *Werner Freiherr Schenk von Stauffenberg. Deutsch-Südwestafrika 1904* (Windhoek, 1994), 137.
93. Raphael Lemkin, *Axis Rule in Occupied Europe* (Washington, DC, 1944), 79.
94. Ibid.
95. See their chapters in this volume. On Lemkin's concept of cultural genocide and its nonconsideration in the UN genocide convention, see also Robert van Krieken, "Rethinking Cultural Genocide: Aboriginal Child Removal and Settler-Colonial State Formation," *Oceania* 75, no. 2 (2004): 125–51.
96. Lemkin, *Axis Rule*, 82–90. See also the contribution of Dirk Moses in this volume.
97. Niels P. Peterson, "Markt, Zivilisierungsmission und Imperialismus," in *Zivilisierungsmissionen. Imperiale Weltverbesserung seit dem 18. Jahrhundert*, ed. Boris Barth and Jürgen Osterhammel (Constance, 2005), 33–54.
98. Helge Kjekshus, *Ecology Control and Economic Development in East African History* (London, 1977), 143.
99. On corresponding plans for GSWA elaborated by the colonial government before 1904, see Bley, *Kolonialherrschaft und Sozialstruktur*, 137–146.
100. Paul Rohrbach, *Deutsche Kolonialwirtschaft*, vol. 1, *Südwest-Afrika* (Berlin, 1907), 285–288.
101. Henning Melber therefore sees the Germans as the inventors of Apartheid. Idem, "Kontinuitäten totaler Herrschaft: Völkermord und Apartheid in 'Deutsch-Südwestafrika'. Zur kolonialen Herrschaftspraxis im deutschen Kaiserreich," *Jahrbuch für Antisemitismusforschung* 1 (1992): 91–114.
102. Tecklenburg to colonial office in Berlin, 17 July 1905, Bundesarchiv Berlin Lichterfelde, R1001/1220, 28.
103. Bley, *Kolonialherrschaft*, 260–62.
104. Zimmerer, *Deutsche Herrschaft*, 68–109.
105. Schaller, *Kolonialkrieg*, 202.
106. National Archives of Namibia (NAN), Bezirksamt Swakopmund (BSW), G.3.s, Dr. Brenner to the district office of Swakopmund, 10. 5. 1913, 6–7.

107. African agency and resistance as well as the restructuring of indigenous societies after the war have long been neglected in historiography. See Krüger, *Kriegsbewältigung*; Gewald, *Herero Heroes*.
108. NAN, Zentralbureau (ZBU), W.III.b.1, letter of the agrarian society Okahandja to the government in Windhoek, 16. 12. 1913, 37.
109. As an experiment, almost two hundred Nama were deported to Cameroon in 1904 and 1910. Most of them died because of tropical diseases. Cameroon was therefore not considered anymore as an ideal destination for deportees. On planned and effectively executed deportations in the German colonial empire, see Schaller, *Kolonialkrieg*, 189–95.
110. Koponen, *Development*, 258–71.
111. Tetzlaff, *Koloniale Entwicklung*, 106.
112. Ibid., 252.
113. Iliffe, *Modern History*, 151.
114. Alison Palmer, "Colonial and Modern Genocide: Explanations and Categories," *Ethnic and Racial Studies* 21, no. 1 (1998): 89–115.
115. Jürgen Zimmerer, "Kolonialer Genozid? Vom Nutzen und Nachteil einer historischen Kategorie für eine Globalgeschichte des Völkermordes," in Schaller et al., *Enteignet, Vertrieben, Ermordet*. 109–28.
116. For a case of "genocidal internal colonialism," see Mark Levene, "The Chittagong Hill Tracts: A Case Study in the Political Economy of 'Creeping' Genocide," *Third World Quarterly* 20, no. 2 (1999): 339–69.

– *Chapter 14* –

INTERNAL COLONIZATION, INTER-IMPERIAL CONFLICT AND THE ARMENIAN GENOCIDE

Donald Bloxham

The "colonization" of the title does not refer to the extension and consolidation of Turkic settlement in the region of Anatolia—the area that forms most of the modern Republic of Turkey and most of the focus of this study. This is a modern story, taking as its point of departure the given fact of the existence of Ottomania as the last in a long line of Middle Eastern imperia (dominated at various times by Christians, Muslims, and rulers of neither faith), not seeking to question the bases or legitimacy of Ottoman rule as established in the late medieval and early modern periods. For the period under consideration, from the mid- nineteenth to the early twentieth centuries, it is not analytically helpful to consider Anatolia as an Ottoman colony, given the thorough mixture of peoples in the region and the way that over centuries they had been more or less absorbed into different levels of the unique Ottoman sociopolitical structure.

The most important factor in the break up of the empire and the accompanying demographic catastrophes around the First World War was the development of essentialist nationalisms harking back to semimythologized pasts and laying spurious claims to sole, authentic land ownership. These nationalisms were in turn expressions of socioeconomic and political conditions stemming from the penetration of European capital, influence, and ideas into the Ottoman polity from the late eighteenth and particularly the mid-nineteenth centuries. The language of colonization, however, remains relevant to the Armenian genocide, the most extreme episode within the wider history of exclusion, destruction, and expulsion in the Near East from c.1912–c.1926, a period beginning with the vicious Balkan wars and concluding with the final acts of the Greco-Turkish "population exchange" conducted in the aftermath of war between the two states.[1] And though for reasons of space little will be written of the matter hereafter, the language of colonization is also relevant to the assault on the collective identity of the Turkish Kurds that began in the mid-1920s, reached its zenith in the late 1930s, and has yet fully to come to an end.

The expulsion during the First World War of the majority of the Ottoman Armenians, including the murder of approximately one million of them, was part of a drive for Ottoman-Turkish population homogeneity in Anatolia—in the eastern provinces of which at the outset of war Armenians formed a plurality with Kurds, with Turks a substantial third minority—and in adjacent Cilicia on the Mediterranean coast. An intrinsic part of this drive, indeed, a trigger at certain points, was the settlement of Muslims in the stead of the Armenians in a sort of "inner colonisation," as one contemporary observer described it:[2] an attempt to consolidate Ottoman control of the land by the installation of "ethnically-reliable" subjects in the stead of "untrustworthy" ones.

This chapter will examine a series of trends that culminated, if not inexorably, in genocide. The first section considers the broader project of state modernization and consolidation into which fits the desire to achieve ever-greater control over lands with substantial Armenian populations. The second considers more specific aspects of late Ottoman history influencing Ottoman population policy, including enforced demographic change and territorial loss. The immediate evolution of genocide during the war occupies the third part.

State Modernization

Inevitably, the story that concluded with the genocide is one of both significant changes in Ottoman attitudes and some important continuities, particularly from the last quarter of the nineteenth century onwards. One very important determinant of late Ottoman population policies—irrespective of the shifts in those policies—and probably the major element of continuity in state ambitions in the final century of the empire, was the attempt to modernize the empire in the interests of its own survival. As in analogous projects elsewhere, this included the attempted development of the state's own industries, the fostering of its own bourgeoisie, the strengthening and expansion (by increased investment and conscription) of its armed forces, and the extension of central control over the imperial peripheries (by, amongst other things, the improvement of the transport infrastructure and increased penetration into the provinces of direct representatives of central government)—both to ensure that they were better protected against the outside world and to assure their allegiance in the face of centrifugal tendencies based around local power networks, separate ethno-religious affiliations, and/or the spread of nationalism amongst subject peoples.

Each of these policy strands was intrinsically related to the others, and each affected in some way the state's relationship with its peoples at both an individual and a collective level. With respect to the development and denouement of the "Armenian question," however, two were more important than the others. The first was the desire to create an Ottoman bourgeoisie, which by the beginning of the twentieth century effectively meant creating a Muslim-Turkish middle class as a driver of nationalism and of the Muslim-Turkish "national economy" at the expense of indigenous Christians. The second, particularly relevant policy strand was the desire to retrench control in the imperial peripheries, which is where eastern Anatolia increasingly came into focus in the nineteenth century. The eastern provinces developed in the Ottoman mind from the comparatively economically and politically insignificant backwater they had been in previous ages into an area that was increasingly precious in the light of huge imperial land losses in the Balkans and elsewhere, but in which at the same time Istanbul's sovereignty was increasingly threatened by Russian encroachment and intrigue and (consequently) also British meddling.

Establishing closer control over eastern Anatolia entailed a protracted struggle with Kurdish tribal leaders and landowners. In a modified form, breaking down Kurdish socioeconomic networks was one of the main aims of the attack on ethnic Kurdishness from the mid-1920s onwards. The nineteenth century watershed of the process was the so-called second Ottoman invasion of Kurdistan in the 1830s and 1840s, a state campaign against the virtually autonomous Kurdish principalities of eastern Anatolia. Many thousands of noncombatants were killed alongside men of fighting age, and the Ottoman military campaign also involved mass conscription of Kurds and commandeering of Kurdish property. It resulted in the alienation from the state of many ordinary Kurds and their traditional leaders, and vigorous resistance led by the greatest of the emirs, Bedr Khan.[3] (Cilicia too from the 1840s saw an assault on Muslim *derebeys*, or "lords of the valley," and attempts to forcibly settle their tribal support base. These measures were initially concluded in 1865 by the iron fist of the Ottoman "reform division."[4])

Given the ethnic mix of eastern Anatolia, it is impossible to extricate the "Armenian question" from this "Kurdish question." The state's confrontation with parts of its Kurdish population was punctuated by periodic attempts, notably at various points from the late 1870s through to the close of the Greco-Turkish war, to appeal to Kurdish sentiment by way of playing Kurds off against the Armenian community. The latter was looming increasingly large as the subject of Armenian nationalist claims, and was simultaneously being ever more exposed as a seemingly "alien" Christian constituency within a Muslim state, as the traditional Ottoman theocracy disintegrated and was replaced by a state doctrine based first on the unity of Muslims and then an increasingly Turkish nationalism. (In light of the development of a specifically Turkish state nationalism from 1908 onwards, Kurds would again be targeted as soon as the "Armenian question" appeared to have been solved, as they were briefly during 1916/17 and again after the establishment of the Kemalist state.) The state's use of Kurds and other, immigrant Muslims during that period as a weapon in the displacement, terrorization, and thinning out of the Armenian population can properly be viewed as a form of internal colonization.

Population Policy and the Armenians in the Late Ottoman Empire

Full consensus has yet to be established about the precise ideology of the *Ittihad ve Terakki Cemiyeti* (Committee of Union and Progress; CUP), the political faction that presided over the Ottoman state in the genocide period. The growing, exclusive Turkish nationalism among CUP leaders in the first decade of the twentieth century still seems to have foreseen, at least as a matter of pragmatism, the coexistence of different Muslim groups under a modernizing Turkish hegemony.[5] For our purposes, "Ittihadism" was only the latest attempted "solution" to the challenges posed by the decline of Ottoman power. The first far-reaching such attempt was the famous *Tanzimat* reform period (c. 1839–76), which brought with it the theoretical introduction of inter-religious equality as well as promises of greater social justice and economic and administrative reform. It was a program of bringing the empire "up to speed" to compete within a burgeoning international system in which the more efficient armies, industries, and administrations of the European powers, informed by the Enlightenment and scientific advancement, and in the French, British, and German cases by nationalism, gave them colossal competitive advantages over the Ottomans.[6] Reforms for non-Muslims were seen as an essential measure in tying the interests of those communities in with the future of the state and thus undermining impulses towards secessionism. Reforming the eastern provinces of Anatolia was increasingly important, since the disastrous Russo-Turkish War of 1828/29 had illustrated quite what a tenuous control the Ottomans had over their border regions.

As we have already seen, key attempts at centralization and reform, as manifested most graphically in the "second invasion of Kurdistan," contributed to a deterioration of relations between Turks and Kurds. Moreover, beyond specific urban centers and regions, the envisaged reforms did not materialize in eastern Anatolia, owing to nonimplementation by Ottoman provincial officials reliant on the support of, or even under the control of, local Muslim notables with an interest in the status quo. "Reform" even resulted in a worsening of the condition of parts of the peasantry, particularly the Armenians. In the case of eastern Anatolia, the comparatively tolerant religious tradition of Bedr Khan was replaced by the rule of often militant sheikhs of Sufi orders. Reforms further affected relations between both groups and Armenians as the delicate, hierarchical balance between Christians and Muslims was upset. Various institutionalized abuses of Armenians, which had always been present as Muslims exploited their religiously determined social superiority over Christians, now intensified as the former perceived the Armenians to be the beneficiaries of the reforms threatening the traditional order.[7] Thus, for instance, the abusive practice of Kurdish nomads "wintering" in Armenian quarters—their unwilling hosts given no say in the matter—persisted despite legislation to the contrary in 1842, for the nomads regarded it is a hereditary right.[8] Meanwhile, the breakdown in the client-protector system meant that many Kurdish tribes simply began to pillage, kidnap, and rape on a much greater scale than before. Such antagonism exhibited by a formerly superordinate group is a common phenomenon when inherently unequal social systems begin to fragment.[9]

The *Tanzimat* also failed to pull Turkey out of its economic mire: for instance, the Ottoman Public Debt Administration was established in 1881, giving Europeans extensive control over Ottoman fiscal policy to ensure repayment of defaulted loans. Moreover, the reforms could not strengthen the empire sufficiently to prevent territorial losses accompanying Balkan nationalist secessions and renewed Russo-Turkish war during the "eastern crisis" of 1875–78. The effective independence of Bulgaria, Romania, Montenegro, and Serbia cost Istanbul its most populous, richest, and most fertile provinces, moved the empire's center of gravity decisively away from its previous location in the southeastern Balkan provinces and into Anatolia, and changed the demographic profile of the empire away from its previous slight Christian majority. In consequence of these developments, many Ottoman leaders and the earliest Turkish nationalists began looking more and more to the east, retrospectively reformulating those regions as the seedbed of the Muslim-Turkish people, and the center for its future renewal. At the same time, the Ottoman loss to Russia of further territories (with substantial Armenian populations) in the Caucasus reminded Istanbul that Anatolia was far from secure. The presence of a mass of Armenians on the Ottoman side of the new border was increasingly problematic for the state because of Russian overtures to the Armenians, which in turn had precipitated the "internationalization" of the Armenian question at the 1878 Congress of Berlin. By stipulating reforms protecting the Armenians in eastern Anatolia (as a British device to forestall further Russian intervention in the area), the Treaty of Berlin simply enhanced Ottoman suspicion about Armenian loyalty to the state. Each of these great shifts provided part of the context for the official endorsement by the last significant sultan, Abdülhamid II, of the doctrine of pan-Islamism, which sought to galvanize the empire's Muslims into a more coherent religious political community and would have negative ramifications for Muslim-Christian and particularly Muslim-Armenian relations.[10]

Armenian grievances at Berlin centered on the many arbitrary cruelties suffered in the rural areas at the hands of local officials and particularly Kurds. Worse was yet to come, for from the Crimean war onwards, but at an accelerated rate from 1875–78, the Anatolian population was being swollen with Muslim refugees from the Balkans and from the Caucasus, the latter including particularly Circassians and "Crimean Tatars" who had been subject to considerable brutality at Russian hands during their expulsion.[11] Such refugees—*muhajirs*—provided an aggressive anti-Christian constituency from which the government made appointments to local administrative posts and that went on to form part of the gendarmerie that would figure prominently in killing Armenians during World War I.[12] They also included some of the foremost proponents of the irredentist ideology of pan-Turkism that was later adopted by some CUP leaders,[13] many of whom themselves originated in peripheral or lost Ottoman lands.[14] While the high death rate amongst these immigrants illustrates that they were not well provided for by the Ottoman government, there was a knock-on effect for many Armenians whose lands were allocated to *muhajirs* and also appropriated in little more than legalized theft by sedentarizing Kurds.[15]

In Turkish ethnic memory, the suffering and dislocation experienced by *muhajirs* in 1875–78 is known as the *sökümü*, the great "unweaving."[16] Not only did most of the refugees head for Anatolia; for many it was their second eviction, if they had originally fled from the Caucasus to the Balkans. The government offered incentives for many of these to settle along rail routes,[17] and the policy of settling *muhajirs* in Armenian areas appears to have become systematic, putting more pressure on the land and increasing Armenian insecurity of life and property.[18] Between 1870 and 1910, some 100,000 Armenians emigrated, and between 1890 and 1910 at least 741,000 hectares of Armenian property were illegally taken or confiscated by representatives of the state.[19]

As it transpired, the failure of the great powers to enforce the reform clauses of the treaty of Berlin, and the worsening plight of provincial Armenians thereafter, led in turn to the formation of Armenian nationalist parties from the 1880s onwards. These parties owed much to radical Russian influences, including the use of terrorism, and they pursued their interpretation of Ottoman Armenian interest without undue concern for the security of ordinary Armenians. Their actions, and the ill-conceived and inconsistent intervention of the European powers, provided the immediate catalysts (though not, of course, the underlying causes and certainly not the justification) for a series of massacres of, in total, at least 80,000 Anatolian Armenians in 1894–96, permitted and tacitly encouraged by Abdülhamid as a sort of combined means of ethnic warning, "punishment," and "cull" of a community that he feared might follow the path of Balkan separatism.[20]

Abdülhamid's pan-Islamism was more properly a pan-Sunniism, an appeal to the majority Muslim grouping of the empire. Groups such as the heterodox Alevis, many of whom were ethnically Kurdish, were subject to an orchestrated attempt to assimilate them into the Sunni community.[21] Pan-Islamism spelt a rapprochement with the majority of the Kurds by way of reversing centrifugal tendencies among them, while Abdülhamid simultaneously promoted a large number of Kurdish leaders in order to prevent intra-Kurdish unity.[22]

One method of establishing central influence over Kurdish tribes was the establishment in 1891 of a number of Kurdish cavalry regiments bearing the sultan's name—the Hamidiye. These rapidly grew in manpower to more than thirty thousand in a region in which regular troops and police were sparse, which was an ominous sign for Armenians who had already suffered so many unlawful attacks. European observers agreed that the Hamidiye had been established in response to the development over the previous years of Armenian revolutionary and self-defense groups, and combating the parties and their actions would certainly form one of the areas of Hamidiye activity.[23] They were gifted grazing areas along the Russian border, underlining their nature as a sort of border militia designed to create an Islamic barrier between Russia and the Armenians.[24] They also took advantage of their effective immunity from prosecution and local control—it is in any case debatable how much central control could realistically have been brought to bear—to plunder and terrorize widely in Armenian villages.

Strategic *muhajir* settlement and the creation of the Hamidiye bear comparison with Russian colonial practices. The use of Cossack and Russian settlers in the Caucasus, Siberia, and central Asia was a standard method of consolidating control of conquered regions. Armed colonists provided willing militias to expel native populations and thereby incorporate their lands into greater Russia.[25] In eastern Anatolia, Ottoman policies were aimed at consolidating Ottoman control over lands whose future disposition had been threatened in the eastern crisis. At the same time, over and above the death toll of the 1894–96 massacres, the Armenian population was declining relative to its own prior growth trajectory as a result of flight, generally to Russian territory.

Despite the hopes temporarily raised by the rise to power of the constitutionalist CUP, the factors that had contributed to this demographic restructuring of eastern Anatolia were not addressed, for at no time was the CUP prepared to alienate its majority Muslim constituency by reforms favoring Christians.[26] Further, almost immediately upon the CUP's assumption of power in 1908, the empire received another major blow as Bosnia-Herzegovina was formally annexed by Austria-Hungary, and Bulgaria declared its full independence. The shock gave impetus to drastic reform measures, including the idea of a new "national economy"—a centrally controlled and independent system, based partly on the ideas of the German theorist Friedrich List.[27] For the CUP, this increasingly implied the removal of Christian economic influence. The year 1909 saw abortive moves to impose trade boycotts against the Ottoman Greeks, as boycotts had been used in reprisal against Austria-Hungary. The rationale was to increase the number of Muslim artisans and merchants at the expense of the Christians.[28]

The need to develop a Turkish middle class was made explicit in CUP policy in 1914, at the climax of a period of de facto economic warfare between some Ottoman Greeks and Muslims. This was concluded in favor of the Muslims in 1913/14 and 1915/16 by a combination of population engineering and economic appropriation, using boycotts, murders, terrorization, and then deportation of parts of the western Anatolian Greek population, which was cast as increasingly suspect by its ties to mainland Greece.[29] At least a million Greeks left western Anatolia with a substantial death toll.[30] Thus, a "new Turkish bourgeoisie" was to be brought into being, complementing the move towards an Islamicized peasantry in the eastern provinces and offering the two vital elements that would hopefully contribute to a modernizing, Muslim-Turkic national economy in Anatolia.[31]

Armenians too might have been awakened to the limited prospects for reform under the CUP when in the spring of 1909 between 10,000 and 20,000 Armenians were murdered in Cilicia against the backdrop of an antiregime insurgency by some liberals and some Islamists.[32] Beyond the massacres, a law on political associations now prohibited the formation of organizations with non-Turkish national aims.[33] Measures of enforced cultural Turkification, revolving particularly around language use, were introduced during 1910 and 1911, and Turkic and other Muslim refugees were encouraged to settle around transport lines, as their predecessors had been after the "eastern crisis."[34]

The Balkan wars of 1912/13 signified the death of any vestige of CUP pluralism.[35] A further coup in January 1913 in the context of Ottoman defeat reestablished the CUP, which had earlier been voted out of office, and made it into an effective one-party dictatorship under the triumvirate of Talât as minister of the interior, Enver as minister of defense, and Cemal as minister of the marine and governor of Syria, guided behind the scenes by the party central committee. This was a triumph for those whom Mehmet Şükrü Hanioğlu identifies as the more ruthless "activists" in the ranks.[36] The wars and their associated ethnic cleansing, with Muslims the primary victims, accelerated the influx of refugees into Anatolia as the remaining key Rumelian lands of Macedonia and even Muslim Albania were torn away. The loss of the latter province—a Muslim one—further encouraged the development of a specifically Turkish ethnic nationalism in the CUP as opposed to a more religiously based Muslim identity. And as the conflicts cast Muslim-Christian relations into the sharpest of relief, with widespread Christian draft evasion and Ottoman Bulgarian and Greek soldiers swapping sides to fight alongside their ethnoreligious brethren, deportations were sanctioned of small groups of Christians from the vicinity of military communications routes.[37] Finally, the end of the wars saw the resurrected vision of externally enforced reform in the eastern Anatolian provinces. Another reform plan was promoted with self-interested Russian support by the Catholicos of All Armenians, whose Holy See was at Etchmiadzin in Russian Armenia.[38] The final package, agreed in February 1914, provided for two European inspectors to oversee reforms including prohibition of further encroachments by *muhajirs* and greater security of Armenian life and property.

The subsequent Ottoman entry into World War I bespeaks firstly a do-or-die effort to eradicate external influences in the empire. On entry, the reform plan was annulled alongside the Public Debt Administration and the "capitulations," those extraterritorial privileges enjoyed by citizens of the great powers living in Turkey and sometimes passed on to individual Ottoman Christians in the service of the powers.[39] Secondly, war provided an opportunity to reinvigorate the empire by the incorporation of Turkic populations to the north and east at the expense of Russia, thus further accentuating the radical change that had already occurred in its ethnic profile. The Armenians were dangerously exposed on all counts.

War and Genocide

By the time of the Balkan wars, the CUP had become obsessed with the twin issues of the ethnic makeup of the empire and potential ethnic-based threats to its integrity. Talât's Ministry of the Interior conducted extensive demographic and ethnological surveys of the population, mapping out Anatolia, Cilicia and the Arab provinces according to the makeup of the population. The titles of the two governmental bodies most closely involved in the ordering and administration of the major Armenian deportations during World War I—that is, those deportations beyond the ones ordered by the military from inside or within the vicinity of actual war zones—reflect the twofold concern with ethnicity and "ethnic security." Both were in the Interior Ministry. One was the Directorate for the Settlement of Tribes and Immigrants (*Iskânı Aşâyir ve Muhacirin Müdiriyyeti;* IAMM), which had been established in 1913 to marshal the settlement of *muhajirs* fleeing the Balkan wars and the new Balkan states. The other was the Directorate for General Security (*Emniyyeti Umumiyye Müdiriyyeti*). Together, as well as overseeing the deportation of the Armenians, these organizations would be involved during the First World War in the movement around the empire of Circassians; Albanian, Bosnian, and Georgian Muslims; Kurds; "Gypsies"; Arabs; and Jews, for various purposes ranging from punishment to assimilation to—in the Circassian case, for example—protection of transport links against attacks by some Arab groups.[40]

Even within this larger matrix of population movement the Armenian fate was clearly different, because of both the extent and murderous intent of the deportations. The destruction of the smaller Christian "Assyrian" population is the closest parallel to the murder of the Armenians, though the latter was somewhat more systematic. Much of the killing, rape, and dispossession of Armenian deportees, parenthetically, was the preserve of the irregular, paramilitary *Teşkilatı Mahsusa*, or Special Organization. Army units were also involved, as were some Kurdish tribes and *muhajirs* who murdered and plundered on their own initiative once the Armenians had effectively been declared fair game by the CUP's decision to deport them. The epithet *genocide* is applicable to the Armenian case specifically because of the combination of the two elements of wholesale deportation, or "ethnic cleansing," and purposive physical destruction by systematic massacre.

Whatever had gone before in terms of the radicalization of the CUP and the exacerbation of the Armenian question, however, the Armenian genocide was not predestined by August 1914, the time of the secret CUP military pact with Germany. That month was marked by the beginning of ruthless war requisitioning, in which the Ottoman Christian communities were disproportionately targeted, in an indirect continuation of the earlier practice of economic dispossession.[41] Direct killing on a large scale by Ottoman forces only developed sporadically in the provinces bordering Russia and Persia from November 1914, and men were initially the prime target.

The great deportations from eastern Anatolia began only in June 1915 (and from Cilicia in April–May), from western Anatolia in late summer, and from Thrace in the autumn. In between, in addition to the aforementioned acts of killing, vicious and repeated arms searches were conducted, Armenian soldiers serving in the Ottoman army were disarmed and assigned to labor battalions from February 1915, and, particularly from late April, Armenian political and communal leaders were incarcerated.

In general terms, genocide developed out of an Ottoman policy of ethnic "reprisal"—meaning deliberately collective "punitive" measures—informed partly by experience and knowledge of links between Armenian nationalists and Entente sponsors, but, more importantly, by simple ethnic stereotypes of Armenian disloyalty. Anti-Armenian policy intensified with every Entente military advance or success. This was the pattern following initial small-scale Russian incursions into Ottoman territory in November, the famous Ottoman defeat at the turn of 1914/15 at the battle of Sarikamish in the Caucasus, the initial Anglo-French assaults on the outer forts of the Dardanelles in March 1915, the near simultaneous Russian successes in Persia, the Gallipoli landings immediately prior to 24 April 1915 (the day commemorated as the beginning of the genocide),[42] and, finally, the Russian advance into the Anatolian interior throughout May and June—indeed, all of the watersheds identified in the genocide historiography.[43]

The broader immediate context was a war in the region that was cast along ethnic lines, with each major combatant trying to stimulate anti-imperial insurgency on ethnic-nationalist grounds in their opponents' territory. Jihad, or holy war, was announced by the Ottoman government (with German encouragement) to arouse the Muslim subjects of Britain and Russia, which was conceptually comparable, for instance, to British sponsorship of the Arab revolt or German appeals to Ukrainian or Georgian nationalists. Russia, too, tried to instrumentalize Armenians, and some Kurds, in Ottoman territory. In September 1914, Armenian volunteer battalions were formed to fight alongside the Russian army.[44] These were composed of men from the territories taken by Russia in 1878, or who had fled to the Caucasus more recently from Ottoman rule. Similar forces were set up on the Persian border. They could provide intelligence and advice on the terrain and, as has been ignored in the literature, a stimulus to their Ottoman Armenian brethren to take up arms.[45]

Yet the element of state "security," however subjectively conceived, clearly should not be singled out in the obliteration of the Armenians. The Russian attempt to incite some Ottoman Armenians against their rulers was not particularly successful, as we shall see shortly; more importantly, no other people suffered as extensively as did the Armenians during the war, so further factors must be taken into account. "Security" only assumed its significance because of the linkage in CUP thought with the drive for ethnic homogeneity and national territorial integrity in the Ottoman "heartlands," and for political and economic independence for Turks as an ethnic-national group. From the CUP's perspective the prospect of *some* Ottoman Armenians joining with advancing Entente forces could be forestalled if the Armenian population as a whole could be removed, but if they could be permanently removed this would render redundant any future British or Russian rationales for intervention or even a protectorate. It would then leave Muslims in sole occupation of the land (and of Armenian property).

As already hinted, the Russian sponsoring of Armenian insurgency bore only limited results, and certainly did not stimulate the "civil war" often invoked in Turkish nationalist literature. For the most part, such eruptions as there were initially in the interior—for example, Armenian assaults on the gendarmerie or the cutting of telegraph cables from late 1914—were comparatively minor, suggesting a lack both of enthusiasm among the wider Armenian population and of large-scale organization.[46] Probably the most discernible phenomenon would have been the widespread desertions.[47] Importantly, the jihad was largely unsuccessful too. Ottoman and German agitation did bear a little fruit in parts of Azerbaijan[48] and other locations in the Caucasus around the turn of 1914/15, where advancing Ottoman forces were joined by several thousand Muslims.[49] The brutal Russian response included expelling suspect Muslim communities over the Ottoman border, and doubtless also massacre.[50] This in itself further exacerbated the ethnic situation inside the Ottoman Empire. From at least early April, for example, the Muslim refugees from Russian reprisals were settled in Armenian dwellings in the Mush district of Bitlis,[51] mirroring a pattern of tit-for-tat expulsions that had occurred in November 1914 on the Persian-Ottoman border.[52]

For their part, the weight and viciousness of Ottoman responses to incidents sparked off internally or by the approach of Russian forces with Armenian volunteer units can be inferred from official references to the dispatch of "militia and tribal forces" or "punishment units."[53] Ottoman forces had no compunction about rationalizing the severest methods to "completely crush" any incidents lest they assume more than "merely regional proportions,"[54] including taking "rigorous measures against the families of deserters and traitors," and punishing "severely peasants who support these outlaws."[55] This policy formed the background to the most contested episode in the prehistory of the Armenian genocide, the large-scale Armenian rising from mid-April in a quarter of the key strategic city of Van, an episode concluded successfully in mid-May with the retreat of the Ottoman besiegers in the face of a Russian advance, but also with the murder of many Muslims as well as Armenians.

At the end of March the governor of Van, Cevdet, accompanied by several thousand soldiers and Kurdish and Circassian irregulars, returned from unsuccessful campaigning in Persia, where Armenian volunteer battalions had been instrumental in his defeat. On 17 April, he responded to a minor occurrence in the Shatakh district of the province by dispatching his forces to annihilate the Armenians there, but the ill-disciplined irregular forces opted instead to attack closer Armenian settlements,[56] and the ensuing chain of massacres drove the Van Armenians to their resistance.[57] Cevdet was attempting to isolate the city from the outlying districts of the province,[58] and crush any sign of trouble with extreme, indiscriminate, vengeful violence. Thus to ascribe the hatching of a plan to either side is thus wrong: in a terrible circularity, the Van Armenians, trying to maintain an escape route towards Persia, were driven to action by the very ethnic "reprisal" measures Cevdet used to crush the putative Armenian threat. The simultaneous development of the Van rising and of the wider war would have even more extreme ramifications.

On 2 May, the Ottoman military leadership requested of the Interior Ministry that Armenians in "rebellious" areas in Van either be forced over the Russian border or dispersed in Anatolia. As well as addressing the problem of insurgency, it was argued, this would provide revenge for the earlier Russian treatment of Muslims, while vacating homes for those refugees.[59] A week later, the Interior Ministry issued corresponding orders for Van and parts of neighboring Erzurum and Bitlis provinces in the face of the Russian advance, thus extending the policy de facto begun in Mush in April.[60] Indeed, from the beginning of May, as Russian troops crossed the border[61] and Cevdet's forces retreated, Armenians were evicted from the rural border regions of the province of Erzurum, whereupon their villages were indeed resettled with Muslims.[62]

During the conclusive days of the Van conflict—16–18 May—the Interior Ministry instructed the governor of Erzurum to deport those Armenians thus far evicted within the province southward to southern Mosul, Der Zor, and Urfa provinces.[63] On 23 May, as the Russians and some Armenian volunteers pushed on from Van towards Bitlis, this decision was extended throughout the provinces in closest proximity to Russian forces: Erzurum, Van, and Bitlis.[64] This was an absolutely critical period in the extension of anti-Armenian measures, as this author has argued elsewhere.[65] On 26 May, the Supreme Military Command contacted the Interior Ministry, referring to an oral decision for the deportation southwards of Armenian from the eastern provinces, and other areas of high Armenian concentration, to the regions south of Diyarbakır province.[66] (In precise contrast to settlement policies involving *muhajirs* in previous years, the deportees were not supposed to settle within twenty-five miles of the railway lines.) Simultaneously, Talât sought the enactment of legislation legitimating deportations. A "provisional law" was promulgated on 27 May, permitting the military to order deportations according to "military necessity."[67] At the beginning of July, as the deportations expanded, so did the reception area for the deportees. It now incorporated the provinces of modern-day Syria, with the stipulation that the Armenians not exceed 10 percent of the overall population, thus the easier to be marginalized and/or assimilated.[68] (This practice of proportionality was also enforced by the IAMM in the settlement of Bosnian and Albanian Muslims in Anatolia.[69])

For many, deportation was a sentence of death by euphemism, meaning expulsion to desert lands where no provision had been or would be made for the deportees. Worse still, however, the defenseless deportees from the eastern Anatolian provinces continued to be met with the massacres, rape, plunder, and theft at the hands of the Ottoman military and irregulars that had by that point become common practice in the ethnic "reprisal" policy. Barely 20 percent would reach their desert destinations. The same is not true of the deportees from the western Anatolian provinces and Cilicia, who passed relatively unmolested to their desert fates of disease and deprivation.[70] A further round of massacres in 1916 accounted for many of the refugees scratching out an existence in the famine-blighted and disease-ridden concentration centers of Syria and Mesopotamia.[71]

The small pockets of Armenians not subjected to deportation, beyond the relatively large numbers left untouched in Istanbul, were somewhat disproportionately composed of Catholics and Protestants, separate from the majority Armenian Apostolic group. In any case, these isolated and traumatized communities were insufficient to form a genuine national presence. Others exempted from the deportations included some who had converted to Islam, though the authorities deported many deemed to have converted only out of necessity.[72] The converted numbered perhaps between perhaps 5 and 10 percent of the Ottoman Armenians, the majority of whom were children and women of childbearing age brought into Muslim households, and who in the process had their names changed by way of absorption into the new national community.[73] The women and many of the girls were to be subject to forced marriage and/or sexual slavery in a horrific form of colonization of the female body.

From June onwards, the Ministry of the Interior directed the auctioning of Armenian property to local Muslims[74] and also the donation of formerly Armenian housing to accommodate Muslims whose own houses had been destroyed.[75] In some places, as we have seen, the Armenian population was replaced en bloc with *muhajirs*.[76] Elsewhere, Armenian land and property was simply taken over by the local Muslim population and/or elites. Overall, of course, the most important aspect of the Armenian genocide for the Ottoman state was the creation of a demographic fait accompli in Anatolia and Cilicia.

Notes

1. Aspects of this chapter are explored in greater detail in Donald Bloxham, "The Armenian Genocide of 1915–16: Cumulative Radicalisation and the Development of a Destruction Policy," *Past and Present*, no. 181 (2003): 141–91; and idem *The Great Game of Genocide: Imperialism, Nationalism and the Destruction of the Ottoman Armenians* (Oxford, 2005).
2. An expression used by a contemporary observer. See Harry Stuermer, *Two War Years in Constantinople* (London, 1917), 164.
3. Hans-Lukas Kieser, *Der verpasste Friede. Mission, Ethnie und Staat in den Ostprovinzen der Türkei 1839–1938* (Zurich, 2000), 41–44, 99–100.
4. Andrew G. Gould, "Lords or Bandits? The Derebeys of Cilicia," *International Journal of Middle East Studies* 7 (1976): 489–90.
5. Mehmet Şükrü Hanioğlu, *Preparation for a Revolution: The Young Turks, 1902–1908* (Oxford, 2001); Erik Jan Zürcher, "Young Turks, Ottoman Muslims and Turkish Nationalists," in *Ottoman Past and Today's Turkey*, ed. Kemal Karpat (Leiden, 2000), 151.
6. Reşat Kasaba, *The Ottoman Empire and the World Economy: The Nineteenth Century* (Albany, NY, 1988), chaps. 3 and 4; Kieser, *Der verpasste Friede*, part 1.
7. On this process of change see Kieser, *Der verpasste Friede*; Stephan Astourian, "Genocidal Process: Reflections on the Armeno-Turkish Polarization," in *The Armenian Genocide: History, Politics, Ethics*, ed. Richard G. Hovannisian (Basingstoke, UK, 1992); idem, "Testing World Systems Theory, Cilicia (1830s–1890s): Armenian-Turkish Polarization and the Ideology of Modern Ottoman Historiography" (Ph.D. diss., UCLA, 1996), esp. 582–601; Kemal H. Karpat, "The Transformation of the Ottoman State, 1789–1908," *International Journal of Middle East Studies* 3 (1972): 243–81.
8. Tessa Hofmann and Gerayer Koutcharian, "The History of Armenian-Kurdish Relations in the Ottoman Empire," *Armenian Review* 39, no. 4 (1986): 10.
9. Susan Olzak, *The Dynamics of Ethnic Competition and Conflict* (Stanford, CA, 1992), 3.
10. On Turkish rhetoric on Anatolia, see David Kushner, *The Rise of Turkish Nationalism, 1876–1908* (London, 1977), chap. 5. On Hamidian policies towards eastern Anatolia, Bayram Kodaman, *Şark Meselesi Işığı Altında Sultan II Abdülhamid'in Doğu Anadolu Politikası* (Istanbul, 1983), esp. 161–81 on the Armenian question.
11. Izzet Aydemir, *Muhaceretteki Çerkes Aydinları* (Ankara, 1991), 43, 152–54.
12. Max von Oppenheim, "Die revolutionierung des Islamischen Gebietes unserer Feinde," folio 36. Yale University Library, Ernst Jäckh papers, file 47.
13. Jacob M. Landau, *Pan-Turkism in Turkey* (London, 1981), 34–35.
14. Wolfdieter Bihl, *Die Kaukasus-Politik der Mittelmächte*, 2 vols. (Vienna, 1975), 1: 143–44; for the background of a key individuals, see Tevfik Çavdar, *Talât Paşa: Bir Örgüt Ustasının Yaşam Öyküsü* (Ankara, 1984), 15–21
15. Astourian, "Genocidal Process," 61–62, 66–67.
16. Karpat, "Transformation," 272.

17. Donald Quataert, *The Ottoman Empire, 1700–1922* (Cambridge, 2000), 115–17.
18. Astourian, "Genocidal Process," 61–62, 66–67.
19. Raymond H. Kévorkian and Paul B. Paboudjian, *Les Arméniens dans l'Empire ottoman à la veille du génocide* (Paris, 1992), 44–45.
20. Kieser, *Der verpasste Friede*, 244–47. Jelle Verheij, "Die armenischen Massaker von 1894–1896," in *Die armenische Frage und die Schweiz*, ed. Hans-Lukas Kieser (Zurich, 1999), is the most sophisticated analysis of these massacres.
21. Kieser, *Der verpasste Friede*, 168–69.
22. Hofmann and Koutcharian, "Armenian-Kurdish Relations," 15–17.
23. Verheij, "Die armenischen Massaker," 80–81.
24. Fadil Rasoul, *Großmachtpolitik und Freiheitskampf: Kurdistan und die sowjetische Nahost-Politik* (Vienna, 1988), 71.
25. Marie Bennigsen Broxup, "Russia and the North Caucasus," in *The North Caucasus Barrier: The Russian Advance Towards the Muslim World*, ed. Abdurahman Avtorkhanov et al. (London, 1992), 5.
26. Astourian, "Genocidal Process," 61–62, 66–67.
27. Feroz Ahmad, "Vanguard of a Nascent Bourgeoisie," in *Social and Economic History of Turkey (1071–1920)*, ed. Osman Okyar and Halil Inalcik (Ankara, 1980), 332–33; Zafer Toprak, *Türkey'de 'Milli Iktisat' (1908–1918)* (Ankara, 1982).
28. Toprak, *Türkey'de 'Milli Iktisat'*; Donald Quataert, *Social Disintegration and Popular Resistance in the Ottoman Empire, 1881–1908* (New York, 1983), 144–45; Hanioğlu, *Preparation*, 69.
29. Taner Akçam, *Armenien und der Völkermord* (Hamburg, 1996), 41–42; Quataert, *Social Disintegration*, 144–45.
30. Akçam, *Armenien*, 43; Zürcher, "Young Turks," 171.
31. Johannes Lepsius, *Der Todesgang des armenischen Volkes* (Potsdam, 1919), xiv–xv.
32. On the pattern of massacre, see Raymond Kevorkian, ed., *La Cilicie (1909–1921)*, special issue of *Revue d'Histoire Arménienne Contemporaine* 3 (1999); Astourian, "Genocidal Process," 63–66.
33. Roderic H Davison, *Turkey: A Short History* (Huntingdon, UK, 1998), 128–29; David McDowall, *A Modern History of the Kurds* (London, 1996), 90–91.
34. Akçam, *Armenien*, 37; Vahakn N. Dadrian, *Warrant for Genocide* (New Brunswick, NJ, 1999), chap. 9; Landau, *Pan-Turkism*, 47–48.
35. Davison, *Turkey*, 132.
36. Zürcher, "Young Turks," 156–57.
37. Fikret Adanir, "Non-Muslims in the Ottoman Army and the Ottoman Defeat in the Balkan War of 1912/13," unpublished paper.
38. Roderic H. Davison, "The Armenian Crisis (1912–1914)," *American Historical Review* 53 (1948): 481–505.
39. Cemal Pasha, *Memories of a Turkish Statesman* (London, 1922), 276.
40. Fuat Dündar, *Ittihat ve Terakki'nin Müslümanları Iskân Politikası (1913–1918)* (Istanbul, 2001), esp. 92–173, for all groups except Jews, for whom see instead Isaiah Friedman, *Germany, Turkey and Zionism, 1897–1918* (Oxford, 1977).
41. Artem Ohandjanian, *Der verschwiegene Völkermord* (Cologne, 1989), 81–82.
42. For the Ottoman view, *Affaires Armeniennes: Les 'Telegrammes' de Talât Pacha: Fait historique ou fiction?*, ed. Sinasi Orel and Süreyya Yuca (Paris, 1983), (hereafter, "*Les 'Telegrammes' de Talât Pacha*") 111–12, Talât to provincial leaderships, 24 April 1915.
43. See Bloxham, "The Armenian Genocide of 1915–16," for further discussion of these issues.

44. G. Korganoff, *La Participation des Arméniens à la Guerre Mondiale sur le Front du Caucase* (Paris, 1927), 20–21; Hratch Dasnabedian, *History of the Armenian Revolutionary Federation Dashnaktsutiun* (Milan, 1989), 117.
45. Boghos Nubar, leader of the Armenian National Delegation established in 1912 to forward the cause of reforms on the international scene, recalled that the battalions were to provide an example for their Ottoman "compatriots . . . in a common action to acquire the rights of autonomy." See Nubar to Kouchakian, 26 October, archives of the Délégation nationale arménienne, Correspondence Arménie 1915, volume I, Bibliothèque Nubar, Paris.
46. Pera, 9 March 1915, in Türkei 183/36, Auswärtiges Amt-Politisches Archiv, Bonn (Political Archives of the German Foreign Office, hereafter, "AAPA").
47. Both Christians and Muslims deserted en masse, given the terrible conditions of service in the Ottoman army and, for the Armenians, doubtless, because of the unpopularity of the war. An indeterminate number of Armenians deserted to join the Russian forces or simply to Russian territory.
48. Gabriele Yonan, *Ein vergessener Holocaust: Die Vernichtung der christlichen Assyrer in der Türkei* (Göttingen, 1989), 111–12; Manuel Sarkisyanz, *A Modern History of Transcaucasian Armenia* (Nagpur, India, 1975), 192; Vahakn N. Dadrian, "The Role of the Special Organisation in the Armenian Genocide during the First World War," in *Minorities in Wartime*, ed. Panikos Panayi (Oxford, 1993), 50–82.
49. Gotthard Jäschke, *Der Turanismus der Jungtürken* (Leipzig, 1941), 14.
50. John Buchan, *A History of the Great War*, I (London, 1921), 173–74, euphemistically on Russian ferocity. Maurice Larcher, *La guerre turque dans la guerre Mondiale* (Paris, 1925), 393 on expulsions. Türkiye Cumhuriyeti, ed., *Osmanlı Belgelerinde Ermeniler (1915–1920)* (Ankara, 1995), (hereafter, "*Osmanlı Belgeler*"), 21 on atrocities against Muslims in Kars and Ardahan.
51. Türkiye Cumhuriyeti, ed., *Osmanlı Belgeler*, 28–29, Interior Ministry to Van and Bitlis, 9 May 1915. For earlier Muslim resettlements, Pera, 15 April 1915, in Türkei 183/36, AAPA.
52. McDowall, *Modern History*, 102–6; Yonan Shahbaz, *The Rage of Islam* (Philadelphia, 1918), 57–61; *The Treatment of Armenians in the Ottoman Empire, 1915–1916. Uncensored Edition*, ed. James Bryce and Arnold Toynbee (Princeton, NJ, 2000), docs. 27, 32, 34.
53. *Documents on Ottoman Armenians*, 3 vols., ed. Prime Ministry Directorate General of Press and Information (first volume simply entitled "*Documents*"), (Ankara, 1982–86), (hereafter, "*Documents*") vol. 1, nos. 11, 17, 21; vol. 2, no. 1903; vol. 3, no. 2001.
54. *Documents*, vol. 3, no. 2001; vol. 1, no. 18 (part 4).
55. *Les 'Telegrammes' de Talât Pacha*, 105, Third Army Command, 11 October 1914.
56. Kieser, *Der verpasste Friede*, 449.
57. Anahide Ter Minassian, "Van 1915," in *Armenian Van/Vaspurakan*, ed. Richard G. Hovannisian (Costa Mesa, CA, 2000), 223–24.
58. Ter Minassian, "Van," 223.
59. Cited in Taner Timur, *Türkler ve Ermeniler* (Ankara, 2000), 33.
60. Türkiye Cumhuriyeti, ed., *Osmanlı Belgeler*, 28–29, Interior Ministry to Van and Bitlis, 9 May 1915. For earlier Muslim resettlements, Pera, 15 April 1915, in Türkei 183/36, AAPA.
61. Larcher, *La guerre turque*, 394; Joseph Pomiankowski, *Der Zusammenbruch des ottomanischen Reiches* (Vienna, 1928), 147; H. Pasdermadjian, *Histoire de l'Armenie* (Paris, 1971), 458.

62. Türkiye Cumhuriyeti, ed., *Osmanlı Belgeler*, 54, Interior Ministry to Erzurum, 27 June 1915.
63. Ibid., 32–33, Interior Ministry to Erzurum, 18 May 1915.
64. Ibid., 33–34, Interior Ministry to Erzurum, Van and Bitlis, 23 May 1915.
65. Bloxham, "The Armenian Genocide of 1915–16."
66. *Les 'Telegrammes' de Talât Pacha*, 115, Talât to Mosul, Urfa, and Der Zor, 23 May 1915.
67. Türkiye Cumhuriyeti, ed., *Osmanlı Belgeler*, 30–32, 30 May 1915; Vahakn N. Dadrian, *The History of the Armenian Genocide* (Providence, RI, 1995), 221.
68. Türkiye Cumhuriyeti, ed., *Osmanlı Belgeler*, 62, Interior Ministry to provincial leaderships, 5 July 1915.
69. Dündar, *Ittihat ve Terakki*, 126–27.
70. Raymond H. Kévorkian, "Le sort des déportés arméniens ottomans dans les camps de concentration de Syrie-Mésopotamie," in *L'Extermination des déportés arméniens ottomans dans les camps de concentration de Syrie-Mesopotamie (1915–1916)*, ed. Raymond H. Kévorkian (Paris, 1998), 11–12, 16; Hilmar Kaiser, *At the Crossroads of Der Zor* (Princeton, NJ, 2001), 10.
71. Taner Akçam, "Rethinking the Ottoman Archival Material: Debunking Existing Myths/General Overview of the Ottoman Documents," unpublished paper.
72. Türkiye Cumhuriyeti, ed., *Osmanlı Belgeler*, 58, Interior Ministry to provincial leaderships, 1 July 1915.
73. Ara Sarafian, "The Absorption of Armenian Women and Children into Muslim Households as a Structural Component of the Armenian Genocide," in *In God's Name: Genocide and Religion in the Twentieth Century*, ed. Omer Bartov and Phyllis Mack (New York, 2001), 209–21.
74. *Les 'Telegrammes' de Talât Pacha*, 117, Interior Ministry to Erzurum, 9 June 1915; more generally on the theft and appropriation of Armenian property, "Confiscation des biens des réfugiés arméniens par le Gouvernement turc" (Paris, 1929).
75. Türkiye Cumhuriyeti, ed., *Osmanlı Belgeler*, 118, Interior Ministry to Urfa, 27 October 1915.
76. In the case of Zeytun and other settlements in Cilicia, Bloxham, "The Armenian Genocide of 1915–16," 174; for other examples of installation of *muhajirs* in formerly Christian settlements, Dündar, *Ittihat ve Terakki*, 156–58.

– *Chapter 15* –

GENOCIDAL IMPULSES AND FANTASIES IN IMPERIAL RUSSIA

Robert Geraci

Raphael Lemkin, who coined the word genocide, defined it as follows in his 1944 book *Axis Rule in Occupied Europe*: "Generally speaking, genocide does not necessarily mean the immediate destruction of a nation, except when accomplished by mass killing of all the members of the nation. It is intended rather to signify a coordinated plan of different actions aimed at destruction of the essential foundations of the life of national groups, with the aim of annihilating the groups themselves." Component actions of such a plan, Lemkin wrote, would be those that pursue "the disintegration of the political and social institutions, of culture, language, national feelings, religion, and the economic existence of national groups, and the destruction of personal security, liberty, health, dignity, and the lives of individuals belonging to such groups."[1] This formulation is spacious and inclusive in at least three notable ways, belying the frequently held notion that the label is only for the most dramatic crimes resembling the Nazi Holocaust: 1) genocide includes not just the physical murder of peoples, but also their cultural and/or moral destruction as well; 2) such destruction may be undertaken or aimed for immediately, or it can be caused to occur gradually over a long period; and 3) genocide is defined by intentions, aims, and objectives as much as (if not more than) by results.

Such a definition undermines the common notion that any investigation of possible genocide in Russian history need be concerned only with the Soviet era. In the tsarist era as well, the list of hardships imposed by the Russian Empire on its constituent peoples contains much that would seem to fall into one or more of Lemkin's categories. It is hardly surprising that the geopolitical, military, and economic challenges of forging and settling an empire that at its apogee would cover one-sixth of the Earth's land would lead to willful actions toward the physical destruction of some peoples and communities. Such actions included outright massacres (usually in border regions being annexed); the serfdom (slavery) of the vast majority of the population, and the low status and extreme poverty of peasants even after its abolition; Slavic encroachment and settlement on the lands of pastoral/nomadic peoples (such as the Bashkirs and Kazakhs); residence, property, and occupational restrictions on certain minority peoples (most consistently on Jews) with repercussions for subsistence; failure to discourage (or even active encouragement of) violent pogroms against minorities; and large-scale, forced relocations from border regions (primarily during wars).

Likewise, the challenge of managing such an enormous multiethnic empire (particularly one connected by land, with no clear distinction between "metropolis" and "colony") all but inevitably gave rise to the pursuit of cultural homogeneity at the expense of minority identities, in the interest of both governability and insurance against national separatism that would threaten the empire's existence. Actions threatening possible cultural or moral destruction of peoples included prohibitions or restrictions on the use of minority languages in schools (most notably Polish) or in the press (the Turkic languages); denial of the very existence of the Ukrainian language; sustained efforts at converting religious minorities to Russian Orthodoxy (by force, by material incentive, or by persuasion); the complete outlawing of some religions (Old Belief, sectarianism, Uniatism); bureaucratic control over all legal minority religions, and the weakening of their institutions through confiscation of property (in the case of the Catholic and Armenian churches); disenfranchisement of most non-Christian peoples in imperial and local administration, and ascription of lower status to them; and the punishment of expressions of minority identity as political crimes.

Close scrutiny of almost any one of these policies or events, however, quickly reveals difficulties in applying Lemkin's definition. Can we always discern when an action truly aims for the "destruction" or "disintegration" of a people or culture, one might ask, as opposed to simply its weakening or (more neutrally) its adaptation to new circumstances? Do we need actual proof of such destructive intentions, or are they self-evident in certain actions and policies?[2] What exactly constitutes a "coordinated plan"—of how many different actions must it consist, and how well must it be organized (are poorly coordinated regimes like tsarist Russia incapable of genocide)? In the absence of documentation, can the genocidal "coordination" of actions be inferred from circumstantial evidence? Are there not single actions (besides actual murder) that seem sufficiently destructive in themselves to constitute genocide? What about actions in which destruction is not exactly intended but is more the result of negligence?

In light of these difficulties (which are not particular to the Russian case), I propose that the study of genocidal impulses and fantasies can be a useful bridge between intentionalist and structuralist approaches to genocide, and a way of rescuing the historical study of genocide from its preoccupation with labeling and moving it further toward meaningful analysis.[3] As expressions of genocidal imagination and desire that might never be acted upon, genocidal impulses or fantasies are certainly not tantamount to crimes. Often, in the psyches of those who express them, they never even rise to the status of intentions. We may think of them, rather, as motivations without immediate intent—in other words, "potential intentions." Usually they are not acted upon directly—often for lack of opportunity (they are usually the expressions of individuals, whereas genocidal actions are normally the work of large groups or institutions, if not a state)—but they can help us to explain why people allow genocidal events to happen, either by "structural" processes or by the actions of *other* people.

This chapter is devoted to describing impulses of this sort that I have come across in my study of tsarist Russia as a multiethnic empire, and some patterns that might be discerned in them. It focuses on the *conceptualization* of genocide more than its realization, by examining three different kinds of expressions: proposals for genocidal or protogenocidal actions that were not acted upon by those who proposed them, the figurative (even subconscious) genocide enacted by linguistic practices, and fantasies about the disappearance of minority peoples through cultural change. Insofar as the Russian state did engage in behavior that can be described as genocidal (by either structuralist or intentionalist definitions, or both), these expressions can be seen as part of an overall landscape or climate contributing to the possibility of genocide during the era of imperialism.

The Imperial Origins of Ethnic Cleansing

One of the most common methods of genocide is the forced physical displacement of peoples. Often designed to rid one ethnically defined community of another's presence, such relocations threaten fundamentally the moral, cultural, and physical well-being of the group displaced. "Even when forced deportation is not genocidal in its intent," writes Norman Naimark, "it is often genocidal in its effects."[4] People are killed when they resist leaving their homes and homelands; those in charge of transporting them in large numbers to a new destination typically have little concern for their welfare. Hunger, disease, cold, and inadequate sanitation may take a significant number of lives. Rare is the case of forced relocation *not* undertaken in a manner that makes mass death inevitable, and even such a case is likely to be extremely destructive in cultural and moral terms.

Considerable attention has been paid to deportations and reprisals against ethnically defined population groups in Soviet history, especially under Stalin.[5] Similar actions committed previously by the tsarist/imperial state, however, have received much less attention. Scholars such as Peter Gatrell and Eric Lohr have recently published pathbreaking works on the behavior of the tsarist state, army, and society during the First World War, when major population groups in the western war zone such as Poles, Jews, and Germans, branded as "unreliable," were subject to violence, expropriation of property, and forced dispersal into Russia's interior.[6] In spite of a developing consensus that World War I was the context in which such systematic population manipulations became habitual in Russia, it appears that new ways of manipulating subject populations were at least experimented with several decades earlier in the imperial borderlands. The most prominent example is the large-scale expulsion and massacre of native mountain peoples from the northwest Caucasus in the early 1860s, which I will discuss shortly.

To be sure, Russian imperial expansion had already for centuries brought violence and death to border-dwelling peoples during conquests, in particular, in the areas of eastward and southward (i.e., Asian) conquest, beginning in 1552 with Ivan the Terrible's "Gathering of the Lands of the Golden Horde"—the conquest of the successor khanates to the Mongol-Tatar empire that had held Russia in dependence from the thirteenth to the fifteenth centuries. By overthrowing the Muslim khanates of Kazan, Astrakhan, and Siberia in a short period of time and annexing their lands and peoples directly to Muscovy, Russia sought the settling of old scores as well as initiating a Christianizing and civilizing mission in Eurasia. These campaigns, in which hundreds and thousands of potential resisters were slaughtered, subjugated, co-opted, and converted by Russia's armies, rulers, and clergy, paved the way for Russia to stretch eastward through the Volga region, the Urals, and Siberia, and then (with the belated overthrow of the khanate of Crimea in 1783) southward to the Caspian and Black Seas, a process that occupied Russia in a long series of wars with the Persian and Ottoman Empires in the eighteenth and nineteenth centuries.[7]

By the nineteenth century, Russia had become the fulcrum of what Michael Geyer and Charles Bright have called a "Eurasian zone of violence, with its focal points in Afghanistan, Transcaucasia, and the Caucasus, and extending westward into the Near East and into Southeastern Europe, where it became the flash point for major European wars."[8] The protracted nineteenth-century war in the Caucasus, which by most accounts began in 1801 and ended only in 1864, was waged essentially to secure the territorial gains Russia had made in Transcaucasia at the expense of the Persian and Ottoman Empires between the beginning of Georgia's protectorate status (1783) and the Treaties of Turkmanchai (1828) and Adrianople (1829). The more the Russians had invested in winning each piece of Transcaucasian territory, the more fiercely they fought to establish control of the mountainous north that connected those conquests to Russia proper; yet the closer their annexations came to the mountain peoples, the more the latter fought off conquest. The Russians' chief challenge was the murid movement: the union of Muslim tribes of the eastern Caucasus (Chechens, Avars, Lezghins, Dagestanis, and others) that in 1829 declared a holy war (*ghazavat*) of resistance against Russia. The movement's most famous leader was the charismatic sheikh Shamil, who took control in 1834 and persisted for twenty-five years until his capture by the Russians in 1859.[9]

The peoples on the northwestern, Black Sea side of the Caucasus (the Circassians, Kabardins, Adyge, Nogais, and others[10]) were somewhat less organized in their resistance to Russia, but beginning in the 1830s, they began to receive support and encouragement from covert operatives of Great Britain, Russia's rival in the "Great Game" for dominance in this Eurasian zone.[11] This situation continued into the Crimean War (1853–55), in which Britain and France allied with the Ottomans to put a check on Russian expansion. Even worse for Russia, during the war Shamil made overtures to the British and French to join forces in their mutual efforts against Russia. Although the Europeans declined the offer, and the Russian army did eventually capture Shamil after the war, the naval defeat at Sevastopol and the ensuing Treaty of Paris (1856) were a disaster for Russia, freezing its longtime ambitions to control the Black Sea and shattering the prestige it had enjoyed in Europe since its role in Napoleon's defeat.

Though historians often refer to post-1855 Russia as a lame duck (in this volume, Mark Levene calls it a "retreating empire"), in fact the empire—though humiliated—continued to advance and grow. Immediately following Shamil's capture and the pacification of his followers, the tsarist army went into the northwestern Caucasus—whose peoples had not joined the murid movement and did not cease their resistance in 1859—to clear the entire area of the mountain tribes, lest these tribes continue to be used by the British to destabilize Russia's presence, and to replace them with Cossacks and other Russian settlers who would be reliably loyal. The brutal last stage of Russia's long war of Caucasian conquest was played out in an accelerated frenzy, an expression of Russia's vengeance not only against the mountain peoples but also, in a sense, against Europe for its efforts to clip Russia's wings in Asia and its condescending dismissal of Russia's claim to be a European power. The expulsion plan, which had been discussed even before 1859, was carried out between 1860 and 1864.[12]

The northwest Caucasus was cleared of virtually its entire indigenous population: historians estimate that during this period as many as 700,000 Circassians, Nogais, Kabardinians, Adygeis, and others emigrated to the Ottoman Empire either "voluntarily" (largely from fear and with strong Russian encouragement) or were forced out, and that anywhere from about half a million to 1.5 million more were slaughtered or perished in the process—including women, children, and entire communities who had never resisted the Russian advance.[13]

As soon as the Circassians were gone, the Russian army continued eastward into the borderland with Persia to begin conquering Turkestan (Central Asia), a stepwise process that took the next twenty years. By many accounts, the bloodiest stage in the conquest of Central Asia was the struggle against the Turkmen nomads east of the Caspian Sea from 1879 to 1881. After a humiliating failed attempt to capture the fortress of Gök Tepe in 1879, the Russians returned under General Mikhail Skobelev on 12 January 1881 and, even after seizing the fortress, proceeded to massacre some 14,000 people, of whom most were either civilians who had been inside the fortress, or soldiers fleeing in surrender.[14] It is perhaps significant that the two-year Gök Tepe episode began on the heels of another diplomatic debacle, the Treaty of Berlin (1878) that, in the view of Geyer and Bright, continued the trajectory begun by Paris (1856) of western European intrusion into what Russia saw as its private affairs along its borders with Asia.[15] There may have been a pattern, then, in the role of diplomatic humiliation by Europe in triggering the most dramatic atrocities against border peoples during these years.

An alternative explanation has been advanced by Peter Holquist, who has argued that the Circassian campaign—and therefore the state brutality against many Russian and Soviet subjects in the twentieth century that it foreshadowed—was the result of the introduction of a modern scientific worldview into the Russian military establishment. According to Holquist, expulsions and exterminations reflected the tsarist army's interest in the strategic importance of certain populations in the empire (which he calls "population politics"), and further asserts that such acts could first be conceived only with the development of a particular way of knowing and thinking about the empire—"population statistics"—in which the military played a leading role. "The idea of extracting 'elements' of the population first became conceptually and practically possible," Holquist writes, "only with the rising concern throughout the nineteenth century for a realm termed 'the social' and with the emergence of technologies for measuring and acting upon this realm. The rise of military statistics, in Russia and throughout Europe, was a critical link in this more general process."[16] By the 1860s, the new scientific mindset had achieved maturity and become operable. "While the Russian empire had earlier practiced 'demographic warfare,'" Holquist asserts, "contemporaries saw [the Circassian] campaign's breadth and systematic nature as marking a new departure. These measures aimed, one participant wrote, to subjugate the Caucasus 'to such a finality of result as had never previously been seen.'"[17] The clarity of intention and precision and thoroughness of execution that Holquist documents in this episode are the same features one would stress in labeling the event an instance of genocide according to Lemkin's definition (though Holquist avoids using the word, referring instead to "extermination").

It makes good sense to stress the role of military institutions in the history of physical genocide (whether one calls it that or not). Virtually by definition, forced population transfers and the like can only be carried out by powerful bodies such as police brigades or armies. War situations can be fertile grounds for ethnic cleansing because they divert the attention of possible objectors, including international public opinion; war may also provide states and politicians with pretexts of state security and reasons for the suspension of normal laws protecting subjects or citizens, and it mobilizes men to commit military violence that may blend seamlessly into extra-military genocidal violence.[18] And indeed, the tsarist military establishment, having played an important role in the long history of state coercion of ethnic minorities, became more accomplished and systematic at this over time, as shown in the works by Lohr and Gatrell on World War I.

But Holquist's explanation does not satisfactorily account for the *conceptual* emergence of genocidal impulses. It overestimates the role of purely military institutions and concerns, by seeming to assume that the imperial-social vision the army was implementing had been incubated entirely within the army itself. And although some kind of modernist account of the emergence of ethnic cleansing is appealing, the one Holquist offers places too much emphasis on statistics as the modern form of knowledge presumably responsible for that vision, without providing any credible evidence of its role in official views of minority populations and decisions to expel or exterminate them. Weaknesses in Holquist's account are laid bare by two sources from the first half of the nineteenth century, which I discuss below. Both advocated genocidal projects in the Russian borderlands well before Holquist's account says such ideas were possible, and outside of the conditions he says were determinative.

Two Apostles of Genocidal Expulsion

Pavel I. Pestel was one of the key participants in the constitutional, anti-autocratic rebellion of December 1825, leading that movement's so-called

Southern Society. In the early 1820s, envisioning a revolution or coup d'état in Russia, Pestel composed a blueprint for Russia's future titled *Russian Justice* (Russkaia pravda), with the subtitle *Instructions to the Temporary (or Provisional) Supreme Administration*. The book of some two hundred pages circulated underground among sympathizers who later participated in the rebellion and became known to history as the "Decembrists." It is well agreed that Pestel's vision was less moderate than that of the Northern Society of the movement. Whereas the Northern Society in St. Petersburg entertained the possibility of a constitutional monarchy (which, because of bungled timing, by the date of the actual uprising on 14 December, turned out to be all the conspirators could reasonably hope to achieve), Pestel was a committed republican who is often described as Jacobin in his embrace of ruthless coercion, and socialist in his vision for nationalizing and redistributing half of the land in Russia.

The program Pestel put forth in *Russian Justice* contained a section on Russia's national minorities that advocated a heavy-handed and potentially genocidal treatment of Russia's Jews, and eerily presaged the genocidal expulsion campaign against the peoples of the northwest Caucasus forty years later. Although Pestel was a military officer (as were most of the Decembrists), his ideas reflected motives not strictly military in nature, and predated by at least fifteen years the era Holquist identifies with the rise of military statistics. The first and second chapters of Pestel's book present, respectively, a geographical overview of the Russian Empire and a survey of its peoples, each followed by administrative recommendations for the new government. A recent Pestel biographer has aptly described this section of *Russian Justice* as amounting to "in effect the first serious consideration and proposed solution of the nationalities problem in modern Russian history."[19] The second, virtually devoid of any statistical information on population groups, expresses the overall insistence that "all the tribes [*plemena*] must be melded [*slity*] into one people [*narod*]."[20] While this ambition was inspired by Enlightenment rationalism as applied to state-building, and seems to express a highly inclusive, civic understanding of the political nation, it turns out that Pestel envisioned this process of melding as not wholly inclusive and not entirely peaceful, just as the transition to his prescribed political-social system would require violent action against the existing autocracy. In his section on the Caucasus, he argues that the warlike nature of some of the region's peoples has left them poor, unenlightened, and "half-savage"—and therefore unfit to exist within the Russian Empire.

> The position of this region next to Persia and Asia Minor could provide Russia with a very significant capability toward establishing the most vigorous and

> profitable commercial relations with southern Asia and therefore toward the enrichment of the state. But all this is completely lost only because the Caucasian peoples are such dangerous and volatile neighbors, such unreliable and useless allies. Taking into account that all efforts have already proved irrefutably the impossibility of inclining these peoples to tranquility by gentle and friendly means, the Supreme Administration resolves: 1) to conquer decisively all the peoples living, and all the lands lying, to the north of Russia's borders with Persia and Turkey, including the maritime part now belonging to Turkey; 2) to divide all these Caucasian peoples into two groups: peaceful [*mirnye*] and unruly [*buinye*]; to leave the former in their homes, and give them Russian [*rossiiskoe*] governance and living conditions [*ustroistvo*], and to relocate the latter by force into the interior of Russia, breaking them down into small numbers among all the Russian districts [*volosti*]; and 3) to start Russian settlements in the Caucasian land, and to distribute to these Russian settlers all the lands taken from the previous unruly inhabitants, and thus to obliterate in the Caucasus every last sign of its previous (i.e., present) inhabitants and to turn the region into a peaceful and comfortable Russian territory [*oblast'*]. All the details of this undertaking are left to the disposal of the Temporary Supreme Administration.[21]

Because it is not clear whether "gentle and friendly means" were really applied toward these peoples *before* they perceived that the Russians were attempting to conquer them and their territory (the war was underway by the time of Pestel's writing), one wonders whether Pestel has identified the "nature" of the Caucasian peoples or simply their stance toward the prospect of subjecthood within Russia.

There are two striking features of the passage. First is Pestel's determination to erase the memory of these people's presence from the Caucasus—every bit as thoroughly as what was achieved in the 1860s and in twentieth-century ethnic cleansings. The chief difference from the Circassian events is that Pestel wanted to banish Caucasians into the interior of Russia rather than out of the empire, but it is clear enough that once "interned" into central Russia in small groups the Caucasian peoples would be expected (or even forced) to assimilate completely. It is not just their presence in one place that needs to be erased, Pestel implies, but their very existence as a group. In his plan, these identities and cultures (though he might not have used the word "culture" to describe peoples he considered half savage) are, simply put, slated for destruction. Since Pestel prescribes destroying the group's identity without actually killing the individuals that constitute it, his impulse is for cultural genocide. But we might also predict that if enacted, the plan might also result in enough deaths to constitute physical genocide.

The second striking fact here is that although Pestel considered some of the Caucasian peoples to be a military threat to Russia, and Russia was already at war with them, his advocacy of ethnic cleansing of "unreliable" peoples in the above passage does not stem primarily from military-security concerns, but rather from his perception that belligerent peoples were hampering the enrichment of the Russian state through commerce. (Many of the Decembrists were similarly concerned with improving Russia's economic productivity and efficiency, and economic arguments played a role in their insistence on the abolition of serfdom—a position that motivated their uprising no less than their desire to change Russia's political system.) This idea contradicts the notion that the desire to rid Russia of certain population elements arose primarily within the institutions and concerns of the military.

About twenty years after Pestel's tract, a different economic argument for the forced relocation of peoples appears in a report to Russia's Ministry of Finance by economic advisor Iulii A. Gagemeister (or Hagemeister, who eventually, in the late 1850s, became director of the ministry's chancellery). Gagemeister was sent to Transcaucasia at least twice, in 1835 and 1844, to survey the regional economy and its role in international trade, and to suggest reforms. Some sections of the reports he submitted after the latter trip are of an ethnographic nature, describing communities in the region and their economic activities and roles—using little or no quantitative data. One report, "The Bases of Popular Wealth in Transcaucasia," described in some detail the economist's concern for eradicating nomadism from the region:

> Nomadism [*kochevanie*] has become so habitual for the Muslim residents of hot places, it is so characteristic for the climate and the mountainous location of the Transcaucasus, and finally is so tempting for everyone that the possibility of settling [*obratit' k osedlosti*] all the residents is hardly foreseeable. In any case, however, order and provisioning [*blagoustroistvo*] are impossible because the time of relocation is always a time of raids and theft, especially in border locations, where it is impossible to track down the perpetrators.
>
> In any case, when hot weather sets in the migration of herds from valleys to mountaintops is unavoidable. But it is more desirable that they be accompanied only by the shepherds. To achieve this it is necessary to give agricultural land to the nomadic residents, so that they don't have to live only by means of their herds, and in time to completely force out [*vytesnit'*] from Russian territory those such as the Kurds who are incapable of settlement [*osedlost'*]. In a short time their place will be occupied by other, more useful, subjects [*polezneishie poddannye*].[22]

Michael Khodarkovsky has argued that Russian antipathy to nomadism was a long tradition: the transformation of frontier steppe lands into imperial borderlands between 1500 and 1800 was essentially the transition from nomadic pastureland to agriculturally or industrially useful land. The reasons were both military and economic:

> While application of Russia's growing military, economic, and political power successfully reduced the threat of raids in the eighteenth century, the need to transform pasturelands into agricultural colonies and industrial enterprises kept the government on a confrontational course with its nomadic neighbors. Whether intent on eliminating nomadic raids or settling and cultivating new lands, the government's experiences dictated the same conclusion: the nomadic way of life eventually had to disappear.[23]

Though Khodarkovsky's account suggests that this project was largely completed in the eighteenth century, Russia of course acquired new nomadic populations in later conquests. The Enlightenment now offered quasi-scientific reasons for stigmatizing nonsedentary, nonagricultural populations: nomads were seen as fundamentally uncivilized and therefore having little importance or value, and were expected eventually either to conform to the march of human progress by settling (adherents of Enlightenment thought generally considered them capable of it) or at least to get out of its way. Given the context of Western challenges to Russian expansion and concerns for both military security and economic development, it is not difficult to see how Russian administrators in the nineteenth century might have grown impatient and frustrated with the slow process of settling nomads and became eager simply to expel them.[24]

Besides a concern for economic development of the empire, negative attitudes toward non-Christian religions also played a role in both Gagemeister's and Pestel's proposals for population expulsions. In his report on Transcaucasia, Gagemeister mentions that "there are no Christian nomads at all, although [Christians] are mixed together with the Muslims. . . . Consequently, although nomadism is appropriate to the climate, it is not a necessity for the geographic position of the Transcaucasian region. In all places where the location has allowed, the Tatars have preserved the habits of their ancestors who came from Central Asia. But they have chosen primarily pastureland, leaving the arable land to the indigenous residents."[25] Gagemeister mentions the Christian population ostensibly to prove that settled agriculture is possible in Transcaucasia and will lead to greater productivity there, but since his statements also imply that Muslims are below Christians on the ladder of civilization (in addition to describing them as immigrants to the region, not the original inhabitants), the information seems intended to assure his superiors in St. Petersburg and Tiflis (the administrative headquarters for Caucasia and Transcaucasia) that it is only Muslims whose expulsion from the empire he is prescribing. Russian authorities could therefore be pleased that the expulsion of Kurds and "Tatars," leading to their replacement by Christians, was both economically and culturally justified and would produce both economic and cultural benefits for the empire. So it appears that in advocating expulsion, Gagemeister was even less motivated by military objectives than Pestel was. He was not even writing about the war zone, but the region to its south, and the Muslims in question were not the same communities whose dispersal Pestel had advocated earlier—though Gagemeister well may have been inspired by a common idea that Muslims did not belong in the Caucasus.

In *Russian Justice*, Pestel's advice to the projected revolutionary government for handling Russia's Jewish population—whom few if any would have portrayed as a military threat in the 1820s—also reads like a recipe for genocide. And as in Gagemeister's thinking, economics and religion loom large here as motivations. Like many imperial officials of this era, Pestel felt that the empire's Jews were a menace to Russia's social and political order because of their hostility to Christians (stemming from their solidarity and the belief of their superiority) and their control of commerce in certain regions, to the detriment of possible competitors and to peasant debtors. "The former government gave them many special rights and advantages that intensified the evil they do," Pestel claimed, with the result that "the Jews constitute, so to speak, their own special, completely separate state within a state, and also now enjoy more rights in Russia than the Christians themselves."[26]

Pestel outlines two possible solutions for correcting the position of Jews to make them less harmful to Russia. The first is a vaguely described gathering of Jewish elites, exhorting them to devise measures to "stop the evil described above and replace it with an order that would correspond in full measure to the general fundamental rules that must serve as the basis of the political edifice of the Russian state. If Russia does not chase out [*vygoniat'*] the Jews," Pestel concludes, "then all the more so must they not put themselves in a hostile attitude toward Christians. The Russian government, although offering every individual protection and mercy, is however obliged first of all to prevent anyone from opposing the state order or the private and social well-being."

The second possible solution, as warned, was to chase the Jews out—or as Pestel then attempts to put it more mildly, "to assist the Jews in the establishment of a special, separate state in some part of Asia Minor." To carry out the plan "it would be necessary to designate an assembly point [*sbornyi punkt*] for the Jewish people and to give them some troops for reinforcement." With more than two million Jews assembled from Russia and Poland, Pestel imagined:

> it will not be hard for such a number of people to overcome all the obstacles that the Turks could pose to them, and traversing all of European Turkey, to go into the Asian part and there, occupying sufficient space and lands, to set up a special Jewish state. But since this gigantic undertaking demands special circumstances and truly ingenious enterprise, it cannot be presented to the Temporary

> Supreme Administration as a specific responsibility. It is mentioned here only to give a hint [*namek*] as to everything that could be done.[27]

In light of twentieth-century history, the potential for serious, widespread violence is not hard to discern. And though this vision may *seem* to have been a century ahead of its time (particularly if one accepts Holquist's claims), in reality—as Pestel himself saw—only the likelihood of its realization was.

The context of both Pestel's and Gagemeister's proposals was broadly military: Pestel was planning a military coup, and Gagemeister was concerned with the development of a region still under military rule. Yet the motives expressed in these texts were not military, but economic and cultural, reflecting not only the kinds of programmatic, utopian social planning that states began to do during the Enlightenment, and without which there might never be a need for anything as categorical and deliberate as a population transfer, but longstanding prejudices against certain religious groups as well.[28] Both Pestel's and Gagemeister's arguments for expulsion, moreover, appear utterly unconnected to quantitative-statistical data or reasoning. It seems more likely that, against Holquist's assertions, ethnic stereotypes already existing in the prestatistical era were perfectly sufficient for inspiring protogenocidal ambitions, and that to the extent that statistical knowledge may have been used to support these stereotypes and these ambitions, it provided nothing more than a veneer of scientific authority. One only has to look at ethnographic or travel literature of the late eighteenth century to know that associating the attribution of qualitative traits to certain population "elements" with the use of statistics is inaccurate; the description of ethnic subpopulations as representing qualitative types was a product of earlier qualitative, not later quantitative, research.[29] In fact, many generalizations about the nature of both Muslims and Jews, and their alienness from Europe, had medieval origins. Even without any serious attempt at scientific-statistical corroboration, these prejudices might, in the context of new ambitions on the part of the Russian state, be invoked as grounds for the exclusion or destruction of these groups. Gagemeister's statement on the Kurds suggests that he thought both factors—the state's ambition for improved economic development, and a group's perceived cultural inferiority or nonbelonging—had to be present to justify removal.

Ethnic Identity Theft: Figurative Genocide

Though specific reform blueprints and policy recommendations such as those of Pestel and Gagemeister certainly reflected genocidal attitudes, such mentalities could also reside in and be conveyed by much vaguer forms of expression. One example is a linguistic convention in imperial Russia—especially in military culture—that I call "ethnic identity theft." Once again the context is the imperial borderlands during the early nineteenth century.

Russian dictionaries, both of the nineteenth century and today, define the word *kavkazets* (plural: *kavkaztsy*) as "Caucasian" or "native of the Caucasus." This is exactly what would be expected from the word's etymology—the name of a region, *Kavkaz* (Caucasus), plus the personalizing suffix *-ets*. The term often includes peoples of the Transcaucasus region as well as the mountain region itself. Yet in historical literature on Russia, one rarely encounters the word used in this way, for in the nineteenth century it became well established as identifying something quite different: a certain subset of the *Russian* military personnel who served the tsarist state in its long campaign to pacify the region.

Literary and memoir sources from the Caucasus—and the historians following them—have often made an issue of Russian officers' adoption of behavior associated with that of the Caucasus mountain peoples (usually known as *gortsy*)—the very populations who were waging guerilla war against the Russian Empire for much of the nineteenth century. As is well known by readers of Mikhail Lermontov's novel *A Hero of Our Time* (1840), many of these officers, most of whom had learned to romanticize the *gortsy* from popular literary works beginning with Aleksandr Pushkin's poem "The Prisoner of the Caucasus" (1822), deliberately adopted the clothing, military accoutrements, and putative value system (freedom, honor, heroism) of the Chechens, Circassians, and other native peoples, as well as (perhaps less consciously) types of behavior that had given the *gortsy* a reputation for savagery such as raiding and kidnapping.[30] According to Dana Sherry's recent study of Russian *kavkaztsy*, a "seeming confusion of identities highlights what may be the most important consequence of service in the Caucasus for the Russian officer—the slow but steady exchange of typical Russian customs and modes of behavior for those attributed to the population indigenous to the Caucasus."[31] But such sources and analyses have almost never commented explicitly on the irony of the Russian officers' appropriation of the label referring to the Caucasus region's inhabitants.

In 1841, Lermontov, whose fiction helped to popularize the phenomenon of officers "gone native" in the Caucasus, wrote a short essay titled simply "*Kavkazets*."[32] A reader previously unfamiliar with the phenomenon might find the essay jarring for the aggressive way in which it seizes that label for the Russians. It begins like an ethnographic study: "First of all, what exactly is a Caucasian, and what kinds of Caucasians are there?"

In reply, Lermontov states: "A Caucasian is a half-Russian, half-Asian being; his inclination for oriental customs takes the upper hand, but he is ashamed of this in the presence of strangers, that is of visitors from Russia." One might still think the author is speaking of Caucasus natives (undergoing Russification), but Lermontov soon dispels this by noting that a *kavkazets* is "usually thirty to forty-five years old," and "if not a staff-captain, then probably a major." In a series of phrases referring to "*real* Caucasians," Lermontov continues to tease the reader into thinking that he will be discussing Caucasian native peoples, but it soon becomes clear that all the distinctions being made are among different Russians who might (and presumably did) call themselves *kavkaztsy*. Thus we learn that "civil *kavkaztsy* are rare; for the most part they are an awkward imitation, and if you meet among them a real one, then only among the regimental physicians."[33]

Of course, even the "real" *kavkaztsy* were Russian poseurs merely imitating (awkwardly or not) native Caucasian men. Lermontov's *kavkazets* is emphatically not native to the Caucasus; he is most likely from Petersburg, where in the Cadet Corps he surreptitiously read Pushkin's "Prisoner of the Caucasus," daydreamed of adventures in the south, and began to sport articles of Circassian clothing. Upon arriving in the south, the "Caucasian" immediately purchases a dagger, with which he never parts, and "as is proper, falls in love with a Cossack girl [*kazachka*]." Here Lermontov finally introduces a sardonic tone by interjecting: "Beautiful! How poetic!" It is important that Lermontov reveal his skeptical attitude toward the officers here, for he now tells us that the typical *kavkazets* begins to dream of subjugating the native peoples, or *gortsy*. "He thinks about capturing some twenty mountaineers with his own hands; he dreams of frightful battles, rivers of blood, and generals' epaulettes."

Such an officer eventually becomes a "real *kavkazets*" by Lermontov's definition only after he befriends some "peaceful Circassian" and from him develops a love for simple, primitive life over the urban, urbane existence he had known in Russia; knowledge of regional customs, folklore, and genealogy; a superficial ability to converse in "Tatar" (although the Caucasian languages are unrelated to Tatar, Russians used this word generically for languages of the region); and a complete Circassian outfit and set of weapons.[34] According to Lermontov, "His passion for all things Circassian reaches an unbelievable degree" and even squelches his interest in women. He becomes a self-appointed authority on "oriental" customs and on the virtues and faults of the various tribes, becomes so attached to his burka that he rarely takes it off, and constantly sings the pleasures of service in the Caucasus. When the *kavkazets* retires from service, according to Lermontov, he takes his identity with him back to Russia proper ("even in

Voronezh province he doesn't remove his dagger or his saber"), where he lives out his days telling exaggerated tales about feats performed during his service. The retired officer's role as popularizer of the war raises the possibility (unaddressed by Lermontov) that the cult of the *kavkaztsy* was as important to civilians outside of the Caucasus as to the officers themselves, and that the civilian public may actually have coined the name.

On one level, the use of a preexisting term for the indigenous mountain peoples to designate the ethnic Russian military personnel fighting against them might be regarded as an innocent coincidence resulting from the structure of the Russian language. In both usages, groups of people are simply named after locations with which they are identified. Officers in the Caucasus war sought to distinguish themselves from their "ordinary" counterparts serving elsewhere in the empire because presumably their burden was greater. For many, identification with the mountain *peoples* too may also have been deliberate, as a way of thumbing their noses at Russian officialdom and authority by expressing admiration for and even solidarity with the enemy, the supposedly inferior object of Russia's civilizing mission—though Sherry's recent collective portrait emphasizes the extraordinary dedication of these officers to the war effort.[35] The same connotations may have been intended even if the term was first coined by civilians.

Whoever was originally responsible for calling the officers *kavkaztsy*, and for whatever conscious purpose, the cumulative and perhaps subconscious *effect* of this usage was pernicious. While the tsarist officers claimed some perceived attributes of "the other," they used a label normally associated with the other but now actually *excluding* all of the true, original members of that group—in effect, stealing the identity. Appropriation of the label made an enormous adventure (even a game) of officers' experience in the war while diverting attention—the public's as well as the officers' own—from the plight of the mountain communities who were killed in large numbers for daring to defend their freedom against the Russians. How else could these men, who claimed to appreciate the mountain peoples and their culture, have abetted their generals in clearing out virtually entire Caucasian populations from the 1830s to the 1860s?[36] Most importantly, the figure of speech implied that Russians belonged in the region whereas many of the peoples living there already did not. By simply declaiming what Pestel and Gagemeister had earlier argued, it both prepared the agents of destruction for their task and conditioned the broader public to accept the Caucasian natives' decimation. Thus the *kavkazets* cult functioned psychologically for Russians as a figurative form of genocide and a mechanism for enabling the actual genocide undertaken militarily.

Identity-formation around the theaters of war and the names of peoples living there persisted through the remainder of the nineteenth century. After the *kavkaztsy*, Russian officers in later wars were known as "*bolgary*" (in the Russo-Turkish War of 1877/78, which was in part a war to liberate Bulgaria from the Ottomans) and "*turkestantsy*" (in the conquest of Turkestan in the 1880s).[37] At first glance, the Bulgarian label seems different because the Bulgarians were not Russia's enemies in the Russo-Turkish War, but it may be key to understanding the other cases. In the Caucasian and Turkestan cases, Russians' use of "enemy" names was appealing because those peoples were being vanquished not so much for offense toward Russia as for resisting Russia's advance, which supposedly was intended to civilize and even liberate them. This linguistic tradition, then, held only in situations where the "others" were traditionally considered inferior (as either "little brother" Slavs or non-Europeans)—so inferior that their existence mattered only insofar as it showed the Russians' higher status.[38] But soldiers' taking of these peoples' names actually helped make the destruction of these peoples palatable. The appearance of new "Caucasians" and "Turkestanis" from Russia helped Russians mentally to begin clearing the regions of these native presences so that the Russians themselves could move in. The trope reemerged, of course, during the 1980s as the Soviet Union attempted to establish control over Afghanistan. Soviet soldiers serving there, and afterwards veterans of the war, became widely known as "*afgantsy*"—"the Afghans."

One final, telling example from the tsarist era appears in a nonmilitary context. Russian students in the Anti-Islam Division of the Kazan Theological Academy in the 1860s were known as "the Tatars" because they were developing knowledge of Tatar culture through linguistic and religious studies. Those who began studies in that division but discontinued became known as "apostates" (*otpadshie*), a wry reference to some of the Tatars they were being trained to convert back to Christianity.[39] By giving themselves the ethnonym of their subjects, the students expressed a certain affinity with the Tatar people, but in effect diverted attention from the very negative effects their future work as missionaries would have on Tatar culture. Indeed, they would be striving to dismantle that culture (since they ultimately envisioned turning the Tatars into Russians through conversion)—but by calling themselves "Tatars" they removed the real Tatars from the story, focused all attention on themselves, and thus masked the destructive aims of their future work.[40]

Great-Power Ventriloquism and Genocide by Assimilation

I have been arguing that the idea of genocide in imperial Russia was far from being limited to the military sphere and its technologies and strategies;

imperial discourses circulating more broadly in Russian officialdom and society also gave play to genocidal fantasies. The genocidal overtones of ethnic identity theft were largely unconscious or subconscious, but closely related ways of thinking were considerably more explicit and more visible. One of these, which I call "great-power ventriloquism," was articulated most famously by Fyodor Dostoyevsky in 1880. Another was assimilatory discourses that envisaged the disappearance of colonized peoples.

The occasion for Dostoyevsky's imperial apologetics was the unveiling of a monument to Pushkin in Moscow (arguably the formal beginning of the Pushkin cult that still flourishes in Russia today).[41] In his speech lionizing the poet, Dostoyevsky claimed that Pushkin's chief virtue was his ability to speak not only for Russians but for the rest of the world: "Pushkin alone, of all the poets of the world, possesses the quality of embodying himself fully within another nationality."[42] Though Dostoyevsky was most concerned with Pushkin's capturing of European mentalities,[43] he also mentioned Pushkin's success in taking on an Eastern voice in one of his poems. Decades earlier, the writer Nikolai Gogol had called attention to Pushkin's ability to capture foreign ethnonational mentalities,[44] but Dostoyevsky took a new turn by attributing this element of Pushkin's genius to the Russian nation as a whole. "The capacity to respond to the entire world and to assume completely the form of the genius of other nations in a reincarnation that is almost total," he said, "is an altogether Russian one, a national one, and Pushkin merely shares it with our entire People."[45] And he made it clear that he saw this capacity as a moral virtue and expression of good will. "Indeed," Dostoyevsky proclaimed, "the mission of the Russian is unquestionably pan-European and universal. To become a real Russian, to become completely Russian, perhaps, means just (in the final analysis—please bear that in mind) to become a brother to all people, a *panhuman*, if you like."[46]

Russians' love for all humanity, according to Dostoyevsky, prevented them from "wall[ing] ourselves off from other nationalities behind our own nationality so that we alone may acquire everything while regarding other nationalities as merely lemons to be squeezed dry (and there really are peoples in Europe who feel this way!)"[47] By invoking European greed and selfishness in opposition to Russian generosity and benevolence, however, Dostoyevsky turned the claim of Russians' empathy and cultural understanding into a narrow-minded ideology similar to the claims of Slavic spiritual-cultural superiority made by racialist neo-Slavophiles. In effect, the virtues claimed for Russians were cancelled out by the arrogance of claiming that *only* the Russian people possessed such traits.

That such an altruistic ideology could have an aggressively self-serving underside became even clearer six months later in one of Dostoyevsky's last pieces of writing. In January 1881, when the Russian army captured the stronghold of Gök Tepe in Turkestan, Dostoyevsky celebrated the event in his newspaper column. He took issue with Russia's "Westernizers" who saw no purpose in the conquest of Central Asia, fearing it would work against Russia's acceptance as a European power. "This shame that Europe will consider us Asians has been hanging over us for almost two centuries now," wrote Dostoyevsky. "This mistaken shame of ours, this mistaken view of ourselves as exclusively Europeans and not Asians . . . has cost us dearly"[48] A newfound engagement with Asia would prove more fruitful:

> [W]hen we turn to Asia, with our new view of her, something of the same sort may happen to us as happened to Europe when America was discovered. For, in truth, Asia for us is that same America which we still have not discovered. With our push toward Asia we will have a renewed upsurge of spirit and strength. . . . In Europe we were hangers-on and slaves, while in Asia we shall be the masters. In Europe we were Tatars, while in Asia we are the Europeans. Our mission, our civilizing mission in Asia will encourage our spirit and draw us on. . . . Every place the "Russ" settles in Asia will at once become Russian land. A new Russia will be created that will also restore and resurrect the old one in time and will clearly show her the path to follow.[49]

Considering this essay together with the Pushkin speech, one is reminded that Russian statesmen often used Russians' putative empathy with other peoples as a justification for imperialism, particularly in the Asian parts of the empire where Russia could play a "civilizing" role. This view described the Russian Empire as a justifiable philanthropic undertaking in contrast to the other European empires that were supposedly illegitimate, coercive, and exploitative. The capacity for ventriloquism, then, was especially important in Asia, where it turned out that the ulterior motive was not the appreciation of non-Russian cultures but a mission to spread *Russian* culture.[50]

This ideology of empire went hand in hand with reigning views of cultural assimilation, which—as the study of Russia's history developed in the nineteenth century—intellectuals were beginning to view as an ubiquitous and central aspect of its past. The motif was present in the work of most of the major historians, but was especially pronounced for those with a more populist bent. Russia's expansion as a land-bound empire, offering ease of Slavic peasant settlement in annexed regions, was frequently cited as a key difference between Russian colonialism and its Western European counterparts. In the eyes of many Russian elites, the resulting possibilities for cultural cross-borrowing made the Russian Empire a more natural, humane, and therefore justifiable undertaking compared with the overseas empires of Britain and France, Russia's key rivals in the nineteenth century. Thus, the

Russian "empire" could be represented as something more benign than an empire: the organic development of a Russian nation-state, ultimately with a homogeneous population.[51] Although those espousing this view of Russian history usually did not deny that cultural assimilation was a two-way process—with the Russians changing as they acquired new cultural traits, habits, and even blood (miscegenation was generally not looked down upon by Russians)—they almost always agreed that Russification was and had to be the dominant trend. Particularly in the eastern and southern parts of the empire, Russian culture was assumed to be superior to the native cultures and therefore was expected to prevail when the peoples mixed. Normatively, assimilation meant Russification.[52]

While many Russians saw expansion and Russian colonization of the empire in a positive light as the mechanism by which Russia established its national character and identity, some people (usually ethnographers) focused on, and lamented, the resultant destruction of minority peoples and cultures. This concern was especially pronounced in Siberia, where the native populations were small, dispersed, and by the late nineteenth century seemed to be dying out because of rampant disease, environmental change, subsistence crises, and poverty. Some revolutionary exiles took up ethnography and devoted themselves to raising public awareness of the crisis. One was Nikolai M. Iadrintsev, who in his book *Siberia as a Colony* (1882) championed the cause of a Siberia free of Russian state domination and blamed the impending extinction of some of the Siberian peoples on the various effects of Russian colonization.[53] Iadrintsev was answered by more conservative commentators such as M. A. Miropiev, who insisted (with some degree of justification) that his colleague had misidentified the process of Russification—through native proximity to Russian settlements—as biological extinction.[54] Although *cultures* may have been dying out, these critics said, it was happening not because large numbers of people were starving, but because they were gradually being transformed into Russians, a process they saw as beneficial in economic and cultural terms ("extinction as survival," in the words of Yuri Slezkine).[55]

The prominent nineteenth-century ethnographer Ivan N. Smirnov painstakingly used linguistic and cultural data to trace the ethnic history of eastern Russia in order to document the gradual assimilation of Russian-Christian culture by several Finno-Ugric, animist peoples—the Mordvins, Cheremisses (Maris), Votiaks (Udmurts), and Permiaks (Komis). In his writings on these peoples, Smirnov argued—in a celebratory tone that is impossible to overlook—that even without the direct intervention of the tsarist state, the language, religion, and customs of the Russians (and eventually their blood too) over time had been so thoroughly absorbed by minority communities in some locales that observers might mistake assimilation for either the out-migration or the biological extinction of those peoples. Smirnov sometimes tried to predict how long it might take before the last representative of this or that Finnic people would become Russian, leaving the tribe's existence as only a vague memory.[56] He might not appear so sinister in simply describing this process if it were not for his role in the notorious Multan human sacrifice case, in which it became evident that Smirnov thought some of the indigenous cultures of the middle Volga region had to be destroyed because they were utterly savage.[57]

Smirnov was one of Russia's chief proponents of evolutionism, the predominant school of anthropological thought in the US and Britain. Although evolutionism was in some regards radically more tolerant of ethnic difference than preceding schools of thought, it could also function as a scientific basis on which to condone or promote genocide. As George Stocking has shown in the case of British scholars and the destruction of the Tasmanians, some evolutionist ethnographers and anthropologists in effect sought the demise (by assimilation when possible, by other means when necessary) of peoples and cultures they considered demonstrably least advanced and thus destined to disappear.[58]

Through the dissemination of ethnographic writings such as Smirnov's, the Russian reading public became familiar with the notion that ethnic groups in Russia might (and rightfully should) disappear over time because of Russification. Russification was seen as the manifestation of the strength of Russian culture, so that the disappearance of neighboring minority groups could be a source of satisfaction. If anything impeded the assimilation process, it might become a subject of heated controversy. This is what happened to the educational project of the famous lay Orthodox missionary Nikolai I. Il'minskii, who founded an enormous network of schools for minorities using native languages and native teachers (rather than the Russian language and Russian teachers) so that the pupils would achieve a deeper understanding of the Orthodox religion and remain within the church. Frequently, the result, even where integration into the Russian church was most successful, was a strengthening of some non-Russian identities that otherwise might have given way to Russification. Amidst the public backlash, at an assembly of Russian aristocrats discussing the schools in Kazan province in 1911, one nobleman waxed nostalgic for the days of aggressive Russification: "In the past, the Russian people were strongly organized, thanks to which we wiped a lot of alien peoples [*inorodtsy*] from the face of the Earth. They fused with the Russians, leaving only their names in history."[59] This statement was a genocidal fantasy not because the disappearance of peoples and cultures happened to be a by-product of the assimilation project the speaker advocated, but because the speaker clearly regarded that disappearance as a desirable goal and a reason to pursue

Russification. Moreover, the very words he used—wiping peoples from the face of the Earth—suggest a willingness to see that goal achieved through violence, so that the minorities might actually be exterminated rather than assimilated. The conflation of cultural and biological genocide here suggests that to some Russians hostile towards a minority ethnic group there might not have been a significant difference between the two; both rid the society of a group perceived as unworthy or troublesome.[60]

Such a mindset also existed within imperial Russia's corridors of power. Konstantin P. Pobedonostsev, the *ober-prokuror* (lay administrator) of the Holy Synod of the Russian Orthodox Church from 1880 to 1905, childhood tutor and thereafter adviser to Tsar Alexander III, and a notorious advocate of coercive Russification policies (by religion and other means), is famously said to have responded to a question about the future of Russia's Jews by predicting, "One-third will die out, one-third will leave the country, and one-third will be completely dissolved in the surrounding population."[61] The statement suggests that Pobedonostsev envisioned the demise of the Jews without sympathy or concern, and perhaps even with satisfaction. Coming from a different person, the prediction might have been made ruefully, but anyone who knew Pobedonostsev's reputation would perceive these overtones. He was concerned only that Russia be rid of the thorny "Jewish question"; his assumption was that it would disappear only when the Jews themselves did. Emigration, assimilation, and extinction were hardly distinguishable in Pobedonostsev's eyes, insofar as they would all contribute to this end. And though we might label this a genocidal fantasy, Pobedonostsev's position made it more than just a fantasy. As one of the tsar's chief advisors, particularly on issues concerning ethnonational minorities, he successfully championed a great number of legal limitations on the rights of these peoples to worship according to their faiths, use their languages in public, participate in civic life, pursue their ambitions, and make ends meet. The Jews faced more restrictions than most (many of the most notorious arising during Pobedonostsev's tenure), including confinement of residence to the Pale of Settlement and to certain places within it, and numerous limitations on property ownership, economic activity, and educational opportunity. Historians of the Jews in Russia would agree that his policies contributed significantly to the decline of Jews and Jewish culture in the Russian Empire—many Jews emigrated, some converted in order to escape restrictions, some died in pogroms that may have been abetted by agents of the government, and many were impoverished as a result of discriminatory policies. Such a set of actions would seem to constitute genocide according to Lemkin's definition, and reportedly Lemkin did include the case of Jews in tsarist Russia in his researches on genocide in history.[62]

Conclusions

The purpose of this chapter has been to examine the range of motivations that can inspire or contribute to genocide, particularly in multiethnic empires such as tsarist Russia. Genocidal impulses and fantasies may be official or unofficial; they may be based on notions that are modern or premodern; they can express concerns that are economic, military, religious, political, or ethnographic; they can be explicitly violent, or seemingly devoid of violence; they can be conscious, specific, and well articulated, or vague and even subconscious. Paying attention to such expressions may not help historians to be more precise in defining and identifying genocide, or in assigning blame for it; it may even work against these *judicial* functions that historians of genocide are sometimes expected to perform. But it can make us more *judicious* as historians by leading away from overly mechanistic conceptions of genocide (a tendency of extreme versions of both the intentionalist and structuralist paradigms) and toward more nuanced, sophisticated, and realistic accounts of causation and agency in human affairs.

It bears reemphasizing that genocidal impulses and fantasies are not tantamount to genocide or even to genocidal "intent." Nor are they mutually equivalent, either in moral terms or in terms of their potential to inspire genocidal actions. Obviously a figure of colloquial speech (like referring to invaders using the name of the people invaded) is not the same as a specific written proposal (like Pestel's or Gagemeister's) to eliminate a population; the desire of a gentry bystander to see Russia's minority peoples undergo extinction is not the same as a similar statement coming from one of the empire's chief policy makers. But while a proposal or official statement might stand a better chance of *directly* inspiring a genocidal event if it strikes the fancy of those with the power to carry it out, an especially pervasive lay opinion or figure of speech could quite possibly play a significant role in motivating genocidal activities or allowing them to be undertaken (even if historians might never be able to measure or even verify that role).

I have presented here in part only several stray examples of genocidal thinking in imperial Russia. Indeed, some of them were made by not particularly prominent individuals. The point is that in a number of realms, in a number of different ways, and for a number of different reasons, many Russians wished for, hoped for, and envisioned the destruction or disappearance of certain subpopulations in their vast empire. But I am emphatically not suggesting—as a Daniel Goldhagen of Russian studies might—that such impulses and fantasies were universal or predominant among Russians, let alone the single *essence* of Russians' imperial vision.[63]

Had that been the case, the history of that enormous conglomeration of peoples would certainly have been many times bloodier, more miserable, and more tragic than it was, and the world would be significantly less diverse today as a result.

Acknowledgement

I wish to thank Eric Lohr, Laurie Manchester, Dirk Moses, and Richard Stites for their thoughtful comments on earlier drafts of the chapter.

Notes

1. Raphael Lemkin, *Axis Rule in Occupied Europe* (Washington, DC, 1944), 79.
2. On distinctions among intent, motivation, and rationalization, see Michael A. McDonnell and A. Dirk Moses, "Raphael Lemkin as Historian of Genocide in the Americas," *Journal of Genocide Research* 7, no. 4 (2005): 510–13.
3. The intentionalist and structuralist approaches are delineated in A. Dirk Moses, "Genocide and Settler Society in Australian History," in *Genocide and Settler Society: Frontier Violence and Stolen Indigenous Children in Australian History*, ed. A. Dirk Moses (Oxford, 2005), 23.
4. Norman Naimark, *Fires of Hatred: Ethnic Cleansing in Twentieth-Century Europe* (Cambridge, MA and London, 2001), 4.
5. Literature from the Cold War period includes Robert Conquest, *The Nation Killers: The Soviet Deportation of Nationalities* (New York, 1970); idem, *Stalin—Breaker of Nations* (New York, 1991); Aleksandr Nekrich, *The Punished Peoples: The Deportation and Fate of Soviet Minorities at the End of the Second World War* (New York, 1978). Post–Cold War contributions include J. Otto Pohl, *Ethnic Cleansing in the USSR, 1937–1949* (Westport, CT, 1999); Terry Martin, *The Affirmative Action Empire: Nations and Nationalism in the Soviet Union, 1923–1939* (Ithaca, NY and London, 2001), esp. chap. 8; Martin, "The Origins of Soviet Ethnic Cleansing," *Journal of Modern History* 70, no. 4 (1998): 813–61; Naimark, *Fires of Hatred*, chap. 3; Amir Weiner, *Making Sense of War: The Second World War and the Fate of the Bolshevik Revolution* (Princeton, NJ, 2002), chap. 3; Alfred Rieber, "Civil Wars in the Soviet Union," *Kritika: Explorations in Russian and Eurasian History* 4, no. 1 (2003): 129–62; Pavel M. Polian, *Against Their Will: The History and Geography of Forced Migrations in the USSR* (Budapest, 2004). See also Peter Holquist, *Making War, Forging Revolution: Russia's Continuum of Crisis, 1914–1921* (Cambridge, MA and London, 2002), chap. 6, which describes de-Cossackization during the Civil War.
6. Peter Gatrell, *A Whole Empire Walking: Refugees in Russia during World War I* (Bloomington, IL and London, 1999); Eric Lohr, *Nationalizing the Russian Empire* (Cambridge, MA and London, 2003). See also Peter Holquist, "Violent Russia, Deadly Marxism?: Russia in the Epoch of Violence, 1905–1921," *Kritika: Explorations in Russian and Eurasian History* 4, no. 3 (2003): 627–52.

7. This process is described broadly by Paul B. Henze, "Circassian Resistance to Russia," in *The North Caucasus Barrier: The Russian Advance towards the Muslim World*, ed. Marie Bennigsen Broxup (New York, 1992), 63–65.
8. Michael Geyer and Charles Bright, "Global Violence and Nationalizing Wars in Eurasia and the Americas: The Geopolitics of War in the Mid-Nineteenth Century," *Comparative Studies in Society and History* 38, no. 4 (1996), 630. Arguably, violence in this zone subsided only after the dissolution of the Russian, Ottoman, and Persian empires and the solidification of new states including the USSR, Yugoslavia, and Turkey, but it re-erupted in the late twentieth century on several fronts—Afghanistan, the former Yugoslavia, and Caucasia/Transcaucasia.
9. Moshe Gammer, *Muslim Resistance to the Tsar: Shamil and the Conquest of Chechnia and Dagestan* (New York and London, 1994); V. V. Degoev, *Imam Shamil': Prorok, vlastitel', voin* (Moscow, 2001).
10. In the tsarist period the peoples known today as Circassians (Cherkes), Kabardians, and Adyge were all referred to by the term Circassian. Ronald Wixman, *The Peoples of the USSR: An Ethnographic Handbook* (Armonk, NY, 1984), 45, 49. I use that broad designation here for the sake of convenience.
11. Peter Hopkirk, *The Great Game: The Struggle for Empire in Central Asia* (New York, 1992), 153–62; M. S. Anderson, *The Eastern Question, 1774–1923* (London and New York, 1966), 91–92; Henze, "Circassian Resistance," 80–87.
12. Peter Holquist, "To Count, to Extract, and to Exterminate: Population Statistics and Population Politics in Late Imperial and Soviet Russia," in *A State of Nations: Empire and Nation-Making in the Age of Lenin and Stalin*, ed. Ronald Grigor Suny and Terry Martin (Oxford and New York, 2001), 111–44; Stephen D. Shenfield, "The Circassians: A Forgotten Genocide?" in *The Massacre in History*, ed. Mark Levene and Penny Roberts (New York and Oxford, 1999), 149–162; Austin Jersild, *Orientalism and Empire: North Caucasus Mountain Peoples and the Georgian Frontier, 1845–1917* (Montreal and Kingston, 2002), chap. 2, esp. 22–27; A. L. Norochnitskii, *Istoriia narodov severnogo Kavkaza (konets XVIII v.–1917 g.)* (Moscow, 1988), 202–212; R. Trakho, *Cherkesy* (Nal'chik, Russia, 1992), 55–64; and Henze, "Circassian Resistance," 102–4.
13. The lower estimate is in Holquist, "Population Statistics and Population Politics," 119, the higher in Shenfield, "The Circassians," 154.
14. Hopkirk, *The Great Game*, 404–09.
15. Russia had won the war against Turkey in 1877/78, but the initial treaty it negotiated, that of San Stefano (1877), so amplified Russian influence in the Balkans through the creation of a "Greater Bulgaria" client/protectorate state that the Western powers refused to accept it and forced Russia to accept the Treaty of Berlin, which reduced the new Bulgarian state considerably.
16. Holquist, "Population Statistics and Population Politics," 111.
17. Ibid., 117.
18. Naimark, *Fires of Hatred*, 187–90.
19. Patrick O'Meara, *The Decembrist Pavel Pestel: Russia's First Republican* (Houndmills, UK and New York, 2003), 82.
20. P. I. Pestel', *Russkaia pravda: Nakaz Vremennomu Verkhovnomu Pravleniiu* (St. Petersburg, 1906), 55.
21. Ibid., 47–48.
22. Iu. A. Gagemeister, "Osnovnye nachala narodnogo bogatstva za Kavkazom," Central State Archive of the Republic of Georgia, Tbilisi, f. 4, op. 2, d. 8, l. 103–103ob. The report was also

published in "Zakavkazskie ocherki Gagemeistera," *Zhurnal Ministerstva vnutrennikh del* (Sept. 1845), 411–39; (Oct. 1845), 32–64; (Nov. 1845), 211–55; (Dec. 1845), 353–99.

23. Michael Khodarkovsky, *Russia's Steppe Frontier: The Making of a Colonial Empire, 1500–1800* (Bloomington and Indianapolis, IL, 2002), 222. It is strange that Khodarkovsky's account of this transformation does not discuss the human toll of this campaign on the nomadic peoples.
24. On the Russian state's aggressive encouragement of Slavic peasant settlement in the Kazakh steppe around the turn of the twentieth century and the disastrous effects on the nomads (described as similar to the American repression of indigenous peoples), see Daniel Brower, *Turkestan and the Fate of the Russian Empire* (London, 2003), chap. 5. According to Brower, Kazakhs' land was protected only if they settled on it and gave up nomadic life; otherwise they faced expulsion. Tens of thousands seemingly chose the former option, leading tsarist apologists to hail the peasant migration as a civilizing influence, but on closer scrutiny it turned out that most of these Turkic communities continued to subsist on pastoral herding, only using newly restricted spaces. In other words, the nomads were not being settled but slowly crowded out.
25. Gagemeister, "Osnovnye nachala," 103ob.
26. Pestel', *Russkaia pravda*, 52.
27. Ibid., 53.
28. See James C. Scott, *Seeing Like a State: How Certain Schemes to Improve the Human Condition Have Failed* (New Haven, CT and London, 1998), 90–93.
29. For a description of such research and the judgments and categorizations it made on the basis of purely qualitative (not quantitative) observation, see Yuri Slezkine, "Naturalists versus Nations: Eighteenth-Century Russian Scholars Confront Ethnic Diversity," in *Russia's Orient: Imperial Borderlands and Peoples, 1700–1917*, ed. Daniel R. Brower and Edward J. Lazzerini (Ithaca, NY and London, 1997), 27–57. Even had statistical thinking been more central to the judgments behind expulsions and ethnic cleanings, Holquist's account would still be misleading in that it seems to overestimate the prominence of the Russian army in the development of statistics as a discipline. The article on the history of statistics in Russia in the most prominent tsarist-era encyclopedia gives much greater emphasis to statistics' use in the study of taxation, agriculture, and commerce by Russia's economic ministries (Finance and State Domains) in the early nineteenth century than by the army. See *Entsiklopedicheskii slovar' Brokgauza i Efrona*, s.v. "Statistika teoreticheskaia."
30. The standard source on this phenomenon and generally on Russian literature of the Caucasus is Susan Layton, *Russian Literature and Empire: Conquest of the Caucasus from Pushkin to Tolstoy* (Cambridge, 1994).
31. Dana Sherry, "*Kavkaztsy*: Images of Caucaus [*sic*] and Politics of Empire in the Memoirs of the Caucasus Corps' Officers, 1834–1859," *Ab Imperio* 3, no. 2 (2002): 191–222 (quotation on 219).
32. M. Iu. Lermontov, *Polnoe sobranie sochinenii*, 4 vols. (Moscow-Leningrad, 1948), 4: 161–64. Writing for a projected literary collection on various Russian social types, Lermontov used his essay to address criticism of *A Hero of Our Time*, including remarks made by Tsar Nicholas I to the effect that the book was too cynical in portraying its protagonist, Pechorin, as a hero. But the censors disallowed the book and so the essay remained unpublished and unknown until 1929. E. E. Naidich, "Ocherk Lermontova 'Kavkazets' v svete polemiki vokrug 'Geroia nashego vremeni'," *Russkaia literatura*, no. 4 (2001): 141–47.
33. Lermontov, *Polnoe sobranie sochinenii*, 4:161.

34. According to Sherry's interpretation of officers' memoirs, the defining feature of a *kavkazets* was his spending his entire military career in the Caucasus, unlike the many officers who served there only for a year or two. Sherry, "*Kavkaztsy*," 197.
35. In fact, Sherry implies, the peculiar group identity of the *kavkaztsy* was in part a way of strengthening these officers' resolve in a situation that required a great deal of self-denial and only limited recognition (a large number of the officers who served in the Caucasus had been exiled to the region as punishment). Sherry, "*Kavkaztsy*," 217.
36. A recent analysis of attitudes of Russian aristocrats toward the Caucasus concludes that indeed, in spite of the mountain peoples' seeming importance to the officers as inspiration for various aspects of their own self-image, "their fate was only secondary and, in effect, was not taken into account." Ia. Gordin, "Russkii chelovek na Kavkaze: Predvaritel'nyi zametki o kavkazskoi utopii," *Zvezda*, no. 7 (2002): 174.
37. Kavad (Karem) Rash, "Derzaite, Rossy!," *Nash sovremennik*, no. 5 (1991). Not having done a search of primary sources, I am unable to cite examples of "*bolgary*" to back up Rash's claim. The use of "*turkestanets*" in this manner, however, is exemplified by D. L. Ivanov, "Iz vospominanii turkestantsa [From the memoirs of a Turkestani]," *Istoricheskii vestnik* 64, no. 6 (1896): 830–59. On "*turkestantsy*," also see Dietrich Geyer, *Russian Imperialism: The Interaction of Domestic and Foreign Policy, 1860–1914*, trans. Bruce Little (New Haven, CT and London, 1987), 95, 107.
38. According to Rash, "even the malevolent enemies of Russia had to admit, when the dust, hysteria, and demagoguery fall aside, that the actions of the Russians in these regions had a progressive-philanthropic influence on the fate of the residents of the region."
39. N. P. Ostroumov, "Vospominaniia o missionerskom protivo-musul'manskom otdelenii pri Kazanskoi Dukhovnoi Akademii," *Pravoslavnyi sobesednik*, no. 1 (1892): 131–42 (2nd pagination).
40. Missionaries trained after the early nineteenth century were not supposed to be imposing Christianity coercively. Beginning in the 1840s, officially the Russian Orthodox Church and the state were adamant that conversion be achieved only by persuasion. But there is evidence that some clergy continued to use coercion, either on their own initiative or with the blessing of local authorities, to convert non-Christians. Use of material incentives remained even more common. Though it would be stretching definitions to say that the missionaries were being trained in genocide, still, missionary work continued to be inspired by fantasies of the minority cultures' disappearance. See Robert Geraci, *Window on the East: National and Imperial Identities in Late Tsarist Russia* (Ithaca, NY and London, 2001), chaps. 2–3.
41. On the event, see Marcus C. Levitt, *Russian Literary Politics and the Pushkin Celebration of 1880* (Ithaca, NY and London, 1989).
42. Fyodor Dostoyevsky, *A Writer's Diary*, trans. and ed. Kenneth Lantz, 2 vols. (Evanston, IL, 1994), 2: 1292.
43. In a sense, this was Dostoyevsky's way of bridging the gaping divide of the decades-old Slavophile-Westernizer debate (Dostoyevsky being decisively on the Slavophile side): Pushkin's putative ability to speak in all national idioms allowed Russia to express affinity with the West without becoming Western*ized*, that is by being in control rather than slavishly importing European ideas and structures. The ability and inclination to mimic, in other words, was a source of strength, not of weakness, and a manifestation of talent rather than of a lack thereof.
44. Quoted in Katya Hokanson, "Literary Imperialism, *Narodnost'*, and Pushkin's Invention of the Caucasus," *Russian Review* 53, no. 3 (1994): 341.
45. Dostoyevsky, *A Writer's Diary*, 2: 1272–73.

46. Ibid., 2:1294.
47. Ibid., 2:1275.
48. Ibid., 2:1369.
49. Ibid., 2:1373–75.
50. The ability of Russians to interact harmoniously with neighboring peoples was sometimes cited as a reason for Russians' "assimilatory capability"—their success in spreading their culture even without the help of state policy. I. N. Smirnov, "Obrusenie inorodtsev i zadachi obrusitel'noi politiki," *Istoricheskii vestnik* 47 (1892): 752–65. But in light of many countervailing examples this affability was also blamed for Russians' tendency oftentimes to become assimilated to the alien languages and cultures, to the point that some elites saw the Russian people as having a weak sense of national identity. N. Kharuzin, "K voprosu ob assimiliatsionnoi sposobnosti russkogo naroda," *Etnograficheskoe obozrenie* 4 (1894): 43–78.
51. Seymour Becker, "The Muslim East in Nineteenth-Century Russian Popular Historiography," *Central Asian Survey* 5, nos. 3/4 (1986): 25–47; idem, "Russia between East and West: The Intelligentsia, Russian National Identity and the Asian Borderlands," *Central Asian Survey* 10, no. 4 (1991): 47–64.
52. See Willard Sunderland, "Russians Into Yakuts? 'Going Native' and Problems of Russian National Identity in the Siberian North, 1870s–1914," *Slavic Review* 55, no. 4 (1996): 824.
53. N. Ia. Iadrintsev, *Sibir' kak koloniia* (St. Petersburg, 1882); see also idem, *Sibirskie inorodtsy, ikh byt i sovremennoe polozhenie* (St. Petersburg, 1891).
54. M. A. Miropiev, *O polozhenii russkikh inorodtsev* (St. Petersburg, 1901).
55. Yuri Slezkine, *Arctic Mirrors: Russia and the Small Peoples of the North* (Ithaca, NY and New York, 1994), 120.
56. I. N. Smirnov, *Permiaki* (Kazan, 1891), 172–73; idem, *Votiaki* (Kazan, 1890), 70, 260. For more on Smirnov's discussion of assimilation, see Geraci, *Window on the East*, 171–76, 195–222.
57. See Robert Geraci, "Ethnic Minorities, Anthropology, and Russian National Identity on Trial: The Multan Case," *Russian Review* 59, no. 4 (2000): 530–54.
58. George Stocking, *Victorian Anthropology* (New York, 1987), 274–83.
59. Russian State Historical Archive, St. Petersburg, f. 846, op. 1, d. 165, l. 28. For more on this controversy regarding the assimilatory effects of schools in Russia, see Geraci, *Window on the East*, chap. 7.
60. Only in the context of strong racialist assumptions about the biological rootedness and heritability of human characteristics (suggesting the impossibility of erasing negative traits by purely cultural means), or extraordinary impatience with waiting cultural change to occur, would physical extermination take on any special appeal. In Russia, such racialist attitudes were not significantly developed (owing probably to the obvious frequency and importance of miscegenation in the country's history), though a sense of urgency was sometimes present.
61. Simon M. Dubnow, *History of the Jews in Russia and Poland from the Earliest Times until the Present Day*, trans. I. Friedlander, 3 vols. (New York, 1975), 3:10. Whether Pobedonostsev said exactly these words is a matter of minor uncertainty. The remark was allegedly made in an unrecorded conversation between Pobedonostsev and a Jewish journalist. More frequently it has been rendered: "A third will be converted, a third will emigrate, and a third will die of hunger." John Klier and others have questioned that particular version, which Klier claims is a later one, on the basis of Pobedonostsev's well-known lack of enthusiasm or hope for the conversion of Jews in Russia. John D. Klier, "State Policies and the Conversion of Jews in Imperial Russia," in *Of Religion*

and Empire: Missions, Conversion, and Tolerance in Tsarist Russia, ed. Robert P. Geraci and Michael Khodarkovsky (Ithaca, NY and London, 2001), 106–7. In spite of Klier's skeptical tone, there is no particular reason to question the veracity of the remark.

62. McDonnell and Moses, "Raphael Lemkin," 502.
63. I am referring, of course, to Daniel Jonah Goldhagen, *Hitler's Willing Executioners: Ordinary Germans and the Holocaust* (New York, 1996).

– *Chapter 16* –

Colonialism and Genocide in Nazi-occupied Poland and Ukraine

David Furber and Wendy Lower

Introduction

In early 1940, SS chief Heinrich Himmler rode through occupied Poland with his friend, the Nazi poet laureate Hanns Johst. Asserting that the Vavel, the centuries-long seat of Polish kings, was a product of Germany's civilizing work in Poland, Johst disparaged Poland with standard colonial rhetoric: "The Poles are not a state-building people. They lack the most basic prerequisites. I drove with the Reichsführer-SS up and down that land. A country with so little sense for artful landscape planning, which cannot even deal with the style of a village, has no claim to any sort of independent political status within the European sphere. It is colonial land!"[1] As the pair drove between Lodz and Warsaw, Himmler kept stopping the car and walking out into the fields, picking up clumps of soil. Rubbing the earth between his fingertips, like the lord and master of all he surveyed, Himmler mused about the coming impact of the "German plough" upon the flat, open landscape. Trees and shrubs would soon be planted, he declared, "hedges will grow rampant, and will shelter the weasels and hedgehogs, buzzards and falcons" that would patrol the fields between the hedges, thereby preventing "the loss of half the harvest to mice and vermin." Predators would clear out field pests "much more naturally and thoroughly than the poison of modern man." Professionals would plant forests, and make the land fertile for the new German settlers from the Baltic, Galicia, and Volhynia. "We stood on the field, held conquered soil in our hands, and looked far and wide across the carelessly neglected plains."[2] In the "rhetoric of empire," this is the language of appropriation.[3]

The Nazis were born into a European world of empire. In keeping with the age, the Nazi jurist Carl Schmitt wrote an essay in 1941 justifying Germany's expansion to the East. The war certainly violated laws applying to wars between European nations, he argued, but not those that applied to colonial wars. Although "colonies have been the spatial element upon which European law is founded," Schmitt believed Germany had been denied and was forced to expand within the colonial space of Eastern Europe.[4] One also finds similar formulations among Germans who experienced the war, asserting that the Nazis were merely applying nineteenth-century colonial methods to Europe.[5] How could the civilized world deny Germany's its "manifest destiny" while proclaiming its own?

As latecomers to the imperial game, the Germans could improve on the model. Thus Johst concluded his story with a comparison to the West's economic colonialism: "The Western world cannot grasp this pure pleasure in duty and work, in sweat and calluses. They think in terms of business deals and turnover, whereas we rejoice in the task itself."[6] Nazi empire builders used the language of colonialism to describe their work in the East, although, as Mark Mazower points out, they rejected the liberalism associated with imperialism of the second half of the nineteenth century.[7]

One of the distinctive aspects of Nazi imperialism was anti-Semitism. Although Jews did not appear explicitly in Johst's racial utopia, anti-Semitism lay clearly at the core of his imperial fantasy. In the Nazi worldview, the abstract Jew represented the "negative aspects of modernity" that had to be eliminated for the regeneration of civilization.[8] Nazis perceived their movement as a struggle for liberation against precisely this "Jewish" influence within German society, Europe as a whole, and the world. When Johst derided the West's tendency to "think in terms of business deals and turnover" rather than "duty and work, sweat and calluses," he meant that this "Jewish spirit" had inhibited the West's prior colonial efforts. The Nazi occupation of Eastern Europe, by contrast, afforded German leaders the opportunity to create their utopia unimpeded by liberal scruples or commercialism; they took colonial fantasies about "race and space" to their radical conclusion. Nazi imperialism thus had a dual genocidal bent: first, as a "total war" to liberate Western civilization from "the Jews," and second as a "colonial war" to wrest *Lebensraum* from the supposedly primitive, inferior, but nevertheless white-skinned Slavs.

The horrific Nazi conquest of the eastern territories took on many forms, as Alexander Dallin wrote in his classic study, mingling "fantasy and realism" and perpetuating the "'white man's burden' in a new and more perverted variant."[9] In Hitler's early writings, wartime secret conversations, and planning meetings with his satraps, he described the lure of the East and the Germans' historic destiny to reclaim the territory. He spoke of a racial paradise, stating that from the newly won territories the Germans must create a "Garden of Eden." Hitler's deputy, Heinrich Himmler, put these ideas into action by managing the SS police's implementation of the Holocaust and mobilizing German institutions and scholars around the "General Plan East," a blueprint for creating the "Garden." Nazi leaders and their enthusiastic developers, racial experts, horticulturalists, architects, landscape designers, agronomists, and ruthless SS police henchmen were empire builders whose common aim was to Germanize the eastern territories.[10] In Nazi thinking, this meant that the *Lebensraum* was theirs to transform however they saw fit, simply because "the law of blood" justified it.[11] Dr. Maurer, Director of the Institute for Horticulture, and "blood and soil" expert serving in Hans Frank's General Government and Alfred Rosenberg's Reich Ministry for the Occupied Eastern Territories, argued that the great achievement of National Socialism was its awakening of Germans to their unique history and destiny as a race. At last, Maurer and other colonizers declared, a unified Aryan race would be able to overcome the chaos in Europe and flourish where Germans were historically rooted, on the fertile terrain of Eastern Europe.[12]

For all the obvious colonial rhetoric in Nazi plans for Eastern Europe, scholars disagree about the relationship between the Holocaust and the Nazi colonial project. Like Hannah Arendt, Enzo Traverso can trace important roots of Nazi imperialism to European overseas colonization, but distinguishes the two by virtue of Nazism's "regenerative" anti-Semitism.[13] Alternatively, Jürgen Zimmerer points out that the most violent aspects of Nazism occurred in the "colonial situation" of the German-occupied East and cannot be divorced from its anti-Semitic worldview.[14] In his words, the "German war against Poland and the USSR was without doubt the largest colonial war of conquest in history . . . if there was a historical precedent, then only the history of colonialism could possibly provide an example of their [Nazi] plans."[15] The thread runs not from Windhuk to Nuremberg, where Nazi racial laws were promulgated in 1935, but from Windhuk to Warsaw, where the Nazis actually practiced genocidal colonialism. For as in German Southwest Africa, the Nazis committed mass murder while constructing a "racially privileged society" of Europeans over Africans.[16]

Both Traverso and Zimmerer illuminate important dimensions of the question, but have yet to provide a satisfactory answer to the complex relationship between colonialism and genocide in Nazi imperialism. Zimmerer's call to analyze "Nazi expansion and occupation policy in the East as colonial"[17] underplays the specificity of anti-Semitism *within* Nazi colonialism, while Traverso does not consider the "colonial situation" that the Nazis created on the ground in the East. Historians of Nazi population policy and the "Final Solution," such as Christopher Browning, Dieter

Pohl, and Götz Aly, who have painstakingly reconstructed the events and underlying decisions, likewise have paid scant attention to the colonial dimension.[18]

This chapter proposes to advance our understanding of the interrelationships between empire building, colonial rule, and genocide in the Nazi-occupied East by illuminating two aspects of this colonial dimension. On the one hand, it highlights how the complex identities of "native" and "colonizer" in Nazi discourse affected the differing treatment of Jews and Slavs. On the other, it focuses on the internal tensions in the Nazi project that led ultimately to the radicalization of policy towards Jews and comparative deradicalization of policy towards Poles and Ukrainians.

Colonial Racism and Anti-Semitism

The Holocaust was not a typical colonial genocide because "the Jew" was not a typical colonial other. Such an other—the "native"—was regarded as stupid, lazy, smelly, ill-clothed, and lacking technical and organizational ability, but able to perform simple work if led. The Slavs filled the role of the colonial "native" in this way. While often depicted as barbarian hordes, they did not arouse fear as such among the Germans. Once deprived of their leadership caste, their residual "Germanic racial elements," and the "living space" required by Germans, they could serve as the slaves for German masters. Such exploitation of the Jews, however, was impossible because they themselves were portrayed as successful colonizers.[19] The Nazis feared the Jews, then, because they regarded themselves as the indigenous people of Central and Eastern Europe who were fighting off Jewish penetration.[20] National Socialism was in its heart a national liberation movement, the swastika its symbol of fertility and resurrection. Even before *Mein Kampf,* Hitler complained that "a nation of poets and thinkers" was being reduced to "a nation of helots." The state created by Bismarck had become "a colony," hardly better off than Ireland, India, or Egypt. In Hitler's eyes, Jews were responsible for godless Bolshevism and soulless Americanism, global capitalism, and the oppressive nature of the Versailles system.[21]

And yet, this telling distinction does not fully capture the place of Eastern Jews in Nazi eyes. For as the German policeman Hans Richter observed, Eastern Jews were oriental in character, especially in their squalor and petty trade in small items. "The Eastern Jew does not rule like the one in the West, as a big capitalist and ruthless dominator of the world market, neither with shares of stock nor the earth's minerals, but in odds and ends and through mass volume."[22] Friedrich Gollert, a Nazi official with the land use planning office in Warsaw, juxtaposed the German and Jewish influence upon that city as a mirror image: what German colonizers had built up over centuries, the Jews took over and ran down. The Nazi assault was "an act of historical justice" because it "took away from the Jew not what he has earned as a fighter and a colonizer, but as a parasite."[23]

What is remarkable about the Nazi treatment of Eastern Jews—and we contend that this accounts for its unrelenting ferocity—is the fact that the Nazis viewed them as natives in the classical colonial sense *and* as pernicious colonizers of supposed ancestral German land. The Jew thereby incarnated both the native other and the colonizing other, combining contempt and fear in a lethal cocktail. This conflation is made plain by the Nazi observation that the seemingly primitive Jews migrated west to replenish the stock of ruthless dominators. H.E. Seifert remarked in 1940 that in Poland, the "Jewish people lives in their native filth," but its danger was not only in its potential to emigrate. "There are not two different kinds of Jews but just different manifestations of the one Jew," he complained. "In Lublin, the ridiculous and the refined are densely concentrated together, the cretin and the would-be intellectual, the Eastern Jew with kaftan and hanging locks and the already Westernized Jew."[24] A page in the 1941 book by the General Government's agricultural minister shows two pictures, one of Jews in a labor gang and one of two Jews standing idly on the street, one wearing a kaftan and the other a suit. "'Lousy times!' Now the time for haggling is over," reads the caption.[25] Here the two racialized others were incarnated in a single image: the Jew appeared as *both* quintessential "native" *and* the greatest threat to the German colonizer. Where Jews edged toward the "native," there was always the reference to the Western Jew through the "breeding ground" argument and, especially in Ukraine, to the Eastern Jew as carrier of "Judeo-Bolshevism" and partisan resistance. The logical outcome of this view was that Jews not be allowed to leave—indeed, that they be exterminated.

Colonial Policy Development and the Contingencies of War

We know from Holocaust research that ideology was not implemented in a mechanical way, but was mediated by a range of wartime and administrative contingencies. We argue that there was a colonial dimension to these contingencies. In colonizing Poland and Ukraine, the Nazis propelled their regime toward genocide. All these dynamics extend in some way from colonialism's basic distinction between settlement and exploitation. Three such dynamics operated in the General Government of occupied Poland and the Reich Commissariat Ukraine. First, although all groups paid homage to the long-term Nazi goal of settling the East with Germans, there were significant conflicts between the exploitation-minded civil administrations and the settlement-minded SS police. The resulting fault lines are remarkably congruent with the traditional distinction between settlement-migration colonialism and occupation-exploitation economic colonialism. As the conflict unfolded, it led both groups to unite over the extermination of Jews while clashing over exterminating non-Jewish, non-German inhabitants. Second, Nazi colonization campaigns and genocide were intrinsically linked in the Nazi concept of *Lebensraum*. "As long as a single Jew remains in the land," wrote a Nazi reporter in May 1942, "the complete fulfillment of the tasks placed before the Government General will hardly be possible."[26] Anti-Semitism was a unifying force among divergent Nazi colonizer groups, each of which pursued its own variant of the colonial mission of building *Lebensraum* in the East. Third, and finally, as the genocide against the Slavs and the Jews progressed in tandem in the occupied Eastern territories, the colonial dynamics related to settlement and exploitation caused the former genocide to progress to its grisly conclusion and the latter genocide to slow down in order to keep the "natives" under control.

Colonialism and Genocide in the General Government (Poland)

The General Government witnessed a conflict between the two ideal types of colonialism, the settlement-oriented SS and the exploitation-oriented civil administration, notwithstanding considerable overlap between them. As the war pushed the clash to crisis stage by 1941, leaders at the center and periphery were able to lay their differences aside regarding colonial concepts and find common ground in the pursuit of destructive anti-Jewish policies. Killing the Jews served the colonial goals of both groups of colonizers. However, a similar consensus was never reached regarding the treatment of Poles. Moreover, the conflict did not begin in 1939, but emerged from the course of colonial rule in the context of war.

In the General Government, exploitation colonialism was the first to emerge, and remained predominant until the summer of 1941. Hans Frank created a full-blown colonial state in order to achieve Hitler's orders to impose order, to alleviate Poland's economic burden on Germany, and to put Poland's land and labor to the service of the Reich. Against Frank's wishes, the General Government also quickly became Germany's Siberia: the dumping ground for "undesirables" from the rest of the empire. Nazi leaders at first intended to create a Jewish reservation around Lublin where "excess" Jews could be worked to death digging anti-tank ditches. In the settlement of ethnic Germans, the General Government served as a "transit land" for the Volhynians and Galicians trekking to the Warthegau, which lay between the General Government and pre-1939 Germany. In 1940, the SS even evacuated 30,000 ethnic Germans from the Cholm region to the Warthegau. Germanization may have been the long-term goal for the General Government; in the first years of occupation, however, the Nazis perceived it as a "labor reserve."[27]

Settlement colonialism soon asserted itself in the General Government. In the first phase of the war, the SS concentrated on Germanizing the so-called incorporated Eastern territories such as the Warthegau. In this context, the General Government was a dumping ground, not a settlement zone. Soon the SS and Police Leader in Lublin, Odilo Globocnik, became convinced that the General Government was ripe for immediate Germanization starting in the District of Lublin. Through 1940, his ethnologists secretly combed the region in a "Search for German Blood." The land surrounding the town of Zamosc they found particularly promising. Yet this entire region was not only a major Jewish cultural center, but also the primary "dumping ground" from the days of the Lublin Reservation. Therefore, the problematic of resettlement and Jewish question went hand in hand in the General Government as elsewhere.

Because Frank's model promised the best utilization of Polish resources in an as-yet-undecided war, his view prevailed until the euphoria of victory overtook the Nazi leadership in the summer of 1941. Operation Barbarossa presented the Nazis with a grand historical opportunity to build their racial empire. By September 1941, Globocnik believed it was time to Germanize Lublin by deporting Jews "to the east" and resettling Poles to make room for test settlements of German villages around Zamosc. On 1 October, he wrote Himmler; the two met for two hours on the thirteenth, after which Himmler approved the construction of a death camp near Belzec and the settlement of seven villages with Germans. Both were initiated in November 1941. Hitler approved the decision and informed Hans Frank, who was in Berlin at the time.[28] Back in Poland, Frank toured the General Government and held meetings with his provincial governors, approving the closing of ghettos, and informing his men that Lublin's Jews would soon be "evacuated across the [river] Bug."[29] Returning to Krakow to celebrate the second anniversary of the General Government, Frank reminded his men that the Nazis' work in the East had a "colonial character."[30] He placed the upcoming evacuation of Jews from the General Government in an imperial context: "The more land we conquer in the East, the greater the probability that we will get rid of the Jews and asocial Poles, that in the course of time the overall settlement program of the East will allow us to arrange to make this land of the Vistula all the way to the Pruth River German settlement land.[31]"

The SS took the lead in the "Final Solution to the Jewish Question" in order to prepare the ground for settlement. Globocnik was working from a local perspective toward the larger goal of Germanization outlined in the SS's emerging, secret colonization plan for the East, the so-called *Generalplan Ost*. Himmler integrated Globocnik's initiative within that broader SS program of extermination and resettlement. During these first two weeks in October 1941, the Wehrmacht was winning stunning victories against the Soviets in the so-called double battle of Vyazma and Bryansk. Soviet defeat appeared imminent; Stalin even contemplated surrender.[32] On 17 October, Hitler relaxed from his position as military commander to explain his decision to Fritz Todt and Fritz Sauckel. For him, it was not a matter of Lublin, but of settlements all the way to the Crimea and the Caucasus. Everywhere, the "natives" (*Eingeborenen*) would be "sifted." The "destructive Jews would be completely excluded." Germany would "not come to the remainder with soft soap," but replace them with Germans and "deal with them like the Indians."[33] Whereas Globocnik sought to build a death camp to further his regional projects in Lublin, Hitler approved the enterprise in an imperial frame of mind. When it happened, the decision to exterminate the Jews was part of a larger Nazi vision of a racial empire in the East.

Although the SS initiated the "Final Solution," Frank's administration supported it for its own reasons. By late 1941, the General Government was suffering from an acute crisis brought on by three factors. First, its thin resources were already overtaxed as thousands more Poles were deported from the Warthegau, which it was attempting to Germanize, and as Jewish transports began rolling in.[34] Second, the Jews in the ghettos were running out of money to finance their upkeep as resources were becoming more scarce, resulting in a health crisis. Third, the extended character of Operation Barbarossa led to increased demands upon the General Government to contribute to the war effort, demands that intensified in 1942 and 1943. There was no way to meet them while maintaining the Jews, whose ability to contribute through labor was by now vastly diminished.[35] This complex of factors motivated administrators to support the murder of Jews while opposing the resettlement of Poles.

Poles deported from the Warthegau were dumped in the General Government, where a police border separated them from their old homes. When the Zamosc villages were settled with Germans in November 1941, the deportees were merely put in a nearby refugee camp. They would show up at night to steal their livestock and otherwise wreak havoc.[36] Then in January 1942, SS men resumed their survey of villages, indicating another resettlement action. As the Governor of Lublin, Ernst Zörner, complained in a letter to Krakow that summarized the complaints of his subordinates, these visits unsettled the Polish peasantry. Some packed up and disappeared; most stopped investing in or caring for their farms; many were ignoring the spring planting—against German orders—because they did not expect to be there for the harvest.[37] The protests went all the way to Himmler and Hitler, who allowed Globocnik to continue on a more limited scale in November 1942. The results were disastrous. By then, German grain requisitions were causing deprivation in the countryside just as military setbacks made the Germans appear vulnerable. Resettlements in Lublin that continued into early 1943 actually sparked a massive partisan movement that required an expensive and disruptive counterinsurgency campaign to suppress.[38]

Resettlement affected agricultural production vital to the war effort, and "seriously threatened the achievement of the final victory [*Endsieg*]," as Frank wrote to Hitler in May 1943.[39] The administrators blamed Globocnik and sought to implement a milder policy that might win Poles over to the German side in return for some cultural autonomy and more indirect rule. Therefore, Frank argued, they should be postponed until after the war. In the event, Hitler gradually came around. Further resettlements were called off; Globocnik was transferred out in September 1943.[40] At the same time, Hitler disavowed Frank's new course on the grounds that Poles could never be reconciled to German rule. Germany had attempted to win Poles to their side in World War I; the Poles instead rose up in November 1918 and expelled the Germans.

Was Frank committed to Germanization? Was this a clash between settlement and exploitation or simply an argument about the timing of settlement? In the propitious circumstances of October 1941, Frank was genuinely excited about Germanization in Lublin, but turned against the settlement aspect when it caused badly timed problems with the Poles. Had the first Zamosc *Aktion* not disrupted the occupation, perhaps he would have continued his enthusiasm. Knowing that Himmler was fully committed to settlement, Frank realized he would get nowhere if he took a stand against Germanization in principle. The appearance of sentimentality toward non-Germans was equally likely to be unproductive in swaying Hitler. Hence the documentary record is strewn with bloodcurdling anti-Polish and pro-settlement statements. At the same time, he liked to be called a "prince of the Italian Renaissance."[41] As "king of the Poles," he announced to all audiences that Poland was a nation of primitive savages unfit for self-government.[42] He believed his "laboratory for colonial administration,"[43] as he sometimes called the General Government, brought peace, order, and just rule to the Poles, albeit in their capacity as racially inferior, second-class subjects. The plans he approved during his heyday as colonial governor, between June 1940 and August 1941, foresaw the transformation of the General Government into a semi-industrialized, agriculturally efficient provider of cheap labor, grain, and raw materials to Germany.

The implantation of German settlers did not figure into these plans on a large scale.[44] Hitler and Frank both wanted to treat the Poles like Indians; although their visions both elided India and North America, Hitler leaned more toward North America and Frank toward India.

Did colonial genocides occur in Poland, the Jewish one remembered and the Polish one ignored—a so-called forgotten Holocaust?[45] Yes and no. Frank and his colleagues in the civil administration arrived in Poland as amateurs, with little knowledge either of Poland or of administration. Experts such as Seifert came forward to educate them on Polish conditions.[46] While expending considerable effort to destroy Polish nationhood as such, they metamorphosed into what was, for the time and circumstances, a typical colonial administration with a mission to educate the "natives" for work. Unrelated to these considerations, Globocnik acclimated to Poland and concluded that Lublin was ripe for German settlement. The SS and civil administration then cooperated or clashed on two different colonial genocides. One, against Poland's Jews, progressed because of a consensus among the colonizers and relative lack of resistance. The other, against the Poles, remained incomplete for the opposite reasons: competing visions and uneconomical resistance. As we will see, the first one progressed because reactions to colonial obstacles, such as black market trading, could be joined to ideological considerations, such as Poland as the "breeding ground" of a racially unified "World Jewry."

The second one elicited no such convergence, but rather a divergence. At first, Nazis conceived of Poles as a unified, Slavic people, but gradually decided there was no such thing as a racial Pole. Instead there were Masovians, Krakovians, "Kurpier, Podlachier, Lubliner, Lasowiaker," and so forth, just as there were no Ukrainians but "Dolynianer, Buzaner, Pidhirianer, Batken," and so on. These were not Slavs but varying admixtures of "Nordic, Subnordic, Dinarian, Praeslavic, and Eastern" racial types.[47] In other words, the Nazis reconfigured or colonized Poland from a European nation into a conglomeration of indigenous peoples. Only a minority of the colonizer community agreed upon the need to exterminate them. A German sergeant at Majdanek about to be hanged in Lublin after the war shouted his regret "at not wiping out the entire Polish population when he had been given the chance."[48]

Jews as Colonial Problem in the General Government

Anti-Semitism heavily influenced how Nazi officials perceived their concrete tasks of colonization and development, and shaped the language of Nazi colonialism. The Nazis in Poland attacked a "Jewish problem" as part of the economic and medical "rationality" of colonial rule. When the district official of Jedrzejow in the Radom District of the General Government arrived at his post in late 1939, the stores were empty, crime ruled the streets, and nobody did any work. The town's one-quarter Jewish population allegedly exacerbated the situation. Order soon appeared after the man had publicly shot on the market square three Jews from whose house snipers had fired at Germans. Then it was "time to revive the economic life of the district." Unfortunately, the official believed this was under the control of Jews who shirked German price restrictions. He placed German trustees in charge of Jewish businesses, but had to move gradually because of the lack of available Germans.[49] The official then called a meeting of Polish priests, teachers, and mayors. He "made it clear that we have not come here as destroyers, but feel responsible for security and calm for the restoration of the economy and orderly life." He warned, however, that Poles and Jews must maintain a "sharp separation of the races." He noted a "particularly keen willingness to cooperate on the part of the mayors, which was also later confirmed in practice during the solution of the Jewish question," which at this time meant expropriation and concentration in preparation for future removal to points as yet undetermined. He characterized the establishment of the ghetto as an economic stabilization measure. "Instead of standing around on the streets, the Jews were organized into labor columns, which marched out at daybreak to road work, debris removal, and other lesser tasks." The unemployed Poles were also pressed into labor gangs, but "were sharply separated from the Jews and given as much as possible more dignified tasks. So far as possible the Jews have been replaced by Aryans."[50]

Officials governing the District of Warsaw also regarded its Jews as a primary development obstacle. The land had to be "liberated from chaos" that stemmed partly from the Poles' perceived natural inability to organize states, and partly from the perceived pernicious Jewish influence that Poles despised but were too weak to counteract.[51] This "liberation" required initiative on the part of the district officials. Already in the spring of 1940, one of them to the west of Warsaw had enclosed "his" Jews in a ghetto to prevent the spread of disease. Officials elsewhere learned from his experience, so that by 1941 all Jews in the Warsaw District resided in ghettos, awaiting future removal.[52] The biggest one was in Warsaw, closed off from the outside world for "public health reasons." Then, in the spring of 1941, the Jews of the western half of the District were evacuated to the Warsaw ghetto, making the region "*judenfrei*." The stated reason were control of epidemics and black market trading, both of which allegedly declined following the removal of the local Jewish populations. These actions were not undertaken with the intention of genocide, but pushed the Germans strongly in that direction. When they removed Jews, they found improvements in health and economy due to less competition for scarce resources in a given area, which led to calls for more removals.

The perceived gains were reinforced by the crisis situation that emerged by the fall of 1941, the crusading mentality that emerged with the war against "Judeo-Bolshevism," and the fact that the ghettoized Jews had run out of money to pay for their upkeep. Instead, German leaders in the General Government hoped that Poland's Jews might be shipped farther east into the soon-to-be former Soviet Union. When these hopes proved to be unfounded and news of mass shootings of Jews in the east filtered into Poland, local German leaders began to think along similar lines.

Jean-Paul Sartre asserted once that colonial regimes shrink from exterminating indigenous populations because they rely on their cheap labor.[53] As General Lothar von Trotha decided to exterminate the Herero of Namibia in 1904, settlement commissioner Paul Rohrbach protested that he was killing the settlers' source of labor.[54] These concerns also abounded in Nazi colonialism, but more with regard to Poles and Ukrainians than to Jews. In the General Government, administrators quickly came to consider Jews a "burden" rather than an economic resource:

> In order to put the work-capable Jews to a useful activity, they were all called to forced labor through a directive of the Governor General. They were primarily put to work on water regulation, road construction, street cleaning, and snow removal, as well as rubble removal in destroyed towns. This effort has definitively proven that the Jew is not in the position to do the simplest physical labor in a reasonable and economically rational way. The average productive capacity of a Polish laborer is far higher than that of the Jew.[55]

At a meeting of the civil administrative leaders in Warsaw in October 1941, the Governor of Warsaw, Ludwig Fischer, announced that the ghetto would be sealed completely to prevent typhus and to decrease black market trade in food. To compensate, ghetto rations would have to be increased to about 1,050 grams of bread per day. He lamented that these amounts of food were still "too little to sustain life." Yet he concluded, "this war is about a confrontation with Jewry in its totality. . . . I believe that threat is answered when we annihilate this breeding ground of Jewry, from which the entire World Jewry continually renews itself."[56]

The Nazi perception of Jews was not only driven by a pragmatic or developmental logic. The colonizers elevated the self-perception of their task to "world historical" by considering Poland the "breeding ground" (*Brutstätte*) of "World Jewry" that they felt was oppressing Germany. "Lublin has been the point of crystallization, the organizational epicenter of World Jewry for centuries," wrote H.E. Seifert in a 1940 book intended for German personnel, *The Jew on the Eastern Border.*[57] In May 1942, as the "Final Solution" was getting underway, Radom governor Erich Kundt wrote in an essay for the *Europäische Revue* that "the territory of former Poland and the broader East can be regarded as the breeding ground of modern world Jewry . . . The Jewish problem therefore posed the German administration from the beginning with special problems."[58] Kundt then recited the familiar litany about typhus, the black market, and the Jewish stranglehold on Poland's economy. While pressing, these problems by themselves do not appear to have fully justified the increasingly harsh treatment and ultimately murder of Poland's Jews. The harsher the treatment became, the more Nazi administrators justified it through the "breeding ground" and similar transcendent arguments.

Nevertheless, the colonial and the metaphysical remained linked. As the policeman Hans Richter wrote in a 1943 memoir, "In the pursuit of its goal to provide the German people with a sufficient, sterilized *Lebensraum*, and over and above that, to achieve the *Neuordnung* of Europe, the Third Reich could not avoid the destruction of this germ cell."[59] As we have seen, even Hitler framed his basic decision in October 1941 to pursue extermination of the Jews of Europe rather than their expulsion from Europe in these biological-racialist, imperial terms.

Nazi Colonization and the Holocaust in Ukraine

To what extent was the Holocaust in Ukraine a colonial genocide? Certainly, the Ukraine was regarded as colonial territory. Whereas in Poland Frank insisted ironically on the essential civility of the Nazi colonizer, in Ukraine his regional counterpart, Reich Commissar Koch, denigrated Ukrainians as "white Negroes" and proudly showed off his unbridled brutality.[60] A self-described brutal dog, Erich Koch relished his newfound power over Ukraine and Ukrainians. Koch condoned the whipping of the "natives," although in a touching gesture toward a code of honor, he thought that German officials who did so while drunk in public were a disgrace to the Nazi uniform. Koch took most of his cues from Hitler, who objected to any civilizing mission in Ukraine. Combining atavistic "blood and soil" notions of utopia with modern state structures and methods, Hitler, Himmler, Walther Darré, and other Nazi ideologues envisioned Ukraine as "a hothouse of Germanic blood," as the future breeding ground of the Aryan race where soldier-peasants tilled the soil, weapons at their side, ready to defend the farm from the "Asian hordes." Hitler summed up the Nazi colonizing mission in Ukraine as follows: "In twenty years the Ukraine will already be a home for twenty million inhabitants besides the natives. In three hundred years, the country will be one of the loveliest gardens in the world. As for the natives, we'll have to screen them carefully. The Jew, that destroyer, we shall drive out . . . our colonizing penetration must be constantly progressive, until it reaches the stage where our own colonists far outnumber the local inhabitants."[61]

Hitler and his cohorts prided themselves as revolutionaries with a radical plan for transforming Ukraine, but their ideas did not develop in a historical vacuum. Thus one finds in Hitler's and Himmler's imaginings of the new Aryan paradise references to the North American frontier, the British Empire in India, and the European exploitation of Africans in the late nineteenth century. Indeed, Ukraine was to be Germany's India. Ukrainians were not to be educated; their nationalistic senses were not to be awakened. They were only to serve their Germans masters like helots and could expect in return, as Hitler put it, "scarves, glass beads and everything that colonial peoples like."[62] In Himmler's SS propaganda publication, *Der Untermensch* (The Sub-Human), one reads about the life and death struggle between Germans and Jews alongside Nazi claims to Eastern European territory, depicted as "black earth that could be a paradise, a California of Europe."[63] Propaganda efforts by the regime, including photos and films, showed ethnic German settlers driving covered wagons adorned with portraits of their Führer.[64] German officials and soldiers in Ukraine wrote home to the Reich that the black marketeering in Ukraine was like trading with "Negro tribes" (*Negerstämmen*) who exchanged ivory for glass beads.[65]

Nazi colonial fantasies—evident in propaganda images, common metaphors, literature that circulated among officials—and the self-fashioning of Nazi leaders (Koch's commissars were ridiculed by Ukrainians and Germans alike for "strutting about like golden pheasants") mingled with an everyday reality of bureaucratic turf wars, power struggles, and ideological clashes over the priorities of *Ostpolitik* (eastern policy). Though much scholarship has dealt with the power struggles between and within Alfred Rosenberg's Reich Ministry for the Occupied Eastern Territories and Himmler's sprawling SS police and racial resettlement agencies, little has been written about the ideological basis of these conflicts. One of the essential divides in the *Ostpolitik* debate was an issue that Rosenberg identified in the 1930s (if not earlier), but was unable to resolve in his capacity as Reich Minister for the Occupied Eastern Territories. More than a decade before the Germans conquered Ukraine, Rosenberg published an editorial in the *Völkischer Beobachter* about Germany's future challenge. Germany had to combine its otherwise divergent *Ostpolitik* and *Weltpolitik* trends, he wrote, in order to satisfy the "peasant" and "Viking" drives of the German Volk. In Rosenberg's mind, the peasant represented the settler, organically and racially tied to the land, while the Viking embodied a Teutonic spirit of conquest. Historian Woodruff Smith has phrased this conflict another way, arguing that Hitler and the Nazi leadership "had to solve the Weltpolitik-Lebensraum dichotomy in the German imperialist tradition. In doing so, they bridged the migrationist and economic driving forces for expansion by developing an ambitious program of resettlement and economic autarky within a Nazi-dominated Europe."[66]

The merger of these two expansionist currents—one focused on settlement, the other on economic extraction—occurred in the Reich Commissariat as it did in Poland, and with similarly disastrous results. Yet for decades, many scholars of the Second World War and the Third Reich, including Smith, concluded that this unusual brand of Nazi imperialist ideology explained how the war began but not why the Holocaust came about, when in fact Nazi expansionism was inherently anti-Semitic and genocidal. Thus, for example, Smith concluded that, "many of the most horrendous of Nazi actions (especially the massacre of the Jews) and many of the self-defeating economic initiatives of the German government before and during the World War had comparatively little to do with the specifically imperialist parts of the Nazi program."[67] His approach also missed significant continuities of German "native" policies in the Kaiser's Africa and Hitler's Eastern Europe.

The causal links between the Holocaust and the Nazi conquest of its *Lebensraum* were forged in the summer of 1941, when the Germans invaded the Soviet Union. According to Christopher Browning, the fateful months of Nazi decision making surrounding the Holocaust coincided with the German war against the Soviet Union in the summer of 1941, as he described it, in a "euphoria of victory."[68] The warfare was not limited to the front lines of battle, but also waged in the rear areas against Bolsheviks, Jews and other "threats." The success of this initial *Vernichtungskrieg* emboldened Nazi leaders to opt for mass murder of all European Jews. But Browning's "euphoria of victory" was also an expression of what historian Elizabeth Harvey has analyzed and Germans at the time called "*Ostrausch*," a colonizing high or intoxication with the East.[69] Even as the military advance slowed in the fall of 1941, the Nazi imperial dream motivated ever more radical genocidal schemes against the Jews and other "natives" trapped behind the lines. By 1942, most of the Europe fell within the sphere of the Nazi empire, but German leaders focused on the East as the central laboratory for genocidal and colonial experiments.

In fact, the now-infamous "Final Solution" order (dated 31 July 1941) that empowered Reinhard Heydrich to pursue a European-wide campaign against the Jews occurred about the same time as Hitler's lengthy discussion with Göring, Bormann, Lammers, Rosenberg, and Keitel about creating a Garden of Eden in the East.[70] This meeting also sealed Erich Koch's appointment as Reich Commissar. Göring nominated Koch by arguing that Koch was the best suited to fully exploit Ukraine's economic resources. Rosenberg objected because Koch was an uncontrollable brute with no appreciation for Ukrainians as a people. Typically, Hitler made the final decision, stating, "the most important region for the next three years is undoubtedly the Ukraine. Therefore, *it will be best for Koch* to be appointed there."[71] Meanwhile, Himmler, whose power was extended over police and security operation in the former Soviet territories, mobilized his resettlement experts to expand the *Generalplan Ost* to include these newly won territories.[72]

As Hitler's right hand man for "Germanization" and security operations, Heinrich Himmler oversaw the development of a new racial and spatial scheme for Ukraine. It was not to be 100 percent Germanized like the annexed territories of the Reich in the Polish Warthegau. Instead, Himmler's planners conceived of Ukraine as a land of *Siedlungsmarken* and *Stützpunkte*, or patches of German settlements. They aimed to consolidate the scattered communities of Volhynian Germans located in west-central Ukraine and residing in the Zhytomyr Commissariat, and the so-called Black Sea Germans located in southern Ukraine, including the Crimea (which Hitler dreamed of as a Nazi Riviera and Robert Ley envisioned as "one large German spa" for his "Strength Through Joy" tourism).[73] The ethnic German settlements and farms were to be placed along the new autobahns, railway lines, and river ways running from east to west and north to south.[74] Such Nazi dreams may very well have inspired Hitler and Himmler to push through a genocidal Final Solution to the Jewish Question. However, most of their subordinates who carried out the killing rarely presented or explained their actions as the first step in German colonization. Instead of referring to vague, utopian notions of a future Aryan paradise in Ukraine, lower-level perpetrators wrote of the immediate security threat posed by Soviet Jews, the so-called bearers of Bolshevism.

Acting under guidelines and instructions from superiors, German soldiers, SS and policemen, and administrative functionaries secured their hegemony over Ukraine through a ruthless campaign of ethnic cleansing and suppression of all forms of resistance. Quickly moving from town to town, shtetl to shtetl, they apprehended and killed Soviet functionaries, Communist Party members, and in ever-increasing numbers, Jews.[75] The Chief of the Reich Security Main Office, Reinhard Heydrich, deployed his *Einsatzgruppen* to penetrate the towns and villages and initiate shooting sprees and pogroms against the intelligentsia and Jewish men with greater force than they had applied in Poland during Autumn 1939. As many as

25,000 Jews died in pogroms during the 1941 invasion of western Ukraine. In Zhytomyr as elsewhere, Nazi secret police stirred up popular anti-Semitism with propaganda campaigns and public demonstrations. Shortly after the Jews of Zhytomyr had been forced into the historic Jewish quarter along Chudnovskaia, a notice appeared in the local Ukrainian paper. Nazi propagandists and officials denounced the Jews as arsonists and blamed them for the destruction of the city center that occurred during the invasion (which had actually been caused by the Luftwaffe bombers). In retaliation, one hundred male Jews were seized, marched along the main square, forced into trucks, transported to the edge of the city and shot on 19 July.[76] Less than two weeks later, Himmler's right-hand man in Ukraine, SS-General Friedrich Jeckeln, sanctioned the killing of women, and pressured subordinates to kill as many Jews as possible.[77] By August 1941, Nazi leaders realized that genocide of all Soviet Jews was possible and began to expand the killing actions against women and children.

As Nazi leaders saw it, the "constructive" work of colonization—the exploitation of Ukraine's racial and economic assets—could not begin until the Reich's political enemies and racial threats had been destroyed and rooted out. Therefore the priority of the advanced squads of mobile killing units such as SS-Colonel Paul Blobel's *Sonderkommando* 4A was to "cleanse" the territory and prepare the way for other Germanization forces operating in its wake.[78] Not far behind Blobel's mobile killing unit was another *Einsatzgruppe* deployed by Himmler, the *Sonderkommando Russland*. In form, the "Special Commando Russia" (less than half the size of an *Einsatzgruppe*) epitomized the conglomeration of security and racial specialists that the SS and police became. It consisted of about 280 men (and a few female assistants, welfare workers, and teachers) from the Reich Commission for the Strengthening of Germandom (RKF), the Race and Settlement Main Office (RuSHA), the Economic and Administrative Main Office (WVHA), the Ethnic German Liaison Office (VoMi), and the Security Service (SD). Many had tested out their methods the previous two years in Poland, concentrating their resettlement efforts in the Warthegau and around Lublin in the General Government. In Ukraine, the *Sonderkommando Russland* established headquarters first in Zhytomyr then Odessa, Nicoleav, Crimea, and Kiev.[79] Thus, while the Sipo-SD *Einsatzgruppen* (C and D) focused on security and intelligence operations, above all anti-Jewish measures, these other SS colonization task forces concentrated on three secret Germanization activities: 1) determination of "valuable German blood"; 2) survey and registration of the land for later SS colonization; and 3) coordination of colonization work with other Himmler agencies in order to secure SS police strongholds in Ukraine.[80] However, only in certain locations where ethnic Germans resided did the unfolding of the Holocaust and Nazi *Volksdeutsche* programs actually coincide, and this overlap occurred mainly in Romanian occupied parts of southern Ukraine.

In the Reich Commissariat Ukraine, the largest concentrations of ethnic Germans were around the Black Sea, Dnipropetrovs'k, and Zhytomyr. In the Black Sea region, which was divided between German and Romanian occupiers, *Sonderkommando Russland* task forces (under Dr. Klaus Siebert's command) registered more than 130,000 ethnic Germans in July and August 1941.[81] Siebert's headquarters was in Landau, a historic ethnic German settlement about fifty kilometers northwest of Nicoleav. From here, his staff managed fourteen settlement centers (*Bereichkommandos*) that stretched across German military, civilian, and Romanian-occupied territory. According to the Tighina Agreement of 30 August 1941 and a November 1941 pact between Romanian Foreign Minister Mihai Antonescu and German Ambassador to Romania Manfred von Killinger, the *Volksdeutsche* colonies in the newly acquired Romanian territory (formerly in Soviet Ukraine) came under the authority of the *Volksdeutsche Mittelstelle* (VoMi), which deployed its SS personnel to the historic settlements of Rastatt, Lichtenfeld, Hoffnungsthal, and Bergdorf, among others. Most of these German communities originated with the migrations of Germans to tsarist Russia in the late eighteenth and nineteenth centuries.[82]

The settlements contained ethnic German mayors, schools, farms, and semi-autonomous German police forces, known as the *Selbstschutz*.[83] With minimal prodding from the Reich German and Romanian authorities, the colonists and their *Selbstschutz* forces were mobilized to assist in the "ethnic cleansing." They massacred Jews and Roma who lived in or near their colonies. According to testimony of a former Romanian prefect in Transnistria, in 1942 the inhabitants of the ethnic German colony Schönfeld killed and burned gypsies on their farms.[84] In the winter of 1941/42, as many as 30,000 Jews were brought from Odessa to Beresovka, located near a cluster of ethnic German colonies. Romanian and German documents as well as eyewitness accounts reveal that a combination of ethnic German *Selbstschutz*, colonists, Ukrainian militia, and Romanian gendarmes shot 18,000 Jews at the death camp of Domanovka south of the Bug River. At the Romanian camp of Bogdanovka, where another 48,000 Jews were forcibly marched, tens of thousands were killed in continuous mass shootings, barn burnings, and with hand grenades. Many succumbed in the freezing temperatures to typhus and famine-related illnesses. [85] In summer and fall 1942, while Himmler was stationed at his Ukrainian headquarters near Zhytomyr, he and his staff toured the *Volksdeutsche* communities and were so impressed with the work of the *Selbstschutz* in southern Ukraine and Transnistria that they formed similar police training schools and activated *Volksdeutsche* police and Waffen-SS units for antipartisan actions in the Reich Commissariat Ukraine.[86]

Besides Himmler, Alfred Rosenberg carved out his area of colonizing activity, which he tried to expand until the last days of the occupation. Dr. Karl Stumpp was Rosenberg's main agent in Ukraine, charged with the registration, rehabilitation, and education of ethnic Germans in Ukraine. But he was not the only agent in the field working on these tasks. Often Stumpp bumped into Nazi Party representatives from the National Socialist People's Welfare Society (NSV) and Himmler's agents from the Ethnic German Liaison Office (VoMi). The overlapping and often confused efforts of the multitude of Nazi colonizers, who had competing visions for developing and exploiting the region, resulted in a failed program of rehabilitating and mobilizing ethnic Germans. There was no Nazi machinery of "construction" in the East that compared in efficiency and inter-agency collaboration with the Holocaust's machinery of destruction.

Stumpp managed a staff of about eighty civilian experts, who were an odd mix of genealogists, ethnographers, racial biologists, geographers, Nazi Party activists, and welfare workers. They combed Ukraine's villages for "pure" and "mixed" Germans, carefully compiling detailed family registers, statistical village reports, and maps depicting the locations of ethnic Germans. Between December 1941 and March 1943, they administered questionnaires to 82,000 inhabitants, representing just under half of the entire *Volksdeutsche* population in the Reich Commissariat Ukraine.[87] In their surveys, they rarely noted anything about the history or presence of Jews in these communities. In a 1943 report on the town of Tschernjachow near Zhytomyr, Stumpp's tabulators, inserted the number 2,662 for the number of Jews living there on 1 June 1941, but left empty the column for Jews remaining in 1943. Thus, as historian Kate Brown has argued, colonizers who were census takers, list makers, surveyors—in short, those who sought to redraw the ethnic map not by bloodying their hands but by rolling up their bureaucratic sleeves—turned a blind eye to the fate of the Jews and instead focused their work and directed their empathy toward the sorry plight of the ethnic Germans. The stark absence of Jews in their detailed demographic reports manifests that by the end of 1942 most Jews in Ukraine had been ghettoized and killed. The Jews were not counted in these inventories of the Reich's racial stock. Instead the *Volksdeutsche* were carefully listed as the racial "material" that would form the foundation of the Nazi empire in the East.[88]

Underlying this fantasy of an Aryan bulwark in Ukraine was the fact that German leaders desperately needed manpower to secure the Reich. Yet as regional chiefs closely examined the ethnic Germans in Ukraine, they realized that the foundation of their empire had many cracks. The economic consequences of the Holocaust in Ukraine were significant since the Jewish population comprised the leading sector of skilled and industrial workers. The Wehrmacht's armaments inspector in Ukraine observed the adverse effects of the killing and complained to his superiors in Berlin that the executions of 150,000–200,000 Jews during the summer and fall of 1941 resulted in the loss of "badly needed tradesmen, who were often indispensable to the armed forces." Furthermore, the inspector wrote: "If we shoot the Jews, let the prisoners of war perish, condemn the urban population in large part to death by starvation, and also lose a part of the farming population in the coming year through starvation, the question remains unanswered: *Who then is supposed to produce anything of economic value here?*" In answering this question, the armaments inspector wrote that the *Volksdeutsche* were "not an element on which the administration and economy of the country can rely."[89]

Indeed, local German officials believed that the *Volksdeutsche* were not strong enough to defend the Reich's frontier because they were economically destitute, had intermarried with Ukrainians and Jews, and lacked basic education including knowledge of German. Most worked as farmers and day laborers, and 40 percent in the Zhytomyr region, were unemployed and lacked skills. Soviet mass deportations in 1937/1938 and 1941 had nearly depleted the male population, leaving behind mostly women, children, and the infirm. The sad state of Ukraine's ethnic German population fell far short of the Nazi racial ideal of the superior Aryan. Instead of finding a population that could administer and defend the Reich's imperial borderlands and colonies, Nazi "Germanizers" discovered a population that became more of a welfare burden than a resource.[90]

Nazi resettlement programs were part of several genocidal colonization schemes for Ukraine. But from the standpoint of most Ukrainians, the most abhorrent of these schemes was neither the Holocaust, nor the *Volksdeutsche* campaigns. The main cause of resistance among Ukrainians (who constituted 80 percent of the population) was the forced labor programs and the Nazi retention of the collective farm system. Decades ago, French scholar Raymond Aron pointed out in his work on European empire that "native" resistance was historically the downfall of empires.[91] While it was not as decisive in the Nazi case (because the Allied armies defeated Germany), it arose nonetheless as a feature of Nazi rule in Europe that resembled partisan or guerilla warfare in the colonies. As in other colonialisms, such resistance revealed that the Nazi overseers had lost their grip over the territory. *Volksdeutsche* households became favorite targets of Ukrainian and Soviet partisan attacks. In the fall of 1942, Heinrich Himmler convinced Hitler that the only way to safeguard the *Volksdeutsche* from further assaults was to create a new colony near the *Reichsführer's* heavily guarded field headquarters at Zhytomyr. Himmler named the colony Hegewald ("preservation forest"). At least 17,000 Ukrainians were rounded up from the area, forced into railway cars and deported to camps in southern Russia or deported to the Reich as forced laborers. Over ten thousand ethnic Germans were moved into Hegewald. Another nine thousand arrived in spring 1943 in the neighboring Försterstadt colony. Many of the children in this colony had been kidnapped from Ukrainian homes and placed in Germanization orphanages. Rosenberg's commissars complained that these resettlement operations and forced labor deportations had driven Ukrainians into the forests where they joined resistance groups, resulting in lower productivity of Ukrainians at work and on the farms. SS General and General Commissar for Zhytomyr Ernst Leyser, who did not hesitate to push through the last killing actions against Jews in the region, voiced his frustration about the German approach to the partisan "menace." Partisans controlled most of his territory. The Ukrainian population proved not to be docile colonial folk. Leyser could not protect his men from regular assassination attempts and attacks. As a result, rural commissars had to limit their travel around the region and barricade themselves in their offices. And perhaps more troubling to Leyser's superiors, they could not guarantee the planting and reaping of the next harvest, which was meant to feed Germans in the Reich and soldiers on the front.[92] The partisan warfare, Nazi-led genocide, and resettlement operations had made it nearly impossible for Leyser and his ilk to develop and exploit the region economically. As it turned out, the Nazi goal of a racially reordered space in Ukraine was nearly accomplished, but Hitler's imperial dreams of German hegemony and autarky in Europe fell apart.

Conclusion

Colonialist thinking shaped Nazi genocidal concepts, rationales, and policies to a much larger degree than prior scholarship has stressed. The Germans discussed here imagined the East as a laboratory to implement the "dirty work" of empire building as well as to experiment with the "constructive" tasks. The theories and practices of Nazi empire builders demonstrate that the Germans found many historical precedents from which to imagine and develop their revolutionary campaign in the East.

Nazi colonialism led to two genocides in Poland and Ukraine respectively: one against the Jews, and another against the indigenous Poles and Ukrainians. Both were implicit in the Nazi ideology of Germanization, *Lebensraum*, and anti-Semitism. As the dynamics of occupation unfolded during the course of the war, the Jewish genocide radicalized until it resulted in the near destruction of the entire victim group. By contrast, the Slavic indigenocide began with a massive Nazi attack upon Polish nationhood in 1939; while remaining murderous, the momentum toward completion of the genocidal act receded as the drive to murder the Jews increased. One went forward as the other fell short, and the reasons shed much light on the nature of colonialism and genocide.

The Jews did not represent a typical colonial other. Nazi anti-Semitism instead portrayed Jews as alien exploiters, the archetypal colonial settlers who must be destroyed if native society was to return to its former state of community and equality. And yet, the overwhelming majority of Jews encountered by the German occupiers lived in such poverty as to fulfill the stereotype of the colonial "native." The colonial ideology thus had to bridge the gap by representing the Polish-Jewish "natives" as the reservoir of exploitative "world Jewry," and Soviet Jews as the agents of "Judeo-Bolshevism." In both cases, anti-Semitism reinforced the Nazis' sense of colonial mission. On the one hand, the Jews had to be exterminated to meet ideological imperatives that transcended colonial rule and influenced Nazi colonizers to see Jews as a problem once they arrived in the colonies. On the other hand, most of the killing took place in the Nazi colonies by colonial authorities motivated to commit genocide because they felt it solved specific problems of colonial rule, such as economic stabilization and public health. This was especially the case in Poland, and less so in Ukraine where Jews formed the artisan and industrial working class. The killing of Jews began in Ukraine as a part of the anti-Judeo-Bolshevik crusade, and reverberated back upon the authorities in Poland, inspiring them to kill Poland's Jews.

The Poles and Ukrainians came closest to the colonial stereotype of the "native." Although genocide of these groups did not progress beyond the stage of de-nationalization and extreme pacification, the result might be considered a "colonial genocide" in the usual sense of the term. Yet for all that, these genocides fell short of their original goals for three reasons typical of colonial genocides. First, the colonizers were absolutely dependent upon the cheap labor and the grain that the indigenous people produced. The war only intensified the situation. Second, the Nazi efforts at "Indian removal," interminable "slave raids," and brutal forced labor practices generated resistance so uneconomical that it persuaded even Hitler and Himmler that the time was not ripe for indigenocide.

Third, these issues led to a struggle between an exploitation-minded civil administration and a settlement-focused police-executive in the form of the SS. This situation is reminiscent of the German genocide of the Herero in 1904: military authority, under General Trotha, was separated from the civil authority under Governor Leutwein. As the civilians urged a negotiated settlement that would preserve the Herero as a docile labor force, the military aimed to exterminate the rebels. For Trotha, it was a race war and a matter of honor for the German Army. Reports of Trotha's genocidal activities had to make it all the way back to Berlin and be countermanded by the Kaiser before the army stopped the killing. Likewise, the Nazis in Poland shared a consensus that Poland was German *Lebensraum*. Because the executive authority was in the hands of the SS, the civilians had to appeal to Berlin, by which time it was possible to stop the resettlement actions but not to save Nazi colonial rule.

Nazi colonial fantasies and dreams of autarky were tinged with anti-Semitism because they sprang from the same source: the basic desire to free the nation from its perceived vulnerability to globalization, whether caused by war and blockade, hyperinflation, or economic depression.[93] The resulting social and economic decay had to be stopped, reversed, and prevented from reoccurring. The Nazis perceived "the Jews" as the primary agent for these disasters seemingly visited upon Germany from the outside, just as the new racial empire would create a safety zone for Germans to flourish in isolation from that cruel world. All empires were built with war; however, in twentieth-century conditions, only total war would suffice to build a total empire.

Acknowledgment

We thank Jason Colby, Konrad Kwiet, Vejas Liulevicius, Dirk Moses, and Roland Spickermann for assistance in the writing of this chapter.

Notes

1. Hanns Johst, *Ruf des Reiches, Echo des Volkes,* 6th ed. (Munich, 1942), 86. See also Michael Burleigh, *The Third Reich: A New History* (New York, 2000), 447.
2. Johst, *Ruf des Reiches,* 87–88.
3. See David Spurr, *Rhetoric of Empire* (Durham, NC, 1993), 28–42; M.L. Pratt, *Imperial Eyes* (London, 1992), 201–5.
4. Quoted in Enzo Traverso, *The Origins of Nazi Violence,* trans. Janet Lloyd (New York, 2003), 69–70. Aimé Césaire makes a similar remark in his *Discourse on Colonialism*, trans. Joan Pinkham (New York, 2000), 36.
5. Robert J. C. Young briefly discusses "fascism as colonialism brought home to Europe" in this context in *White Mythologies: Writing History and the West* (London, 1990), 8–9, 128; and idem, *Postcolonialism: An Historical Introduction* (London, 2001), 2. For an example within Nazi Germany, see Theodor Oberländer, "Bündnis oder Ausbeutung," in *Der Osten und die deutsche Wehrmacht: Sechs Denkschriften*

aus den Jahren 1941–43 gegen die NS-Kolonialthese, ed. Alfred Schickel (Asendorf, 1987), 124. For an original analysis of the history of German migration and specifically Germanization in Poland, see Sebastian Conrad, *Globalisierung und Nation im Deutschen Kaiserreich* (Munich, 2006).

6. Johst, *Ruf des Reiches*, 88–89.
7. Mark Mazower, *Dark Continent: Europe's Twentieth Century* (New York, 1998), 71–72.
8. Traverso, *Origins of Nazi Violence*, 140.
9. Alexander Dallin, *German Rule in Russia, 1941–1945: A Study of Occupation Policies* (London, 1957), 254 and 454.
10. See Michael Burleigh, *Germany Turns Eastward: A Study of Ostforschung in the Third Reich* (Cambridge, 1988); Rolf-Dieter Müller, *Hitlers Ostkrieg und die deutsche Siedlungspolitik* (Frankfurt am Main, 1991); Jürgen Zimmerer, "Im Dienst des Imperiums: Die Geographen der Berliner Universität zwischen Kolonialwissenschaften und Ostforschung," *Jahrbuch für Universitätsgeschichte* 7 (2004): 73–100. Also see, for example, the discussion of empire-builders who callously disregarded the lives of non-Germans in the *General Plan Ost* meeting notes of Dr. Wetzel from 7 Feb 1942. Among the participants in this discussion over the Baltics was the famous racial scientist Eugen Fischer of the Kaiser Wilhelm Institute. U.S. National Archives and Record Administration (NARA), Record Group (RG) 238, International Military Tribunal at Nuremberg (IMT), NO-2585.
11. The Nazi worldview derived from various strands of thought that had become especially popular as of the late nineteenth century. See Woodruff Smith, *The Ideological Origins of Nazi Imperialism* (Oxford, 1986); Holger Herwig, "*Geopolitik*: Haushofer, Hitler and Lebensraum," *The Journal of Strategic Studies* (1999): 218–41; Alan Steinweis, "Eastern Europe and the Notion of the 'Frontier' in Germany to 1945," in *Germany and Eastern Europe: Cultural Identities and Cultural Differences*, ed. Keith Bullivant, Geoffrey Giles, and Walter Pape, *Yearbook of European Studies* 13 (1999). As Hitler put it to his subordinates: "Out of the eastern territories, we must make a Garden of Eden; they [the eastern territories] are vital to us . . . [overseas] colonies play an entirely subordinate role." See Bormann's notes of the July 16 1941 meeting, NARA, RG 238, IMT, Document 221-L, reprinted in volume 38, 86–94.
12. See Dr. Maurer's files, records of the Reich Ministry for the Occupied Eastern Territories, United States Holocaust Memorial Museum (USHMM), RG 14.017M, fiche R6/7. On the significance of the landscape in German colonization see, Joachim Wolschke-Bulmahn, "Heinrich Himmler and Landscape Planning in Nazi Germany," German Historical Institute, Washington DC, 11 November 1999; Elizabeth Harvey, *Women and the Nazi East: Agents and Witnesses of Germanization* (New Haven, CT, 2003), 118–20.
13. Traverso, *Origins of Nazi Violence*, 73–75, 153. See the recent critique of Arendt, which aptly points out that her focus on the British South African model does not suit the German case of imperial rule in Eastern Europe, she fails to appreciate the influence of American expansionism on Nazi thinking, and she wrongly privileges the nation-state as the only protector of basic human rights and "fundamentally at odds with imperialism," among other interesting insights. Pascal Grosse, "From Colonialism to National Socialism to Postcolonialism: Hannah Arendt's 'Origins of Totalitarianism," *Postcolonial Studies* 9 (2006): 32–52.
14. Jürgen Zimmerer, "Von Windhuk nach Warschau. Die rassische Privilegiengesellschaft in Deutsch-Südwestafrika—ein Modell mit Zukunft?," in *Rassenmischehen—Mischlinge—Rassentrennung. Zur Politik der Rasse im deutschen Kaiserreich*, ed.

Frank Becker (Stuttgart 2004), 97–123. Birthe Kundrus, "Kontinuitäten, Parallelen, Rezeptionen—Überlegungen zur 'Kolonialisierung' des Nationalsozialismus," *WerkstattGeschichte* 43 (2006): 45–62. For more on colonialism, see Jürgen Osterhammel, *Colonialism: A Theoretical Overview*, trans. Shelley Frisch (Princeton, NJ, 1997).

15. Jürgen Zimmerer, "Colonialism and the Holocaust: Towards an Archaeology of Genocide," in *Genocide and Settler Society: Frontier Violence and Stolen Indigenous Children in Australian History*, ed. A. Dirk Moses (New York, 2004), 49.
16. Jürgen Zimmerer, "Kolonialer Genozid? Vom Nutzen und Nachteil einer historischen Kategorie für eine Globalgeschichte des Völkermordes," in *Enteignet-Vertrieben-Ermordet: Beiträge zur Genozidforschung*, ed. Dominik Schaller et al (Zurich, 2004).
17. Jürgen Zimmerer, "Colonialism and the Holocaust," 49–76. For a more systematic explanation of the Nazi occupation as a colonial enterprise, see David Furber, "Near as Far in the Colonies: The Nazi Occupation of Poland," *International History Review* 26, no. 3 (2004): 541–79. For an historiographical overview of the Nazi occupation and the Holocaust in Poland, see Dieter Pohl, "War, Occupation, and the Holocaust in Poland," in *The Historiography of the Holocaust*, ed. Dan Stone (Houndmills, UK, 2004), 88–119.
18. Christopher Browning with Jürgen Matthäus, *The Origins of the Final Solution: The Evolution of Nazi Jewish Policy September 1939–March 1942* (Lincoln, NE, 2004); Götz Aly and Susanne Heim, *Architects of Annihilation: Auschwitz and the Logic of Destruction*, trans. A.G. Blunden (Princeton, NJ, 2002); Götz Aly, *"Final Solution": Nazi Population Policy and the Murder of European Jews* (New York, 1999); Also see Christian Gerlach, *Kalkulierte Morde: Die deutsche Wirtschafts-und Vernichtungspolitik in Weissrussland 1941–1944* (Hamburg, 1999), and chapters in *National Socialist Extermination Policies*, ed. Ulrich Herbert (New York, 2000).
19. See Joseph Goebbels, "Why do we oppose the Jews?" (1932) reprinted at http://www.calvin.edu/academic/cas/gpa/haken32.htm. Compare Jeffrey Herf, *The Jewish Enemy: Nazi Propaganda During World War II and the Holocaust* (Cambridge, MA, 2006) with Ghassan Hage, "The Anatomy of Anti-Arab Racism," *Australian Financial Review*, 15 August 2003. Reprinted as the foreword in Scott Poynting, Greg Noble, Paul Tabar, and Jock Collins, *Bin Laden in the Suburbs* (Sydney, 2004).
20. See Alan E. Steinweis, *Studying the Jew: Scholarly Antisemitism in Nazi Germany* (Cambridge, MA, 2006) and Mahmood Mamdani, *When Victims Become Killers* (Trenton, NJ, 2001), 9–11.
21. Adolf Hitler, "Der völkische Gedanke und der Partei," Institute for Contemporary History, Munich, Fa 52.46, 3.
22. Hans Richter, *Einsatz der Polizei* (Berlin, 1943), 30.
23. Friedrich Gollert, *Warschau unter deutscher Herrschaft* (Cracow, 1942), 175.
24. H.E. Seifert, *Der Jude an der Ostgrenze* (Berlin, 1940), 12.
25. Hellmut Körner, *Zwischen Warthegau und UdSSR* (Berlin, 1941), plate XV.
26. Gustav Andraschko, "Die 'Lehranstalt der Weisen Lublins,'" *Krakauer Zeitung*, 31 May 1942.
27. See Czeslaw Madajczyk, *Die Okkupationspolitik Nazideutschlands in Polen 1939–1945*, trans. Berthold Puchert (1970; reprint, Berlin, 1988), 46–142, on German occupation policy in the General Government.
28. Christopher Browning, "Initiating the Final Solution: The Fateful Months of September–October 1941," *Ina Levine Annual Lecture*, 13 March 2003, United States Holocaust Memorial Museum, Washington, DC, 2003, 8; Bogdan Musial, *Deutsche Zivilverwaltung und Judenverfolgung im Generalgouvernement* (Wiesbaden, 1999), 203–8; Hellmut Mühler, "Lagebericht," 15 October 1941, in *Die*

faschistische Okkupationspolitik in Polen (1939–1945), ed. Wolfgang Schumann and Ludwig Nestler (Cologne, 1989), doc. 95, 208.

29. Bogdan Musial, "The Origins of 'Operation Reinhard': The Decision-Making Process for the Mass Murder of the Jews in the *Generalgouvernement*," *Yad Vashem Studies* 28 (2000): 116.
30. "Parteieinsatz kolonialen Charakters," *Krakauer Zeitung*, 26 October 1941.
31. Hans Frank, Speech to Nazi Party Organization, 23 October 1941, in *Diensttagebuch des deutschen Generalgouverneurs in Polen 1939–1945*, ed. Werner Präg and Wolfgang Jakobmeier (Stuttgart, 1975), 444.
32. Richard Overy, *Why the Allies Won* (New York and London, 1995), 19. On the significance of the "double battle," see Browning, *Origins of the Final Solution*, 314–30.
33. Adolf Hitler, *Monologe im Führerhauptquartier 1941–44*, ed. Werner Jochmann (Hamburg, 1980), 90–91.
34. The Warthegau was a province carved out of western Poland in 1939. Half of it had belonged to Germany before 1918 as the Province Posen, and half had been under Russian rule. The Nazis were attempting to Germanize it and the other provinces they annexed from Poland, such as Danzig-West Prussia and East Upper Silesia. See Richard Lukas, *The Forgotten Holocaust: The Poles Under German Occupation* (Lexington, KY, 1986), 1–39, for a concise description of the different territories. On resettlement in the Warthegau, see Aly, *"Final Solution."* On East Upper Silesia, see Sybille Steinbacher, *"Musterstadt Auschwitz": Germanisierungspolitik und Judenmord in Ostoberschlesien* (Munich, 2000); on Danzig-West Prussia, see Carl Tighe, *Gdánsk/Danzig: National Identity in the Polish-German Borderlands* (London, 1990), 154–77.
35. Musial, *Deutsche Zivilverwaltung*, 208–12.
36. Kreishauptmann of Zamosc to Governor Ernst Zörner, 4 April 1942, USHMM, RG 15–068M, reel 1.
37. Governor Ernst Zörner to State Secretary Josef Bühler, 13 February 1942, USHMM, RG 15–068M, reel 1.
38. Police major Erich Schwieger on resistance to resettlement, 4 March 1943, in *Die faschistische Okkupationspolitik*, doc. 135, 255–56.
39. Hans Frank, memorandum to Hitler, 25 May 1943, in *Die faschistische Okkupationspolitik*, doc. 148, 273.
40. Präg and Jakobmeier, "Introduction," 28.
41. Curzio Malaparte, *Kaputt*, trans. Cesare Foligno (New York, 1946), 64.
42. For example, see Hans Frank, "Das Generalgouvernement in der Neuordnung Europas," *Europäische Revue* 18 (May 1942): 233–35.
43. Hans Frank quoted in Dieter Rebentisch, *Führerstaat und Verwaltung im Zweiten Weltkrieg* (Stuttgart, 1989), 174. On the "colony as laboratory" see Dirk van Laak, "Kolonien als 'Laboratorien der Moderne'?" in *Das Kaiserreich transnational—Deutschland in der Welt 1871–1914*, ed. Sebastian Conrad and Jürgen Osterhammel (Göttingen, 2004), 257–79.
44. See the protocol of the meetings on economic policy, 7 June 1940 and 22 July 1941, in *Diensttagebuch*, 224–26 and 389–90.
45. Lukas, *Forgotten Holocaust*, ix.
46. See Aly and Heim, *Architects of Annihilation*.
47. John Connelly, "Nazis and Slavs: From Racial Theory to Racist Practice," *Central European History* 32 (1999): 18–19.
48. Waldemar Lotnik, *Nine Lives* (London, 1999), 125.
49. *Kreishauptmann* in Jedrzejow, "Bericht über die Aufbauarbeit," 25 February 1941, USHMM, RG-15.045, reel 1: 1–3.

50. Ibid., 6–7.
51. Gollert, *Deutsche Herrschaft in Warschau*, 72–74.
52. Ibid., 88.
53. Jean-Paul Sartre, *On Genocide* (Boston, 1968).
54. Isabel Hull, "Military Culture and "Final Solutions," in *The Specter of Genocide*, ed. Robert Gellately and Ben Kiernan (Cambridge, 2003), 145.
55. Gollert, *Deutsche Herrschaft in Warschau*, 98.
56. Ludwig Fischer, presentation at meeting of Government General, 14–16 Oct 1941, USHMM, RG 15–008M, reel 4.
57. Seifert, *Der Jude an der Ostgrenze*, 11.
58. Erich Kundt, "Der polnische Staat und seine Minderheiten," *Der Europäische Revue* 18 (May 1942): 255. A copy can be found in the Bundesarchiv Berlin, R 52/250, 28., mirrored in the USHMM in RG-14.025M.
59. Richter, *Einsatz der Polizei*, 31.
60. On Koch, see Karel Berkhoff, *Harvest of Despair: Life and Death in Ukraine under Nazi Rule* (Cambridge, 2004), 37–38 and in passim.
61. Monologue of 17 October 1941, *Hitler's Table Talk, 1941–1944: His Private Conversations* trans. Norman Cameron and R. H. Stevens (London, 2000), 68. Also see *Generalny Plan Wschodni: Zbior dokumentow*, ed. Czeslaw Madajczyk (Warsaw, 1990), 69.
62. Quotation of Adolf Hitler from the Bormann letters, monologue of 17 Sept 1941. Adolf Hitler, *Secret Conversations 1941–1944*, trans. Norman Cameron and R.H. Stevens (New York, 1972), 29.
63. NARA, RG 238, NMT, NO-1805. Reprinted in Ihor Kamenetsky, Appendix II, *Secret Nazi Plans for Eastern Europe: A Study of Lebensraum Policies* (New York, 1961), 189–92.
64. Also see Alan Steinweis, "Eastern Europe and the Notion of the 'Frontier' in Germany to 1945," in *Germany and Eastern Europe*, ed. Keith Bullivant, Geoffrey Giles, and Walter Pape, *Yearbook of European Studies* 13 (1999): 56–69; Horst Grill and Jenkins, "The Nazis and the American South in the 1930s: A Mirror Image?," *Journal of Southern History* 58 (1992): 667–94. Gert Gröning and Joachim Wolschke-Bulmahn, *Der Drang Nach Osten: Zur Entwicklung der Landespflege im Nationalsozialismus und während des 2. Weltkrieges in den ‚eingegliederten Ostgebieten'* (Munich, 1987), 132. For photos of migrating Volhynian Volksdeutschen in covered wagons see, Maximilian du Prel, ed., *Deutsche Generalgouvernement Polen: ein Überblick über Gebiet, Gestaltung und Geschichte, mit 12 Karten und 33 Abbildungen*, 1940.
65. NSDAP report of 3–23 June 1942 trip, NARA, RG 242, T454/R 92/000193–000199.
66. Smith, *The Ideological Origins of Nazi Imperialism*, 241. The connection between the Teutonic model of German Ostkolonisation and the Nazi Lebensraum (as contrasted with British imperialism) was explained by the economics advisor to the Nazi Party in Berlin, Dr. Heinrich Hunke ed. *Hanse, Downing Street und Deutschland's Lebensraum* (Berlin, 1940). On the German "civilizing mission" of *Ostkolonisation*, also see the exhibit catalogue and film, *Das Sowjet Paradies* (Berlin 1942), excerpts available at http://www.calvin.edu/academic/cas/gpa/paradise.htm.
67. Smith, *The Ideological Origins of Nazi Imperialism*, 255; Wendy Lower, *Nazi Empire-Building and the Holocaust in Ukraine* (Chapel Hill, NC, 2005).
68. Browning, *Origins of the Final Solution*, 314–30. The "Final Solution" was the result of several regionally oriented decisions by Nazi leaders who concentrated their assaults on the different Jewish populations across Europe. In 1941 the lack of resistance to the mass murder in the Soviet territories made the genocide of all European Jews thinkable.

After the bolshevized Jews, the Reich Jews were next in line, as the Nazis saw it, hence the October–November 1941 deportations of German Jews to the mass shooting sites in Minsk and Riga, as well as plans for deportations of Reich Jews to Ukraine in early January 1942. See Lower, *Nazi Empire-Building,* 89. For a later dating of a general decision to kill Europe's Jews, see Peter Longerich, *The Unwritten Order: Hitler's Role in the Final Solution* (London, 2003).

69. Harvey, *Women in the Nazi East*, 125.
70. Browning, *Origins of the Final Solution,* 312–13.
71. Underlines in original notes. Bormann Meeting Notes, NARA, RG 238, IMT, 221-L (published in volume 38, 86–94).
72. On 24 June, Himmler instructed Konrad Meyer and staff of the Reich Commission for the Strengthening of Germandom to incorporate the Soviet Territories into the General Plan East. See Peter Witte, et al, eds., *Der Dienstkalender Heinrich Himmlers 1941/1942* (Hamburg, 1999), 179.
73. See Dallin, *German Rule in Russia*, 253–57.
74. Meir Buchsweiler, *Volksdeutsche in der Ukraine am Vorabend und Beginn des Zweiten Weltkrieges—ein Fall doppelter Loyalitaet?* (Tel Aviv, 1984).
75. See pre-Barbarossa orders such as the "Guidelines for Conduct of Troops in the East," in *Verbrechen der Wehrmacht: Dimensionen des Vernichtungskrieges 1941–1944,* ed. Hamburger Institut für Sozialforschung (Hamburg, 2002); Gerhard Hirschfeld, ed., *The Policies of Genocide: Jews and Soviet Prisoners of War in Nazi Germany* (London, 1986).
76. Viktor Trill, statement of 25 June 1960 and of 8 June 1965, Trial of Kuno Callsen et. al., Ludwigsburg 207 AR-Z 419/62. Trill was one of the drivers of the three vehicles in the *Vorkommando.* The executions, explained as retaliation for arson are reported in *Ukraïns'ke Slovo* (Zhytomyr), 19 July 1941. Newspaper Collection ZSA, Ukraine. These killings were also recorded in the *Ereignismeldung* of 19 July 1941 and of 22 July 1941, see Yitzhak Arad, Shmuel Krawkowski and Shmuel Spector, eds., *The Einsatzgruppen Reports,* 41.
77. See Jeckeln's Einsatzbefehl of 25 July 1941 for Novohrad-Volyns'kyi, NARA RG 242, T 501/R5/000559–60. See also Browning, *Origins of the Final Solution*, 309–13.
78. The German People's List (DVL) consisted of four categories: Group I represented those deemed racially Aryan and willing to be Germanized; Group II racially pure Germans who lacked a will to be Germanized but were capable of being Germanized; Group II those with mixed but predominantly Aryan blood and capable of being Germanized, and who could apply for temporary Reich citizenship and then live under racial political surveillance for ten years before receiving citizenship; Group IV were those with only some German blood, assimilated to other groups and unwilling to become German citizens or considered unfit for Germanization; persons in this last category were handed over to the Gestapo, sent to camps, or liquidated on the spot. Those who fit into categories I and II were immediately eligible for Reich German citizenship. See Ingeborg Fleischhauer, "The Ethnic Germans Under Nazi Rule," in *The Soviet Germans: Past and Present,* ed. Ingeborg Fleischhauer and Benjamin Pinkus (New York, 1986), 96–97.
79. On Sonderkommando Russland, see Isabel Heinemann, *"Rasse, Siedlung, deutsches Blut": Das Rasse-& Siedlungshauptamt der SS und die rassenpolitische Neuordnung Europas* (Göttingen, 2003), 418–20. Also see Aly, *"Final Solution,"* 189.
80. Parts of this essay appeared in Wendy Lower, "Hitler's 'Garden of Eden' in Ukraine," in *Gray Zones: Ambiguity and Compromise in the Holocaust and its Aftermath,* ed. Jonathan Petropoulous and John K. Roth (New York, 2005), 179–204. Priorities

as RuSHA chief Otto Hofmann defined them. See Heinemann, "*Rasse, Siedlung, deutsches Blut*," 422.

81. See the war crimes investigation of Dr. Siebert and his staff, Zentralstelle Dortmund gegen Dr. Siebert und andere, 45 Js 26/62, "Verfuegung," 15 January 1974, 1–27.
82. The "pacifistic" Mennonites comprised a large number of them. Nazi ethnographers such as Karl Stumpp traced German migration history further back to the medieval conquests of the Goths: Karl Stumpp, *Ostwanderung: Akten über die Auswanderung der Württemberger nach Russland 1816–1822* (Leipzig, 1941). This study was the second volume in a series: *Sammlung Georg Leibbrandt, Quellen zur Erforschung des Deutschtums in Osteuropa*. Leibbrandt was Rosenberg's chief of the political department in the Ostministerium, July 1941–1943. See the recent analysis of Stumpp's and Leibbrandt's work in Ukraine and their postwar fate, Eric Schmaltz and Samuel Sinner, "The Nazi Ethnographic Research of Georg Leibbrandt and Karl Stumpp in Ukraine and its North American Legacy," *Holocaust and Genocide Studies* 14 (2001): 28–64.
83. On Nazi-Romanian diplomacy vis-à-vis the Holocaust in Transnistria, see Jean Ancel, *Transnistria, 1941–1943: The Romanian Mass Murder Campaign* (Tel Aviv, 2003).
84. Radu Ioanid, *The Holocaust in Romania: The Destruction of Jews and Gypsies under the Antonescu Regime, 1940–1944* (Chicago, 2000), 232–37; see Zentralstelle Dortmund gegen Dr. Siebert und andere 45 Js 26/62; on the persecution of Roma by ethnic German farmers, see International Office of Migration Restitution Claims, Roma Testimony, Geneva Switzerland office.
85. Dalia Ofer, "The Holocaust in Transnistria," in *The Holocaust in the Soviet Union: Studies and Sources on the Destruction of the Jews in the Nazi-Occupied Territories of the USSR, 1941–1944*, ed. Lucjan Dobroszycki and Jeffrey Gurock (New York, 1993), 136–87. On German involvement in Transnistria, see Ioanid, *Holocaust in Romania*, 187–201. Iaonid estimates that 75,000 Jews were killed in the Golta region.
86. Plans for increasing the *Selbstschutz* materialized at Hegewald, where Commander von Oelhafen placed about 2,500 ethnic German men into police formations, established four *Selbstschutz* schools, and began training an additional one thousand men. Compare with the sixteen *Selbstschutz* schools in Transnistria, which trained seven thousand men. See undated report, NARA RG 242, T-175/R 72/2589180. See also Valdis Lumans, *Himmler's Auxiliaries: The Volksdeutsche Mittelstelle and the German Minorities of Europe, 1933–1945* (Chapel Hill, NC, 1993), 246–47.
87. Stumpp, "Abschliessender Bericht," USHMM, RG 31.002M, reel 11. Also see the records of the Deutsche Auslands-Institut, NARA, RG 242, T-81, R/739/0006 and R/740/0010. We are grateful to Timothy Mulligan for providing the DAI materials.
88. Kate Brown, *A Biography of No Place: from Ethnic Borderland to Soviet Heartland* (Cambridge, 2003), 195.
89. Report to Georg Thomas from Armaments Inspector Ukraine, 29 Nov 1941, NARA, RG 238, 2174-PS. Emphasis in original.
90. Wendy Lower, "A New Ordering of Space and Race," *German Studies Review*, no. 25 (2002): 234.
91. Raymond Aron, *The Dawn of Universal History: Selected Essays from a Witness to the Twentieth Century, Raymond Aron*, trans. Barbara Bray (New York, 2002), 33–34, 103–8.
92. Leyser report to RmfdbO, Berlin. 12 Feb 1943, NARA, RG 242, T-175/R140/2667589–593.
93. See Harold James, *The End of Globalization* (Cambridge, MA, 2001), 188–89.

– Section III –

Subaltern Genocide

– *Chapter 17* –

Genocide from Below

The Great Rebellion of 1780–82 in the Southern Andes

David Cahill

Introduction

In the late eighteenth century, mass rebellion swept like a firestorm throughout southern Peru and Bolivia, with secondary outbreaks ignited in Argentina and northwards as far as Venezuela.[1] The rebellion was long in coming. It followed nearly two decades of mounting protest revolts in the highlands and more serious urban insurrections. Those open, violent protests were directed generally against the deleterious consequences for colonial subjects of the Bourbon reform program after c. 1740 that aimed at a root-and-branch restructuring of the empire, and specifically against the heavy-handed and venal implementation of successive reforms by provincial governors and their local allies. Tax imposts had increased dramatically, exponentially so in the case of the indigenous poll-tax or tribute, and their felt impact was exacerbated by the abrupt and occasionally brutal manner of collection. Especially burdensome was the hated *repartimiento de mercancías*, the forced sale of mostly unwanted merchandise at inflated prices to the indigenous and mixed-race peasantry. That this rising tide of unrest culminated in mass rebellion was due to the catalytic effects of three major, divisive legal and jurisdictional disputes that sharpened rivalries and divided loyalties, and gave rebels-in-waiting cause to think that any declaration of insurrection would receive spontaneous support from all social sectors, bar the European-born, peninsular Spaniards (*chapetones*), who were seen as the natural adversaries of the Crown's American subjects.

The core rebellion comprised two separate movements, in Peru and Bolivia respectively, that gradually merged until they fused into one Great Rebellion from mid-1781; it was extinguished by 1782.[2] José Gabriel Túpac

Amaru, a minor provincial chieftain (*cacique*) who claimed to be of royal Inca blood, was leader of the northern rebellion. The southern rebellion was led by an indigenous petty merchant, the self-styled Túpac Catari, whose authority however derived in large part from his invoking the name of his northern counterpart. Túpac Amaru has a preeminent place in the pantheon of the great heroes of Latin American history. His 1780 uprising against Spanish misrule is considered by nationalist historians to be the birth of the Latin American Independence process between 1808 and 1826.[3] This line of interpretation casts the insurgent Inca as having welded disparate races and classes into a modern nation. While many historians reject the allegedly nationalist character of the rebellion, there is widespread consensus among historians that his rebellion was the most momentous event during the long interval between the wars of conquest in the early decades after 1492 and the onset of the Independence wars after 1800. For reasons of space, this chapter will concentrate on the northern Túpac Amaru rebellion in the southern highlands of Peru rather than the Catarista rebellion in Bolivia. Moreover, these two mass rebellions shared several key characteristics but also evinced many significant differences, and therefore require discrete analysis before broader comparisons can usefully be made. For all that, the one provides the contextual counterpoint of the other.

Despite the historiographical salience of the rebellion, few scholars have dwelt at length on its violence per se beyond recording numerous instances of atrocities by both rebels and loyalists, and remarking the level of sanguinary mortality. In the rebellion of 1780–82, a contemporary mortality estimate of 100,000 Indians and 10,000 non-Indians has been widely accepted. This estimate will be discussed later in this essay, but whatever its merits, the incidence of mortality and the racial nature of the conflict invite its interpretation as an instance of genocide. Within a large rebellion or war, there may be isolated genocidal instances and related genocidal discourse, without the whole uprising or war necessarily being genocidal. A distinction can be drawn between isolated genocidal instances within a broader movement and the concerted, or directed implementation of a core genocidal policy. In the rebellion of 1780, two clear orders of Túpac Amaru were repeated serially, and were manifestly genocidal in their intent and execution—the orders to kill all peninsular Spaniards and all provincial governors (corregidores). Historians have not hitherto thought to categorize these commands as genocidal, perhaps because the number of victims was small in relation to the overall mortality occasioned by the rebellion, but genocidal these instances assuredly were. The targeting of any specific racial/ethnic group, irrespective of political allegiance or combat status, would appear to fall within even the most stringent definition of genocide and call for extended explanation as to its genesis.

In spite of the obvious value of the 1780 rebellion as a case study for testing theories of genocide and colonialism, it was not until the appearance in 2002 of Nicholas Robins' study of the Túpac Catari rebellion in Bolivia that genocide was used as the theoretical framework for the rebellion, and by implication casts the cognate Túpac Amaru movement in a similar light.[4] The theoretical scenario, then, is one in which a large population group, usually considered as victims of colonialism, invert the existing order so that colonial authorities and allied ruling elites now become the victims. John Docker has drawn attention to Raphael Lemkin's remarking "the strange transformation of genocidal victim[s] into genocidists."[5] A necessary point of departure is to understand the extent to which native peoples of Latin America had been, for some 250 years, the principal victims of colonialism. Specifically, they were the victims of violent armed conquest, severe epidemic-driven depopulation, extirpation of religious customs, and so forth. On the eve of the 1780 rebellion, native Andeans remained subject to multivalent colonial oppression, whence their liberationist efforts transcended the norms of military context and descended into genocidal war, one that was as much a civil war as an anticolonial enterprise. What commenced as a cross-racial movement in 1780 curdled into caste war—genocide from below.

This essay will explore the nature and incidence of violence in the Túpac Amaru rebellion. In particular, it will seek to allocate responsibility for the rebel atrocities increasingly evident as the rebellion progressed. Both armies committed atrocities, sometimes as the concomitant of military campaigns, and sometimes during ad hoc forays by avenging loyalist patrols and rebel bands—but what is in question here is the extent to which subaltern violence may be categorized as genocidal. Numerous vignettes of such violence—some concerning massacres of innocents, women, children, the old and the infirm—are well known to historians.[6] This allocation of responsibility for rebel depredations is necessary because it impinges on our understanding of the nature of the movement and therefore of the character and leadership of José Gabriel Túpac Amaru, his command over rebel violence, and the extent to which this was influenced by the flow of events in the crucial first three months of the rebellion. New evidence calls into doubt the traditional view that "in reality, the *tupamarista* leaders were incapable of preventing excesses," and provides the basis for a fresh reading of older narratives.[7]

What follows goes beyond a reevaluation of the vast historiography on the 1780–82 rebellion, by advancing a new interpretation of the very nature of the rebellion, based on new archival data. Indeed, the following discussion of the genocidal nature of the rebellion depends on this new interpretation. It hinges on a closer, even microscopic examination of racial and ethnic identities, the way these combined and separated, and the chronology of such changes—variable in Peru and Bolivia—especially by way of a social *cum* ethnic analysis of the victims of violence. The origins of this change in the nature of the movement will necessarily involve some attention to the political mechanics within the rebellion, to non-indigenous rebel cadres, as well as radically revising the accepted chronology of the rebellion. Specifically, in light of the fact that atrocities committed by both sides manifested a certain ethnic selection, it is first necessary to set in place a brief conspectus of colonial ethnic categories. Second, given that the rebellion has been interpreted principally as an Indian uprising, a brief analysis of the rebellion's leading creole cadres will suggest that the rebellion was cross-ethnic in leadership as well as in participant affiliation.[8] Third, a hitherto overlooked mutiny within rebel ranks, which split the rebel army and rebel loyalties along ethnic lines, will be especially highlighted because—it will be argued—this led to a revenge phase that translated into a radical change in the nature of the rebellion and to a very great degree explains the consequent escalation in rebel violence.

Recognition of this mutiny and immediate reprisals necessarily recasts the long-accepted chronology of the movement that divided the rebellion into two distinct phases: from November 1780 to April 1781 when Túpac Amaru was captured by rebel forces, and from April 1781 to mid-1782, a disintegrative phase in which the rebellion unraveled even while the Peruvian and Bolivian movements fused into one great rebellion. The new chronology divides the first phase of the northern rebellion into two, the failed siege of Cuzco and subsequent mutiny in rebel ranks in early January 1781 marking a distinct middle period, in which the character of the rebellion changed radically. The southern Catarista movement had displayed clear signs of retributive caste war almost from its inception in January 1781—a separate rebellion but one that recognized the overarching sovereignty of the new Inca. Such deference to Túpac Amaru's authority was unavoidable because the Catarista leadership needed to reinforce its own fragile authority, given its followers' millenarian belief in a revenant Inca King, whom they identified with Túpac Amaru. Finally, this chapter will attempt to apportion responsibility for the ethnically targeted rebel violence.

Social Classifications

Racial or ethnic tensions compromised the rebellion from its inception. A clear grasp of the complex social stratification of colonial Andean society is essential to an understanding of the true nature of the depredations visited upon loyalist and rebel forces alike, and to the social and cultural targets of their sanguinary ire. The complex social gradations of the Incan empire on the eve of the Spanish conquest were further parsed by introduced Spanish social categories broadly pertaining to class, race, and estate, thereby rendering some strata of the precolonial social hierarchy anachronistic and immeasurably complicating the meaning of introduced Spanish social categories.[9] Moreover, processes of *mestizaje* and hybridized customs and practices demanded the creation of new social categories to express the reality of such social and cultural nuances; this led to the creation of a complicated racial index in order to calibrate miscegenation by birth.

It is probable that the population of the viceroyalty had been increasing slowly during several decades prior to the rebellion. According to the 1795 census of the Viceroyalty of Peru, 58 percent of the population was "Indian"; in the Cuzco region, the figure was 73 percent.[10] These were underestimates. Cuzco was a smallish city of some 25,000 in the late eighteenth century, a clear majority being creoles and mixed-race groups, principally the mestizos of mixed Spanish and Indian ancestry; the Indians were located overwhelmingly in the provinces. A snapshot view of southern Andean society on the eve of rebellion would limn four salient groups. The first comprised a Spanish and Creole aristocracy: counts and marquises; *mayorazgos* of entailed estates; the *noblesse du robe* of the great military orders of Santiago and Alcántara; and the minor nobility of hidalgos and caballeros. To these were added an Incan nobility, and there was significant interaction and also miscegenation between creole aristocrats of Cuzco and its numerous Inca nobles.[11] These elites sat atop an ethnically diverse, middling group in which non-creoles overwhelmingly predominated.

In the cities and large towns, deracinated Indians and creoles, mestizos, and castes blended into an embryonic proletariat. However, the inhabitants of the countryside overwhelmingly were both the main victims and main perpetrators of the massacres of 1780 and 1781. Most were peasants (campesinos)—indigenous, mestizo, and creole—spread throughout a vast mosaic of inalienable, indigenous community lands, private smallholdings, haciendas and estancias, and numerous small towns and hamlets. A network of caciques, male and female, controlled these rural underclasses, assisted by the mayors and aldermen of the myriad town and village councils. Many rural creoles and mestizos resided in the towns as well as on smallholdings. Colonial censuses reveal little about them, but we know from qualitative documentation that they were numerous. Their identity is sometimes conflated and in fact they differed little in fortune and lifestyle.

Crucial to the argument of this essay is the definition of "*español*." There is frequently confusion in the modern historiography of the rebellion between "creole" and "peninsular." In the local documentation of the period, *español* refers to creoles and sometimes mestizos; as one prominent

Crown official pointed out, "*mestizo*" was also a synonym for ""*español*" in the southern provinces.[12] Reference to *español* is almost always reference to Americans of Spanish descent, but not peninsular Spaniards.[13] There is no doubt that the rebel leader intended the physical destruction of both the peninsular Spaniards (also pejoratively known as *chapetones* or *pucacuncas*) who were relatively few in number but disproportionately influential and wealthy, and the exploitative provincial governors (corregidores), most of whom were in any case peninsulars. Rebel victims, however, were overwhelmingly creoles and mestizos. In what follows, creole will be employed as the synonym for *español*.

Estimates of Mortality

The mortality attendant upon the 1780 rebellion remains unclear. A contemporary estimate of around 100,000 indigenes (Indians) and 10,000 creoles in the combined Peruvian and Bolivian insurgencies is widely accepted. This estimate comes from a 1784 treatise on the rebellion by the presbyter Rafael José Sahuaraura Tito Atauchi, an Inca noble who lost a close relative at rebel hands.[14] Sahuaraura was thus keenly aware of the intensity of violence, but at the same time perhaps more prone to overestimate its impact for reasons both emotional and rhetorical. This figure has been challenged by Magnus Mörner, who noted that the "limited and secondary effects of Early Modern warfare" tended to be relatively modest, and drew attention to quantitative and qualitative demographic indicators of the late colonial period that suggest the 1780–82 death roll also fell within this pattern (he implies an upper limit of 10,000 deaths).[15] Mörner uses Indian tribute lists to support his thesis of low mortality, but these ipso facto exclude non-indigenous groups, yet many rural victims belonged to the rural creole and mestizo underclasses, suggesting that Mörner's own estimate of mortality needs to be revised significantly upward. Most historians recognize that mortality in the Bolivian movement was proportionately higher than in Peru, but a few provinces of the Túpac Amaru rebellion witnessed similar levels of bloodshed, especially in the territories around Lake Titicaca.[16] There, precisely where the two movements met, horrific massacres in the towns of Chucuito, Puno, Juli, and Sorata consumed adults and children alike, a true hecatomb. Similar rebel atrocities closer to Cuzco were sporadically reported, most notably the massacre of creole loyalists at Sangarará and the infamous slaughter of non-combatants in Calca by rebel troops in retreat from the unsuccessful siege of Cuzco. So, too, massacres by loyalist forces are reported both before and after the siege of Cuzco.

Some observations are in order concerning reported estimates of mortality and the size of loyalist and rebel armies. Reporting of battles and massacres tended to be apocalyptic, given the panic and fear that gripped those placed in the path of one army or another, and because survivors sometimes strove too hard to convey a sense of what living in the eye of the storm felt like. Thus the massacre of rebels at the hacienda *La Angostura* on the eve of the siege fluctuated from 100 deaths in one account, to 130 in another, and reached 300 in still another testimony.[17] More striking are the varying estimates of troop numbers. One example is that of the enormous number of troops amassed for the siege of Cuzco in January 1781. In one account, Túpac Amaru is said to possess an army of 30,000 soldiers, creole and mestizo as well as indigenous.[18] Yet the wife of a cacique of the high provinces claimed to have a letter from the rebel chief, in which he rued that he had set out for the siege with a great army, but that after four days' march he had been left with only 3,000 troops.[19] After the siege, he reportedly still had 3,000 troops, but his dead numbered 11,000.[20] Yet another logical explication of inflated troop estimates comes from a local testimony discounting reports that the Inca had a large army. This witness claimed, to the contrary, that the rebel army in late 1780 consisted of no more than 1,800 "among Indians and creoles"—the small number was due to the fact that Túpac Amaru had to pay them a "salary" from limited and dwindling resources; put simply, he could not afford any more soldiers. Exaggerated mortality reports were understandable; according to one eyewitness, because "the other Indians who occasionally join up are from those towns immediate to the passage [of the rebel army] who follow him, to rob or sack the place" and, their booty won, disengage.[21]

Victims and Ethnicity: Creoles, *Chapetones*, and *Castas*

Túpac Amaru's relationship with the several ethnic groups in colonial society and under his command was complex. That he championed the interests of the indigenous majority is not in doubt, but his attitude to creole and mixed-race groups is rather more difficult to discern, because he had to court their participation in the rebel army—he needed modern armaments, military prowess, and money—and while he counted some creoles as friends, his most inveterate enemies were prominent creoles. Túpac Amaru's reputation as a nationalist champion of creole and mestizo interests is nevertheless well supported by the primary sources pertaining to the first two months of the insurgency. He himself was mestizo by birth and his extended family, many of whom participated as rebel cadres, were of mixed mestizo and indigenous ancestry.

Túpac Amaru increasingly emphasized his own Indian and noble Incan identities in the years immediately prior to the rebellion, but even then he continued to look wistfully to his creole roots. Contemporary testimony had it that he spoke Latin, and dressed in fine Hispanic style, though this too was loaded with ambiguity, because any descendant of the Incas was ipso facto regarded as an hidalgo, and vice versa. Orphaned at an early age, he was raised partly by Antonio López de Sosa, his local parish priest and a creole besides, notwithstanding that Túpac Amaru always had his extended family around him. Moreover, prior to the rebellion he seems to have believed that he had some special rapport with creole elites. He sought the company of prominent creoles, even, according to one source, arranging "orgies" for them.[22] However, once the rebellion was underway he was quickly disabused of any idea of creole solidarity, because none of the leading creole elites would support his cause (at least overtly). Moreover, Túpac Amaru, profoundly religious, had in vain counted on support from creole clergy and especially from the Bishop of Cuzco, regarded as a champion of creole interests vis-à-vis peninsular interests, and who was at the time locked in furious dispute with Crown representatives in the region.

The rebel leader's attitude towards the creole and mixed-race groups is a fundamental matter that goes to the root of the nature of the movement. Conversely, it is an issue that has attracted little attention from researchers. That he felt a visceral hatred toward peninsular Spaniards has long been established. So, too, it is well known that the rebel "indios" were wont to kill creoles on the spurious pretext that they were peninsulars disguised as creoles, because for reasons of phenotype it was difficult to tell the difference anyway, and because (as one source put it) some rebels bore an aversion to "*chapetones* and their descendants," i.e., they regarded peninsulars and creoles as generically equivalent.[23] The reason is not far to seek: mestizos and "insolent" indigenes acted against "white men, especially against the Europeans."[24] For some rebels, the rebellion simply pitted white faces against indigenes, and this was to a degree an apprenticeship in hatred and therefore collective violence: Túpac Amaru's order, early in the rebellion, to torch the church of Sangarará and slay its creole occupants appears to have been at least partly a reprisal for a (false) rumor of a massacre by the mainly creole expedition: "the *chapetones* had decapitated all the village women."[25]

The conflation of creoles and *chapetones* is here most notable. In any case, it was not easy in the heat of battle to distinguish the one from the other: there were just "indios" against "blancos." Identification as a *chapetón* meant death, but this might also be a property distinction; in one vignette, a resident argued with rebel indigenes over whether a rapidly abandoned hacienda belonged to a *chapetón* or a creole, for this fact alone determined whether or not they would destroy it.[26] It is clear that Túpac Amaru would spare no *chapetón*. His order to kill any corregidores who might be captured is well known, and was paralleled by another order obliging caciques to erect gallows in their villages "to hang all *chapetones*."[27] There is even a suggestion that the caudillo allowed his antipeninsular hatred to affect his judgment. Historians have long remarked his delay in marching on the city of Cuzco—from the outset in early November until the first week of January—explicable perhaps by logistical and recruitment needs, but in hindsight probably a strategic mistake. One witness recorded that Túpac Amaru first marched south to the high provinces (altiplano) because "there are reports that some *chapetones* remain [there] and they are to be entirely destroyed"—hardly a priority given the imminent arrival of a counter-insurgent viceregal army.[28]

The rebel leader's protestations that his rebellion was not directed in any way at creoles, and that he regarded himself as championing their rights and welfare, are well known. They are set out, again and again, in his numerous proclamations of the first two months of the uprising. In the light of such protestations, historians have generally exculpated Túpac Amaru from direct responsibility in the many reported massacres and atrocities in the movement. It is the "Indians" who allegedly were to blame. Certainly, there is evidence of a certain lack of control, with rebel patrols acting increasingly erratically; the rebellion in part represented a series of local uprisings, to greater or lesser extent spontaneous. There is apparent, too, a division between Túpac Amaru's wider vision and program, on the one hand, and the limited aims of many of his followers, some of whom seem to have been inspired by little more than vengeance and rapine.

Yet there is some indication that a certain disenchantment with his Hispanic identity and with his "beloved creoles" antedated the rebellion. The loss of his litigation over the succession to the Marquisate of Oropesa appears to have eroded his regard for Spanish legal and judicial institutions, no less than his private and public humiliations by several corregidores of the province of Tinta had alienated his respect for Crown office-holders.[29] Some remarkable documents of 1779 throw into relief his attitude to creoles and mestizos shortly before the rebellion. The gist of these was that Túpac Amaru had usurped the royal prerogative by meting out justice at the urging of indigenous complainants; yet the rebel chief was then an insignificant cacique of three small villages. Recording the details of this episode would spring the bounds of this essay, but several are relevant for present purposes. The first that compels attention is the extreme brutality with which he acted: assaulting, flogging, imprisoning, or placing in stocks his adversaries, their relatives, and "infinite Indians." The second aspect is that, "having come to his house some Indians with their complaint because of the news that the said Don José Tupa Amaro was the last Inca of Peru,"[30] he grandly sat in judgment on their case. Finally, even more extraordinary is testimony that "it is notorious that he flogs those creoles with white faces." On New Year's Day, 1779, Túpac Amaru publicly instructed the village mayors (*alcaldes*) that, "outsider mestizos must leave the village and [even] locally born mestizos were to relocate to Cuzco and that no mestizo should remain in the town."[31] The complainants petitioned that he be restrained from inflicting damage on "the creoles."[32] Commenting on this case in 1785, the Intendant intendant of Cuzco noted that, in rural areas, *mestizo* was a synonym for *español* and this for creole.[33] This testimony thus puts a very different gloss on his proclamation to his "beloved creoles," a protestation that appears in retrospect to have been little more than a recruiting ploy. The fact was that for his rebellion to succeed, he needed creoles and their resources, armaments, and military, and technical expertise. More than eighteen months before his rebellion, then, his disenchantment with creoles was already well advanced.

The Creole Leadership: The Castelo Clan

The rebellion of 1780–82 is conventionally presented as a complex uprising headed by a charismatic Inca leader, assisted by his extended family and a small commissariat, mostly staffed by captured functionaries who were creoles and mestizos. At rebel headquarters, there were also several captive peninsulars. Yet, as one witness remarked, of those peninsular prisoners—despite the Inca's anti-European crusade—only one was executed, the victim being the provincial governor of Tinta, Antonio de Arriaga.[34] This ethnic mix at rebel headquarters has been seen as an earnest of the rebellion's cross-ethnic nationalist aspirations. Other interpretations downplay the roles of this non-indigenous commissariat—they were apparently all captives—and consider the movement (like the Catarista movement in Bolivia) to have been essentially nativist in character: in short, an "Indian rebellion." In the first two months of the rebellion, for example, there were many episodes of well-armed creoles and mestizos in the rebel army as well as in the initial mustering of troops.

However, the movement's organization and cadres during the first two months of the rebellion suggests that, initially, it was even more multiethnic than hitherto suspected. New evidence suggests that creoles played a more crucial leadership role at the outset of the rebellion than present historiography allows. The later sundering of this multiethnic leadership group witnessed a radical transformation in the nature of the rebellion from multiethnic alliance to genocidal caste war. To understand this switch in character, it is first necessary to identify the principal Creole cadres, their fall from grace, and the retribution meted out to them and to other, non-indigenous participants and bystanders. Most worthy of remark, and all but ignored in the historiography, was the central role of the Castelo family, a prominent creole clan. Their involvement was such as to suggest that the rebellion could well be seen as a joint conspiracy of Túpac Amaru and the Castelos. That is to say, rather than the leadership having consisted of a charismatic Inca leader and a small nucleus of lieutenants, the rebellion was rather the creation of a ruling Inca-Creole Junta with Túpac Amaru allocated the starring role—in effect, a joint venture of the Túpac Amaru and Castelo families—given that his stature as Inca made him a lodestar for Indian recruitment. The role of the Castelos was absolutely pivotal in the watershed events that marked a change in the character of the northern movement. Given their salience in rebel affairs, a short sketch of the clan is necessary in order to grasp the clan's importance in provincial affairs, its relationship to Túpac Amaru, and its members' activities during the rebellion.

The rebel leader shared his insurrectionary intentions with them; it is probable that the Castelos helped formulate the overall strategy and tactics. Their intimacy was of long standing; their closeness to the rebel warlord was well attested. Long before the rebellion, Melchor Castelo assiduously promoted José Gabriel's Incan credentials throughout the province, not least by referring to him as the "Inca King" and prophesying, "gentlemen, look at that Indian, well there is coming a time when he will rule."[35] Melchor was the undisputed clan head who, with his "six sons, their brothers-in-law, and many relatives of the same name" ("such a numerous lineage") constituted the backbone of the rebel military staff and commissariat.[36] After the rebellion, the Crown investigation concluded that the Castelos had been the "principal caudillos of the sacrilegious traitor."[37] They were deeply involved in the initial stages of the insurgency and "commanded the rebel party in such a way that the insurgent Tupa Amaro played no other role than that of making himself leader [and] calling himself Inca."[38] This is extraordinary testimony, tantamount to saying that the rebellion was the undertaking of a cross-ethnic Junta, in which Túpac Amaru was primus inter pares only by virtue of his widely acknowledged Incan identity.

Notable is the Castelos' central role in commanding the ranks of the militiamen and directing operations at rebel headquarters. They dragooned and managed the recruitment of rebel levies, deploying them throughout the rebel stronghold at Tungasuca—transformed within the space of days into a holding camp for massed troops—at the outset of the uprising, controlling and sorting the crowd into ranks, and distributing cash and provisions among the new recruits. The new rebel army was arrayed on three sides of the plaza, each formation in three loose ranks: in the first rank, the creoles; then, the mestizos; at the back, the "Indians." Here, then, in the context of a supposedly nativist liberation movement, we find a synopsis of the colonial caste system as its army's essential inner framework—an anti-colonial movement that had paradoxically ingested colonial racialist logic. Cash allowances to these soldiers were also based on caste distinctions: six *reales* for creoles, four *reales* for mestizos, and two *reales* for Indians.

Historians have glossed over the question of how Túpac Amaru financed his uprising. It is clear that the rebel host was paid and provisioned from the booty seized on campaign. However, the insurgency needed initial capital to set it in train, cash for soldiers' rations, and as much powder and shot as possible. These could only have been obtained at considerable outlay; supplementary resources would fall to the rebel army as it marched. Some resources, especially firearms, powder, and shot, were in finite supply, as became glaringly obvious following the siege of Cuzco, when the rebel army was left almost entirely without firepower.[39] The rebellion was financed from several sources; we know of Indian tribute tax monies held by the rebel leader and the executed provincial governor's private and official cash reserves, impounded by the rebels. On the eve of rebellion, however, Túpac Amaru was effectively bankrupt; by contrast, the Castelos were wealthy by provincial standards. There is some reason to think they were initially the movement's principal financiers: many testimonies insist that the material fortunes of the Castelos underwent a quantum leap at the outset of the rebellion when they opportunistically skimmed off "as much as possible" rebel booty, perhaps only recouping monies they had already advanced to the rebel cause.

This was interpreted as incontrovertible proof of the Castelos' culpability as co-instigators of the insurgency. The rebel army itself was split into three forces led respectively by José Gabriel Túpac Amaru, Diego Túpac Amaru, and Antonio Castelo (proxy for his aged father Melchor).[40] Here, then, is a military triumvirate—these three plus the Inca's consort, Micaela Bastidas, provided the generalship of the rebellion, with Andrés Mendigure, alias Andrés Túpac Amaru, attaining a similar rank in 1781. In such manner, then, the Castelos loomed large in the rise of José Gabriel Túpac Amaru and the launching of his rebellion. Their subsequent betrayal foredoomed his decline and fall.

The Great Mutiny: From Rebellion to Caste War

What can only have been a deteriorating belief in the steadfastness of creole support was dealt a final blow at the siege of Cuzco (5–8 January

1781). With the rebel host facing an unexpectedly committed loyalist defense, and caught in a torrential downpour that lasted for days, the creole and mestizo components of the rebel army decamped with most of the available firepower. This was a full-blown mutiny, aggravated when the deserters returned to their base in the large town of Sicuani—they were, effectively, the provincial militia—and announced a counter-rebellion. There is a suggestion that this betrayal preceded the failure of the siege, rather than merely reflecting a growing realization by creole and mestizo rebels of the ramifications of having chosen the wrong side. As one loyalist witness pointed out, prior to the siege, one of the "captain-generals of that rebel, had made a pact with our band."[41] This creole perfidy was a welcome surprise to hard-pressed loyalist forces, and its timeliness won an immediate pardon for its perpetrators, now deploying their flintlocks in the King's name. Theirs was a double treason, first betraying their King and then their Inca. Their mutiny was a watershed in the rebellion. For José Gabriel Túpac Amaru, this creole betrayal fatally undermined any remaining chance of success in his venture, and was all the more bitter because the turncoats were his closest friends.

As the siege of Cuzco disintegrated, the creole contingent of the rebel army peeled off and fled, taking most of the firepower with them. Then Antonio Castelo and "almost all of the creoles" as well as "various Indians from other provinces" made haste to Sicuani, bent upon organizing armed resistance to the rebel army.[42] Quite how long they deliberated is unknown, but it is evident that faced with impending loyalist reprisals, some immediate turncoat initiative was called for to stave off the gallows. Accordingly, the Castelos and "all the creoles" of the town composed an edict announcing that Túpac Amaru had deceived them and that he was a rebel and traitor to the King.[43] This exculpatory edict was simultaneously a call to arms, exhorting residents, "as loyal vassals," to unite in order to punish, kill, or capture the rebel chief and any of his followers. This edict was promulgated in both Spanish and Quechua throughout the towns of the high provinces, and a copy sent with a passing friar to the *Junta de Guerra* (Junta of War) in Cuzco. This last act was designed to secure for them the benefit of the doubt from vengeful, royalist counter-insurgent commanders.

Three days later, a second edict appeared, embellishing the traitors' tale. By the time they realized the rebel leader was a traitor, it ran, "it was at a time when our forces couldn't halt those of the Traitor because of the infinite Indians who followed his colors."[44] This new edict threatened the faint-hearted with summary execution. It announced that a list was being drawn up of the loyal subjects of Sicuani, and that those residents not present would be deemed insurgents. This was cruel irony, in that the absent residents were precisely those who had fled rather than betray the King, while almost all on the loyalty list were those who had taken part in the Sangarará slaughter and then laid siege to Cuzco. Within days, an emissary from the *Junta de Guerra* arrived from Cuzco bearing a pardon. However, this was no moment for celebration, because of their fear of Túpac Amaru's inevitable reprisals. The second edict announced that all residents were to decamp further south, there to make their "fortress." En route, Melchor, Antonio, and Eugenio Castelo, and some dozen followers died in a nocturnal ambush; their fellow mutineers had already deserted them.

Those edicts were patently a farrago of lies and half-truths. If nothing else, the intervening rebel slaughter of the "flower of creole youth" at Sangarará would have disabused the Sicuani creoles and mestizos of any notion that they were engaged in doing the King's will. There was abundant testimony, during and after the rebellion, that the Castelos had been co-instigators and facilitators of the insurgency. One of Túpac Amaru's inner circle noted that "all the creole residents of all the towns that favor him, serve him voluntarily and for their own interests," thus undermining the standard excuse that they were forced; self-interest and compulsion were doubtless in many cases combined.[45] This well-placed witness, Túpac Amaru's scrivener or clerk José Esteban de Escarcena, emphasized that "the most cruel and damaging [were] all the creoles or mestizos of [the] town of Sicuani and particularly the said Castelos."[46] Moreover, the siege of Cuzco commenced on 4 January and it rapidly became obvious that the attempt was doomed, yet the first edict of the Sicuani mutineers was not composed until 11 January. Their decision to defect should perhaps be dated to 3 January, the day preceding the onset of the siege, when the rebel vanguard commanded by Antonio Castelo suffered a devastating defeat at Saylla, with rebel losses estimated at one thousand dead.[47] This was a shameful and ignoble loss, which presaged the eventual collapse of the enterprise against an adversary now well prepared, after the shock of the Sangarará massacre. The Castelos manifestly deserved no royal pardon. Double traitors, they merited the death penalty, twice over. Only a handful of the clan survived the rebellion and the official recriminations that followed, luckier than many whose transgressions had been comparatively benign but received the death penalty.

Genocidal Revenge

Túpac Amaru immediately responded by launching reprisals against the Sicuani creoles; few of them appear to have survived. It is at this point that contemporary accounts, some of them from the rebel camp, report that the caudillo had ordered his troops not to spare any creole and even mestizos, where once he had ordered his followers to kill only peninsular Spaniards. This mutiny in his ranks marked a turning point in the rebellion that has been missed by historians. It marked the transformation from a multi-ethnic, multi-class rebellion to a caste war—ironically, given that Túpac Amaru and his family were mestizo, as were some of his remaining staff at rebel headquarters. Nonetheless, the movement became xenophobic and racialist with a corresponding increase in its innate nativistic tendencies. From this point on, the rebellion, now a lost cause, becomes increasingly vengeful, violent and iconoclastic.

The numerous testimonies to this effect are emphatic and convincing, not least because many stem from the high provinces of the altiplano, heartland of rebellion and its major killing ground, and most are taken from the private correspondence of those who were stranded there or else had recently fled for their lives. Because of the betrayal of the creoles and mestizos, Túpac Amaru "has given the order to his [troops] that they kill every creole that they find . . . and they are carrying it out to the letter;"[48] "he returned from Cuzco totally angry with the creoles . . . [and] . . . is killing creoles, women, children, burning houses of the indigenous male and female Indians, no-one has escaped;"[49] "he has given orders to kill in the towns and roads any creoles that [the Indians] find."[50] The full story is encapsulated in the following testimony: "in the other provinces by order of the traitor they are annihilating the creoles and mestizos because those whom he had in his company abandoned him, betraying him, and at present the traitor finds himself without any creole because all have withdrawn taking with them all the firearms."[51] Moreover, the wife of the rebel chief, Micaela Bastidas, who was in charge of operations at headquarters during her husband's absence on campaign, sent messengers to the provinces with orders "to join forces . . . to destroy the creoles calling them traitors to his cause [with the intent] that this race be entirely destroyed, saying that as soon as the rebel gives the order to the Indians, no white face would remain alive."[52]

Not all the testimonies of the order to kill all creoles and mestizos are fully in accord: a few accounts indicate that the order to kill them referred just to those who had abandoned Túpac Amaru at the siege of Cuzco.[53] Yet in giving this order Túpac Amaru knew full well that he was unleashing a chain reaction of atrocities, because from the inception of rebellion he had had great difficulty in restraining his indigenous troops, prone to kill any "*cara blanca*" they came across. Indian detachments carried out with alacrity Túpac Amaru's order to kill any creoles that they found, with appalling results: thus the notably fierce rebel detachments from Carabaya and the Collao region each "brought loads of heads from creoles in honor of the rebel [chief]" to his headquarters in Tungasuca.[54] Violence against creoles and mestizos, manifestly on the rise the longer the rebellion went on, was neither random nor adventitious, not just the product of maverick rebel outriders or over-enthusiastic looters. It responded rather to a declared change of rebel aims and targets by Túpac Amaru, reacting furiously against the inconstancy and "treason" of his erstwhile creole and mestizo allies.

The Verdict

The defection of the creole and mestizo components of the rebel army at the siege of Cuzco marked a watershed in the nature of the 1780 rebellion, one hitherto overlooked in its vast historiography. There was an abrupt switch from Túpac Amaru's insistence upon exempting creoles from violence, a policy that he had urged (in the face of ad hoc infringements by his indigenous troops) preceding the siege of the city of Cuzco. After the ignominious retreat of his ethnically mixed army from the heights of Cuzco and the desertion of his non-indigenous troops with most of the firearms, the rebel leader pronounced a policy of summarily executing creoles and mestizos, in addition to the peninsular Spaniards who had been targeted for killing from the inception of the rebellion. Of course, it is difficult to assess how far the order to kill creoles and mestizos was generalized, and for how long its implementation endured. Túpac Amaru may, after all, have intended that it be directed solely against the mutineers and sundry other deserters—as several testimonies suggest—and lasted only until such time as those miscreants had been exemplarily slain. If so, it was a vain hope, because it led to the immediate and widespread slaughter of creole and mestizo deserters and non-combatants—men, women, and children. The ethnic hatreds that for long had simmered in colonial life were brought unambiguously to the boil once the order to kill was given, and nothing short of crushing the rebellion militarily could hope to stem the "blood-dimmed tide."

Túpac Amaru's rebellion patently underwent a metamorphosis from a broad-based alliance against the colonial system and *chapetones* generally, to an insurgency that bore all the hallmarks of xenophobic caste war. The key to that revised image is the set of testimonies from within the eye of the rebellion, which coincide in alleging that Túpac Amaru had switched from ordering the death of peninsular Spaniards while sparing creoles, to a general order to put all creoles to the sword. That violence now became indiscriminate was due not just to maverick rebel troops or indigenous marauders and plunderers, but rather as a direct consequence of a radical change of policy coeval with a change in the very nature of the rebellion. José Gabriel Túpac Amaru was the author of the spiraling violence that marked the post-siege phase of the rebellion. Rebel perpetrators of atrocities were, then, at least from January 1781, "just following orders."

As the rebellion wore on, creoles and mestizos increasingly became victims of rebel violence, irrespective of whether these were loyalist or rebel sympathizers or just non-aligned fence-sitters. The conventional explanation for rebel atrocities has been that indigenous rebels were beyond the control of the leadership, whose pleas (in the first two months of the uprising) to spare non-combatant creoles and mestizos were ineffectual in the face of the bloodlust and depredations of rebel troops, and in part due to communication difficulties innate to the vast expanses of rough terrain across which the rebellion ebbed and flowed. Yet this traditional exculpation of Túpac Amaru from the most egregious rebel atrocities has always rung somewhat hollow. How could an unequivocally charismatic leader with unsurpassed authority have had such little control over his supposedly purblind followers? Were the many atrocities and summary killings of creoles and mestizos simply due to maverick rebel outriders? Or were they an integral part of rebel military strategy? Manifestly, on the evidence presented here, the post-siege violence was directed principally by the rebel caudillo, rather than being merely a reflection of disintegrating rebel leadership after the failure of the January 1780 siege of Cuzco, and the attendant random violence by retreating, rebel soldiers and marauding rebel outriders.

The Túpac Amaru rebellion of 1780–82 thus stands revealed as a genocidal movement orchestrated by its charismatic leader. Rebel atrocities, manifestly genocidal in character, thus appear not as regrettable excesses within a generally noble nationalist and anticolonial war, but rather as episodes true to the very nature of the rebellion. These were not the "scattered attacks" of Charles Tilly's typology of collective violence, but rather pertained to a policy of "coordinated destruction" that went well beyond the "license to kill" of conventional warfare, not least in its targeting of civilians along ethnic lines.[55] The Túpac Amaru rebellion was, in effect, a regional eighteenth-century expression of total war in which no one was exempt from intentional death; in such manner, the rebellion abrogated the norms of early modern warfare. At least from January 1780, genocidal intentionality and coordinated, ethnically targeted destruction of combatants and non-combatants alike were present in the rebellion. It was, like its even more sanguinary Bolivian counterpart, a genocide from below in which the long-suffering indigenous victims of Spanish colonial rule unleashed their long-awaited reprisals against their exploitative Other. Unlike the Catari rebellion, however, the principal architect of genocide was its charismatic leader.

Genocide from below in 1780 sprang from a colonial crisis whence subalterns reacted against burdens that, already deemed intolerable, continued to worsen. Among the targets of rebel resentment and clamor for reform were numerous issues that many contemporaries considered to be just claims, morally righteous. Among the most pressing were relief from crushing economic and fiscal burdens; the social dislocation attendant upon forced mine labor; usurpation of indigenous community lands by outsiders; rough handling (especially floggings) by clergy and district officials; state offices being given to outsiders, especially the hated peninsular Spaniards; corruption by royal officials; and the severe difficulty of winning judicial redress of grievances. There was a whole kaleidoscope of different world-views, beliefs, behaviors, and culpabilities apparent within the rebellion. Rebel agendas of social justice, legal redress, moral economy, and representative government should not be obscured by an undue focus on collective violence, targeted or not. The genocide from below was perpetrated by long-suffering victims of colonial exploitation who, after the killing was over, reverted to the former status; still victims, still exploited at roughly the same levels as hitherto, for all that the rebellion forced some concessions from the Crown. In 1780, a mass rebellion was launched in order to overthrow or at least reform radically an oppressive colonial system. That it eventually degenerated into a genocidal caste war should not preclude a historical understanding of the negotiated complexities of colonialism in the Andes nor the "emic" perspectives of the rebels; such an understanding would embrace aspirational mass rebellion as well as its vengeful aftermath—due acknowledgement that its perpetrators were also victims, and therein lay the wellsprings of that genocide from below.

Notes

1. Modern Bolivia was until 1825 variously called Charcas or Upper Peru (*Alto Peru*), and in 1776 moved from the jurisdiction of the Viceroyalty of Peru to the new Viceroyalty of Río de la Plata. Argentina was similarly a postcolonial creation, having also from 1776 been part of the latter viceroyalty, effectively independent from 1810 and formally so from 1816.
2. There is an immense bibliography on eighteenth-century Andean rebellions. The best introduction to the Túpac Amaru rebellion is Charles Walker, *Smoldering Ashes: Cuzco and the Creation of Republican Peru, 1780–1840* (Durham, NC, 1999), chap. 2. For the Catarista rebellion, see especially Sinclair Thomson, *We Alone Will Rule: Native Andean Politics in the Age of Insurgency* (Madison, WI, 2002). Of great importance are Boleslao Lewin, *La rebelión de Túpac Amaru y los orígenes de la independencia de Hispanoamérica*, 3rd rev. ed. (Buenos Aires, 1967). Scarlett O'Phelan Godoy, *Rebellions and Revolts in Eighteenth-Century Peru and Upper Peru* (Cologne and Vienna, 1985); Ward Stavig, *The World of Túpac Amaru: Conflict, Community and Identity in Colonial Peru* (Lincoln, NE, 1999), chap. 8; Serge Serulnikov, *Subverting Colonial Authority: Challenges to Spanish Rule in*

Eighteenth-Century Southern Andes (Durham and London, 2003); Nicholas A. Robins, *Genocide and Millenialism in Upper Peru: The Great Rebellion of 1780–1782* (Westport, CT, 2002).

3. Excellent introductions to Spanish American Independence are: John Lynch, *The Spanish American Revolutions 1808–1826*, 2nd ed. (New York and London, 1986); Jay Kinsbruner, *Independence in Spanish America: Civil Wars, Revolutions, and Underdevelopment* (Albuquerque, NM, 1994). For Brazilian Independence, see Leslie Bethell, "The Independence of Brazil," in *The Independence of Latin America*, ed. Leslie Bethell (Cambridge, 1987), pp. 155–94. See also the wide-ranging revisionist essay by Brian R. Hamnett, "Process and Pattern: A Re-examination of the Ibero-American Independence Movements, 1808–1826," *Journal of Latin American Studies* 29, no. 2 (1997): 279–328.
4. Robins, *Genocide and Millenialism in Upper Peru*, whose work is informed especially by Jan Szeminski, "Why Kill the Spaniard? New Perspectives on Andean Insurrectionary Ideology in the 18th Century," in *Resistance, Rebellion, and Consciousness in the Andean Peasant World, 18th to 20th Centuries*, ed. Steve J. Stern (Madison, WI, 1987), 166–92. Szeminski similarly highlights the millenarian influence as context and cause of rebel violence.
5. John Docker, "Are Settler-Colonies Inherently Genocidal? Re-reading Lemkin" (in this volume), citing Raphael Lemkin.
6. Iván Hinojosa, "El nudo colonial: La violencia en el movimiento tupamarista," *Pasado y Presente* 2, nos. 2–3 (1989): 73–82, for a selection of such incidents, some of which are also recorded in Lewin, *La rebelión de Túpac Amaru*.
7. Hinojosa, "El nudo colonial," 76, whose argument has merit up to a certain point, but although noting that some atrocities were committed within the context of military actions commanded by rebel leaders, does not consider the possibility that some of those "excesses" stemmed directly from explicit orders of Túpac Amaru. Robins, *Genocide and Millenialism*, 2, from the outset of his study exculpates the rebel leader from the charge of genocide, arguing that the rebellion "quickly escaped his control and exceeded his vision." This was true of the southern movement, but not of the northern, which to a large extent remained under the control of Túpac Amaru.
8. The names and functions of many non-indigenous cadres have long been known, for which see O'Phelan, *Rebellions and Revolts*, 299–309, for a list of captives who were tried for treason after the rebellion. However, this essay brings some of these individuals out from the shadows and advances the names of still others, all of whom were much closer to the eponymous leader and who themselves carried out clear leadership functions, rather than just executing orders.
9. Note that ethnicity was a subset of race in this society, in which the indigenous population comprised multiple ethnic groups, corresponding to the myriad polities that existed prior to the Spanish conquest. These continued to maintain separate ethnic identities after 1532. However, for present purposes, "ethnicity" will be used as a synonym for "race."
10. For a summary of the 1795 census, see John R. Fisher, *Government and Society in Colonial Peru: The Intendant System 1784–1814* (London, 1970), 251–53. The city of Cuzco numbered 24,842 and the Intendancy of Cuzco totalled 208,791, the most numerous of the Viceroyalty's seven intendancies.
11. David Cahill, "A Liminal Nobility: The Incas in the Middle Ground of Late Colonial Peru," in *New World, First Nations: Native Peoples of Mesoamerica and the Andes under Colonial Rule*, ed. David Cahill and Blanca Tovías (Brighton, Sussex, 2006),

169–95. For the nobility of Early Modern Spain, see the seminal work of Antonio Domínguez Ortiz, *La sociedad española en el siglo XVII*, vol. 1: *El Estamento nobiliario* (Universidad de Granada, facsimile edition, 1992 [1963]).

12. Archivo General de Indias (hereafter AGI), Audiencia del Cuzco, Leg. 35, Benito de la Mata Linares (Intendant of Cuzco) to José de Gálvez (No.18), 12 October 1785.
13. Peninsular Spaniards were variously rendered as "Europeans," "of the kingdoms of Spain," "of the kingdoms of Galicia," "of Vizcaya," "the Andalusian," "the Galician," and so forth.
14. Rafael José Sahuaraura Tito Atauchi, "Estado del Perú (1784)," in *Colección Documental de la Independencia del Perú*, vol. 2, tomo 1 (Lima, 1971), 331–415.
15. Magnus Mörner, *Perfil de la sociedad rural del Cuzco a fines de la colonia* (Lima, 1978), 123–25. See also Oscar Cornblit, *Power and Violence in a Colonial City: Oruro from the Mining Renaissance to the Rebellion of Tupac Amaru (1780–82)*, trans. Elizabeth Ladd Glick (Cambridge, 1995), 111, which suggests that the mortality reached between 100,000 and 140,000 on the rebel side alone, with some "tens of thousands" on the loyalist side.
16. José Tamayo Herrera, "Las consecuencias de la rebelión de Túpac Amaru y la decadencia económico-social del altiplano," in *Actas del coloquio internacional: "Túpac Amaru y su tiempo"* (Lima, 1982), 599–607.
17. AGI, Audiencia de Lima, Leg. 1052, folios 88v, 90v and 77r, respectively.
18. Ibid., fol. 166v, testimony de Eugenio Canatupa Sinanyuca, cacique of Coporaque, and prisoner of Túpac Amaru in the first few weeks of the rebellion, before escaping to Arequipa, whence his loyalty was rewarded by the Crown.
19. Ibid., fol. 115r, testimony of Antonio Zanabria, referring to the wife of Blas Pacoricona, rebel cacique of Lampa.
20. Ibid., fol. 89.
21. Ibid., fol. 158v, remarking that "it is false that Tupa Amaro has many soldiers."
22. *Colección documental del bicentenario de la revolución emancipadora de Túpac Amaru*, tomo 1, 526.
23. Ibid., fol.3v. This aspect is discussed by Hinojosa, "El nudo colonial," 77, who emphasizes that "the order [to kill *chapetones*] . . . would be carried out with great distortions" [my translation].
24. AGI Lima 1052, fol. 32; cf. Juan Carlos Estenssoro F., "¿Historia de un fraude o fraude histórico?", *Revista de Indias* LVII, no. 210 (1997): 566–78, esp. 571, who wrongly argues that "white" (*blanco*) was not used as a descriptive racial term in colonial. For racial/ethnic categories in the colonial era, see Magnus Mörner, *Race Mixture in the History of Latin America* (Boston, 1967); Claudio Esteva Fábregat, *El mestizaje en Iberoamérica* (Madrid, 1988); David Cahill, "Colour by Numbers: Racial and Ethnic Categories in the Viceroyalty of Peru, 1532–1821," *Journal of Latin American Studies* 26, no. 2 (1994): 325–46.
25. AGI Lima 1052, fol. 102. The massacre of loyalist forces—hundreds dead, many creoles and mestizos, and some twenty peninsulars—was a point-of-no-return event. The scale of the rout and its attendant mortality made clear that this was no mere jacquerie, but rather an uprising of a magnitude previously unknown, and of a nature calculated to overturn the colonial state and social order. For an excellent account of Sangarará, see Walker, *Smoldering Ashes*, 36–39.
26. Ibid., fol. 33r.
27. Ibid., fol. 18v.
28. Ibid., fol. 37r.

29. For more details, David Cahill, "First among Incas: The *Marquesado de Oropesa* Litigation (1741–1780) en route to the Great Rebellion," *Jahrbuch für Geschichte Lateinamerikas*,no. 41 (2004): 137–66.
30. AGI, Audiencia del Cuzco, Leg. 35, Mata Linares to Gálvez, 12 October 1785 (No.18), enclosing complaints by Lorenzo de Zuñiga, Estévan de Zuñiga, and Felipe de Vejar, with a response from "Don José Tupa Amaro Inga."
31. Ibid.
32. Ibid.
33. Ibid.
34. "La verdad desnuda," in *Colección documental de la Independencia del Perú*, tomo 2, vol. 1: *La rebelión de Túpac Amaru*, ed. Carlos Daniel Valcárcel (Lima, 1970), 461–650, esp. 575. The author of this anonymously published tract was Eusebio Balza de Berganza, nephew and unofficial deputy of Arriaga, whose capture and execution by the Inca leader marked the beginning of the rebellion. Balza estimates there were ten to twelve *chapetón* prisoners at rebel headquarters in Tungasuca.
35. Ibid., testimony of Don Cipriano Órué.
36. Of these, the principal family protagonists were the brothers Antonio, Eugenio, Ignacio, and Manuel, and nephew Feliz Castelo.
37. "Expediente relatibo," Mata Linares to Croix, 23 May 1787.
38. Ibid., testimony of Don Cipriano Órué, a cacique and Arriaga's *alguacil mayor* in Sicuani.
39. *Colección documental del bicentenario*, III:1, 152, testimony of José Gabriel Túpac Amaru.
40. Ibid., fol. 65r.
41. AGI Lima 1052, fol. 87v.
42. Ibid., fol. 106r.
43. Ibid.
44. Ibid., fol. 106r–107r.
45. *Colección documental del bicentenario*, V:III, confession of José Esteban Escarcena de Villanueva, 141.
46. Ibid.
47. Atilio Sivirichi Tapai, "Cronología de la revolución de los Túpac Amaru (1780–81)," in Alejandro Seraylán Leiva, *Historia General del Ejército Peruano: El Ejécito durante la dominación española del Perú* (Lima, 1981), 688.
48. AGI Lima, fols. 82v–83r.
49. Ibid., fol. 95v.
50. Ibid., fol. 97r.
51. Ibid., fol.111r.
52. *Colección documental del bicentenario*, IV:II, 8–9.
53. For example, *Colección documental del bicentenario*, V: 3, 235, testimony of Manuel Gallaguillos; *Colección Documental de la Independencia*, III:1, 509, declaration of Francisco Molina.
54. *Colección documental del bicentenario*, V:III, 538, testimony of Don Genuario Castro.
55. Charles Tilly, *The Politics of Collective Violence* (Cambridge, 2003).

– *Chapter 18* –

THE BRIEF GENOCIDE OF EURASIANS IN INDONESIA, 1945/46

Robert Cribb

Introduction

During the closing months of 1945 and the first months of 1946, a small and little-known genocide took place in Indonesia. The victims were members of Indonesia's mixed-race Eurasian community, the perpetrators were ethnic Indonesian nationalists, and the context was the difficult aftermath of the Japanese occupation of the Netherlands Indies that included the declaration of Indonesian independence in August 1945 and attempts by the Dutch to restore the colonial authority of the Netherlands Indies. The genocide was one of history's small number of genocides directed against a settler community at a time of dramatic political change. They were part of a process by which indigenous peoples recovered control of their own country from outside rulers after an interval of imperial domination.

Every genocide has its own characteristic forms of horror. The Indonesian genocide of 1945/46 was not an affair of gas chambers and methodical extermination like the Holocaust, but rather a time of unpredictable violence carried out with deliberate savagery and intimidation. The victims were seized in their houses late at night, ambushed as they walked to the morning market, hauled off trains in broad daylight. They were seldom held long in detention by their killers. Instead, they were murdered quickly, stabbed, strangled, beheaded, or hacked to death, and their bodies were buried in hastily dug graves, tipped into wells, flung into rivers or canals, or simply left on the spot as a frightening reminder to passers-by.

The agents of the genocide were a multitude of independent militias, known at the time as *badan perjuangan*, "struggle organizations," which sprang up in the days and weeks after the independence declaration. Fiercely proud of their country's fresh independence, they had neither patience with nor understanding of the national leadership's cautious strategies. Rather, they were convinced that the passionate commitment to the cause and a willingness to die for their country would overcome all obstacles.[1] There was much of a swaggering bravado among these militias: in order to put the humiliation of colonization behind them, they cultivated an air of arrogance and confidence. Intensely suspicious of Dutch plots and enormously sensitive to slights and insults, they reacted violently to perceived threats and challenges. To Westerners still smarting from the deliberate humiliations that had been heaped upon them during the Japanese occupation, this swagger was an extra source of shame.

In the memories of survivors, the violence seemed all the worse because it came after nearly three and a half years of Japanese occupation in the Indonesian archipelago. The Japanese, in a hurry to set their mark on their new territory, had consigned the most European-looking of the Western population to internment camps, where conditions had ranged from tedious to appalling. The bulk of the Eurasian population had not been interned, but life outside the camps had been terribly difficult as well. Acute shortages of food, clothing, and basic utensils,[2] together with the insecurity produced by a nervous and trigger-happy occupation force, made the occupation years a time of prolonged difficulty for most Eurasians, but their hopes for better times after the Japanese had left were shattered by the outbreak of the nationalist revolution.

As this brief description suggests, the genocide of the Eurasians in Indonesia was not a state-sponsored affair. Although the Indonesian republic had been formally created on 18 August 1945, a day after the independence declaration, for weeks the new state barely existed as an institution. Only gradually did officials in government departments transfer their allegiance from the Japanese occupation authorities, and only on 5 October did the leaders of the republic finally declare the creation of an army. This diffidence arose from the desperate desire of President Sukarno and other nationalist leaders to avoid what they feared would be an unwinnable military struggle with the Dutch. Instead, they hoped that the Atlantic Charter, which had promised self-determination for all subject peoples, would deliver them a smooth transition to independence. Thus they sought to appeal over the heads of the Dutch to the victorious Allies by promising an economy open to Western business interests and a peaceful social environment to allow postwar reconstruction to begin at once. For the national leaders of the republic, therefore, there was no reason to want a massacre that would only reinforce the Dutch argument that the republic had to be crushed if law and order were to be restored.

Whether they had emerged from the camps or simply tried to pick up the thread of their old lives from the old residences, the Eurasians of the Indies were profoundly shocked by the violence they encountered. Indeed, one of the striking features of late colonial European and Eurasian society was its relative lack of anxiety over native violence. The prewar Netherlands Indies had cultivated a myth of peace and order in the colony,[3] a perception that benevolent Dutch development policies in the twentieth century had aroused a profound sense of affection for the colonial rulers amongst the vast majority of Indonesians. The Dutch therefore attributed the violence largely to the experience of the Japanese occupation when, in their eyes, their former subjects had been inculcated with a hatred of all things Western and with a "bushido" culture that glorified violence.[4] For these observers, the violence irremediably tainted the republic, making it unfit to be the bearer of national aspirations. In scholarly studies of the nationalist revolution, by contrast, the violence against the Eurasians has been largely ignored, regarded as a marginal phenomenon, a regrettable but minor and understandable consequence of Indonesian resentments accumulated during the colonial era.[5] The violence of the militias toward their victims in 1945/46 was a profound shock to the Western community in Indonesia, and the almost universal explanation offered at the time was that it was a consequence of malignant brutalizing policies carried out by the Japanese occupation forces.

But scholarship no longer treats any violence as unproblematic, and it is important to understand the violence inflicted on the Eurasians, both as an element in the history of violence in Indonesia and as a case of indigenous revenge against a settler community. The puzzle in the case of the Eurasians of Indonesia is that there was very little sign of violent antagonism towards Eurasians in colonial Indonesia. It is hard to present the violence of 1945/46 as the consequence of long-simmering, specific antagonisms. By contrast, the violence that took place against Chinese residents of Indonesia slightly after the period of violence against the Eurasians is easy to locate in a longer history of indigenous resentment of the Chinese.[6]

Rather, the genocide of the Eurasians was a consequence of a two-stage process. First, during the course of the twentieth century, the Eurasian community in the Netherlands Indies parted company with the Indonesian nationalist movement that it had helped to found. Then, at the time of Indonesia's independence declaration, the weakness of the two aspirant states in the postoccupation archipelago brought the issue of loyalty to the fore, precisely at a time when Eurasians were especially vulnerable to attack.

Colonial Society and Ethnic Categories

To understand that the violence of 1945/46 was not simply a consequence of colonial-era social antagonisms, it is necessary to begin with an exploration of the tangled racial politics of the Netherlands Indies. The Dutch colonial order, from its origins in the commercial ventures of the Dutch East Indies Company (VOC) in the seventeenth century until its overthrow by invading Japanese forces in 1942, consistently divided its subjects into ethnically defined groups. The categories into which people were classified and the practical social and legal significance of that classification changed repeatedly during the long colonial period. In the late colonial era, however, the dominant system of classification divided residents of the Indies between three categories: "Europeans," "Natives" (*Inlanders*), and "Foreign Orientals" (*Vreemde Oosterlingen*).[7]

Many scholars have been inclined to see these categories as having a profound effect on Indonesian views of the world, introducing a fundamental racial consciousness to societies where such consciousness had not previously existed, and dooming the Foreign Orientals in particular (notably Indonesia's substantial Chinese minority) to exclusion from "nativeness" and thus ultimately also from being accepted as Indonesian. These scholars have given less attention to the fact that the sharp legal classification of Netherlands Indies residents into three ethnic categories concealed not only a complex array of ethnic identities in the colony, but also ambiguities and blurred boundaries. Formal ethnic status was principally a function of paternal ancestry. That is to say, the child of a European man automatically acquired European status, provided either the mother was also European or, if there was no marriage, the father recognized the child as his own. Until 1838, the colonial authorities had banned interracial marriages, but European men had routinely lived with indigenous and other Asian women, and the children of these relationships had European status as long as they were recognized by the father. After 1838, when interracial marriage became legal, wives took the ethnic status of their husbands. The category "European" (*Europeaan*), therefore, included not only people of unambiguously European birth and descent but also many people with a high degree of indigenous ancestry. It also encompassed Japanese, who became a significant presence in the commercial and service sectors in the late nineteenth century and who achieved "European" status in the early twentieth century after a long diplomatic struggle by Japan.[8] *Europeaan*, too, were people of non-European descent who had been legally assimilated (*gelijkgesteld*) to European status.[9]

Even setting aside the Japanese and the *gelijkgestelden*, the category *Europeaan* was not only enormously diverse but also divided into several loosely defined and overlapping subcategories. European newcomers to the colony were commonly called "import-Europeans"; if they expected to leave the colony in due course, they were called *trekkers* ("movers"), if they chose to stay there, they became *blijvers* ("stayers"). Those who were more purely European in culture and appearance were called *totoks*. In the early nineteenth century, the colonial authorities distinguished between *mestiecen* (mestizos, i.e., Europeans of mixed race) and *creolen* (creoles, i.e., those who were locally born of exclusively European ancestry), but by the late nineteenth century these terms had largely disappeared in favour of *Indo-Europeaan* (sometimes abbreviated as *Indo*), which generally implied mixed ancestry but that could also include *totok blijvers* who had adopted significant elements from the local cultures. There was often a social distinction between *totoks* and *Indos*, but the terms of this distinction varied enormously. In parts of eastern Indonesia such as Ambon and Kisar, Indo-Europeans were distinguishable from Christian indigenes only by their surnames.[10] In parts of Java, *Indos* were a liminal group, seen as combining European self-confidence with "native" superstition, fecundity, hygiene, and shiftiness. Yet they could also be portrayed as classically small-minded burgers, conventional in their tastes, conservative in their values, and verging on racist in their views of the world. Depending on circumstance, physical appearance, accent, fluency in one or more indigenous languages, family name,[11] occupation, and cultural attributes such as clothing and food, might or might not be defining features of a local *Indo* identity.[12] The introduction of steamships and the opening of the Suez Canal in 1869 led to a sharp increase in the number of European women traveling to the Indies, and therefore to a sharpening of the racial distinction between pure Europeans and the mixed-race community. Nonetheless, the distinction between different sections of the European community was never formalized and never absolute.

"Foreign Orientals" were an even more diverse community, encompassing the many different communities and individuals who had settled in the Indies from other parts of Asia. The most important group within this broad category was the Chinese, and colonial statistics often made a distinction between Chinese and "other" Foreign Orientals, of whom the most numerous were Indians and Arabs. All these groups themselves, however, were internally divided along a variety of cultural, religious, and class lines. In particular, different degrees of assimilation to indigenous cultures gave rise to a distinction between relatively unassimilated *totoks* or *singkeh* and the more thoroughly indigenized *peranakan*, a distinction comparable to that between *totoks* and *Indos* amongst the Europeans. The

Chinese were also divided into dialect groups and the Indians were divided both regionally and between Hindus and Muslims.

Under these circumstances, it is not surprising that those whom the Dutch classified as *Inlanders* were not all indigenous in the strict sense of the word. As we have seen, during the colonial era, the child of a European father and an indigenous mother became European only if formally recognized by the father. This recognition was by no means always forthcoming, and so there was a significant proportion of people with indigenous status who nonetheless had some European ancestry and who were well aware of the fact. Marriages between native men and mixed-race women with European status were not uncommon and had the same consequence. Even before the colonial era, moreover, during the great age of commerce in Southeast Asia beginning in about 1200, Chinese, Indians, Persians, Arabs, Siamese, Japanese, Vietnamese, Armenians, and many others had settled permanently in coastal cities and towns of the archipelago, often marrying local women and leaving progeny who were gradually absorbed into local societies. As a consequence, a great many "indigenous" Indonesians possessed some foreign ancestry.

Whereas the simple tripartite division of the legal system gives the impression of a society segmented into large, relatively coherent racial blocks, the social reality was very different. Skin color in all its shades, along with eye shape, created a finely gradated social hierarchy that was always modified to some extent by class, culture (including religion), and wealth. The Netherlands Indies legal system, privileging paternal ancestry over physical signs of race, saw nothing anomalous in the fact that a "European" might have considerably darker skin than a "native." Nor, at least after 1838, did the law place any obstacle in the way of interethnic marriage. Law and social prejudice never coincided closely in colonial Indonesia.

Nor, it seems, was the pattern of daily racial discrimination in the Netherlands Indies as pervasive as that in apartheid South Africa or in the United States South before the civil rights movement. There was no formal segregation of the races in public transport or in places of public entertainment such as swimming pools and theaters. Occasional mention has been made of signs that announced that certain public facilities were "forbidden for dogs and natives" (*verboden voor honden en inlanders*), but no photographs of these signs seem to exist and they are strikingly absent from contemporary critiques of Dutch colonialism. It seems likely that the anecdote has been transplanted from elsewhere, perhaps China, and has taken on life as an urban myth because it seems consistent with the character of colonialism.[13]

Netherlands Indies society was profoundly unequal in terms of wealth and power, but these disparities did not closely follow ethnic lines. A striking feature of the photographs of public events such as horse races and dances from the first half of the nineteenth century is the significant sprinkling of Chinese and indigenous faces in the crowds.[14] None of this is to disregard the reality of ethnic consciousness and ethnic discrimination in the Dutch colony. Europeans were the lords of society and indigenes were not. The system of government was autocratic and at best paternalistic. Public expenditure was perceived to favor the interests of the Europeans and, even when it was ostensibly for the interests of Indonesians, to reflect a European sense of priorities. Color and culture created a painful hierarchy within the European community. Eurasian girls, above all, were under pressure to marry men with paler skins to "rectify," as they sometimes put it, the mistake of their ancestor in marrying, or coupling with, an Indonesian.[15] The overall picture of ethnic identity and ethnic classification in the colony was one of baroque complexity and overlapping categories. In short, the ethnic categorizations of the colonial era do not point to the violence of 1945/46.

I do not want to discount the significance of ethnic discrimination in colonial Indonesia. This system had given rise to a range of discriminatory practices that were amongst the most important grievances against the colonial system. Nonetheless, the structure of ethnic categorization in the Netherlands Indies did not separate the Eurasians as a special category symbolic of the system's injustices to the poor who eventually spearheaded the massacres of 1945/46. One would not have expected such intense hostility to Eurasians in 1945/46 simply on the basis of racial prejudices simmering in the late colonial order. Prejudice did simmer, but there is no evidence of a vast reserve of animosity that might explain the genocide.

Not only was the genocidal violence against Eurasians in 1945 unprecedented in Indonesian history, it was also without sequel. Although civil violence remained at a relatively high level in Indonesian society until the military-imposed order of the Suharto era, Eurasians were never again specially targeted as victims. The Dutch citizens who were expelled from Indonesia in 1959 as part of the shrill nationalism of the Sukarno era were removed because of their nationality; the many Eurasians who had adopted Indonesian citizenship suffered no such discrimination. And today, although Eurasians are as subject to stereotyping as other Indonesian ethnic groups (they are seen as being mainly entertainers, criminals, and policemen), there is no hint of the venom that blights attitudes toward Indonesia's other contentious exogenous community, the Chinese Indonesians.

Ethnicity and Indonesian Nationalism

Although the urbane nationalists who created the Indonesian republic in August 1945 may have been innocent of the massacres, the exclusion of

Eurasians from the Indonesian polity was not simply the work of men of violence lurking in bamboo groves close to European habitations. The Indonesian constitution, drafted in the difficult weeks before the end of the Second World War in 1945, contains a curious contradiction. On the one hand, the document specifies that there shall be no legal discrimination between Indonesian citizens.[16] This formulation may appear worthy and unremarkable but in fact it marked a revolutionary transformation by ending at a stroke the complicated system of ethnic discrimination that, as we have seen, had underpinned the legal system in the Netherlands Indies for more than three centuries. The abolition of ethnicity as a legal category, therefore, was an unequivocally revolutionary act by the nationalists who declared Indonesian independence in 1945.[17]

On the other hand, the abolition of ethnic classification in the 1945 constitution was incomplete. Article 6.1 of the constitution contradicted the bold new principle of equality by specifying that only those who were *asli*, a term normally translated as "indigenous," were eligible to become president of the republic.[18] This small gesture has generally attracted little attention in analyses of the history of ethnic relations in Indonesia, but it is significant as the first formal act of ethnic discrimination by independent Indonesia. In view of the troubled history of ethnic relations and the persistence of gross ethnic discrimination in the archipelago since independence, despite the formal abolition of ethnic classification, explaining Article 6.1 may help us to understand both the genocide of Eurasians in 1945 and the complex nature of ethnic prejudice in Indonesia more generally.

In the context of Indonesian nationalism, moreover, the fact that Article 6.1 of the constitution excluded nonindigenes from the possibility of contributing a president to the new nation is puzzling. The idea of Indonesia, after all, was determinedly multiethnic and multireligious, encompassing hundreds of indigenous ethnic groups, including Papuans who were physically very different from the Austronesian majority. Especially in the years around the declaration of independence, moreover, the idea of Indonesia was a modernizing one, open in principle to ideas from anywhere in the world. Of course, many different ideas contended for the soul of Indonesian nationalism, including Islam and Marxism, but nationalist discourse was generally free of overt racism and of appeals to blood and ancestry of the kind that has often underpinned Western racism and nationalism.

Nonetheless, this admirable universalism of the Indonesian nationalist ideals concealed elements of racial antagonism. Since early in the colonial period, there had been tension between metropolitan Dutch and locally-born Eurasians. In 1721, an alleged conspiracy by the Eurasian Peter Erberfelt was suppressed with special brutality. The first modern political party in the Netherlands Indies, moreover, was the *Indische Partij* (Indies Party) founded in 1911 and led by a Eurasian, E. F. E. Douwes Dekker, and two Javanese intellectuals, Suwardi Suryaningrat and Tjipto Mangoenkoesoemo. The party's key slogans were "the Indies for those who make their home there" and "the Indies free from Holland." The party's program was progressive and particularly hostile to aristocratic authority.[19] Tjipto was famous for having suggested that the archipelago would be better off if the Javanese language, with its multitude of levels of speech that made it virtually impossible to conduct a conversation without one side being designated as superior to the other, were extinguished.[20]

The emergence of a mixed-race community as leaders of a local settler or creole nationalism was no unusual phenomenon. It had been characteristic of Latin America, bore important resemblances to settler nationalism in Australasia and North America, and was the central element in anti-Spanish nationalism in The Philippines. There the term "Filipino," which was originally applied to Spanish born in the colony, as opposed to the *peninsulares* from Spain itself, expanded in meaning to encompass all residents of the archipelago, including the indigenous peoples who had previously been called *Indios*. The *Indische Partij*, with its commitment to social democracy and its repudiation of ethnicity as a basis for nationality, lay firmly in this broad tradition.

In the course of the twentieth century, however, two main factors worked to marginalize Eurasians from the developing Indonesian nationalist movement.[21] First, the colonial authorities, acutely aware of the fact the creole nationalism in The Philippines had come close to toppling Spanish power, and probably would have done so if the Americans had not stepped in and toppled it themselves, took sharp repressive measures against the *Indische Partij*, exiling its leaders and restricting its activities. More important, in constructing a rationale for continued colonial rule in the twentieth century, when developments all around the Netherlands Indies were pointing in the direction of a colonial retreat, the Dutch increasingly portrayed their rule as being essential to protect vulnerable groups in Indies society from exploitation or oppression by other parts of the same society. Whereas the rationale for colonialism in earlier times had been the alleged benefits it brought in terms of civilization, economic development, or welfare (especially peace, law, and medicine), the rationale of the late colonial state was more negative. It involved identifying both "dangerous" groups in society and the vulnerable groups that might be their victims. This protective rationale was manifest in a growing attention to the welfare of supposedly "primitive" indigenous peoples of West New Guinea, to the preservation of traditional Hindu culture and religion in Bali, and to the protection of indigenous Indonesians from Eurasians and Chinese.[22]

The construction of Eurasians and Chinese as dangerous to the rest of Indonesian society took different paths. The classification of the Chinese as a group distinct from the Dutch ruling elite had much older roots than the sharp social distinction between Eurasians and metropolitan Dutch. The Chinese, moreover, had been a central element in the colonial system of revenue farms, in which the right to collect tax in a particular segment of the economy was auctioned off to the highest bidder, who then used private gangs of enforcers to extract tax from the public. Working at the sharp edge of colonial exploitation, these Chinese (though a tiny minority of the total Chinese population) were deeply hated. By the beginning of the twentieth century, the revenue farm system had been done away with in favor of more modern systems of tax collection, but the Dutch now drew increasing attention to the supposedly destructive effects of Chinese moneylending in the countryside. Chinese lenders, whose practices were indeed extortionate by today's standards, were excoriated as bloodsuckers and exploiters of simple-minded peasants in the countryside. It is notable that anti-Chinese riots in the Netherlands Indies only began in the early twentieth century at the time when this official vilification of usury began to take form.[23]

The Eurasians, by contrast, were constructed primarily as the enemies of the modern Indonesian elite. This elite took shape in the first decades of the twentieth century as a result of the expansion of modern education beyond European society and beyond the high aristocratic elite most closely involved in colonial rule. As the economy and society of the Indies grew more complex, so too grew the need for literate, articulate middle-ranking employees and government officials. The colonial establishment fostered a discourse in which the interests of this new elite were set against those of the Eurasians who had tended, following the color hierarchy, to occupy the middle reaches of the colonial civil service. Eurasians were increasingly portrayed as clever and cunning, with the arrogance and ambition of Europeans but none of the European sense of noblesse oblige. By the end of the colonial era, the radical, inclusive nationalism of the *Indische Partij* was overshadowed by the antinationalist conservatism of the *Indo-Europeesch Verbond* (IEV, Eurasian Association), representing a community that feared Indonesian nationalism and stood firmly behind the colonialist hard line of the 1930s and early 1940s.

Indonesian nationalism was always a hugely diverse movement. It was never united in a single organization, and even periods of domination by a single organization were no more than brief. The movement included radical Muslims and communists who envisaged violent revolution against the colonial state, as well as conservative gradualists who imagined long eras of tutelage during which the Dutch would slowly relinquish control to a trusted, indigenous elite. For all this division, however, these diverse forces saw themselves as a single movement (*Pergerakan*) ultimately sharing the same goal. Precisely because Indonesian nationalism saw itself as inclusive of those who regarded the Indies as their home, the pro-colonial views of the IEV seemed deeply and contemptibly disloyal to most Indonesian nationalists. The European Dutch were a powerful and dangerous enemy, but the IEV were traitors who had betrayed their homeland to uphold its subordination to foreign rule.

During the final decade of colonial rule, hostility to the IEV and to Eurasians in general was mitigated by the fact that they did not play any pivotal role in maintaining the colonial order. The colonial parliament, the *Volksraad*, was heavily weighted with government supporters and had relatively few powers. The colonial state's capacity to censor, to spy, to exile, and to imprison was far more important to its survival than the small chorus of support coming from the IEV. In 1945, however, the perception of Eurasian disloyalty suddenly moved to the center of the political stage.

Loyalty and the Critical Moment, 1945

Indonesian independence was declared by the two most prominent nationalist leaders, Sukarno and Mohammad Hatta, on 17 August 1945, two days after the Japanese surrender. In the previous weeks, both leaders had been members of a committee sponsored by the Japanese occupation authorities to prepare for Indonesian independence under Japanese auspices. The Japanese intention, although they did not come to it until late in the war, was to create an Indonesian republic as a puppet or client state alongside other states in the so-called Greater East Asia Co-Prosperity Sphere—Manchukuo, Wang Ching-wei's China, The Philippines, Burma, Vietnam, Cambodia, and Laos. The preparations for Indonesian independence, however, had been short-circuited by the end of the war and by the obligation that the Allies placed upon Japan to maintain the political status quo in occupied territories. The Indonesian nationalists thus had two reasons to abort the independence process: they risked suppression by the Japanese authorities, and they risked having their claim for independence tainted by its association with Japanese imperial plans.

After considerable hesitation, the Indonesian leaders chose to create what we would now call a virtual republic. Rather than seeking to create state institutions or to take over institutions from the Japanese, they focused on winning expressions of loyalty from the people of the archipelago. They were hopeful that the Allies would recognize the principle of self-determination as set out in the Atlantic Charter and that the promise of an independent Indonesia open to Western interests would outweigh any sense of obligation to the Dutch, whose performance in resisting both the Germans and Japanese had been hardly impressive. In particular, the new government declined to transform Japanese-trained local armed units into a national army for fear that such a move would brand the republic with the then-pejorative term, "made in Japan."

Indonesians outside the central nationalist elite, however, generally viewed this strategy with alarm. They were immediately aware that the Europeans in the archipelago regarded the Japanese defeat as a victory and expected that the colonial order would be restored. They remembered how obdurate the Dutch had been in resisting the claims of Indonesian nationalism before the Second World War. Whereas The Philippines under the United States had acquired a high degree of internal autonomy as a commonwealth with its own Filipino president, and Burma had achieved responsible parliamentary government under British tutelage, the Dutch in Indonesia had set their caps firmly against any significant movement toward independence. Even after the fall of the Netherlands to Germany in 1940, the Dutch had promised no more than a constitutional convention to consider changes to the relationship between colony and metropolitan power. And during the Second World War, the Dutch had made it clear that they planned to reestablish the colonial order before contemplating ways in which it might be modified.

With apparently nothing but moral force standing between the new Indonesian republic and a return to Dutch colonial rule, many Indonesians resolved to take matters into their own hands, forming the *badan perjuangan* (struggle organizations) mentioned above, and fired with a determination to use any means at hand—bricks, stones, sharpened bamboo stakes, even poisonous snakes—to resist the return of colonialism.[24]

But Dutch forces did not land on the coasts of Indonesia in the days after the Japanese surrender. The Netherlands itself had been occupied by Germany until the very end of the Second World War, and the colonial government-in-exile based in Australia had virtually no forces at its disposal. It was to be six weeks or more in fact before the first substantial Allied forces were to arrive in the main islands of Java and Sumatra. In the immediate aftermath of the war, therefore, the Netherlands Indies was as weak as the republic whose existence it refused to acknowledge. This weakness had much the same effect on European residents in the archipelago as the weakness of the republic had had on Indonesian nationalists. Like the nationalists, the Europeans began to flaunt signs of their loyalty to the Netherlands, waving flags, singing patriotic songs and generally behaving as if a return to the colonial era was imminent. Like the nationalists, though on a lesser scale, they began to form militias, partly to maintain local law and order, partly as a surrogate colonial army.

This situation put tens of thousands of ordinary people in the front line of the monumental struggle between colonialism and nationalism. The struggle was not delegated to formal armed forces, but rather conducted by patriotic individuals whom the extraordinary circumstances drove to action. It was not carried on through institutions, but rather as a contest over manifestations of loyalty. The enemies of the Netherlands Indies were not soldiers of a yet-to-be-formed Indonesian army, but ordinary Indonesians who had chosen for the republic. The republic's enemies in turn were not the returning soldiers of the colonial army but rather the ordinary people, Dutch, Eurasian, and Indonesian, who wanted to see the Dutch tricolor flying again. Those who perished in 1945/46 died for their beliefs, rather than for their skin color or their formal ethnic status.

Yet ethnicity was important. Eurasians suffered more than any population group in this period. The recorded death toll is around 5,000, based on recovered bodies, but an estimated 20,000 Eurasians were noted as missing by the time the Dutch authorities were in a position to begin compiling records.[25] Out of a total European population of around a quarter of a million, this was a substantial proportion, even allowing for the likelihood that many of those registered as missing had in fact managed to escape or to survive. By contrast, the Chinese of the archipelago, four times more numerous than the Europeans at the time, probably suffered between one fifth and one tenth of the casualties.

The acute victimization of the Eurasians probably arose partly from sheer physical factors. Whereas Chinese tended to be clustered in so-called *Chineesche wijken* (Chinatowns) that were somewhat more easily defended, Eurasians were more widely scattered and tended to be more vulnerable. Europeans, still in Japanese internment camps, were paradoxically protected by the fact of being concentrated in defensible encampments.

The genocide of the Eurasians in Indonesia in 1945/46 has largely been forgotten within Indonesia, and memory of what took place is kept alive mainly by aging survivors in the Netherlands.[26] The broader significance of the genocide lies not in the fact that on this occasion a settler community was the victim of genocide instead of the perpetrator, but rather in the tangled relationship between ethnicity, nationality, class, and political affiliation that led to the genocide.

The colonial legal, social, and cultural system did not itself mark out Eurasians as likely victims of violence with the departure of colonialism. Rather, despite early involvement in shaping the idea of Indonesia, Eurasians developed an ambiguous, and then an antagonistic, relationship with the Indonesian nationalism movement. During the colonial period itself, this antagonism had little significance beyond colonial elite circles, though it was ultimately to lead to the otherwise puzzling provision of the

Indonesian constitution that insisted the nation's president be of indigenous descent. In 1945, however, this separation became fatal. Both the new Indonesian republic and the recovering Netherlands Indies were in a state of utter weakness, and their respective capacities to command loyalty became the single most important attribute of the state. In these times, those who were perceived to be disloyal paid a heavy price. Just as Eurasians could not be trusted in the presidential palace, they had to be eliminated from the streets as potential traitors.

Acknowledgement

Research for this chapter was carried out with the assistance of research grants from the Netherlands Institute of War Documentation (NIOD) within the program "Indonesia Across Orders, 1930–1960" and from the Australian Research Council.

Notes

1. For a powerful evocation of this belief, see Benedict R.O'G. Anderson, *Java in a Time of Revolution: Occupation and Resistance, 1944–1946* (Ithaca, NY, 1972), 125–31.
2. There is evidence that hundreds of thousands of people died of hardship and starvation during the occupation, while clothes were so scarce that some families had only a single sarong, which they took turns in wearing in order to be able to emerge from the house. See Pierre van der Eng, "Bridging a Gap: A Reconstruction of Population Patterns in Indonesia, 1930–61," *Asian Studies Review* 26 no. 4 (2002): 487–509, and Shigeru Sato, "Japanization in Indonesia Re-examined: The Problem of Self-sufficiency in Clothing," in *Imperial Japan and National Identities in Asia, 1895–1945*, ed. Li Narangoa and Robert Cribb (Richmond, UK, 2003), 270–95.
3. J.S. Furnivall, *Colonial Policy and Practice: A Comparative Study of Burma and Netherlands India* (Cambridge, 1948), 271–73.
4. For a gripping literary evocation of this conviction, see Hella S. Haasse, *Oeroeg* (Amsterdam, 1961); for a recent exploration of perceptions of the Japanese period, see Remco Raben, ed., *Representing the Japanese Occupation of Indonesia: Personal Testimonies and Public Images in Indonesia, Japan, and The Netherlands* (Zwolle, Netherlands, 1999).
5. See for example, Anderson, *Java in a Time of Revolution*; Audrey R. Kahin, ed., *Regional Dynamics of the Indonesian Revolution: Unity from Diversity* (Honolulu, 1985); William H. Frederick, *Visions and Heat: The Making of the Indonesian Revolution* (Athens, OH, 1989).
6. Takashi Shiraishi, 'Anti-Sinicism in Java's New Order' in *Essential Outsiders: Chinese and Jews in the Modern Transformation of Southeast Asia and Central Europe*, ed. Daniel Chirot and Anthony Reid (Seattle, 1997), 187–207.

7. C. Fasseur, "Cornerstone and Stumbling Block: Racial Classification and the Late Colonial State in Indonesia', in *The Late Colonial State in Indonesia: Political and Economic Foundations of the Netherlands Indies 1880–1942*, ed. Robert Cribb (Leiden, 1994), 31–56.
8. Fasseur, "Cornerstone and Stumbling Block," 40.
9. *Gelijkstelling* involved demonstrating either a thorough assimilation to European culture or a pressing practical (usually commercial) reason to have European status. Those who made this transition were expected also to take European names. An Indonesian named Prawiraningrat, thus might take a name such as "Tom Praaning" on becoming a European.
10. Ernst Rodenwaldt, *Die Mestizen auf Kisar* (Batavia, Dutch East Indies, 1927).
11. All Europeans had European family names, but French surnames were common among people of mixed descent, probably as a result of Huguenot (French Protestant) settlement in the archipelago after the revocation of the Edict of Nantes in 1685.
12. Paul W. van der Veur, "Cultural Aspects of the Eurasian Community in Indonesian Colonial Society," *Indonesia* 6 (1968): 38–53; the novels of Pramoedya Ananta Toer provide a powerful, though not always reliable, picture of ethnic relations in the colonial period. See, for example, *This Earth of Mankind: A Novel* (Melbourne, 1982).
13. The most explicit reference to this sign is provided by H.C. Beynon, *Verboden voor honden en inlanders: Indonesiërs vertellen over hun leven in de koloniale tijd* (Amsterdam, 1995). Beynon's introduction refers to "private swimming pools" where the sign was allegedly displayed, while the chapter of Abdul Haris Nasution, entitled "Honden en inlanders," refers specifically to a high school (HBS) in Bandung where the swimming pool was labeled in this way. I have argued elsewhere, however, that Nasution is an unreliable historical source and I am reluctant to accept his unsupported testimony in this case. On the persistence of urban myths as bearers of an important and plausible message about the way in which society functions, see Jan Harold Brunvand, *The Vanishing Hitchhiker: Urban Legends and Their Meanings* (London, 1983).
14. The idea that Netherlands Indies society was infused with racial consciousness also owes a good deal to the writings of J.S. Furnivall, who coined the term "plural society" and described Netherlands Indies as socially segregated along ethnic lines, with its different groups meeting only in the marketplace. See Furnivall, *Colonial Policy and Practice*, 303–12. Recent work by Coppel, however, has pointed out how misleading Furnivall's description is as an account of day-to-day experience in Indies colonial society. See Charles A. Coppel, "Revisiting Furnivall's 'Plural Society': Colonial Java as a Mestizo Society?," *Ethnic and Racial Studies* 20, no 3 (1997): 562–79.
15. Van der Veur, "Cultural Aspects."
16. Bab X Pasal 27.1: "Segala warga negara bersamaan kedudukannja didalam hukum dan pemerintahan dan wadjib mendjundjung hukum dan pemerintahan itu dengan tidak ada ketjualinja." The 1989 translation reads: "All citizens have equal status before the law and in government and shall abide by the law and the government without any exception."
17. Fasseur, "Cornerstone and Stumbling Block," 54–55.
18. Bab 3, Pasal 6.1: "Presiden ialah orang Indonesia asli." The official 1989 translation reads: "The President shall be a native Indonesian citizen." Although there have been occasional attempts to argue that the exception laid down in Article 6.1 was a translation of Article 6.1X of the United States Constitution, which requires the president to have been born in the United States, there has always been a general political consensus that the article was directed at members of Indonesia's substantial communities of nonindigenous descent, regardless of where they were born.

19. E.F.E. Douwes Dekker, "The Indies Party: Its Nature and Objectives, 1913," in *Indonesia: Selected Documents on Colonialism and Nationalism, 1830–1942*, ed. Chr. L.M. Penders (Brisbane, 1977), 228–32; Robert van Niel, *The Emergence of the Modern Indonesian Elite* (The Hague, 1970), 63–66.
20. Takashi Shiraishi, "The Disputes between Tjipto Mangoenkoesoemo and Soetatmo Soeriokoesoemo: *Satria* vs. *Pandita*," *Indonesia* 32 (1981): 93–108.
21. Religious difference was significant, of course—the Christianity of most Eurasians was a barrier between them and the Muslim majority. This element can be only part of the explanation, however, because indigenous Christians were an important part of the nationalist movement.
22. Henk Schulte Nordholt, "The Making of Traditional Bali: Colonial Ethnography and Bureaucratic Reproduction," in *Colonial Subjects. Essays in the Practical History of Anthropology*, ed. Peter Pels and Oscar Salemink (Ann Arbor, MI, 1999), 241–81.
23. Shiraishi, "Anti-Sinicism."
24. Robert Cribb, *Gangsters and Revolutionaries: The Jakarta People's Militia and the Indonesian Revolution 1945–1949* (Sydney, 1991), 38–69.
25. Okke Norel, *En . . . hoe was het daarbuiten: buiten de Japanse kampen en in de bersiap* (n.p., 2001), 8.
26. See H.Th. Bussemaker, *Bersiap!: opstand in het paradijs: de Bersiap-periode op Java en Sumatra 1945–1946* (Zutphen, Netherlands, 2005).

– *Chapter 19* –

Savages, Subjects, and Sovereigns
Conjunctions of Modernity, Genocide, and Colonialism

Alex Hinton

> Although the Lord hath given the earth to children of men . . . the greater part of it [is] possessed and wrongfully usurped by wild beasts, and unreasonable creatures, or by brutish savages, which by reason of their godles[s] ignorance, and blasphemous Idolatrie, are worse than those beasts which are of most wilde and savage nature.
>
> —Robert Gray, 1609[1]

> I killed those Indians because I knew that the government would not reprimand us nor make us pay for the crime that was committed.
>
> —Colombian settler, 1967[2]

The savage. The subject. The sovereign. These notions mark significant contours in the conjunction of genocide and colonialism. We have "savages," such as the Taino of Española, who are excluded as subjects and hunted down by colonial powers like "rabid" animals. We have "savages" who are marked for transformation into colonial "subjects"—like so many Native American tribes and the Aborigines—and, in the process, lose their lives, family members, and distinctive traditions. And we have colonial "subjects" who aspire for sovereignty and, upon attaining it, turn back upon their own newly perceived "subjects" and engage in mass murder—frequently using the very discourses of the colonial power they displaced. Cambodia and Rwanda certainly fit this case.

As such examples suggest, and as this book demonstrates, colonialism and genocide are closely interlinked. In this essay, however, I want to suggest that in order to more fully understand the relationship of colonialism and genocide, we must take into account broader and related processes associated with modernity, which are intimately tied to savages, subjects, and sovereigns. Along the way, I argue that we need to constantly keep in mind that encounters with modernity are always local ones, at once transforming and transformed, as the relationship between colonialism and genocide illustrates. I draw extensively on my ethnographic research in Cambodia to illustrate these points.

Modernity

What is modernity? While some scholars prefer a distinctly local definition of modernity along the lines of "the desire to be modern," others, including myself, view modernity as a set of interrelated processes that generate distinct formations through time and place.[3] Economically, modernity is associated with the rise of the large-scale market exchange that was catalyzed by the Age of Exploration and, later, the Industrial Revolution and Fordist production. Private property, monetarized exchange, wage labor, mass production and consumption, capital accumulation, and the search for new markets (with its corollary, the generation of new desires) have been central to this process. Modernity is often driven by new technologies, ranging from the invention of guns and faster ships to ergonomics to electronic media and the Internet.

Politically, modernity is linked to increasing secularization, the rise of the nation-state, imagined communities of citizens bound to a legitimate authority, notions of sovereignty and Westphalian law, fixed territorial boundaries, and centralized state surveillance and control. Socially, modernity is related to new types of social differentiation and organization, ranging from categories of race, class, gender, ethnicity, and related stratifications to bureaucracy and new divisions of labor. Culturally, modernity is associated with often antireligious ideologies of rationality, progress, faith in science, human emancipation, human nature, and individualism—notions that coalesced in the Enlightenment. On a more abstract level, modernity has been tied to the collapse of time and space, as people, money, ideas, technologies, images, and commodities move increasingly quickly, a tendency that has culminated in globalization and late capitalist dynamics.

While scholars like Max Horkheimer and Theodor Adorno[4] and Hannah Arendt[5] made important early contributions to our understanding of the relationship between modernity and the Holocaust, Zygmunt Bauman[6] has perhaps made this argument most forcefully, linking Nazi atrocities to modern metanarratives (of progress, rationality, race), centralized political control, technologies of death, rational design and a project of social engineering, and bureaucratic efficiency. This association between modernity and genocide, however, has less frequently been applied to other genocides, including those associated with colonialism.[7] Here, it is useful to return to the conceptual triad mentioned above: savages, subjects, and sovereigns.

Savages

The Age of Exploration, poised on the cusp of modernity, posed a key problem for Europeans. While Europeans were familiar with "others" in places like the Middle East and India, they were suddenly confronted with new lands and new peoples that pushed the limits of the preexisting understandings.[8] Were they, like the "others" with whom they were already familiar, "degenerates" who had "fallen" far from the Garden of Eden, but were still human? Or, were they something else entirely, closer to devils and monsters?

Driven by the desire to procure wealth and new lands, many explorers, including Columbus, chose the second answer. If these newly discovered creatures were subhuman, then they had no right to their lands and, like wild beasts, could be killed without a qualm. These beings were animals, a nuisance to be gotten rid of, particularly since they stood in the way of riches and glory. The history of this tragic moment is well known. Millions of indigenous peoples in the "new world" perished from diseases, the military superiority of the Europeans, or outright execution.

Christopher Columbus himself was intimately involved in these genocidal practices. As the viceroy of Española (Haiti and the Dominican Republic), he oversaw a program of enforced slavery and mass murder that, coupled with disease, reduced the native Taino population from as many as 8 million to 100,000 by the time he departed in 1500.[9] According to the missionary-activist Bartolomé de Las Casas, the Spaniards perpetrated all sorts of horrors upon the Tainos—hacking, roasting, burning, and working them to death. When, in response to this brutality, the Tainos attempted to defend themselves, the Spanish response was brutal and overwhelming:

> They forced their way into native settlements, slaughtering everyone they found there, including small children, old men, pregnant women, and even women who had just given birth. They hacked them to pieces, slicing open their bellies with their swords as though they were so many sheep herded into a pen. They even laid wagers on whether they could manage to slice a man in two at a stroke, or cut an individual's head from his body, or disembowel him with a single blow of their axes. They grabbed suckling infants by the feet and, ripping them from

> their mothers' breasts, dashed them headlong against the rocks . . . They slaughtered anyone and everything in their path.[10]

Within 50 years, the Tainos had been eradicated from the face of the earth,[11] a pattern that was repeated through the "new world." Over the following centuries, the number of indigenous peoples throughout the world declined by perhaps 50 million people—some estimates put the number at 100 million or more—from precontact levels.[12] Here, at the dawn of modernity, we find a number of processes at work that would reappear in genocides through the ages: the expansion of Western states into distant locales, mass death driven by greed and facilitated by new technologies, and the construction of the victims as dehumanized "others" who are depicted as the binary opposite of the perpetrators.

Savages into (Primitive) Subjects

During the sixteenth century, a dispute broke out over the existential status of the newly discovered "savages." The two sides were epitomized by the 1550/51 Valladolid debates between a Spanish chaplain and royal chronicler, Juan de Sepúlveda and the activist missionary Father Bartolomé de las Casas, over the legitimacy of the Spanish "war" against the Indians—with Sepúlveda arguing vehemently in the affirmative because, he claimed, American Indians, like Africans and other "animals," were naturally inferior beings who lacked "souls," and de las Casas refuting this claim based on his first-hand observations of the Indians.[13] Ultimately, de las Casas asserted that Indians were capable of salvation and therefore should not be obliterated.

Both strands of thought—the savage as subhuman versus the savage as "primitive" but still human and therefore capable of salvation—have persisted through time, albeit in different incarnations (we now talk of "development" and "progress" instead of salvation), legitimating genocide in different ways. During the Enlightenment, for example, the salvation argument was secularized based partly on the principle of the psychic unity of mankind. Given that "savages" were humans and therefore partook of the same "nature" as the "civilized" Europeans, Enlightenment thinkers had to explain their seemingly irrational behavior. This was done through stage theory, which posited "savages" at the bottom of a hierarchy leading to "civilization." Bound up with the spirit of human emancipation, the "civilized" were responsible for helping these "child-like," "uncultivated," "irrational" beings to "progress." While human, the "savage" was placed on the bottom end of a series of binary oppositions:[14]

Civilized: Savage
Rational: Irrational
Cultivated: Uncultivated
Progressed: Degenerate
Science: Superstition
Advanced: Backward
Developed: Underdeveloped
Adult: Child-like
Strong: Weak
Law: Uncontrolled
Knowledge: Ignorance

These discourses buttressed colonial policies that, while aimed primarily at economic exploitation and territorial aggrandizement, could be legitimated in terms of the "white man's burden." The colonizers would beneficently help transform savages into more civilized subjects. In most cases, the colonizers developed a complex "apparatus" to promote this project of social engineering.[15] The power of the colonial government was gradually expanded, usually by means of force. As it encompassed locals, they were "liberated" through a Western education that taught them a certain set of values and types of knowledge. These understandings often disparaged and discouraged—and sometimes directly outlawed—the "savage" customs of the "primitives." Moreover, locals were interpellated and incorporated into the capitalist system, through enticements and inducements, including a taxation system that forced indigenous peoples to engage in wage labor. As subjects of the colonial administration, they were required to follow "civilized" systems of "law" and "justice."

This production of colonial subjects has been associated with physical and cultural genocide in a number of instances. In numerous cases, including mass murder in the Americas, local ways of life have been diminished (or made illegal) and groups have been forcibly evicted from their native lands. Sometimes, children have been removed from their families and given to new parents who will allegedly provide them with a "better" life. In still other cases, the ideology of the "white man's burden" has worked in tandem with discourses about the incorrigible savage to foment genocide. The genocide of many Native Americans tribes (for example, the Sioux, Cherokees, Ottawas, and Mandans) fits this model, as governmental assimilationist policies coexisted with officially or unofficially sanctioned campaigns of war to eradicate, diminish, or forcibly evict the "savages."[16] Infamous cases in the Americas include the Cherokee "Trail of Tears," Lord Jeffrey Amherst's intentional infection of the Ottawas with smallpox to "extirpate this execrable race,"[17] and the massacres at Sand Creek (1864) and Wounded Knee (1890). Sometimes the profit motive was clear-cut, as was the case with the slave labor, torture, and massacre of Putumayo Indians in Peru or natives in King Leopold's Congo (1885–1908).[18] And, who can forget General Roca's "Conquest of the Desert" in Argentina, the annihilation of the Herero in Southwest Africa, or the destruction of the Aborigines in Australia.[19] Such genocides are not a thing of the past: they continue today in a variety of locales, ranging from the Yanomami of Brazil to the Chittagong Hills people of East Pakistan.[20]

Savages into Sovereigns

As these last two examples illustrate, one of the ironies of contemporary genocides is that they are often perpetrated by former colonial subjects who, upon attaining independence, have turned upon their own subjects and "savages" to perpetrate genocide. Yet another irony is the fact that these acts are often motivated by discourses of modernity, as the newly liberated sovereigns remain subjugated by colonial regimes of truth—a paradox of "double-consciousness" that was recognized by W. E. B. DuBois[21] and Franz Fanon.[22] Palimpsests of the new are inscribed upon local and colonial traditions of the old.

This double consciousness has played out vividly in Rwanda and Burundi, where Hutu and Tutsi demagogues forged their messages of hate out of all-too-modern notions of race and ethnicity. German, and later Belgian colonial authorities combined pseudoscientific notion of race and stage theory to legitimate their "civilizing mission" and the administrative structure they imposed to maintain their dominance and economic exploitation.The minority Tutsi were constructed as the lost descendants of Ham (thus explaining the complex sociopolitical and cultural system that existed in the area) and placed in positions of authority over the "negroid" Hutus. What had been far more fluid ethnic categories were crystallized into rigid racial differentiations. Through the generations, as they were educated in colonial schools, many Rwandans came to believe in the truth of this "Hamitic hypothesis." Tutsis could legitimate their rule by invoking their racial superiority; Hutus, in turn, could argue for the removal or elimination of these Tutsi "invaders from the North." Such racist discourses have provided fodder for genocidal demagogues in Rwanda and Burundi. As a side note, I should stress that these modern discourses are always localized—they are played out in local idioms and in culturally patterned ways. Thus, genocidal perpetrators in Rwanda fused ideological notions of racial difference with local conceptions of kingship, exchange, and bodily health—including conceptions of blockage and flow that Christopher Taylor has argued patterned much of the violence in Rwanda in 1994.[23]

A similar argument could be made for Pol Pot's Cambodia.[24] On the one hand, the Khmer Rouge line was specifically geared to eliminate colonial and imperialist influences in Cambodia, particularly the "privatism" of capitalism. On the other hand, their revolutionary discourses were strongly influenced by Marxist-Leninist ideas that top cadre, including Pol Pot, had learned in Paris. Like Maoist and North Vietnamese communists, the brand of communist ideology the Khmer Rouge promoted was saturated with modernist thought, including an extreme faith in rationality, social engineering, progress, and human emancipation.

In September 1977, for example, Pol Pot gave a speech to commemorate the seventeenth anniversary of the founding of the Communist Party of Kampuchea (CPK) that devoted a great deal of time to describing how the Party's "correct [strategic] line" had been ascertained by preliminary "research" and "scientific analysis" of the "real nature of Kampuchean society at that time."[25] Specifically, the party line held that there were two major socioeconomic "contradictions" that needed to be "defined" and "resolved"—first, the contradiction between Cambodian society and imperialism, particularly US imperialism; and, second, internal class contradictions.

Pol Pot's speech is suffused with high-modernist notions of science and progress. His description of the Khmer Rouge class analysis repeatedly invokes such words and phrases as: "answer questions," "conclusion" of "analysis," "definition," "resolve" or finding "solutions," "scientific analysis," "social science," "correct resolution," drawing "lessons" from history, "self-examination," and so forth. As the one who uses scientific analysis to accurately diagnose and resolve "contradictions" though its "correct line," the party is portrayed as all knowing, as the "correct and clear-sighted" leadership that "sees" the truth. Such insight enables it to "diagnose" the "contradictions" that create social woes, to construct a blueprint that will overcome such problems by creating a new utopian society, and to "guide" the people to this revitalizing future. Ultimately, this program of social engineering led to genocide, as certain "impure elements" of the population were deemed incorrigible and, in order to prevent them from contaminating the revolution, targeted for eradication.

As in Rwanda, such modern ideas and aspirations were localized within a specific historical and sociocultural context. Thus, the Khmer Rouge frequently invoked Buddhist notions.[26] Like Buddhists who had achieved enlightenment, the Khmer Rouge leadership had attained secret knowledge that would transform Cambodia and enable its inhabitants to reach a higher state of being. In fact, the Khmer Rouge ideology often invoked the theme of enlightenment when depicting Angkar through metaphors of clairvoyance and omniscience. Key revolutionary concepts also played upon or were directly translated using Buddhist terms and ideas. Thus, revolutionary "consciousness" (*sâtiarâmma*) was directly derived from the Buddhist concept of "mindfulness"—like a monk who mindfully acts in accordance with dhamma, a proper revolutionary would "mindfully" act in accordance with Khmer Rouge doctrine.[27] Among other things, a proper consciousness required "renunciation" (*leah bang*). Just as a monk renounces worldly desires and attachments, a proper revolutionary should renounce "the garden of the individual," ranging from the desire for material goods to attachment to one's family members. Even mourning a loved one who had died or been arrested could raise suspicion that one had a "regressive" consciousness. In fact, one of the greatest displays of devotion to the party involved a willingness to arrest or even kill a family member or spouse who had been accused of being an "enemy"; a cadre who did this evinced the highly valued ability to "cut off their sentiment" (*dach chett, chett dach, pdach/legn manosânhchetâna*) from the enemy, regardless of former ties to that person.

Local Modernities: An Example from the Cambodian Case

As the above examples of localization illustrate, we must be careful to recognize that "savages," colonial "subjects," and postcolonial "sovereigns" are not simply swept along by the modernity, but actively help form it. Modernity, in other words, does not unfold in a teleological manner but is always localized, thereby yielding distinct formations. The colonial encounter and its aftermath constitute one powerful moment in which this process of localization unfolds, as "subject" populations—like their subjugators—are transformed by the exchange. Elements of the old are mixed with the new, yielding new landscapes of understanding, the contours of which continue to shift as subjectivities are made and remade.

One of the interesting dynamics that emerges in this convergence of modernity, colonialism, and genocide is the important role of preexisting local knowledge in a given context. Not only does it provide an emotionally salient basis for genocidal ideologies, but it may also serve as the basis for "antimodern" discourses—that usually coexist, at times paradoxically, with "modern" discourses—or motivate patterns of behavior that, while transformed by the encounter with modernity and colonialism, may nevertheless subvert or undermine certain "modern" aspirations of the perpetrator regime. This tension is evident in the Cambodian genocide,[28] which blended a yearning for the past with a distinctly modern project of social engineering.

Patronage relationships, for example, constituted a key point of tension during DK.[29] On the one hand, the Khmer Rouge leadership explicitly condemned such relationships of personal dependency, viewing them as a threat to the Party Center's authority. Accordingly, upon attaining power, the Khmer Rouge set out to destroy "enemy" networks, including former members of the Lon Nol military, police, and government. Throughout the country, ties of friendship, family, community, and vocation were undermined by communalization, new patterns of cooperative labor, the banning of Buddhism, population relocations, common dining, the abolition of money and markets, and other structural changes.[30] The Khmer Rouge party line explicitly denounced such ties of personal dependency as a manifestation of "privativism" and a sign of a regressive consciousness. On the other hand, patronage networks remained central to sociopolitical organization during DK, as numerous cadre placed their friends, former associates, relatives, and family members in key positions of power. This pattern did not just occur on the local level: the power of almost every high-ranking Khmer Rouge leader was, at least in part, predicated upon the creation of such networks.[31] Not surprisingly, the confessions of alleged enemies concluded with a detailed list of their "string of traitors."

* * *

To understand both how DK came to be characterized by this paradoxical juxtaposition of the old and the new and how patronage ties were transformed by modernity and colonialism, however, we need to explore how Cambodian patronage relationships were transformed at various historical junctures. Looking back through history, we find that the political dynamics in the territories within and nearby what is now called Cambodia were often characterized by patterns of patronage that are reminiscent of those that exist today, including the attraction of followers to powerful leaders and the frequent instability of the resulting political formations.

While little is known of the pre-Angkorean period, scholars have speculated that local "men of prowess," thought to be infused with mana-like energies such as *sakti*, attracted large entourages of followers, thus enabling them to expand their orbit of influence. These polities are often referred to as "mandalas" because of the cosmological symbolism associated with them and because these rulers were heavily influenced by Indian political theory, which used circular imagery to portray political process and strategy.[32] Moreover, the idea of the mandala, which emphasizes center-oriented space and the control of people as opposed to fixed territorial boundaries, is more fluid than the Western notion of the "state." These centers of power were somewhat fragile, expanding and contracting in accordance with the accomplishments, demise, and death of a charismatic leader.

The political dynamics of the ancient Khmer empire of Angkor (AD 802–1431), like other great Southeast Asian mandalas, was characterized by a similar pulsating pattern.[33] On the one hand, the kingdom underwent periods of turmoil and fragmentation as local chiefs vied for power. Surviving inscriptions metaphorically reference such fragmented eras by stating that the empire was shaded by "many umbrellas" as opposed to just one.[34] On the other hand, powerful monarchs such as Jayavarman I, Suryavarman I, Suryavarman II, Jayavarman II, and Jayavarman VII were able to unify the factions and to greatly expand the influence of the domain. For example, Suryavarman I (AD 1011–1050), the son of a lord from the northeast who had a weak claim to the throne, defeated his rival, Jayaviravarman, after a long civil war. A key to Suryavarman's victory was his ability to form coalitions "by force, marriage, and cajolery . . . that enabled the pretender to reduce or buy off the power of local chiefs."[35] After being proclaimed king, Suryavarman I expanded the frontiers of the Angkorean empire by annexing the kingdom of Louvo (contemporary Lopburi in central Thailand) and colonizing the western part of the Tonle Sap lake. If Suryavarman's reign was characterized by an expanding pulsation, that of his next few predecessors gradually shrank in size.

A number of scholars have discussed the expansions and contractions of these Southeast Asian polities.[36] Stanley Tambiah, for example, has argued that this pulsating pattern of such "galactic politics" was generated from a number of overlapping dimensions of political ideology and practice.[37] Cosmologically, mandala myths and imagery provided a sought-after ideal of sociopolitical organization in which a potent center encompasses and brings abundance to the surrounding periphery. This prosperity was dependent upon a leader's ability to establish a parallelism between the earthly and the divine realms, which was signified by the universal monarch's feats of conquest, ritual connection to the gods, association with mandala symbols and motifs (for example, the sunshade, wheel, lotus, axis mundi, world tree, naga), and construction of magnificent Hindu-Buddhist monuments that replicated the cosmos and placed the ruler and his capital at its center. Just as these gods resided at the summit of Mt. Meru in Hindu cosmology, so too did the Angkorean king live at the center of the world, ensuring the flow of cosmic energies to the earthly realm he encompassed.

These cosmological motifs were mirrored by topographical conceptions of the structure of galactic polities, often portrayed as comprising concentric rings of influence that radiated outward from the capital core. Thus, Angkor ideally exerted strong control over a ring of nearby regional capitals, including Bhavapura, Indrapura, Phimai, Hariharalaya, Isanapura, Sambhupura, Aninditapura, and Amoghapura, and weaker influence over a more distant circle of tributary states such as Louvo.[38]

Each of these regional capitals was controlled by great landed families who had local power bases and, periodically, might vie for ascendancy to the Angkorean throne. These topographical relations were often idealized by complex geometric designs that assigned a cosmological place and rank—sometimes inscribed on umbrellas—to each of the great families and realms that had been encompassed by the Angkorean galactic polity. Externally, this galactic polity was threatened by neighboring power centers, which might be willing to wage war against Angkor, or vice versa, to affirm their own claim to being the center of the world.

Faced with both internal and external threats, Angkorean kings remained in a somewhat precarious position. One of their key mechanisms for potentially solidifying control was a form of decentralized patrimonial domination. As the most powerful patron in the empire, an Angkorean king controlled key resources—the right to distribute land, titles, prestigious court appointments and ceremonial roles, war booty, and lucrative government positions—that enabled him to maintain a network of loyal clients and to potentially expand his power through increased revenues or conquests.[39] The king's clients, in turn, used the authority and resources they had been given to maintain their own patronage circles, some of which were powerful enough to threaten the throne during times of weakness. In order to stay in power, the king had to be careful to contain these local warlords while still providing them with enough benefits to maintain their loyalty and support.

Despite such measures, Angkorean kings were faced with the threat of revolt, betrayal, and usurpation.[40] A successful king therefore had to reward his loyal clients with resources, but not to the point that their power bases grew to threaten his own. Because no fixed rules of succession existed, anyone could conceivably claim to have the divine sanction that entitled him to be king. While the ruler could attempt to solidify his position by creating overlapping roles and fostering crosscutting loyalties among his subordinates,[41] he nevertheless constantly feared attacks from without and betrayal from within. The chronic insecurity and distrust that pervaded Angkorean kingship was reflected by the Sanskrit *sastras* "which at some points seem almost paranoid in their preoccupation with secrecy, identification of traitors, and apprehension by all manner of ruses of what are called 'thorns', public enemies, who are . . . to be found in the royal service, in the palace, even in the king's family."[42] Such court intrigue increased after the decline of the Angkorean empire. Kings had to be constantly on their guard as usurpation was common, and a rival might seek the military patronage of Thailand or Vietnam to support their claim to the throne.[43]

All of these factors—cosmological, topographical, administrative, and political—helped to generate a pulsating pattern as a galactic polity's sphere of influence grew and shrank.[44] At times, powerful rulers were able to subdue their rivals through alliance or defeat and to strengthen their control over peripheral realms. As increased revenue flowed to the royal coffers, the king was able to expand his patronage network, initiate more war campaigns, and build projects that symbolically established his capital as the center of an expanding galactic polity. Such moments of expansion, however, were transient. If kings prospered during these periods of strength, so, too, did the principalities they encompassed. Sometimes, a covetous rival would attempt to usurp the throne during a king's lifetime. In other situations, a number of princes would battle for ascendancy after the death of the ruler. Over time, then, a galactic polity like Angkor tended to resemble an oscillating mandala, expanding in size under a universal monarch before contracting during periods of infighting.

Clearly, Southeast Asian political dynamics have undergone enormous change since the Angkorean era, particularly in the wake of European colonialism. Stanley Tambiah has argued that we should not view the modern era as one in which Southeast Asian countries simply adopted "more advanced" Western political ideas. Instead, we should see it a period of dialectical culture contact, in which earlier political formations were transformed while maintaining continuities with the past. Specifically, he argues that Southeast Asian galactic polities were often transformed into "radial polities" that resembled the strongest form of a galactic polity.[45] This metaphor conveys the idea of a dominant political core that directly controls peripheral regions and subordinate administrative units through its "spokes" of highly centralized authority. Thus, in late-nineteenth-century Thailand, King Chulalongkorn initiated a series of reforms that reorganized the government into functionally differentiated ministries, expanded Bangkok's control of the provinces, and revamped the system of taxation and revenue collection—all of which served to at least partially undermine the involuting authority of traditionally powerful families and officials. The resulting radial polity nevertheless came to resemble a patrimonial bureaucracy, in which power was concentrated and relationships of personal dependency remained key.

Cambodia's path during this period was somewhat different. From the fall of Angkor in the mid-fourteenth century to the colonial era, the Khmer empire was characterized by a number of trends, including: diminished political influence and tributary status to galactic polities in what is now Thailand and Vietnam; the increasing importance of commerce and trade; the eventual relocation of the capital to Phnom Penh, which was more strategically located in terms of trade and distance from the encroachments of the Thai kingdom of Ayudhya; the continued ascendancy of Theravada Buddhism, though animist and Hindu influences remained strong; expanding foreign involvement in Khmer affairs; and the enduring salience of patronage and factional maneuvering in Khmer politics.[46] These latter two trends had devastating effects in the century before French colonialism, as the Cambodian court was rent by infighting, rebellion, and war. A dismal cycle eventually began in which contending rivals for the throne would seek backing from either Bangkok or Hue (the ancient capital of Vietnam), paying for this military patronage with money, land, manpower, and foreign domination. The size and power of the Khmer empire shrank as the court lost territory and revenue, ultimately leading Cambodian kings to seek French protection from the encroachments of these neighbors. Cambodia became a French protectorate in 1863.

Over the next eighty years, the French authorities initiated a number of reforms that gradually centralized administrative control and transformed Cambodia's economy and infrastructure. Phnom Penh's influence over the provinces grew as new roads, public works, and lines of communication were built. Moreover, many of the French reforms—like the abolition of slavery, the streamlining of the taxation system, the placement of French bureaucrats in the provinces, the functional reorganization of the government administration, and the institutionalization of land ownership—undercut the power base of the provincial elite, who periodically expressed their displeasure through revolts. Many officials adapted to this situation by taking civil service positions, finding new ways to skim off government revenue, and exercising authority in the many areas of local governance that the French had left largely undisturbed. Meanwhile, Cambodian peasants, who received few benefits during this process, shouldered much of the cost of French colonial rule and resource extraction through corvée labor and taxation.

Cambodia's transformation into a more centralized radial polity was completed by Prince Sihanouk who, after leading Cambodia to independence in 1953, quashed an incipient democratic movement and dominated a patrimonial bureaucracy that was run from Phnom Penh and staffed by centrally appointed administrators. While many of these officials were from elite families, others came from a small yet growing middle-class that had taken advantage of new economic and educational opportunities. Sihanouk's rule illustrates two key tendencies of the radial polity. First, increased centralization is potentially conducive to despotism, as a potent center firmly encompasses and dominates the surrounding periphery. For many years, Sihanouk established himself as just such a dominant political force, quashing all dissent and demanding obedience in return for the protective "shade" he offered to his "children." And, second, relationships of personal dependency constitute a key structural component of patrimonial bureaucracies, thereby potentially giving rise to political instability and factional strife. Sihanouk's regime was rife with such patronage networks, which often engaged in corrupt practices and schemed for greater power—as illustrated by Sihanouk's ouster by a former subordinate, Lon Nol, whose own rule was characterized by despotism, patronage, and endemic corruption.

In some ways, however, this newly formed radial polity in Cambodia was less expansive than in Thailand insofar as the Cambodian governmental bureaucracy continued to have a minimal effect on peasant life. If more formalized patronage ties constituted a key sociopolitical mechanism in government bureaucracies and urban life, relationships of personal dependency remained much more limited and informal in the pre-DK villages where, as May Ebihara noted, the family and household remained "the only enduring and clearly defined units. . . . There are no larger organized kin groups and no formal associations or clubs, while groupings such as friendship cliques, work parties, or factions tend to have shifting or ill-defined membership and to be temporary coalescences."[47] One of the major sociopolitical shifts that has taken place since DK—particularly during the socialist eras—has been the expansion of radial government control and programs into the village level and greater opportunities available for villagers to gain access to more formalized patronage networks. Cambodian patronage networks, then, have varied in terms of the degree of their formality across time and place, with an increase in formality paralleling the increased centralized control of the polity.

Throughout this process of historical transformation, patronage relationships have remained a crucial part of sociopolitical life in Cambodia. James Scott has argued that the lasting importance of patronage ties in Southeast Asia is linked to: "(1) the persistence of marked inequalities in the control of wealth, status, and power . . . (2) the relative absence of firm, impersonal guarantees of physical security, status and position, or wealth, and (3) the inability of the kinship unit to serve as an effective vehicle for personal security or advancement."[48] Nevertheless, the structure of patronage relationships has changed in important ways. During the colonial and postcolonial periods, the resource base of patrons has been revamped, with land ownership, bureaucratic office, political position, business contracts, development programs, and military office serving as bedrock of power within the radial polity. In addition, local patronage networks have become more directly linked to the national center of the radial polity though, as discussed above, these connections have only recently made an impact upon Cambodian village life. And, finally, patronage ties have become increasingly fluid and unstable due to the vagaries of politics, the limitations of specialized office, the proliferation of and increased competition between patronage circles, and the growing instrumentality of patron-client relations.

Like its Southeast Asian neighbors, then, Cambodia's encounter with modernity should not be viewed as a story of linear "progress" ending with the adoption of a more "advanced" Western legal bureaucracy. These encounters lead to distinct sociopolitical formations, as local understandings are blended with new ideas. The radial polity represents just such an amalgam, combining the centralizing and bureaucratic tendencies of modernity with local understandings of power, hierarchy, and relationships of personal dependency. In contrast to the legal bureaucratic authority that is prevalent in many Western societies, the government bureaucracy in radial polities tends to rely more on a form of patrimonial authority that is centered on powerful leaders, structured in terms of the diffuse, particularistic, horizontal ties of patronage, and prone to competition and fragility.

If one looks through Cambodian history, it is evident that patronage has been an important structural element in Cambodian life for centuries, though often to a greater degree in the political domains than in everyday village life.[49] During the DK period, the reach of the state was greatly expanded on the village level and traditional patronage networks were eliminated. Nevertheless, patronage continued to be a key dynamic in DK politics, as illustrated by the frequent references to patronage networks in Khmer Rouge documents and the arrest of scores of suspected enemies and their networks. It is only through examination of Cambodia's past, particularly the country's encounter with modernity and colonialism, that we may understand why patronage relations remained so pervasive during DK and, ultimately, served as one of the key fulcrums of violence.

Conclusion

To conclude, I want to stress two points. First, to understand the relationship of genocide and colonialism, we must be attuned to more than the colonial encounter as described by the colonizers: we need to examine the dynamism of the encounter on the local level, as cultural knowledge was transformed—again, this is true both for the colonizer and the colonized—and the historical legacy of this encounter was reworked in the postcolonial period.

The Cambodian case illustrates this point. The Khmer Rouge were influenced by French colonialism in a number of crucial ways. Some Khmer Rouge leaders, like Pol Pot, Khieu Samphan, and Ieng Sary, had gone to high school as Cambodia's independence movement was intensifying, and studied in France where they were first exposed to communist doctrine; others, such as Ta Mok, Ke Pauk, and Sao Phim were former Khmer Issarak who had taken up arms against the French prior to independence.

Such formative experiences were later reflected in Khmer Rouge doctrine, which contained a sense that the impossible might be possible (at one time, few Cambodians could imagine overthrowing the French, just as initially few would have imagined that the Khmer Rouge could "defeat" the United States) and stressed the "contradiction" created by foreign oppression and domination, extreme nationalism, and the importance of independence and self-reliance.

At times, the anticolonialism (or neocolonialism) of the Khmer Rouge was expressed in terms of a longing for a lost past or a lost purity. Khmer Rouge propaganda repeatedly contrasted the decadent lives of those corrupted by capitalism to the more pure and idyllic peasant traditions, including farming which constituted a means of improving one's revolutionary consciousness. Pol Pot even took up the pen name "the original Khmer" when publishing his first tracts in Paris. In many ways, the Khmer Rouge resembled a revitalization movement,[50] combining an idyllic imagined past with a curative program for change in the present.

This longing for the past was also strongly influenced by French colonial rule, in particular the "discovery" of Angkor Wat by French archaeologists in the 1850s. (While the Angkorean empire had not been forgotten, it was remembered more through ritual than historical accounts.)[51] By "returning" this lost past to Cambodians, the French both legitimated their own "civilizing mission" (since they could claim to be helping this "fallen" race to its regain its lost glory) and helped to create a sense of deserved grandeur that Cambodian politicians, including Pol Pot and his associates, were to later invoke.[52] By providing a "history" of Cambodia's "decline" that was linked to the covetous designs of its neighbors, particularly the Vietnamese, the French also provided Cambodians with a powerful narrative that subsequent leaders reworked to meet the needs of a given historical moment. These discourses were all manifest in Khmer Rouge ideology, ranging from the regime's grandiose claims and invocation of the Angkorean past, to the sense of constant threat from perceived internal and external "enemies burrowing from within."

The second concluding point I want to emphasize is that we must constantly keep in mind that the juncture of genocide and colonialism is one set in the broader backdrop of modernity. My discussion of Cambodian patronage provides one illustration of this point. Modern discourses of the savage, the Great Chain of Being and other stage theories, progress, rationality, human nature, and human emancipation have figured prominently in a variety of colonial and postcolonial situations, including Cambodia. Such genocides have also taken place in the context of capitalist expansion and increased political centralization that, in some cases, have been conducive to explicit programs of social engineering. Consequently, the world has seen the mass murder of untold numbers of savages and subjects, often by postcolonial sovereigns who are inspired by modernist ideologies and practices to physically or culturally eradicate those regarded as incorrigible subjects or savages.

Acknowledgment

I would like to thank Dirk Moses for his comments on this chapter and for his work as editor of this volume. I am also grateful to Nicole Cooley for her thoughtful comments and suggestions.

Notes

1. Quoted in Jacob Pandian, *Anthropology and the Western Tradition: Toward an Authentic Anthropology* (Prospect Heights, IL, 1985), 67.
2. Quoted in John H. Bodley, *Victims of Progress* (Mountain View, CA, 1999), 34.
3. Anthony Giddens, *The Consequences of Modernity* (Stanford, CA, 1990); Stuart Hall, David Held, Don Hubert, and Kenneth Thompson, eds. *Modernity: An Introduction to Modern Societies* (Cambridge, MA, 1995); and David Harvey, *The Condition of Postmodernity* (Malden, MA, 1989).
4. Max Horkheimer and Theodor W. Adorno, *Dialectic of Enlightenment* (New York, 1944).
5. Hannah Arendt, *Eichmann in Jerusalem: A Report on the Banality of Evil* (New York, 1963).
6. Zygmunt Bauman, *Modernity and the Holocaust* (Ithaca, NY, 1989); Zygmunt Bauman, "The Duty to Remember—But What?" in *Enlightenment and Genocide, Contradictions of Modernity*, ed. James Kaye and Bo Strath (Brussels, 2000), 31–57.
7. But see Bodley, *Victims of Progress*; Robert Gellately and Ben Kiernan, eds., *The Specter of Genocide: Mass Murder in Historical Perspective* (New York, 2003); Alexander Laban Hinton, "Introduction: Genocide and Anthropology," in *Genocide: An Anthropological Reader*, ed. Alexander Laban Hinton (Malden, MA, 2002), 1–23; Alexander Laban Hinton, ed., *Genocide: An Anthropological Reader* (Malden, MA, 2002); James Kaye and Bo Strath, eds., *Enlightenment and Genocide, Contradictions of Modernity* (Brussels, 2002); and Dan Stone, "Modernity and Violence: Theoretical Reflections on the Einsatzgruppen," *Journal of Genocide Research* 1, no. 3 (1999): 367–78.
8. Pandian, *Anthropology*.
9. Ward Churchill, *A Little Matter of Genocide: Holocaust and Denial in the Americas 1491 to the Present* (San Francisco, CA, 1997).
10. Bartolomé de Las Casas, *A Short Account of the Destruction of the Indies* (New York, 1992), 15.
11. Frank Moya Pons, "The Politics of Forced Indian Labour in La Española 1493–1520," *Antiquity* 66 (1992): 130–39.
12. Bodley, *Victims of Progress*.

13. William Adams, *The Philosophical Roots of Anthropology* (Stanford, CA, 2001); Churchill, *A Little Matter of Genocide*; Lewis Hanke, *All Mankind Is One: A Study of the Disputation Between Bartolomé de Las Casas and Joan Ginés Sepúlveda on the Religious and Intellectual Capacity of the American Indians* (DeKalb, IL, 1974).
14. Hinton, "Introduction."
15. Bodley, *Victims of Progress*; Michel Foucault, *Power/Knowledge* (New York, 1980).
16. Churchill, *A Little Matter of Genocide.*
17. Ibid., 236.
18. See Bodley, *Victims of Progress*, 27–28; Micheal Taussig, *Shamanism, Colonialism, and the Wild Man: A Study in Terror and Healing* (Chicago, IL, 1987).
19. See David Maybury-Lewis, *Indigenous Peoples, Ethnic Groups, and the State* (Boston, MA, 2001); A. Dirk Moses, ed., *Genocide and Settler Society: Frontier Violence and the Stolen Indigenous Children in Australian History* (New York and Oxford, 2004).
20. Bodley, *Victims of Progress.*
21. W. E. B. DuBois, *The Souls of Black Folk* (Las Vegas, NV, 2001).
22. Frantz Fanon, *The Wretched of the Earth* (New York, 1963).
23. Christopher C. Taylor, *Sacrifice as Terror: The Rwandan Genocide of 1994* (Oxford, 1999).
24. Alexander Laban Hinton, *Why Did They Kill? Cambodia in the Shadow of Genocide* (Berkeley, CA, 2005).
25. Pol Pot, *Long Live the 17th Anniversary of the Communist Party of Kampuchea. Speech by Pol Pot, Secretary of the Central Committee of the Kampuchea Communist Party Delivered on September 29, 1977* (Phnom Penh, 1978).
26. Hinton, *Why Did They Kill?*; François Ponchaud, *Cambodia, Year Zero* (New York, 1978).
27. Hinton, *Why Did They Kill?*
28. Hinton, *Why Did They Kill?* John Marston, "Democratic Kampuchea and the Idea of Modernity," in *Cambodia Emerges from the Past: Eight Essays*, ed. Judy Ledgerwood (DeKalb, IL, 2002), 38–59.
29. Hinton, *Why Did They Kill?*; Marston, "Democratic Kampuchea"; John Marston, "Cambodia 1991–1994: Hierarchy, Neutrality and Etiquettes of Discourse" (Ph.D. diss., University of Washington, 1997).
30. May Ebihara, "Revolution and Reformulation in Kampuchean Village Culture," in *The Cambodian Agony*, ed. David A. Ablin and Marlowe Hood (Armonk, NY, 1990), 16–61.
31. Hinton, *Why Did They Kill?*; Ben Kiernan *The Pol Pot Regime: Race, Power, and Genocide in Cambodia under the Khmer Rouge, 1975–79* (New Haven, CT, 1996); Serge Thion, *Watching Cambodia: Ten Paths to Enter the Cambodian Tangle* (Bangkok, 1993).
32. Charles Higham, *The Archaeology of Mainland Southeast Asia* (New York, 1989); O. W. Wolters, *History, Culture, and Region in Southeast Asian Perspectives* (Ithaca, NY, 1999). On "center-oriented" versus "bounded" notions of space, see Stanley J. Tambiah, *Culture, Thought, and Social Action: An Anthropological Perspective* (Cambridge, MA, 1985).
33. What follows is based upon David P. Chandler, *A History of Cambodia* (Boulder, CO, 2000); G. Coedès, *The Indianized States of Southeast Asia.* trans. Susan Brown Cowing, (Honolulu, HI, 1968); D. G. E. Hall, *A History of South-East Asia* (London, 1981); Higham, *Archaeology of Mainland Southeast Asia*; Ian Mabbett and David Chandler, *The Khmers* (Cambridge, MA, 1995); Wolters, *History, Culture and Region.* On the "many umbrellas," see Chandler, *History of Cambodia*, 59, 75.

34. Chandler, *History of Cambodia*, 59, 75.
35. Ibid., 42.
36. Benedict R. O'G. Anderson, *Language and Power: Exploring Political Cultures in Indonesia* (Ithaca, NY, 1990); Clifford Geertz, *Negara: The Theatre State in Nineteenth-Century Bali* (Princeton, NJ, 1980); Robert Heine-Geldern, "Conceptions of State and Kingship in Southeast Asia," *The Far Eastern Quarterly* 2, no. 1 (1942): 15–30; Higham, *Archaeology of Mainland Southeast Asia*; Soemarsaid Moertono, *State and Statecraft in Old Java: A Study of the Later Mataram Period, 16th to 19th Century* (Ithaca, NY, 1968); Stanley J. Tambiah, *World Conqueror and World Renouncer: A Study of Buddhism and Polity in Thailand against a Historical Background* (New York, 1976); Wolters, *History, Culture and Region.*
37. Tambiah, *World Conqueror*; Tambiah, *Culture, Thought, and Social Action.* Tambiah's discussion of the "galactic" and "radial polity" has influenced several parts of my argument in the following section.
38. In nineteenth-century Cambodia, the Cambodian polity, centered at Udong, encompassed five surrounding *di*, or "earths"—Tboung Khmum, Ba Phnom, Trang, Pursat, and Kompong Savay. Mandala space was signified in terms of a set of toponyms that "proceed in a clockwise spiral, beginning to the east of Udong and gradually enclosing it within a . . . circle," David P. Chandler, *Facing the Cambodian Past, Selected Essays 1971–1994* (Chiang Mai, Thailand, 1996), 28.
39. See Chandler, *History of Cambodia*; I. W. Mabbett, "Kingship in Angkor," *Journal of the Siam Society* 66, no. 2 (1978): 1–58; Mabbett and Chandler, *The Khmers*; Milton Osborne, "Notes on Early Cambodian Provincial History: Isanapura and Sambhupura," *France-Asie*, no. 186 (1966): 433–49.
40. Chandler, *History of Cambodia*; Coedès, *Indianized States of Southeast Asia*; Hall, *History of South-East Asia*; Mabbett and Chandler, *The Khmers*; Wolters, *History, Culture and Region.*
41. Mabbett, "Kingship in Angkor."
42. Ibid., 46.
43. Chandler, *History of Cambodia*; Thion, *Watching Cambodia.*
44. Tambiah, *Culture, Thought, and Social Action.*
45. Tambiah, *World Conqueror*; Tambiah, *Culture, Thought, and Social Action*; Charles F. Keyes, *The Golden Peninsula: Culture and Adaptation in Mainland Southeast Asia* (Honolulu, 1995); David Joel Steinberg, ed., *In Search of Southeast Asia: A Modern History* (Honolulu, 1985). See also Thongchai Winichakul, *Siam Mapped: A History of the Geo-Body of a Nation* (Honolulu, HI, 1994) on the administrative and conceptual transformations that took place in Siam during this period of contact with European colonial powers.
46. Chandler, *History of Cambodia.* For a detailed description of Cambodian history from the fall of Angkor to French colonialism, see Chandler, *History of Cambodia*; Chandler and Mabbett, *The Khmers*; Hall, *History of South-East Asia*; Marie Alexandrine Martin, *Cambodia: A Shattered Society* (Berkeley, CA, 1994); Steinberg, *In Search of Southeast Asia.* The following survey of Cambodian history draws from all of these sources, particularly Chandler, *History of Cambodia.*
47. May Mayko Ebihara, "Svay, a Khmer Village in Cambodia" (Ph.D. diss., Columbia University, 1968), 186–87. On the transformation of patronage ties from the pre-DK period into the present; see also Marston, *Cambodia 1991–94* and Thion, *Watching Cambodia.*
48. James C. Scott, "Patron-Client Politics and Political Change in Southeast Asia," in *Friends, Followers, and Factions: A Reader in Political Clientelism*, ed. Steffen W.

Schmidt, Laura Guasti, Carl H. Landé, and James C. Scott (Berkeley, CA, 1977), 132. The discussion in this paragraph draws heavily on Scott's detailed analysis of the structure and historical transformation of patronage ties in Southeast Asia. In particular, see Scott on the "secular trends in the nature of patron-client ties in Southeast Asia."

49. Ebihara, "Svay," 186–87. For an analysis of these differences and of the ways in which patronage ties have changed in Cambodia's recent past, see Caroline Hughes, *The Political Economy of Cambodia's Transition, 1991–2001* (New York, 2003); Judy Ledgerwood and John Vijghen, "Decision-Making in Rural Khmer Villages," in *Cambodia Emerges from the Past: Eight Essays*, ed. Judy Ledgerwood (DeKalb, IL, 2002), 109–50; Marston, *Cambodia 1991–94.*
50. Anthony F. C. Wallace, "Revitalization Movements," *American Anthropologist* 58 (1956): 264–81.
51. Chandler, *Facing the Cambodian Past.*
52. Ibid.; Penny Edwards, "Imagining the Other in Cambodian Nationalist Discourse Before and During the UNTAC Period," in *Propaganda, Politics, and Violence in Cambodia: Democratic Transition under United Nations Peace-keeping*, ed. Steve Heder and Judy Ledgerwood (Armonk, NY, 1996), 50–72; Panivong Norindr, *Phantasmatic Indochina: French Colonial Ideology in Architecture, Film, and Literature* (Durham, NC, 1997).

Select Bibliography

Agamben, Giorgio, *Homo Sacer: Sovereign Power and Bare Life* (Stanford, CA, 1998).

Aldrich, Robert, *Greater France: A History of French Overseas Expansion* (London, 1996).

Aly, Götz, *"Final Solution": Nazi Population Policy and the Murder of European Jews* (New York, 1999).

——— and Susanne Heim, *Architects of Annihilation: Auschwitz and the Logic of Destruction* (London, 2003).

Anderson, Benedict R.O'G., *Java in a Time of Revolution: Occupation and Resistance, 1944–1946* (Ithaca, NY, 1972).

Anderson, David, *Histories of the Hanged: Britain's Dirty War in Kenya and the End of Empire* (London, 2004).

——— and Johnson, Douglas H., eds., *Revealing Prophets. Prophecy in Eastern African History* (London, 1995).

Armitage, Andrew, *Comparing the Policy of Aboriginal Assimilation: Australia, Canada, and New Zealand* (Vancouver, 1995).

Armitage, David, *Ideological Origins of the British Empire* (Cambridge, 2000).

Arendt, Hannah, *The Origins of Totalitarianism* (New York, 1966).

Arneil, Barbara, *John Locke and America: The Defence of English Colonialism* (Oxford, 1996).

Attwood, Bain and Foster, S. G., eds., *Frontier Conflict, the Australian Experience* (Canberra, 2003).

Barta, Tony, "Relations of Genocide: Land and Lives in the Colonization of Aboriginal Australia," in *Genocide and the Modern Age: Etiology and Case Studies of Mass Death,* ed. Isidor Wallimann and Michael N. Dobkowski (Westport, CT, 1987), 237–52.

———, "Discourses of Genocide in Germany and Australia: a Linked History," *Aboriginal History* 25 (2001): 37–56.

———, "Mr. Darwin's Shooters: On Natural Selection and the Naturalising of Genocide," *Patterns of Prejudice* 39, no. 2 (2005). Reprinted in Moses and Stone, *Genocide and Colonialism*, 20–41.

Bauman, Zygmunt, *Modernity and the Holocaust* (Cambridge, 1989).

Becker, Felicitas, and Beez, Jigal, eds., *Der Maji-Maji-Krieg in Deutsch Ostafrika 1905–1907* (Berlin, 2005).

Belich, James, *Making Peoples: A History of the New Zealanders from Polynesian Settlement to the End of the Nineteenth Century* (Auckland, 1996).

Berkhofer, Jr. Robert F., *The White Man's Indian. Images of the American Indian from Columbus to the Present* (New York, 1979).

Betts, Raymond, F., *Assimilation and Association in French Colonial Theory, 1890–1914* (New York, 1961).

Bley, Helmut, *South-West Africa under German Rule 1894–1914* (London, 1971).

Bloxham, Donald, *The Great Game of Genocide: Imperialism, Nationalism and the Destruction of the Ottoman Armenians* (Oxford, 2005).

Bodley, John H., *Victims of Progress* (Mountain View, CA, 1999).

Bordewich, Fergus M., *Killing the White Man's Indian: Reinventing Native Americans at the End of the Twentieth Century* (New York, 1996).

Braddick, Michael J., *State Formation in Early Modern England, c.1550–1700* (Cambridge, 2000).

Brantlinger, Patrick, *Dark Vanishings: Discourse on the Extinction of Primitive Races, 1800–1930* (Ithaca, NY, 2003).

Brown, Kate, *A Biography of No Place: from Ethnic Borderland to Soviet Heartland* (Cambridge, 2003).

Browning, Christopher R. (with Jürgen Matthäus), *The Origins of the Final Solution: The Evolution of Nazi Jewish Policy, September 1939-March 1942* (London, 2004).

Buck-Morss, Susan, "Hegel and Haiti," *Critical Inquiry* 26, no. 4 (2000): 821–65.

Cain, P. J. and Hopkins, A. G., *British Imperialism: Innovation and Expansion, 1688–1914, London* (New York, 1993).

Canny, Nicholas, *Making Ireland British, 1580–1650* (Oxford, 2001).

Carranco, Lynwood ,and Beard, Estle, *Genocide and Vendetta: The Round Valley Wars of North California* (Norman, OK., 1981).

Césaire, Aimé, *Discourse on Colonialism* (New York, 1972 [1955]).

Chandler, David P., *A History of Cambodia* (Boulder, CO, 1983).

Chu, Wen-Djang, *The Moslem Rebellion in North-West China 1862–1878, A Study of Government Minority Policy* (The Hague and Paris, 1966).

Churchill, Ward, *Indians Are Us? Culture and Genocide in Native North America* (Monroe, ME, 1994).

———, *A Little Matter of Genocide, Holocaust and Denial in the Americas: 1492 to the Present* (San Francisco, CA, 1997).
Cooper, Frederick, *Colonialism in Question: Theory, Knowledge, History* (Berkeley, CA, 2005).
Crosby, Alfred W., *Ecological Imperialism* (New York, 1986).
Dallin, Alexander, *German Rule in Russia, 1941–1945: A Study of Occupation Policies* (London, 1957).
Daniels, Christine and Kennedy, Michael, eds., *Negotiated Empires: Centres and Peripheries in the Americas, 1500–1820* (New York, 2002).
Darian-Smith, Eve, and Fitzpatrick, Peter, *Laws of the Postcolonial* (Ann Arbor, MI, 1999).
Daunton, Martin and Halpern, Rick, ed., *Empire and Others: British Encounters with Indigenous Peoples, 1600–1850* (London, 1999).
Davis, Mike, *Late Victorian Holocausts: El Niño Famines and the Making of the Third World* (London, 2001).
Debo, Angie, *A History of the Indians of the United States* (Norman, OK, 1970).
Denoon, Donald, *Settler Capitalism: The Dynamics of Dependent Development in the Southern Hemisphere* (Oxford, 1983).
Dippie, Brian W., *The Vanishing American: White Attitudes and US Indian Policy* (Middletown, CT, 1982).
Docker, John, *1492: The Poetics of Diaspora* (London, 2001).
Douglas, Bronwen, *Across the Great Divide: Journeys in History and Anthropology* (Amsterdam, 1998).
Dowd, Gregory Evans, *A Spirited Resistance: The North American Indian Struggle for Unity, 1745–1815* (Baltimore, MD, and London, 1992).
Drechsler, Horst, *Let Us Die Fighting! The Struggle of the Herero and the Nama Against German Imperialism (1884–1915)* (London, 2001).
Dussel, Enrique, *The Invention of the Americas: Eclipse of "The Other" and the Myth of Modernity* (New York, 1995).
Elkins, Caroline, *Britain's Gulag: The Brutal End of Empire in Kenya* (London, 2005).
Evans, Raymond, *Fighting Words: Writing About Race* (Brisbane, 1999).
Fanon, Frantz, *The Wretched of the Earth* (New York, 1963).
———, *Black Skin/White Masks* (New York, 1967).
Ferrer, Ada, *Race, Nation and Revolution, Cuba 1868–1898* (Chapel Hill, NC, and London, 1999).
Ferro, Marc, *Colonization: A Global History* (London, 1997).
Fieldhouse, D.K., *Colonialism 1870–1945: An Introduction* (London, 1983).
Fitzmaurice, Andrew, *Humanism and America. An Intellectual History of English Colonisation, 1500–1625* (Cambridge, 2003).

Fixico, Donald L., *Termination and Relocation: Federal Indian Policy, 1945–1960,* (Albuquerque, NM, 1986).

Flannery, Tim, *The Eternal Frontier: An Ecological History of North America and its Peoples* (Melbourne, 2001).

Foucault, Michel, *The History of Sexuality, vol. 1: An Introduction*, trans. Robert Hurley (Harmondsworth, 1984).

Francis, Daniel, *The Imaginary Indian: The Image of the Indian in Canadian Culture* (Vancouver, 1992).

Friedrichsmeyer, Sara L., Lennox, Sara, and Zantop, Susanne M., eds., *The Imperialist Imagination: German Colonialism and Its Legacy* (Ann Arbor, MI, 1998).

Furber, David, "Near as Far in the Colonies: The Nazi Occupation of Poland," *International History Review* 26, no. 3 (2004): 541–79.

Gammer, Moshe, *Muslim Resistance to the Tsar: Shamil and the Conquest of Chechnia and Dagestan* (New York and London, 1994).

Gascoigne, John, *The Enlightenment and the Origins of European Australia* (Cambridge, 2002).

Gellately, Robert, and Kiernan, Ben, eds., *The Specter of Genocide: Mass Murder in Historical Perspective* (Cambridge and New York).

Gerlach, Christian, *Kalkulierte Morde: Die deutsche Wirtschafts-und Vernichtungspolitik in Weissrussland 1941–1944* (Hamburg, 1999).

Geraci, Robert P., *Window on the East: National and Imperial Identities in Late Tsarist Russia* (Ithaca, NY, 2001).

——— and Khodarkovsky, Michael, eds., *Of Religion and Empire: Missions, Conversion, and Tolerance in Tsarist Russia* (Ithaca, NY, 2001).

Gewald, Jan-Bart, *Herero Heroes: A Socio-Political History of the Herero of Namibia 1890–1923* (Oxford, 1999).

Geyer, Michael, and Bright, Charles, "Global Violence and Nationalizing Wars in Eurasia and the Americas: The Geopolitics of War in the Mid-Nineteenth Century," *Comparative Studies in Society and History* 38, no. 4 (1996): 619–57.

Gladney, Dru C., *Dislocating China: Muslims, Minorities, and other Subaltern Subjects* (Chicago, 2004).

Gosden, Chris, *Archaeology and Colonialism: Cultural Contact from 5000 BC to the Present* (Cambridge, 2004).

Green, L. C. and Dickason, Olive P., eds., *The Law of Nations and the New World* (Alberta, 1989).

Guillaumin, Collette, *Racism, Sexism, Power and Ideology* (London, 1995).

Hannaford, Ivan, *Race: The History of an Idea in the West* (Baltimore, MD, 1996).

Harris, Cole, "How Did Colonialism Dispossess? Comments from an Edge of Empire," *Annals of the Association of American Geographers* 94, no. 1 (2004): 165–82.

Herbert, Ulrich, *National Socialist Extermination Policies: Contemporary German Perspectives and Controversies* (New York, 2000).

Hennessy, Charles Alistair Michael, *The Frontier in Latin American History* (London, 1978).

Hinton, Alexander Laban, *Why Did They Kill? Cambodia in the Shadow of Genocide* (Berkeley, CA, 2005).

———, ed., *Annihilating Difference: The Anthropology of Genocide* (Berkeley, CA, 2002).

Hochschild, Adam, *King Leopold's Ghost: A Story of Greed, Terror and Heroism in Colonial Africa* (London, 1998).

Honour, Hugh, *The New Golden Land: European Images of America from the Discoveries to the Present Time* (New York, 1975).

Horsman, Reginald, *Expansion and American Indian Policy 1783–1812* (East Lansing, MI, 1967).

Iliffe, John, *Tanganikya under German Rule, 1905–1912* (Cambridge, 1979).

Ivison, Duncan , Patton, Paul, and Sanders, Will, eds., *Political Theory and the Rights of Indigenous Peoples* (Cambridge, 2000).

Jennings, Francis, *The Creation of America: Through Revolution to Empire* (Cambridge and New York, 2000).

Jersild, Austin, *Orientalism and Empire: North Caucasus Mountain Peoples and the Georgian Frontier, 1845–1917* (Montreal and Kingston, 2002).

Kasaba, Resat, *The Ottoman Empire and the World Economy: The Nineteenth Century* (Albany, NY, 1988).

Kaye, James, and Stråth, Bo, eds., *Enlightenment and Genocide: Contradiction of Modernity* (Brussels, 2000).

Keegan, Timothy J., *Colonial South Africa and the Origins of the Racial Order* (London, 1996).

Kepple-Jones, Arthur, *Rhodes and Rhodesia. The White Conquest of Zimbabwe 1884–1902* (Kingston and Montreal, 1983).

Khodarkovsky, Michael, *Russia's Steppe Frontier: The Making of a Colonial Empire, 1500–1800* (Bloomington and Indianapolis, IN, 2005).

Kiernan, Ben, *How Pol Pot Came to Power: Colonialism, Nationalism, and Communism in Cambodia, 1930–75*, 2nd edn (New Haven, CT, 2004).

———, *The Pol Pot Regime: Race, Power and Genocide in Cambodia un der theKhmer Rouge, 1975–1979*, 2nd edn (New Haven, CT, 2002).

———, *Blood and Soil: Genocide, Conquest, Cultivation, and History, 1400–2005* (New Haven, CT, 2007).

King, Richard, *Race, Culture, and the Intellectuals, 1940–1970* (Washington, DC, and Baltimore, MD, 2004).

——— and Dan Stone, eds., *Hannah Arendt and the Uses of History: Imperialism, Nation, Race, and Genocide* (Oxford and New York, 2007).

Koebner, Richard and Schmidt, Helmut Dan, *Imperialism: The Story and Significance of a Political Word, 1840–1960* (Cambridge, 1964).

Koponen, Juhani, *Development for Exploitation: German Colonial Policies in Mainland Tanzania, 1884–1914* (Münster, 1995).

Kuper, Leo, *Genocide: Its Political Use in the Twentieth Century* (New Haven, CT, and London, 1981).

Ledonne, John P., *The Russian Empire and the World, 1700–1917: The Geopolitics of Expansion and Containment* (New York, 1996).

Lenman, Bruce, *England's Colonial Wars, 1550–1688* (London, 2001).

Lemkin, Raphael, *Axis Rule in Occupied Europe: Laws of Occupation, Analysis of Government, Proposals for Redress* (Washington, DC, 1944).

Levene, Mark, *Genocide in the Age of the Nation- State*, 2 vols. (London, 2005).

——— and Penny Roberts, eds., *The Massacre in History* (New York, 1999).

Levine, Robert M., *Vale of Tears: Revisiting the Canudos Massacre in Northeastern Brazil, 1893–1897* (Berkeley and Los Angeles, CA, 1992).

Lieven, Dominic, *Empire: The Russian Empire and its Rivals* (London, 2000).

Lincoln, W. Bruce, *The Conquest of a Continent: Siberia and the Russians* (New York, 1994).

Lindqvist, Sven, *"Exterminate all the Brutes"* (London, 1998).

Lohr, Eric, *Nationalizing the Russian Empire* (Cambridge, MA, and London, 2003).

Lower, Wendy, *Nazi Empire-Building and the Holocaust in Ukraine* (Chapel Hill, NC, 2005).

MacDonagh, Oliver, *States of Mind: A Study of Anglo-Irish conflict, 1780–1980* (London, 1983).

MacDonald, Helen, *Human Remains: Episodes in Human Dissection* (Melbourne, 2005).

Madley, Benjamin, "Patterns of Frontier Genocide 1803–1910: the Aboriginal Tasmanians, the Yuki of California, and the Herero of Namibia," *Journal of Genocide Research* 6, no 2 (2004): 167–92.

———, "From Africa to Auschwitz: How German South West Africa Incubated Methods Adopted and Developed by the Nazis in Eastern Europe," *European History Quarterly* 33, no. 3 (2005): 429–64.

Malik, Kenan, *The Meaning of Race: Race, History and Culture in Western Society* (London, 1996).

Mamdani, Mahmood, *When Victims Become Killers: Colonialism, Nativism, and the Genocide in Rwanda* (Princeton, NJ, 2001).

Mann, Michael, *The Dark Side of Democracy: Explaining Ethnic Cleansing* (Cambridge, 2005).

Martin, Terry, *The Affirmative Action Empire: Nations and Nationalism in the Soviet Union, 1923–1939* (Ithaca, NY, and London, 2001),

———, "The Origins of Soviet Ethnic Cleansing," *Journal of Modern History* 70, no. 4 (1998): 813–61.

Maybury-Lewis, David, *Indigenous Peoples, Ethnic Groups, and the State* (Boston, MA, 2001).

McLoughlin, William G., *Cherokee Renascence in the New Republic* (Princeton, NJ, 1986).

McDonnell, Michael A. and Moses, A. Dirk, "Raphael Lemkin as Historian of Genocide in the Americas," *Journal of Genocide Research* 7, no. 4 (2005): 501–29.

McGregor, Russell, *Imagined Destinies: Aboriginal Australians and the Doomed Race Theory, 1880–1939* (Melbourne, 1997).

Memmi, Albert, *The Colonizer and the Colonized*, intro. Jean-Paul Sartre (Boston, [1957] 1965).

Moor, J.A. de and Wesseling, H. J., eds., *Imperialism and War: Essays in Colonial Wars in Asia and Africa* (Leiden, 1989).

Morris, Alexander, *The Treaties of Canada with the Indians of Manitoba and The North-West Territories* (Toronto, 1971).

Moses, A. Dirk, ed., *Genocide and Settler Society: Frontier Violence and Stolen Indigenous Children in Australian History* (New York, 2004).

———, "The Holocaust and Genocide," in *The Historiography of the Holocaust*, ed. Dan Stone (London, 2004). 533–55.

———, "Conceptual Blockages and Definitional Dilemmas in the 'Racial Century': Genocides of Indigenous People and the Holocaust," *Patterns of Prejudice* 36, no. 4 (2002): 7–36. Reprinted in Moses and Stone, *Genocide and Colonialism*, 148–80.

———, and Stone, Dan, eds., *Colonialism and Genocide* (London, 2007).

Moses, John A. and Kennedy, Paul M., eds., *Germany in the Pacific and Far East 1870–1914* (Brisbane, 1977).

Muldoon, James, *Popes, Lawyers, and Infidels: The Church and the non-Christian World, 1250–1550* (Philadelphia, PA,1979).

———, ed., *The Expansion of Europe: The First Phase* (Philadelphia, PA, 1977)

———, *Empire and Order: The Concept of Empire 800–1800* (London, 1999).

Naimark, Norman M., *Fires of Hatred: Ethnic Cleansing in Twentieth-Century Europe* (Cambridge, MA, 2001).
Nederveen Pieterse, Jan, and Parekh, Bhikhu, eds., *The Decolonization of Imagination: Culture, Knowledge and Power* (London, 1995).
Nekrich, Aleksandr, *The Punished Peoples: The Deportation and Fate of Soviet Minorities at the End of the Second World War* (New York, 1978).
O'Brien, Sean M., *In Bitterness and in Tears: Andrew Jackson's Destruction of the Creeks and Seminoles* (Westport, CT, 2003).
Osterhammel, Jürgen, *Colonialism: A Theoretical Overview*, trans. Shelley Frisch (Princeton, NJ, 1997).
Palmer, Alison, *Colonial Genocide* (Adelaide, 2000).
Pohl, Dieter, "War, Occupation, and the Holocaust in Poland," in *The Historiography of the Holocaust*, ed. Dan Stone (Houndmills, 2004), 88–119.
Pohl, J. Otto, *Ethnic Cleansing in the USSR, 1937–1949* (Westport, CT, 1999).
Porter, Bernard, *The Lion's Share: A Short History of British Imperialism, 1850–2004*, 4th edn (Harlow, 2004).
———, *The Absent-Minded Imperialist: Empire, Society, and Culture in Britain* (Oxford, 2004).
———, *Empire and Superempire: Britain, America and the World* (New Haven, CT, 2006).
Preston, Diana, *A Brief History of the Boxer Rebellion: China's War on Foreigners, 1900* (London, 2002).
Ranger, Terence O., *Revolt in Southern Rhodesia 1896–97: A Study in African Resistance* (London, 1967).
Rawson, Claude, *God, Gulliver, and Genocide: Barbarism and the European Imagination, 1492–1945* (Oxford, 2001).
Reece, R.H.W., *Aborigines and Colonists: Aborigines and Colonial Society in New South Wales in the 1830s and 1840s* (Sydney, 1974).
Reynolds, Henry, *The Other Side of the Frontier: Aboriginal Resistance to the European Invasion of Australia* (Sydney, 1981).
———, *The Fate of a Free People* (Melbourne, 1995).
———, *An Indelible Stain? The Question of Genocide in Australia's History* (Melbourne, 2001).
———, *The Law of the Land* (Melbourne, 1987).
Roberts, Tony, *Frontier Justice: A History of the Gulf Country to 1900* (Brisbane, 2005).
Robinson, Ronald Edward, *Africa and the Victorians: The Official Mind of Imperialism* (London, 1961).
Robins, Nicholas A., *Genocide and Millenialism in Upper Peru: The Great Rebellion of 1780–1782* (Westport, CT, 2002).

———, *Native Insurgencies and the Genocidal Impulse in the Americas* (Bloomington and Indianapolis, 2005).
Rowley, Charles, *The Destruction of Aboriginal Society* (Melbourne, 1970).
Russell, Lynette, ed., *Colonial Frontier: Indigenous-European Encounters in Settler Societies* (Manchester, 2001).
Ryan, Lyndall, *The Aboriginal Tasmanians* (Sydney, 1981).
Said, Edward, W., *Orientalism* (London, 1978).
———, *Culture and Imperialism* (London, 1993).
Samek, Hana, *The Blackfoot Confederacy 1880–1920: A Comparative Study of Canadian and U.S. Indian Policy* (Albuquerque, NM, 1987).
Schaller, Dominik J. et al, eds., *Enteignet-Vertrieben-Ermordet: Beiträge zur Genozidforschung*, ed. (Zürich, 2004).
Shaw, Martin, *War and Genocide: Organized Killing in Modern Society* (Malden, MA, 2003).
Sheehan, Bernard W., *Seeds of Extinction: Jeffersonian Philanthropy and the American Indian* (Chapel Hill, NC, 1973).
Slezkine, Yuri, *Arctic Mirrors: Russia and the Small Peoples of the North* (Ithaca, NY, and New York, 1994).
Smith, Woodruff D., *The German Colonial Empire* (Chapel Hill, NC, 1978).
———, *The Ideological Origins of Nazi Imperialism* (New York, 1986).
Spies, S.B., *Methods of Barbarism: Roberts and Kitchener and Civilians in the Boer Republics, January 1900- May 1902* (Cape Town, 1977).
Spurr, David, *Rhetoric of Empire* (Durham, NC, 1993).
Stern, Steve J., ed., *Resistance, Rebellion, and Consciousness in the Andean Peasant World, 18th to 20th Centuries* (Madison, WI, 1987).
Sternhell, Zeev, *The Founding Myths of Israel: Nationalism, Socialism and the Making of the Jewish State* (Princeton, NJ, 1999).
Serulnikov, Serge, *Subverting Colonial Authority: Challenges to Spanish Rule in Eighteenth-Century Southern Andes* (Durham, NC, and London, 2003).
Stasiulis, Daiva, and Yuval-Davis, Nira, eds., *Unsettling Settler Societies* (London, 1995).
Stannard, David E., *American Holocaust: Columbus and the Conquest of the New World* (New York, 1992).
Stone, Dan, ed., *The Historiography of the Holocaust* (Houndmills, 2004),
———, *History, Memory and Mass Atrocity: Essays on the Holocaust and Genocide* (London and Portland, OR, 2006).
———, ed., *The Historiography of Genocide* (Houndmills, 2008).

Suny, Ronald Grigor, and Martin, Terry, eds., *A State of Nations: Empire and Nation-Making in the Age of Lenin and Stalin* (New York, 2001).

Taylor, William B. and Pease, Franklin G. Y., *Violence, Resistance, and Survival in the Americas: Native Americans and the Legacy of Conquest* (Washington, DC, 1994).

Thompson, Leonard M., *The Political Mythology of Apartheid* (New Haven, CT, 1985).

Thomas, Nicholas, *Colonialism's Culture: Anthropology, Travel and Government* (Melbourne, 1994).

Thomson, Sinclair, *We Alone Will Rule: Native Andean Politics in the Age of Insurgency* (Madison, WI, 2002).

Thornton, Russell, *American Indian Holocaust and Survival: A Population History Since 1492* (Norman, OK, 1987).

Traverso, Enzo *The Origins of Nazi Violence* (New York, 2003).

Trigger, David, and Griffiths, Gareth, eds., *Disputed Territories: Land, Culture and Identity in Settler Societies* (Hong Kong, 2003).

Todorov, Tzvetan, *The Conquest of America: The Question of the Other* (New York, 1984)

———, *On Human Diversity: Nationalism, Racism, and Exoticism in French Thought* (Cambridge, MA, 1993).

Tuck, Richard, *The Rights of War and Peace: Political Thought and the International Order from Grotius to Kant* (Oxford, 1999).

Tully, James, *An Approach to Political Philosophy: Locke in Contexts* (Cambridge, 1993).

Turnbull, Clive, *Black War: The Extermination of the Tasmanian Aborigines* (Melbourne, 1965 [1948]).

Valentino, Benjamin A., *Final Solutions: Mass Killing and Genocide in the Twentieth Century* (Ithaca, NY, 2004).

Vandervort, Bruce, *Wars of Imperial Conquest 1830–1914* (London, 1998).

Veracini, Lorenzo, *Israel and Settler Society* (London, 2006).

Wallace, Anthony F.C., *The Long Bitter Trail, Andrew Jackson and the Indians* (New York, 1993).

Wallerstein, Immanuel, *The Modern World-System: Capitalist Agriculture and the Origins of the European World-Economy in the Sixteenth Century* (New York, 1976).

———, ed., *Social Change: The Colonial Situation* (New York, 1966).

Walker, Charles, *Smoldering Ashes: Cuzco and the Creation of Republican Peru, 1780–1840* (Durham, NC, 1999).

Weaver, John C., *The Great Land Rush and the Making of the Modern World, 1650–1900* (Montreal and Kingston, 2003).

Weitzer, Ronald, *Transforming Settler States: Communal Conflict and Internal Security in Northern Ireland and Zimbabwe* (Berkeley, CA, 1990).

Weeks, Theodore R., *Nation and State in Late Imperial Russia: Nationalism and the Russification of the Western Frontier, 1863–1914* (Dekalb, IL, 1996).

White, Richard, *The Middle Ground: Indians, Empires and Republics in the Great Lakes Region, 1650–1815* (Cambridge, 1991).

Williams, Robert A., *The American Indian in Western Legal Thought* (Oxford, 1990).

Wolfe, Patrick, "Nation and MiscegeNation: Discursive Continuity in the Post-Mabo Era," *Social Analysis* 36 (1994): 93–152.

———, *Settler Colonialism and the Transformation of Anthropology: The Politics and Poetics of an Ethnographic Event* (London, 1999).

———, "Land, Labor, and Difference: Elementary Structures of Race," *American Historical Review* 106 (2001): 865–905.

———, "Race and Racialisation: Some Thoughts," *Postcolonial Studies* 5, no. 1 (2002): 51–62.

———, "History and Imperialism: A Century of Theory from Marx to Postcolonialism," *American Historical Review* 102 (1997): 389–93.

Zimmerman, Andrew, *Anthropology and Antihumanism in Imperial Germany* (Chicago, 2001).

Zimmerer, Jürgen, *Deutsche Herrschaft über Afrikaner: Staatliche Machtanspruch und Wirklichkeit im kolonialen Namibia*, 3rd edn (Münster, 2003).

———, "Colonialism and the Holocaust: Towards an Archaeology of Genocide," in *Genocide and Settler Society: Frontier Violence and Stolen Indigenous Children in Australian History*, ed. A. Dirk Moses (New York, 2004), 49–76.

———, "The Birth of the *Ostland* Out of the Spirit of Colonialism: a Postcolonial Perspective on the Nazi policy of Conquest and Extermination," *Patterns of Prejudice* 39, no. 2 (2005): 197–219. Reprinted in Moses and Stone, *Genocide and Colonialism*, 101–23.

———, *Von Windhuk nach Auschwitz? Beiträge zum Verhältnis von Kolonialismus und Holocaust* (Münster, 2010).

———, "Colonial Genocide: The Herero War, Australia and Beyond," in *The Historiography of Genocide*, ed. Dan Stone (Houndmills, 2008).

———, "The First Genocide of the Twentieth Century: The German War of Destruction in Southwest Africa (1904-1908) and the Global History of Genocide," in *Lessons and Legacies VIII*, ed. Doris L. Bergen (Evanson, IL, 2008).

———, and Zeller, Joachim, eds., *Genocide in German in South-West Africa: The Colonial War of 1904–1908 and Its Aftermath* (London, 2008).

Contributors

Donald Bloxham is Professor of History at the University of Edinburgh. He is author of *Genocide on Trial: War Crimes Trials and the Formation of Holocaust History and Memory* (2001); *The Great Game of Genocide: Imperialism, Nationalism, and the Destruction of the Ottoman Armenians* (2005); (with Tony Kushner), *The Holocaust: Critical Historical Approaches* (2005); and *The Final Solution: A Genocide* (2009).

David Cahill is Professor of History, School of History, University of New South Wales, Sydney. His recent publications include *From Rebellion to Independence in the Andes: Soundings from Southern Peru 1750–1830* (2002), and (with co-author Peter Bradley) *Habsburg Peru: Images, Imagination and Memory* (2000).

Robert Cribb is Professor of Pacific and Asian History at the Australian National University. His research is on modern Indonesian history. He is author of *Gangsters and Revolutionaries* (1991) and *Historical Atlas of Indonesia* (2000), and editor of *The Indonesian Killings of 1965–1966* (1990), *The Late Colonial State in Indonesia* (1994), and (with Li Narangoa), *Imperial Japan and National Identities in Asia* (2003).

Ann Curthoys is ARC Professorial Fellow in History at the University of Sydney. She has written on many aspects of Australian history and historical writing, including Aboriginal history, colonial debates over Chinese migration, Australian feminism, national identity, and media history. Her award-winning book, *Freedom Ride: A Freedomrider Remembers* appeared in 2002. Her latest books are *Is History Fiction?* (2005), with John Docker, *Rights and Redemption: History, Law, and Indigenous People* (2008) with Ann Genovese and

Alexander Reilly, and *How to Write History that People Want to Read* (2009), with Ann McGrath.

John Docker is Honorary Professor in the Department of History, the University of Sydney. He has published in various fields: Australian literary and cultural history; contemporary theories of culture, identity, colonialism, and diaspora; Orientalism and exoticism; monotheism and polytheism; and genocide in relation both to the Enlightenment and colonialism. His most recent books are *1492: The Poetics of Diaspora* (2001), with Ann Curthoys, *Is History Fiction?* (2005), and *The Origins of Violence: Religion, History, and Genocide* (2008).

Raymond Evans is an Adjunct Professor with the Centre for Public Culture and Ideas at Griffith University, Brisbane, and Honorary Reader in History and the Australian Studies Centre at the University of Queensland. His recent publications include *Fighting Words: Writing About Race* (1999), *Radical Brisbane: An Unruly History* (2004), and the *Concise History of Queensland* (2007).

Norbert Finzsch teaches North American History at the University of Cologne. His major publications include *Die Goldgräber Kaliforniens* (1982), *Obrigkeit und Unterschichten* (1990), *Von Benin nach Baltimore: Die Geschichte der African Americans* (1999), and *Konsolidierung und Dissens: Geschichte Nordamerikas von 1800 bis 1865* (2005).

Andrew Fitzmaurice teaches in the Department of History at the University of Sydney. He is the author of *Humanism and America* (2003) and is currently working on two books, a history of anticolonial thought and a history of *terra nullius*.

David Furber received his Ph.D. in modern European history from the State University of New York at Buffalo in 2003. Specializing in the history of the Nazi occupation of Poland, he is working on a book on the colonial dimensions of that occupation and its impact on German behavior.

Robert Geraci is Associate Professor of History at the University of Virginia. He is the author of *Window on the East: National and Imperial Identities in Late Tsarist Russia* (2001), and editor (with Michael Khodarkovsky) of *Of Religion and Empire: Missions, Conversion, and Tolerance in Tsarist Russia* (2001). He is currently writing a book on commerce and ethno-national identities in the Russian empire.

Alex Hinton is Director of the Center for the Study of Genocide and Human Rights and Associate Professor of Anthropology and Global Affairs and at Rutgers University, Newark. He is the author of *Why Did They Kill? Cambodia in the Shadow of Genocide* (2005) and five edited or co-edited collections, *Genocide: Truth, Memory, and Representation* (Duke, forthcoming), *Night of the Khmer Rouge: Genocide and Democracy in Cambodia* (2007), *Annihilating Difference: The Anthropology of Genocide* (2002), *Genocide: an Anthropological Reader* (2002), and *Biocultural Approaches to the Emotions* (1999). He is currently working on several other book projects, including an edited volume on *Local Justice*, a book on 9/11 and Abu Ghraib, and a book on the politics of memory and justice in the aftermath of the Cambodian genocide.

Ben Kiernan is the Whitney Griswold Professor of History and Director of the Genocide Studies Program at Yale University (www.yale.edu/gsp). He is the author of *Blood and Soil: A World History of Genocide and Extermination from Sparta to Darfur* (2007), *Genocide and Resistance in Southeast Asia: Documentation, Denial and Justice in Cambodia and East Timor* (2008), *How Pol Pot Came to Power: Colonialism, Nationalism and Communism in Cambodia, 1930–1975* (1985, 2004), and *The Pol Pot Regime: Race, Power and Genocide in Cambodia under the Khmer Rouge, 1975–1979* (1996, 2002), and coeditor of *The Specter of Genocide: Mass Murder in Historical Perspective* (2003).

Mark Levene attempts to combine being Reader in Comparative History at the University of Southampton, and in the Parkes Centre for Jewish/non-Jewish Relations, with peace and environmental activism. His works include *War, Jews and the New Europe* (1992), for which he was awarded the annual Fraenkel Prize in Contemporary History, and with Penny Roberts, ed., *The Massacre in History* (1999). The first two volumes of his projected four-volume work, *Genocide in the Age of the Nation-State*, appeared in 2005 with I.B. Tauris. He is cofounder of the Crisis Forum (The Forum for the Study of Crisis in the 21st Century: http://www.crisis-forum.org.uk).

Wendy Lower is a DFG Research Fellow at Ludwig Maximilians University, Munich. She is the author of *Nazi Empire-Building and the Holocaust in Ukraine* (2005). She was formerly a program director, historical consultant, and research fellow at the United States Holocaust Memorial Museum, Washington, DC. She is currently working on a book on perpetrators.

A. Dirk Moses teaches history at the University of Sydney, and writes about genocide and postwar Germany. He is the author of *German Intellectuals and the Nazi Past* (2007), editor of *Genocide and Settler Society: Frontier Violence and Stolen Indigenous Children in Australian History* (2004), and (with Dan Stone) of *Colonialism and Genocide* (2006). With Donald Bloxham, he is editing the *Oxford Handbook on Genocide*. He is an associate editor of the *Journal of Genocide Research*.

Dominik Schaller teaches history at the Ruprecht-Karls-Universität Heidelberg, Germany. He is contributing coeditor of *The Origins of Genocide: Raphael Lemkin as a Historian of Mass Violence* (2009) and *Late Ottoman Genocides* (2009). Schaller is the co-editor of the *Journal of Genocide Research*.

Dan Stone is Professor of Modern History at Royal Holloway, University of London. He is author of *Breeding Superman: Nietzsche, Race and Eugenics in Edwardian and Interwar Britain* (2002), *Constructing the Holocaust: A Study in Historiography* (2003), *Responses to Nazism in Britain, 1933–1939: Before War and Holocaust* (2003), and *History, Memory and Mass Atrocity: Essays on the Holocaust and Genocide* (2006); and editor of *The Historiography of the Holocaust* (2004), *Hannah Arendt and the Uses of History, Imperialism, Nation, Race and Genocide* (with Richard H. King, 2007), and *The Historiography of Genocide* (2008).

Blanca Tovías is a University of Sydney Postdoctoral Fellow in History, and editor (with David Cahill) of *Élites Indígenas en Los Andes: Nobles, Caciques y Cabildantes bajo el Yugo Colonial* (2003), and *First Nations and the Colonial Encounter: Native Peoples of Mesoamerica and the Andes under Colonial Rule* (2006).

Lorenzo Veracini is QEII Senior Research Fellow at the Institute for Social Research, Swinburne University, Melbourne. His research interests include the comparative history of colonial systems, settler colonialism, settler societies, and Australian history and historiography. He is currently writing a global history of settler colonialism.

Patrick Wolfe is Charles La Trobe Research Fellow in History at La Trobe University. In 2009–2010, he is also Charles Warren Fellow in US History at Harvard University. In 2008, he was appointed to the Organization of American Historians' Distinguished Lectureship Program. He has written, taught and lectured on race, colonialism, Aboriginal history, genocide, and the history of anthropology. He is currently working on two books: a comparative history of racial regimes that Europeans have sought to impose on colonized peoples in Australia, Brazil, Palestine, and the USA; and a history of settler colonialism in the nineteenth-century US West.

Index